IN THE SHADOW OF ROCK

A HISTORY OF THE GIBRALTAR METHODIST CHURCH

SUSAN I. JACKSON

Wesley Historical Society
2009

First published in Great Britain in 2009
Wesley Historical Society
22, Broadway Road
Evesham
WR11 1BG

ISBN 978-0-9554527-5-8

Printed in Great Britain by the MPG Books Group.

Front cover illustration – *North Front from the cemetery showing the Galleries embrasures.* Photograph by Grace Torres.

Rear cover illustration – *The author in Spain with Gibraltar in the background.* Photograph by Mavis Sykes.

Beneath the Cross of Jesus
I fain would take my stand -
The *shadow of a mighty rock*
Within a weary land;
A home within a wilderness,
A rest upon the way,
From the burning of the noontide heat
And the burden of the day.

Upon that Cross of Jesus
Mine eye at times can see
The very dying form of One
Who suffered there for me.
And from my stricken heart, with tears,
two wonders I confess -
The wonders of redeeming love,
And my own worthlessness.

I take, O Cross, thy shadow,
For my abiding-place!
I ask no other sunshine than
The sunshine of His face;
Content to let the world go by,
To know no gain nor loss -
My sinful self my only shame,
My glory all - the Cross.

Elizabeth Cecilia Clephane, 1830-69

Dedicated to my parents who are part of this story and who first took me to Gibraltar; and to the unsung heroines of Methodism, the ministers' wives.

CONTENTS

Acknowledgements   *ix*

Preface   *xi*

1   Setting the Scene -   1
    (Up to 1769)

2   Foundations and Beginnings -   6
    Soldier Preachers and Lay Leaders (1769-1804)

3   Ministerial Oversight -   18
    The Building of Providence Chapel (1804-11)

4   Growth and Consolidation -   28
    Tension and Division (1812-21)

5   Evangelisation -   46
    A Mission to the Spanish on the Rock (1821-8)

6   The Fever Epidemic of 1828 and its Aftermath -   66
    A New Missionary is Sent (1828-32)

7   The Ministry of William Harris Rule (1) Expansion -   77
    A System of Education Forays into Spain (1832-6)

8   The Ministry of William Harris Rule (2) Cádiz -   96
    The First Spanish Methodist Society (1836-9)

9   The Ministry of William Harris Rule (3) Back to Gibraltar -   121
    More Rights for Soldiers;
    Mission Premises at the South (1839-42)

10 Maintaining the Ground -   148
    A New Initiative is Begun (1842-8)

11 Opposition -   163
    Retrenchment (1848-53)

12 The Ministry of George Alton (1) Into Spain with the Bible   176
    Society -
    Hopes soon Dashed (1853-8)

13 Spain -   201
    The Fate of Escalante and the Work in Cádiz (1858-63)

14 The Ministry of George Alton (2) Gibraltar –   221
    Work with the Sanitary Commissioners;
    Openings in Portugal and Spain (1863-9)

15 Marking Time in Gibraltar -   240
    Developments in Oporto and Barcelona (1869-74)

16 Official Recognition of the Work in Gibraltar -   260
    A New School is Built (1875-85)

17 Further Hopes for Work in Spain -   280
    A Mission in La Linea (1885-96)

18 The Soldiers and Sailors take Precedence -   306
    The Welcome Home is opened (1896-1903)

19 Under New Management -   318
    Increased Work and Staff (1903-19)

20 The Welcome is Finally Purchased -   345
    Brown Returns to the Rock (1919-36)

21 The Ministry of Padre Brown Continues -   361
    The Spanish Civil War and the Second World War (1936-52)

22 A Successor to Brown -   385
    The Work Unites on One Site (1952-61)

23 Problems with Spain -   407
    The Border is Closed (1961-81)

24 Changes in Gibraltar -   424
    The Border Re-opens and the Troops begin to Leave (1981-97)

25 Another New Beginning -   441
    Into the Future (1997 onwards)

Early Leaders and Ministers of the Gibraltar Methodist Church   446

Bibliography and Source Material   448

Index   453

ILLUSTRATIONS

Map of Spain	xiii
Map showing Gibraltar and nearby towns and cities	xiii
Plan of Gibraltar circa 1888	xiv
General view of Gibraltar	1
George Whitefield	3
James Gill	28
William Croscombe	52
James Dixon	53
William Harris Rule	79
Henry and Mary Nicholson	146
Thomas Trevor N. Hull	148
Cemetery	163
George Alton	221
Christiana, Martha Octavia and Margaret Lyth	241
Richard Burdsall Lyth and Mary Ann Lyth	243
Eastern view of Gibraltar	252
Wesleyan School House	266
John Ridgeway Griffin	268
William Harris Rule	270
John Grimshaw	281
Families of Terry Coppin and John Righton	294
William Henry Sarchet	306
The Welcome	311
Methodist premises on Prince Edward's Road	319
Alfred Barrett Sackett and Lydia Anne Sackett	322
Lydia Sackett with her children Barrett and Dorothy May	323
South Branch of the Welcome	325
Ronda Party	327
Providence Chapel before renovation	330
Opening of the renovated Church	331
The Renovation Committee	332
Memorial Windows	333
The renovated Church	334
Outing to the cork woods	335
Lydia and Barrett Sackett	341
Alfred Barrett Sackett	344
Frederick Edmund Brown	349
King Edward VII Soldiers' and Sailors' Institute	352
Soldiers at the Manse	369
Gibraltar Club founders	371
Padre Brown and Miss Halsey at the first Reunion	375
Robbie and Mildred Emerson	376
Frank Wilson and Padre Brown	379

Group photo including Frank Wilson and Richard Cavilla 382
The Jackson family 386
Group tour in Spain 389
Roy Dalton 390
John Jackson and Dr W. Edwin Sangster 398
New Church at Wesley House 399
Sunday School outing 400
Trip to the cork woods 401
The Welcome boat 402
The canteen with the book section 403
Adele Dalton with Rene Jackson in Ronda 404
Toy Service at Ronda 405
The Jefferies family 417
Norman and Isobel Berryman 420
Anne and Dougie Dennis 430
Paula and Leila Mears 433
Brian Beck and Paul Mears with the RAF 436
Frank and Mavis Sykes 440
Wilf and Doreen Pearce 442
Mary and David Dolding 444

Colour section:
Methodist premises
Words Aflame Bookshop
Carpenter's Arms
Methodist Church
Fidel and Sheila Patron
Group taken at the Church weekend in 2009
Road map of Gibraltar

ACKNOWLEDGEMENTS

A great many people have given me invaluable help with this research and my thanks go to them all although it is not possible to mention everyone by name. However, without all the help so willingly given, this work would never have been completed.

In Gibraltar thanks go to: Jon Searle at the Garrison Library and later Lorna Swift; Thomas Finlayson, Gibraltar's archivist, and later Denis Beiso; the staff at Land Property Services and many members of the Methodist Church especially Mary and David Dolding, who have passed on numerous useful contacts to me; Lucille Rodríguez for her translation of the Escalante papers; Douglas Cumming for help and support over the final hurdles; Paul Cosquieri and 123 printers for the use of the road map of Gibraltar; and Peter and Sheila Lee for putting me up so often. Thanks also to those who allowed me access to the records at the Cathedral of the Holy Trinity, St. Andrew's Church of Scotland and King's Chapel.

In England thanks go to: Rosemary Seton at the School of Oriental and African Studies; Peter Nockles at John Rylands Library; Ingrid Roderick of the Bible Society for permission to use their archives and Alan Jesson and Rosemary Matthew at Cambridge University Library for their unfailing help in doing so; Peter Forsaith of the Oxford Centre for Methodism and Church History, Oxford Brookes University; and above all to Joy Fox, the former Methodist Missionary Society Archivist, whose help and encouragement was so great that without it the work would probably never have been finished.

Thanks are also due to those who have been willing to share their own researches with me: Francisco Quirell for information on John Quirell; Arthur Langford and the family of J.W.V. Cumming for their researches on Henry Ince; Martin Eayrs for his research on Henry Nicholson; Catharine Crawford and her family for information on Richard and Mary Ann Lyth and Edmund and Robert Sackett for sharing their family memoir about Alfred Sackett and their photographs.

Others have helped me track down books or lent them to me, particularly Geoffrey Milburn, Edwin Thompson and Matthew Hill of the Spanish Gospel Mission. Thanks also go to all those named in this account who were willing to share their time and stories with me, particularly past and present members of the church, the ministers and their wives and the lay workers. Also to members of the Gibraltar Club for making me welcome, for sharing their stories and for allowing me access to their archives.

Family and friends too have been most helpful and supportive: my parents; particularly my sister Dorothy Carling, her husband Peter, and also Emma, Ruth and Hannah for putting up with my many research visits; Elizabeth Gardner for similar help with visits; my brother, Richard Jackson, for the use of his pictures; Gerald Burt for advice and guidance; Joan Chilton, for her support and encouragement; and to Sheridan Gilley, who was my supervisor for the first half of this story, for his advice at the beginning and for his help and encouragement in the difficult times which kept me going.

Finally to Richard Jones for his much appreciated preface and, last but not least, Norma Virgoe, the WHS editor for all her hard work on the text as well as her general support and encouragement to me.

PREFACE

In 1997 I was staying for the weekend in Gibraltar to share in an unusual celebration. The Methodist Church there – housed in the same premises as "The Carpenter's Arms" – was to be given its proper autonomy like any other society within Methodism, and to become part of the then London South West District. That was odd, but sensible, since it had previously been a special outpost of the Forces Board. But now it has ended up as Circuit 36/15 in the recently formed South East District and sits alongside such very English places as Hastings or Hove. It has, one might say, become slightly more normal, and the process is described in the last two chapters of this book.

That weekend was redolent with history, with the stories of the first Methodists in Gibraltar, serving soldiers who were treated as dangerous cranks by their officers, misunderstood and oppressed for their distinctive religious passion. However, they ended up being respected, not least because of the stature and military prowess of men like Sergeant Ince. So the first Methodist seeds were well sown. Previously, when we held a brief service in the cemetery, laid out on a piece of flat ground with the great Rock towering over it, that history seemed etched into every stone. And every time one talked to the people there who had brought many warm memories, one sensed that a unique and rich history was woven into everything that was happening. Better still, one of the guests told how she was writing up that history …

It is salutary and inspiring to have it all here, set out for us by Sue Jackson. All Christian living rests upon a momentous world-changing power and passion that moulds so much of the last twenty centuries making today's churches impossible to understand without the Story. It begins in the backwaters of the Roman Empire and lands us in places like Gibraltar, once famous in the annals of the British one. It begins with Jesus Christ and ends up with today's women's meetings and Sunday services and strong hymns and lively songs, with local preachers and class leaders and ministers, with open doors and cafés and bookshops, with collections for the Relief and Development Fund and petitions for Making Poverty History, with prayer meetings and alpha courses and lots of ordinary Christians making their witness to their faith. The great history feeds all this discipleship today.

Ah, but we live in a time when so many quietly despise history. One sometimes imagines that many Christians today wish that the faith had been devised some fifty years ago by a telegenic preacher, preferably American, strumming a guitar like Bob Dylan, wearing a beard and dark sun glasses. No, no! The faith comes to us via countless saints and unsung ordinary Christians through twenty centuries of bravery, wisdom, faith, prayer and guts. This book is a strong reminder of all that, of a little outpost of the faith that has nurtured thousands of doughty disciples and is vibrant today. So read this finely crafted and thorough study, and then thank God for the Church Militant on Earth, Triumphant in Heaven, to be spotted in the Carpenter's Arms in the Main Street, under the massive Rock, almost opposite the somewhat pretentious entrance to the Governor's residence, most noticeable in the people who sing and pray there.

Richard G. Jones

Spain

Gibraltar and nearby towns and cities

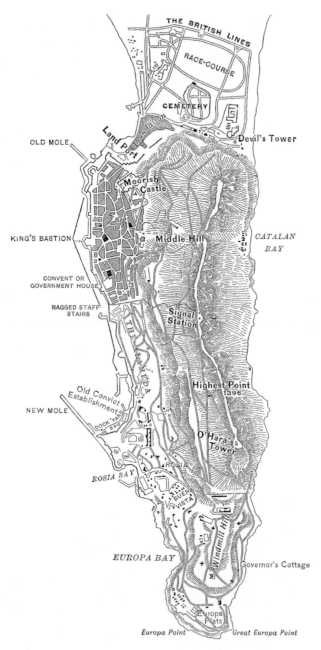

PLAN OF GIBRALTAR CIRCA 1888

CHAPTER 1   SETTING THE SCENE
Up to 1769

Although Gibraltar once became a symbol of strength and security, it is today probably best known for its apes and for its population's desire to remain British in the face of Spain's claim to sovereignty. Much of its rich history has been forgotten and few people know that there is a Methodist Church there, one of the oldest in Methodism and the second oldest Protestant Church on the Rock itself.

Methodism in Gibraltar had small and humble beginnings, but it gradually came to play a significant part in the life of the community. Its development is a remarkable story of persecution, opposition and perseverance as Methodists sought to point people to a different kind of Rock - a God who is indeed a safe and sure stronghold.

The towering Rock of Gibraltar dominates its locality although it is only a small promontory, about two and a half square miles in size and fourteen hundred feet high. It was originally known as Calpe and it formed, with Mount Abyla in North Africa, the Pillars of Hercules, one of the wonders of the ancient world. Many visitors landed on its shores – Neanderthals, Phoenicians, Romans, Vandals and Visigoths, but it was the Moors who arrived in 711 AD under the leadership of Tarik-ibn-Zeyad who named it Gibel Tarik, Mountain of Tarik, which developed into the modern name, Gibraltar. They were the first to settle on the Rock and remained in possession of it for nearly 600 years until, in 1309, the Spanish besieged Gibraltar, in the first of fourteen sieges. Gibraltar changed hands several times in the following years but, in July 1502, after Queen Isabella of Spain gained Gibraltar for the Crown, it received its coat of arms, the Castle and the Key, still in use today.

THE ROCK
(From the collection of J. Richard Jackson)

The mosque was converted into a church, which was later completely rebuilt and called St Mary the Crowned. Eventually there were fifteen places of worship for the population of five to six thousand, including the shrine of our Lady of Europa near Europa Point. The Franciscan friars completed their Convent around 1531.

At this time relationships between Protestant England and Catholic Spain were not good. The Spanish Armada set sail and was defeated in 1588. Adventurers like Drake, Hawkins and Raleigh attacked Spanish shipping, occasionally with the aid of the Dutch. In 1625 Cádiz was attacked by the English, but the raid failed. However, in 1662, England acquired Tangier which gave them a base in the area for over twenty years. As Spanish power declined and France's increased there was much speculation as to who would ascend the Spanish throne after the death of Charles II. The prospect of Spain coming under French rule led to a declaration of war between France and England in 1702. Two British and Dutch fleets were prepared for action. Admiral Sir George Rooke was appointed Commander-in-chief of the smaller force and was instructed to take Cádiz or possibly Gibraltar. The attempt on Cádiz failed and so, in the summer of 1704, one year after the birth of John Wesley in England, Rooke attacked Gibraltar.

Some two thousand marines under Prince George of Hesse-Darmstadt landed almost unopposed on the isthmus separating the Rock from Spain, but Don Diego de Salinas, the Governor, refused to surrender. A bombardment from the ships began and other landings took place. When the women and children, who had fled to take refuge at the shrine of our Lady of Europa, became cut off from the town and were captured, the Governor did agree to surrender. The garrison was allowed to leave but civilians were given a choice. They could leave with their belongings or stay if they were prepared to swear allegiance to Charles III of Spain in whose name the Rock had been taken. All but seventy of the inhabitants left and settled where they could. A parish priest, Juan Romero, and a few others stayed behind and saved St Mary the Crowned from desecration, the fate of other places of worship, and some of the monks at the Convent also stayed on.

However, Spanish and French forces soon began gathering in the area and laid siege to Gibraltar in October 1704. The siege was abandoned in the spring of 1705 but the French and Spanish continued to blockade the Rock until November 1712 when an armistice was agreed between Britain and Spain. Then, under the Treaty of Utrecht of July 1713, Britain recognised Philip as King of Spain and Gibraltar became British. From then on, as a garrison town, British soldiers formed a large part of the population. They successfully defended the Rock against the Spanish during a further siege in 1727. After this the monks at the Convent left for San Roque and the English Governor took over the Convent as his residence. It has retained this use and its name to the present day. Its chapel was named 'The King's Chapel' and became the first and only Protestant place of worship in the Garrison. It was served by military chaplains, though both the troops and civilians were allowed to worship there.

Meanwhile, in England in 1725, John Wesley had been ordained in the Church of England, and the following year he was elected a fellow of Lincoln College, Oxford. From 1727 to 1729 he served as a curate in Lincolnshire, on behalf of his father, the vicar, who was ill. On his return to Oxford he took over the leadership of the Holy Club which met regularly 'to study the classics and to seek a serious Christian way of life'.[1] They gained the nickname 'Methodist' because of the methodical way in which they ordered their lives. One of the members of this Club was George Whitefield who sailed to Georgia in February 1738 in the *Whitaker*, which called at Gibraltar so that troops could be embarked for Georgia to aid in the defence of the colony.

George Whitefield

Whitefield went ashore on 20 February 1738 and was 'delighted with the prospect of the place'.[2] The following day he was welcomed by the Governor, Lieutenant General Joseph Sabine, and was invited to dine with him. He also visited 'both the ministers of Gibraltar' who warmly welcomed him and offered him the use of their pulpit in the King's Chapel. He attended public prayers which seem to have been a frequent, if not a daily, occurrence and were attended by many officers and soldiers. On 24 February Whitefield moved into lodgings ashore and the following day at six in the morning, he went to the church to meet a small society of soldiers which had been in existence for twelve years. At first the soldiers had met in caves and dens, but the Governor had then allowed them to use the church where they met three times a day 'to read, pray and sing psalms.' They had encountered some persecution and were 'in derision called, the new lights'. There was also another society of the Scottish Church nicknamed 'dark lanterns'. Whitefield was more impressed with the former group and was also impressed with Governor Sabine, writing in a letter that 'Gibraltar is blessed with a governor, who hath not absented himself from public worship, unless when he was sick, for these seven

---

[1] John Pudney, *John Wesley and his World*, Thomas & Hudson: London, 1978, p.32.
[2] George Whitefield, *Journal of a Voyage from London to Savannah in Georgia*, no publisher: 1826, vol. xix, pp.50-63.

years, and yet is very moderate towards the dissenters.'[3] On Sunday 26 February Whitefield joined the soldiers at the church between five and six in the morning. Later in the morning he preached to a congregation of officers and soldiers and found the church, 'though very large, was quite thronged'. After evening prayers he joined the society again and had nearly thirty hearers. On the evening of Wednesday 1 March, Whitefield's congregation was 'near two hundred people, amongst whom were many of the officers, and of the honourable women not a few' and on 4 March about a thousand people attended. Several people were visibly moved by his preaching, and on Sunday 5 March one person 'was so affected, that he wished himself a despised methodist'! Whitefield received the sacrament that morning along with Governor Sabine and Lieutenant General Francis Columbine, the Lieutenant Governor, plus about fifty others. On 6 March, his last day in Gibraltar, many came to see him bringing presents for his journey. He was accompanied to the ship by nearly two hundred people all sorry to see him go. He sailed the following day.

One of Whitefield's biographers, reporting on this remarkable visit, described the 'new lights' as 'a little group of pious soldiers, who, for twelve years, had been the *methodists* of Gibraltar'.[4] It is unlikely that they could have been Methodists as early as this but they did continue to meet as attested by Robert Poole, a Christian doctor, who visited Gibraltar in October 1748.

After visiting the King's Chapel, Poole reported that 'a society of soldiers, I am informed, meets here every night at a set hour, to assist each other in the exercise of religion, prayer, reading etc. This society is said to have subsisted these sixteen years, though they are now much reduced to a very small number, and several of them little better than indifferent Christians'.[5] He referred to them as the 'New Lights' which must have been a continuation of the earlier group despite the discrepancy in the number of years of its existence.

Whitefield had returned to England in December 1738 and had soon become renowned for his preaching. When he was banned from London pulpits he went to Bristol. When doors there also closed to him, he began to preach in the open air instead with thousands flocking to hear him. He had promised to return to Georgia and so he asked John Wesley to take over his work in Bristol. Wesley eventually agreed and thus began his itinerant ministry which was to take him all over Britain, meeting with opposition and persecution as well as a great deal of success. Wesley founded religious societies throughout the country which he intended to be

---

[3] *Letters of George Whitefield for the period 1734-1742*, The Banner of Truth Trust: Edinburgh, 1976, p.38.

[4] Robert Philip, *The Life and Times of the Rev. George Whitefield, M.A.*, George Virtue: 1837, p.64.

[5] Robert Poole, 'Gibraltar in 1748', *Gibraltar Heritage Journal,* no.3, 1996, pp.61-90.

part of the Established Church, but the seeds of separation were really sown at the beginning of his work. Wesley's open-air preaching, distinctive message, itinerant life style, use of lay preachers, development of the class system and building of separate preaching houses were all innovative ways of working which were likely to arouse suspicion, opposition and condemnation from more traditional Anglicans. Developments after Wesley's death also contributed to the gradual establishment of Methodism as a separate denomination.

One group of people who particularly concerned Wesley were soldiers, whose lives were often hard. Watkins in his book *Soldiers and Preachers Too*, stated that 'there was no class of the community to which John Wesley was more drawn or of which he records with greater pleasure signs of spiritual awakening than the soldiery. His letters and his Journal abound with references to these men, over whom his heart yearned, and whose spiritual destitution was so great'.[6] Wesley preached to them as often as he could and many responded to his preaching and became Methodists, forming themselves into small Methodist Societies within the army which could continue to meet wherever they were posted. In addition, in the early years when Wesley and his followers were much persecuted, some Methodists including preachers were deliberately press-ganged into service. They too then either began or joined in these soldiers' societies and so the word spread. Thus it is not surprising that it was soldiers who first took Methodism to Gibraltar which 'for nearly a hundred years was to be the chief seat of Methodism in the army'.[7] The first of them was Henry Ince.

---

[6] Owen Spencer Watkins, *Soldiers and Preachers Too*, Methodist Church: Reprint, 1981, p.1.

[7] William Harris Rule, *An account of the Establishment of Wesleyan Methodism in the British Army*, T. Woolmer: London, 1883, p.20. Watkins, op. cit., p.1.

CHAPTER 2 FOUNDATIONS AND BEGINNINGS
Soldier Preachers and Lay Leaders (1769 - 1804)

Henry Ince is thought to have been born in 1736 in Penzance; to have been 'brought up to the trade of a nailor' and to have later 'acquired some experience as a miner'.[1] In 1755 he enlisted into the Second Queen's Regiment of Foot then stationed in Galway. He served with them in Ireland until June 1765 when the Regiment moved to the Isle of Man. In March 1768 it went to Gibraltar where, on 4 July 1768, Henry Ince was listed on the muster rolls of Captain Nickson's Company with the rank of Sergeant.[2]

On 3 April 1769, Ince wrote to John Wesley from Gibraltar:

> At our first coming to this place, I found a people of such abominable practices, as I never before had seen. However, I and two or three more took a room to meet in, and we were soon joined by some of the Royal Scotch: but this continued only a short time; the reason was, they would not allow your hymns to be sung, neither your works to be read. Upon this I was obliged to declare, that while I could get any of your writings to make use of, I would use them; since I had found them agreeable to the word of God. And as God gave me a word to speak, I cared not who heard, so He might be glorified. On this many were offended, and separated from us. Yet, in about two months, we were thirty-seven in number, till a little persecution came, then we were reduced to about eighteen. But, blessed be God! he is reviving his work again. We are now thirty-two, fifteen of whom can rejoice in the pardoning love of God, and most of the others are pressing hard after it. Several Officers come to hear, and God gives favour in the sight of all men. There is one Gentleman of the town who has joined us lately, and is a very great help to us.
>
> As to myself, God is ever gracious to me, who am less than the least of his children. I am astonished that he should work by me! O, that I may be found faithful unto death! and that he may carry on his work in this barren place! So prays your unworthy Friend, Henry Ince.[3]

From the way in which this letter was written, it seems likely that Ince had met Wesley who had first visited Cornwall in 1743, and returned several times, so that the young Ince might well have heard him preach or met him there. He might also have met Wesley in Ireland which he visited on five occasions during the time Ince was serving there and often preached to soldiers. On one occasion he noted in his journal, 'I was well pleased to see a little army of soldiers there, and not a few of their officers. Nor did they behave as unconcerned hearers, but like men that really desired to save

---

[1] T.W.J. Connolly, *History of the Royal Sappers and Miners,* 2 vols. Longman, Brown, Green, Longmans & Roberts: London, 1857, vol. i, p.31.
[2] A. Langford, 'Henry Ince (1736-1808) A Research Appreciation', *The Cornish Methodist Historical Association Journal,* October, 1975, p.30.
[3] *Arminian Magazine,* February, 1784.

their souls.'[4]

The persecution, mentioned in the letter, was to be a continuing and deepening problem and on 3 June 1769 Fortress Orders stated that: 'Whereas divers soldiers and inhabitants assemble themselves every evening to prayer it's the Governor's Order that no person whatever presume to molest them nor to go into their meeting to behave indecently there'.[5] It seems that the Governor, Lieutenant General the Honourable Edward Cornwallis, was sympathetic to the cause and was prepared to support the Methodists against their persecutors.

Others soon began to help Ince with his task. In 1769 soldiers from a Methodist Society in Winchester were posted to Gibraltar and, on 23 November, one of them wrote a letter saying,

> We have between thirty and forty joined in the Society from the different regiments, besides some townsfolk and one officer. Our proceedings are as follows. We have preaching every night and morning. We have three nights set apart for Class-Meeting after the sermon, and on the Sabbath day, at eight in the morning, two in the afternoon, and six in the evening; and for our speakers we have Henry Ince of the IInd Regiment, Henry Hall of the Royal Scots, and Brother Morton, under whom the work seems to prosper.[6]

Meanwhile, as Spain had not given up her claim to the Rock, attention had turned to Gibraltar's defences. In 1769 William Green, the Senior Engineer, visited England to seek permission for the implementation of his plans for strengthening them. This work was being done by civilian workers who had little regard for discipline and progress had been slow. Green suggested that the problem could be solved by forming a company of military artificers who would work under military authority and discipline. Permission was granted and members were recruited from regiments already in Gibraltar. On 30 June 1772 the Soldier Artificer Company was mustered and included Sergeant Henry Ince whose occupation was given as miner.[7] Extensive work on Gibraltar's fortifications began which was well timed as, in June 1779, Spain once again declared war against Britain and soon laid siege to Gibraltar. This fourteenth siege, later known as the Great Siege, lasted more than three-and-a-half years.

Forces gathered on the isthmus and began to bombard the town. The Governor, George Eliott, later to become Lord Heathfield of Gibraltar, ordered the streets to be ploughed up and steeples and other landmarks pulled down, to try and limit the effectiveness of the enemy's

---

[4] Nehemiah Curnock, *The Journal of John Wesley,* Epworth Press: London, 1938, vol. iv, p.398.

[5] Garrison Orders, WO284 vol. 05.

[6] William D. Lawson, *Wesleyan Local Preachers*, William D. Lawson: Newcastle upon Tyne, 1874, p.277.

[7] Connolly, op. cit., p.5.

bombardment. The main problem, however, was food. People were encouraged to leave, but as the blockade tightened this became almost impossible and the shortages increased. The gardens of the garrison were situated on the isthmus and soon came under threat. Supplies did arrive from time to time, but food was very scarce causing sickness, including scurvy, to break out. In May 1781 Drinkwater reported that 'the buildings in town, at this time, exhibited a most dreadful picture of the effects of so animated a bombardment. Scarce a house, north of the Grand Parade, was tenantable; all of them were deserted. Some few, near South-port, continued to be inhabited by soldiers' families, but in general the floors and roofs were destroyed, and the bare shell only was left standing.'[8] The Church of St Mary the Crowned had been severely damaged by fire and the Convent had also been hit.

In November 1781 a successful sortie into enemy lines took place which included some of the Artificer Company. The enemy's guns were spiked and magazines blown up. In May 1782, the Governor, along with Green, was inspecting some of the defences and apparently offered a thousand dollars to anyone who could suggest a way of getting guns to bear on the enemy from a position called the notch. It was Ince, now Sergeant-Major, who suggested tunnelling through the Rock and he was then given the job of overseeing the work, which began immediately. When a hole was blown out to provide ventilation for the miners it was realised that this too would provide a gun emplacement and so more were made. By June 1783 Spilsbury reported that 'Ince's gallery got to within a few yards of the notch, and a gallery is now making to it on the outside from the furthest embrasure'.[9]

However, by this time the siege was over. In September 1782, the Spanish had used floating batteries to launch an all-out attack, but Gibraltar's defences held and the use of red-hot shot proved very effective even though the Spanish thought their batteries were fire proof. After this, hostilities gradually declined in intensity and it became clear that the siege was drawing to an end. At the beginning of February 1783, the Duke de Crillon, Commander of the Spanish forces, informed Eliott that peace was being negotiated between Britain and Spain. The two met and toured each other's defences, including Ince's Galleries, which astonished and impressed the Duke.

Henry Ince had played an important part in the siege. Connolly said of him, 'He was active, prompt and persevering, very short in stature, but wiry and hardy in constitution; was greatly esteemed by his officers, and frequently the subject of commendation from the highest authorities at

---

[8] John Drinkwater, *A History of the late Siege of Gibraltar*, no publisher: London, 1835, p.161.
[9] Captain Spilsbury, *A Journal of the Siege of Gibraltar 1779-1783*, Garrison Library: Gibraltar, 1908, pp.107 & 109.

Gibraltar.'[10] He received special pay and privileges as a result of the high esteem in which he was held, not only because of his work on the defences, but also for his help with the food shortage. Half way up the Rock are the ruins of a property called Ince's Farm, which was eventually granted to Ince in January 1787. The original grant stated:

> Whereas Henry Ince Sergeant Major in the Royal Military Artificer Company having at his own expense, during the late blockade and with my consent and permission for the improvement and benefit of the place, enclosed and cultivated a certain extent of ground situated on the center of the Hill above the town ... which ground the said Henry Ince hath partly planted with trees, erected some buildings thereon and otherwise improved and converted the same into kitchen garden for raising greens and other esculent plants and roots for market, that have ever since proved to be of great utility to the Garrison in General. Wherefor for the encouragement of so usefull an undertaking and the increase of vegetables, roots and fruits for the benefit and consumption of the Troops and Community, as well as the increase of the King's Revenue, I do, by virtue of the power and authority to me given by His Majesty hereby let and grant the said ground and appurtenances unto the same Henry Ince ... for the space and term of forty one years.[11]

Although it is generally believed that the farm was given to Ince in recognition of his work on the defences, there is no mention of this in the grant. In addition, Methodist tradition, referred to on a plaque in the present church, states that, after receiving the farm, Henry Ince 'gave his old home in Prince Edward's Road as the first regular meeting place for the Methodist Society in Gibraltar,' but there is no evidence to support this belief.[12]

When Ince wrote to Wesley, he said he took a room to meet in and his name is not mentioned in the original lease of the Prince Edward's Road site, granted in January 1788, or in subsequent transactions.[13] Ince probably lived on the farm during the siege which would have been a much safer place for him and his family. Although there are no records of any marriage in Gibraltar, several children were born there whose baptisms are recorded at the King's Chapel.

In 1791 Ince was discharged from the Artificer Company but continued as Overseer of the works. In February 1796 he was commissioned as an Ensign in the Royal Garrison Battalion and was promoted to Lieutenant in March 1801. In 1802 the regiment was disbanded. On 1 January 1803 the

---

[10] Connolly, op. cit., p.31.

[11] Crown Lands (Series M) Register of Leases no.1 (1802-4) p.21.

[12] B.D. Crofts, A.K. Stanley, P. & K.R. Jefferies, *Upon this Rock: A Short History of Methodism in Gibraltar written and published to commemorate the Bicentenary of the Founding of the Church*, Gibraltar, 1969, p.2.

[13] File Mark no. 542 and Letters Patent 13.

lease on Ince's Farm was renewed for another sixty-six years 'on account of his former and meritorious services'.[14] Ince had actually lost the original grant which may explain why the lease was renewed early. Some time afterwards he left Gibraltar 'having worn himself out in the service of the fortress' and retired to Devon.[15] It is not clear why or exactly when he decided to leave especially when it involved leaving family members behind. He died, at the age of 72, in Gittisham on 9 October 1808 and was buried in the churchyard there on October 14.

After the end of the Great Siege, life in Gibraltar was so disrupted by indiscipline and drunkenness amongst the troops that many civilians began to feel Spanish rule might be preferable. However, their plans were discovered and over a thousand people were expelled from the Rock. In 1802 Prince Edward, Duke of Kent, was appointed as Governor and instructed to deal with the problems amongst the soldiers but, in December 1802, the soldiers rebelled against his strict regime. However, their plot was not successful either and several were court-martialled. Some were shot and others transported. Kent was recalled to England and left in May 1803. He never returned to Gibraltar although he retained his title and salary as its Governor until his death seventeen years later. Until then Gibraltar was ruled by a series of Lieutenant Governors, the first of whom was Major-General Sir Thomas Trigge. The other powerful figure of the time was Major-General Charles Barnett.

It is against this background that the story of Methodism unfolds. No information about the work has been found from 1769 until 1787 when Andrew Armour, a young man of just eighteen years, arrived in Gibraltar with his regiment. He was born in Glasgow in 1769 and in 1786 enlisted in the army. Whilst serving in Ireland, he attended a Methodist meeting and then joined the Wesleyan Society. After his arrival in Gibraltar, he and another soldier met together to read the Bible and talk about spiritual matters. Armour's faith deepened and some feel it was here in Gibraltar and not in Ireland that he was actually converted. He and his friend were eventually joined by others,

> ... and a Methodist Class-meeting was formed in which the members told one another of their spiritual experiences. Armour was the 'Leader' of this meeting. They met in a small place near the Governor's house, and for a time refrained from singing, lest they should alarm or disturb others. More and more soldiers joined the Class, and Armour became a Local Preacher. They now began to sing and soon got talked about, till Armour was summoned to Government House to explain the strange doings. His explanation was accepted, and the meetings were formally sanctioned.[16]

---

[14] File Mark no. 774.

[15] Connolly, op. cit., p.32.

[16] L.E. Blaze, 'Andrew Armour', *D.B.U. Journal*, reprinted April 1941, p.3.

It is not clear from this account exactly when these developments took place. However, a letter written in November 1801 seems to refer to the same events and places them in 1792. It stated:

In March 1792, the 46th, 51st and 61st regiments arrived at Gibraltar from Ireland. In them there were ten or eleven persons who feared God, one of whom preached, and two exhorted. They first met in a private room, not knowing they would be permitted to meet in public. But, when they began to sing, people flocked about the door, entreating to get in; to which they consented. Fearing, however, that they might incur the displeasure of the Governor, [Lieutenant-General Sir Robert Boyd] they petitioned him for permission to assemble together to worship God. Hearing they belonged to the Methodist connection, he readily consented, hoping they would not neglect their duty as soldiers. Immediately after this, a large room was taken; but it could not contain one half of the people; another, about twice as large, was immediately taken at one guinea per month. Many now began to be concerned about the salvation of their souls; and some of them did not rest until they knew, in their experience, that Christ had power on earth to forgive sins. Our number soon increased to about fifty. Before the war broke out in 1793, our number was one hundred and twenty...

All this time, however, the enemy was not idle; for he stirred up much opposition from every quarter. Two or three gentlemen importuned the governor to put a stop to our meetings; but the Lord, in whose hands are the hearts of all men, soon overthrew their counsel. General O'Hara [Governor from December 1795] is said to have replied, "Let them alone; I wish there were twenty for one of them, and we should have fewer court-martials in the garrison than we have". Nevertheless, the persecution did not cease; for we were reproached on every hand, and all manner of evil spoken against us falsely. This had one good effect; for such as did not receive the seed into good ground, soon withered away; but the hands of the faithful were strengthened, and their hearts united by the love of God, and we frequently found the Lord present in our little assemblies.... Our Society seemed now well settled; but the war soon occasioned the removal of the troops ... by which in about twelve months, our numbers reduced to twenty, yet we continued to meet regularly, there being always some to give a word of exhortation. In August 1796, the 28th regiment arrived from England; among whom there were some who preached. At the same time there came also a young officer, who preached. The novelty of an officer preaching, drew many to hear the Word ... Our Society increased, the house was far too small for the congregation, and we then took a larger room; but with this revival the enemy stirred up fresh persecution. The commanding officer of a regiment gave out an order, that no man belonging to his regiment was to attend the Methodist meetings, upon pain of being punished for disobedience of orders. Application was made in vain to have the order done away; however, the regiment was soon ordered for England, as was also the young officer mentioned above. But there being some left to speak in the name of Christ, their labour was not in vain; for the number of those continued to increase who sought redemption in the blood of Christ. It was then thought advisable to build a chapel, as we were at this time paying above two guineas per month. The chapel was accordingly built without delay, the expense of which amounted to upwards of £120 sterling. Our brethren were so desirous of the prosperity of Zion, that each gave freely of what the Lord had blessed him with; and when the house was finished, there was not a farthing of debt on it. This was a great encouragement to us. Our number at this time was about fifty, and our congregation commonly between two and three hundred.[17]

Further regimental changes soon reduced the numbers in the Society to about fifteen, but despite this and continued opposition, the chapel remained open for worship. When the letter writer left Gibraltar in June 1801, the Society numbered 35 and the congregations around 200. Preaching took place on Sundays and Thursdays and on the other nights there were exhortations or prayer meetings. The writer also noted;

And that every thing may be done decently and in order, we have a committee, consisting of eleven members, one of whom is the leader, and another the steward. These meet as often as occasion may require, to consider the best methods of conducting both the spiritual and temporal affairs of the Society.... Our leader is set apart to his office by solemn prayer, and he also administers the Lord's Supper to the Society once a month. Farther, no one is admitted a member amongst us till he has been two months on trial (unless we knew that he has been serious before;) then, if there be no objection to him, he is admitted with public prayer. This we think a prudent way to prevent reproach from being brought on the cause of God by unworthy members. We were led to this from having suffered much from this quarter in times past. If any amongst us walk disorderly, we admonish him, and bear with him for a season; but if he still continue to walk disorderly, and contrary to the Gospel, we then at a public meeting, declare him to be no more of us.

In a second letter, the writer reported that contact had been made with ships in the bay and sometimes the Society sent a preacher to preach on board ship and distribute pamphlets. A library of about one hundred and fifty books had been established to which many owed 'a great deal of their knowledge in the ways of God.'[18]

Clearly, this was a well organised Society, but the events described occurred nearly twenty-three years after the beginnings of 1769 and the account does seem to describe a new work and not a continuation of a Society already in existence. Findlay and Holdsworth in their *History of the Wesleyan Methodist Missionary Society* regarded this as the start of

---

[17] *Methodist Magazine,* vol. xxv, July 1802, pp.323-5.
[18] Ibid., pp.326-7.

Methodism in Gibraltar and do not refer to the earlier beginnings of 1769.[19] In 1814 Armour himself referred in a letter to his time in Gibraltar (1787-98) saying, 'I was made instrumental in establishing a society, which I am happy to understand remains till this day'.[20] This certainly sounds like a completely new venture, so what had happened to Ince's initiative? It is odd that he is not mentioned or referred to in this account or in subsequent events as he was so well known in Gibraltar. One can only speculate. Perhaps the Great Siege put a stop to meetings. Perhaps the persecution proved overwhelming. Perhaps Ince lost his faith or transferred his loyalties to the Established Church which would have been much more acceptable to a man in his new position of importance.

The later persecution continued initiated by the Garrison Chaplain, the Rev. Mr Wetherell, and the Rev. Mr Hughes, Chaplain to the Governor, the Duke of Kent. They threatened to suppress the Methodist meetings largely because of their practice of administering the sacrament without an ordained minister. In October 1802 the Methodists, hearing that they had been represented to the Governor as 'disaffected persons' holding 'improper meetings', sent a memorial to the Governor. They wished to put the record straight and assured the Governor of their loyalty to King and country. They referred to the previous memorial sent to Sir Robert Boyd, the Governor in 1792, in which they had asked leave for freedom to worship God in their own way, which had been granted. Since then, not wishing to take the sacrament from a minister of the Established Church, they had chosen a person to administer it, but only to their own members, which they claimed was the practice elsewhere. They asked for permission to continue. The memorial was signed by John Byrn, a schoolmaster and local preacher, Robert Brand and Michael Caulfield, who were leaders of the Society.[21]

The outrage of the Garrison Chaplains at the Methodist practice of administering the Lord's Supper was understandable. The view of the Established Church was that only an ordained priest was authorised to do this and a similar controversy had also occurred in Britain. As already stated the early Methodist Societies were not intended to be separate from the Church of England and members were expected to attend services at their local parish church and to take communion there.

Sometimes they were not made welcome and eventually some exceptions were made. After Wesley's death in 1791, many Societies wanted greater independence and the Methodist Conference of 1795 laid down various regulations for the administration of the Lord's Supper. By this time

---

[19] G.G. Findlay and W.W. Holdsworth, *The History of the Wesleyan Methodist Missionary Society,* Epworth Press: London, 1921, vol. iv, pp.417-8.

[20] Blaze, op. cit., p.5.

[21] *Some account of the Opposition to the Religious Instruction of the Soldiers at Gibraltar,* Butterworth: London, 1805, pp.11-12.

Methodism was developing into a separate denomination with its own travelling preachers or ministers some of whom were now authorised to administer communion. As the Society in Gibraltar had no such preacher appointed to them, it is possible that the Methodist authorities in England would not themselves have been happy with their practice, although the Society was clearly well disciplined and concerned to do things properly.

An immediate reply to the memorial of October 1802 was sent, stating that the Governor did not want to interfere with their forms of worship, or privileges previously granted, as long as they continued 'to merit the same, by a correct and faithful adherence to the true spirit and tenets of the Christian religion.' The final sentence stated that the Governor did not wish that their 'meetings should be so much frequented by the military part of this garrison'.[22] Although this reply was somewhat guarded, the memorialists were encouraged by it as they were to be allowed to continue to worship in their own way. Wetherell was not happy with this outcome but there was little more that he could do.

After receiving the letter from the Governor, the work prospered and the chapel 'could not contain all that attended'.[23] About thirty members of the Queen's Regiment joined the Society despite a 'bitter persecution'. But almost as soon as the Duke of Kent had left Gibraltar in May 1803, the persecution increased and it seems that only the support of the Governors had kept it at bay. On 26 May 1803 Lieutenant-Colonel Ramsay, the commanding officer of the Queen's Regiment, issued the following regimental order:

> It having been observed, that a great number of the men are constantly attending the Methodist Meetings, and have induced the youngest boys of the regiment to do the same, Lieutenant-Colonel Ramsay is determined to put a stop to it; it will therefore be considered as a standing order of the regiment, that no man will ever attempt to preach, or attend the Methodist Meetings, or induce others to do the same, under pain of being tried for disobedience of orders, unless a particular permit is granted by the Commanding Officer.

On 29 May Major-General Barnett summoned John Byrn to his office and told him he was not to hold any more meetings, threatening him with prison and expulsion from the town if he did. On hearing this, Robert Brand with three friends went the same day to see Barnett, hoping he would change his mind. Brand described him as showing 'an overbearing tyrannical spirit which refuses to see reason', and he would not listen to anything they had to say. So a memorial was then sent to Sir Thomas Trigge giving the history of the dispute, and asking for permission to meet for worship. The answer came dated 3 June. No objection was made to the

---

[22] Ibid., p.13.
[23] Ibid., pp.15-9.

townsfolk meeting for worship, but he would not allow 'any assembly or association, of which the soldiers of the garrison, under his command, are to form a part. Mr Robert Brand's manner of speaking to Major-General Barnett is a strong reason against it, in addition to many others.'

Soldiers of various regiments therefore began to meet at the house of a man called Ballantine, but Colonel Ramsay issued a verbal order to his regiment forbidding any three Methodists from walking or talking together. Some of them wrote to him to protest and he sent for them, denying that he had made the order. When they asked for permission to meet together to read the Bible and pray he refused, but then said they could meet where they liked, but if Mr Byrn preached to them he would be sent to prison. They therefore joined the others at Ballantine's house and met there for five nights. On the sixth night, as they left, five of them were arrested. They were court-martialled the following day, 11 June 1803, charged with 'unsoldier-like conduct, in attending a Methodist Meeting, contrary to regimental orders'. The prisoners were Corporals James Lamb and Richard Russell and Privates James Hampton, John Reeves and John Fluccard, one of whom was only fourteen years old. At the hearing, Sergeant-Major Wright, who had arrested the men, explained that when he had asked James Hampton what he had been doing, he had answered that 'he had been to meeting', which was hardly the reply of a man with something to hide. The prisoners all acknowledged this, saying that they had received the Colonel's verbal permission. He denied giving this and, according to Robert Brand, any further attempts by the prisoners to speak in their own defence were halted by the words 'Hold your tongues, we don't want you to preach to us.' The men were all found guilty and sentenced to five hundred lashes apiece with the two Corporals also being reduced to the ranks.

That same evening James Lamb and Richard Russell were reduced to the ranks and each received two hundred lashes. The rest of the sentences were suspended on condition that the men did not attend another Methodist meeting. Robert Brand's great distress at what had happened comes over strongly in his account of events and he claimed that Colonel Ramsay had gone to the guardhouse before the trial and told the corporals that 'he certainly would flog them'. It does not sound like a fair trial. It was the usual procedure for the convening of a court martial to be announced in Garrison Orders. An account of the proceedings followed with the sentence given, which the Governor then either confirmed or altered. If the sentence was a flogging then notice of this too was given, as such punishments were usually carried out on the Grand Parade 'in the presence of the whole of the detachment for guard'.[24] There is no mention whatever of the Methodist court martial in Garrison Orders which does suggest that it was a very hole-in-the-corner affair, especially as the floggings were

---

[24] Garrison Orders, WO284, vol. 13.

carried out the same evening.

Information concerning these events reached England and, on 9 November 1803, Joseph Butterworth, Secretary of the Methodist General Committee, wrote to the Rt Hon. Charles Bragge, Secretary at War, 'to submit a remonstrance upon some late proceedings, which have infringed upon the liberty of conscience'.[25] An acknowledgement of the letter was sent on 11 November indicating that the matter had been referred to his Royal Highness, the Commander-in-Chief. There appears, however, to have been no further correspondence. The Government was very much involved in the Napoleonic war against the French and, no doubt, religious affairs in Gibraltar were not felt to be of national significance. In addition, Methodist missionary work was not yet well organised which may also have hindered the matter from being pursued.

It was Dr Thomas Coke who developed the missionary work. He had become an Anglican priest in 1772. He then met, and was influenced by, a number of Methodists before he finally met Wesley himself in August 1776. Shortly after this, he was forced to leave his parish and he then joined the Methodists. Coke worked closely with Wesley himself as his assistant, and Wesley acknowledged his evangelical zeal by commissioning him to 'go out, and preach the Gospel to all the world.'[26] The work overseas had already begun to develop mainly in America and the West Indies which Coke visited as often as he could.

When Wesley died in 1791, Coke was in America and, on hearing the news, he hurried back to England. The years following Wesley's death were somewhat turbulent and Coke was very much involved with British Methodism. He served as Secretary of the Conference for a number of years and as President in both 1797 and 1805. He was also often appointed as President of the Irish Conference. Yet, despite these commitments, Coke still continued to oversee all the missionary work. He was aware of the situation in Gibraltar and at the Conferences of 1798 and 1800 enquiries were made to see if any preacher was willing to go there, but it seems that no-one could be found.

In 1804 Conference appointed a Committee of Finance and Advice to oversee the missionary work. This consisted of all the London preachers with Coke as President. Since the preachers changed from time to time and Coke was often away, it was hard for the Committee to be efficient. In addition some tension was bound to occur because Coke was used to dealing with missionary affairs on his own. Although he was given the power of making final decisions, at times he found it irksome to have to go through the Committee. It was before this Committee that 'all letters and communications whatever from the Missionaries shall be laid from time to

---

[25] *Opposition to the Religious Instruction of the Soldiers*, op. cit., pp.25-34.
[26] Findlay & Holdsworth, op. cit., vol. ii, p.14.

time, and their advice taken upon the same.'[27]   So from autumn 1804, letters from Gibraltar were placed before the Committee but before this, in February 1804, Brand had written to report the state of the Society.

There had been no further trouble but they were still obliged to turn away the soldiers from the chapel.   Some were meeting at a friend's house and a few more had joined them.   The meetings were not known to the authorities.   A few of the inhabitants attended the chapel but Brand felt there was little prospect of achieving much amongst them.   He went on to say, 'You will judge what our feelings are, in being obliged to turn away our friends from the means of grace, and in being prevented from preaching to the only people who are willing to hear.'[28]   Byrn was still under the threat of imprisonment and banishment if he preached to the soldiers and they felt nothing would change while General Barnett remained in Gibraltar.

In view of these continuing difficulties, a minister was once again sought for Gibraltar.   The Rev. James McMullen, from Ireland, volunteered his services.   It is likely that Coke, through his connections with Ireland, recruited him.   He had been accepted on trial as a travelling preacher in 1788.   By 1804 he had had twelve different appointments in Ireland and had served as Chairman of the District in Dublin and Cork.   He sailed for Gibraltar in August 1804 with his wife Susanna and their little daughter Annie.

---

[27] Ibid., vol. i, p.68.
[28] *Opposition to the Religious Instruction of the Soldiers*, op. cit., pp.35-6.

CHAPTER 3 MINISTERIAL OVERSIGHT
The Building of Providence Chapel (1804 -11)

After all the persecution and the long wait for a minister, the beleaguered Society in Gibraltar awaited the arrival of James and Susanna McMullen with considerable hope and expectation.   However, their passage out proved both difficult and dangerous as a severe storm forced the ship to take shelter in a bay off the African shore.   They survived the storm and arrived in Gibraltar on Sunday 17 September, in some relief, believing that all danger was past.   However, on landing, they discovered Gibraltar to be in the grip of a yellow fever epidemic which had broken out in August in a tenement near the garrison library.   By September it had spread throughout the town.   McMullen described events in a letter to Dr Coke dated 1 October 1804;

> The disorder ran through the garrison like an armed man, whose footsteps are marked with certain death.   The streets were cleansed, the garrison guns were fired again and again; fires, by the Governor's orders, were lighted in the streets and lanes: and all this to purify the air.   The garrison was drained of vinegar, the dock-yard was whitewashed with lime slaked with vinegar, which deprived the inhabitants of this useful article.   The garrison was removed to camps, pitched among the rocks, and along the sea shore, the mortality being dreadful among them, nor did this measure appear to retard its progress.   Rain, which used to pour down in torrents at this season, was now withheld, and all appearance of it vanished; and instead thereof, a constant blaze of sun, and a fiery atmosphere, parched up all our juices.   To heighten our misfortunes, the water of the garrison failed; so that that indispensable article of life could not be had unless it was fetched more than a mile.... provisions are very scarce.... This day we had to make a dinner of a little barley boiled, and God only knows whether we shall be able to get that to-morrow, for the shops are all closed up.... My little child was seized with the disorder about five days after we landed.   As we could get no house (except we would go into a house deserted or emptied by the plague,) I was in a friend's house, [Michael Caulfield] when my child was taken ill.   What an hour of distress!   A stranger without an habitation! my child ill of the plague, and myself and wife expecting to be obliged to take up our lodging to abide in under a rock! For I could not hope that any one would suffer me his house, at almost certainty of infecting his own family.   Yet I had no sooner intimated my purpose of departure, than my affectionate host declared I should not stir; that he would run all risks, as also did his kind wife.   Such an instance of friendship, I believe, is very rare.   The captain, with whom I sailed, has sent me word, if my family be in health, he will take me on board; but my family is not in health.   My child is but just able to creep about, and my wife complains of a pain in her head to-day, which is the first symptom of the disease....

Our Society here consists of only twelve, three of whom have been carried off in a few days. Many of the soldiers were in the society, but dare not come to meet. I waited on Sir Thomas Trigge, as is the custom, to inform him, that I meant to reside some time in the garrison; he received me with courtesy. I had a note from him, informing me, that the Health Committee judged it necessary to shut all places of worship, lest the infection should be communicated by large numbers assembling together. In this note he submitted the measure to my own consideration. I knew the orders were general; therefore complied, but obtained liberty for a select number to meet in a private house. From the courtesy of both the notes, and my reception, I hope I shall be able to obtain liberty for the soldiers, if God's hand should be removed, and myself be spared. But at present none will assemble together. Indeed our friends cannot spare an hour from the sick and dying. This day we have observed as a day of fasting and prayer in our respective houses. Where this awful desolation will end, God only knows![1]

The real horror of this situation is hard to imagine. Benady, quoting from contemporary accounts of events, described how carts were stationed outside the Spanish church to receive the bodies, which were then taken to the neutral ground for burial in pits dug every morning by the soldiers.[2] Often bodies were left in the streets and were picked up as the carts passed by. Hundreds of people were buried in this way and it was impossible to keep an accurate account of names and numbers.

James McMullen soon developed the fever himself and died on Wednesday 17 October. It is clear from his obituary that he had suffered ill health before because he was described as 'truly disinterested in worldly views, labouring with his hands, without burdening the Connexion when unable to travel through debility of body'.[3] He had been a minister for sixteen years. Caulfield wrote,

It appears to me, it is not the will of God his gospel should be preached here, where it has been so long rejected; for besides Mr McMullen, two of the three local preachers, four more of the society, (inhabitants) as also several of the pious soldiers, have been taken off. The writer of this was taken from the very gates of death, he believes, in answer to the very faithful prayers of Mr McMullen, in order to pay some little attention to dear sister McMullen, in her now most unpleasant situation, occasioned by want of even the common necessaries of life. It is entirely impossible to describe the distress; it is only known to God and the sufferers.[4]

Although Susanna McMullen appeared at first to have only a slight touch

---

[1] *Methodist Magazine,* vol. xxviii, 1805, p.93.

[2] Sam Benady, *Civil Hospital and Epidemics in Gibraltar*, Gibraltar Books Ltd.: Northants-Gibraltar, 1994, pp.75-6.

[3] *Minutes of the Methodist Conference*, vol. ii, 1805, p.270.

[4] *Methodist Magazine*, vol. xxxiv, 1805, p.94.

of fever, she died on Sunday 28 October. The McMullen's daughter, Annie, who was seven years old survived. Caulfield planned to leave Gibraltar and return to Ireland, his native land, taking the little girl to a Mrs Morris of Waterford as requested by her mother.[5] However, he must have changed his mind about leaving and it is not certain who, if anyone, accompanied the child back to England. In April 1805 the Committee commended Michael Caulfield's care of all the McMullens and decided it was 'best that Miss McMullen who is now at Mrs Tyler's should remain in London till Dr Coke go to Ireland.'[6] It is not clear if Annie ever did go to Ireland. She became Dr Coke's ward and was given some financial support by the Committee. On Coke's death Dr Adam Clarke gave her a home and treated her like one of his own daughters. She wrote some years later of his loving heart and thanked God for him. Her parents' effects had been packed into a trunk and kept at City Road. It was not until Annie was grown-up that she was taken to look into the trunk as fear of yellow fever had prevented anyone opening it earlier. She later obtained a post as a governess and she married John Harrison Rigg, a Methodist minister, in 1818. One of their sons, James Rigg, also became a Methodist minister serving twice as the President of Conference. Annie died at Southport on 3 June 1869 at the age of 72.

Under the circumstances, McMullen had been able to achieve very little in the few short weeks of his ministry in Gibraltar. He seems to have made a favourable impression on the Governor but had no opportunity to plead for soldiers' rights. He baptised Samuel James Caulfield on 23 September, the son of Michael and Sophia, which forms the first entry in the baptismal register. He preached twice in the Caulfield's house because the chapel had been closed. Of the twenty people or so at the meetings, eight had died including Brand and Byrn. Corporal James Lamb, Henry Ince's son, Thomas, and Major-General Barnett were also among the dead. The *Gibraltar Chronicle*, which ceased publication when the epidemic was at its height, did not re-appear until Saturday 23 March 1805. In that issue the total number of deaths was given as 5,946. It had not been possible to name all those buried by the chaplain, but the burials register at the King's Chapel includes the words: 'The Reader will see what dreadful havoc has been made in this small place - but of the misery that accompanied this scene of desolation, no one, without being an actual witness, can form an idea.'

The whole of Gibraltar was devastated by the epidemic fever and it is clear from the newspaper articles that the cause, spread and treatment of the fever was not understood. Those who now remained in the little Methodist Society struggled to understand how God could have allowed such a thing to happen. Thomas Davis, the only remaining local preacher, wrote in

---

[5] Ibid., p.95.
[6] *WMMS Home and General Minutes 1798-1837*, fiche 1.

December 1804,

> Our dear and Rev. Mr McMullen was received with thankfulness and
> with great expectations of much good being done by him but this the
> Lord thought fit to disappoint us in ... and we know not if we ever can
> so expect another blessing of this nature from Britain. But the will of
> God be done.[7]

Davis had written to the Governor for permission to re-open the chapel.
This had been granted 'under the usual restrictions of not allowing the
soldiers to meet with us, nor encouraging them to attend Divine Service in
that place'. Under these restrictions, meetings were carrying on through the
week and Davis tried to preach twice on a Sunday. He reported that the
congregations were 'truly small' but that they hoped for better things when
the new Governor arrived.

The new Governor was Lieutenant-General the Honourable Henry
Edward Fox. On 4 January 1805 a memorial was sent to him signed by
Thomas Davis, Michael Caulfield and Zachary Ledger, asking for the
restrictions to be lifted and for the soldiers to be allowed to worship at the
chapel.[8] The Governor sent for the three men and gave them full liberty to
carry on their meetings, adding that he did not wish them to turn a single
soldier out of the chapel, 'as long as they conducted themselves properly'.
This news was transmitted to London by Davis who felt there was 'now
every prospect of doing good'. However, he hoped another minister would
be sent as he was 'the only person left to speak to them of the things of
God; and my time is much occupied in secular concerns.' He reported that
the chapel had been put 'into decent order, by whitewashing, painting etc.
and the army, and some of the inhabitants begin to crowd our meetings, so
that we have a comfortable prospect of much good being done, May God
grant it.'[9]

Meanwhile Britain, France and Spain were still occupied with war but in
Gibraltar there were good relations between General Fox and the Spanish
General Castaños. In late 1806 Fox was succeeded by General Sir Hew
Dalrymple who maintained this friendship. It was even possible for the
inhabitants of Gibraltar to obtain permission to travel into nearby Spain.
However, in October 1807, the Spanish were given orders from Madrid to
close the border. Spanish resentment against the French domination of
their country began to grow and, in May 1808, the people of Madrid
rebelled. The rest of Spain followed suit, but this only marked the
beginning of a long struggle and, by December 1808, the French had
occupied Madrid and were pushing south. British help was sought and

---

[7] *WMMS Correspondence Gibraltar, 1804-1902.* Davis to Committee, 6 December 1804,
fiche 635, no.1.
[8] *Opposition to the Religious Instruction of the Soldiers*, op. cit., pp.46-8.
[9] Ibid., pp.46-8.

Gibraltar became an important and busy port, repairing ships, and replenishing stores at the New Naval Victualling Yard at Rosia Bay which was built in 1808. The Rock proved a useful base for aiding the Spanish until Napoleon was finally defeated.

During these years, despite their lack of a minister, the little Methodist Society carried on its work. In 1806 the Committee received a letter from Gibraltar 'informing us that the Society have renewed the lease of their Chapel, speaking of a prospect of good and entreating the Committee to send a Missionary'.[10] It was agreed that the Secretary would reply saying that 'they may expect a Missionary, if a proper person can be found', but once again this seems to have proved a difficult task. In the same year the following annual report on the work in Gibraltar was given to the Conference:

> This impregnable Rock is of vast importance in a religious view. The Missionary, who may be stationed here, must not expect much of the honour which comes from man. For when, under the blessing of God, he has formed a large Society, they may, on a sudden, be ordered to another part of the world; and he may have to begin a new work, perhaps among a new people. But when we consider that, by these means, the divine fire may be scattered through all the quarters of the globe, the object rises very high in its value! One missionary would, probably, be always sufficient; but the expense might be considerable, as every thing there is so very dear ... the Superintendent and Committee have it deeply at heart to find out a proper person for this important post. We have, at present, a small Society and a good congregation, composed chiefly, of the military. The preachers are soldiers. But many of the proper inhabitants say, that they will sit constantly under the preaching of the gospel, if we send them a regular minister.[11]

In March 1804 the British and Foreign Bible Society, known today as the Bible Society, was formed in London with the aim of supplying Bibles and New Testaments, without note or comment, on a world-wide basis. In 1807 the Society supplied Bibles to Gibraltar. It is not clear how the contact was initially made as the whole correspondence has not survived, but Joseph Butterworth, a Methodist who supported Methodist missionary work, was also on the Bible Society's Committee and was probably the link.

The earliest surviving letter, dated 10 November 1807, is from Joseph Tarn of the Bible Society to Davis and Caulfield. This referred to sending out 600 English Bibles and Testaments, plus 200 Spanish Testaments, and also mentioned a previous consignment of 500 Spanish Testaments. Instructions regarding distribution were given as follows:

---

[10] *WMMS Home and General Minutes,* fiche 1.
[11] *WMMS Reports,* vol. i, 1789-1820, 1806, p.19.

The Committee having the fullest confidence in your zeal and fidelity, have taken the liberty of placing the above at your disposal; the English Scriptures for the Garrison or for Troops or Seamen who may occasionally touch at your Port, and the Spanish Testaments for distribution among the Spaniards with whom you may have opportunities of communicating.[12]

Free distribution was allowed, but it was suggested that recipients would value the books more if they had paid something for them and that the Spanish would then be more likely to keep them from their priests. The 500 Spanish Testaments arrived in mid-March 1808 but as Davis and Caulfield explained,

... since October 1807 all communication between this Garrison and Spain by land has been entirely cut off unless by a flag of truce, which will effectually deprive us of the opportunity of forwarding anything in the Book way there at present, but have hope that we may be able to meet with some of the masters of the small craft which frequently arrive here who will be prevailed with to accept some of them gratuitously. The foreigners in the Garrison we have reason to believe will purchase many of them, as we have already had an order for fifteen ... [13]

The second consignment of books arrived on 28 April and Davis and Caulfield called a few friends together to discuss plans for distributing them. By June 1808 the problems at the border were easing and it did prove possible to get some scriptures into Spain, but in August Davis and Caulfield reported that there was 'little probability of much good being done with the Spanish Testaments till things are in a more settled state'.[14] In a postscript to the letter they wrote: 'Please mention to Mr Butterworth that our minister is safely arrived with us.'

A minister, William Griffith, had finally been appointed to Gibraltar. He was born in 1777 and towards the end of the century had become a Methodist. In 1801 he became associated with the 'Community' in London which was a Christian association formed for work among the poor, in particular through visiting the workhouses. Dr Coke encouraged him to offer for missionary work and he was appointed to Gibraltar. He was not at this time a travelling preacher though probably was a local preacher. He set sail with his wife, Ann, and their young son, William, in June 1808. Their accommodation on board ship was not good, the voyage was slow and their water supply nearly failed. Ann Griffith suffered from seasickness and was also nearing the end of a pregnancy. They were both anxious in case she went into labour during the voyage. However, they arrived safely on the Sunday afternoon of 16 July 1808 and were 'gladly

---

[12] Tarn to Davis & Caulfield, 10 November 1807, *Miscellaneous Book no.2*, p.127.

[13] *Home Correspondence In,* Davis & Caulfield, 17 March 1808.

[14] Ibid., Davis & Caulfield, 8 August, 1808.

received by Brother Davis and the Society who were the more thankful as they had entirely given up all hopes of a Preacher at least for the moment', which implies that word of the appointment had not reached Gibraltar.[15] The following day they went to stay with Zachary Ledger and a son, Samuel, was born there on 23 July.

Griffith felt that 'the work of God in this place is at a low ebb'. The Society numbered thirty-six, mostly soldiers, and few others attended services for there were many other attractive diversions particularly on a Sunday. Griffith visited most of the Society and described three classes. These were a Friday men's class which met at the chapel, a Monday women's class and a further class of soldiers who met in a cave about two miles from the chapel 'as they cannot attend with us'. The reason for this was not given. They were led by a 'pious man of the regiment'. Griffith met with them but shortly afterwards they received embarkation orders and left Gibraltar, diminishing the Society even further.

The work of distributing the scriptures continued and Griffith soon also became involved in this as Davis and Caulfield reported:

> A few days since our minister Mr Griffith taking a few of the Testaments to market where the Spaniards mostly resort, he offered one of them to a man who at first declined accepting it thinking he wished him to purchase it, but when he found he might have it gratuitously he received it and went from one to another showing it who in their turn applied to Mr Griffith that they might have one also. He went for twelve more which he soon distributed and numbers of people followed him to our chapel, where in consequence of not being able to converse with them, he was obliged to lock himself in till they dispersed, a number of whom attended in the evening. Next day being Sunday we had no sooner opened our chapel than they began to flock in, many of them remained during the sermon, after which we supplied them that were present, but the members of our church having been detained to partake of the Lord's Supper and those who had received books having informed their acquaintances, our house was so surrounded with men, women and children that we were obliged to open the door and let them continue while we were engaged in that ordinance, after which we distributed Spanish Testaments as far as we could, and it gives us pleasure to say they received them with the greatest eagerness.[16]

Links were also made with a Captain Gourly of the Royal Navy who stated, 'This unsettled way of life has given me many, very many opportunities of scattering the Scriptures far and wide.'[17] Supplies for him were sometimes sent to Gibraltar. He worked closely with Griffith and Davis, although he was not a Methodist, saying 'we are fellow servants and

---

[15] *WMMS Correspondence*, Griffith to Committee, 8 August 1808, fiche 635, no.2.

[16] *Home Correspondence In,* Davis & Caulfield, 16 November 1808.

[17] Ibid., Captain Gourly, 30 September 1809.

have one master and his glory is our chief desire.'[18]

Griffith soon realised that the Society's main need was for a proper place for worship as services were being held in

> ... a kind of temporary shed, the sides of which are formed of boards, and the roof of canvas; but being only nine feet in height, and contracted in its limits, it is neither wholesome nor commodious. In addition to this, the passage which leads to it is frequently blocked up with materials belonging to other buildings, or with lumber, which proves a great annoyance to the people. Above all our holding in it will expire in 1811.[19]

The £120 chapel had served its purpose and it was time to build a new and bigger one and to build a Mission House to provide a home for the missionary and his family. The report went on to say, 'to accomplish this, we have reason to believe that we can procure a spot of land in a convenient place'. Financial help from 'our wealthy friends in England' was sought and local people were already promising to help. The Society was growing. Membership had increased to forty and the Sunday congregation had nearly doubled, with the week-night congregation nearly quadrupled since the previous year. Many soldiers were unable to attend the services in the chapel 'being prevented by the rules of military discipline from leaving their quarters at the regular hours of worship.' Griffith had therefore been preaching to them weekly 'at a place called the South', which was out towards Europa.

It was necessary first to seek permission to obtain the land. A memorial was therefore sent to the Governor, now General Sir John Craddock, which was transmitted to the Secretary of State in London on 7 July 1809, requesting permission to lease land for the purpose of building a chapel and a house. However, a favourable reply was clearly expected as on the same day a document confirming the 'assignment of property from Francis Fau, Ann Fau and Luigi Danino to Thomas Davis, Zacharias Ledger and William Griffith' was signed by General Craddock, subject to the terms and conditions of the original lease.[20]

The land in question was situated on Prince Edward's Road and covered an area of 1,889 square feet. Permission from London to purchase and build was finally received in Gibraltar on 25 September and Griffith 'immediately opened a subscription towards the expense of the buildings'.[21] He reported: 'Besides our own Society, several of the inhabitants who at present have no connection with us, have contributed liberally. A Roman Catholic gave us 15 doubloons or £54 - another two. And I doubt not

---

[18] Ibid., Captain Gourly, 7 July 1809.
[19] *WMMS Report*, 1809, p.22.
[20] File Mark no.542 & Letters Patent 13.
[21] Thomas Coke, 23 October 1809, PLP/28/17/16.

others will yet further assist us in the work.' On 29 November 1809, the Governor, now Major General Sir Colin Campbell, granted formal permission for the work to go ahead subject to two conditions.[22] Firstly, that if the land was 'demanded for the service of Government' it would be handed over without any compensation though the Society would have the right to remove any building materials. Secondly, that at the expiration of the lease, (on 1 January 1829) the chapel and the ground would become the property of His Majesty. These were similar to the conditions laid down in most leases of the day so the Society had little choice but to accept them. Nevertheless, it seems a risky undertaking to commit so much money to so uncertain a future.

On 24 January 1810 Griffith reported that 'the work is begun and I expect the first stone to be laid tomorrow'. No exact accounting of the expense involved has survived but it was more than the local Society could afford. All possible sources of financial help were approached and in February 1810 Davis wrote to the Bible Society.

> I sincerely thank you in the name of the little church here for the active part you have taken in our behalf with Mr Butterworth, and also for your kind contribution towards the chapel which is going on fast, and will be completed in a very few months if all things continue as they now are, but would thank you to say to Mr Butterworth as from me, that yesterday we had a meeting and that after doing our utmost we find that we are about 950 dollars [about £143] short of our first payment, which will become due about Monday next, which sum we have been forced to borrow on interest and that in less than one month from this date, we expect the second payment will become due which we will have to borrow in like manner, and at a much higher rate (as cash is very dear here at present) unless we have remittances from England.[23]

He hoped, once the chapel and house were completed and the work better established, that collections and monetary contributions would enable them to defray the expenses of the preacher without depending on income from England. He apologised for 'speaking so freely to you on this subject for that you do not belong to the same branch of Christ's Church that we profess to belong to, yet sir, you have the one common cause at heart, and will I hope use all your influence in our favour.'

The work in Gibraltar was discussed at the Methodist Conference of 1810 when it was agreed that Gibraltar would be considered a regular circuit under the same regulations as circuits in Britain. The sum of £500 was granted from Mission funds towards the building costs but, even so, there was still a shortfall and the consequent debt was a great burden to the

---

[22] File Mark no.542 & Letters Patent 13.
[23] *Home Correspondence In,* Davis, 26 February 1810.

Society for many years.[24]

The old chapel was sold and the new one was finished by the summer and named Providence Chapel. On 27 June 1811 Ann Griffith was born at the Mission House. She was baptised by her father in Providence Chapel on 14 July. Griffith performed his last baptism in Gibraltar on 11 August 1811 and some time after this, he and his family returned to England where he was ordained. Griffith became a supernumerary in 1850 and died on 24 February 1860 in his eighty-third year.

Griffith's successor did not immediately follow him, but presumably Davis and Caulfield supervised the work, as they had before, until he arrived.

---

[24] *Minutes of the Methodist Conference*, vol. iii, 1810, p.155.

CHAPTER 4   GROWTH AND CONSOLIDATION
Tension and Division (1812 -21)

The new missionary, James Gill, had been accepted on trial as a travelling preacher in 1795 and Gibraltar was his twelfth appointment. He was advised to delay his departure because of fears about the plague in Cartagena and so he did not leave Portsmouth until Christmas Day. Unfortunately, sailing at this time of year meant a stormy passage was more likely and Catharine Gill was extremely seasick throughout the voyage. Whilst still off the coast of England, she begged her husband to take her ashore and to 'make no other attempt for Gibraltar', but the seas were running too high to make this possible.[1]

James Gill

They arrived in Gibraltar on 9 January 1812 and found to their anger and dismay that the house was empty of all furniture; the plaster on the walls and ceiling had fallen down and they felt that the house was very badly planned as the stairs were outside and they had to go out of doors to go to bed. Gill engaged a mason and carpenters to make some alterations. He also bought furniture, insisting that he had only bought absolute necessities, but prices were high and altogether it proved a costly business. Although Gill expected help from London with these expenses, it is unlikely that assistance was given as the local debt was considerably increased. Gill also wished that they had brought an English girl with them as a servant, because local wages were very high and 'it is impossible to do without one in this hot country'.

Gill reported that Griffith had been much respected and had done much in building the chapel and house, although he felt the chapel was very small. He also referred to 'a dreadful battle fought at Tarifa a small distance from us a few days before we came'. The French were still fighting the Spanish and in January 1810 the old Spanish lines, forts and batteries at Gibraltar had all been dismantled and destroyed to prevent the French making use of them. The French reached San Roque a few days later and, by the end of February 1810, only Cádiz, Tarifa and Gibraltar had escaped French occupation. The Governor of Gibraltar, Sir Colin Campbell, sent help in the defence of Tarifa which resulted in a French withdrawal, but two British officers were killed in the action. In April

---

[1] *WMMS Correspondence*, Gill to Committee, 30 January 1812, fiche 635, no.4.

1812 Gibraltar's troops returned to the Rock with the thanks of the Spanish. Gradually the French withdrew from Andalucia and by the summer of 1812 they had left the area of Gibraltar altogether. When the Napoleonic Wars ended in 1815, Gibraltar began to enjoy more peaceable times with friendlier relations with Spain.

Contact with the Bible Society continued. Shortly after his arrival Gill was asked to make enquiries about the language used in the Spanish version. He began to learn Spanish; made 'enquiries of some respectable Spanish gentlemen', and also purchased a Spanish Bible, printed in Madrid, to compare with the Society's version.[2] He concluded that the Society's Bible contained some inappropriate language and needed improving. Gill was also involved in the work of distribution which he felt 'has been a principal cause in this place of the success of my mission'.[3] Once word went out that he had books for distribution his 'house was crowded with soldiers, soldiers' wives and soldiers' children, pressing upon each other with the greatest eagerness, to obtain the sacred volume.' Many soldiers after receiving them became 'regular attendants on the ministry of the word, and were reformed in their conduct.' Gill estimated that there were about 5,000 troops in Gibraltar with about 300 Bibles among them. He therefore wanted more to distribute particularly the pocket Bibles, which were a more convenient size. He gave scriptures to the crews of ships, placed them in different barracks, supplied the hospital, the orphan house, the guard houses, the Signal House, the Regimental schools, and regiments leaving Gibraltar, as well as individuals and families. Some Spanish, Portuguese, Italian, Arabic, German, French and Welsh books were also distributed.[4]

During this time there was further anxiety about yellow fever. There had not been an epidemic for several years, although a few cases were reported in 1810, but in 1813 an epidemic claimed the lives of 883 civilians and 461 soldiers. In a moving account Gill described how Catharine fell ill in September with a feverish cold. She then developed yellow fever and became so ill she was not expected to recover. Their servant was ill and left them. 'Our friends in the south with their families, were ordered into the dock-yard, to prevent their communication with the garrison, and the soldiers' wives being prohibited going into the house of an inhabitant, I could receive no assistance from them; and persons in health were afraid of approaching the sick.'[5] It was Caulfield, 'that good man', who came to their aid with his sister-in-law but then she too became ill, as did her mother, and much of Caulfield's time was taken up in nursing them. For a while Gill was without help until a Mr Gillfilang, a member of the Society,

---

[2] Gill, 19 September 1812, *Correspondence Book No. 5,* pp.14-9.
[3] Ibid., Gill, 16 September 1812, pp.28-32.
[4] *Home Correspondence In,* Gill, 17 September 1814.
[5] *Methodist Magazine,* vol. XXXVII, May 1814, p.386

came to his aid. Then Gill caught the fever himself but thankfully was less seriously affected and he was very grateful that they had the best of medical care from Dr Gilpin, the Deputy Inspector of the Hospital, who had travelled to Gibraltar on the same ship as the Gills. Their friendship, which had developed on shipboard, had continued in Gibraltar. Thankfully both the Gills did recover.

Gibraltar itself was much affected by the epidemic and for thirteen weeks all churches were closed and so there were no services, prayer meetings or class meetings. Finally, on 12 December, the churches were re-opened for a day of thanksgiving that the outbreak was over and Gill reported the chapel to be well attended. Only a few members had died but several had fallen away and the chapel finances were also much affected. However, it seems that Methodism gained greater recognition and acceptance at this time as the Missionary Report for 1815 recorded that 'His Majesty's government has allowed our missionary, for a limited time, two rations from the king's stores, which will prove very useful, especially in cases of fever, siege, or war with Spain'.

The Gills left Gibraltar on 7 July 1814 on the transport brig *Sceptre* and landed at Deal on 6 August. Once again Catharine suffered from severe seasickness and so they travelled along the coast to Portsmouth, their next appointment, in easy stages. James Gill never served abroad again and fulfilled a further twelve appointments, serving on several occasions as Chairman of the District. His last two appointments were as a supernumerary, but he continued to be 'diligent in preaching and pastoral visiting till within three months of his decease.'[6] He died on 1 May 1844 at the age of 74.

The Gills had been able to meet their successors, Benjamin and Esther Wood, who had arrived in Gibraltar on 28 June 1814 after a voyage lasting twenty-three days. Benjamin was born near Sheffield in 1784. As a child he worshipped in the Established Church but at the age of seventeen he heard Methodist preaching and eventually became a travelling preacher himself being accepted on trial in 1806 and serving in Shaftesbury before being posted to Gibraltar. It is perhaps remarkable that he and his wife were willing to go to Gibraltar at all because they arrived in what was, by then, acknowledged to be the fever season. Wood expressed their anxiety about this in his first letter from the Rock, but felt it was right to have undertaken the work.[7] On arrival they were given a 'kind reception'. Few soldiers were attending the chapel but Wood reported that it 'was well attended by attentive and respectable inhabitants'.

In August 1814 fever did break out. Spain immediately placed Gibraltar under quarantine and various measures aimed at combating the spread of the disease were enforced. These included an order to close the chapel,

---

[6] *Minutes of the Methodist Conference*, vol. x, 1844, pp.12-13.
[7] *WMMS Correspondence*, Wood to Committee, 8 October 1814, fiche 635, no.7.

along with other places of worship. A number of 'respectable inhabitants not as yet members of our Society' attempted to find the Woods a safe place to live in Spain, but they were prevented from going there by the quarantine. They went instead to a bay nearly two miles from the Garrison, probably Catalan Bay which Wood reported had been unaffected by the previous epidemics. There was some criticism of his move to a safer area, but Wood felt that most people approved and he himself felt it was the right thing to do.

On 5 November they were allowed to re-open the chapel and the Woods returned to town. In all 114 troops and 132 inhabitants had died, considerably less than in the previous epidemics, but Wood reported that Gibraltar's economy was affected and that 'every branch of business has been nearly at a stand'.[8] This was also due to Ferdinand VII's 'rigorous measures to prevent British manufactures from being imported into Spain', introduced partly to combat smuggling. The economic situation affected the financial state of the Society. The chapel debt stood at $4,500, about £675. Local income was not sufficient to pay the interest on the loan and the preacher. Wood had to ask for help from London with his own expenses, particularly the £3 12s a month paid to a wet nurse as Esther Wood had been too ill to feed their daughter, Harriet, born on 21 November 1814. They had, however, begun to receive rations from the Government stores. The church drew up a strategy for dealing with the chapel debt, but it was unlikely to be successful because of the limited local resources.

Links with the Bible Society continued, helped by Mrs Caroline Nicklin, a shopkeeper, who supported the work by sending an annual subscription and by distributing scriptures through her shop.[9] On 20 January 1815 the Rev. Dr Symons wrote to the Bible Society from Portsmouth where he was about to embark for Gibraltar to serve as a chaplain there. He had discovered that on board the ship were some cases of Bibles destined for Wood. He wrote,

> I think it right to inform the Committee that there are at Gibraltar two clergymen of the Established Church - Government chaplains - either of whom would be happy to distribute these Bibles - I am at this time on the point of embarkation to succeed the Rev. M. Hughes as chaplain to the garrison and shall have great pleasure in distributing the Bibles now about to be sent there.[10]

He therefore asked for Wood's Bibles to be placed at his disposal instead and the Bible Society complied with his request! Needless to say, Wood was not pleased with this decision and it hindered his work of distribution. The Bible Society explained that Dr Symons had been urged 'to use his

---

[8] Ibid., Wood to Committee3, 27 March 1815, fiche 635, no.9.
[9] *Home Correspondence In,* Nicklin, May 1814.
[10] Ibid., Rev. Dr Symons, 20 January 1815.

best exertions to promote the establishment of a Bible Society at Gibraltar'.[11] Perhaps it was felt that he would be in a more influential position than Wood to do this, but the Governor, General Don, would not allow a Bible Society to be formed, appearing to think that this would be provocative to the many staunch Roman Catholics. When Dr Symons left Gibraltar he left the majority of the Bibles at the garrison library. They were eventually taken into the care of the Methodists who were instructed by the Bible Society to distribute them 'as though they had been originally granted to you' which indeed they had![12]

Unfortunately, this was not the only occasion of dispute between the Methodists and the garrison chaplains at this time. On 25 September 1815 the Rev. Mr Mackereth refused to bury the child of Methodist parents as he did not consider the child's baptism to be valid. He also told the parents and Wood that he felt their actions over the baptism exposed them to the risk of expulsion from the garrison by the Governor. Wood therefore wrote to the Governor, to lay the matter before him, and sent copies of his letters to the Missionary Committee in London.[13] He argued that their baptismal registers had been recognised as legal and he linked the problem with the lack of a Methodist burial ground. In his previous appointments, the dead had been buried by clergymen of the Established Church for a fee, a perfectly satisfactory practice to all concerned, and one which he stated he would be quite happy to follow in Gibraltar. It is evident from the letters that the child's parents were caused great distress. Wood also reported that Dr Symons had come to 'brow beat' him, and had told Wood that the matter would be determined against him. The Governor appears to have forwarded copies of all relevant documents to London presumably for advice on what to do.

This problem had also arisen in England as Methodists began to perform their own baptisms. As late as 1840 an article appeared in the *Wesleyan Watchman* quoting a letter from an Anglican clergyman complaining about being expected to bury children baptised by Methodists.[14] The article however quoted the case of Wickes of 1811, when the court had stated that it was the duty of the parish minister to bury all persons dying within his parish unless they had been excommunicated, and also acknowledged the validity of baptisms by the laity.

During the summer of 1815 the Woods once again moved to the bay where they had stayed the previous year. They remained there for two months and Wood reported that 'the garrison has not been visited with the

---

[11] John Owen to Benjamin Wood, 13 February 1815, *Correspondence Book No.7*, pp.60-1.

[12] Ibid., Joseph Tarn to Davis, 20 March 1818, *No.10*, pp.12-3.

[13] *WMMS Correspondence*, Wood to Lieutenant Governor, 26 September 1815 and 9 October 1815 to the Committee 20 October 1815, fiches 635-6, nos. 11-13.

[14] *The Wesleyan Watchman,* vol. vi, 15 April 1840, p.126.

malignant fever this year thank God'.[15] In January 1816 another daughter, Mary, was born and the family left Gibraltar in July to return to England. After a further eleven appointments Wood became a supernumerary in Birmingham in 1845. For twenty more years he 'continued to work for Christ' though for the last ten years he 'was disabled from active service'.[16] He died on 17 September 1875 in his ninety-first year.

Meanwhile changes had been made to the management of Methodist Missions following the unexpected death of Thomas Coke in May 1813. In 1817 Conference approved a plan for a General Wesleyan Methodist Missionary Society with a Mission House in London as headquarters. The following year various laws and regulations governing the Society were adopted to provide a systematic and efficient plan for the support of foreign missions. A General Committee for the management of missions was appointed by Conference along with a General Treasurer and three General Secretaries, one of whom resided at the Mission House. From this time onwards the missionaries in Gibraltar corresponded directly with one or other of the General Secretaries. Their letters were then placed before the Committee for discussion, following which one of the Secretaries would write a reply. A missionary magazine, *Missionary Notices*, was also published with the aim of publicising Methodist missionary work around the world. Missionaries were expected to keep journals and quotations from these and their letters were often printed in the magazine, to encourage interest in the work and support for it through prayer and gifts of money.

The next minister to be appointed to Gibraltar was Thomas Davis. He had been accepted on trial in 1808 and, after several appointments, he was posted to Gibraltar and arrived in mid August 1816 with his wife Jane. He did not overlap with Wood who had left about a month before. It is a little confusing that he had the same name as Davis, the local preacher. Several days after his arrival he 'waited upon General Don and received strong marks of attention and kindness'. He went on to say, 'the General has been of very great use here' and he also proved to be a good support to the Methodist cause.[17]

Lieutenant-General Sir George Don was Lieutenant Governor from 1814 until he retired in 1831. Ellicott described him as 'The Father of Modern Gibraltar' and there is no doubt that he achieved a tremendous amount during his period of office.[18] The Duke of Kent was still officially Governor and when he died in 1820 the Earl of Chatham succeeded him. However, he did not spend much time in Gibraltar and Don was, in effect, in charge of Gibraltar's affairs until the Colonial Office appointed General

---

[15] *WMMS Correspondence,* Wood to Committee, 20 October 1815, fiche 636, no.13.

[16] *Minutes of the Methodist Conference,* vol. xx, 1876, p.11.

[17] *WMMS Correspondence,* Davis to Committee, undated, fiche 636.

[18] Dorothy Ellicott, *Our Gibraltar*, Gibraltar Museum Committee: 1975, p.106.

Sir William Houston to succeed him in May 1831.

Don's measures probably helped to lessen the incidence of fever after 1814. He improved the water supply and ordered the building of a sewage system. Commissioners for Paving and Scavenging were appointed, who levied a rate for the cost of paving, repairing and cleaning the streets and for making and repairing sewers and drains. Vaccination against smallpox was encouraged and a register was made of all civilian medical practitioners. Don set up a system of District Inspectors who, with the help of a Sergeant and Medical Officer, supervised conditions and reported disease. In the summer months he encouraged people to move out of the overcrowded town and he built a hospital for the civilian population. It was not only in the field of health that he brought about change and reform. In previous years British Governors had had little power over civilians other than to expel them from the garrison, but Don set up a Supreme Court which was empowered to try both civil and criminal cases. Alameda gardens were laid out, and the first garrison schools opened which the children of civilian inhabitants could attend on payment of a small fee. Some of Don's actions were less popular than others. He prohibited slave ships from fitting out at Gibraltar and also set up a Commission to settle the titles to land in Gibraltar.

At this time, only Protestants were allowed to own property. This measure had been taken to encourage Protestants to settle on the Rock, but it had led to Protestant nominees being used for property actually owned by Jews or Roman Catholics. Don's Commission caused anxiety in case titles were found to be invalid because everyone, including the Methodists, had to justify their claim to property. Davis reported that it had cost $90 to make the claim, and the person from whom they had purchased the lease also claimed it, but this claim was rejected and the matter was settled satisfactorily.[19] By 1825 all titles to property had been reviewed and confirmed and ownership of land was no longer limited to Protestants. It was also during General Don's period in office, in 1830, that the status of the Rock was changed from a garrison town to the Crown Colony of Gibraltar. This meant that from then on Gibraltar's affairs were the responsibility of the Colonial Office and not the War Office.

General Don also helped to provide another Protestant place of worship. The King's Chapel was not big enough for the inhabitants to worship with the garrison on Sundays and Don supported the building of Holy Trinity Church which began in 1825. It was completed in 1832 though it was not consecrated for a further six years. In 1842 it was designated a Cathedral. General Don did not live to see the church finished, but he is buried within it. As the Cathedral guide book says, 'it was fitting that he should be buried in front of the spot where the High Altar was to stand in the church

---

[19] *WMMS Correspondence*, Davis to Committee, 11 April 1818, fiche 636, no.25.

he had done so much to bring into existence.'[20]

It is not surprising therefore that Thomas Davis was so impressed with General Don. He described him as a 'very sensible, mild, active moral man', but did go on to say that it was 'a pity he should suffer the Lord's Day to be so dreadfully profaned'.[21] Sunday was the main market day and Davis felt Don could have stopped this trading if he had wanted to do so.

Davis had arrived in Gibraltar with considerable energy and enthusiasm. He wrote, 'I bless God for my appointment. Kind friends, prosperity in God's work, and plenty to do, with the Divine smile, this is sufficient to cause any man to rejoice'. He felt there were many proofs that the appointment was from God: 'favour in the eyes of the Governor and men in authority; the love of the little flock here; an additional number of hearers; above one hundred souls added to the society, many of whom are converted to God and a mind composed and thankful'.[22] The increase in numbers was clearly due to his energy and commitment to the task. He took every opportunity to meet with, and preach to, the soldiers. When a group of over a thousand black soldiers landed from St Kitts in early 1817, he obtained permission to visit them in their barracks. He asked for suitable tracts for them and hoped to arrange for other soldiers to go and read to them as few could read.

Davis made quite an impact on several regiments - the Royal Artillery, the 67th Regiment and notably the 26th Regiment of Foot. The head doctor and two captains of this Regiment came to the chapel, met with Davis in his home, and professed themselves keen to be involved. Indeed the doctor, Dr Coldstream, offered to treat Davis and his family free of expense during their stay. One convert from this regiment was Captain Tripp who first went to the Methodist chapel in the spring of 1817. At the beginning of the following year he made a firm step of commitment to faith in God and decided to speak at the first love-feast he ever attended in July 1818. These were special services when a simple meal was eaten, hymns were sung and money collected for the poor, but the most important aspect was the sharing of personal Christian testimony. Tripp was extremely nervous about speaking and prayed for strength to do so. He said, 'I think I never was more embarrassed. I had just power to speak, almost all I wished. However I sat down quite content and happy. The next day I enjoyed much heavenly favour'.[23] He was then twenty-seven years old.

In the summer of 1818 the army moved to camp on the neutral ground as a precaution against the fever. Tripp went with them and Davis preached to them weekly. In addition he had 'taken a room at the South of the Rock

---

[20] Dorothy Ellicott, *A Short History of the Cathedral*, no details, p.4.

[21] *WMMS Correspondence*, Davis to Committee, undated, fiche 636.

[22] *Missionary Notices*, vol. i, 1816-18, p.146 (quoting Davis's letters of 25 March & 10 April 1817).

[23] *WMMS Special Series (biographical) Europe*, fiche 13.

about two miles from our chapel in which a class of soldiers meet who could not get into the garrison in the evening as the gates are closed and the gun fires before they could return'.[24] Davis preached to them there once a week and also held regular prayer meetings. Thomas Davis, the local preacher, also visited them weekly when possible so that there was frequent preaching. Davis also encouraged the soldiers of the 26th Regiment to set up a small library through monthly subscriptions, recommending books to them and helping them to run it. The success of the work among the inhabitants was never as great as they had hoped. Nevertheless, in August 1817, membership was 102 consisting of 35 inhabitants and 67 military, the largest total so far recorded. In addition, the chapel was described as being well attended by a number of other 'respectable persons'.[25]

The work of Bible distribution continued and Davis also gave out religious tracts. He wrote,

> My common method of giving for tracts is to send them by the ship-boats, which come to water-port in our market, early in the morning. I have sent a good number of Spanish tracts into Spain, through those who come to our market out of Spain and by Spanish Boat-men.[26]

Concern about the chapel debt increased 'owing to the breaking up of the Dock-yard which has thrown most of our members out of employ'.[27] Times were very hard because of the low state of trade in Gibraltar and merchants were 'daily emigrating'.[28] However, the recession was short-lived for, when Spanish American colonies declared their independence and severed the trading links between Spain and South America, both sides used Gibraltar as a neutral port and 'the traffic was large and profitable'.[29] Davis was also due to lose his ration because of an order from England to issue no more rations to any except the army but General Don supported his case and, by the end of the year, he was allowed to draw one ration for the next twelve months, although this was a less valuable field ration.

Opposition from the garrison chaplains continued which Davis felt was partly because of the success of their mission. The chaplains claimed that he had no right to visit the hospital or baptise any child belonging to the army. However, Davis appealed to General Don who granted him full liberty to do these things, and Davis reported that, 'the chaplain is much lessened in the General's esteem by such unnecessary opposition.'[30] However, it seems that there were continuing problems over burials and so,

---

[24] *WMMS Correspondence,* Davis to Committee, 29 September 1818, fiche 637, no.31.

[25] Ibid., Leaders and Stewards to Committee, 25 August 1817, fiche 636, no.20.

[26] *Missionary Notices,* vol. i (1816-18), p.146 (quoting Davis's letter 10 April 1817).

[27] *WMMS Correspondence,* Davis to Committee, 16 February 1817, fiche 636, no.16.

[28] Ibid., Davis to Committee, 11 April 1818, fiche 637, no.25.

[29] William G.F. Jackson, *The Rock of the Gibraltarians; a History of* Gibraltar, Associated University Presses: London & Toronto, 1987, p.226.

[30] *WMMS Correspondence,* Davis to Committee, 10 November 1817, fiche 636, no.22.

on 1 December 1817, a memorial was sent to Don asking for a separate piece of ground in which to bury their own dead. Don wrote back the following day saying,

> As it is not yet ascertained what ceremonies the clergyman of your persuasion is authorised to perform, it will not be in my power to sanction a deviation from what has hitherto been the practice here until I receive a reply to a communication which I intend to make to His Majesty's Government on the subject.[31]

In June 1818, the church leaders wrote to say that General Don

> a few days since sent for Mr Davis and told him he had received directions from Earl Bathurst to grant our request (consequently a piece of the present burying ground is marked out for us) and that Mr Davis is at perfect liberty to administer the sacraments of baptism and the Lord's Supper as also to bury the dead.[32]

They were delighted by this news and went on to say,

> We who have been a number of years here and recall having frequently to rise from our knees and turn out His Majesty's subjects from a Protestant public place of worship, are constrained to exclaim 'what hath God wrought' in the course of a few years, in having given us favour in the eyes of our superiors and in having sent us faithful pastors who care for our souls, may we ever be kept humble and thankful.

This measure of independence took away many of the weapons of the garrison chaplains but the Methodists were only too well aware that the support of General Don had made all the difference. They had previously written to say that 'His Excellency has given every proof of his readiness to patronise our cause in this place - and behaved in the most kind manner to both Mr Davis and his predecessor Mr Wood, his favour renders access to the troops more easy in many cases, and is highly desirable.'[33]

The ministry of Thomas Davis was very much appreciated. The church leaders informed the Committee that 'since the arrival of our worthy and well beloved brother and pastor the Rev. Thomas Davis, God has been carrying on a good work amongst us'.[34] They described Davis as 'highly respected' and even quoted General Don as saying, 'Mr Davis there is one thing in your rules that I do not approve of, which is the changing of your Ministers so soon when they are found very useful, and much good is being done by them, were my opinion asked I should say you ought to remain

---

[31] General Don to Davis, 2 December 1817.
[32] *WMMS Correspondence*, Davis, Caulfield etc. to Committee, 4 June 1818, fiche 637, no.28.
[33] Ibid., leaders and stewards to Committee, 25 August 1817, fiche 636, no.20.
[34] Ibid.

longer'. This letter was accompanied by one from the forty-five Methodists of the 26th Regiment who stated their love for their pastor and praised God 'for sending such a man amongst us as our present preacher'.[35] They all wanted Davis to stay another two years, but the writers acknowledged the impossibility of this because of Jane Davis's health, which was not 'equal to the heat of the climate'. Perhaps the Committee did not fully understand what they were saying, for Davis then received a letter from London informing him that he was to stay another year. The church leaders were quite concerned about this and wrote again to say that Davis had not been prepared for such news. They stated that they felt 'some misunderstanding has arisen among the Committee relative to the allotted time for the stay of the Missionary in this place' and went on to say 'the disappointment to both himself and partner on receipt of your letter was therefore great especially as Mrs Davis suffers much during the summer months from the heat of the climate the which she almost dreads again encountering.'[36]

However, by then Davis had replied to the Committee, showing his commitment to the work and his sense of humour. He wrote,

> Although I fully expected to be relieved this April (as I was not told when in London anything about the appointment being for three years) yet as the friends here continue to urge me to remain with them and God's work prospers my dear wife and myself after much thought and prayer have concluded to venture upon another year in the name of the Lord.... After preaching to the same people ever since I arrived I am surprised they should desire to hear me another year for I am truly tired of hearing myself and engage with them to be their preacher for another year (if spared) with much fear. Lord help! If the Lord don't the chapel will be emptied and Society dissolved.[37]

Further letters to the Committee describing the importance of the work in Gibraltar and in appreciation of Davis's ministry were sent by Captain Tripp and Dr Coldstream.

However, the decision to stay was a costly one. On 10 January 1817, Thomas and Jane Davis had a son, Thomas Spencer, and in October 1818 Davis reported that his wife was expecting their second child. Although there is no account of any baptism in the register it seems the baby was born, but Jane's health was further affected and, just before they left the Rock, Davis referred to the 'very great and long affliction of my dear wife'.[38]

Davis was still in Gibraltar when his successor, Owen Rees, arrived.

---

[35] Ibid., Methodists in the 26th Regiment of Foot to Committee, 30 August 1817, fiche 636, no.21.

[36] Ibid., Davis, Caulfield etc. to Committee, 26 January 1818, fiche 636, no.24.

[37] Ibid., Davis to Committee, 12 January 1818, fiche 636, no.23.

[38] Ibid., Davis to Committee, 21 April 1819, fiche 637, no.33.

Rees, a Welshman, had been accepted on trial in 1809 and had served in several appointments. However, once in Gibraltar it became clear that he had always preached in Welsh. This raises the question about his motives in wanting to become a missionary and about the Committee's wisdom in selecting him, for unfortunately his ministry in Gibraltar, while fruitful in some ways, was to be dogged by dissension and division.

Rees set sail with his wife and son, Thomas, in April 1819. They experienced a difficult voyage with 'contrary winds and strong gales' in a 'little brig' which he reported 'had not been accustomed to take passengers which rendered our situation far from comfortable'.[39] So he was grateful the voyage had only taken nineteen days. They arrived on Sunday 25 April and immediately sent word to Davis who came on board and arranged for them to come on shore. Rees reported that the Society was in a prosperous state and could not speak too highly of Davis whose 'whole conduct has been such as merits the highest commendation ... he is immensely respected and great regret has been expressed by all classes at his leaving the Rock'. A few days after his arrival, Davis took Rees to meet General Don who was actually residing at San Roque at the time. He reported:

> I was equally surprised and pleased on my introduction to His Excellency the Governor to observe the kindness and freedom with which he conversed with us, and the high terms in which he spoke of Brother Davis's conduct during his residence upon the Rock, also expressing the greatest regret at his departure at the same time telling me that he should be very happy at all times to serve me in any way, saying that his sole object was to do good in general, that religion was the first thing in this world, as well as for that which is to come. And looking at Mr Davis observed that that had been their mutual object during Mr Davis's residence in the Garrison.[40]

The Davis family left the Rock in May 1819. On his return to England, Davis reported fully to the Missionary Committee. As a result, a letter of thanks was sent to General Don in July 1819, signed by all three of the General Secretaries. In this letter Don was thanked most warmly for his help and kindness to Davis and the hope was expressed that 'Mr Rees will continue to deserve for himself and the Society under his care the protection and kindness with which his predecessor has been honoured.'[41]

Davis served in several appointments in England, the last in Durham in 1828. In 1829 the *Minutes of Conference* recorded that he had 'desisted from travelling'. No reason was given. One is left to speculate about the reasons, to wonder about Jane Davis's health and to mourn the loss to

---

[39] Ibid., Rees to Committee, 4 May 1819, fiche 637, no.34.

[40] Ibid., Rees to Committee, 4 May 1819, fiche 637, no. 34.

[41] *WMMS Correspondence, Home & General Outgoing 1816-1914*, Bunting, Taylor & Watson to General Don, 15 July 1819, fiche 1132.

Methodism of a truly gifted man whose ministry in Gibraltar was so fruitful and so greatly appreciated.

The Committee also sent books to both Caulfield and Davis, the local preacher, in appreciation of their work in Gibraltar. Caulfield was thanked for his 'services in the cause' and for his 'kindness and attention to their Missionaries appointed to that station'.[42] Davis was thanked for his 'faithful and diligent labour as a Local Preacher for many years past' and the hope was expressed 'that your example, prayers and ministry will long benefit the Society and Congregation at Gibraltar'.[43] Rees felt Mr Herbert should also have received a book, as he was the chapel steward, 'a man on whom devolves all the business and everything that belongs to this Society, he has had all to do now for seven years and to him all look up as to Mr Davis and Mr Caulfield.'[44]

In the summer of that year there were concerns and alarms about the fever but there was no major outbreak. Rees soon set about establishing an Auxiliary Methodist Missionary Society in Gibraltar, but he ran into some opposition from Davis and Caulfield in particular. They were concerned about the high prices in Gibraltar; the extent of the chapel debt and the difficulties in raising money. Rees described them 'as the most inactive men I have ever met with whatever they have been in years that are past'.[45] He later said they were 'the weakest men I ever saw'.[46] He seemed to have lost his high opinion of them already. He went ahead anyway without their support, held meetings, got subscription cards printed and spoke to the Governor. The result was that he obtained seventy collectors, appointed Captain Tripp and Mr John Pyne, a solicitor, as treasurers and raised £106 in the first half year. Rees was clearly delighted with this success despite the fact that he had been unable to obtain the Governor's patronage, although he does not seem to have opposed what Rees had done. The formation of the Auxiliary Society was reported with enthusiasm both in the Missionary Society's Report for 1820, and in *Missionary Notices*, and a warm congratulatory letter was sent from the Committee to Captain Tripp.

As time went on there were continued differences of opinion between Rees and the leaders and stewards, namely Davis, Caulfield, Herbert, Gilbert, Barnard and Gillfilang. Several incidents took place and as Captain Tripp explained, 'Mr Rees from his first arrival was never popular with the class leaders in general'.[47]

After Wesley's death, many lay people were heard to say: 'Mr. Wesley was our father; the preachers are our brethren and they have no right to rule

---

[42] *WMMS Correspondence Outgoing,* Taylor to Caulfield, 15 July 1819, fiche 1132.
[43] Ibid., Taylor to Davis, 15 July 1819, fiche 1132.
[44] *WMMS Correspondence*, Rees to Committee, 6 August 1819, fiche 637, no.36.
[45] Ibid., Rees to Committee, 4 September 1819, fiche 637, no.37.
[46] Ibid., Rees to Committee, 11 November 1819, fiche 638, no.40.
[47] Ibid., Tripp to Committee, 8 February 1820, fiche 638, no.44.

over us.'[48] This tension between the preachers and laity was clearly part of the problem in Gibraltar. The leaders tried to find out what Rees had done before, knowing that Davis had formerly been a bookbinder. Rees refused to answer their questions and had possibly, in view of his age and years in the ministry, never had other employment. Rees felt the leaders regarded themselves as equal to the minister and 'boldly assert that in the Church of Christ all should be on a level and that to pay respect to their minister is only the remains of Popery. The plausible argument on which they build their system is that the preacher is only the servant of all, and as such he ought to be considered.'[49] He did not agree with this view and even suggested that his predecessor had been too lenient with them. Rees saw himself as the leader and decision maker and perhaps failed to see that this would be a particularly sensitive issue in Gibraltar, where the church had been established by lay people and often maintained by them in the absence of an appointed preacher.

The leaders' main cause for complaint concerned Rees's ability to preach. Everyone acknowledged that, as he had not been accustomed to preach in English, he made grammatical errors. His preaching was described as plain, and there seems to have been agreement that he was not the best of preachers. However, the leaders also criticised the content of some sermons, and said that they could not always follow his train of thought. They felt he had no calling to preach and that they received no benefit from his preaching. Others disagreed, and Pyne wrote that 'a complaint of this kind issuing from the source it does - persons in low stations of life and having no pretension to learning I conceive - becomes rather ridiculous when men of education such as Captain Tripp, Mr Coldstream and others are not offended'.[50] This was the first time that more educated men had been part of the church, which may have threatened the leaders who came from humbler backgrounds different from those of the new arrivals.

The leaders did not criticise Rees's doctrine or moral standing. They did not deny that much good was being done, although they were critical that this was only with the military. They did feel that Rees was extravagant and that he took more than his due in his allowances, a view the Committee seems to have shared as he was ordered by it 'to bring his ordinary expenditure within the allowances made by those regulations of the Committee made in May 1819'.[51] They found him high-handed and overbearing and felt he did not listen to, or understand, their point of view. Discussions within the leaders' meetings became very heated at times.

---

[48] John Walsh, 'Methodism at the end of the Eighteenth Century,' in Davies, Rupp (eds.) *A History of the Methodist Church in Great Britain*, Epworth Press: London, 1965, vol. i, p.282.

[49] *WMMS Correspondence,* Rees to Committee, 29 May 1820, fiche 638, no.54.

[50] Ibid., Pyne to Committee, 11 February 1820, fiche 638, no.45.

[51] *WMMS Correspondence Outgoing,* Taylor to Rees, 1 March 1820, fiche 1136.

Davis and Caulfield withdrew for a while, but were persuaded to return by Coldstream who tried to adopt a mediating role on several occasions. Finally, matters came to a head on Sunday 6 February 1820. The leaders did not stay for the morning communion service. They felt unable to participate because of the tension existing between themselves and Rees. However, this was the first time that Lieutenant Bailey and Pyne had taken part in the sacrament, so it was a special service of public commitment for them. Rees therefore felt that the leaders' action was rude and also made everyone present aware that there was a problem. So he decided to lay the whole matter before the Society. The leaders urged him not to, feeling that 'he would make a breach he could never heal'.[52] He went ahead anyway and, after the Sunday evening service, discussed all the issues before the Society as a whole, quoting from private conversations and from those that had taken place within the leaders' meetings which they felt was a breach of confidentiality. They also felt they had little time to defend themselves as Rees kept talking close to the time the soldiers had to leave to be back in barracks.

The leaders met together, by themselves, on 9 February to discuss matters and drew up a list of resolutions which they sent to Rees and to the Committee. They had decided to meet separately as a class but to continue attending the chapel. They also resolved to lay the whole matter before the Committee, which they did in a lengthy report. Rees did not reply to their letter but, since they were meeting separately in class, he regarded them as having left the Society and in due course other leaders were appointed to their positions. Rees also wrote a full report to the Committee and Captain Tripp, Mr Pyne, Lieutenant Bailey and Dr Coldstream all wrote in his support. A letter signed by seventy-five soldiers and wives was also sent, though a few of the soldiers later retracted their support, saying that many had not known what they were signing. The leaders were aware of Rees's support saying, 'we are not ignorant that Mr Rees has the interest and influence of two or three individuals of note and who from real pure motives are led to act but who are altogether ignorant of real facts as it respects his behaviour to us.'[53] After these events the leaders gained the impression that Rees would not administer the Lord's Supper to them and so wrote to ask him if he would, as they did not want to be denied the sacrament at the actual service. He refused to do so saying he could not give it to those 'who have evinced a conduct so gross and unworthy'.[54] They did, however, continue to attend the chapel although they reported Rees making pointed observations about them in his sermons and prayers. All of this was reported to the Committee and thus the matter was fully laid before it and a decision was eagerly awaited by both sides.

---

[52] *WMMS Correspondence,* Davis etc. to Committee, 18 February 1820, fiche 638, no.48.

[53] Ibid., Davis etc. to Committee, 18 February 1820, fiche 638, no. 48.

[54] Ibid., copy Rees to the leaders, 3 March 1820, fiche 639, no.51.

Meanwhile the work of the Mission continued and the work of Bible distribution. Rees was wary of giving Bibles away particularly after one soldier attempted to sell on one he had been given. He and Coldstream distributed Bibles and tracts in Spain and were thrown out of the church in San Roque for not bowing to the altar. Rees engaged two people to sell Bibles in the market. He liaised with a Dr Parker, who was involved in supplying Bibles to a contact in Málaga, and with Mrs Nicklin who continued to sell books through her shop. She reported in a letter that 'Mr Rees and other gentlemen have exerted themselves in forming a Bible Society but they have not yet succeeded'.[55] They were all hopeful that opportunities of doing work in Spain would improve. Rees also suggested that a young probationer minister should be appointed, in addition to the married preacher, to learn Spanish and to work with the twelve to fourteen thousand souls on the Rock who spoke Spanish. Such a person might also be able to branch out into neighbouring Spanish towns. So, despite the rift with the leaders, Rees's ministry did continue to bear fruit.

However, this time of waiting was clearly very difficult for both sides, who were each convinced that they were in the right. Everyone in the Society, and some people outside it, were aware of what had happened. The leaders were bewildered by Rees's treatment of them, reminding the Committee of their years of work and lack of problems with previous ministers. They sent a memorial to Conference, dated 17 July 1820, in which they asked for Rees to be removed and suggested that either Davis or Griffith be asked to return. It may not have arrived in time and they did not receive a reply. They later expressed the hope that 'a kind and loving man' would be sent to them.[56]

Rees also expressed his feelings about his difficult situation and the rugged path he had to tread, feeling both angry and upset about what had happened. Although he sought the Committee's opinion, overall he felt he was in the right stating, 'what a support and consolation is a clear conscience'.[57] He did not express any loving concern for these men who were in his pastoral care. Instead, he was reported to have referred to them as villains and ignorant fellows who were activated by a diabolical spirit. He made no attempt to seek a reconciliation and several times expressed the view that the Society was better off without them. 'It is my firm opinion ... that whilst such characters had anything to do as leaders and stewards it would never prosper. In losing them I hope it will ultimately prove an everlasting blessing to the cause in this place.'[58] The whole affair must have been very difficult for Mrs Rees too and in July she was reported to be unwell. She eventually spent some time in San Roque and by

[55] *Home Correspondence In,* Mrs Nicklin, 27 May 1821.
[56] *WMMS Correspondence*, Davis to Committee, 1 December 1820, fiche 640, no.69.
[57] Ibid., Rees to Committee, 29 May 1820, fiche 639, no.54.
[58] Ibid., Rees to Committee, 17 February 1820, fiche 638, no.47.

October was back in Gibraltar apparently much better.

So they awaited the Committee's decision, both sides sure it would be in their favour. Yet it is hard to see what the Committee could do. It had received conflicting accounts, communication was slow and there was no possibility of sending out an arbitrator. The tragedy, however, was that months went by without a decision of any kind.

Finally, in June, Rees informed the Society that the Committee had told him it hoped to write in July as at present it 'had business of more importance to attend to' but by the end of September no word had come.[59] The leaders saw in the *Minutes of Conference* that Rees had been appointed to Gibraltar for another year and, as all their letters to the Committee had gone unanswered, they were still denied communion and their 'feelings were constantly hurt in his [Rees's] public discourses as also by his slanderous assertions for these past eight months', they felt they had had enough.[60] So, they separated from the Society along 'with those who feel with us' and on 25 September took a room to meet in. Shortly afterwards a Mrs West, who had been in the Society for many years, was expelled by Rees because she had met with them in their room.

It later transpired that the Committee had written on 30 June, but these letters never arrived. Duplicates were finally sent and appear to have arrived in November. Although at the time of writing the leaders were still attending services they were regarded as having left the Society and they were criticised for having done so. They denied this, arguing that Rees had thrust them out and that they would never have completely left in September if the Committee had written earlier. The Committee argued that some of the matters were trivial and that not profiting from preaching could sometimes be caused by a want of prayer, which they also denied. The Committee urged reconciliation stating that they had 'laid it upon Mr Rees to throw no obstacle in the way' and adding 'do not plead that you have been grieved, none of us can keep our place in religious society, without being at times grieved'.[61] The leaders still wanted Rees removed and altogether were very disappointed in the Committee's response.

Rees was criticised too, firstly for having the public discussion on a Sunday evening after a service of communion and secondly by too often placing himself in situations likely 'to excite and court opposition'.[62] He was reminded that the former leaders had 'been for years steady and useful members of the society and for this you should give them credit at all times.' He was urged to open the way to their return and whenever they did to promise that past grievances would not be mentioned. However,

---

[59] Ibid., Davis etc. to Committee, 5 June 1820, fiche 639, no.57.

[60] Ibid., Davis & Herbert to Committee, 16 October 1820, fiche 640, no.66.

[61] *WMMS Correspondence Outgoing,* Taylor to Davis, Caulfield, etc. 30 June 1820, fiche 1137.

[62] Ibid., Taylor to Rees, 30 June 1820, fiche 1137.

Rees seems to have found the letter almost irrelevant stating that it 'arrived too late to prevent the mischief which was done.' He felt their observations arose 'either from a misconception or a misrepresentation of the subject' and did not seem willing to accept any blame either.[63] By this time the Committee had another preacher in view for the station. This was referred to in a letter to Coldstream, so Rees was naturally upset and perplexed as to why the Committee had not mentioned it to him.

The stalemate between the two sides continued and a reconciliation was not even attempted. In February 1821, the leaders reported to the Committee that Rees had been found drunk and had been unable to take his class meeting. Gillfilang then sent him a copy of a pamphlet Rees had himself written on drunkenness. Rees threatened to take him to the magistrate, but took no further action apart from telling the Committee. He did not state his guilt or innocence, but he was, in fact, completely innocent and the whole affair was based on a misunderstanding. However, the incident proves what a sorry state of affairs now existed. The months prior to their departure must have been very difficult for the Rees family and in March 1821 Mrs Rees was again reported to be unwell both because of the climate and 'the treatment we have received'.[64]

So Rees prepared to leave Gibraltar but, before he did, he received news of the death of Captain Tripp who had left the Rock in March 1820 because of ill-health. Rees paid tribute to this courageous young man who had worked so hard for the cause of Methodism and felt he 'lived on in the hearts of all who knew him'.[65] In January 1820 Tripp had written about his increasing ill-health in his journal, describing his feelings about this in relation to his faith in God. He was much affected by a sermon Rees preached on the text 'This year shalt thou die', but despite all he felt he had not 'lost the divine peace which passeth understanding'.[66] He spent time in San Roque, considered to be healthier, but was forced to return to England where he died in December 1820 at the home of his mother in Sussex, shortly after his thirtieth birthday.

However, his contribution to the Society in Gibraltar was not finished for he left them a large legacy of £600 to pay off the debt on the chapel. He also bequeathed £50 to the Mission Fund, £100 to the Rev. Thomas Davis, £50 to Rees and £20 to Caulfield whose circumstances were apparently very difficult. This legacy relieved the chapel of most of its burdensome debt and could hardly have come at a better time, with a new preacher coming and the prospect of a fresh beginning.

---

[63] *WMMS Correspondence,* Rees to Committee, 12 December 1820, fiche 640, no.70.

[64] Ibid., Rees to Committee, 1 March 1821, fiche 640, no.75.

[65] Ibid., Rees to Committee, 23 March 1821, fiche 640, no.76.

[66] *WMMS Special Series,* fiche 13.

CHAPTER 5 EVANGELISATION
A Mission to the Spanish on the Rock (1821-28)

For the first time, the person appointed to Gibraltar was an experienced missionary. William Croscombe was born in Tiverton in Devon. He was accepted on trial in 1810 and soon went to Canada where he worked on five different stations over the next eight years, returning to England because of problems with his health. In 1819 he was stationed in Nottingham and was then appointed to Gibraltar. Prior to leaving England, he visited the Mission House and read most of the recent correspondence from Gibraltar. He was given strict instructions not to make any decisions without reference to the Committee.

William Croscombe with his wife, Ann, and their family journeyed to Falmouth. They were delayed on the way and arrived there in April 1821 after a trying journey. Unfortunately, the delay meant that Ann was advised, at the last minute, not to sail with her family. She was in the last stages of pregnancy and to embark so late on was too risky. Croscombe expressed his great distress at this separation in his first letter to the Committee.[1] They were eventually re-united in good health and spirits, on 21 June. In his letter Croscombe wrote of his safe arrival in Gibraltar with his 'dear little children' after a passage of thirteen days. Rees had come on board to meet him and Croscombe had been joyfully received by him, his wife, Coldstream, Bailey and Pyne, but he reported a great deal of anxiety about what he would do about the division in the church. The former leaders expected Croscombe to call Rees to account, believing they would then be vindicated and restored to their former positions in the Society. Davis asked to see him soon after his arrival and expressed this view, placing the blame for the division firmly on Rees. Croscombe acknowledged that his position would have been very difficult indeed had he not been given clear instructions which, he told Davis, were to receive the Society from Rees and not to undo anything he had done without consulting the Committee. Davis was bitterly disappointed and saw this decision as an endorsement of Rees's actions. However, this plan did give Croscombe time to make his own assessment of the situation and, as it was the Committee's decision, it freed him from any responsibility for it, enabling the former leaders to blame the Committee and remain free to make up their minds about Croscombe himself. Nevertheless, they were very disappointed and Herbert wrote a final letter to Rees signing himself 'Your much injured brother in the gospel'.[2] He sent a copy to the Committee with a covering letter, endorsed by Caulfield, Gilbert, Gillfilang and Barnard, in which he went over many aspects of the dispute and clearly

---

[1] *WMMS correspondence*, Croscombe to Committee, 10 May 1821, fiche 640, no.71.
[2] Ibid., Herbert to Rees, 21 May 1821, fiche 641, no.78.

felt misjudged and upset by the Committee's decision.[3]

Croscombe and Rees spent several weeks together. They appointed five new trustees, including Pyne and Bailey. One of their first jobs was to write to the Committee to ask permission to raise the preacher's house by one storey as it was not big enough to accommodate the whole Croscombe family.[4] In addition the drains passed directly through the house and so Croscombe had been encouraged to move to a rented house temporarily. The Society was anxious to receive instructions and 'mailed packet after packet in hopes of receiving some communication in answer to the suggested alterations'.[5] When they still heard nothing they finally decided to go ahead with a cheaper scheme. A store-room in the chapel yard was converted into a vestry. By raising this to the height of the house an extra bedroom was added and a cellar was built under the vestry. The work was finished by the end of October and the Croscombes returned to the Mission House. The work cost about £100 which was added to the chapel debt, which was now very much lower as a result of Tripp's legacy.

Croscombe had taken charge of the station on 25 May 1821. Rees and his family left Gibraltar on 1 June and were stationed at Shepton Mallet for two years, followed by seven appointments in England, the last five of which only lasted one year. In 1832 Rees returned to Wales. By then his health was declining and he died on 22 August 1832 while only in his forty-fourth year and his twenty-fourth year of ministry. A brief obituary appeared in the *Conference Minutes* of 1833.

Soon after Rees left Gibraltar, Croscombe informed the former leaders that the way was open for their return to Society, on condition that they were willing to acknowledge the impropriety of their conduct. Davis, Caulfield, Gilbert and Mrs West applied at different times to return, but all continued to justify their conduct and blame Rees for what had happened. Indeed Caulfield said he would rather jump over the ramparts of Gibraltar than acknowledge wrong conduct on their part! However, they were all attending chapel regularly and professing to gain much benefit from doing so. They were still unhappy about the Committee's standpoint, but all parties seem to have accepted Croscombe. There is a difference in the tone of his letters, and it seems the Society had been sent the kind and loving man they had asked for, but it was still difficult to find a way to resolve the situation.

A breakthrough came towards the end of 1821, when Croscombe discovered that the allegation of drunkenness had been made against Rees, which he had not read about in London. The charge had been false. Rees had fallen whilst painting his house, and the fact that he had needed to be helped indoors and was unable to meet with his class had been

---

[3] Ibid., Herbert to Committee, 31 May 1821, fiche 641, no.81.
[4] Ibid., Trustees to Committee, 31 May 1821, fiche 641, no.80.
[5] Ibid., Pyne to Committee, 20 October 1821, fiche 641, no.83.

misinterpreted. Croscombe explained this to the Committee in a letter which was taken to England by Coldstream who had obtained leave of absence for a few months.[6] Before he left Gibraltar, he had taken an affectionate leave of all the former leaders and advised them most earnestly to return to the Society. Davis discussed the allegation of drunkenness with Croscombe and acknowledged that he should have made more careful enquiries before reporting to the Committee. He put this in writing for Rees and the Committee saying, 'this act with some others I now see to have been unwise and improper and would have been better left undone, but all I can do now is to express my deep regret'. He also expressed his 'earnest desire to return to the Society', acknowledging his 'sincere sorrow for the unpleasant things which have taken place some of which as far as I have been concerned I see to have been unwise and improper'. The leaders' meeting agreed to his return and Croscombe therefore wrote to the Committee, recommending its agreement.[7] Others, including Caulfield, followed suit, sending similar apologies and requests. Croscombe reported that they were all showing a much better spirit, but gave no reason for the change. Time may have played its part and a growing confidence and trust in Croscombe whom they clearly liked and respected. Perhaps there was a recognition that the division had not been entirely their fault and it was easier to link the apology to a specific incident where they had been in the wrong. Whatever the reason, it was time to go forward and engage in the work of mission which was seen to be the primary role of the church. When, in due course, all had returned to the Society, they played their part in this work.

At this time links with the Bible Society were strengthened largely through the efforts of John William Bailey, who was a lieutenant in the Royal Navy and Agent for Transports at Gibraltar. He first wrote to the Bible Society in April 1821 asking for a supply of books, because he felt his situation gave him a very good opportunity of conversing with people from many different nations.[8] He reported French, Spanish, Portuguese, Italian, German, American, Greek, Arabic and Turkish people as continually in Gibraltar. The Bible Society agreed to send some scriptures and requested Bailey, Coldstream, Croscombe, Pyne and Dr Parker to act as a committee for their distribution and to supply Mrs Nicklin. They were asked to sell the books, wherever possible, however low the price. Bailey had hoped to form an Auxiliary Society, but as there was already an Auxiliary to the Society for Promoting Christian Knowledge, supported by the garrison chaplain, Dr Hughes, permission from the Governor was not forthcoming and so a Corresponding Committee was formed instead. By the following year, the committee had circulated 3,175 copies of the

---

[6] Ibid., Croscombe to Committee, 23 November 1821, fiche 641, no.86.
[7] Ibid., Croscombe to Committee, 25 December 1821, fiche 642, no.88.
[8] *Foreign Correspondence In,* Bailey, 27 April 1821, 1821 p.25, letter A.

scriptures.

Bailey became the committee's secretary and sometimes also its treasurer. He wrote numerous letters to the Bible Society reporting on progress and ordering stock. He used a room in his own home as a depository, sending books as required both to Mrs Nicklin and the Methodist Mission House. He made contact with a friar in Tangier and had high hopes that he would write an Arabic translation. He kept in touch with him, even visiting him, but the translation was never produced. He had a variety of other correspondents and sought to circulate the scriptures as widely as possible, though it was difficult to get them into Spain as such books were prohibited by Spanish law.

One means of distributing the scriptures was on board ship. In August 1821 Croscombe reported:

> We held a meeting on board ship, for the first time in the Bay of Gibraltar. This is intended as a preparatory step towards forming a Society for the religious benefit of seamen in this Garrison, similar to those formed in the sea-port towns of England. Of the importance of such a Society at Gibraltar there can be no doubt where, it is said, more than 3,000 sail of shipping anchor annually, a considerable part of which are English or American.[9]

The result of this was the formation of the Bethel Society in September 1821. The Committee consisted of Croscombe, Parker, Coldstream, Bailey, Pyne and five others. They linked with the parent Society in London, printed notices to advertise themselves and organised a depository for their Bethel flag. Any ship willing to host a service collected the flag and flew it to advertise the fact that a service would be taking place so that others could join if they wished. Services were held every Sunday, weather permitting, and occasionally on weekdays. Tracts, scriptures and other publications were sold and distributed. Davis and Caulfield joined the Committee in 1823 and Herbert the following year. In 1824 the preaching extended to the lateen craft, small Spanish and Portuguese trading vessels, with ten to fifteen people on board. Three or four were visited on Sunday afternoons and Croscombe felt this was a very useful opportunity as there were 'at no time less than <u>one hundred</u> of these craft not more than a pistol shot from the shore.'[10]

Work with the soldiers continued, although the frequent regimental changes were hard on the missionary. There was also continued opposition. Several soldiers of the 64th Regiment joined the Society after their arrival in Gibraltar and in August 1822 Croscombe reported on a

---

[9] *WMMS Correspondence,* Croscombe to Committee, 17 December 1821, fiches 641-2, no.87. Also *Missionary Notices,* vol. iii, (1821-2), p.235.
[10] *WMMS Correspondence,* Croscombe to Committee, 23 April 1824, fiche 644, no.20.

small revival amongst them.[11]   A sergeant, who was 'much alive to God', had worked hard to encourage and strengthen the five or six men belonging to the Society by inviting them to his room for prayer.   More had joined them until the room was full.   'Then to their astonishment another sergeant came forward and offered his room for prayer and when that room was filled, a third came forward in like manner.'   The result was that the men showed a great desire to hear the word of God and the preaching room at the South became crowded with them.   More than twenty were admitted to the Society, but this led to opposition.   The room at the South was considered 'a very important auxiliary to this Mission in consequence of its being in the very centre of three of the regiments stationed here'.[12] However, it was also near to the hospital where two or three medical officers lived who were opposed to Methodism.   They complained that the sound of singing and prayer four times a week was offensive to them and an annoyance to the patients.   The patients, however, expressed the opposite view; nevertheless Croscombe was sent for by the chief magistrate.   He seems to have held his own well during the meeting and left feeling that there was nothing the civil authorities could do.   The medical officers then turned their attention to the regimental commanders.   The colonel of the 27th Regiment issued an order forbidding the men from attending worship, which affected thirteen members of the Society.   They were not forbidden to attend the chapel in town, but in fact were unable to do so because of the distance from the barracks and the nature of their military duties.   The 64th Regiment was then removed from its barracks at the South and quartered in several different barracks which meant that the opportunity to meet with the sergeants was lost and several had 'backslidden'.   Croscombe does not say whether this move had anything to do with the opposition to the Methodists, but he did report that the Garrison chaplain was hostile to their cause and that 'Our own good friend the Doctor [Coldstream] has had a dreadful time of it since his return from England.'[13]   The result of all this was that attendance at the room at the South lessened, although the chapel in town was reported to be well attended.   An attempt was made to obtain a plot of land on which to build their own place of worship at the South, but permission was withheld.

In the autumn of 1822, Coldstream and his regiment, the 26th, left Gibraltar.   This involved a loss of sixteen members of the Society, including three leaders, which meant for Croscombe the loss of many whose fellowship and support he valued.   He often kept in touch with soldiers after they left and tried to arrange for their continued support so he placed a small group in the 80th Regiment under the care of a young corporal when they were sent to Malta.

---

[11] Ibid., Croscombe to Committee, 17 August 1822, fiche 642, no.3.

[12] Ibid., Croscombe to Committee, 16 September 1822, fiche 642, no.4.

[13] Ibid., Croscombe to Committee, 16 September 1822, fiche 642, n. 4.

The Auxiliary Missionary Society continued to raise money with some success, despite lack of support from England as regular supplies of *Missionary Notices* and other publications were often not sent, despite being requested. In March 1822 a Sunday school had been formed with Bailey as Superintendent. Despite feeling that it was 'an office quite novel to me', he had accepted the post, working with a committee of nine members.[14] By October, the Town branch had 108 scholars but the removal of the 26th Regiment left only 49. At the South, average attendance was between ten and fifteen. There were some difficulties at first with the children's behaviour, but these were soon overcome. Special anniversary services were held in 1823 and 1824. There were then 103 children with twelve teachers and an average attendance of about 80.

There were also practical matters to be considered such as the need for a water cistern at the Mission House. Croscombe wrote,

> Persons not acquainted with Gibraltar can scarcely conceive the difficulty the inhabitants labour under in obtaining a regular supply of good water, especially at the hot season of the year this invaluable article is the most wanted. All the tanks within the Garrison belong to the Government and are filled with rain water. The troops, the navy and all persons in government employ are supplied from this source and if there is any surplus the inhabitants can have it by paying for the carriage of it. But in the event of a dry season we have no access to it and are reduced to the necessity of using water brought from Neutral ground which is in general brackish.[15]

Most houses of any size or respectability had their own cistern 'even if they have to build them under their sitting rooms, which is frequently the case'. The cost of building one was estimated at about £50 which in the long run would be much cheaper, as they had to pay between 2s 6d and 3s a week with the 'inconvenience of being at the <u>Mercy</u> or <u>Caprice</u> of your waterman'.

Finally, there was interest in opening up work amongst the Spanish-speaking population. In February 1823 Croscombe reported that a Benevolent Society had been formed in the garrison with the aim of assisting sick and distressed foreigners. One of the main visitors was John Quirell whom Croscombe described as 'just beginning in the good way'.[16] Quirell was often asked by the Spanish to read the scriptures and to pray in Spanish and had asked them if they would like a missionary of their own who would learn their language. This idea, first suggested by Rees, had been well received and Croscombe, Bailey and Pyne each wrote to the

---

[14] *Correspondence, rules and regulations of the Gibraltar Sunday School instituted 17 March 1822.*

[15] *WMMS Correspondence,* Croscombe to Committee, 26 September 1822, fiche 642, no.5.

[16] Ibid., Croscombe to Committee, 21 February 1823, fiche 643, no.10.

Committee in support of it. In addition, Quirell had been asked for tracts by people from the interior of Spain, which led to the hope that work could also be done there, especially in nearby towns like San Roque.

Thus, under Croscombe's ministry, the work of evangelisation expanded considerably with several new initiatives. He reported that the Society was in a settled state, 'all is harmony and love'.[17] He later wrote that 'a most happy degree of unity and affection presides among us.'[18] He had healed the divisions and enabled people to work together to take the church forward in many different ways. In June 1823 he began to think about his own next appointment. His health had been good most of his time in Gibraltar. There were no serious fever outbreaks although in 1821 there was sickness among the children and, although the Croscombe's children survived, others died from scarlet fever, measles and other complaints which had been 'alarmingly prevalent among the children in this Garrison'.[19] It is not clear how many children the Croscombes had, possibly five including Elizabeth Emma who was born on 17 December 1822. Croscombe wanted to return to Nova Scotia but, in fact, was offered a post in Newfoundland which he accepted. He then received some distressing news of his family in England and wanted to visit them. Permission was not granted which Croscombe accepted with amazing equanimity, seeing it as the will of Providence.

The Croscombes hoped to leave Gibraltar at the end of May 1824, but in March they were told that a successor had not yet been found. They had already partly packed but agreed to stay on a few months. However, Croscombe cautioned the Committee 'against sending a man to Gibraltar in whose preaching abilities and sound judgement and experience of mankind you have not the fullest confidence' as it was 'on some accounts a difficult station.'[20]

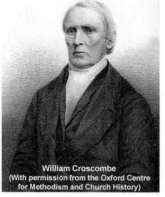

William Croscombe
(With permission from the Oxford Centre
for Methodism and Church History)

In June Croscombe heard that James Dixon had been appointed, but he was very concerned about the planned timing of his arrival. 'I almost tremble for himself and family as the summer is extraordinarily hot'.[21] Croscombe had hoped, and had been instructed, to welcome Dixon before leaving, but opportunities of passage to Newfoundland became scarcer as time went on. In the end he was forced to leave shortly before Dixon arrived. He sent a last letter

---

[17] Ibid., Croscombe to Committee, 8 April 1823, fiche 643, no.11.

[18] Ibid., Croscombe to Committee, 23 August 1823, fiche 643, no.15.

[19] Ibid., Croscombe to Committee, 25 April 1822, fiche 642, no.1.

[20] Ibid., Croscombe to Committee, 19 April 1824, fiche 644, no.19.

[21] Ibid., Croscombe to Committee, 12 June 1824, fiche 644, no.22.

from Cádiz in August explaining this.[22] He was delayed there for several days but then sailed on to Newfoundland, where he was soon serving as the Chairman of the District. He remained in Canada for the rest of his life. He retired in 1851 and died in 1859. Findlay and Holdsworth said of him that 'scarcely any man has inspired more affection amongst all classes of people'.[23] His ministry certainly turned round a very difficult situation in Gibraltar and enabled the church to move forward together.

The new missionary, James Dixon, was born on 28 October 1788. He became a Methodist at the age of twenty and then spent several years studying. He was accepted on trial in 1812 and Gibraltar was his seventh appointment. He arrived with his wife, Mary, and their children in late July or early August 1824. Unfortunately, the fears often expressed previously about the foolishness of sending missionaries to arrive in the summer were all too quickly realised in their case. Pyne reported to the Committee that

> Our new missionary, Mr Dixon, appears to give satisfaction to the Society and congregation but I am sorry to say he has suffered much from the climate having come here in the middle of the summer.... strangers from England coming here during the sultry months have enough to do to maintain tolerable health and have seldom energy enough to attend to any labours.[24]

James Dixon

His health needs and those of his family were to predominate in the short time they were in Gibraltar and there are few records of Dixon's work there. A long letter from him appeared in *Missionary Notices* focusing almost entirely on plans for a Spanish Mission. By then, Conference had agreed to send a second missionary for this work.

The key figure in this new development was John Baptist Quirell, (known also as Juan Bautista). He was born in Gibraltar on 4 August 1795, although his parents, Claudio and Anne Rose Bremon, were both French. He married Antonia Cerudo from Tarifa on 25 February 1818 in the Roman Catholic Church in Gibraltar. Later he became involved with the Methodist Society and four children were baptised in the Methodist chapel, three daughters born in 1821, 1824 and 1830 and a son born in 1832. Dixon described Quirell as 'a man of deep piety and an excellent spirit' and reported that he visited between a dozen

---

[22] Ibid., Croscombe to Committee, 3 August 1824, fiche 644, no.24.

[23] Findlay and Holdsworth, op. cit., vol. i, p.342.

[24] *WMMS Correspondence,* Pyne to Committee, 10 September 1824, fiche 644, no.23.

and twenty families, sometimes with some of their neighbours, to read and expound the scriptures and to pray. He was also involved in visiting Spanish ships in the Bay, working with the Bethel Society Committee from spring 1824. Weekly Spanish services had just begun, one in the chapel and one at the South, at which Quirell preached. Although attendance had not been good, it was hoped it would form the basis of a greater and permanent work. Those who understood Spanish reported that Quirell's preaching 'both as to matter and language is highly respectable' and Dixon added that he thought 'from his excellent spirit he is likely to be of great use in the work'. Dixon himself was attempting to learn Spanish, but 'owing to my engagements and afflictions I do not make the progress I desire'. Dixon also urged the formation of a Spanish school and recommended Quirell be attached to the Mission 'as a schoolmaster or Assistant Missionary' and felt he would be very useful in either or both these roles.[25]

Thus there were already the beginnings of work for the new missionary to build on. The person appointed was William Barber. He was born in Bristol on 25 April 1799 into a Christian family. In June 1814 he and his brother, Aquila, gained a more personal sense of joyful salvation whilst being prayed for at a private prayer meeting. William was already a Sunday school teacher and in 1816, when nearly seventeen years old, he became a local preacher in the Bristol Circuit. In 1818 he was unanimously recommended to Conference to become a minister. He himself was drawn to missionary work, but his mother's opposition and ill health caused him regretfully only to offer for work at home. However, although he was accepted by Conference, he was put on the reserve list so, in the meantime, he accepted a teaching post. Unfortunately, his health then began to decline and he developed a serious chest condition. The Conference of 1819 passed with no appointment for him because of financial problems within the Methodist Connexion. His health deteriorated further but he opened a school in Gloucester and also continued preaching and leading a class. On 19 February 1822 he married Anne Howell who, unlike her husband, had always had very good health. They lived at the school together and were clearly very happy there but, after only six months of marriage, Anne died of typhoid at the age of twenty-one. One of the ministers who visited her during this illness was James Dixon and William kept in touch with him afterwards regarding him as a very good friend. William was devastated by grief and as the typhoid outbreak occurred at the school it had to be closed. He found comfort in his faith and managed to continue his teaching career in the hope of earning enough to pay off his debts, incurred because of the closure of the school.

However, he really wanted to be a missionary and when he heard that

---

[25] *Missionary Notices,* vol. iv, (1823-5), March 1825, p.428.

Dixon was going to Gibraltar, he wished he could go with him, little knowing that the way was opening up for him to do just that. His doctor urged him to go to warmer climes, the family rallied round to help with the debt, and his mother had died so her wishes no longer needed consideration. In September 1824, William was summoned to London to meet the Missionary Committee, and was appointed to Gibraltar as a missionary to the Spanish-speaking population of the Rock. He was delighted with this chance of a new beginning, but he was still in poor health, still grieving and by nature a little prone to depression and doubts about his own worth.

On 17 November 1824 Barber was ordained in London and he sailed from Blackwall on Sunday 28 November. An accident on the river meant they had to stop at Gravesend for repairs and Barber went ashore to find the local Methodists. He preached to them in the evening and felt much blessed at receiving the sacrament. Although happy with his appointment, he was anxious about the voyage and was missing family and friends. He had arranged with Aquila to remember each other in prayer every day at 4 o'clock in the afternoon.

Windy weather delayed their departure from Gravesend. However, they reached the Downs in safety, although once anchored there the gales returned with a ferocity that alarmed everyone on board and caused Barber to be seasick. The captain had to put out a second anchor as the first was dragging. Other ships did likewise including a large convict ship bound for Botany Bay. The cables on a nearby brig parted; it drifted away and Barber feared it was lost. They finally left the Downs but conditions were so adverse that more than two weeks passed before they reached the Lizard. They entered the Bay of Biscay on Sunday 19 December. Barber preached to the sailors on deck, but gales soon struck them again. Barber was obliged to lie flat on his cabin floor unable to sit, stand or kneel because of the motion, and even so was thrown about the cabin, though he found he could stand 'in the companion-stairs'.[26] He prayed earnestly for deliverance from the storm and believed his prayers were answered. They finally sailed into Gibraltar Bay on Wednesday 5 January 1825 after what had been a long and hazardous journey. The ship, the *Edward Protheroe*, was lost later in the year.

Barber had been given a letter of introduction to Pyne. After reading it, Pyne welcomed him warmly and sent his son to show him the way to the Mission House. Dixon was not expecting him as the letter informing him of the appointment had not yet arrived. They greeted each other with great warmth and affection; Barber reporting it to be 'one of the most memorable

---

[26] Aquila Barber, *A Brother's Portrait or Memoirs of the late Rev. William Barber Wesleyan Missionary to the Spaniards at Gibraltar*, no publisher: London, 1830, p.258. (Letter to his family, 10 January 1825.)

and affecting days of my life'.[27] He described Dixon as being 'much esteemed and beloved here, the people know and value his worth.' They soon began to study Spanish together and Barber felt warmly welcomed by the whole family and reported that the people generally were delighted by his arrival.

Barber explored the Rock and sent back descriptions of the town. 'Its houses are crowded, its streets narrow, its windings intricate, and its population swarming'. It had no appearance of order unlike 'The South' with its 'superior pleasantness' which was 'the result of British arrangement and labour'. The distance between the two was 'nearly an hour's walk'. He referred to General Don, the Lieutenant-Governor, 'who has conducted himself here with the most manly and liberal public spirit, and thus won the gratitude and esteem, I should think, of every body'. He was impressed with the recent improvements he had made in laying out a 'grand parade and beautiful public gardens'.[28]

As to the Society, members were mostly ordinary soldiers and non-commissioned officers. Life was very hard for Christian officers and he felt that 'the existence of vital piety in an officer is very precarious; - his situation becomes distressing; - and the persecution he has to endure is very galling: in fact, he must either resign his commission, or almost every comfort of existence.'[29] In addition he felt 'Methodism is not here what, in England, it is commonly supposed to be. I had a most erroneous expectation regarding this. Our cause is despised, and shut out from mixing at all with the world … few or no persons of influence and responsibility in the world's estimation give us their decided countenance.'[30] However, despite this, the congregation was between two and three hundred on a Sunday morning and the chapel was filled at night. In the South there was 'erected a neat room' where preaching took place on Thursday evenings. He reported on Quirell's work in similar terms to Dixon, describing his visiting and his preaching in Spanish at the chapel on Thursdays which eight to twelve people attended. Quirell was also of the opinion that there were four or five people who would join a class if a Spanish Society was formed.

Barber's main priority was to learn the language, but he also assisted Dixon and helped with the work of the Bethel Society. He soon reported that Quirell had formed a Spanish class which neither he nor Dixon had known anything about, but he felt it was a pleasing development. Barber's health continued to cause concern, not helped by an incident at the end of February when he had to run hard to escape from a runaway mule. The result was that he began to cough blood and had to curtail his activities for

---

[27] Ibid., p.262. (Letter to his family, 10 January 1825.)
[28] Ibid., p.265. (Letter to Aquila, 21 January 1825.)
[29] Ibid., p.267. (Letter to Aquila, 21 January 1825.)
[30] Ibid., p.279. (Letter to his father, 17 May 1825.)

a while. As the year wore on he became further debilitated, but he was also very concerned about the Dixon's state of health as 'neither of them has ever been well since their arrival'.[31] He felt it was impossible for Mary Dixon to live in Gibraltar and that the family would have to return home.

In fact Dixon wrote to the Committee in May 1825 to inform them that his wife's state of health was such that, without a speedy improvement, they would have to leave the Rock. She had spent time at the South and San Roque where it seems the whole family had lived for a time, but all to no avail. Soon Dixon informed the Committee that he was returning. He enclosed a doctor's letter confirming that he felt a return to England was essential for Mary.[32] The children had also been adversely affected, one had recently had dysentery and another, Eliza, had a painful eye condition. Dixon was distressed at having to take this course of action, but felt he had no choice and that Barber could supply the station, with the help of Davis, until another missionary could be sent.

The family left Gibraltar on 13 July 1825. Mary rallied on the voyage but relapsed again later. She never regained her health and died in the summer of 1828. Dixon spent the rest of his ministry in England serving in many major cities. 'In due time he became one of the most able preachers and speakers of the day' and 'one of the most prominent men in Methodism.'[33] In 1841 he served as President of Conference. Gradually however his eyesight failed until he was totally blind, but for a further nine years he still preached. He died in Bradford on 28 December 1871 aged 83.

So Barber was left alone on the station rather overwhelmed by the responsibility and also very lonely. He had never before lived without family prayers and so invited others to join him early in the morning for this purpose, with some small success. Quirell agreed to sleep at the house which gave Barber more opportunities to speak Spanish and he hoped that Antonia Quirell and their two children might join them there. He and Davis agreed to take services in the chapel alternately with Barber doing the Bethel preaching in addition but, soon after Dixon left, Davis developed such a severe attack of gout that his life seemed to be in danger and all the work therefore fell on Barber. He managed as best he could until Davis was restored to health when they shared the duties 'with great cordiality till Mr Pratten's arrival' just over three months later.[34]

Joseph and Fanny Pratten arrived on 20 October 1825 after 'a very long and rough passage of five weeks', during which both suffered from seasickness although their little girl, Elizabeth, was reported to be an

[31] Ibid., p.277. (Letter to Aquila, 16 May 1825.)

[32] *WMMS Correspondence,* Dixon to Committee, 14 May 1825, fiche 644, no.28.

[33] *Minutes of the Methodist Conference,* vol. xviii, 1870-1872, 1872, pp.496-8.

[34] Barber, op. cit., p.300. (Letter to Dixon, 27 December 1825.)

excellent sailor.[35] Pratten was born in 1792 and joined a Methodist Society at the age of fourteen. He was accepted on trial in 1815 and Gibraltar was his seventh appointment.

Once they had arrived Barber could again concentrate on the Spanish work. He had reported earlier in the year that Quirell's class was 'dissipated and his congregation entirely gone' although he did not state the reasons for this.[36] He expressed his discouragement about the work. However, he also had some ideas about the need for a separate place of worship for the Spaniards who were reluctant to go to a Protestant chapel which was, in any case, only free for them in the afternoons, a time dedicated to the siesta! However, his first priority was to become more proficient in Spanish. He therefore engaged a Spanish master which he should have done earlier but he had been worried about the expense. On 8 December 1825 he read his first sermon in Spanish on a stormy evening with only five people present. However, the following week there were thirty-five in the congregation. He was keen to preach extempore and contemplated a visit to Cádiz to practise his Spanish. In the end he did not go, but he did visit Algeciras for a few days in March 1826. However, by this time he had made better progress. On 24 February he had begun a Spanish prayer meeting at Quirell's house when about twelve people were present and he had then managed a short extempore address.

Work amongst the English congregation had continued much as before including the Sunday school and the Auxiliary Missionary Society. The work of the Bethel Society was much reduced in 1825 when one of its key supporters left leaving them with the boat hire, which was beyond their means, but links with the Bible Society had continued through Lieutenant Bailey. However, in October 1824 he reported that his wife was 'alarming ill' and he feared for her life.[37] She lived for a while but died in early 1825 and shortly afterwards Bailey left Gibraltar for a new post in the Isle of Wight where he continued his links with the Bible Society. Dixon first took over as secretary of the Corresponding Committee, and later Barber, with Pyne acting as treasurer, but communication lessened once Bailey, who had been so energetic in this work, had gone. He was also a great loss to the Methodist Society.

In February 1826 the Bible Society wrote to all its contacts to say that it would no longer be supplying copies of the scriptures with the apocrypha. The Gibraltar Committee reacted with dismay at this news which they felt would 'in a great measure terminate their usefulness with reference to the Spanish population', who usually wanted the apocrypha.[38] Despite their protestations they finally accepted the decision and had to return the books

---

[35] *WMMS Correspondence,* Pratten to Committee, 2 November 1825, fiche 645 no.32.

[36] Barber, op. cit., p.282. (Letter to Committee, May 1825.)

[37] *Foreign Correspondence In,* Bailey, 23 October 1824, p.188.

[38] *Minutes of the Corresponding Committee of the BFBS,* 4 August 1826.

they had in stock. The committee at this time included Pyne, Mrs Nicklin, Pratten, Barber and Dr John Hennen in whose house the meetings were often held. He was the Principal Medical Officer in Gibraltar but it is unlikely that he was actually a member of the Methodist Society. However, he was clearly in sympathy with them and gave free professional services to the missionaries and their families. Barber became very friendly with him and his family and obviously valued his support and friendship very much indeed. The Missionary Committee sent Dr Hennen a set of books in gratitude for his services to Methodism. In his letter of thanks he stated his particular pleasure that the books had included one on 'the life of the venerable founder of your Society, for whose name and virtue I have ever felt the most sincere respect, and whose person is still present to my recollection, although it is nearly forty years since I saw and heard him.'[39]

The Committee also sent gifts of books to Davis, now clearly fully restored to favour, and to Quirell in recognition of their contributions to the work. Meanwhile Fanny Pratten's health was causing concern, although Pratten had earlier written that he was 'much inclined to believe that her health will improve in this climate.'[40] However, in April 1826, he reported that she was nearing the end of a pregnancy and described her as a 'considerable sufferer' in these circumstances.[41] There is no record of any baptism but it seems a second daughter was born. However, after the birth, Fanny Pratten's condition gradually declined and eventually the doctors judged her to be in the last stage of consumption. She died on 10 November 1826 at the age of 33. Her funeral was held the following day when Barber officiated.

By this time Quirell was building a house in apartments and, with the approval of Pratten and Pyne, Barber felt it would be helpful for him to move there. Quirell 'gained a livelihood by teaching English to the Spaniards, an employment which keeps him fully engaged from morning to night', and living under the same roof would enable the two to work more closely together.[42] The building would also provide a more acceptable meeting place for the Spaniards. A watchnight service had been held there on 31 December, with about twenty-five Spaniards present, which Barber reported as 'the first Methodist watch-night service ever held on the Continent of Europe, in the Spanish language.'[43]

However, before Barber could move Pratten fell ill. It is not clear how much his illness was physical and how much he was affected by grief. He himself later wrote that 'there is reason to believe that my illness was more

---

[39] *WMMS Correspondence*, Hennen to Committee, 14 June 1827, fiche 646, no.47.
[40] Ibid., Pratten to Committee, 2 November 1825, fiche 645, no.32.
[41] Ibid., Pratten to Committee, 29 April 1826, fiche 645, no.34.
[42] Barber, op. cit., p.341. (Letter to Dixon, 19 September 1826.)
[43] Barber, op. cit., p.355. (From Barber's Journal.)

from domestic afflictions than from the climate', but he does seem to have had physical problems including an asthmatic condition.[44] Dr Hennen advised him to spend some time away from Gibraltar and he therefore went to Lisbon via Cádiz and was away for about six weeks, returning much restored in health.

Pratten left Davis to cover for him whilst he was away so that Barber could continue the Spanish work. Davis preached a few times and then fell ill again with another attack of gout and Barber had to shoulder most of the work himself. He coped much better on this occasion, and enjoyed preaching in English for a change which he found much easier than Spanish. At the same time, in January 1827, he moved into Quirell's house where he had 'the use of two excellent rooms' and was clearly much happier there feeling that the move was of great benefit to his work amongst the Spanish.[45] As soon as Pratten returned, he began an additional Spanish service at the house on Sunday mornings. On the first occasion about thirty attended and, by then, the Thursday evening congregation had increased to about fifty.

Then, in April 1827, Barber received unexpected instructions from the Committee to leave Gibraltar immediately and to move to Malta. At the same time William Harris Rule was ordered to leave his post in Malta and take over from Barber. The news appears to have caused some consternation in Gibraltar, and it gradually became clear that the reason for the orders was because Barber had consistently played down his progress and sent rather discouraging and negative reports to London. His tendency to depression and doubts about his abilities, together with a somewhat mistaken view of the need for humility, lay behind this and he was instructed by Pratten and Pyne to send a more accurate account to the Committee about his work and to present a case for staying.

Barber did so, describing the many evenings spent talking with Spaniards in private houses; the regular meetings - the Thursday evening service, the Friday prayer meeting and the Sunday morning service, which were all increasingly well attended. He also pointed out that a move at this stage would be a waste of all his hard work in learning Spanish. By August Barber had conducted a Spanish communion service for the first time when seventeen Spaniards participated, including Quirell and his younger brother. This was a big step forward as evidence of real commitment and conviction was required before anyone could be admitted to the Lord's Table. Quirell also wrote to the Committee asking that Barber be allowed to stay, and it seems that no one in Gibraltar thought he should leave. Once the Committee had the facts and felt more encouraged about the progress of the work, Barber was ordered to stay and his salary, which had been very low, was increased. However, by this time, Rule was already on his way to

---

[44] *WMMS Correspondence,* Pratten to Committee, 10 May 1827, fiche 646, no.46.
[45] Barber, op. cit., p.357. (Letter to his sister, 7 February 1827.)

take up the post! He left Malta on 31 May 1827 and arrived in Gibraltar on 9 July after a forty-day voyage. He spent thirty-six days there and was very well received, making quite an impact on the people. Both Quirell and Pyne wrote to the Committee to say that they felt Rule could be very useful in Gibraltar. Pyne wrote,

> We are very sorry to lose Mr Rule after so transient a visit to us. He appears to be a young man of much ardent piety and of a steadiness and solidity beyond his years; and I have no doubt that both he and his partner would be very useful in this place. They have already highly commended themselves to the people belonging to and connected with the Methodist Society here and I would humbly suggest that on a future occasion the Committee could hardly send to Gibraltar a more suitable missionary than Mr Rule.[46]

This is indeed what eventually happened, but that comes later in the story.

One of the difficulties for the whole Society at this time was the lack of a female missionary. The wife of a missionary was expected to play her part in the work though little reference was ever made to this. Now that Pratten and Barber were both widowers the lack was keenly felt. Barber lamented the loss of Mrs Rule 'because a pious and affectionate female missionary such as Mrs Rule is so much needed here and would be very valuable - there is no one to lead the female young persons of our congregations - we have no female leader'.[47] Barber himself had given much thought to the question of marrying again. He was very lonely and felt that a wife would be a great support and help in his work. He even contemplated returning to England to seek a wife, but was not sure how he could set about this. Then, in August 1827, visitors arrived.

Lady Georgiana Wolff and her husband Joseph, who were missionaries though not Methodists, called at Gibraltar on their way to Jerusalem. They were warmly received by General Don and his wife and Mr Wolff preached several times in the Methodist chapel. They were in Gibraltar for about three weeks waiting for the packet to take them to Malta. Lady Georgiana had a companion, Miss Eliza Duck, who was in fact a Methodist. At the time of their arrival, Barber was staying with the Hennens and so it was a few days before he met them. When he did, he was immediately drawn to Miss Duck. Eventually he discussed his feelings with his friends in Gibraltar, with Lady Georgiana and presumably with Eliza herself. The outcome was a happy one though only concluded a few hours before the party left for Malta. Eliza went too, to give Lady Georgiana time to find a replacement and for everyone concerned, Eliza's family and the Committee in London, to give their permission for a marriage to take place. Barber

---

[46] *WMMS Correspondence,* Pyne to Committee, 11 August 1827, fiche 646, no.52.
[47] Ibid., Barber to Committee, 11 August 1827, fiche 646, no.51.

therefore wrote most joyfully to the Committee expressing his delight that 'a kind and gracious Providence has heard my prayer and pitied my unhappiness ... and has kindly sent me most unexpectedly the very person whom he has selected for me.'[48] He described Eliza in glowing terms and asked permission to marry her, as he was obliged to do under the terms of his contract.

The Committee refused permission because Barber was still on probation, which he had assumed was drawing to a close as it was usually for a term of three years. He was bitterly disappointed. It seems that the Committee planned to keep him on probation until he received a medical testimonial that he was fit to work anywhere in the world, which he thought was never going to be possible as certain climates did not suit him. He therefore felt he was being condemned to a life of probation and celibacy. Barber also pointed out that Pratten had been ordered by the doctor to leave before the summer because he was unwell, 'while I the weak gloomy brother have gone on so regularly that I suppose I have not missed six services in all since the short illness I had soon after landing.'[49] He added that on several occasions he had been left alone on the station to carry out the whole work. Nevertheless, he knew he had no choice but to comply and he therefore sent a copy of the Committee's letter to Eliza, with a 'suspension of the engagement for the present on my part - with the option of making it final on hers'.

There is no record of the private correspondence between the two, but Eliza was by then living with the Rev. and Mrs John Keeling, the Methodist missionaries in Malta, who reported that 'this unhappy intelligence came to Malta; and I believe it has caused considerable pain to both parties.'[50] When Lady Georgiana left Malta, Eliza remained behind as she 'had reason independent of her connection with Mr Barber for going no higher up with Lady Georgiana, which would abundantly justify her in your judgement.' Lady Georgiana had given her the money for a passage to England, but Keeling invited her to stay with him and his family and told the Committee, 'I can assure you we esteem it a privilege to have her in the house'. He had thought this the best plan in case Conference did permit the marriage. Eliza had belonged to the Methodist Society for about four years. She attended Mrs Keeling's class throughout her stay in Malta and seems to have made herself useful there. Keeling described her as 'exceedingly active, tidy and industrious, and both pious and polite in her manner - and every way adapted for a missionary'.

Dr Hennen wrote to the Committee to support Barber's cause, stating that he felt Barber's health and vitality would be considerably improved as a

---

[48] Ibid., Barber to Committee, 2 September 1827, fiche 646, no.53.
[49] Ibid., Barber to Committee, 26 November 1827, fiche 647, no.56.
[50] *WMMS Correspondence Malta*, Keeling to Committee, 30 January 1828, fiche 1057, no.24.

result of any marriage. He felt he was a man who particularly needed the comforts of home life which had been shown by the striking improvement in his health that summer whilst he had been staying with the Hennens. He added that he and his family held Barber 'in a very high degree of respect and esteem'.[51] Pratten also wrote in support of him, explaining how hard he had worked in Gibraltar. He acknowledged the limitations of his constitution but ended by saying, 'I can only say that in Gibraltar or a similar climate he is <u>able</u> to do the work of a regular missionary'.[52]

So Eliza waited in Malta and life went on in Gibraltar. In May 1827 a memorial had been sent to the Governor asking for a renewal of the chapel lease which was due to expire in 1829. This was signed by Pratten, Pyne, Barnard, Herbert, Caulfield and Davis. Further correspondence about the lease was mostly handled by Pyne who kept the Committee informed of events but was clearly disappointed at times by the lack of response from London. Eventually Mr Bell, the Deputy Receiver General, was instructed to liaise with the Methodists about the renewal, but was planning to do so 'on the terms of a fair and equitable rent according to the value of the property, as would be the case if let to any other individuals'.[53] This would have involved the chapel in paying a much higher rent, which they could not afford, and Pyne was worried that as Bell was 'no friend to the cause, I do not expect he will be disposed to shew favour on the present occasion.'[54] Pyne therefore wrote to General Don, in December 1827, to plead their case and stated also that they still had a debt of £400 (about $1,845). Pyne also wrote to the Committee saying,

> It would have been a comfort to us to have heard from the Committee on this subject ere this, as I can assure you we have been in considerable trepidation as to the issue of this affair: there are several persons to whom the Lieutenant Governor is in the habit of referring matters of this kind, who are no friends of ours, who would thwart us if they could; but I took the liberty of pressing on Sir George Don the propriety of his bestowing his own sole personal attention on the subject and he has done so.[55]

In fact General Don wrote to the Secretary of State for the Colonies recommending a further lease of twenty-one years at the same rent of $1 or 4/4d per annum. The reply, when it eventually came early in 1828, was favourable so Methodism was once again indebted to Don for his support. In April 1828 Pyne submitted a list of seven trustees in whose name the lease would be granted. These were Dr Hennen, Davis, Pyne, Herbert,

---

[51] *WMMS Correspondence,* Hennen to Committee, 26 November 1827, fiche 647, no.56.
[52] Ibid., Pratten to Committee, 29 November 1827, fiche 647, no.58.
[53] Ibid., Pyne to Committee, 12 December 1827, fiche 647, no.59.
[54] Ibid., Pyne to Committee, 11 August 1827.
[55] Ibid., Pyne to Committee, December 1827, fiche 647, no.60.

Robert Barnard the younger, Henry Stokes and John Nicklin. The names were all approved and plans went ahead to renew the lease before its official expiration on 1 January 1829.

In March 1828, Pyne wrote to the Committee about the future of the work in Gibraltar. He was aware that there had been a reduction in the Missionary Society's income and wondered if Gibraltar actually needed two missionaries, suggesting therefore that one who could preach in both English and Spanish might be sufficient. This view was later endorsed by both Pratten and Barber. Pyne felt that the best person for the job would be a 'steady, middle aged married man, with few or no children, a master (grammatically) of the English language and if already acquainted with the Spanish so much the better'.[56] He also felt it would be better if the three-year rule could be waived so that the missionary, if acceptable, could stay longer. He somewhat reluctantly went on to say that, while he had a great respect for Barber, he did not think he was the man for the job as his preaching was not liked. 'He consumes in discussion and definitions a great part of that time which ought to be employed in admonishing and exhorting sinners and in edifying and comforting the people of God'. If his sermons were anything like his extremely long-winded and detailed letters it is hardly surprising that Pyne was worried about the congregation falling away! Pratten also expressed a similar view and stayed a little longer in Gibraltar than he had originally intended, despite his poor health, because he was worried about the effect on the congregation of Barber only doing the preaching. To be fair, it is clear from his correspondence that Barber himself was aware of the problem and hoped to improve.

In April 1828 Barber went into Spain on a visit to Almería and Granada. His passport, dated 9 April 1828, still exists in the church archives. In it Barber was described as being tall with brown hair, grey eyes and a regular nose! He returned in good health. So, Dr Hennen wrote again to the Committee to report the improvement, saying, 'He has made a tour to Granada, from which he has recently returned, apparently, in a state of perfect health.'[57] One wonders how much this improvement was due to his hopes for a future with Eliza, still faithfully waiting for him in Malta. Anyway, Conference did fully admit William Barber into the ministry in July and he was therefore free to marry Eliza.

Pratten's appointment was drawing to a close. He hoped to stay in Gibraltar until his successor arrived, unless he had not come by the end of June when he planned to travel overland to England. As no one did arrive, he presumably followed this course of action and left for England, where he was appointed to Swansea. He had feared his state of health might necessitate his resignation from the ministry, but it must have improved for he served in a variety of other appointments, working as the Chairman of

---

[56] Ibid., Pyne to Committee, 25 March 1828, fiche 647, no.2.
[57] Ibid., Hennen to Committee, 19 May 1828, fiche 647, no.3. Barber, op. cit., p.407.

the District for a good number of years. In 1854 he retired because of ill health and went to live in Carmarthen where he died on 16 June 1862 in his seventieth year.

So Barber was once again left alone in Gibraltar, although he did have the assistance of Davis. He moved back into the Mission House. However, before long he had much more serious matters to deal with for once again fever struck the Rock.

CHAPTER 6   THE FEVER EPIDEMIC OF 1828 AND ITS AFTERMATH
A New Missionary is Sent (1828-32)

On 10 October 1828 Barber wrote to the Committee to describe events as the epidemic took hold. The alarm was first raised at the end of August 'by the successive illness of several of the members of a very respectable family, in the habit of attending our chapel.'[1] The family's servant became ill and died. Another woman before this had concealed her illness till it was too late to do anything about it. Benady states that the disease did indeed start in the area near the Methodist chapel and that the inhabitants there tried to keep it secret, as they did not want their possessions to be burnt in an attempt to limit the spread of infection.[2] Barber reported that 'alarm began to spread about the 4th of September; and on the 5th, an order was issued from the Government, that every individual living in the district infected, should immediately leave home, and encamp on the Neutral Ground, tent-equipage being provided for them there'.[3] This was a sensible measure though, at the time, no one understood the cause of the yellow fever. It is spread by mosquitoes which probably bred in the water supplies in the town but, as they are poor fliers, they were less likely to affect the people camped on the neutral ground, or indeed at the South, who fared much better. As the Mission premises were at the centre of the infection Barber had moved to the South to stay with Mr Barnard and his family, whom he described as 'very dear and kind friends'. His servant, Paulo, had insisted on staying at the Mission House, but paid a heavy price for doing so, as he caught the fever and died soon afterwards. Barber reported that nearly 2,500 cases had already occurred and more than 450 people had died.

On 7 September the chapel was opened for the last Sunday services (an order to close all public meeting places was to take effect from 9 September), 'but the congregation was so diminished, that we occupied no more than the lower part'.[4] In the morning Davis preached while Barber administered the Lord's Supper, and baptised the son of Sergeant and Mrs Grey of the Royal Artillery. He described it as a happy occasion for they were close friends of his, but he also recalled that 'our circumstances were very solemn; we apprehended that it was the last time the chapel would be open; and everyone seemed to feel the uncertainty of ever meeting in it again'.[5] In fact, not long afterwards, both Mr and Mrs Grey died though the baby survived. Barber spent much time with them during their illness

---

[1] *WMMS Correspondence,* Barber to Committee, 10 October 1828, fiche 648, no.6.
[2] Benady, op. cit., p.83.
[3] *WMMS Correspondence,* Barber to Committee, 10 October 1828, fiche 648, no.6.
[4] Ibid., Barber to Committee, 10 October 1828, fiche 648, no.6.
[5] Ibid., Barber to Committee, 10 October 1828, fiche 648, no.6.

and acknowledged that he felt their loss keenly.

The Governor had requested the use of the chapel as an emergency hospital and, after consulting some of the leaders, Barber agreed to this. The Rev. Robert Hatchman, Chaplain to the Forces, died of the fever on 12 October at the age of 31. As soon as he became seriously ill, Barber offered to take on his duties, despite the risk to himself. His offer was accepted by General Don and his name appeared in Garrison Orders as Acting Chaplain to the Forces. He refused to accept any payment for this service, asking for it to be donated instead for the relief of the poor living on the neutral ground. The duties meant that twice a day he had to officiate at burials. He went 'to the ground on horseback, at 8 o'clock in the morning and at four in the afternoon. He likewise had to visit the sick in the hospital, which was running a great risk; but as he saw that it was the path of duty, he did not shrink from it.'[6]

He was, of course, aware of the danger he was in, and told the Committee:

> I feel deeply at the possibility, that this is the last letter I shall write to you; for I have no constitution to stand against a violent attack of fever. But should that be the case, I now leave my deliberate testimony, that I believe salvation by Jesus Christ to be the true and only worthy object of human life as a whole.[7]

In a letter to his father, he referred to the congratulations he had received from friends in England on being fully accepted as a Methodist minister, but added,

> What do they all avail now? - Eliza, dear lovely girl, is, by a special Providence, detained, and that in a remarkable manner, at Malta; and, by this time, she must have received my letter, to direct her to wait sometime longer in safety, where she is. But now, after all, I shall, perhaps, have to leave her *an unmarried widow*. Should that, unhappily, be the case, I am sure, that I shall not commend her in vain to your earnest affections, if you should ever see her.[8]

On 16 October both Hennen and Barber wrote to John Pyne who had gone to England on a visit, and happily for him had been detained there away from all danger. Hennen reported that there had been 566 deaths noted in the official returns (daily statistics were in fact printed in the *Gibraltar Chronicle*) but he felt it was likely a hundred more had died without being reported to him. Five medical men were already dead. His wife had been ill but was now better. He ended his letter with the short but

---

[6] Barber, op. cit., p.426. (Letter from Mrs Barnard to Pratten, 5 November 1828).

[7] *WMMS Correspondence,* Barber to Committee, 10 October 1828, fiche 648, no.6. Barber, op. cit., p.420.

[8] Barber, op. cit., p.423. (Letter to his father, 12 October 1828).

telling sentence: 'Do not come here'.[9] Barber's letter to Pyne included the following distressing and moving account of what was happening to him in Gibraltar.

> Every remaining friend is to us, now, very dear indeed. What a scene surrounds us! What a scene have I before me every day on the Neutral Ground! .... no man can calculate upon a single hour; and deaths are very, very numerous, at three or four days illness ... I have lost some of my most intimate friends in the Society, to whom my warmest affections were linked, for their piety and love. Great God! how terrible is this! A fierce disease, which you can neither see, nor hear, nor touch, springs invisibly on its victims; and not by ones or twos, but by scores and hundreds, we are putting them into the grave. The number of dead is so great, that to bury them in single graves is impracticable. Trenches are dug, and the coffins (for, thank God, as yet coffins can be had, though only by the most praiseworthy vigour of the Government) are laid side by side, in regular and most afflictive order. Yesterday, for example I read the funeral service over nineteen bodies in the Protestant Ground. More than that number, of course, were likewise interred in the grounds of the Catholics and Jews. This morning I had to discharge the same melancholy duty for ten more; and how many will follow in the afternoon, I cannot guess ... never have I had duties so melancholy to discharge. The burial ground and the hospitals are spots of intense infection, and I am every moment with my life in my hand. But, 'What do ye more than others?' There are very many who deserve infinitely higher praise, if praise at such a moment can be thought of with innocence, than I. With a very, very sinful heart, and a life that looks to me only in the light of something worse than a blank, I fling myself at the feet of Jesus, and hope for every thing through His atonement alone.[10]

Barber continued his duties but on the evening of Tuesday 21 October, after returning from visiting a sick man in the hospital, he complained of feeling ill himself. William Thornton, a diarist of the time, described Barber's commitment to his work when he wrote,

> This young man is supposed to have taken the Fever whilst attending a patient in the Hospital who wished to confess something and being very much exhausted, Mr B. was obliged to lean quite over him to hear what he had to say, and from that circumstance supposed he took it.[11]

Later that night his condition worsened and a doctor was sent for, but he too was ill and unable to come. Indeed he later died. However, Dr Hennen came with a colleague. He returned the next day with three other medical

---

[9] Ibid. (Letter from Hennen to Pyne, 16 October 1828).

[10] Ibid., pp.424-5. (Letter to Pyne, 16 October 1828).

[11] L.A. Sawchuk and S. Benady, *Diary of an Epidemic: Yellow Fever in Gibraltar, 1828*, Gibraltar Government Heritage Divison: 2003, p.63.

men but there seemed to be little hope. On the Wednesday night, Mr and Mrs Herbert sat up with him and he seemed a little better in the morning. Barber was clearly given the best nursing and medical care available, but his constitution was against him. On Saturday night the Barnards sat up with him and early on Sunday morning Davis and Caulfield visited him. He gave good testimony to his faith and died at quarter to four in the afternoon on Sunday 26 October in the presence of many of his friends. He was twenty-nine years old. Mrs Barnard wrote, 'It was a great trial to part with one, who had lived seven weeks under our roof, and who was become as one of the family. We all loved him much.'[12]

The following day, at 8 o'clock in the morning, Barber was buried near the grave of Fanny Pratten as he had requested. Many of the Society were present. Davis officiated as there were now no clergymen left alive, and he reported that many were in tears. A plaque in memory of William Barber was placed in the chapel and eventually a tombstone was erected in the burial ground, although no trace of this can be found today.

Shortly afterwards, another tragic death occurred, for Dr Hennen too became a victim of the fever. He died on 3 November at the age of 49. There is a plaque in his memory in the King's Chapel giving these details and adding the following words:

> This tablet is erected by his personal friends, not with a view of perpetuating his name, for that lives in the more imperishable memorials of his own Genius but as a testimony of Regard for a man whose zeal was indefatigable and who, in the day of great calamity sacrificed all consideration of his own safety for the public weal.

He had apparently continued to work until the day before his death. His passing was a great loss to Methodism too and to the cause of the Bible Society.

So, once again the Society was ravaged by an epidemic fever and left to try and make sense of it all. News of the tragic loss of William Barber was sent to London, to his family and also to Eliza Duck waiting vainly for him in Malta. It was particularly tragic, after so much sadness in his life, that he should die when his work was bearing fruit; he had regained his health and found someone else to marry. It was also a tragedy for Eliza. She stayed on in Malta until December when Keeling reported that she was leaving for England.[13] He felt she would have been very useful in their Mission School but she wanted to go to Bristol where one hopes she had some family to comfort her, or perhaps she had gone to William Barber's family there. Barber's books were later sent on to her.

The *Gibraltar Chronicle* gave the final death toll as 1,618 but other

---

[12] Barber, op. cit., p.428. (Letter from Mrs Barnard to Pratten, 5 November 1828).
[13] *WMMS Correspondence Malta*, Keeling to Committee, 30 December 1828, fiche 1057, no.28.

estimates gave a figure of 2,300. Whatever the final figure, it was considerably lower than that of the 1804 epidemic probably because of the measures both Hennen and Don had implemented. Nevertheless, the Rock had been devastated by the disease. Many members and friends of the Society had died and once again those who remained were left without a missionary, but the ever faithful Thomas Davis stepped in to lead as best he could. His long letter to the Committee in November 1828 ended as follows:

> I would beg leave to call your attention to the distressed state of the little church in this place - we are, you perceive left without any visible head or guide, and like sheep scattered on the tops of the mountains. As to the chapel, the sick are removed from it, but in order to prepare it for the reception of the sick, they removed the pulpit and reading desk, broke down the backs of the seats in the galleries and built two platforms for the sick to be placed on, and also made two windows in the back part of the chapel. In this state they have left it, and what government intends doing towards replacing these damages I do not know but I believe it is thought by all who know anything of the real state of the chapel, that we will not be able to open it when permission is granted, till it goes through a general repair. I hope then Rev. Sir, both you and the Committee will see the great necessity of sending us a missionary to take the oversight of the Church, and to superintend these repairs. As to myself I promise to do what I can when this trying scene is over, to gather the little flock together and to keep them together. My intention is to open the room in the South for public service as soon as it will be permitted, until a preacher arrives among us, but please remember Sir, I am now an old man and only fit to be laid by.[14]

The official termination of the epidemic was finally announced in a proclamation from General Don, printed in the *Gibraltar Chronicle* on 12 January 1829. Don ordered all places of worship to open on 16 January so that the day could 'be set apart as one of Solemn Thanksgiving for the mercy here vouchsafed to us, and to propitiate a continuance of the Divine favour.' Shops and places of public business were to be closed. All public meeting places re-opened on 17 January and so, on Sunday 18 January, Davis was able to open the room at the South where he preached to a crowded congregation. He continued to do so, both Sundays and Wednesdays, until Sunday 8 February when he was finally able to open the repaired chapel in town. He took both morning and evening services there, the latter taking the form of a memorial service for William Barber. Classes had been meeting since then and Davis had tried to meet with the leaders of them once a fortnight as was customary, but had not been able to meet with them all. Caulfield had been taking care of the Mission House and the chapel had been repaired by the government. Davis and two others

---

[14] *WMMS Correspondence*, Davis to Committee, 30 November 1828, fiche 648, no.8.

had 'waited on the proper authorities' and were 'most graciously received'. They were thanked for giving up the chapel to be a hospital and condolences were given on the loss of Barber. Perhaps his willingness to serve the garrison encouraged the authorities to be generous in their turn for the chapel had been returned to them in 'the most handsome state of repair'.[15]

Quirell continued the work with the Spanish congregation. He reported progress to Dixon and asked him to approach the Committee on his behalf. He first expressed his sorrow at 'losing my dearest friend', William Barber, and said that some of the Spanish flock had also died.[16] He had visited some when they were ill and felt those who had died had done so as Christians should, professing their faith. On 18 January the group had met for worship in his house for the first time since August. Congregations on Sundays, Thursdays and Fridays amounted to between forty and fifty people and between twelve and fourteen of them were accustomed to take the sacrament. Quirell had to work long hours to earn a living which meant he could not 'pay all the attention that is necessary or as I would wish to the little flock which grieves me very much, for the Lord knows the Spanish cause lies at the centre of my heart'. He was anxious to know if the Committee was willing to continue paying the rent for the Spanish meeting room in his house and also offered to work for the Mission himself, or to work alongside a new missionary.

At the end of February word came that Joseph Stinson had been appointed. He was born in Leicestershire into a Methodist family, and was himself converted by the age of twenty. He became a local preacher and was accepted, in 1823, to be a missionary and was appointed to East Canada. Later he returned to England where he was stationed in Manchester for one year before being appointed to Gibraltar. He set sail with his wife, Hannah, arriving on 4 May 1829 after a voyage of thirty-four days. No mention is made of any children sailing with them but a daughter, Selina, was born in April the following year. In his first letter from Gibraltar, written just a few days after landing, Stinson reported that they 'were very affectionately received by our friends who had been long and anxiously looking for us.'[17]

The very next day he held his first leaders' meeting and began a record of these in a new minute book which continued in sporadic use until 1895. Both Caulfield and Davis were present at the meeting, and Herbert was unanimously appointed as Society and chapel steward. As a result of the epidemic, membership had declined and was given as fifty-nine. The Committee had sent Davis another book in appreciation of all he had done.

On 6 May Stinson met General Don and thanked him for his help with

---

[15] Ibid., Davis to Committee, 4 March 1829, fiche 648, no.10.
[16] Ibid., Quirell to Dixon, 21 January 1829, fiche 648, no.9.
[17] Ibid., Stinson to Committee, 7 May 1829, fiche 648, no.11.

the chapel repairs and with the lease. He was well received and felt there was 'every reason to conclude that he will continue to exercise towards us that kindness which has so marked His Excellency's conduct'.[18] The renewal of the lease had in fact been delayed because of the epidemic and the death of Hennen, who had been proposed as a trustee. Pyne had returned to Gibraltar after the fever had abated and in April he submitted a new list of trustees. These included the three secretaries and the treasurer of the Missionary Society, Stinson, Pratten, Davis, Pyne, Herbert, Robert Barnard the younger, Henry Stokes and John Nicklin. The lease was eventually drawn up in their names, signed by General Don on 15 May 1829 and registered in the court, as required by law, on 4 June under the same conditions as the original lease.

Stinson reported that he felt the Spanish cause was rather low as a result of Barber's death and other losses to the group. He promised to give another more informed opinion as to 'the propriety of making Brother Quirell a regular allowance for his labours'. Quirell was apparently under the impression that the Committee was likely to do so and Stinson reported that 'he is to all appearances a very pious man and I should think a very fair preacher in his own language'.[19]

Stinson was rather disappointed to find the Mission House 'in a most uncomfortable state'. It had never properly been cleaned since the epidemic when Barber's servant had died in it. There was little furniture and 'the roof is broken in several places, the water spouts are split - the plaster is off the walls and altogether it presents a most dreary aspect'. He planned to repair and furnish the house as cheaply as possible. Finally, he reported that Pyne was to leave Gibraltar and would be greatly missed. No reason is given for his departure but it may well have been because of the epidemic.

Gradually Stinson, with the help of the leaders, began the work of building up the church and, in July 1829, he reported that membership had increased to seventy-three. He described the Society as one that was 'as affectionate and united as ever I saw' adding 'I believe that the leading members of our little church are particularly anxious that the end for which this mission has been established may be fully answered and I do receive from them that sympathy, that kindness and that co-operation which is so necessary for the comfort and success of a missionary'.[20]

In July Quirell was unanimously appointed to act as a local preacher at the leaders' meeting but the Spanish cause remained low. Stinson commented,

> Although Brother Quirell is a pious and active person - yet truth obliges

---

[18] Ibid., Stinson to Committee, 7 May 1829, fiche 648, no.11.

[19] Ibid., Stinson to Committee, 7 May 1829, fiche 648, no.11.

[20] Ibid., Stinson to Committee, 14 July 1829, fiche 648, no.12.

me to say that he has not talent to command a Spanish congregation - as is evidenced from the fact that he seldom has more than twelve or fourteen hearers whereas Mr Barber used to have sixty and seventy - on this account I have resolved not to pay anything for a separate room but get him to meet them in the chapel when it is not occupied by the English congregation. That he may be useful in distributing religious books and visiting people from house to house I have no doubt - and if the Committee allow him 4 or 5 dollars per month for doing this it might be well - but this if granted at all, should only be continued until I am able to do the work myself which I hope will be before too long.[21]

It is not clear how accurate this assessment was. The work had been more successful under Barber, though the figures of sixty to seventy are a little high. Some members of the Spanish congregation had died during the epidemic and others had left Gibraltar afterwards, fearing further outbreaks. In addition, Quirell's time for the work was limited and Stinson does not seem to have understood the difficulties of expecting the Spaniards to meet in a Protestant chapel, which had proved a problem in the past. Stinson did not say what Quirell thought about all this and sadly he was soon in trouble. At the leaders' meeting in August 'a charge was brought against Brother J. Quirell by Mr T. Rich for taking fixtures from the House which he lately occupied which did not belong to him, and for defamation of character, the latter having called the former an old rogue'.[22] As a result Quirell was forbidden to preach to any congregation and was excluded from the Society for three months.

The summer passed without a fever outbreak. Stinson reported that 'all strangers were strongly recommended to spend three months on the neutral ground where the troops were encamped' and that this was the reason he took 'part of a shed'.[23] Membership continued to increase and in October he opened a new and 'very large room in the South', as the previous one had proved too small.[24] Further thought was given to building their own preaching place there but nothing came of it.

In November 1829 Quirell appeared before the leaders' meeting and was re-admitted to the Society on trial. In February the following year, it was unanimously agreed that he be allowed to preach to the Spanish congregation but not to the English. In March of that year Stinson wrote to the Bible Society. The Corresponding Committee, which had been temporarily suspended as a result of the epidemic, had been revived and new members were coming forward to take the place of those who had died. The committee had 'employed a person who understands the Spanish, Portuguese and French languages to visit the poor people in the

---

[21] Ibid., Stinson to Committee, 14 July 1829, fiche 648, no.12.

[22] Chapel minute book.

[23] *WMMS Correspondence,* Stinson to Committee, 12 January 1830, fiche 649, no.14.

[24] Ibid., Stinson to Committee, 30 October 1829, fiche 648, no.13.

Garrison and to go on board the small vessels which lie in the Bay - to sell or give away copies of the Scriptures as circumstances may require'.[25] This person was later named as Quirell. He was paid $4 a month, but the proceeds from the sale of books were only just sufficient to pay him and maintain a depository. Many Spaniards were reported as being keen to receive the scriptures despite the strict watch of others opposed to the 'spread of divine knowledge'. Stinson felt there was evidence that many Spaniards, supplied from Gibraltar, regularly read the Bible and persuaded others to buy one. He used every opportunity to send Spanish scriptures and tracts into Spain. In 1830 a ship's captain took some up the coast to Almería and found that Barber's visit there was still remembered. He soon distributed his stock and could have sold many more.

Stinson also began some new work, reporting that they had 'established an evening school for Spanish children in which they are taught to read in English and that about 40 attend every Tuesday from 7 till 9 o'clock'.[26] This was in addition to the Sunday schools which continued to thrive and also included Spanish children. By July 1830 Stinson reported that nearly seventy Spanish children were attending the sabbath and week schools where they were taught to read the Bible.

There were continuing problems over the finances and various schemes, mainly of collections and subscriptions, were devised to help clear off the debt and to raise money for a new roof. However, insufficient money was raised by these means for either purpose.

In January 1831 Stinson reported that his wife was not in good health: 'she has been so ill that I have thought of sending her home next spring as I fear if she does not gain strength now it is cool she will not be able to bear the hot weather'.[27] He reported his own health to be 'generally good' but as so often happened it seemed to be the wife who suffered the most. He does not give the cause of her problems, but clearly was concerned about the heat of the summer. She did not improve and in the summer Stinson described his wife and little daughter as 'almost always ill'.[28]

In February 1831 Quirell was once again in trouble and the leaders' meeting unanimously agreed that he should be excluded from the Society. In April Stinson informed the Committee, referring to the earlier suspension 'for defaming the character of a gentleman with whom he was connected in business and in then denying it, in the face of the strongest evidence of his guilt'. Now he had been called to account for 'a similar offence, only attended with more deliberate wickedness. I brought him before the person whose character he had endeavoured to injure (a very respectable female). He so far acknowledged his guilt as to ask her pardon,

---

[25] *Foreign Correspondence In,* Stinson, 1 March 1830, 1830 Box 1, p.117.
[26] *WMMS Correspondence,* Stinson to Committee, 19 April 1830, fiche 649, no.16.
[27] Ibid., Stinson to Committee, 17 January 1831, fiche 649, no.20.
[28] Ibid., Stinson to Committee, 15 July 1831, fiche 649, no.25.

and she was by that means prevented taking him before the courts.'[29] He had, however, refused to attend the leaders' meeting saying that he was not accountable to them and that he would no longer remain in the Society. This inevitably injured the Spanish cause and Stinson felt their main hope of converting anyone was now through the schools. He himself had made good progress in learning Spanish and preached to the Spaniards on Tuesday evenings in a private room which he now realised suited them better than the chapel. Average attendance was about ten. He reported that they had nothing to do with Quirell, who was calling himself a reformed Catholic, and was still preaching in his own house to about a dozen people, including his own family.

Discipline was strict throughout the Society and no one was exempt. In June 1831 the following resolution was passed unanimously: 'that the conduct of Brother [Michael] Caulfield had been in many respects very inconsistent with the Christian character: but that in consideration of his age and long standing in the Church he shall not at this time be excluded the Society'.[30] Instead he was prohibited from taking any part in prayer meetings, class meetings or leaders' meetings. It was hoped his future conduct would be more circumspect and justify these more lenient measures.

So Stinson's time in Gibraltar drew to an end. His wife had not returned to England; indeed in January 1832 he had written to say that his 'dear partner and two little daughters are much better than usual'.[31] This is the first mention of a second daughter but it is not clear what age she was - there is only a record of one child being born in Gibraltar. The improvement was only short-lived though, because in March he referred to his wife as 'far from being well', so it was probably a good thing that the family was about to leave.[32] During their time in Gibraltar the membership had almost doubled and under Stinson's leadership much of the work, so badly affected by the epidemic, was revived and taken forward. Throughout his ministry in Gibraltar no major opposition was reported, though Stinson did mention 'some petty opposition from without', but gave no details about it.[33] Unfortunately the Spanish cause did not revive. It never recovered from the loss of Barber whilst Quirell, who had worked so hard for the cause, was also lost to it. However, the start of the school was seen to be an exciting new venture and provided education for some Spanish children.

Meanwhile in England a new missionary had been appointed, William Harris Rule, who of course had already visited Gibraltar and therefore

---

[29] Ibid., Stinson to Committee, 18 April 1831, fiche 649, no.22.

[30] Chapel minute book.

[31] *WMMS Correspondence,* Stinson to Committee, 11 January 1832, fiche 650, no.20.

[32] Ibid., Stinson to Committee, 20 March 1832, fiche 650, no.31.

[33] Ibid., Stinson to Committee, 17 January 1831, fiche 649, no.20.

knew something of the work. He arrived in February 1832 before Stinson left, so they were able to work together and had 'many very serious conversations' about the work considering the best way of going forward. As a result of these conversations, Rule wrote to the Committee to 'express our conviction that there is an opening for more extensive <u>effort</u> and probably for more extensive <u>usefulness</u> among the foreigners on this rock', and the development of this work was to be Rule's first main aim.[34]

Stinson left Gibraltar in mid April and returned to England for one year. In 1833 he resumed his work in Canada where he served at times as the General Superintendent of Missions and as President of the Canadian Conference. He returned to England in 1842 and served in a number of different appointments before returning to Canada where he was re-appointed as President of the Canadian Conference in 1858. His health began to deteriorate in 1861 and, after some months of illness, he died on 26 August 1862 in Toronto in his 61st year.

Meanwhile, back in Gibraltar, Rule had begun his ministry which was to last for ten years and was to take the work forward in several ways.

---

[34] Ibid., Rule to Committee, 9 April 1832, fiche 650, no.32.

CHAPTER 7 THE MINISTRY OF WILLIAM HARRIS RULE (1)
EXPANSION
A System of Education, Forays into Spain (1832-6)

William Harris Rule was born in Penryn in Cornwall on 15 November 1802. His father, a surgeon in the navy, did not see his son until he was nearly three years old. They did not get on and William was thrown out of his home by his father when he was seventeen. He and some friends then formed the Falmouth Philosophical Society, and one in Truro, for the purpose of reading and debating together. One friend was Richard Treffry whose father was a Methodist minister. His whole family welcomed William into their home and he was impressed by them. Later he left Cornwall and lived as a student, earning a basic living as an artist, and ending up in London. The Treffry family moved to Rochester and Richard sent William a Bible in the autumn of 1822, informing him of his own conversion. William decided to read it for Richard's sake but was soon reading in earnest for his own sake. At Christmas he went to Rochester for a week and was much impressed by the Methodists he met there. He returned to London and some months later after 'anxiously seeking peace with God', he found it at a prayer meeting in Exeter and 'left the house of God rejoicing'.[1]

Later, Richard Treffry senior encouraged him to give up his itinerant life and so, instead of following his cherished plan of touring the continent as an artist, he became a village school master, preaching two or three times every Sunday. Three months later he was accredited as a local preacher and offered as a candidate for the ministry. In 1825 he was accepted on trial and summoned to London to wait for an appointment as a missionary. He spent the next few months studying. In February 1826 he married Mary Ann Dunmill, after receiving permission from the Missionary Committee to do so. On 14 March he was ordained in London and on 22 March he and his wife set sail for Malta. Rule had been sent there to prepare for a mission in Palestine but the project had to be abandoned when war broke out and so, in 1827, he was directed to Gibraltar.

After discovering that they were not needed in Gibraltar the Rules returned to England. In November 1827 they set sail for the West Indies but, by the beginning of 1831, Mary's health was so poor her husband felt that there was 'no hope of her living much longer' if they remained.[2] They left in March, but Mary was so weak she had to be carried onto the ship. By this time they had a son, 'a fine little boy not yet three years old, whom we loved most tenderly'. It was not a good voyage, the captain was often drunk, provisions were scarce and their little boy suddenly fell ill and died

---

[1] W.H. Rule, *Recollections of my life and work at home and abroad*, T. Woolmer: London, 1886, p.14.

[2] Ibid., p.60.

in his father's arms on 27 April. He was buried at sea and just a few days later on 3 May they landed in England, seeking 'among the sympathy of our nearest friends to rise above the sorrow, but it was too heavy'.

Rule expected to be disciplined by the Committee for disobeying orders, by returning to England without permission, but he was in fact received with much kindness. It seems that Mary was pregnant and at some stage a daughter was born. Rule was given a 'nominal appointment to the Sevenoaks circuit' which he held from August until January.[3] Here he began preparing for his next appointment in Gibraltar.

The family embarked at Falmouth on 10 February 1832 and completed the voyage to Gibraltar, including a visit to Lisbon, in an amazing six days. This was because the ship was a steam packet and Rule believed that he was the first missionary to have the advantage of travelling aboard such a ship. On arrival they were kept in quarantine for five days on a ship in the bay. There was cholera in London and the authorities did not want it brought into Gibraltar. However, some of the congregation came out to visit them, surely making a nonsense of the notion of quarantine! Rule unwittingly upset some of them by failing to call them 'brother' or 'sister' referring to them instead as 'Mr' or 'Mrs'. They apparently called a special prayer meeting afterwards to pray for him! He reported that not everyone shared this view, but nevertheless they 'had great trouble in consequence' of it.[4] He obviously won the day for in the minute book the use of 'brother' and 'sister' largely ceased. Stinson wrote to the Committee to report the safe arrival of the Rule family saying that Rule 'is very acceptable to the people and is likely to be very useful'.[5]

However, this controversy marked a somewhat difficult beginning for Rule, and in many ways his time in Gibraltar was characterised by opposition and controversy. Physically small in stature, he was large in vision and possessed phenomenal zeal, commitment and enthusiasm for his work as a minister of the gospel, but he found it hard to accept those who did not share his energy or his viewpoint. He favoured a more formal approach to worship and apparently even had a vestry built near the entrance to the chapel to display his gowns! He was well educated and later gained a doctorate. He was also a natural linguist and by the end of his life was said to be able to read eleven languages and converse in several. He soon mastered Spanish. He was extremely energetic and dynamic as well as forthright and outspoken in his views and it was perhaps, therefore, inevitable that some would not like his approach. In addition he was a born missionary and, unlike most of his predecessors for whom the English cause had come first, Rule's passion was for the Spanish cause both in Gibraltar and Spain. There were some who did not like this

---

[3] Ibid., p.63.

[4] Ibid., p.65.

[5] *WMMS Correspondence,* Stinson to Committee, 20 March 1832, fiche 650, no.31.

emphasis and many of those who had been so impressed with him in 1827 were no longer in Gibraltar. Letters were sent to England complaining about Rule acting with an 'iron hand'.[6] His sermons were criticised and the dull formal prayer meetings which now lacked 'earnestness and fervency in prayer'.[7] He was compared unfavourably with Stinson and John Allen, speaking for several members, urged the Committee to remove Rule. Rule, on the other hand, was clearly most distressed by their complaints which gave him 'unspeakable pain in my own mind'.[8] He did his best to talk with those concerned, to understand their position and to put things right.

The controversy continued for several years causing division in the church. He was described by some as a 'little tyrant', and exception was taken to the tightening up of discipline. Rule insisted that members of the Sunday School Committee be approved by the leaders' meeting and all those 'engaged in the singing pew'! The choirmaster, Mr Rich, was so incensed by this that he and his singers said they would withdraw if this measure was insisted upon. Rule accepted his resignation acknowledging 'his indefatigable attention to the advancement of the singing during the last four years'.[9] However, Rich must have relented as shortly afterwards he was requested to form a choir and from then on the names of those wishing to belong to it were submitted for approval to the leaders' meeting.

William Harris Rule
(With permission from the Oxford Centre for Methodism and Church History)

General discipline continued to be strict with cases of drunkenness and theft usually leading to exclusion from the Society. One of the leaders, Mr Newman, 'having repeatedly manifested a quarrelsome disposition at our meetings, is no longer to be a leader', though he was eventually restored to the position.[10] Michael Caulfield was re-instated as a class leader in March 1835, after an absence of nearly four years.

At this time the Rule family itself was not without its own troubles. Rule reported in January 1833 that he had had to undergo an operation, though

---

[6] Ibid., Allen to Stinson, 22 January 1833, fiche 651, no.2.
[7] Ibid., French to Rule, 13 August 1832, fiche 650, no.36.
[8] Ibid., Rule to Committee, 29 March 1833, fiche 651, no.5.
[9] Chapel minute book.
[10] Ibid..

he did not give any details. He described his wife as suffering 'a long and severe attack of bowel complaint, which has been here a prevalent and sometimes fatal disease'.[11] The result of this illness was the premature birth of their son, Barrow, born on 14 January 1833. Two days later their daughter died. It seems she too had been ill for some time, but there is no mention of her death in the burials' register. As a result of all this, Mary Rule was ill for some months.

Rule does seem to have done his best to weather the storm of criticism and continue with his work, but a small group left the Society in September 1834, including John Allen and his wife. Although the reasons for the rift were never explicitly stated, Rule did refer to the group as Warrenites. In England, this group wanted 'lay representation in the Conference and self-government for local congregations'.[12] The issue of lay representation caused many problems in England after the death of Wesley. There were other disagreements too which led to a number of breakaways and developments, including that known as Primitive Methodism, but Gibraltar remained Wesleyan until the different branches of Methodism united in 1932. However, the question of lay involvement was an issue in Gibraltar where the work had been founded, developed and sometimes continued by lay people in the absence of a minister. Those missionaries who understood this and were prepared to work with the lay leaders fared best, but those like Rees and Rule who took a more authoritarian stance ran into difficulties. However, opposition aside, Rule's ministry was certainly a dynamic one, and the work developed during his ten years in Gibraltar in many different ways. The first main development was an unplanned one in the field of education.

It has sometimes been said that Rule began the first schools in Gibraltar but this is not strictly true. Traverso's work on the history of education shows that even in the early days of the British occupation there were some private educational establishments.[13] Then, at the end of 1802, or early 1803, the Duke of Kent recommended the establishment of regimental schools which were gradually set up. Around 1816, General Don re-organised them into two schools, one for the Northern District on Castle Road and the other at Buena Vista in the South, but in 1828 they were closed because the premises were required for other purposes.

Wesley himself had always stressed the importance of education and the first Methodist Societies in London, Bristol and Newcastle all had schools attached to them. He expected his preachers to follow a course of study long before formal training colleges were established and is reported to

---

[11] *WMMS Correspondence,* Rule to Committee, 1 January 1833, fiche 651, no.1.

[12] John Kent in Davies, Rupp, op. cit., vol. ii, p.233.

[13] Albert Austin Traverso, 'A History of Education In British Gibraltar 1704-1945', MA Thesis, University of Southampton: 1980. E.G. Archer & A.A. Traverso, *Education in Gibraltar 1704-2004,* Gibraltar Books: Gibraltar, 2004.

have said that 'if the Methodists were not a reading people the work of grace would die out in a generation'.[14] Education was seen as a means of social reform but it was also seen as a means of proselytising, which was certainly Rule's intention in Gibraltar.

Rule attributed the start of his educational work to his wife, who was always a strong support to him. She too became a fluent Spanish speaker. When they arrived in Gibraltar, the Rule family went into lodgings, as the Stinsons were still occupying the Mission House. About a month after their arrival, one of their neighbours approached Mary Rule and asked her if she would teach her eldest child to read, hoping this would enable her daughter to find better work in the future. Mary agreed and the little girl came every morning for a lesson. Her brother soon joined her and, as the word spread, more parents sought lessons for their children until Rule himself had to help his wife 'to teach no inconsiderable school the first letters'.[15] The children were at first mainly Roman Catholic but soon Jewish children joined them and when the numbers became larger they were taught in the chapel, 'for want of a more suitable place'.[16] Thus Rule felt he 'became, unawares, founder of the first charity-school in the garrison'.[17] It is not clear what happened to Stinson's evening school, which may have been for older working youngsters.

Rule then began to consider how religion should be taught in his school, which had really developed in an unplanned way. Somewhat unusually for him, he felt it was wise to be cautious and so there were no prayers at school, only a morning reading class from the Bible. However, as time went on, he became more and more unhappy with this approach and sought for an opportunity to change it. The Jews finally removed their children anyway, as the rabbis were not happy about them attending a Christian school. Then a new educational initiative was suggested for Gibraltar itself and a meeting was convened to consider setting up a proper free public school. The meeting was chaired by the Lieutenant Governor, now Lieutenant General Sir William Houston. Rule felt this initiative was a result of his efforts and it may well be that his work had prompted the authorities to re-establish the schools of the past. Anyway, a public school, funded by local voluntary subscriptions, was opened in September 1832 in a building, situated on Flat Bastion Road, which the government provided free of charge. Rule transferred his children there immediately. A managing committee was set up which included the heads of the Catholic and Protestant churches along with lay representatives of the Catholic Church, the Church of England and the Jewish community, although the

---

[14] John T. Smith, *Methodism and Education 1849-1902*, Clarendon Press: Oxford, 1998, p.1.

[15] Rule, *Recollections*, op. cit., p.69.

[16] W.H. Rule, M*emoir of a Mission to Gibraltar and Spain*, John Mason: London, 1844, p.95.

[17] Rule, *Recollections*, op. cit., p.69.

Jews apparently later withdrew. Methodism was not represented and, because of the different religious backgrounds of the children, it was agreed that religion would not be taught. Rule was unhappy about that and felt it opened the way for him to open a proper Mission School and he announced this plan in October 1833.

This time he made it clear that religious education would be a compulsory part of the curriculum and, most controversially, that the children would be required to attend the Sunday morning services in the Methodist chapel. At first only two children were brought to the school, but after three months there were ten and by the end of the first year there were thirty pupils. No exceptions were made to the rule of attending Sunday worship and, as most of the children were Roman Catholics, it is not surprising that this stirred up considerable opposition from the priests who tried hard to persuade parents not to send their children to the school. Their opposition was not just aroused because of the school, but also because of Rule's growing work amongst the Spanish-speaking population.

Rule had reported this work to be at a low ebb. Quirell's work was still developing and he had also gathered together a Sunday school. After investigation, Rule felt there was a possibility that Quirell had been misjudged and so he decided to give him the benefit of the doubt. He therefore began to preach to the Spaniards at Quirell's house and reported at first that he had no reason to regret this decision. In May 1832 he baptised the Quirell's son, Juan. By this time Quirell was regarded by the Spanish 'as a sort of priest' and had even been administering communion, but Rule insisted that he be acknowledged as their sole pastor and as such he undertook to pay 'the trifling expenses of lighting his room, and any such incidental cost'.[18] However, after a trial of two months, Rule ceased to preach at Quirell's house because, as soon as he had developed a good congregation, Quirell took a room 'to set up for himself'. Rule felt it was clear that as 'I have no hope of establishing with him a Christian Society, I must be disencumbered of him and avail myself of that co-operation of a few good people among ourselves who willingly give encouragement to this infant cause without wishing to be at the head of a party or desiring pay as assistant missionaries'.[19]

Perhaps it is not surprising that Quirell took this course of action, as he had been leading the people for twelve months and presumably enjoyed his success and status as their leader. His congregation continued to increase and sometimes amounted to two hundred. However, they continued to call themselves Methodists, which caused problems for Rule because people could not differentiate between the two groups. Quirell then preached against the Catholics with the result that all Methodists were denounced at each mass held in Gibraltar one Sunday. Rule tried to explain that Quirell

---

[18] *WMMS Correspondence,* Rule to Committee, 25 May 1832, fiche 650, no.34.
[19] Ibid., Rule to Committee, 26 June 1832, fiche 650, no.35.

and his followers were not Methodists, and felt he convinced some, yet he worried that Quirell might gain from the publicity of his open opposition. He therefore decided that his best course of action was to establish a proper Spanish Methodist Society himself, but he argued that he would need an assistant in order to do the work properly.

What happened to Quirell's Spanish congregation is not known. He continued teaching and, in August 1832, the planned opening of an academy 'under the auspices of a Mr J.B. Quirrel' was reported in the *Gibraltar* Chronicle.[20] In 1836, a final reference to him in the Methodist correspondence, stated, 'John Quirell has got a situation, he is now clerk in the Protestant Church, so both brothers are now employed there'.[21] His brother, Luis, had in fact continued as a Methodist. After Quirell's wife died, he married Rosa Nogueras Sanclaudio on 28 July 1857 in the Protestant Cathedral and they later moved to Cádiz with Quirell's son, Juan, who opened a shop there. A daughter, Rosa, was born there in October 1859. She eventually had eleven children so there are many descendents of Quirell alive today. He himself died in Cádiz on 16 February 1866 aged 71.

Meanwhile, as the Catholic opposition in the South was strong, Rule concentrated his efforts in town. He held two Spanish services every Sunday in the chapel, one at mid-day and one in the evening after the English congregation had left. Ten to fifteen Spaniards attended and in the evening some of the English congregation stayed, presumably to add their support. Rule visited the Spanish and talked and prayed with them. He had six communicants and formed a small class in January 1833. The workload was heavy, particularly on Sundays when he had four services altogether. He felt his engagements on that day 'are more than I can well get through and attention to them generally leaves me in a state of painful exhaustion.'[22] There were few local preachers at this stage. In April 1832 Rule had reported 'old Mr Davis has resigned, his days of labour being past', but it seems he continued to help out as the following year, when Rule was under a lot of pressure, he reported that 'there are remaining old Mr Davis, who is quite worn out and two sergeants each of which are in situations which render their attendance at any time precarious indeed and often quite impracticable.'[23] Rule continued to plead for a second missionary to be sent and in the meantime tried to do all the work himself.

Rule reported that it was the custom for the Roman Catholic preachers during Lent to preach against Protestantism. They 'usually closed that part

---

[20] Traverso, op. cit., p.18.

[21] *WMMS Correspondence,* Thomas to Garrett, 20 January 1836, fiche 657, no.18.

[22] Ibid., Rule to Committee, 29 May 1833, fiche 651, no.5.

[23] Ibid., Rule to Committee, 9 April 1832, fiche 650, no.32 and 21 May 1833, fiche 652, no.6.

of their mission by collecting Bibles and burning them'.[24] Rule therefore sought a 'friendly interview' with the Lenten preacher for 1833 but was not successful, so instead he became a 'frequent hearer' at his services.[25] This action was rather provocative and, as it brought Rule more public attention, he decided to advertise his own preaching in the *Gibraltar Chronicle* with the result that 'a large multitude of people' came to hear him and there was not enough room for them all in the chapel. However, they were disappointed that Rule did not use the opportunity to speak against their own preacher, choosing instead to preach an ordinary sermon - it was, in fact, Good Friday. So, as much interest had been generated, Rule decided to give a course of lectures 'bearing directly against the whole scheme of popery'.[26] He advertised them and they took place in the Methodist chapel from April to July 1833. However, all this took up even more of his time and he was therefore delighted when the news came that another missionary had been appointed.

John Garrett arrived in Gibraltar around the end of October 1833. He had been accepted on trial in 1829. Little information about his ministry in Gibraltar has survived. He appears to have written only one letter to the Committee, shortly after his arrival.[27] In it he described his voyage from Falmouth to Gibraltar. On arrival he was informed that he would have to spend time in quarantine, but he was able to speak with Rule and his wife before being sent to Malta for fourteen days quarantine there. When he returned the Rules welcomed him with great kindness. As there was no room at the Mission House lodgings were arranged for him in the home of Mr Keys, a member of the congregation and a builder. Here Garrett had the exclusive use of two rooms.

Garrett had been appointed solely to work with the English congregation but Rule had overall responsibility as the superintendent minister. Rule rarely commented on Garrett's work, but he reported in early 1834 that, despite suffering from rheumatism in his feet, Garrett had entered into the spirit of his work and he felt he would be an assiduous pastor.[28] Rule also later reported that those who were critical of his ministry welcomed the arrival of Garrett and 'flew to him as to their Saviour' in the hope that he would support them against Rule whose removal they were still seeking. 'But all was in vain. Mr Garrett saw their unholy spirit and told them what he thought of them'.[29]

By this time, Rule had begun negotiations with the Governor about the possibility of enlarging the chapel, which he had several times described as

---

[24] Rule, *Recollections*, op. cit., p.87.

[25] *WMMS Correspondence,* Rule to Committee, 3 May 1833, fiche 651, no.6.

[26] Ibid., Rule to Committee, 3 May 1833, fiche 651, no.6.

[27] Ibid., Garrett to Committee, 23 December 1833, fiche 652, no.10.

[28] Ibid., Rule to Committee, 18 January 1834, fiche 652, no.12.

[29] Ibid., Rule to Committee, 7 February 1835, fiche 654, no.25.

small, inconvenient and often excessively hot. His first memorial for a grant of land adjoining the premises was rejected. This land had in fact been unoccupied for several years. After the epidemic of 1828 it was cleared as a health measure to improve the ventilation of the area and reduce overcrowding. There was a reluctance to reverse this policy because of a continuing fear of epidemics. However, Rule had some health concerns of his own and was therefore advised to memorialise the Governor again. He pointed out that 'one half of the dwelling house is almost entirely enclosed. Not even an outlet could be found for a drain, but by carrying it under the ground floor of the house, nor any free channel for the passage of air through the premises.... The stagnant atmosphere of the house is loaded with a noxious effluvium from the drain which flows beneath it'.[30] He felt this was a health hazard and indeed it could help to explain the repeated illnesses of so many of the missionary wives. The chapel was too small and the atmosphere within it also became very oppressive.

The premises were therefore inspected and the inspector agreed with Rule and so a small piece of the adjoining land was granted to them, sufficient to enlarge the chapel, but leaving the rest unoccupied as before. Rule hoped that the enlargement might also provide enough room for Garrett to live on the premises. However, there was still the problem of paying for the work, estimated at £585, when there was also a debt of about £227 on the premises. Rule outlined a plan to the Missionary Committee of repaying the debt over ten years from seat rents and special subscriptions but he asked them to advance the £585 in the first instance.

It was some time before Rule received an answer to his request. Indeed communication between himself and London often seemed particularly slow and caused him several times to express his annoyance and frustration. He sent a Spanish hymn book to London for approval and seems to have had to wait about two years for permission to print it, despite numerous reminders. On this occasion, seven months after sending his request, he wrote to say he felt they were in danger of losing the grant because of the excessive delay. 'The result of this must be either to stifle the work of God for want of room, or after all this trouble, to make fresh memorials, abandon the premises, and go to some other part of the garrison. In such a case, the whole inconvenience and <u>expense</u> will have been the consequence of <u>procrastination</u>'.[31] Just over three weeks later he wrote again saying, 'We look for a letter on that subject like they that wait for the morning.'[32]

In fact a letter giving permission to go ahead was already on its way though the Committee did not agree to advance the money. This had to be

---

[30] Ibid., Rule to Committee, 3 May 1833, fiche 652, no.6.

[31] Ibid., Rule to Committee, 26 December, fiche 652, no.11.

[32] Ibid., Rule to Committee, 18 January 1834, fiche 652, no.12.

raised by local loans instead and moreover Rule had, by then, prepared a slightly different and more expensive plan, as he wanted to incorporate a class-room into the building too. The school was still meeting in the Mission House which must have been very inconvenient for everyone. His proposals meant that the chapel would end up measuring 46 by 36 feet. There would be four rooms underneath which would provide a classroom, a room for class meetings and general purposes and 'two light, dry and airy rooms for the second preacher'.[33] In addition space was found for a much needed depository for the Bibles and tracts. This plan seems to have been approved and the work began, with Mr Keys as the builder. The lease was drawn up to expire at the same time as that on the original premises. The trustees were again a mixture of London officials and people in Gibraltar. The latter were Rule and Garrett, Osler, Davis, Elms, Humphries and Guilbert.

The work went ahead and the congregation moved to temporary accommodation. This was difficult to find and added to the expense, costing $50 a month with the agreed term being five months. Rule managed to raise much of the money but found himself urgently short of $1,000, about £220. He therefore took the difficult and highly irregular step of drawing on the Committee without seeking permission first. He sent urgent letters explaining his reasons for doing this and acknowledged that he did it 'with a trembling apprehension of being exposed to your censure'.[34] The Committee's reply is one of only two letters to Rule to have survived. The Missionary Society's Treasurers refused to take responsibility for the bill but the Committee finally and very reluctantly agreed to do so, but only as a loan and 'on the express condition that it shall be repaid <u>as early as possible</u>'.[35]

The new chapel was opened on Sunday 5 October 1834. Rule reported, 'The building was admired, I believe without any exception and what is far better, was <u>well filled</u> and in the evening more than filled.'[36] It was also a happy day for the Rule family for their son Martin Luther, who had been born on 5 July, was baptised by Garrett.

Garrett had only stayed in his lodgings with Mr Keys for a few weeks and then found alternative lodgings for himself. After a short while he moved again insisting that living at the South was necessary for the good of his health. This meant that he did not immediately move into the rooms on the Mission premises but he did do so around April 1835 thus saving his rent of $10 a month. Now that the enlargement of the chapel was completed and Garrett was in post, Rule could turn his attention more fully to the Spanish cause, which provoked further opposition.

---

[33] Ibid., Rule to Committee, 21 February 1834, fiche 652, no.14.

[34] Ibid., Rule to Committee, 21 August 1834, fiche 653, no.18.

[35] *WMMS Correspondence Outgoing,* Bunting to Rule, 10 October 1834, fiche 1167.

[36] *WMMS Correspondence,* Rule to Committee, 10 October 1834, fiche 653, no.20.

In Lent 1834, the Lenten preacher had announced his intention of speaking about the errors of Protestantism. Rule decided to go and listen, so he could defend his own position, and in order to do so effectively he felt he needed to take notes. This was felt to be provocative and, on the second night, men were positioned near him to prevent the note taking by force if necessary. Afterwards Rule informed the magistrate that he anticipated further trouble and asked for protection. So, on the third evening, policemen were sent to the church and the men trying to prevent Rule from taking notes were quietly removed. Father Zino, the Vicar Apostolic, then marched towards him asking him not to break the peace and, when he made no impression on Rule, he called out an order to turn him out. Several men armed with bludgeons rushed out of the vestry to do just that. Only one blow struck Rule and only slightly as it was turned aside by someone else. Others were not so lucky and two young Englishmen were dragged to the ground and beaten. The police sergeant suggested Rule left and he did so. The service then continued and Rule 'walked quickly home and saw through all how deeply I had been indebted to the providential care of our Heavenly Father'.[37]

The Governor was appealed to and seems to have supported the priests. Rule remained totally unrepentant and told the Committee that although there were some repercussions following this incident he did not have time to relate them and 'all is now as though it had never been', which seems rather unlikely. In fact elsewhere he reported that by this time the Pope had warned 'the clergy of Andalusia to be on their guard against the heretic in Gibraltar who was acting, he said, against the Catholic religion'.[38] Rule saw even this as a good thing as he felt it gave him increased influence as a preacher amongst the local inhabitants.

The work of the school continued. From time to time the Roman Catholic priests threatened the parents with excommunication if they let their children attend, and some children were withdrawn, but there were always more to fill their places. Rule reported, 'There is a public school patronised by the hierarchy of the place, where poor children are taught gratuitously but they send them here in preference.'[39] So why did Catholic parents send their children to schools openly teaching Methodist doctrine? It may have been the quality of the education, for even the opposition acknowledged that the education provided was good and that the children were well disciplined. Traverso suggested it might have been due to Rule's personality, or the fact that the classes were smaller than elsewhere, or that it was a 'reflection of liberal and anti-clerical factors' which had begun to show themselves in Spain.[40] It is also probable that there were still not

---

[37] Ibid., Rule to Committee, 6 June 1834, fiches 652-3, no.16.

[38] Rule, *Recollections*, op. cit., p.90.

[39] *WMMS Correspondence,* Rule to Committee, 16 June 1835, fiche 654, no.29.

[40] Traverso, op. cit., p.19.

enough school places for everyone who wanted one. Whatever the reasons the school flourished and, by May 1835, there were fifty pupils. Rule therefore decided to take on an assistant, on a small salary, as the task was becoming too much for him and his wife. Girls and boys were always taught separately and so Mary's help was invaluable.

The assistant was Salvador Negrotto, one of the very first pupils to have attended the school. Not all the children in the school were Spanish. In fact, Gibraltar's population was very mixed as H.W. Howes described at length in his book *The Gibraltarian*. Indeed he felt that 'far too much has been made of the idea of the alleged complete domination of Spanish influences on the population of Gibraltar, and not enough of the Portuguese, and above all the Genoese'.[41] Rule's evangelical spirit embraced everyone, including the Jews, and his work amongst the 'Spanish' was rather more generic than the name implies. Negrotto's parents were Genoese struggling to make a living, but prepared to sacrifice Salvador's help to gain an education for him. However, when he decided he wanted to become a Protestant his parents tried hard to dissuade him, and his father occasionally whipped him. Father Zino apparently offered him a job but Negrotto persisted in his intention. He was fifteen years old when he became an assistant at the school. During the previous eighteen months, without being asked, he had come an hour early each day to help with the preparations. Soon his mother and sister also attended the Spanish services. He later became a master in the school and in May 1841 he married Catherine Parody who had been a pupil in the girls' school.

By June 1835 there were fifty-five children in the school and Rule reported that they were having to turn children away. He wanted to erect a school house and possibly also a chapel to provide separate premises for the Spanish work. He memorialised the Governor on several occasions for the remainder of the land adjacent to the premises. The authorities seem to have found his persistence in doing so rather irritating and he was never successful. The fear of further epidemics was still strong and the decision to keep the land cleared was strictly adhered to. In fact there were no further yellow fever epidemics, but in June 1834 cholera struck Gibraltar for the first time and 380 people died. Spain suffered much more severely. There were 5,231 deaths in Madrid in just one fortnight. So it is understandable that health fears were still strong in Gibraltar, although Rule gives only a passing mention to the cholera in his letters to the Committee.

Rule also began looking for a master for the school and in September 1835 he appointed James Lyon. He had arrived in Gibraltar in 1834, aged 25, with the rank of pay sergeant in the 92nd Highland Regiment. He did not come from a Methodist background, but soon became a class leader and

---

[41] H.W. Howes, *The Gibraltarian - the origin and development of the population of Gibraltar from 1704*, Mediterranean Sun Publishing Co. Ltd. [reprint]: Gibraltar, 1991, p.95.

went on trial as a local preacher. As a boy in Glasgow, he had had some teaching in Latin and Greek and he now began to learn Spanish. He obtained his discharge from the army in order to take up the position in the school. Shortly afterwards he and Rule also began a Sunday school for Spanish children, separate from the day school. Together they had gone out one Sunday afternoon, and gathered forty-two names of prospective pupils. Lyon was to superintend this but in the beginning Rule reported, 'I must take charge of it until he [Lyon] can use the language, and we get the wild children into some order.'[42]

Any new development was bound to increase Catholic opposition but, by this time, the Catholics had decided that the best way to oppose Rule was to open their own school. Accordingly two Christian Brothers from Ireland, Patrick O'Flaherty and Thomas Anthony, arrived in Gibraltar in November 1835 as the teachers. Caruana gives a detailed account of what happened next in his book *The Rock under a Cloud*, but in essence it seems that the decisions about the school were made by a Junta of Elders, supposedly working with Father Zino, but in reality wielding the power.

From the start there were disagreements about the type of school and about the way it was to be run. The school opened in February 1836 when 'so many destitute candidates turned up that not even one half of them could be accommodated' but, by the end of the month, there were 260 children in the school and Rule had lost half his pupils to it.[43] However, this meant that more staff were needed. In addition most of the children did not speak any English and the Brothers did not speak Spanish. There were also problems over discipline. Then the Junta decided the school would not close for a summer holiday which meant the Brothers could not take a break. They threatened to leave. Various discussions followed and a new Junta was elected, but the main points of difference were not really resolved, although another Brother, Francis Corcoran, was sent to help. By 1837 the Brothers had been in post for over a year, without a break, and their health was beginning to suffer. However, as no other schools had holidays, there was a continued reluctance to change the policy which it was thought would give an advantage to the Methodists. Brother O'Flaherty, after taking advice from his order, took matters into his own hands and dismissed the pupils, ordering them to take a holiday. The Junta responded by telling the Brothers that their services were no longer required and measures had been taken to find new teachers. They therefore left Gibraltar in the summer of 1837. The school did continue but no longer provided much of a threat to Rule's work which once again prospered.

During all this time Rule had not lost interest in Spain itself. He had also continued the links with the Bible Society, but at first reported little success

---

[42] *WMMS Correspondence,* Rule to Committee, 16 November 1835, fiche 655, no.36.
[43] Charles Caruana, *The Rock under a Cloud*, Silent Books: Cambridge, 1989, p.51.

in the work of distributing Bibles. 'The poverty of the foreigners here, their <u>indifference</u> to all that is good, and the diminution of the floating population of the bay from decay of commerce, have reduced the sale of Scriptures'.[44] In fact it was so low that they had stopped paying a distributor. Books were still available from the Mission House and Mrs Nicklin's shop. The Committee met regularly and for a time at least included 'both the military and civil chaplains'.[45] Rule had 'studiously cultivated a friendly correspondence with the chaplains' and seems, at first, to have had better relations with them than many of his predecessors, though there was some opposition later on.[46] Every opportunity to distribute Bibles was taken and, at some stage, Rule 'canvassed the whole town, in order to ascertain who of the humbler classes had copies of the Holy Scriptures, and who had not. Many families were supplied; *a very few* declined accepting them; but the remainder were furnished with Spanish, Italian and Portuguese Testaments'.[47]

In the summer of 1834, Rule obtained the addresses of thirty-five booksellers in the principal towns and cities of Spain, from newspaper advertisements. He wrote to them to ask if they were willing to receive Bibles from the Bible Society to sell on commission. He received a surprising number of favourable replies, which he found encouraging, but there was one insurmountable problem. All books printed outside Spain were prohibited so it was difficult to get them into the country and dangerous to sell them. Rule managed to get a few books taken to Cádiz, Granada and Madrid by private means, but that was all. He therefore decided that he needed to visit Spain to try and discover for himself what opportunities there were. After receiving permission from the Committee, he set out at the beginning of January 1835, leaving his wife and Garrett in charge of affairs in Gibraltar.

Rule arrived in Cádiz on 11 January. The Consul, John Brackenbury, was away, but he met his son the Vice-Consul, who was also called John. Both men were correspondents of the Bible Society. Brackenbury introduced Rule to Manuel Barleta, editor of the *Diario*, a Spanish newspaper in Cádiz, who had once worked in England as a translator. He and Rule had several discussions about ways of introducing the Bible into Spain and a useful relationship was formed. Rule visited several booksellers in Cádiz and then travelled on to Seville. He had been persuaded, rather against his will, to travel incognito as travelling openly as a Protestant clergyman was thought to be rather dangerous. However, at Jerez, where they stopped to eat he was recognised and addressed by name! He reported from Gibraltar some weeks later, 'It is known all over Spain

---

[44] *Foreign Correspondence In,* Rule, 20 May 1833, 1833 Box 2, p.108.
[45] Ibid., Rule, 30 August 1833, 1833 Box 4, p.32.
[46] *WMMS Correspondence,* Rule to Committee, 14 September 1835, fiche 655, no.33.
[47] Rule, *Memoir,* op. cit., p.110.

that this is a Bible Society and a Mission station and enquirers begin to make their appearance.'[48] His fame was clearly spreading. His fellow travellers to Seville were five young students from the University there. Rule entered into animated discussions with them about religion and their openness left him with the impression that a considerable opportunity existed for work amongst them.

Rule reached Seville on 14 January and called to see Ramírez, a tradesman, who had some months previously visited Gibraltar. He had heard Rule preach and had subsequently had several deep conversations with him. He insisted that Rule stayed with him and his family and he took him round Seville. Ramírez felt there were many Spaniards interested in Protestantism. Rule left Seville rather reluctantly for Madrid on 18 January, arriving four days later having narrowly escaped being robbed on the way. Again he visited booksellers but it seemed impossible to resolve the difficulty of getting a supply of books to them. He also twice visited Don Félix Torres Amat, Bishop of Astorga, and translator of the Bible into Spanish. He had spent many years working on his translation and had struggled against considerable opposition to get it published. 'Only the financial assistance of Anglican friends in London allowed the work to appear between 1833 and 1835 after numerous delays'.[49] According to Rule, the work had been rigorously examined and Amat had had to add several notes and say that the reading of the Bible was not necessary for salvation. He gave Rule a copy plus some of his other writings. Amat had also examined Protestant versions of the Bible and reported favourably on them to the Pope. He had encountered some hostility because of his work and views, and he and Rule held a long and interesting conversation on the subject of religion and the hope of more liberal attitudes developing in Spain.

Rule had hoped to visit Granada and Málaga but this would have been expensive and time consuming. It would also have been dangerous as a proper escort was not available. Spain was actually in a state of civil war and travelling alone was not recommended. He therefore returned to Seville and finally reached Gibraltar via Cádiz on 5 February. The return journey gave Rule time to think carefully about the situation in Spain. At this time, all Spanish Bibles had to be printed with notes and Rule felt what was needed was a new version accompanied by a carefully written commentary. He soon began translating the four gospels in this way. He did finish them and the work was printed in Gibraltar in June 1841. In addition, Rule used the press extensively to produce school books, hymn-books and a variety of religious books, some of which he wrote himself or translated into Spanish. As a Protestant it was not possible for Rule to

---

[48] *WMMS Correspondence,* Rule to Committee, 16 March 1835, fiche 654, no.26.
[49] William J. Callahan, *Church, Politics and Society in Spain 1750-1874*, Harvard University Press: Cambridge, Massachusetts, London, 1984, p.143.

preach openly in Spain at this time, but he discussed with Barleta the possibility of printing books there, wondering if it might also be possible to gather people together in one's own home for conversation, fellowship and prayer.

In July 1835 Rule wrote to the Committee asking to be relieved of the task of superintending the English side of the work in order to concentrate on the Spanish work. However, he felt that he could not recommend Garrett for the task, partly because of his health problems, and partly because Rule felt his ministry was not acceptable. He had not criticised Garrett before, but explained this by saying that some of the facts had only just come to light and he had not wanted to pass on suspicions without proof. He was also very much grieved by the necessity of having to do so.

Rule stated that concern had been expressed when Garrett arrived in Gibraltar. The captain and fellow passengers had reported that his conduct on board ship had been 'highly discreditable to his profession', although Garrett denied this.[50] Some concerns were expressed about the company he kept in Gibraltar and about his personal appearance. Although intending to study he never managed to do so. Rule had tried meeting with him for conversation and prayer but after a few attempts the meetings were abandoned. Rule reported that Garrett had avoided the Mission House despite invitations and said he could not walk far because of the pain in his feet, yet he was usually out when Rule called to see him. Rule felt Garrett suffered from hypochondria and there were allegations of drunkenness and also of being in debt. Rule quoted from a letter Garrett had sent him describing himself as

> ... one of the most inconsistent and restless beings in the world; a well without water, a cloud without rain. I cannot rest in company at home or from home. I make resolutions and then break them. When I shall be more consistent I know not. But if I cannot read, write, pray, study or preach as I once did and as I long every day to do, I will not disturb any brother or friend who can.[51]

Rule thought that in England a special district meeting would be convened to discuss such a case which he could not do in Gibraltar, but he could no longer work with Garrett. He did state that 'all things considered I hope his return will not be regarded as censurable' but later he seems to have changed his mind because of his concern as to how Garrett might behave in England.[52] In October 1835 Garrett's doctor recommended that he should leave Gibraltar on health grounds. He referred to Garrett's rheumatism and an eyesight problem which had caused the temporary loss

---

[50] *WMMS Correspondence,* Rule to Committee, 17 October 1835, fiche 655, no.34.

[51] Ibid., Garrett to Rule, fiche 657, no 18 [23 letters and papers concerning the case of John Garrett 1836].

[52] Ibid., Rule to Committee, fiche 655, no.35.

of sight in one eye. His general health was also affected. Before leaving, Garrett sent a letter to the leaders' meeting asking them if they considered him worthy and to state either their joy or sorrow at his departure. The reply stated that they unanimously recommended that he did not press the matter.

> Should an investigation take place, there is no doubt, but that much information would be elicited which would be disagreeable not only to your feelings, but also to ours. Under all the circumstances of the case, we consider that the best plan you can adopt will be to leave Gibraltar for England agreeably to the medical recommendation.[53]

Garrett did this, leaving in the middle of November and Rule was once again left in sole charge of the work. He expressed the 'distress with which I find our hands weakened when we need them for the work's sake to be strengthened. However, I am at present favoured with tolerable health and trusting in divine goodness for a continuation of this blessing I will strain every nerve to hold on <u>until you can relieve me</u> by an English preacher'.[54]

Despite being on his own, he still continued to take any opportunity which arose. So when Nicolas Lovero and his wife, members of his Spanish class, moved to San Roque he decided to visit them there. After several visits Rule hired a room for himself in the hope of assembling a small congregation. On 29 December 1835 he arrived at San Roque, having issued some private invitations to friends to meet with him. However, the woman to whom he had entrusted the invitations had informed the authorities. On his arrival, Rule felt that all was not well and, having heard rumours that the authorities were planning to take action against him, he decided to forestall them and went to see the chief alcalde, or mayor, of the town. In a short space of time, the Judge of First Instance, the Vicar Apostolic, the military commander of the district and the parish priest had been notified as well and all gathered together to confront Rule. Thus the civil, military and ecclesiastical authorities were united against him. A reasonably amicable conversation followed in which Rule was asked to obey Spanish law which prohibited the exercise of the Protestant religion. Rule acknowledged their right to uphold the law but pointed out that he acted under the higher command of Jesus Christ who had instructed his disciples to preach to all the world. He agreed to take further advice on the matter and was allowed to leave.

After this, Rule knew he could not continue any work in San Roque but he did send a letter of remonstrance to the authorities in Madrid. He did not receive a reply but reported that Lovero and his wife were not directly persecuted as a result of these events. He kept in touch with them and occasionally visited them. However, some four years later Lovero was

---

[53] Ibid., Leaders to Garrett, October 1835, fiche 657, no.18.
[54] Ibid., Rule to Committee, 19 October 1835, fiche 655, no.35.

apparently imprisoned on a trumped-up charge brought by the vicar.

In January 1836 Rule was informed that a married man, Edward Sweetman, had been appointed to Gibraltar to take charge of the English work, and to his delight Rule was at last appointed solely to the Spanish work. Edward Sweetman was born in Aynhoe in Northamptonshire on 12 April 1793, and was therefore older than Rule. After becoming a local preacher, he was accepted on trial in 1834 and was sent with his wife, Sarah, to Australia. However, they were shipwrecked on the way and returned to England, serving for a few months on the Isle of Wight and in France at Calais and Boulogne, before travelling to Gibraltar which they reached on 26 April 1836. They stayed at first in the Mission House with the Rules and then found a house of their own. In his first letter Sweetman reported that there had been a great deal of unpleasantness in the church but that many of those involved were now attending his services. Some months later he was able to report 'that those days of discord and disgrace have apparently passed away. The people have received me with great kindness and are willing to do their utmost to assist me to build up the waste places of Zion'.[55] In addition to his ordinary duties, he paid special attention to the Sunday school which he felt had been rather neglected and he also hoped to revive the Missionary Society. His wife wanted to help too and had two classes under her care.

Meanwhile Garrett was still under investigation and evidence was requested from Gibraltar, where he had some support because there were those who felt he had been harshly treated by Rule. Rule and Sweetman together interviewed a number of people and took several statements which certainly seemed to provide overwhelming evidence of drunkenness on several occasions. Garrett had returned to his family in Bradford and while there soon became involved in preaching and his behaviour gave no cause for concern. His letter to the Committee is a much more coherent one than that written to Rule and in it he protested his innocence. Perhaps his behaviour in Gibraltar had been out of character. He certainly had a great deal of freedom there and many tempting opportunities. Perhaps, he did not get sympathy and understanding from Rule who wanted a competent assistant so that he could get on with his work amongst the Spanish. It certainly seems odd that it took two years for any criticism to come to light.

The Conference of 1836 finally made its judgement taking into account all the factors mentioned above as well as Garrett's poor health and the divided state of the Society. Garrett was not found guilty of 'those acts of intemperance with which he has been charged' but was felt not to have 'acted with that wakeful caution which is requisite' in such a community as Gibraltar. It was 'resolved that he be placed under the care of a Superintendent in whose house he shall reside'.[56]

---

[55] Ibid., Sweetman to Committee, 14 November 1836, fiche 656, no.14.
[56] Ibid., fiche 659, no.18.

Rule was not at all happy with this verdict and felt he had been portrayed as a 'vexatious litigant' and that his own reputation had been questioned.[57] However, the Conference judgement did not entirely clear Garrett of blame and it seems unlikely that that was the end of the matter for him because in 1838 he retired from the work. However, in 1839 he was once again accepted on trial and was stationed at Bangalore. Here he managed a printing press which he operated for seventeen years without leave and was reported to have done 'excellent work in this department', being regarded by many as a missionary of great ability, standing in for the Chairman of the District in his absence.[58] However, when he did finally return to England in 1856, his financial records in India came under scrutiny, and were found to be unsatisfactory. Garrett protested his innocence and returned to India to justify himself but was unable to do so. In 1858 he resigned from the ministry.

In Gibraltar, Garrett's successor, Sweetman was now established and well accepted in his post but the church lost two of its older members. Mary Anne Davis, wife of Thomas Davis, died in February 1836 at the age of 67. She had lived through so many trying times supporting her husband in his work and was clearly well thought of and much missed. Then in August Caroline Nicklin died, aged 73. She had been a staunch supporter of the Bible Society, selling Bibles in her shop, and was a great loss to this work.

Rule could now at last turn his attention to Spain. On hearing of his appointment to the Spanish work, he had written,

> I know not what to say, for it seems to introduce me into a field so dear to me and at the same time so important, and, except through divine help, so far above me, that I can only offer my devout thanks to God for the favour and honour he confers on me, and express the gratitude, yet deep beyond expression, with which I receive this token of confidence on the part of the Committee.[59]

He already knew working in Spain was no easy task, but perhaps his enthusiasm caused him to underestimate the obstacles in his way.

---

[57] Ibid., Rule to Committee, 10 September 1836, fiche 656, unnumbered.

[58] Findlay and Holdsworth, op. cit., vol. v, p.209.

[59] *WMMS Correspondence,* Rule to Committee, 19 January 1836, fiche 655, no.2.

CHAPTER 8   THE MINISTRY OF WILLIAM HARRIS RULE (2)
CÁDIZ
The first Spanish Methodist Society (1836-39)

Roman Catholicism had become Spain's official religion in 589, although in later years Muslims and Jews were also allowed to practise their faith there.   After Ferdinand of Aragon and Isabella of Castille married in 1469, their joint reign united the two kingdoms of Spain. They eventually became known as the Catholic Monarchs because of their desire to protect the Catholic faith and the Inquisition was set up to eradicate heresy and to guide people back into the Church through repentance and a public act of faith. The first auto-da-fé, or act of faith, was held in 1481 in Seville when six people were burnt at the stake. Only those who refused to repent were executed, and many an auto-da-fé took place without any burnings, but it still meant that purity of faith and uniformity of belief was achieved through a climate of fear and repression.

Eventually both Jews and Muslims were expelled from Spain and the process of achieving religious conformity was complete.   It was the practice of Catholicism which united Spain and brought political unity and social stability to what had been a divided and restless country. The result was that Spain became a powerful nation and the explorations of Columbus soon opened up a whole new world.

The Roman Catholic Church became a wealthy and powerful institution. However, there were divisions within it particularly between the wealthy clerical elite and the humble parish priests, who were often inadequately trained and paid; and also between the Church and the religious orders. As the years went by, the Church's power did come under attack and there were calls for reform which included a desire to improve the status of the parish priests and reduce the influence of the religious orders. However, both sides, reformers and traditionalists, were united in their desire to see an increase in faith amongst the population.

The fight against the French led to change too. The Church's wealth was used in the struggle and many of the religious houses were suppressed by the French.   In 1833 King Ferdinand VII died.   His infant daughter, Isabella, came to the throne with her mother, María Cristina, acting as regent.   She turned to the more moderate liberals for support.   However, there was another contender for the throne, Don Carlos, Ferdinand's younger brother, who promised a more traditional regime.   The Carlist movement was formed to support him. A bitter civil war broke out. There were clerical supporters on both sides, with some of the dispossessed monks and friars supporting the Carlists. It was the hope of more liberal attitudes gaining ascendancy in Spain which spurred the Methodists and others to seek opportunities to establish Protestant work there. However, they may well have failed to realise that, despite the political differences, there was an overall consensus regarding the importance of the Catholic faith itself.

Rule had kept in correspondence with the Bible Society sending reports of his efforts, information about Spain and details of his hopes for the future. Together they watched and waited for a chance to develop work there. Eventually three people entered the country, Lieutenant James Newenham Graydon, George Borrow and Rule himself and, because the work of each affected that of the others, and contributed to the developing situation in Spain, each of their stories needs to be told. In due course the Rev. Andrew Brandram, Secretary of the Bible Society from 1823 until his death in 1850, had the task of corresponding with all three of them, and sometimes must have found it very difficult to deal with the differing views and behaviour of these three very different personalities.

Graydon was the first to work in Spain. He was one of nine children. His mother was the daughter of an Irish baronet and his father a colonel in the army. Graydon entered the navy at the age of fourteen and during the Peninsular War served on the coast of Spain. After the end of the war he petitioned the Admiralty for work on the Spanish Main because he spoke Spanish, but his services were not required anywhere and he was pensioned off on half pay. He retired to the Continent, partly for reasons of economy, and at some stage 'was brought to a knowledge of the truth by the simple reading of the Bible'.[1] He lived for a time in Berne and then returned to Ireland and settled in Dublin. Here he involved himself in raising funds to provide a chapel for sailors and, when the project was completed, he looked for other opportunities of service. During an after dinner conversation with a friend in London, John Radley, who was a member of the Bible Society's Committee, the suggestion was made that Graydon might work for the Society in Spain which would put his knowledge of Spanish to good use. As he had some means of support, Graydon was willing to work without a salary, providing his additional expenses were met and the books supplied for distribution. Towards the end of 1834, after an interview and the receipt of satisfactory references, Graydon was appointed. He decided to start out from Marseilles as he had a cousin, the Swedish Consul, there who 'would give me no doubt much needful assistance in the way of procuring me friends in Spain.'[2] In addition, Graydon was introduced to the Courtois brothers who were bankers in Toulouse and agents of the French Bible Society. They too had some Spanish contacts.

So, although Graydon was not a regular paid agent of the Bible Society, he was certainly sent off on his mission with its sanction and approval. However, many of Borrow's biographers seem unaware of this, taking their cue from Knapp who, quite incorrectly, stated,

---

[1] *WMMS Correspondence,* Graydon, 16 January 1837, with biographical details from Radley, fiche 659, no.1.
[2] *Foreign Correspondence In,* Graydon, 11 November 1834, 1834 Box 41, No.4, p.86.

In the course of his wanderings, Lieutenant Graydon landed at Gibraltar in 1835 and made soon after the acquaintance of Mr Rule. From that moment he became interested in Spanish evangelisation and, being an independent gentleman, seeking neither money nor office, he easily drifted into relations with the Bible Society.[3]

Possibly as a result of Knapp's statement, many of Borrow's later biographers assumed that Graydon had worked 'in the warmth and security of Gibraltar' which is simply not true.[4]

Graydon left England in December 1834. He decided to travel as a private individual rather than as an official of the Bible Society as this was thought to be safer, and most of his early correspondence was sent to Radley rather than to Brandram. Graydon planned to make contacts, to see if he could establish Bible depots and find a way to introduce the Bible into Spain. He visited Paris where he was given some books to take with him and the Courtois brothers gave him advice and introductions to people in Madrid and Barcelona. At Perpignan he tried to organise a supply of Bibles for Spain through a bookseller there. Graydon reached Marseilles on 23 December and Barcelona early in 1835. Here he met Prat, the translator of a Catalan New Testament, and on his recommendation placed a few books with a bookseller, but some of this stock was seized by the censors. However, he did manage to sell a few books himself and placed others with another bookseller. An offer to supply books to schools was turned down on the grounds that 'things were not sufficiently ripe for such a step' as 'the posture of the national affairs were too precarious'.[5]

Graydon left Barcelona on 14 March 1835, travelling with an armed escort because of the unsettled state of the country. He reached Valencia a few days later and spent three weeks there, making contact with booksellers and schools. Again his offer to supply the schools was turned down, but he felt he could have distributed many more books than he had been able to carry with him. He reached Madrid on 5 April, having again travelled with an armed escort. Here he visited Razola, a bookseller Rule had also contacted, but the problem of getting supplies into the city still remained. Graydon felt quite disheartened about his lack of progress and therefore enquired into the possibility of printing an edition himself. He met with the Count de Toreno before he came to power as head of the government in June 1835. He was well received but in the end no help was forthcoming. He also met with Sir George Villiers, later Earl of Clarendon, the British Minister in Madrid and asked for his help in getting books into Spain. This was reported to be a friendly interview but Villiers felt he could not help.

---

[3] William I. Knapp, *Life, Writings and Correspondence of George Borrow*, 2 vols, John Murray: London, 1899, vol. i, p.277.

[4] David Williams, *A World of his own - The Double Life of George Borrow*, Oxford University Press: 1982, p.111.

[5] *Foreign Correspondence In,* Graydon, 1 May 1835, 1835 Box 43, No.2, p.127.

All in all, Graydon thought that there was little he could do in Madrid and so he returned to Barcelona arriving on 27 June, after another difficult and dangerous journey.

Graydon went on to Perpignan to organise a fresh supply of scriptures. Two hundred Catalan New Testaments had been sent there for him. He divided them into small packages and sent four parcels off by coach. They never reached Barcelona because the coach driver from Figueras was too scared of the priests to take them. However, Graydon was able to send more to Figueras in the hope that he could get them to Barcelona later.

The weather was hot and Graydon was feeling unwell. There were fears of a cholera epidemic in Barcelona and so Graydon decided, on the advice of a doctor, to go to Switzerland for a few weeks rest. He was also rather discouraged by his lack of success, feeling that he had very little to show for the expense to the Society. The Bible Society does not seem to have shared his view, and Brandram wrote to him in August to say that he felt his journeys had been of considerable importance, even if no great results had flowed from them because they now had more information about Spain.[6]

While Graydon was away, further political changes took place in Spain. Juan Alvárez Mendizábal came to power heading a more radical and liberal regime. On hearing the news, Graydon decided to return immediately and obviously hoped that the political changes would enable him to make better progress with his work. He also now openly acknowledged his connection with the Bible Society.

In many cities, revolutionary juntas had been formed and Graydon petitioned the one in Barcelona seeking permission to introduce scriptures into Spain. His request was refused and his difficulties in importing books continued but he reported growing evidence of anticlerical feeling and of the diminishing power of the Church which he hoped would aid his cause. He thought the way was opening up to print books and he obtained some estimates from a printer and bookseller called Antonio Bergnes. At the end of 1835, Graydon received the Committee's authorisation to print 5,000 copies of the Catalan New Testament, although in the event it seems only 3,000 were printed.

It is not clear when printing began because Graydon's letters of this time have been lost. However, he went to Madrid in May 1836 to seek permission to print Bibles and had two interviews with Isturitz, Mendizábal's successor. Formal permission was denied but Graydon claimed that he was given informal, verbal permission to print quietly in some provincial city, though he was warned not to print a Bible without notes or the apocrypha.[7] Printing must have started some time after this.

---

[6] *Foreign Correspondence Out,* Brandram to Graydon, 18 August 1835, 1835 Box 13, No.2, p.63.

[7] *Foreign Correspondence In,* Graydon, 21 September 1839, 1839 Box 59, No.3, p.193.

At some stage in 1836 Graydon visited London and probably also continued his travels in Spain. In November, Rule reported that a 'great step has been gained on the eastern coast by Mr Graydon and I am thankful to be engaged in handing onward to him when being confined by duties to this Garrison, I cannot do more myself'.[8] He was involved, when possible, in sending scriptures on to Graydon. In the four months up to January 1837 Graydon and his agents distributed 556 copies of the scriptures, chiefly by sale. Shortly afterwards the printing of the Catalan New Testaments was completed and Graydon was authorised to print 2,000 New Testaments and 3,000 Bibles. Bergnes also agreed to act as depot keeper as well as printer. The Catalan New Testaments proved very popular and were soon selling well and, although Graydon reported 'that a great opposition had been raised against the printing of the Bible at Barcelona', the work does seem to have proceeded.[9]

Meanwhile the Bible Society had appointed a paid agent to Portugal and Spain. It is not clear why it took this step, but Graydon's activities and hopes may have influenced the decision, along with the changes in the political situation, and the availability of a suitable person who was George Borrow. Much has been written about this somewhat eccentric and controversial man. He was born in July 1803 and, as his father was in the army, he spent a rather nomadic childhood without the benefit of a regular and settled education. He became interested in languages and also in the gypsy way of life. In 1819 he was articled to a solicitor for five years but seems never to have planned to practise as a lawyer and, as soon as these years had passed, he went to London in the hope of developing his interests in languages and writing. In December 1832 he was introduced to the Bible Society by the Rev. Francis Cunningham, Vicar of Lowestoft, who described Borrow as able 'to read the Bible in thirteen languages. He is independent of circumstances, of no very exactly defined denomination of Christians, but I think of certain Christian principle'.[10] Collie commented 'Borrow's christianity remained conveniently ill-defined throughout his life' and, although he did excellent work for the Bible Society, many of his biographers acknowledge that there was a conflict between this work and Borrow's desire to be an adventurer, explorer and writer.[11] His first appointment was to St Petersburg where he produced a Bible in Manchu. He was then asked to go to Portugal to investigate opportunities there and if possible to consider the situation in Spain. In the event he devoted all his energies to Spain.

Borrow sailed to Portugal in autumn 1835, landing at Lisbon and eventually travelling on to Madrid. He too hoped to get permission to print

---

[8] Ibid., Rule, 20 November 1836, 1836 Box 3, p.108.
[9] *Minutes of Committee Book No.26*, 8 March 1837, p.150, minute 54.
[10] Michael Collie, *George Borrow, Eccentric*, Cambridge University Press, 1982, p.64.
[11] Ibid.

Spanish New Testaments to overcome the problems of importing prohibited books. He unsuccessfully sought an interview with Mendizábal, the Prime Minister. He then met Sir George Villiers whose help and support was to prove invaluable. Through his influence, a meeting between Borrow and Mendizábal was arranged but permission to print was not forthcoming. However, before long, Mendizábal's government fell and Isturitz came to power. Again Villiers offered his help and around July 1836 permission to print was given. The law still prohibited Bibles without notes being published but Borrow reported that 'measures have been taken by which the rigor of the law can be eluded and the printer be protected, until such time as it shall be deemed prudent to repeal the law made, as is now generally confessed, in a time of ignorance and superstitious darkness'.[12]

Borrow briefly visited England for consultation with the Bible Society. In November 1836 he returned to Cádiz which he found in a very unsettled and dangerous state because of the war. However, he travelled on safely to Madrid and, with the support of Villiers, made preparations to print New Testaments. He also obtained the help of Don Luis de Usoz y Río a man of noble birth, who was very much in sympathy with the aims of the Bible Society, and later became one of its subscribers. He held the chair of Hebrew at Valladolid and was an editor of *El Español*, one of the main newspapers in Spain. He had connections all over the country and was a valuable help and support to Borrow in getting the books edited and printed. Borrow also began preparing copies of St Luke's gospel in the Romany and Basque languages which were eventually printed.

Thus, by the end of 1836, both Graydon and Borrow were establishing their work in Spain and both were involved in printing the scriptures. At the same time, Rule began to develop his own work equally undeterred by the difficulties and dangers. In May 1836 he made another journey into Spain visiting Cádiz, Málaga and Granada. He met Brackenbury again and discussed with him the possibility of starting a mission in Spain. Rule felt Cádiz could provide a useful and legitimate starting point because the port was frequently visited by British and American ships, and there were a few hundred British, American and German Protestants living in the area. The only form of worship available to them was the reading of prayers at the Consul's house where a sermon was also preached on Sundays whenever possible. However, attendance was poor and Rule felt that the provision for their spiritual needs was inadequate. Brackenbury offered his support in such matters as gaining access to the hospital, but he counselled caution as the authorities were bound to suspect Rule's motives in doing this work. He did, of course, plan to look 'for opportunities to make the Gospel

---

[12] T.H. Darlow (ed.), *Letters of George Borrow to the British and Foreign Bible Society*, Hodder and Stoughton: London, 1911, p.162. (Quoting Borrow's letter of 30 June 1836.)

known to the inhabitants of the city', and to circulate the scriptures.[13] Rule met Barleta again who introduced him to Don Pedro Urquinaona, the Governor of Cádiz, 'well known in Spain as a tried friend of civil and religious liberty' who promised Rule support and protection if he went to Cádiz provided that he did not gather together a public congregation of Spaniards which was against the law.[14]

Rule went on to Málaga where he met William Mark the Consul there. He had been doing everything in his power to aid the circulation of the scriptures and Rule was much impressed with him. He travelled on to Granada where he stayed with yet another of his correspondents. He spent several days exploring the city, entering into conversations whenever possible. He felt there were opportunities in all three cities but Cádiz seemed the most promising of all.

In June 1836 Rule sent a full report to the Committee in which he suggested that James Lyon be sent to Cádiz 'to act there as the Society's agent for <u>Seamen</u>'.[15] Rule felt he could take over much of Lyon's work in Gibraltar now he was freed from the English work. He was also willing to go to Cádiz himself and the reason he suggested Lyon is not clear. Rule obviously thought very highly of him and may have felt his arrival would be less likely to arouse immediate interest as of course Lyon did not have the reputation Rule had gained for himself. The bishop of Cádiz was well aware of the events at San Roque because he was in charge of the vicar there. Probably Rule was most needed in Gibraltar where Mary was also needed to teach the girls.

As usual Rule had to wait as patiently as he could for the Committee's decision. He urged them to grant permission and insisted that if they were worried about the political situation or his safety they should trust in God. He did not tell them, however, what he reported to the Bible Society in November 1836: 'A horde of Carlists has just been here. We have watched their columns from our windows ... Their object seems not to be victory, but plunder', but he thought that this would 'work together for the advancement of the gospel' because the behaviour of these 'dragoon-friars shall have demonstrated in every corner of the land that their religion is characterised by bloodshed'.[16] He seemed unconcerned about his and Lyon's personal safety. Rule reminded the Committee of Graydon's work writing, 'Is there not now in Catalonia ... an active and devoted agent of the Bible Society, well known and highly successful? <u>There is</u>. He affords the precedent which I had hoped we should have provided'.[17]

While he waited to hear the Committee's decision Rule was not idle. In

---

[13] Rule, *Memoir*, op. cit., p.192.

[14] Ibid., p.192.

[15] *WMMS Correspondence,* Rule to Committee, 13 June 1836, fiche 656, no.9.

[16] *Foreign Correspondence In,* Rule, 20 November 1836, 1836 Box 3, p.108.

[17] *WMMS Correspondence,* Rule to Committee, 17 November 1836, fiche 656, no.15.

the autumn of 1836 he rode out again to San Roque, this time to distribute Bibles there. They were so well received that he returned a few days later with some more. However, the authorities were prepared for him this time and a burly constable appeared to escort him to the Judge of First Instance. Rule, and a companion who was probably Lyon, were in a carriage so the constable, carrying a large club, walked beside the horse. Rule later reported,

> At the proper moment, just when we should have turned off short into town, I gently tickled with my whip at once the horse's right ear and the man's left, for the two ears were not very far apart. Man and beast, both startled, shied away in different directions, - the horse forward, the man sideward, - and we were on our way to the Rock again before the bewildered constable could recover full consciousness of his position.[18]

For the next few days soldiers were stationed on the road to prevent Rule from making any further visits and Sweetman was summoned to see the Governor's civil secretary. He was informed that as people connected with the garrison often went to San Roque for relaxation the Governor did not want any 'variance between that town and this', and he was requested not to allow any more books to be taken there. Sweetman agreed and reported to the Committee that he thought the Spanish would 'probably kill him [Rule] the next time they can take him in Spain'.[19]

However, Rule seemed undeterred and when the Committee finally gave its permission for a six months' trial, he and Lyon immediately set out for Cádiz even though it was Christmas time. They travelled on horseback on 22 December as no ships were available. Lodgings were found and Rule stayed with Lyon for a few days, writing to the Committee to report their delight over the decision, their progress so far and the fact that the Consul was assisting them.[20] On the last Sunday in December 1836, they raised the Bethel flag in the bay and the work in Cádiz began.

Lyon sometimes attended morning service at the Consul's house on Sundays, preaching in the bay to the sailors in the afternoon. He soon began a small Bible class, after discussing the matter with Barleta who was keen to send his own two children. The first meeting was attended by three boys and two girls and they continued to meet two evenings a week. In addition Lyon sought out booksellers to sell Bibles and managed to find outlets in Port St Mary, La Isla and later in Jerez. People also began coming to him to buy Bibles and tracts. Soon Lyon began to read a sermon or tract in Spanish to a few neighbours in his lodgings and, as his Spanish improved, he began preaching sermons of his own. Once people heard that he had been a schoolmaster in Gibraltar he was encouraged to open a

---

[18] Rule, *Recollections*, op. cit., p.160.
[19] *WMMS Correspondence,* Sweetman to Committee, 14 November 1836, fiche 656, no.14.
[20] Ibid., Rule to Committee, 27 December 1836 from Cádiz, fiche 657, no.16.

school. Children were brought to him rather than being sought out and by August 1837 there were seventeen children. The number soon increased to twenty-six, despite the fact that the children would receive religious education. Most of them were from the middle classes but it is not clear whether or not they paid a fee. Lyon was aware of the risks he was taking but kept consulting friends, including Brackenbury and Rule. The bishop of Cádiz was reported as saying, 'I have no objection to the school, provided he teach nothing contrary to our doctrines; but to preach on Sundays is another thing. I wish I could put a stop to it'. When it was suggested that he had the power to stop the preaching, the bishop apparently replied, 'O that I could! The civil authorities of Cádiz will not support me. They say it would prove that we are not yet free'.[21]

By this time Graydon had written to Rule at length pressing the case for Barcelona, where he felt there were good opportunities for preaching the gospel. Rule therefore asked for more workers to be appointed who could either undertake work in Spain or go to Gibraltar thus freeing the Rules to go to Spain. He felt his wife particularly needed a change. He reported,

> Mrs Rule does her utmost, but she is very feeble. Often she has been overcome by the effort of teaching in the school, and often fainted in it from exhaustion, for she is <u>very</u> weak. And now she is near confinement again, so that I know not what to do. She will willingly give her last grain of strength to a cause so dear to her as it is to me, but after all I must ingenuously confess that I should like her to be delivered from the climate of this rock, having resided here five years without the least change and with severe afflictions.[22]

In Gibraltar the school had continued to grow and in March 1837 there were sixty-five pupils. Rule again petitioned the Governor for the waste ground alongside the chapel 'notwithstanding repeated denials'.[23] A further rejection meant that even he had to give up this plan. Instead he proposed the demolition of the Mission House and a complete rebuilding to incorporate the Spanish congregation and the school, as well as the missionary's quarters, which could be achieved partly by building under the chapel and by adding an extra storey to the building. As this did not involve the acquisition of any more land there were no objections from the authorities and Rule went speedily ahead, with work starting as soon as Mary had had the baby, Melancthon, who was born on 26 April 1837. By 31 May the house was down and the new walls were rising. The work cost $2,300 (or about £500) which the Missionary Committee paid. By October the new building was in use though some work was still going on fitting it

---

[21] Ibid., Rule to Committee, 13 September 1837, fiche 661, no.18. Rule, *Recollections*, op. cit., p.176. Rule, *Memoir*, op. cit., p.214.

[22] *WMMS Correspondence*, Rule to Committee, 17 February 1837, fiche 660, no.18.

[23] Ibid., Rule to Committee, 18 March 1837, fiche 660, no.7.

out. By then there were ninety-seven children in the school. In November the Rev. Thomas Hull and his wife stayed briefly in Gibraltar on their way to Malta. He preached in the chapel and reported, 'I have been highly gratified with the very neat and commodious chapel and dwelling house which have been so recently completed - they do much credit to our cause and your liberality'.[24]

Rule continued to urge the Committee to send out new workers, and also wanted some kind of recognition for Lyon who was doing such good work in Cádiz. In addition to the request from Barcelona and the on-going work in Cádiz, Rule thought there might be opportunities in Valencia because of a contact made there by Graydon who had gone to the city to distribute scriptures. Here Graydon had met Don Pascual Marin y Candado, a Roman Catholic priest. Marin had been thinking deeply about religion for some time when he met Graydon and, after their conversations, he obtained leave of absence from his bishop. Graydon paid his fare and gave him a letter of introduction to Rule in Gibraltar.

Marin arrived in June 1837 and for over a month he and Rule studied and talked together. Rule welcomed him into his home, shared family prayers with him and wrote to the Committee that he was 'most anxious to have him as a fellow labourer in Spain'.[25] Marin had to return to Valencia to look after his mother, but he decided he would then leave the priesthood. He had a doctorate in law which he hoped might enable him to earn a living, and Rule wrote to the Committee, the Bible Society and the European Society to ask if any of them would employ him. On his last Sunday in Gibraltar, Marin preached a farewell message to Rule's Spanish congregation 'couched in the most cautious language so as not to give a handle to the Papists'.[26] However, when he returned to Valencia events overtook him. He was stripped of his priestly office, because the Vicar Apostolic in Gibraltar had laid a charge of heresy against him. Apparently, some of this information had come directly from Rule's own household through a servant who had eavesdropped on their private conversations. Rule thought Marin might well have been thrown into prison had it not been for the new Constitution.

The previous Constitution of 1812 had stated, 'The religion of the Spanish nation is, and shall be perpetually, the Catholic, apostolic, Roman, only true. The nation protects it by wise and just laws, and prohibits the exercise of any other'. However, under a new Constitution of 1837 the article relating to religion now stated, 'The nation obliges itself to maintain the worship and Ministers of the Catholic religion, which the Spaniards profess'.[27] The prohibition of any other religion had been lifted and Rule

---

[24] Ibid., Hull to Committee, 2 November 1837, fiche 662, no.23.

[25] Ibid., Rule to Committee, 9 June 1837, fiche 661, no.11.

[26] Ibid., Rule to Committee, 8 August 1837, fiche 661, no.17.

[27] Rule, *Memoir*, op. cit., p.218.

felt the new Constitution 'may be so interpreted as to allow the liberty of conscience'.[28] On the other hand it could be interpreted that any means to maintain the Catholic religion were justified, and in fact no law had been passed granting religious toleration.

The theologians of Valencia met to consider Marin's case and declared him to be a 'mixed heretic'. They demanded that he recant and do penance. Marin refused to submit to this judgment and appealed to the Cortes. There were liberals within the Cortes so he had some support there, and letters were sent on his behalf, including one from Rule, making it clear that Marin's sermon in Gibraltar had in no way been anti-Catholic. Rule desperately wanted to visit Marin but felt he could not do so without permission from the Committee. After discussion with Sweetman, he sent him some financial support as Marin was now without pay. The Committee did in fact later authorise Rule 'to afford him [Marin] such aid as would enable him with his own resources to keep from want', but cautioned against extravagance.[29]

The Cortes referred Marin's case to the Ecclesiastical Commission which reported in September 1837. It felt that 'the ecclesiastical governor of Valencia should not have regarded the business as one of those cases which are of the greatest importance'.[30] The matter was therefore referred to the Government, which was busy with many other matters and could not do anything for Marin unless he recanted and was reconciled to the Church, which he was not prepared to do. However, the Cortes would not allow him to be punished, which in previous years could have meant imprisonment, exile or death. It could not of course prevent the ostracism and petty persecution which was meted out to Marin, but he stayed in Valencia and began to write and to try and gather together a congregation, keeping closely in touch with Rule by letter.

In September 1837 problems also arose in Cádiz. On hearing of the difficulties, Rule immediately went there and found that there had been a meeting of the Board of Public Instruction to discuss the fact that Lyon was running a school, whilst unqualified, which was against the law. Various meetings and discussions took place and Brackenbury advised that the school be closed until the law was satisfied. So, the school was closed and a petition was drawn up to present to the Civil Governor, not now Urquinaona. Rule was hopeful of ultimate success. He preached several times to the small congregation Lyon had gathered and was encouraged by the progress of the work. Lyon had now been in Cádiz for nine months but no word had been received from the Committee, despite numerous letters from Rule.

---

[28] Ibid., p.219.

[29] *WMMS Correspondence,* Rule to Committee, 2 December 1837, fiche 662, no.26.

[30] Ibid., Rule to Committee, 19 October 1837, fiche 662, no.22. Rule, *Memoir,* op. cit., pp.230-1. Rule, *Recollections,* op. cit., pp.100-1.

The Board of Instruction referred the matter to a municipal body which did not want to place any difficulty in the way of the school, 'believing that it will be useful and convenient to the public, since the youths of this city may avail themselves of the commendable talents and good methods of instruction which it is so well known adorn the preceptor'.[31] The Governor forwarded this favourable decision to a provincial body who did not oppose it but felt that the matter should be discussed in Madrid. Rule was hopeful of a positive outcome there too and, in the meantime, Lyon was allowed to reopen the school. Rule continued to urge the Committee to send another couple as a female missionary was desperately needed. He feared a new attack might be made on the school on the grounds that Lyon was teaching girls. Boys and girls were never taught together in Spain. His letters got more desperate as time went on. 'What would I not give to hear your mind as to Spain'.[32] As he still heard nothing he authorised Lyon to take a larger house as the school had risen to forty pupils.

Rule continued a detailed correspondence with the Bible Society and introduced Lyon to it encouraging him to maintain a depository and to use ships' captains to help in the work of circulating the scriptures. Thirty New Testaments were given for the use of the children in the Cádiz school. Sometimes Rule was sent books to be forwarded on to Graydon and, as this was not always successful, Graydon visited Gibraltar in October 1837, to see if he could persuade the Spanish Consul there to release some of them. He was not successful, but he did visit Rule who did not quite know what to make of him. He wrote,

> Our kind brother paid me a curious visit. He came on us quite unawares, after having rapturously embraced Mrs Rule as his 'dear sister in Christ' he gave me the osculum caritatis ... However we were, are and I trust ever shall be, good friends, and I cannot but love him as a good man, although rather anomalous.[33]

No word came from the Missionary Committee, so Rule and Lyon continued as before until early in 1838 when Lyon travelled to Gibraltar to consult Rule. The Spanish Government had made an unfavourable judgment about the school and the Governor of Cádiz, 'the <u>third</u> Governor since the matter has been on hand', had ordered the school to be closed. The Government decree stated that Lyon could not be allowed to teach unless 'he lose the character of foreigner, with which the authorised exercise of that calling was incompatible'.[34] Rule notified the Committee

---

[31] *WMMS Correspondence,* Rule to Committee, 13 November 1837, fiche 662, no.24.

[32] Ibid., Rule to Committee, 28 November 1837, fiche 662, no.25.

[33] *Foreign Correspondence In,* Rule, 16 November 1837, 1837 Box 4, p.62.

[34] *WMMS Correspondence,* Rule and Sweetman, 24 February 1838, fiche 663, no.3. Postscript, Rule, 3 March 1838. Rule, *Memoir,* op. cit., p.233. Rule, *Recollections,* op. cit., p.180.

of this development and also stated that he and Sweetman wished to recommend Lyon as a candidate for the ministry. They had examined him together on 23 February 1838 and strongly recommended him, sending a statement from Lyon giving an account of his faith and experience. As far as the school was concerned Rule felt that the only course of action open to him was to go to Madrid in person to argue their cause. He felt it was a matter of some urgency and so did not wait for the Committee's permission. He informed them of his plans and also proposed visiting Valencia and Barcelona to see for himself what opportunities there might be in these cities.

Rule went by sea to Cádiz landing there on Sunday 11 March 1838. He found everything in order at the Mission House and in the afternoon preached to a few people there. In the morning he attended the service at the Consulate. Barleta gave him a letter of introduction to the Under-Secretary of State and Brackenbury a letter to Sir George Villiers. With Brackenbury he 'had some interesting conversations as to the principles in which we have to conduct our Mission here, and whose scruples and apprehensions I endeavoured to remove'.[35] This is the first hint of any concern from Brackenbury who thought Rule 'was doing wrong in coming into Spain', and it was only with reluctance that he gave Rule the letter of introduction.[36] This sounds like a change of heart but in fact the previous contact and support had all come from the Pro-Consul, Brackenbury's son. On this occasion Rule refers to meeting the Consul-General, John Brackenbury. Presumably father and son did not agree about what Rule was doing in Spain.

Rule travelled on to Seville by steamer and was delayed there for several days trying to find a way of getting to Madrid. However, he did not waste time. He engaged a bookseller to sell Bibles, met and conversed with students, and visited establishments looking after abandoned and orphaned children. He was eventually able to travel on, often with an armed escort, through countryside showing the ravages of war. It was a dangerous and uncomfortable journey but he arrived safely in Madrid on 29 March.

As soon as he could, he visited Razola, the bookseller, who directed him to Borrow where he received 'a most cordial welcome'.[37] Rule later reported that 'It was rather amusing to find him receiving a morning visit, and taking wine with two gipsy ladies, whom he did me the honour to introduce, one as "an accomplished highwaywoman", and the other as "an expert pickpocket".'[38] He felt Borrow was 'somewhat anomalous in habits

---

[35] *WMMS Correspondence,* Rule to Committee, journal extracts, 12 March-13 April 1838, fiche 663, no.5.

[36] Rule, *Recollections*, op. cit., p.182.

[37] *WMMS Correspondence,* Rule to Committee, journal extracts, 12 March-13 April 1838, fiche 663, no.5.

[38] Rule, *Memoir*, op. cit., p.248.

and predilections' but seemed impressed that he had written a history of the gypsy race and published Luke's gospel in their language. Borrow described Rule as 'a gentleman who has much interested me, and of whose zeal, piety and discretion I have formed the highest opinion'.[39] They talked at some length on many subjects, including Marin, who had already written to Borrow twice. He had replied to the first letter 'very cautiously' but, after discussing the situation with Rule, he sent Marin 'a small sum on my own account to relieve the pinch of utter need, till more can be known of him'.[40]

Rule also met Villiers who received him well and promised to help by using his influence with the Prime Minister, now the Conde de Ofália. He soon discovered that 'the representation adverse to the Mission did not proceed from Cádiz but from Gibraltar'.[41] After various discussions, Rule decided 'to place the school under the ostensible direction of a Spaniard'.[42] As long as he had the necessary qualifications it was felt there could be no objections. Rule was very grateful to Villiers, informing the Committee that 'we are greatly indebted to the British Minister for valuable advice, and for the cordial sympathy he has manifested in the interests of our mission'.[43] Rule also met Don Luis de Usoz y Río who was helping Borrow. He was very impressed with him and his offer of 'assistance to any of our Christian Societies'.[44]

Rule decided against visiting Barcelona but did go to Valencia to see Marin. He found him living in poverty with his mother who 'ceased not from pouring on him the bitterest reproaches'.[45] Marin showed him round Valencia including the church, where his former room had been emptied of furniture and the plaster stripped from the walls. His name had been erased from the priest roll and he was subjected to much petty persecution. Rule had thought about taking him back to Gibraltar but Marin felt there would be a problem in obtaining a passport and was concerned about his mother. They decided instead that he should go to Madrid where Rule hoped he might be able to help with the work of distributing the scriptures and begin to gather together a congregation. Rule gave Marin his fare and a letter of introduction to Usoz. He wrote to Borrow directly who was furious when he received Rule's letter and did not want any responsibility for Marin. Rule expected Borrow to help Marin financially in the short term because he did not have enough money with him to do much more than pay his fare, but he held himself responsible for Marin's expenses and only invited

---

[39] Darlow, op. cit., p.288. (Quoting Borrow's letter of 30 March 1838.)

[40] Ibid., pp.290-1. (Quoting Borrow's letter of 30 March 1838.)

[41] *WMMS Correspondence,* Rule to Committee, journal extracts, 12 March-13 April 1838, fiche 663, no.5.

[42] Ibid.

[43] Ibid., Rule to Committee, 5 April 1838 from Madrid, fiche 663, no.6.

[44] Ibid., Rule to Committee, journal extracts, 12 March-13 April 1838, fiche 663, no.5.

[45] Rule, *Recollections,* op. cit., p.102.

Borrow 'to assist us by your advice as long as you may be in Madrid', believing that they were both engaged in a 'common cause'.[46] Rule hoped that the Bible Society might offer some allowance for any work done there. It had previously authorised Graydon 'to engage his services for a few months at a suitable remuneration' if he could 'be usefully employed on behalf of this Society' but, on this occasion, the Society did not agree to employ Marin.[47] Borrow was an individualist and certainly did not want to be saddled with him, especially as his own circumstances were becoming increasingly difficult. Rule was, however, only doing what Graydon had done to him and seems to have been rather surprised by Borrow's reaction.

By this time Borrow had completed printing the New Testaments and had spent time travelling round Spain distributing them, and organising depots. After returning to Madrid, he opened a shop there in November 1837 to sell his remaining books. He put up a sign to say it was a depot of the Bible Society. He advertised his stock widely throughout the streets of the city and in journals and periodicals. The Spanish authorities were not happy about this and eventually ordered that the shop be closed and the stock seized. In May 1838 Borrow was arrested and imprisoned. It is unlikely that he was in a great deal of danger. He had the support of Villiers and the Spanish did not want to antagonise Britain to any great extent, but selling Bibles without notes was still illegal in Spain. Marin arrived whilst Borrow was in prison and visited him there. Borrow was not in the least impressed with him as he 'favoured me with a scene of despair, abject despair which nearly turned my brain. I despised the creature, God forgive me, but I pitied him; for he was without money and expected every moment to be seized like myself and incarcerated'.[48] He, of course, would have had none of the protection available to Borrow as a British subject. Borrow did, however, give him some financial help and Brandram also sent £10. As soon as he heard what had happened, Rule sent Marin some money and also asked the Committee if it would pay him a small salary. Borrow was eventually released from prison after a stay of about twelve days.

Meanwhile Rule had returned to Gibraltar and found himself travelling on the same steamer as Graydon who was on his way to Málaga, and other southern cities including Cádiz. They thus spent two or three days together, but Rule was not impressed with Graydon's state of mind describing him as 'in a perfect fervour - irritable and restless to an extreme', and he resolved to have no further personal correspondence with him.[49] In fact both Rule and Borrow had written to the Bible Society asking it to stop Graydon visiting Cádiz, which Rule felt might hinder his

---

[46] Darlow, op. cit., p.296. (Quoting Rule's letter of 12 April 1838.)

[47] *Minutes of Committee No.26,* 4 September 1837, p.358, minute 34.

[48] Darlow, op. cit., p.303. (Quoting Borrow's letter of 11 May 1838.)

[49] *Foreign Correspondence In,* Rule, 10 May 1838, 1838 Box 2, p.120.

work, and Seville where Borrow had contacts. Rule thought he might cause the sort of opposition which had occurred in Valencia.

In August 1837 Graydon had reported 'that a complete stop had been put to his operations in Valencia'.[50] Unfortunately, without his letters for 1837, details of what happened there have not survived, but both Borrow and Rule seem to have attributed the problem to Graydon's advertisements. The Committee did caution Graydon on the language he used in them, which was probably anti-Catholic. Graydon remained unrepentant, arguing that his advertisements were the cause of his success and, as he was not a salaried agent, he felt he could only compromise himself and not the Society. He was so upset by the Society's criticism that he suggested someone else should be sent in his place. Placatory letters were sent to him but he was reminded of the importance of not departing from the Society's 'one simple and well defined object', that of circulating the scriptures.[51] In this role Graydon was very successful. By August 1837 he had distributed 2,800 copies that year alone mostly by sale. He, too, had established contacts and depots in several cities and was convinced he would be equally successful in Cádiz. He was therefore extremely upset at being asked not to go there, which probably explains his state of mind on the steamer.

In Málaga, Graydon visited the Consul and on 24 April 1838 advertised his Bibles for sale in the local paper. The editor was a friend and the depot keeper. The result was that in the first hour alone he sold nearly 100 copies. The bishop tried to stop the sale because the Bibles lacked the apocrypha. Graydon, with the support of the Consul, William Mark, refused to accept any authority other than that of the civil authorities. However, the bishop found a judge willing to order a suspension of the sale and Graydon was forced to stop selling. The bishop published his views in the paper on 26 April and declared his intention of informing the Queen's government. As it happened, he was himself arrested a few days later as a conspirator against the Queen, but he did send a despatch to Madrid which caused quite a stir there. Graydon was aware that it was 'most unfavourable to me both in respect to the government and our ambassador.'[52]

A jury met to consider the nature of Graydon's advertisement and agreed unanimously that he should be prosecuted on the grounds that it was subversive to the Constitution. The judge did not arrest or imprison Graydon but accepted his promise not to leave Málaga until the affair was settled. The judge visited him several times at home and Graydon could not speak too highly of the civil authorities. He was anxious to emphasise

---

[50] *Minutes of Committee No.26,* 4 September 1837, p.358, minute 34.
[51] *Foreign Correspondence Out,* Brandram to Graydon, 3 February 1838, 1838 Box 18. No.1, p.42.
[52] *Foreign Correspondence In,* Graydon, 18 May 1838, 1838 Box 54, No.2, p.160.

this as he felt 'it is highly probable that this affair in Málaga will be blazoned forth in an untrue light'.[53] He was also grateful for the support he received from the Consul.

On 8 May Graydon was acquitted by a jury vote of eleven out of twelve. The jury also ordered that a copy of their finding be sent to the Madrid papers, which it was hoped would counteract the reaction to the bishop's despatch. The Consul also promised Graydon that he would explain the true state of the case to the ambassador. Graydon still faced a charge of selling books without a licence but, at the beginning of June, the charge was dropped and Graydon was free to go. He paid the costs of his lawyer with regard to the advertisements himself, seeing this as solely his affair.

The Spanish authorities now acted more decisively. The sale of Bibles without the apocrypha and without notes was still prohibited in Spain and so a Royal Order was passed that all such books should be seized, packed and sealed for their owners to export from the country. Borrow was furious and blamed Graydon for all the difficulties, writing in the strongest terms to the Bible Society about him. He urged the Society to recall Graydon, claiming that he was insane, indiscreet, the cause of all the difficulties and in personal danger. He even quoted Villiers as saying that Graydon was 'the cause of my *harmless* shop being closed at Madrid and also of my imprisonment'.[54] This is extremely unlikely. Borrow's shop was raided on 16 April before the events at Málaga occurred. He had, in fact, already stored most of his books elsewhere because of persecution. He had also opened the shop without consulting Villiers, who later wrote that he had told Borrow that 'such a measure will render the interference of the Authorities inevitable, and so it turned out'.[55] Borrow was also angry with Rule claiming that the authorities attributed Marin's conversion to him, bringing him even more adverse attention. It is difficult to assess the truth of all this but it was probably the combined activities of all three men which proved too much and provoked the authorities into taking a more decisive stand against Protestantism.

Graydon was clearly surprised by Borrow's reaction and the urgent letters of recall sent to him expressing concerns for his personal safety. He had never felt in any danger at all and said that he would, in similar circumstances, act in the same way again though he thought he would make a minor alteration to the advertisement. He sent a copy of it to the Bible Society. Borrow also accused him of circulating tracts and Graydon acknowledged that he had sold four tracts at times, including one about the differences between Protestants and Catholics, and one entitled 'The true history of the Virgin Mary'. He claimed that he had always sold them

---

[53] Ibid., Graydon, 8 May 1838, 1838 Box 54, No.2, p.159.
[54] Herbert Jenkins, *The Life of George Borrow*, John Murray: London, 1924, p.250.
(Quoting Borrow's letter to Brandram, 13 May 1838.)
[55] Ibid., p.215. (Quoting letter from Villiers to Lord Palmerston, 5 May 1838.)

discreetly and only in response to requests for them; always making it clear that he did so as an individual and not as an agent of the Bible Society, though it is doubtful whether buyers would have understood such a distinction. Graydon does seem to have regretted doing this to some extent and the Bible Society was unlikely to be happy about it.

Graydon was recalled. After his return to England Brandram and the Superintendent of the Editorial department 'had an interview with him, which had proved highly satisfactory'.[56] The following resolution was passed:

> Resolved that while this Sub Committee regretted that Mr Graydon should have issued the advertisements and tracts, which have been made the subject of so much unpleasant remark at Madrid, they yet feel that he has done so much towards promoting the Society's objects in Spain, that they cheerfully recommend to the General Committee to present to Mr Graydon a gratuity of fifty guineas as a small acknowledgment of his valuable services.[57]

While he was in England, Graydon kept in contact with many of his agents in Spain, and was told that in many areas the civil authorities had not put into effect the Royal Order to seize the books. He spent some months in Liverpool and then announced his intention of returning to Marseilles or Geneva. The Committee authorised him to do his best to secure his stocks in Spain through correspondence but, in April 1839, he returned to Spain to visit his depots and make the arrangements himself.

Meanwhile Borrow had continued to try and distribute his books despite the increasing difficulties. The Bible Society recalled him in early August and some weeks later he travelled to England. He managed to persuade the Society to let him return to Spain, partly because he had left some papers and property there. He reached Cádiz again at the very end of December 1838.

By mid 1838 therefore the work of both Borrow and Graydon had largely come to a halt, but what of Rule? He had returned to Gibraltar at the end of April 1838 and Lyon, who had been overseeing the Spanish work there, returned to Cádiz. However, they agreed that for the time being they would not try to re-open the school. Instead Lyon continued preaching in the bay and privately in his house. Rule had sent full reports of his journey into Spain to the Committee, asking yet again for its views on Spain; what to do about Marin and raising the possibility of developing work in Madrid. He still heard nothing and in May wrote an anguished letter to the Committee regarding its long silence. Apart from one brief letter he had not heard from it for eighteen months. He also reported on Lyon's disappointment: 'he has not yet been encouraged by one word of

---

[56] *Minutes of Committee Book No.27,* 6 August 1838, p.299, minute 6.
[57] Ibid., 6 August 1838, p.299, minute 7.

any sort from the Committee. I know he is often much distressed by this, and as I cannot censure your proceedings to him, I am obliged to be silent. Yet the question in both our minds is, do you approve of our proceedings?' Marin too would have liked to hear from them. 'And if I could have any clue as to your views with regard to him it would relieve me from great concern.' The responsibility for Marin weighed heavily on Rule, and for all the work and the decisions, and so he was 'most desirous to hear from you, and to be relieved from the painful perplexity which attends every effort to form or execute a plan with regard to Spain. May I say, but in the most respectful and affectionate manner, that it is only from my own society that I can obtain no correspondence?'[58] Even this letter did not elicit an immediate reply.

In June 1838, perhaps not surprisingly, Rule admitted to some health problems. An attack of pleurisy in December 1837 had left him with a weak chest. He had managed to carry on but was clearly also weighed down by the volume of work and the responsibilities he carried. He had not had a break for over six years and reported that he had now 'lost every sensation of health'.[59] He felt he needed to come to England but did not know how the work could be covered in his absence. Mary's health was also poor and later a medical report was sent recommending 'a thorough and complete change of air' for them both.[60] The Committee agreed to a return to England and also authorised Rule to make a monthly allowance to Marin. Rule immediately sent off money to cover the months of April to July, thus backdating the wage. He was very grateful to the Committee although these matters seem to have been the only subject of the correspondence and all other questions remained unanswered.

In the end, Rule felt unable to leave either station unmanned until relief was sent. As he could no longer stay in Gibraltar, he went to Cádiz in mid July with his family and Salvador Negrotto and Lyon returned to the Rock. The doctor had not recommended Cádiz because of the heat there but, after a week, Rule reported that he felt a little better though still stated 'it is a fact that our health is shattered'.[61] But he soon got down to work, and by the end of July had appointed a Spanish master, José María Perez, and had seven boys and a few girls in school. Shortly afterwards they moved to a much bigger house with plenty of room for separate boys' and girls' schools as well as a chapel. A Spanish mistress for the girls was also appointed. Brackenbury senior did not approve of what they were doing, which had depressed Lyon but seems to have left Rule unperturbed. He warned the Committee that he thought Brackenbury represented their mission as 'a failure, or at least as a hopeless, improvident and unlawful undertaking' in

---

[58] *WMMS Correspondence,* Rule to Committee, 25 May 1838, fiche 663, no.9.

[59] Ibid., Rule to Committee, 7 June 1838, fiche 664, no.10.

[60] Ibid., Charles Foote MD to Committee, 5 July 1838, fiche 664, no.13.

[61] Ibid., Rule to Committee, 19 July 1838 from Cádiz, fiche 664, no.15.

his correspondence.[62]

Rule taught for a time in the school but his health finally failed and he was forced to return to England. He left on 1 September and in England it was found that 'pulmonary disease had advanced so far that recovery was doubtful'.[63] Mary remained in Cádiz to oversee the work and also made a brief visit to Gibraltar to check on the girls' school there. However, a few weeks later, she too returned to England, with the children, as she was 'almost exhausted with fatigue and anxiety'. Rule's health did improve with good medical care and, perhaps equally helpful, he was able at last to meet with the Committee and discuss his work and plans for Spain. Although the reason for the long silence is not reported, presumably the Committee had approved of Rule's actions or else letters would have been sent earlier. Missionary work around the world was expanding at a considerable rate and the Committee was probably facing more work than it could handle. This also put an enormous strain on financial resources which meant that difficult choices had to be made about priorities.

Rule was advised to avoid a British winter and, as he was feeling much restored in health, he and his family embarked for Cádiz. With them went George Dowty, a young single probationer minister, who had been appointed to work alongside Rule. They reached Cádiz on 27 November and found everything in good order. The Spanish staff, with Negrotto, had kept up the school in their absence and by 10 December Rule reported that they had sixty-seven children in the school and numbers were increasing all the time. He had by then been there for two Sundays and also reported that 'the congregations have been very pleasing'.[64] Much furniture and equipment was still needed and he set about acquiring this as cheaply as he could. Lyon continued his work in Gibraltar, and Negrotto, who was no longer needed in Cádiz, returned to the Rock to work in the schools there.

Several letters from Marin were waiting for Rule. He was now better settled in Madrid and had found more suitable lodgings where he could hold meetings. Borrow's last reference to him was in July 1838 when he stated that 'the unfortunate M. is dying of a galloping consumption, brought on by distress of mind. All the medicine in the world would not accomplish his cure'.[65] Borrow was a little prone to exaggeration, and although Rule was aware of this illness he did not report it as life threatening and certainly Marin survived it. Instead Rule reported Marin to be writing, wanting to establish a congregation and start a school in Madrid. His allowance was still being paid, though it was barely sufficient for his needs. The Committee had also allowed Rule £10 to spend on

---

[62] Ibid., Rule to Committee, 31 July 1838 from Cádiz, fiche 664, no.16.

[63] Rule, *Recollections*, op. cit., p.196.

[64] *WMMS Correspondence*, Rule to Committee, 10 December 1838 from Cádiz, fiche 665, no.20.

[65] Darlow, op. cit., p.335. (Quoting Borrow's letter of 14 July 1838.)

books for Marin to use in Madrid.

So the Rule family settled back into life in Cádiz but they were soon hit by tragedy, for their youngest child, Melancthon, died in convulsions about two weeks after their return. Mary Rule had never been well enough to breast feed him and a Spanish wet nurse had been engaged who had gone to England with them. It seems that she was suffering from breast soreness and the Spanish mistress of the school gave her some ointment. This ointment consisted of white lead and oil and it poisoned the little boy who had previously been in excellent health. There is no suggestion of deliberate intent in Rule's letter to the Committee, but in his autobiography he stated his belief that this was an act of murder and that the woman had also been in secret correspondence with the priests about what they were doing. She left the school immediately but could not be brought to justice. As there was no Protestant burial ground in Cádiz, Rule had to smuggle out the body of his son in a packing case, bribing the custom's officials, and taking him back to Gibraltar where he was buried in the cemetery by Sweetman on 19 December. He was just nineteen months old. The Rules had now lost three of their children, but characteristically Rule did not dwell on this, throwing himself once more into the work. He did not comment on Mary's feelings. She had not even been able to attend the funeral.

While in Gibraltar, Rule was able to liaise with Sweetman and Lyon and felt the work was progressing well there. The girls' school was not doing so well because of the absence of Mary Rule, but they were training up a young girl, Catalina Parody, in the hope that she would be able to become its mistress. Rule also met with the Governor who seemed rather cool. While in England Rule had taken the opportunity of memorialising the Secretary of State, Lord Glenelg, yet again asking for the waste ground next to the chapel on which he wanted to build a school house. Lord Glenelg seems to have offered his support to the plea but the authorities in Gibraltar, probably rather irritated by Rule's persistence and attempt to go over their heads, were adamant in their continued refusal. He was offered another site but, as it was at a distance from the rest of the Mission, he did not feel it to be suitable. However, the Governor's wife had given them a subscription and a variable government grant was also awarded, which was calculated in proportion to the amount raised by subscriptions. This proved to be a great help over the years, though even so there was often a shortfall which the Missionary Committee made up. This development brought official recognition of the schools and in 1839, for the first time, they were mentioned in Gibraltar's blue book of statistics and from then on full details of all the Mission schools were given there.

In Cádiz the work seemed to progress well. By the end of January there were nearly one hundred children in the school despite the fact that religious instruction was given and attendance at Sunday services was required. A girl from Gibraltar came to help Mary with the girls. Dowty was reported as throwing himself into the work and was preaching in the bay. He was learning Spanish but not with great speed. There were two services on Sundays and, as numbers grew, they had to enlarge the room they used as a chapel.

Then, to Rule's delight, a young girl of about thirteen, Enriqueta Martínez, came to him of her own accord asking to become a 'Methodist Protestant'. Her mother, who had been attending the services, had no objection and so Rule formed a small class consisting of Enriqueta, Margarita Barea, a servant in their house, her son Federico González and Mary Rule. Enriqueta's mother later joined them along with a few others and the nucleus of the first Spanish Methodist Society was thus formed. By the end of the March quarter recognition was given to twenty-five class members and a memorable evening service of Holy Communion was held for them, which the entire congregation stayed to witness. Rule was overjoyed by these events.

Meanwhile Marin was working on plans to establish a school but, as he did not have any experience in running one, Rule suggested that Dowty should go to Madrid to work with him, which he also thought would help him to learn Spanish more quickly. Dowty was willing but expressed some anxiety about the journey itself but, as he would travel with an armed escort, Rule felt there would be little danger. Rule had had some concerns about Dowty 'who seemed to be rather out of his element at first', but now felt, 'he has lately appeared to catch the spirit of his work in a way I feared at first he would not have done.'[66] The Committee agreed to the plan and Dowty left Cádiz on 29 March 1839 arriving safely in Madrid on 15 April. By then Rule was rather concerned about Marin feeling that he had suffered much, 'that his spirit is soon cast down and every little disappointment arouses his fears. It is therefore important that he should not be alone'.[67]

On the Sunday before Dowty left Cádiz, 24 March, which was the day of the Communion Service already mentioned, Rule was visited by a member of the Municipal Assembly of the city. A charge had been laid against him and more information about the school was required. However, the civil authorities seemed quite favourably inclined towards them and Rule was not too perturbed, but it was the season of Lent which seems to have been the most dangerous time for opposition to manifest itself.

The following Sunday which was Easter Sunday, 31 March, an article appeared in one of the daily newspapers denouncing the school and congregation and attacking the authorities of Cádiz by implying that they were supporting Methodism by not opposing it. The next day their Spanish master was ordered to appear before one of the alcaldes and then Rule was summoned too. The alcalde declared the school to be illegal because it was

---

[66] *WMMS Correspondence,* Rule to Committee, 27 March 1839 from Cádiz, fiche 666, no.9.
[67] Ibid., Rule to Committee, 18 April 1839 from Cádiz, fiche 666, no.12.

a Protestant establishment. Rule argued it was not unconstitutional and was therefore legal. They parted without agreement but Rule, fearing that the school would be closed, decided to suspend it himself and he informed the authorities that he intended to establish a grammar school instead. Since his visit to Madrid the previous year, a Royal Order had been passed in 1838 giving permission for any individual of 25 years of age and above, who was of good moral standing to open such a school. So Rule now prepared to use the Order to re-open the school. The authorities acknowledged the Order but would not allow Rule to open the school until they had received some proofs of his good character, which he immediately set about providing.

In the meantime Rule continued to consult with Brackenbury who sent details of the affair to the acting Minister in Madrid. Villiers was away in England. He also met with the new Governor of Cádiz who did not show any sympathy for their cause. A Spaniard was questioned by the authorities because his daughter had been seen to enter Rule's house and, on 4 April, the bishop addressed the alcaldes in support of the newspaper article, begging them to put an end to Rule's preaching and the school.

On the next Sunday, 7 April, Rule was sent a note from an alcalde stating that as he was holding religious meetings in his house which were not in harmony with Catholic worship, he was breaking the law. He was warned to stop the meetings or measures would be taken against him. Rule immediately replied stating his surprise at receiving the note as the meetings had been held for such a long time and he did not believe them to be contrary to the present Constitution of Spain, but he agreed to stop them for the present. The congregation assembled as usual that evening but an alcalde and others were also present. Rule entered the pulpit, read the two notes to the assembled people adding only the following words, "You are Spaniards, I am an Englishman. I am free; and I pray that the time may soon come when you also shall be free".[68] He then pronounced the benediction and left the pulpit. The people had no choice but to disperse. Out in the street they discovered a group of soldiers with fixed bayonets which reduced their murmurings to silence. Sentries were placed outside the house for the next few days.

Rule decided that he would not stop his own family worship and on the following Sunday he invited a few friends to join him. He conducted a service but they did not attempt any singing. The next Sunday, 21 April, a similar group gathered, some coming early to the house to avoid detection but as soon as they had started the doorbell rang. The door was answered and an alcalde with some soldiers forced their way upstairs to the door of the chapel. Despite the effect on the assembled group, Rule continued the service, even preaching the sermon. The alcalde stood at the door, the

---

[68] Rule, *Recollections*, op. cit., p.208.

soldiers inside with drawn swords pointing to the floor, but they made no attempt to stop the proceedings. Afterwards Rule refused to speak to the alcalde until he had dismissed the soldiers, on the grounds that he was a British subject and they had no right to force their way into his home. The following day Rule received a further note to say that it was known he had continued to hold services and if he repeated such a scandal severe measures would be taken against him. Rule denied having 'open doors' worship and felt he was entitled to do what he liked in the privacy of his own home.

Then early next morning, 23 April, Rule was informed verbally by Brackenbury that the Spanish Secretary of State for Foreign Affairs had sent a note to the British Minister that the Queen wanted Rule to leave Spain immediately and if he did not do so she was determined to treat him as a criminal. The law prohibited the exercise of any religion other than the Catholic and the penalty for breaking it was death. Rule had no choice but to leave. Brackenbury expected him to go within forty-eight hours but as a steamer was due the next day, Rule decided to go even earlier and used the short time that was left to prepare for departure. So, on 24 April 1839, the whole Rule family with their servants walked through the city to the steamer 'greeted on the way with many friendly salutations and loud expressions of respect and sorrow'.[69]

Later a Royal Order dated 30 April was sent to Cádiz in which the Queen commanded that Rule be forbidden to open any kind of school or to have any meetings in his house and should he persist in doing so contrary to their laws he should be expelled from the province. Rule had of course by then been ordered out by Brackenbury, but on terms a little different from those stated in the Royal Order. He was therefore rather suspicious of Brackenbury's role in the affair, especially as his information had only been given verbally.

Rule sent full details of the events to the Missionary Committee, begging them to take up the matter with the British Government, arguing the case for the British seamen in Cádiz and for his right to work there. He based his arguments on the Constitution of 1837 and, even though he had to acknowledge that the old laws had not formally been repealed, he felt they 'are regarded as obsolete by all who are not immediately interested in their revival, and were virtually superseded in the revisal of the Spanish Constitution in the year 1837'.[70] However, whatever the new Constitution stated, it seems that the old laws could be successfully used to crush any threat to Catholicism.

Rule did not give up and, whilst he had to accept that he could no longer work in Cádiz, there was no such prohibition on Lyon. So, by the beginning of May, Lyon was once again in Cádiz, preaching in the Bay and

---

[69] Ibid., p.211.
[70] *WMMS Correspondence,* Rule to Committee, 23 April 1839 from Cádiz, fiche 666, no.13.

meeting privately with some of the Spaniards in their own homes. He proceeded very cautiously but his presence was of course known to the authorities. Their Spanish master, who was by now much in sympathy with them, also continued his work teaching small groups of children in a variety of venues, and Lyon gave some religious instruction to them when he could. Together they thus tried to keep the nucleus of the Mission alive, in the hope that it could be revived at a more favourable time.

Despite these developments Rule did not lose hope and still felt optimistic about their prospects in Spain. The Committee, however, does not seem to have shared his views and it is unlikely that any representation was made to the British Government on Rule's behalf. It seems to have felt that the obstacles in Spain were now too great and that it was time to retrench rather than advance. These differing views inevitably led to tension in the relationship between Rule and the Committee which worsened as Rule's time in Gibraltar drew to an end.

CHAPTER 9 THE MINISTRY OF WILLIAM HARRIS RULE (3)
BACK TO GIBRALTAR
More Rights for Soldiers; Mission Premises at the South
(1839-42)

Information about the activities of Borrow, Graydon and Rule had been sent to Lord Palmerston, the Foreign Secretary, by both Villiers and Ofália. In October 1838 the Bible Society had received a letter from the Foreign Office stating Villiers' observation that

> The present moment is peculiarly unpropitious for such an effort as that which the Bible Society seem desirous to make in Spain; because the Clergy have taken alarm at what they consider to be an intention to convert the people from Catholicism, and will not be slow to use their powers with the Government by a display of severity against those whom they term Heretics; that, moreover, it should be the object of the Agents of the Bible Society to avoid exciting the attention of the Public, because they can scarcely take a step without infringing some existing Law of Spain; and thereby placing themselves in the power of the Ecclesiastical or Civil Authorities; and that if by their Acts they do thus infringe the Laws of the Country, it will be impossible for the British Minister at Madrid successfully to defend them with the Spanish Government, or to afford them that protection which as British Subjects, and as Men engaged in a work of difficulty and danger, they may consider themselves entitled to claim.[1]

Palmerston therefore advised the Society to stop its agents working, hoping that when the civil war was over they would have a better chance of success.

However, despite this letter, Borrow had been authorised to return to Spain to deal with his remaining stock. He arrived in Cádiz on the last day of 1838 and travelled on, via Seville, to Madrid where he did manage to dispose of some of his books, but the work became too difficult and he returned to Seville to try and distribute them there. He set up house with Mary Clarke and her daughter Henrietta, although he did not tell the Bible Society, and began gathering together material for a book. At the end of July 1839, the Bible Society ordered his return but Borrow did not receive the letter as he had set off on his travels again. He called at Cádiz where he met Brackenbury, who was very impressed with Borrow. Brackenbury agreed to organise the shipping out of Borrow's remaining stock of books, which would otherwise have been at risk of confiscation, and wrote to the Bible Society expressing his pleasure at meeting Borrow and his sorrow at the disruption of his work. Without mentioning their names, Brackenbury implied that the blame for Borrow's difficulties lay with Graydon and Rule.

---

[1] Darlow, op. cit., p.358. (Quoting letter from the Foreign Office of 6 October 1838.)

This was certainly Borrow's opinion which he expressed quite forcefully at times.

Brackenbury wrote that previously the circulation of the Word of God had not been illegal and was 'countenanced by the Government itself', but there is little evidence to support this view.[2] He went on to say that Bible Society agents 'should neither be Sectarian Ministers of the Gospel, who by teaching and preaching, strive to make Proselytes ... nor private individuals who consider it to be their duty to combat on Spanish ground the errors of Popery', referring of course to Rule and Graydon.

Borrow travelled on to Tangier via Gibraltar and returned to Cádiz on 21 September, calling again on Brackenbury who gave him a letter of recall from the Bible Society. Brackenbury had also received a circular from Palmerston forbidding British Consuls in Spain and their assistants 'to afford the slightest countenance to religious agents'.[3] Borrow returned to Seville to put his affairs in order but seems to have been in no hurry to leave Spain. He was briefly imprisoned again because of difficulties with his passport and did not return to England until April 1840. He married Mary Clarke shortly after landing. His employment with the Bible Society was then terminated and eventually Borrow wrote his highly successful book *The Bible in Spain*. Despite his earlier outbursts against them, in the preface he paid tribute to Graydon and also to Rule and Lyon, describing them as 'two last brave disciples of the immortal Wesley'.[4] Borrow continued to write and published several more books. However, he never again found a role that fulfilled his adventurous spirit in the way that the work for the Bible Society had done. Mary died in January 1869 and Borrow himself in July 1881.

Meanwhile Graydon had also returned to Spain reaching Barcelona in April 1839, where he delivered a special Bible to Bergnes, the printer, which the Bible Society presented to him in appreciation of all his hard work. Graydon visited several places along the coast but was detained in Murcia until orders could be received from Madrid, which in fact expelled him from Spain 'for circulating small books containing opinions contrary to the religion of the country'.[5] He claimed this referred to the Bible but later stated that the order expelling him declared him 'to be a disturber of the public peace, by circulating tracts containing doctrines in contradiction to those believed in by all Spaniards.'[6]

Despite this, Graydon travelled on to Málaga where he reported on a friendly meeting with William Mark, the Consul. He arrived in Gibraltar on 28 June meeting up with Rule again and reported that 'The Cádiz affair

---

[2] Ibid., pp.448-9. (Quoting Brackenbury's letter of 29 September 1839.)
[3] Eileen Bigland, *In the Steps of George Borrow*, Rich and Cowan: London, 1951, p.245.
[4] George Borrow, *The Bible in Spain*, Collins: London, no date, pp.8-9.
[5] *Foreign Correspondence In,* Graydon, 4 July 1839, 1839 Box 59, No.3, p.30.
[6] Ibid., Graydon, 26 July 1839, 1839 Box 59, No.3, p.79.

has sounded throughout Spain and elicited most bitter articles in the public papers. Mr Rule has published therefore 'A Defence of Methodism'!! ... He is expelled also!!'[7]

Graydon returned to Barcelona calling in at the major cities along the way to contact his depot keepers and make arrangements for his books. He then left Spain, arriving in Marseilles on 24 July 1839. The civil war ended that year but the situation regarding Bible distribution remained unchanged. However, in November 1840, the Bible Society gave permission for Graydon to return to Spain as Bergnes thought that he would not be at risk if he wished to circulate the scriptures remaining there. Graydon sold some Bibles in Barcelona and then travelled down the coast visiting his depots on the way, but in Cádiz, his books were seized under the Royal Order of May 1838. It seems Graydon was thought to be in league with Rule, though he had deliberately not visited him, despite calling at Gibraltar on the steamer. He did meet him on his return journey and also visited Mark in Málaga. Both Bergnes and Graydon had hoped to recommence printing but these events put an end to their plans and Graydon left Spain on 31 May 1841.

He moved to Switzerland and in 1845 began working for the Bible Society becoming its agent for Switzerland and North Italy in 1851. By this time he had married, but in 1860 he resigned because his wife was unwell. A letter of appreciation for his twenty-five years of service was sent to him, along with a gratuity. In 1861 the Bible Society asked Graydon to visit Spain and Gibraltar again but this did not lead to any further work there. In 1864 Graydon's offer to work in South America was declined but in 1866 a gratuity of £50 was sent to him as he was in financial difficulty. He died in Bonn on 21 June 1869.

Graydon's contribution to the work in Spain has largely been ignored because of the publicity given to Borrow's work and because of Borrow's strongly outpoken criticism of him. Both had circulated a large number of Bibles and Testaments though Graydon was probably more successful in terms of sheer numbers, and also generally managed to dispose of copies by selling them rather than by giving them away. In addition he printed some whole Bibles for which there was always a great demand in Spain, and Borrow came to regret that he had only printed New Testaments. Because Borrow himself was so negative about Graydon his biographers have tended to portray him in the same way, as an impetuous and reckless amateur. He was clearly not an amateur, but certainly his advertisements and distribution of tracts was indiscreet and in the end caused considerable problems. However, Borrow too was rather foolish in opening his shop and advertising it so widely in Madrid, and it is too simplistic to blame Graydon for all Borrow's difficulties.

Borrow's biographers also tend to be rather dismissive of Rule whose

---

[7] Ibid., Graydon, 4 July 1839, 1839 Box 59, No.3, p.31.

attempts at missionary work were far more provocative. Graydon and Rule felt much more passionately about their faith than Borrow, and perhaps it was their keen desire to share this faith which caused them both to be a little unrealistic about what could actually be achieved in Spain at this time. However, overall the political situation in Spain was against them all and in the end proved too strong for each of them, and it should not be forgotten that, whatever changes were taking place in Spain, they had all broken the law.

It is not clear whether the Methodist Missionary Society received a similar letter to that sent to the Bible Society by the Foreign Office, but it would undoubtedly have been aware of Palmerston's views. In July 1839, the Missionary Committee informed Rule of its decisions. Sweetman was recalled to England; Rule was to take over as superintendent of both the English and Spanish work, and Dowty was ordered to leave Madrid and work alongside Rule in Gibraltar. Rule immediately wrote back to argue the case for Madrid. He felt that the Committee had based its decision on the rather negative reports from Dowty. Shortly after reaching Madrid, Dowty had reported that he and Marin had to proceed very cautiously indeed as the newspapers were full of the events in Cádiz and they did not want to provoke action against themselves. In the meantime, Dowty continued to learn Spanish and on his first Sunday he and Marin had 'celebrated divine worship for the first time in Madrid'.[8] Two months later he reported that their 'downfall (as it is here termed) at Cádiz is the general topic of conversation in Madrid and the public printers are constantly attacking us so that we have done but little as yet in this capital'.[9] Parents were reluctant to send them their children and they only had one little boy whom they were both teaching. On Sundays Dowty accompanied the singing on his flute and two or three Spaniards did attend their services using 'the strictest precautions', but in general he felt 'little can be done in this country until Spain … possesses the right of religious liberty'.

Rule insisted that Dowty's most recent letter to him had been more encouraging and that some progress was being made and would surely continue. He did not think Dowty had enough money to return so Rule did not send him any, arguing that it might be lost if Dowty had already left Madrid, as Marin was away. This was clearly a delaying tactic in the hope that the Committee might reconsider. Rule did not feel Dowty would be useful in Gibraltar as he could not yet preach in Spanish and was too inexperienced to cope with the English work. Whatever the decision regarding Madrid, Rule asked them not to send Dowty to Gibraltar. Instead he urged them to send a suitable successor to Sweetman as soon as possible.

---

[8] *WMMS Correspondence*, Dowty to Committee, 27 April 1839 from Madrid, fiche 666, no.14.

[9] Ibid., Dowty to Committee, 24 June 1839 from Madrid, fiche 667, no.20.

Dowty was on his own in Madrid as Marin had gone to Valencia on 22 July for a holiday because he was ill. Even Rule admitted to feeling some alarm at what he heard of Marin's health. It seems he had a chest condition but Rule thought his illness had been 'induced by long anxiety'.[10] As Dowty did not have the money to leave he had to stay in Madrid alone, but he wrote to the Committee to express his pleasure at being sent to Gibraltar. He felt Marin could continue the work and that he could use the time in Gibraltar to assist Rule in the schools, to do some English preaching and become more fluent in Spanish in preparation for future work in Spain.

The Committee did not change its mind so Rule had to make arrangements to receive Dowty in Gibraltar. Dowty left Madrid at the end of September. Marin was still in Valencia but was thought to be on his way back. Dowty arrived in Cádiz in the middle of October but felt unable to proceed to Gibraltar, writing to Rule instead to confess a sin. He wrote,

> Having no friendly adviser whose counsel I could follow, being bereft of all the public means of grace and surrounded by those temptations of the world to which youth are especially exposed, I found myself placed in a perilous situation. But until the last month I have been enabled to hold fast my profession by the grace of God and resist the adversary of souls, but alas for me in an evil hour, I listened to the enemy's suggestions, and am undone. My peculiar temptation was an ardent desire to attend the Opera.[11]

He was truly distressed by what he had done, feeling he could no longer count himself a minister and that he had let everyone down. He did not know what to do and was even wondering about trying to get a job in Spain. Rule sent the letter to the Committee with a note on the bottom saying that Dowty had had the support of Marin, conveniently forgetting Marin's long absence, and adding that he had 'had private and <u>social</u> means of grace in abundance' which is highly unlikely. His next letter was a scathing condemnation of Dowty, believing him guilty of far worse than attending the opera and certainly not wanting him in Gibraltar. He treated his letter as one of resignation. He did not believe in the genuineness of his repentance and suggested that Dowty remain in Cádiz until the Committee issued further instructions.

At the end of October Dowty wrote a long letter to the Committee pleading his youth and inexperience; the lack of support from Marin, because of his absence, and from Rule. Dowty was a young, inexperienced man in his first appointment, in a strange and dangerous country with no fluency in the language, and had felt out of his depth in Madrid, where he had been alone for two months. The Committee's instructions to go to Gibraltar had seemed like an answer to prayer, but Rule had intervened and

---

[10] Ibid., Rule to Committee, 17 July 1839, fiche 667, no.24.
[11] Ibid., Dowty to Rule, 17 October 1839 from Cádiz, fiche 668, no.36.

the longer stay and his friendship with other Englishmen had proved his undoing. He placed himself at the mercy of the Committee and begged to be given another chance but, if so, he asked to be placed 'under the direction of one to whom I can look as a Father'.[12] Rule was not the man to nurture young, inexperienced probationers, especially those who disagreed with him over Spain.

So Dowty was ordered home and landed at Gravesend towards the middle of December. No doubt he met with the Committee but no details of any meeting have survived. He did not serve in Methodism again. In his autobiography, Rule added a rather scathing footnote to say that Dowty 'afterwards obtained ordination in a diocese of the Church of England. The Bishop asked no questions, but took him at hazard, for better or for worse'.[13] It was in 1841 that Dowty began his training for the Anglican priesthood. He was ordained deacon in 1842 and priest in 1843 and served as curate at Todmorden from 1842 to 1844. He served in subsequent appointments as a perpetual curate and senior curate before becoming rector in Stockleigh English in the diocese of Exeter in 1878. No information about him is recorded after 1888 when he must either have died or retired. Dowty did not have the best of opportunities to prove his worth in Methodism under Rule, but hopefully found fulfilment in the Anglican church.

Rule did not question Sweetman's removal and plans went ahead for his departure. There are no detailed reports of his work in Gibraltar as he only wrote brief occasional letters to the Committee. The work continued much as before although in 1839 Sweetman reported his involvement with a Temperance Society which had 150 members, not just Methodists, which he felt was much needed as drunkenness was a considerable problem in Gibraltar.

After ten months in post, Sweetman complained that he had not yet had a letter from the Committee, but he was not as isolated as many of his predecessors as he had Rule as a colleague. They seem to have got on very well and on several occasions Rule reported discussing issues with Sweetman whom he described as 'a man of angelic goodness, and very diligent and much beloved in his own circle, and by no one more than myself'.[14] Towards the end of Sweetman's stay he said, 'A person of more gracious and lovely spirit than Mr Sweetman could scarcely be found', but added 'another class of excellence seems to be wanted now' and thought that "a man of energy and life" was needed.[15] Perhaps he meant someone like himself!

However, Sweetman had healed the breach in the church and one of the

---

[12] Ibid., Dowty to Committee, 30 October 1839 from Cádiz, fiche 669, no.39.
[13] Rule, *Recollections*, op. cit., p.198 (footnote).
[14] *WMMS Correspondence*, Rule to Committee, 19 July 1838 from Cádiz, fiche 664, no.15.
[15] Ibid., Rule to Committee, 4 January 1839 from Cádiz, fiche 665, no.1.

last things he did was to restore John and Susan Allen to membership. The leaders' meeting in July 1839 agreed to their request to return on condition that they acknowledge their faults and did not try to justify their past behaviour, despite provocation. This does seem to indicate a recognition that there had been faults on both sides, but presumably they agreed to these conditions because they were soon both back in positions of leadership. When Rule heard he was to take over the superintendence of the English work, he was concerned about the reaction of those, especially the Allens, who had so strongly opposed him in the past. He invited Allen to meet him and was delighted and astonished at the change in him and from then on they worked well together.

A son, Edward Merson, was born to the Sweetmans on 10 July 1837 and baptised by Rule in August. The following summer Sarah Sweetman was not well. She planned to go into Spain for a while but the rain and cooler weather came early, reviving her. In January 1839 Sweetman wrote to the Committee, assuming that his three-year appointment was ending, to say that he intended to send his wife on ahead and wait himself for his successor. However, the Committee instructed him to stay which he accepted without question despite his worries about his wife who was pregnant and the summer was approaching. Sarah Harriet was born on 5 April 1839. However, the delay in departure cost them dearly for, at the same time as they received the Committee's letter ordering their return to England, Edward died after a short illness. He was buried the following day, 16 July, by Rule. They were devastated and Sweetman wrote,

> It has pleased Almighty God to take to himself my dear, my lovely little boy, my first born. He died on the 15th inst. aged 2 years and five days. In intense suffering of soul we desire meekly to submit to the divine will. We feel fewer ties to earth and fresh inducement to long and prepare for heaven; and from deeper conviction than ever of the uncertainty of life, we hope to live more than ever to the glory of God.[16]

They left Gibraltar on 25 July arriving in England at the beginning of August. Soon afterwards they went to Australia, as they had very first intended, and on this occasion arrived safely. They served in several appointments there and three more children were born. Findlay and Holdsworth described Sweetman as a saintly man 'one of nature's noblemen ... of grave and dignified mien, affable and courteous manner, deep and unaffected piety - a Preacher of a very superior order'.[17]

In 1854 Sweetman asked the District Meeting for permission to return to England on account of his wife's health. Permission was given and the family left for England in May. However, Sarah died on the voyage. As the Missionary Committee itself had not given permission for their return,

---

[16] Ibid., Sweetman to Committee, 17 July 1839, fiche 667, no.25.
[17] Findlay and Holdsworth, op. cit., vol. iii, p.56.

it refused to pay the cost of the voyage and the expenses in London which Sweetman claimed and the *Conference Minutes* of 1855 record that Sweetman had withdrawn from the ministry. He went to his wife's family in Sampford Peverell in Devon and died there, after a period of ill-health, on 4 November 1856 at the age of 63. Some insurance money may have been paid by the Committee in 1857 but it seems rather harsh treatment of a grieving man who had served Methodism well.

Although Rule accepted Sweetman's removal without question, he was very concerned about the amount of work he would have to do.

> My spirit is willing, but my flesh is weak, and unless my mind be quite at ease, and I can move on without undue pressure, I am sure that I shall break down again. But if I have to superintend the English department, which needs at this juncture the extraordinary effort of an entire man, I fear that that and I shall sink together.[18]

His health kept up fairly well at first but he continued to plead on numerous occasions for a replacement for Sweetman. In the meantime, the better spirit now prevailing in the church certainly helped, and Rule prioritised the work, reporting that some things had to be left undone because he simply could not do everything. However, even so, Rule continued to expand the Spanish work and on 1 July 1839 opened a new school in the South. By early August it had thirty pupils, all boys. Rule did not seek the Committee's permission, announcing instead, when things were well under way, that he had planned a three-month trial and then to lay the case before them. What he really had in mind was a separate mission in the South, with its own congregation, chapel and school. The town school was now run by Negrotto and the new South school by Richard Deacon. Little is known about his background but, before long, a girls' school was also established in the South run by Deacon's wife, Mary Ann. By September there were seventy children in the South schools.

In addition, in October 1839, an evening school for working young men was opened. Allen and Stevenson, another church leader, volunteered to teach in it. Shortly afterwards Negrotto was appointed to run a young persons' Spanish class and the following year a small evening school for women was also begun. Finally, an English fee-paying school for young ladies was opened, again without waiting for the Committee's permission. A Miss McCrindell was appointed to run it. She was a native of Guernsey and was well educated herself, speaking several languages. She arrived in Gibraltar at the end of February 1840 and the school opened the following month. Pupils were only accepted on condition that they attended the English service in the chapel on Sundays, which did not always please the Anglicans. Rule sent the Committee several very favourable reports about

---

[18] *WMMS Correspondence,* Rule to Committee, 17 July 1839, fiche 667, no.24.

Miss McCrindell and her school.

The year 1839 was Methodism's Centenary year and plans went ahead in Gibraltar to celebrate the occasion along with the rest of Methodism. On Friday 25 October, after a prayer meeting in the morning, all the children in the schools and Sunday schools, about 400 in number, were assembled in the chapel. They were then marched to the Governor's house, with Rule at their head, accompanied by their teachers and members of the Society. Religious processions were normally banned as likely to be divisive, but on this occasion the Governor, General Sir Alexander Woodford, had given his permission and he and his wife received the party at the Convent where the school choir sang a verse of the National Anthem specially translated into Spanish for the occasion.

The procession then continued through the town to the neutral ground. A white banner was held aloft bearing the inscription '*Hasta aquí el Señor nos ha socorrido*' (Hitherto the Lord has helped us). This was carried by Thomas Davis, their oldest member, who rightly deserved this place of honour. One of the youngest members supported him, and the class leaders carried the British Ensign. At the neutral ground a shed had been loaned for the occasion and here the children had tea. Afterwards they moved outside, were formed up in their schools, and 'whilst a multitude of inhabitants made a broad circle around us,' they sang hymns and Rule spoke to them in Spanish.[19]

After giving three cheers, they marched back through the town to Gunners Parade, surrounded by numerous spectators, parents and friends, and here the children were dismissed. Although the police were in evidence throughout the day, the priests were not, and the day of celebration was enjoyed by all and unmarked by trouble of any kind. The Centenary celebrations continued over the next three days, with prayer meetings, special sermons on the Sunday and a tea meeting on the Monday. A collection in aid of the Centenary Fund was held and tracts were distributed in Spanish and English.

The procession, however, provoked a negative response from both the Catholics and the Anglicans, and Rule felt it had a direct bearing on events which soon occurred in the army when two soldiers were subjected to persecution. Religious persecution had lessened over the years, and in July 1839 General Lord Hill, Commander-in-Chief, had issued a General Order stating,

> Commanding Officers of Regiments are to be particularly attentive that no soldier, being a Roman Catholic, or of any religious persuasion differing from the Established Church, is to be compelled to attend the Divine worship of the Church of England; but that every soldier is to be at full liberty to attend the Worship of Almighty God according to the

---

[19] Rule, *Recollections*, op. cit., p.76.

forms prescribed by his own religion, when military duty does not interfere.[20]

However, little attention seems to have been given to this order in Gibraltar and, on 4 November, Rule was informed that two Methodist soldiers were under arrest in their barracks. It was already late and the barracks were shut for the night but, before six o'clock the next morning, Rule was at the gates to gain admission as soon as they were opened. He spoke to the men, one of whom was Corporal Henry Nicholson. He was born in Eniskillen on 29 September 1817 and had come to Gibraltar with his regiment, the 46th. In February 1839 Nicholson was given the post of clerk to the Garrison Chaplain because he was felt to be well qualified for such a job and he appears to have done it well. He was known to be a Methodist but his duties meant that he often had to worship within the Church of England. However, Major Garrett, who was temporarily commanding the 46th Regiment, had called all the non-commissioned officers together and let it be known what he thought of Methodism, threatening anyone who attended a Methodist chapel with his displeasure. He singled out Nicholson, accusing him of hypocrisy by pretending to belong to the Church of England when he was in fact a Methodist. Later that day Nicholson was released from confinement but deprived of his post.

Rule immediately wrote to the Governor to express his concern at Nicholson's treatment which he felt was 'solely and expressly on account of his being a Methodist'.[21] The Governor returned his letter, declining to interfere in a military matter, but pointing out that Nicholson himself had a right to bring the complaint before him. As the mail packet was about to leave for England, and it was clear that Rule was not going to find any support in Gibraltar, he decided to appeal directly to Lord Hill himself. He therefore wrote to him, stating Nicholson's case, and claiming his right to religious liberty as stated in the General Order. He enclosed copies of the correspondence between himself and the Governor. He informed the Governor of what he had done and sent him a copy of his letter. The Governor therefore had time to delay the mail boat and send his own report and a statement from Major Garrett, which meant that all the facts from both sides were presented to Lord Hill at the same time.

The reply from Horse Guards was dated 4 January 1840 and referred to discrepancies in the two accounts of events. The letter quoted the General Order and added that there should be an abstention 'in conformity with its spirit and letter, from every measure that might even in appearance, have a tendency to violate the rights of conscience; so long as the conduct of the

---

[20] W.H. Rule, *An Account of the Establishment of Wesleyan Methodism in the British Army*, T. Woolmer: London, 1883, p.25.

[21] *WMMS Correspondence,* Rule to Committee, 5 November 1839, fiche 669, no.40. Chapel minute book, November 1839.

soldier was in strict accordance with a preservation of good order and discipline'.[22] Since this reply seemed to be a positive outcome for Rule, he asked the Governor to make the General Order known to the garrison which he had not done before. The Governor did not reply to Rule's letter and so Rule read out the letter from Horse Guards to his congregation to inform them of the outcome of his representations. He was then accused of having 'spoken contemptibly of Major Garrett'.[23] Several members of the Society were interviewed at the Military Secretary's office and the leaders of the church drew up a statement in which they strongly denied that Rule had ever spoken out against Garrett. By this time the Governor had also sent a letter to all the regimental commanding officers forbidding any soldier from being involved in preaching and exhortation, as this 'renders them inefficient for the Service'.[24]

Rule was therefore forced to stop his three military local preachers from preaching which left him with only Michael Caulfield, who had become a local preacher in later life. This meant his own work-load was even further increased and he did not know how he could keep up the usual services. He decided therefore to write again to Lord Hill seeking his intervention. He pointed out that soldiers had been preaching for many years in Gibraltar without their duties being adversely affected. He was particularly worried about the prohibition of exhortation, being aware that a wide interpretation of this could limit almost any religious activity. Rule also urged the Committee to take up the matter, as did the leaders who stated 'the whole of us being either military men, or holding situations under Government, it is impossible for us to address his Lordship directly'.[25] Rule reported that the affair had 'produced great excitement among our people, and I fear will keep many soldiers from the Chapel'.[26]

A reply was received from Horse Guards but, as it really only re-stated the substance of the previous letter, it was of little help. Rule therefore wrote to the Governor assuming that the decision now rested with him. He was then asked to call at the Military Secretary's office. He did not see the Governor in person but was shown a written message from him. In this, Rule was requested not to communicate further with him on this matter as he was only acting under orders. It now transpired that the explicit order prohibiting preaching and exhortation had actually been issued by Lord Hill himself. Clearly there was nothing the Governor could do, nor indeed Rule, who only wished he had been aware of all the facts before he had written to Lord Hill. The Governor's message contained many favourable

---

[22] Rule, *Account*, op. cit., p.28. Chapel minute book, January 1840.

[23] Chapel minute book, January 1840.

[24] *WMMS Correspondence*, Trustees & Leaders to Committee, 21 January 1840 [incorrectly dated 21 June 1840], fiche 671, no.21.

[25] Ibid., Trustees & Leaders to Committee, 21 January 1840, fiche 671, no.21.

[26] Ibid., Rule to Committee, 22 January 1840, fiche 670, no.3.

comments about Methodism and the tenor of the meeting was positive, but local preaching could not be allowed. The only hope now lay with the Committee. In the meantime Rule had been visiting the barracks to collect the names of Wesleyan soldiers and to suggest that they sought permission to attend their own chapel on Sunday mornings. He was refused permission to enter the Artillery barracks and so appealed to the Governor who informed him that he had been trespassing. Rule accepted the Governor's authority in this matter but in further discussions the Governor stated that he now intended to march the Wesleyans to their own services on Sunday mornings. The following year he agreed to publish information about Methodist worship in Garrison Orders which was a considerable step forward in gaining rights for the Methodist soldiers.

By this time, Corporal Nicholson had found his position in the army so difficult, because of continued persecution, that he had bought himself out and Rule gave him a position as a teacher in the schools. He felt that the offer of his help was 'peculiarly seasonable' when he had so many calls on his time.[27]

As the repercussions from these events died down, a new threat appeared on the horizon, for once again Lent was approaching bringing with it the likelihood of renewed attacks in Cádiz. Lyon had continued his work there and Rule wrote often of him in glowing terms asking the Committee to recognise his work and recommending him as a candidate for the ministry. He reported that 'Brother Lyon is well adapted for the English, as well as for the Spanish work ... his English sermons have always been very acceptable'.[28] They were both pleased therefore in September 1839 to hear that Lyon had been accepted on trial as an assistant missionary and his name duly appeared in the *Minutes of Conference*. Shortly after hearing the news, Lyon himself wrote to the Committee to report on the progress of his work in Cádiz.[29] He preached twice every Sunday to a small congregation of Spaniards, only inviting those who were truly interested, and proceeding with great caution. He met with a small class of four people. Perez was still teaching nearly fifty children from house to house and once a week Lyon met with about fifteen of them to talk to them about the gospel. Three of them also came to his house for deeper study. He continued to distribute Bibles and tracts whenever possible and preached every Sunday in the bay, weather permitting. He found the need for caution necessary but frustrating.

By this time Rule was aware of Palmerston's warning that no protection could be given to religious agents and so he drafted a letter to Palmerston to appeal against this, sending the letter to England for printing. The Committee discovered this plan; Rule was reprimanded and the letter was

[27] Ibid., Rule to Committee, 14 November 1839, fiche 669, no.41.
[28] Ibid., Rule to Committee, 18 April 1839 from Cádiz, fiche 666, no.12.
[29] Ibid., Lyon to Committee, 12 September 1839 from Cádiz, fiche 668, no.32.

not sent. However, Rule continued to insist that things were settling down in Spain although he did acknowledge the vulnerability of Lyon's situation.

In December 1839 Rule reported that he had been confined to the house for four weeks with a badly ulcerated leg and that Lyon had come to help him. This had given them an opportunity to discuss the work in Cádiz which they felt could now be expanded and in March 1840, Rule reported that all was going well and Lyon had recently had 'a famous congregation' which had included the Vice Consul from Port St Mary.[30]

However, on 6 April 1840, Lyon arrived in Gibraltar having been ordered out of Cádiz. It seems that a temporary alcalde had watched Lyon's house. When he knew several people were assembled in it, he had demanded entry and later reported the matter to a higher authority, stating that Lyon had been about to preach to the people. Lyon had therefore been charged with breaking the law and the Royal Order, which prohibited Rule from holding meetings in his house, was invoked to justify this action. Lyon had liaised with the Consul and informed Rule of developments. Rule had ordered him to stay in Cádiz unless he was expelled by force or given a written order of expulsion. The Governor of Cádiz did give Lyon such a document, which he received from the Consul, and so he felt he had no choice but to leave. Rule wrote to the Committee to inform them of these events and to ask for their instructions. He also enclosed a copy of a letter he had written to Lord Palmerston and he hoped they would not disapprove of his action in doing so. In this he stated the history of events in Cádiz; argued for protection against obsolete laws which were inconsistent with the Constitution of Spain, and stated the case of the British seamen now left without the preaching they had enjoyed for over three years.

Later in April, Rule visited Cádiz himself, reporting that ten adults and five youths were meeting in class, openly declaring themselves to be Methodists. On Sunday 26 April, fifteen to eighteen people gathered together for prayer but, just as Rule was speaking to them, an alcalde arrived. Rule met him on the stairs to give the group time to conceal the books and themselves if necessary. One person, who was in public employment, wisely went on to the roof. The rest remained and their names were taken. Rule placed Margarita Barea, his former servant, who had 'a most courageous, fervent and devoted spirit' in charge, with Josefa Martínez as her assistant.[31] He arranged to send a weekly pastoral letter 'to contain the substance of a sermon' to be read out on Sundays when they met together, and Rule continued to do this until he left Gibraltar. The group planned to change venues to avoid detection and hoped to continue the work of tract distribution.

On his way to the steamer, Rule preached to about fifty people on board

---

[30] Ibid., Rule to Committee, 5 March 1840, fiche 670, no.8.
[31] Ibid., Rule to Committee, 27 April 1840, fiche 671, no.14.

a ship in the bay. It later transpired that the authorities were planning to arrest him, but were detained at a bullfight on the Sunday afternoon and so, when they arrived on the Monday morning, they discovered that he had already left. However, an inventory was taken of all the property in the house and Rule feared for a time that this would be seized.

In May, Margarita Barea was ordered to appear at the police office where she was fined for providing Rule with lodgings and for having permitted him to hold meetings in her house. She was willing to go to prison as she did not have the money to pay the fine and she refused to recant saying that even 'if they would give me millions of money, I could not give up such a lovely religion as that which is engraven on my heart.'[32] Friends lent her the money so she avoided prison and Rule later re-imbursed this, as well as the amount of the three or four fines which were imposed on others. A letter of support and encouragement was sent from all the leaders in Gibraltar, led by Allen, to their 'Brothers and Sisters in Christ' in Cádiz, urging them to persevere in prayer and Bible study.[33]

By this time, the Committee was not happy with some of Rule's actions and in May 1840 he was reminded of its displeasure at his earlier attempt to write to Palmerston and about his letters to Lord Hill and it was made clear that the Committee was most unhappy that he had written to Palmerston on this occasion. He was instructed that in future he must always go through the Committee itself. He was firmly told that the Committee 'will not submit that any Missionary should in despite of rule and remonstrance proceed in this way'.[34] Rule was unrepentant, claiming that the Committee had not previously given him such explicit instructions and that he had not therefore disobeyed orders. However, he stated that he would regard 'the injunction in the last letter as binding', but he did not obey the rest of the instructions in the letter, which were to sell the furniture in Cádiz and give up the work there. [35] He had previously been told that another missionary was to be sent but he was now told that he and Lyon could do the work between them. They were both ordered to keep to the station and not to visit Spain. Rule was also informed that the Missionary Society funds were in such a poor state that expansion anywhere was now impossible. In fact it had a debt of £30,000.

Despite these instructions Rule continued to argue the case for a missionary for Cádiz. He sent on a petition from 489 seamen and residents there asking for a continuation of the ministry that had been given to them, supported by the reply to his letter to Palmerston which made it clear that

---

[32] Ibid., Rule to Committee, 21 May 1840, fiche 671, no.18, enclosing a letter from Margarita Barea of 14 May 1840.

[33] Chapel minute book, copy of a letter from the Leaders to the Society in Cádiz, 8 May 1840.

[34] *WMMS Correspondence Outgoing,* Beecham to Rule, 29 May 1840, fiche 1173.

[35] *WMMS Correspondence,* Rule to Committee, 8 June 1840, fiche 672, no.19.

there was unlikely to be any objection to work among the seamen in Cádiz, though Rule of course planned wider work than this. So Rule did not inform the people in Cádiz that the station was to be given up and reported them to be 'full of courage, hope and confidence, and in an admirable spirit'.[36]

Over the next few months, Rule continued to put the case for Cádiz, arguing that Spain was undergoing further changes with more hope of religious liberty, and that the people in Cádiz were confident that the Committee would not desert them. He even pursued the possibility of employing a native agent but without success, and towards the end of the year he was finally ordered to close the mission. Rule expressed his anguish about this saying that he had been placed 'in the most distressing situation in which a missionary can be placed. I am persuaded that this suppression of an infant church, and abandonment of a perishing people is not sanctioned by God. The Committee acts under its own impression that my zeal has gone beyond knowledge - that my precipitancy ought to be checked - that this door is shut against us'.[37] He did not agree, and so did not immediately obey, using one more delaying tactic by stating, 'if by four weeks from this time I should hear the Committee are determined to cast off those whom God has given them in Spain, and who are now under my pastoral charge, and think themselves to be in communion with our church, I will endeavour to do what is required of me'. But if this was the case he wanted to return to England.

The Committee did not change its mind and agreed to Rule's request to return to England at the next Conference. Rule went to Cádiz in January 1841 to sort out affairs there. He reported that the school and oratory furniture would have only fetched a nominal sum, so he had arranged for its storage instead! He met twelve people in class, who continued to meet every Sunday at noon to pray and read his weekly letter. They also met for reading and prayer every Thursday. He asked for permission to make a quarterly visit to give out the class tickets. Margarita Barea wrote to the Committee, and a separate letter signed by fifteen Spaniards was sent stating their gratitude for the truths they had been taught, their desire to persevere in faith and a plea for further help.

By this time, the work in Madrid had also ended. After Dowty left, the Committee clearly had doubts about the viability of operations there. Rule, being aware of this, explored the possibility of having Marin working alongside him in Gibraltar, but the Governor would not allow him to live there on the grounds that he had received orders from England to 'sanction nothing that might seem unfriendly to the Papists'.[38] By October 1839, Marin had returned to Madrid in the hope of continuing work there but, by

---

[36] Ibid., Rule to Committee, 22 June 1840, fiche 672, no.22.
[37] Ibid., Rule to Committee, 18 December 1840, fiche 673, no.33.
[38] Ibid., Rule to Committee, 10 September 1839, fiche 668, no.31.

the end of November, Rule reported that he was no longer as satisfied with Marin as he had been. He urged him to more decisive action and began to feel that Marin was not qualified to set up an establishment on his own. Rule was still reluctant to give up Madrid as there had been no persecution there, but finally decided that it would be best for Marin to go to Cádiz, even though he was anxious that this might provoke opposition from the priests there. However, when Marin did not reply to his letter suggesting this plan, he concluded that he had ceased to correspond with him and from February 1840 he stopped sending his allowance.

Towards the end of February 1840 Marin wrote directly to the Committee. He reported that although life had become more difficult for him in Madrid, he had been unable to obtain a passport for Cádiz, being known as a heretic. The authorities would only issue one for his home town of Valencia and he had therefore gone there. He also reported that 'in consequence of the old laws being revived, every Spaniard must be a Catholic'.[39] In fact he had been imprisoned on the order of the archbishop in a convent in Valencia where he had been forced into writing a profession of faith which was likely to be published. He claimed, however, that he still held the real truth in his heart. He did have the support of a few friends, one of whom wrote to Rule and stressed that the profession of faith had been 'extorted from him by violence, that no regard whatever is to be paid to it'.[40] Rule did not feel it appropriate to send Marin money as he felt he would have no use for it in prison but assured Marin's friend that if he could be 'extricated from that situation and will honestly disown the involuntary act he has committed' he would pay him his salary.[41] He told the Committee that he felt he could not acknowledge 'an agent who does not seem to have resisted the solicitations and threatenings of the priesthood, who according to the constitution of the country, could not have deprived him of his liberty, if he had appealed against them as he did with perfect success on a former occasion'.[42] He did add that it grieved him to have to act in this way towards one whom he regarded with brotherly affection. However, once again Rule based his arguments on the Constitution of Spain rather than its laws, and seemed to forget that Marin was in a very different position from himself, being a Spaniard. He had suffered severe anxiety for years which had affected his physical health. He had also been much perturbed by the events in Cádiz concerning an Englishman, who was in a much more secure position than he was as a Spaniard. He had no protection whatsoever against the legal processes of Spain should his fellow countrymen choose to enforce them.

Marin's friend wrote again to Rule and requested some financial help

---

[39] Ibid., Marin to Committee, 23 February 1840 from Valencia, fiche 670, no.7.
[40] Rule to Committee, 5 March 1840. (Only copy in church archives.)
[41] Ibid.
[42] *WMMS Correspondence,* Rule to Committee, 27 April 1840, fiche 671, no.14.

which Rule felt he could not send. Then in April, after being released from prison, Marin wrote to Rule himself. This was a coherent and reasonable letter in which he stated his distress at the belief that he had only wished to receive money. He reminded Rule of all he had given up and lost and was sorry that he had not lived up to expectations but felt that circumstances were against him. He did not believe that there was civil or religious liberty in Spain, although he hoped that one day there would be. He had 'embraced a cause which, according to my conscience is just and true. It is my own choice'.[43] He did not ask for money but Rule sent him some anyway. He was clearly impressed with this letter and asked the Committee if it could get permission for Marin to live in Gibraltar. However, the Committee instructed Rule to close the connection with Marin, authorising him to send a parting gift if he wished. There was further contact from Marin in 1844 when he wrote to the Committee from Madrid sending the prospectus of a Spanish academy of ecclesiastical sciences which he thought would be of interest to the Missionary Society. He also asked if employment could be found for him. The Committee was unable to offer him a job but did send him £5. In 1855, George Alton, who was then the missionary in Gibraltar, met Marin in Madrid and commented, 'I believe he continues faithful to the convictions which have subjected him to so many long years of persecution', but he does not say what Marin was doing and what finally happened to him is not known.[44]

So, for the time being, the work in Spain had come to an end and Rule and Lyon had to confine their activities to the work in Gibraltar. In July 1840 another son, Ulric Zuinglius, was born to the Rules. Rule sorted out a number of issues relating specifically to the English side of the work. He refused to pay the tax levied on the chapel because other places of worship were exempt. He continued to fight for soldiers' rights. In September 1841 young sergeant Weatherburne died and the military chaplain made the arrangements for his funeral. Rule intervened and the Governor supported him so that he was enabled to carry out the funeral himself. He recorded the incident in the chapel minute book as proof that Methodist ministers could not 'be excluded from the performance of any part of their duty'. When a marriage law was passed in England allowing Methodists to officiate at weddings, Rule claimed and won the right to do so in Gibraltar. The first marriage he conducted took place on 16 April 1840 when Henry Richard Nicholson married Mary Pottash.

In January 1841 a Presbyterian church was begun in Gibraltar under its first minister, William Strauchan. He had apparently been a schoolmaster in Gibraltar and was also a member of the Bible Society's Corresponding Committee. Rule had encouraged him to qualify for the ministry and to go to Scotland for ordination, possibly out of pique at the strong opposition

---

[43] Ibid., Marin to Rule, 22 April 1840 from Valencia, fiche 671, no.16.
[44] *Missionary Notices*, vol. xiv, (1854-6), March 1855, p.33.

from the Anglicans. Rule allowed him the free use of the Methodist chapels in town and at the South on Sunday afternoons as the Presbyterians did not have a chapel of their own. He also encouraged Strauchan to seek permission to have his men marched to the services.

In the autumn of 1841 Thomas Davis died at the age of 73. He was buried by Rule on 19 October. His death was not noted in the minute book or reported to the Committee. He had not attended a leaders' meeting since April 1839 although he had taken part in the Centenary celebrations, but after that the only mention of his name was as a trustee of the property, so he may have been ill for some time. It seems that he had been a drummer boy in the Great Siege and that he had worked in the sail loft in Gibraltar. His contribution to Methodism had been immense. So his death should be marked for, apart from the difficulties experienced during the ministry of Owen Rees, he had given much to the cause in Gibraltar, as class leader, trustee and local preacher sometimes taking sole leadership responsibility in the absence of any minister. The church might well have had to close at times without him and his faith, loyalty and commitment provided a strong foundation and example on which future generations could and did build.

In June 1840, Rule passed on to the Committee Lyon's request that he be allowed to go to England to be examined and ordained. There is no record of any answer to this request and Rule did not mention Lyon again until April 1841, when he commented on the situation in Gibraltar before Conference and the decisions that would be made there regarding the station. He reported Lyon's services as invaluable as regards the daily work with the schools expanding, but added,

> As an English preacher he is equal to <u>many</u>, but not at all calculated to <u>keep</u> a congregation. As a Spanish preacher I can scarcely at all employ him, beyond addressing the schools. He can engage the esteem of persons in conversations and visits, but he cannot preach acceptably a Spanish sermon. I <u>necessarily</u> state this as if you should remove me under the impression that he can attend to the foreign congregation, the Committee will be disappointed, and the work fail.[45]

This is in marked contrast to Rule's previous reports about Lyon who at various times had been left in sole charge in Cádiz and of the Spanish work in Gibraltar. Indeed Rule had often sent glowing reports of his abilities and progress to the Committee. Lyon and Rule had worked together for nearly six years, and it is hard to believe that in all that time Rule's judgement of him had been wrong. By this time, Rule seemed less keen to leave Gibraltar and perhaps these comments were made to justify the need for him to stay. In his next letter Rule was more positive, hoping that the Committee's opinion of Lyon when he went to England would support this better report. He spoke positively of Lyon's advances in study, his good

---

[45] *WMMS Correspondence,* Rule to Committee, 29 April 1841, fiche 674, no.10.

character and the fact that he was 'now more than ever devoted to his work'.[46] Rule's health was not very good and Lyon was 'a hard-working man with a healthy constitution, and our principal school, and many other matters, are stayed by his diligence'.

Lyon also wrote to the Committee giving his reasons for wanting to visit England.[47] He wanted to meet the Committee and be ordained. He also wanted to learn more about Methodism and about educational methods in England. He hoped to look for a wife and to have an opportunity to see his family. Since he had left home both his parents and a brother and sister had died. His remaining sister was unwell and a missionary brother was about to leave for India.

Although Rule now seemed rather ambivalent about leaving Gibraltar, he wrote to the Committee again in July 1841 as both he and Lyon were anxious to know what had been decided. Rule now reported that he was far from well and was not sure he should spend another summer in Gibraltar. He felt any successor would need to come out before he left to ensure a proper handover. Then, most unexpectedly, Rule informed the Committee that Lyon had left Gibraltar. He reported that 'since his return from Cádiz, a nearer acquaintance and closer observation had led me to hope less confidently for his usefulness as a Minister of the Gospel'.[48] So he had told Lyon that he could no longer recommend him as a candidate for the ministry. He had not changed his opinion about 'his diligence in teaching etc. and the strict propriety of his moral character'. He denied that they had had any sort of argument and when Lyon had requested Rule's written permission to return to England at his own expense, he had given it to him. Rule did not want to prefer any charges against him and stated that he had not dismissed him, but remained silent as to the details merely saying that 'he is not qualified for the office of <u>Pastor</u>'. He was prepared to give more information if requested. He now felt his work load was impossible, but did not express any regret at Lyon's departure.

The leaders then wrote to the Committee saying that they did not want Lyon back 'in consequence of his very incautious and unprudent conversations with many members of the Society ... giving existence to a partizanship to the prejudice of Mr Rule's character rather than to spread the Gospel'.[49] They went on to state 'We do not wish unnecessarily to prejudice Mr Lyon's case, and therefore use the mildest language possible' but they nevertheless felt his return would be injurious. Presumably they had had enough of divisions.

The Committee does not seem to have asked Rule for more information but it did receive two unsolicited letters on Lyon's behalf which shed some

---

[46] Ibid., Rule to Committee, 19 May 1841, fiche 674, no.12.
[47] Ibid., Lyon to Committee, 19 May 1841, fiche 674, no.13.
[48] Ibid., Rule to Committee, 29 September 1841, fiche 675, no.24.
[49] Ibid., Leaders to Committee, 7 October 1841, fiche 675, no.25.

light on what had happened. One was from Guilbert, a former leader of the church and a trustee who was clearly distressed by what he believed was Rule's betrayal of Lyon. He felt that the members of the Society would all support Lyon if they were asked for their opinion.[50] The other was from Captain Robert Steward who had been a Methodist for over twenty years and had been sailing between London, Gibraltar and Cádiz for the previous eight years and, as he therefore knew both parties involved, he felt he was well qualified to speak. It was on his ship that the Rules and Dowty had travelled to Cádiz from England when he had observed for himself Rule's 'overbearing spirit'. Lyon had often preached on his ship at Cádiz and he had watched over him 'with all the tenderness and anxiety of a parent'.[51] He stated his high opinion of Lyon and that he felt Rule had been jealous of him. He also believed that Rule had tried to hold him back since he had left Cádiz:

> It so frustrated the plans of the <u>Great little man</u> that he never since could look on Mr Lyon with complacency although it did not nor would it have failed in Mr Lyon's hands, it is generally believed had Mr Rule never come to Cádiz we might have had a Mission here to this day. Mr Rule thought of ruling these Spaniards, but they are not to be ruled but led.

Rule certainly was displeased with Lyon for leaving Cádiz, because he later wrote,

> I had instructed him to act as seamen's missionary, and to refuse obedience to any *irregular* order from a Spanish authority alone, beyond suspending meetings with Spaniards, if that became necessary, but to claim his rightful freedom to minister to his fellow countrymen in the Bay. Had he followed this plain course he could not have been easily expelled, but he did not even mention his vocation as missionary to seamen.[52]

Neither had Rule mentioned this when he was expelled from Spain and it is unlikely that Lyon had had any choice in the matter, nevertheless Rule was not a man to be crossed. Lyon may well have been indiscreet in his comments about him, but it seems a real tragedy that, after all this time, Lyon was lost to the work. He had laboured long and hard wherever he was sent, without complaining. He had never had a holiday, had suffered grievous losses amongst his family in England and had always earned Rule's praises until he was ordered out of Cádiz.

The Committee did plan to send Lyon back to Gibraltar. Rule could not

---

[50] Ibid., John Guilbert to Steward, [sent to the Committee by Steward] 14 October 1841, fiche 676, no.28.

[51] Ibid., Captain Steward to Committee, 21 October 1841 from Cádiz bay, fiche 676, no.29.

[52] Rule, *Recollections*, op. cit., p.214.

understand this decision as he had not been asked for a report on him. So he wrote again using stronger language about Lyon's 'moral unfitness' for the work of a minister.[53] A few weeks later the leaders also wrote more strongly to say that they did not want him back. So Lyon did not return. His name does not again appear in the *Minutes of Conference,* so he could not have been ordained. There is no further information about what happened to this man who had worked so hard for Methodism both in Gibraltar and Cádiz. One can only hope he was able to see his siblings and that he found other satisfying work.

Lyon's going did, of course, enormously increase Rule's workload. The Spanish services had to be suspended as Rule could not carry out the usual four English services and two Spanish services on a Sunday. The weekly Spanish service was also suspended. There were only two local preachers as the military were still banned from preaching. It is not clear when this ban was finally lifted as there is no further surviving correspondence on this subject but it is unlikely that it was during Rule's time in Gibraltar.

In the summer of 1841 Miss McCrindell was ill and it soon became obvious that she would have to return to England. She planned to return at her own expense, as she had not been there for three years, and she also refunded the money for her passage out so that it was available for her successor's fare. Rule had always reported very favourably on her work and her school had attracted some more respectable people to their English congregation. The school paid for itself and so Rule was very anxious that a suitable successor was appointed, especially as the Civil Chaplain had recently set up a similar school in opposition to theirs. Miss McCrindell was willing to continue as long as possible to allow a successor to be found to teach 'a sound English education, including Geography, Astronomy, History and Ornamental Needle Work' and preferably a language as well.[54] A suitable young lady from St Ives in Cornwall was found but the Committee did not appoint her as it could not pay for her passage. Rule was furious because the Committee had been told about the refunded passage money. Nevertheless when Miss McCrindell left Gibraltar, the school was closed.

By this time, relationships between Rule and the Committee had become very strained. At the beginning of 1841 when he sent the accounts for the previous year, Rule wrote,

> I had anticipated the pleasure of drawing up a report accompanying the accounts which would have represented the Gibraltar station as in a prosperous, and most interesting condition, but on turning over the letters received since my return from Cádiz, I find that I stand so far out of the estimation of the Committee as a prudent or judicious missionary,

---

[53] *WMMS Correspondence,* Rule to Committee, 31 January 1842, fiche 677, no.1.
[54] Ibid., Rule to Committee, 23 June 1841, fiche 675, no.15.

that I cannot be expected to suggest any favourable report of my labours. Still, I will spend and be spent in the cause which is so dear to me, and enjoy an approval which fills me with confidence in the daily discharge of my various duties.[55]

But he still continued to act without seeking the approval of the Committee first.

In June 1841 Rule announced that he had 'set up another branch of our Mission in Spain' and hoped that the Committee would not censure him for doing so, although he must have known that it would. This involved Henry Nicholson whom Rule described as a 'warm Irish lad, a fervent Christian and most willing and docile servant' who 'had worked in the hot atmosphere of day and night schools, much beyond his strength, so that he was laid up sick.'[56] By reorganising the schools, he could dispense with Nicholson's services there without incurring additional cost and he had sent him to Algeciras, with his wife and young son, Richard Francis, who had been born in February 1841. The plan for Algeciras had been formed with the main alcalde, the chief civil authority there, so that

> Mr Nicholson should receive from him sanction, (license is not required) to establish himself there as 'Professor of the English Language'. That he should teach at low prices so as to obtain a larger number of pupils. That he should watch every opportunity to enlarge the circle of his operations, but should at first chiefly labour to form connexions. And that I should take the sole superintendence of his proceedings, with the concurrence of the civil authority, by whose advice from time to time we might be so guided as to avoid any infraction of existing laws respecting public instruction, and be protected from the opposition of the parish priest, who declared at the same time that he would do his utmost to frustrate our plans, and this in obedience to the repeated commands of the Bishop of Cádiz to be on the watch against me and my emissaries.[57]

Nicholson received the same allowance as he had in Gibraltar with the addition of $4 a month for house rent. He had taken his own furniture but was already making $8 or $9 a month teaching English which soon rose to $15. He was making good progress with learning Spanish and Rule felt this 'cheap agency, likely to pay itself, might be adopted more extensively in Spain, and would serve as a seminary for missionaries'. Rule had clearly not given up his hopes for Spain and was paying a weekly visit to Nicholson which was in direct disobedience to his orders from the Committee to stay in Gibraltar. It may have sanctioned a quarterly visit to Cádiz and in July 1841 Rule went there, having missed the previous quarter. He had given class tickets to thirteen people and preached there as

---

[55] Ibid., Rule to Committee, 11 January 1841, fiche 673, no.2.
[56] Ibid., Rule to Committee, 14 June 1841, fiche 674, no.14.
[57] Ibid.

usual. He was convinced the door to Cádiz was wide open and later reported that he had found people willing to offer financial support to a missionary school-master in Cádiz if the Committee would appoint someone.

Nicholson continued to work in Algeciras, but the parish priest soon began to oppose him, quoting the Royal Order against Rule which he claimed should be put into effect as Nicholson was under Rule's supervision. Despite the support he did have in some quarters, Nicholson was arrested in the street one mid-day and imprisoned. After a night in prison, he was marched at bayonet point to the border and thus escorted back to Gibraltar. Presumably his wife and son followed, after what must have been an anxious night for them. Rule does not seem to have informed the Committee of these developments, unless his letter has been lost, but in November 1841 he mentioned that he had received 'another unmerited censure'.[58]

By then Rule was in further trouble for having purchased a property at the South, which he had bought in January 1841, for the sum of $650. He claimed the Committee had provisionally sanctioned the plan and, as the money needed to purchase the land and to build on it would all be raised in Gibraltar, it would cost the Missionary Society nothing and would eventually bring in a profit. In addition to this expense, Rule had ordered the printing of his Spanish Gospels with commentary, knowing that he did not have the means to pay for it. He asked the Committee for a loan, offering his library as collateral. They refused and in the end the printing costs of $2,000 were added to the cost of the new venture at the South and loans were sought to cover the whole amount. Rule did commit himself to pay the $2,000 back and was not therefore expecting the local Society to pay, but nevertheless it added to their financial burden, when they still had a debt on the main chapel. Steward in his letter about Lyon reported that every time he visited Gibraltar all he heard about was 'the pride and extravagance of Mr Rule. And really they have a just cause of complaint, he is so burdening them with debt and so determined in his ways that all the Trustees can say to him cannot drive him from his purpose'.[59]

The purchase of the property at the South actually caused several problems. The Governor refused to sanction the names of the trustees suggested by Rule and so he bought the property in his own name. This meant that these official Methodist premises were legally owned by Rule. The property itself was quite extensive. It consisted of a large building containing two rooms measuring 50 feet by 25 feet to be used as school-room and chapel. There were three dwelling houses to provide rent and another building had been converted into a house for a 'gentleman's family'

---

[58] Ibid., Rule to Committee, 22 November 1841, fiche 676, no.32.
[59] Ibid., Captain Steward to Committee, 21 October 1841 from Cádiz bay, fiche 676, no.29.

which had already been let for $16 a month.[60] The total cost of purchase and work done on the site had come to $7,650 plus the $2,000 for his commentary, about £2,000. The Society tried to cover this enormous debt through lots of loans, and there are many receipts in the church archives relating to them, but the cost was so great that in August, Rule was forced to ask the Committee for help. He stressed he was only asking for a loan and not a grant but an instalment of $800 was due and Rule reported that if it could not be paid, he would be fined $500, the work would have to stop and the credit of the Mission would be ruined.

Although the Committee's reply has not survived, it is clear from Rule's letters that his proceedings had not met with approval. He was acting very independently and seemed to have forgotten that he was under the authority and discipline of the Missionary Society, which would have been in real difficulties if all its missionaries had behaved like this. Rule had been instructed to economise and the Committee did not have the money to help him now, because of the Missionary Society's debt. In his reply Rule referred to the 'mingling of kindness towards myself and evident misunderstandings of my proceedings and of the character and exigencies of this Mission strengthens my convictions that both yourselves and the Committee are misled by other representations than those of my letters'.[61] He went on to say, 'With your views of my proceedings (inexact as I feel them to be) you ought to provide another missionary, and I, for my part, ought not to consent to occupy a station which has suffered severely by a withdrawal of your sympathies from my best and really most useful efforts'. He ended the letter by saying, 'In resigning my connexion with the Missionary Committee I retain a heightened feeling of love to the work itself, and unutterable compassion for the <u>scattered, fainting flock in Spain</u>'.

Rule does not seem to feel that he had done anything wrong at all and at this stage one cannot help wondering about his state of mind. He was clearly physically unwell and he had pushed himself extremely hard during his years in Gibraltar. His wife had been ill and two of their children had died. Perhaps he was simply burnt out. There is sometimes a note of desperation in his letters particularly when writing about Spain. He still did not believe that Spain was closed to them, despite all the evidence to the contrary. He felt he was a lone voice and indeed he was. He could not accept the Committee's ruling to cease activities in Spain, which may well have affected his dealings with Lyon. He seemed unable also to accept the Committee's request for economy and, whereas a property in the South was a desirable means of extending their work there, it was an enormous expense and involved them in overseeing properties which were of no direct use to the Mission other than in providing an income.

Rule did manage to raise further loans in Gibraltar but there was worse to

---

[60] Ibid., Rule to Committee, 12 August 1841, fiche 675, no.19.
[61] Ibid., Rule to Committee, 16 September 1841, fiche 675, no.22.

come because Solomon Benlisha, the previous owner, complained first to Rule and then to the Committee about the way the property had been sold. Benlisha had mortgaged the property to a Mr Grain who had subsequently taken Benlisha to court for failure to meet the mortgage repayments. The court had ordered Benlisha to pay Grain by a due date and if he did not do so the property was to be transferred to Grain. As he had not paid, Grain was entitled to sell the property, which was valued at $650. It was sold at a public auction but Grain and Rule had come to a private agreement that if the price went beyond the $650, Grain would refund the money and if for less, Rule would make up the difference. Rule insisted that no secret was made of this agreement and that it was drawn up by Grain's lawyer, because he was regarded as the real purchaser. It did mean though that no one else had a hope of purchasing the property and Benlisha claimed his friends bid as far as $1,220 but it was knocked down to Rule for $1,240 although he only actually paid the $650.

The whole sorry affair was one the Committee could have done without and a special sub-committee was convened to consider the matter largely because Benlisha had written to the Missionary Society complaining about Rule's behaviour and was seeking redress. He even called at the Mission House in London. Rule had offered to let him stay on his property as a tenant at a low rent but he declined to do so.

It seems that in the early stages of the negotiations, when matters had looked fairly straightforward, the Committee had given permission for the building of a schoolroom at the South but only on condition that there was no cost to the Missionary Society which could not be responsible for any borrowed money either. The Committee certainly did not feel permission had been sought or granted for the purchase Rule had actually made. It was therefore the unanimous opinion of the sub-committee that 'The Committee did not authorise the purchase nor did they consider the manner of it seemly or even equitable'. It was felt that Rule 'appears (though mostly from indiscreet zeal, and not for the sake of any personal advantage) to have lost sight of the obligation to "think on whatsoever things are of good report" and to abstain from appearances of evil'.[62]

As far as Benlisha was concerned, as the Missionary Society had not been in any way party to the purchase, it could not be held responsible and Benlisha was advised to seek redress from the mortgagee. Rule was surprised by this as he did not regard himself as the owner. However, he said he would accept it as 'treasure trove', adding that he and his family would benefit from the income derived from the property in years to come![63]

In March 1842 Rule reported that 'a beautiful congregation is now

---

[62] *WMMS Home and General Minutes 1842-3,* fiche 55.
[63] *WMMS Correspondence,* Rule to Committee, 10 December 1841, fiche 676, no.33.

established at the South'.[64] The school there was still functioning but the girls' teacher, Mary Ann Deacon, had died at the age of 28. Just over two months later her baby son of five months also died. Her husband, Richard Deacon, did continue to teach but moved to the town school, and Henry and Mary Nicholson took over the schools at the South.

Henry Nicholson
(With permission from Martin Eayrs)

Mary Nicholson
(With permission from Martin Eayrs)

Nothing further had been heard of a successor for Rule and he became more and more concerned about how he could cope through another summer. In May he reported that his son Barrow had a disease of his knee joint and that the doctors thought the leg would have to be amputated. He sent a medical certificate in which the doctor stated that a change of climate was necessary for the safety of the limb and to obtain a professional opinion in London. Finally, in June, Rule reported that he planned to return on 14 July. 'I have no strength left and dare not venture any longer'.[65] He regretted taking this step but felt that the Committee had had abundant time to provide for the station and was clearly worried that he could not survive much longer in Gibraltar.

Rule did leave in July as planned and thus his ten-year ministry in Gibraltar came to an end. He had achieved a great deal during this time, very ably supported by his wife. For the first time, the missionary's wife was not only a support but had a distinctive role of her own in the girls' schools. As a result of their work, Methodism now occupied a very different place in the life of Gibraltar than it had before. Maybe only a person with Rule's determination, energy and zeal could have achieved this, yet had these qualities been tempered with a little more humility and understanding, fewer people might have been hurt. The cost to himself,

---

[64] Ibid., Rule to Committee, 31 March 1842, fiche 678, no.5.
[65] Ibid., Rule to Committee, 14 June 1842, fiche 678, no.8.

and to his family, was enormous and he may well have left Gibraltar a broken man. He was certainly physically unwell and does not seem to have been thinking very rationally. He remained unable to face the truth about prospects in Spain, maintaining until the end that the country was open to evangelisation. He was also unable to accept that any of his actions had been wrong, even when he was disobeying the Committee's orders. The Committee was not without fault. Instructions and correspondence had been so infrequent at times that Rule had been forced to act without waiting to hear from London. Latterly he did not even seem to make an attempt to gain permission before acting. He probably did not intend to leave Gibraltar permanently, but the Committee would not agree to his return and he never served abroad again. It seems sad that he was lost to missionary work because he had a missionary heart but the relationship between him and the Committee had been very badly damaged and he had, of course, sent in a letter of resignation.

Once back in England, Rule served in a variety of appointments, the first of which at Manningtree only lasted a year. One suspects it was not a happy time for he said, 'I was not well prepared for the prescribed movements of a Circuit at home, and the manifold exigencies of official discipline'.[66] He continued to write and for six years became one of the Connexional Editors. Barrow's leg was not amputated but he walked with a limp for the rest of his life. Two other children were born to the Rules, Philip Melancthon and Mary Ann. Both Ulric and Martin were ordained into the Anglican Church. Ulric served for many years in Newfoundland; Martin later became a Roman Catholic. He even returned to Gibraltar where he became vice-principal of St Bernard's Roman Catholic college which did not please his father.

Rule's own connections with Gibraltar did not cease, since he was the legal owner of the South property and also because of his later work fighting for soldiers' rights. He also retained an interest in missionary work particularly in Spain and in later life he re-visited both the Rock and Spain.

---

[66] Rule, *Recollections*, op. cit., p.218.

CHAPTER 10   MAINTAINING THE GROUND
A New Initiative is Begun (1842-8)

Thomas Hull
(With permission from the Oxford Centre
for Methodism and Church History)

So the Methodist Church in Gibraltar was left without a minister until the Committee appointed Thomas Trevor N. Hull. He was born at sea in August 1806. His father was a British army officer and Thomas spent his very early years in Egypt. The rest of his childhood was spent in Ireland. It was here that he was converted and became a probationary minister just before his twentieth birthday, being fully accepted into the Methodist ministry in 1830. He continued to serve in Ireland but, because of his wife's health, he sought work in a milder climate. He was sent to Malta in 1838 and stayed briefly in Gibraltar on the way, as already mentioned. Four years later, the Hulls returned to England and were not free to go to Gibraltar until October. In the meantime, John Jenkins had been appointed to Malta and so the Committee asked him to visit Gibraltar on the way.

Jenkins landed on 12 September 1842 just over eight weeks after Rule had left. His ship had stopped at Cádiz but, despite making enquiries there, he was unable to contact any of the Methodists. The voyage from Cádiz to Gibraltar took eight hours and he was impressed with the view of the Rock from the ship and also the extensive views over the bay from the Mission House. He stayed in Gibraltar for two weeks and in that time visited several classes, met with the leaders, preached at services in the Town and at the South, visited the schools and baptised two children, one of whom was Mary Eleanor, the Nicholson's second child.

He felt the Society had suffered some losses in the absence of a missionary but was generally impressed with what he saw. He met the Governor who commented favourably on their work and Mission and spoke highly of Rule.   Jenkins felt the Mission had been 'conducted with considerable vigour and zeal. Mr Rule must have been a most laborious Missionary' but he commented, 'how far the purchase of the entire property [at the South] was prudent I know not' though the congregation there was quite large.[1]   Nicholson and his wife continued to teach at the South schools and he was also now in charge of the Spanish class and was preaching at the Spanish services. Jenkins concluded that no one person could carry on the work 'without killing himself' and that no missionary

---

[1] *WMMS Correspondence,* Jenkins to Committee, 15 September 1842, fiche 678, no.10.

could work efficiently without a knowledge of Spanish. He therefore hoped the Committee would not leave Hull to work there on his own.

Thomas Hull and his wife arrived in Gibraltar late on Friday 7 October, about ten days after Jenkins had left. They moved into the Mission House the following day and Hull preached twice on the Sunday though the congregations were small and largely composed of the military. He reported that Jenkins' visit had been much appreciated and had also relieved him a little from the 'press of duties'.[2] He had hoped to discuss school affairs with Negrotto and was disappointed to find that he had left for South America with his wife. The Negrottos settled in Buenos Aires and were soon running a school there. Negrotto held several offices in the Methodist Episcopal Church and in 1855 wrote to Rule enclosing £5 for the Missionary Society and saying, 'I think it will gratify you to know that the seed you kindly and generously sowed in this poor stony heart, in my childhood, is now, blessed be God, yielding some fruit'.[3] Since his departure Deacon and Nicholson had taken over the evening school as well as continuing their duties in the day schools. Hull was very impressed with the schools and saw these 'nurseries of Protestantism as laying the foundation of a very important work' and he hoped the Committee would soon either re-appoint Rule or some other missionary for the Spanish work.[4]

Although Hull did take Spanish lessons, he had not been appointed to work in depth in the Spanish department. As well as his other duties, it was hard for him to have to follow Rule who had worked so hard and energetically in so many different ways. In addition, because Rule was the legal owner of the South property, he was still involved in Gibraltar affairs. Allen and Nicholson both kept in touch with him and this, at times, proved undermining to Hull.

As regards the South property, Hull found it difficult to understand why Rule had taken on such a huge commitment with the house and cottages and thought it would have been much more sensible to have just acquired the premises they needed themselves. He felt the decision about the South property could only be accounted for 'on the grounds of Mr Rule's extreme anxiety, coupled with an unfounded confidence in the resources of our Treasurers'.[5] Hull did not know what to do, believing Rule must be 'at his wit's end for pecuniary resources'. Allen had agreed to act as his agent in his absence and reported that, just before Rule's departure, one person had sought repayment of $300 and already had a police warrant in his pocket in case of refusal. Allen was clearly in considerable difficulties in meeting the claims, some of which he seems to have had to pay out of his own pocket,

---

[2] Ibid., Hull to Committee, 18 October 1842, fiche 678, no.13.

[3] *Missionary Notices,* vol. xiv (1854-6), March 1855, p.33.

[4] *WMMS Correspondence,* Hull to Committee, 18 October 1842, fiche 678, no.13.

[5] Ibid., Hull to Committee, 19 October 1842, fiche 678, no.14.

at least in the short term. In addition, those who had lent money believed Rule had purchased the property on behalf of the Committee, and that it would guarantee the repayments. Rumours that this was not true were now causing concern, increasing the likelihood of further loans being withdrawn. By this time Hull had revised his opinion that it would be appropriate for Rule to return, feeling that, with some few exceptions, 'it was an appointment that would not meet with general acceptance' as people in Gibraltar were concerned about what they termed his 'building mania'![6]

Matters soon became even worse when a wall at the South premises gave way. The schoolroom was flooded and two pillars partly supporting the vestry were knocked down. Thankfully the premises were unoccupied at the time, so no one was hurt but it meant further expense. Both Allen and Nicholson told Rule what had happened and Allen reminded him that he had pointed out at the time of building that there was too much sand in the mortar. Allen did not want to have anything more to do with the property management. He was extremely busy at work and had not fully recovered from a serious illness. He suggested Nicholson should take over.

The special sub-committee met at length to consider the options. The Committee did not want to take over management of such a large property when it had not authorised its purchase. Selling was not an option as it would not raise enough money to pay off the creditors. Neither could the Missionary Society afford to purchase the property itself. In the end the Committee agreed to guarantee the loans 'out of respect to the motives and character of those who have advanced to Mr Rule the sums he has expended' and presumably to protect the name of Methodism.[7] It also planned to liaise with Rule over the future management of the property.

This decision was relayed to Hull in December 1842 when he was also informed that the Committee did not feel it suitable to re-appoint Rule to Gibraltar or even to send him on a visit, but suggested instead that an agent could see to his interests.[8] Nicholson did take over as agent, the wall was eventually repaired and finally, in October 1843, Hull reported that all the cottages and the house were let.

Hull was also concerned about the Presbyterian use of both the Methodist chapels, which had resulted in fewer soldiers attending the Methodist services, and also meant that the chapels were 'not only used but exceedingly abused by the men'.[9] In view of the enormous Methodist debts, Hull could not believe Rule had allowed free use of the chapels. He reported that the people generally had been reluctant to agree and the Trustees had 'acceded simply because Mr Rule as their pastor proposed it to them'. Hull was angry about having to deal with so many consequences

---

[6] Ibid., Hull to Committee, 17 November 1842, fiche 679, no.15.
[7] *WMMS Home and General Minutes 1842-3,* fiche 55. (SOAS)
[8] *WMMS Correspondence Outgoing,* Hoole to Hull, 15 December 1842, fiche 1174.
[9] *WMMS Correspondence,* Hull to Committee, 15 November 1842, fiche 679, no.21.

of Rule's actions and felt his behaviour so went against 'every principle of justice and prudence for our own interests, that I am frequently obliged to restrain my feelings, or I should sometimes break through the laws of Christian charity'.[10]

Hull felt that Strauchan's ability was not such that he would draw away too many Methodists but thought that if he were replaced by someone of 'more pulpit ability, - of a more enterprising spirit - and of a less friendly heart' the Methodist cause would suffer further.[11] Hull felt he had to protect Methodist interests but did not want to be compared unfavourably with Rule. In fact the Presbyterians soon gave them £50 in gratitude for their kindness and did begin to make a regular payment for the use of the chapels. Hull and Strauchan remained on friendly terms, working together on occasions, and no doubt valuing the fellowship in what Hull, at least, found to be a rather isolated post.

The work of the English department continued much as before. Hull felt they had all the 'necessary machinery for success' and only needed 'more decided piety, more of the spirit of prayer, and a richer outpouring of the Holy Spirit, to render all more efficient'.[12] In October 1843, a day was set aside for special prayer for revival. Hull had, by this time, achieved a recognition not previously given, for, on being invited to dine with the Governor, he was called upon to act as chaplain at the dinner table. He commented 'had I consulted my own feelings I should much rather have gone without my dinner than have it on such terms but under all the circumstances of the case, being the first time a Wesleyan Missionary has been in so formal a manner recognised in Gibraltar ... I thought I would not have been justified in rejecting the invitation'.[13] Despite his nervousness, he was grateful for the recognition because the Anglicans had been working hard 'to draw away every respectable person from our ministry'.

Hull also established a Tract Society in 1843. He divided the South into three districts and organised teams to distribute the tracts and to enter into conversations with those whom they met. He also revived interest in the Mission library which had fallen into debt and only had three subscribers. The following year he organised a special Juvenile effort to arouse interest in missionary work around the world amongst the young people and to raise money for the schools.

Unfortunately the climate of Gibraltar did not suit Mrs Hull and early in 1843, even before the summer, Hull reported that she was not well. She remained unwell for most of their time there and her illness worsened the longer they stayed. In February 1844 Hull reported that there was 'much sickness on the Rock, and we have had a great number of very sudden

---

[10] Ibid., Hull to Committee, 13 December 1842, fiche 679, no.18.

[11] Ibid., Hull to Committee, 15 November 1842, fiche 679, no.21.

[12] Ibid., Hull to Committee, 17 November 1842, fiche 679, no.16.

[13] Ibid., Hull to Committee, 9 March 1842, fiche 679, no.24.

deaths'.[14] According to Benady, an epidemic 'among the poorer sections of the civilian population in the winter of 1843-44' was probably a form of meningitis.[15] Hull stated that '400 persons of the Romanist community alone died during the first two months of the year - many of these died of brain fever and suddenly'.[16] There had been unusually little rain and the medical men were hoping for a heavy downfall, fearing that without it the troops would have to be encamped on the neutral ground for the summer.

Little was reported about Cádiz. Jenkins had told the Committee that a small group was meeting every Sunday for prayer but gave no further details. In the autumn of 1843 Rule asked Hull to arrange the sale of the remaining Mission property in Cádiz and give up the room there, though it is not clear why this request came from Rule and not the Committee. Hull wrote to Cádiz requesting this be done but, as he was not sure what was happening there, he sent Nicholson on a visit. The furniture had been sold and the proceeds had just covered the debt on the room. Hull reported that

> Our friend spent a few days among them and took the opportunity of praying and conversing with them and on the whole reports favourably of them, particularly of a good old woman who had been a servant of Mr Rule's [Margarita Barea] who seems not only to hold fast the form of sound words but in a truly missionary spirit distributes all the tracts and Bibles she can become possessed of among the poor families she visits and takes every opportunity of pointing them to 'the Lamb of God which taketh away the sin of the world'.[17]

Hull planned to supply them with books when he could and suggested making an annual pastoral visit but, if this happened, no reports of his visits have survived.

In July 1844 Margarita Barea's son, Federico, arrived at Gibraltar's border, but was not allowed into the garrison as he did not have a passport. Instead, he was accommodated on a hulk in the harbour which was used as a wine store. He had fled from Cádiz to avoid being conscripted into the army but, as there was an agreement between Gibraltar and Spain to return deserters, he was soon likely to be handed over. His mother followed him. She was allowed into Gibraltar and stayed with the Hulls who were most impressed with her and, after 'consulting with all our friends here', they felt they could not refuse help 'to this aged and useful disciple - who not only supports openly her own principles, but as far as she can the Methodist cause and has suffered persecution for the Name and Word of Christ'.[18] The police authorities granted Federico a pass for the day to discuss his

---

[14] Ibid., Hull to Committee, 9 February 1844, fiche 680, no.2.

[15] Benady, op. cit., p.90.

[16] *WMMS Correspondence,* Hull to Committee, 27 March 1844, fiche 680, no.4.

[17] Ibid., Hull to Committee, 9 February 1844, fiche 680, no.2.

[18] Ibid., Hull to Committee, 17 July 1844, fiche 681, no.8.

situation and it was decided that he should travel to England. The agent of the steamer company agreed to take him as a deck passenger to Southampton at the reduced fare of £4. Hull hoped a situation could be found for him in England or that he could be placed in Rule's care as Federico had expressed the hope that Rule might make him into a preacher of the gospel. As there was no time to be lost Federico left immediately. He needed to be out of the country for three years to avoid conscription, but Hull said the Society would hold themselves responsible for his return fare if arrangements could not be made for him in England. Federico probably went to the Rules as Rule asked the Committee to support him. The Committee refused to do so but several members of it agreed to provide his passage money when he was ready to return to Gibraltar. Perhaps this is what happened as no other reference to him was ever made.

In the autumn of 1844 Rule wrote to the Committee giving an unfavourable view of what he believed was happening on the Rock, largely gained from his correspondence with Nicholson and Allen. It is not clear why he did so unless he was trying to present a case for his return or to protect his financial interests in the South. Hull was most upset at what he felt was implied criticism of his work. Membership had decreased from 76 to 64 but, as nine members had left with their regiment for the West Indies and two had died, this could hardly have been prevented. The Spanish class was largely the same, but there were problems at the South schools which were soon to come to a head. However, these could not be attributed to Hull's management. They were due to forces way outside his control.

In view of Rule's interference, Hull suggested that one of the Missionary Society's Secretaries should visit Gibraltar to assess the situation. Hull thought that a second missionary was needed, but realised this might not be possible because of the Missionary Society's continuing debt. As he was nearing the end of his three year appointment, he suggested that Conference might feel it more appropriate to appoint someone else. His wife's health was not good and he would have sent her back to England for the summer had passages not been so expensive. Hull continued to request a Secretarial visit but no-one came and he was left alone, feeling the burden of responsibility for the work.

In June 1845 Hull suggested that the South schools be given up. His letter was accompanied by a statement from Nicholson who described the history of the schools and seemed to agree to their closure because of Catholic opposition. The Anglican school had already closed. In 1839 Dr Henry Hughes had been given the title of Bishop of Heliopolis and appointed to Gibraltar. He arrived around the beginning of 1840 and his time was at first taken up in a clash with the Junta of Elders whose power he disputed. They took him to court in Gibraltar and won their case. Then in March 1842, when the bishop tried to retaliate, he was actually imprisoned for contempt of court. These internal squabbles occupied his attention for some time, but he was also very concerned about the effect of Protestant education on Catholic children.

He began his opposition by visiting parents in their homes and threatening them with excommunication. He also collected the children together and informed them that they were heretics and could not expect the benefits of the church in case of death. In October 1841 he opened his own school and in that month many children were removed from the Methodist schools leaving them in a low state. Thus, when Rule left Gibraltar in July 1842, there were just forty-nine children of both sexes in the South schools, though he does not appear to have reported this to the Committee. However, these measures had proved short lived in the past and, soon after Hull arrived, the numbers began to pick up so that by October 1843 there were seventy-two children in the school.

However, in January 1844, when the Catholic parents complained about the quality of the teaching in their own school, the bishop brought 'an active, zealous friar from Cádiz to superintend his school'.[19] Nicholson felt he was far more suitable than any of his predecessors and shared the affections of his people for 'his zeal and amiability'. Even so, the Protestant school was not too badly affected. However, Lent was approaching. On weekday evenings the Catholic children had been going to their own church for instruction but the friar now decided to exclude those attending the Protestant schools. The children were upset by this and the name-calling which followed. They begged their parents to withdraw them from the Protestant schools. Then in March 1844, during the fever outbreak, Antonio Victor died. He had attended the Methodist school from its beginning, so the bishop decided to deny him the rites of Catholic burial as he had previously threatened to do. No one had really believed that he would actually do this, but his wishes were carried out, horrifying the parents of Antonio and the other parents whose children attended the Protestant school. This, more than anything, contributed to the decline of the South schools. By June 1845, Hull felt it was clear that things were not going to improve. By then there were twenty-four boys and ten girls in the school but only about twelve of them were Spanish, the others being English. Hull felt this was not the purpose of a Mission school and that it was difficult to justify the expense. The annual expense of the South schools was more than £110 and Hull was being expected to work within a total Mission budget of £500 which he was finding very difficult. Perhaps surprisingly the Town schools remained unaffected. Apparently the priests did not have so much influence there and there was still no good alternative school. The boys' school met in a rented room on Governor's Parade and the girls' school met in the Mission House. In Gibraltar's blue book of statistics for 1845, the total number of pupils in the town and evening

---

[19] Ibid., Nicholson's statement attached to Hull to Committee, 4 June 1845, fiche 682, no.17.

schools is given as 284.

By this time Nicholson himself was ill. After Negrotto left, he and Deacon had been teaching at the night school on alternate nights, which Hull reported to be 'a great additional tax on their time and energies, indeed greater than they can well bear during the summer season ... but I thank God they are willing labourers'.[20] In addition Nicholson was 'the chief prop of the Spanish Society' meeting with the Spanish class and preaching at the Spanish services. This was a very heavy work load, not helped in the summer of 1843, when the Spanish congregation was subjected to harassment from local people making 'outlandish noises' and throwing 'lighted cigars and other missiles into the room' where they were meeting.[21] An appeal was made to the police office and peace was restored but, by the summer of 1844, Nicholson's health gave way. Hull felt he was 'not of a naturally robust constitution' and referred to the previous breakdown in health when Rule had sent him to Algeciras.[22] This time he went to San Roque, presumably with his family, and the South schools were suspended for a month plus the Spanish evening service and the evening school which Deacon felt unable to continue on his own.

Hull discussed Nicholson's future with him in the event of the South schools' closure. He thought that his father-in-law would set him up in a grocery store by lending him some money. Hull therefore suggested that he be given three months notice with an extra payment of £20 in appreciation of all his hard work. He also thought that a small annual allowance would secure his future services in the Spanish department. All this would of course affect Rule who received £18 a year in rent for the use of the schoolroom, but Hull suggested it was best to leave his 'interests as they may be affected by this decision in the hands of the Committee'.[23]

Rule, as might have been expected, did not agree with the suggestion of closure, aided by the receipt of an adverse report on the subject from Allen, who seems to have blamed Hull for the schools' decline. Hull was furious at this interference. He reminded the Committee of Allen's earlier defection, when he had actually established separate meetings in his own house and even administered communion adding,

> I have often had sufficient discrimination to see through the petty jealousy of both Mr and Mrs A. and their little efforts at detraction but have not appeared to notice either to prevent the recurrence of what probably would have taken place under the regime of a more pugnacious spirit, or of one who at the time of the first secession it was often complained to me on my first coming ruled with a rod of iron.[24]

---

[20] Ibid., Hull to Committee, 17 November 1842, fiche 679, no.16.

[21] Ibid., Hull to Committee, 12 September 1843, fiche 680, no.28.

[22] Ibid., Hull to Committee, 20 November 1844, fiche 681, no.12.

[23] Ibid., Hull to Committee, 4 June 1845, fiche 682, no.17.

[24] Ibid., Hull to Committee, 5 July 1845, fiche 682, no.18.

Hull acknowledged that he did not have 'the aptitudes of Mr Rule for the details of the school department' and that he was not a fluent Spanish speaker. Nevertheless he had spoken with the teachers almost every week, visited the schools frequently, heard the children read, examined their books, administered reproofs and had every confidence in the teachers themselves. He felt that Allen's facts were not correct, and was very hurt too by the fact that Nicholson had also commented to Rule that they would soon not have a Society or congregation at the South instead of the 'flourishing classes' he had left. Nicholson did admit in later conversation that the statistics did not bear this out. Hull felt that Nicholson had acted without thinking, under the influence of Allen and out of regard for Rule, whom he admired so much that he named his fifth child, born in 1846, William Harris Rule.

However, for Hull, it was just about the last straw. He was very grateful that the Committee expressed confidence in him and satisfaction with his work, but he asked to be removed at the next Conference. After twenty years in the ministry, he felt almost ready to resign and even suggested Rule himself ought to return to sort things out, adding,

> I am sure that no other minister having a proper self respect will be willing in the knowledge of the facts to undertake this mission with a self constituted superintendent at Lynn [where Rule was currently stationed] or elsewhere who is capable of writing so personally ... as Mr Rule has done and who is in the practice of keeping up a correspondence with local agents and others.[25]

In fact the Committee decided not to close the South schools, hoping that a further trial might give time for them to pick up. Hull asked Nicholson to visit the parents whose children had been withdrawn, which he did, but none of the children returned. As Hull stated,

> The circumstances of Gibraltar have completely altered from the time Mr Rule commenced his operations 15 years ago. He certainly has the honor and the satisfaction, of having provoked into <u>existence the public gratuitous schools of Gibraltar,</u> <u>his</u> were the <u>first</u> but they have naturally called forth others, so that in addition to our own four schools, there are not less than five or seven others, independent of <u>many</u> on private account at moderate rates.[26]

Then, on 13 December 1845, three Loreto nuns and a lay sister arrived to establish schools. Caruana reported,

> The whole town turned out to receive them. The Cathedral bells rung with joy, the troops lined Waterport Street up to the Cathedral and His

---

[25] Ibid., Hull to Committee, 5 July 1845, fiche 682, no.18.
[26] Ibid., Hull to Committee, 25 August 1845, fiche 683, no.19.

Excellency the Governor together with the Bishop and the Junta of Elders waited on them to give them a formal welcome.[27]

They were to play an important part in the education of girls in Gibraltar and today still run a small private school on the Rock. Hull was surprised that 'we retain as many as we do and often while I rejoice at it, I rejoice with trembling! Our work however is with our God, and our reward is from him'.[28]

The South schools continued to decline and in November 1845, Hull reported that the children were all English and could receive education elsewhere. At the beginning of 1846, he sent his annual report to the Committee. It gives a clearer picture of the work than just the return of seventy-four members does.[29] Average attendance at Sunday worship, including the school children, was given as 598. There were four day-school teachers and six Sunday school teachers for forty-nine scholars, three local preachers and seven class leaders. By March 1846 Hull reported a slight improvement in the South schools as two or three Spanish children had returned. The Town schools continued to flourish.

By then, Hull had also developed some new work. Links with the Bible Society had lapsed but in 1844 Hull had written to report that he and Strauchan, plus a few officers, had formed a committee for the purpose of establishing a depository for the sale of the works of the Religious Book and Tract Society, and wanted also to promote the objects of the Bible Society. Fifty Spanish New Testaments were granted to the schools which were much appreciated and, in March 1845, the Corresponding Committee was formally revived. A Mrs Bull agreed to run a depository, situated near the Convent, and an advertisement was placed in the *Gibraltar Chronicle* in September 1845 to announce that she had Bibles for sale there. In 1846 the committee formed themselves into small groups of two or three and visited ships in the bay whenever possible to sell and distribute tracts and Bibles. Several reports of these visits have survived.

No decision had been made about Hull's own appointment in Gibraltar and in June 1846 he again asked to be removed as soon as possible. He felt he had 'as Mr Rule's successor, and as a consequence of some of his plans suffered much both in body and mind, more so than the Secretaries or any person not on the spot can well understand or estimate'.[30] This, in addition to the overall responsibilities of the work, had affected his 'general health and spirits' particularly since Rule's last letter to the Committee. Relationships with Allen continued to be strained and, although he was very grateful for the Committee's support, he felt to stay any longer would

---

[27] Caruana, op. cit., p.68.

[28] *WMMS Correspondence,* Hull to Committee, 25 August 1845, fiche 683, no.19.

[29] Ibid., Hull to Committee, 14 January 1846, fiche 684, no.1.

[30] Ibid., Hull to Committee, 17 June 1846, fiche 684, no.5.

injure his constitution. In addition, his wife was far from well and he was very worried about her.

Conference passed with no change of appointment for Hull and in September 1846, he wrote to the Committee from Cádiz, as the doctor had felt a change of air was essential for Mrs Hull who had 'a low fever, with a return of pain in side and chest attended with cough and expectoration'.[31] Hull had intended to return to Gibraltar himself but the providential visit of the Rev. Dr Baird from New York enabled him to stay with his wife as Baird agreed to preach in his place. They spent a few days in Cádiz and then travelled on up river to Seville for a further few days. Mrs Hull's fever and cough abated and Hull himself found the break very beneficial 'after four years uninterrupted labour and preaching four times a week to the same people with scarcely the exception of one service'.[32] They seem to have stayed in a private house in Cádiz but Hull made no mention of any of the former Cádiz Society. He did hold a service on the two Sundays he was there but only mentioned an English family by name, although he did report that he felt the barriers were giving way and that liberty of worship would come to Spain within a few years.

Whilst he was in Cádiz, a Baptist minister, the Rev. Mr Brooks, arrived to work with the resident English there. Rule seems to have played a part in this appointment and Brooks had been led to believe that there were between two and three hundred resident English people apart from the seamen. On contacting the Consul, he discovered that there were just two English Protestant families in Cádiz and no more than one hundred English people throughout the whole area of Cádiz, Port St Mary and Jerez, some of whom were Catholics. They talked and prayed together and Hull shared in Brooks' disappointment at this state of affairs. They must have kept in touch because in March 1847 Hull reported that Brooks had returned to England 'bitterly disappointed with the exaggerated statements of the extent of the English population and the cheapness of living etc. in that station'.[33] In fact, in 1844, Rule had tried to find a missionary for Cádiz. The Committee was not happy about this plan, reminding him 'of the difficulties into which you plunged yourself and the Committee by your unauthorised proceedings in Gibraltar ... Have you forgotten that if the Committee had not interfered for you, your position would have been a very painful one?'[34] He was told that if he proceeded with his plan to send a missionary to Cádiz disciplinary action would be taken against him. As no further correspondence has survived, it is impossible to know what the committee thought of these later events.

At the beginning of January 1847, Hull sent his annual report and

[31] Ibid., Hull to Committee, 28 September 1846, fiche 684, no.7.
[32] Ibid.
[33] Ibid., Hull to Committee, 15 March 1847, fiche 685, no.11.
[34] *WMMS Correspondence Outgoing,* Hoole to Rule, 19 November 1844, fiche 1139.

accounts. He felt they had coped well financially as it had been a year of 'much depression in the mercantile community of Gibraltar and provisions generally have advanced in price'.[35] The leaders had recently discussed ways of improving military attendance, with the result that Methodist soldiers now went to the barracks an hour before services to invite other soldiers to go with them to church. There were 331 pupils in the schools and seven or eight young people were meeting voluntarily on Friday evenings for Bible study. A Society tea meeting focusing on missionary work had been held at the South on New Year's Eve with seventy people present. Allen spoke at the meeting and Caulfield spoke about the past, rejoicing in the freedom the military now had to worship with them. Bad weather prevented the tea-meeting for the young missionary collectors from taking place the following day and it was postponed until 4 January, when sixty-three collectors attended and 105 youngsters sat down to tea. Delight was expressed at the total collected - £12 0s 3d.

Correspondence with the Bible Society continued and Hull was asked for his opinion about Spain. In January 1847 he suggested that there were openings there ideally for an English person who spoke Spanish. He did not think such a person should go as a formal agent to be judged on what scriptures he sold or distributed, but that he should have a wider, fact-finding mission to acquire knowledge of people and places in preparation for a more systematic effort in the future. 'Such a man permitted for two years to move about Spain, might do an immensity of good'.[36] He reported that friends visiting nearby parts of Spain usually took tracts and scriptures with them which were well received, as were those taken by military friends on excursions further afield to Cádiz, Seville, Granada and Málaga. It was still illegal to import scriptures into Spain although customs officers could apparently easily be bribed because of their low pay, but Hull wondered about further attempts to print Bibles in Spain. He felt the suspension of their work in Cádiz was not what the people wanted but was a result of the jealousy of the clergy there.

The Bible Society followed up on this idea and appointed the Rev. Dr James Thompson for a period of two years. The overall results were disappointing.

> In the first of the two years he travelled extensively, and endeavoured to get the Scriptures printed in the different towns in Spain, but uniformly failed. Arrangements were several times all but completed, when some evil influence interposed, and deterred the printer from proceeding. The importation of copies has been found all but an impossibility.[37]

By 1847, the Missionary Society had managed to overcome the worst of

---

[35] *WMMS Correspondence,* Hull to Committee, 8 January 1847, fiche 684, no.10. (SOAS)
[36] *Foreign Correspondence In,* Hull, 12 January 1847, 1847 Box 1, p.30.
[37] BFBS Report 1849, p.xc.

its financial difficulties. Dr Baird's favourable reports on the work in Gibraltar, which were widely published when he reached England, encouraged the Committee to consider expansion. So, in March, Hull was informed that two missionaries were to be appointed to Gibraltar, one to take his place and the other to work in the Spanish department. Hull was pleased about this, only wishing he had had such a colleague himself. He hoped the appointment would be made soon as he was seriously concerned about his wife. He felt she would have died had they not gone to Cádiz and the doctor urged them to leave as soon as possible. Hull wanted to wait for his successor but in the end was forced to leave in mid August. However, in Southampton he met Thomas Dove, the man appointed, who reported that he had greatly benefited from their conversation.

So the Hulls left Gibraltar after what had really been a difficult appointment for them, although Hull had achieved a great deal in maintaining the ground despite the severe financial constraints placed upon him. In the circumstances, the Committee deferred their next appointment and so they had time to recuperate and to visit family and friends in Ireland. They later went to Australia where Thomas Hull 'came to be regarded by many as the ablest Minister with which the Australian Church had been favoured ... He walked with God, and drew men thither too'.[38] Mrs Hull died there and in 1853, after her death, Hull returned to Britain and was sent to Cornwall where, under his ministry, revival broke out. He then returned to Ireland and retired in 1867, though he continued to play an active part in Methodism. He preached his last sermon at the age of 90 and died on 6 December 1903 aged 97.

Thomas Dove, who had been appointed to the English department, was born and brought up near Maidstone in Kent. He was converted in early life and soon became a local preacher and eventually offered to serve on the mission field. He was sent to West Africa in 1833 and returned to England on leave three years later. In 1837 Dove was appointed to Sierra Leone, where he became the General Superintendent of the Mission. However, there were many deaths on the station including that of Mrs Dove in June 1840. Dove himself carried on until 1845 when he returned to England, when he may have been given extended leave as he appears not to have been stationed. At some stage he re-married and he arrived in Gibraltar with his wife on 3 September 1847 after a pleasant voyage. Soon after they anchored in the bay several people went on board to welcome them. Dove felt that the Society was in a low state and he commented that he was expected to preach to the same people four times a week. He called a series of special prayer meetings to pray 'for the outpouring of the Holy Spirit and for a revival of the work of God'.[39]

The man appointed to the Spanish side of the work was George Alton.

---

[38] Findlay and Holdsworth, op. cit., vol. iii, pp.113-14.
[39] *WMMS Correspondence*, Dove to Committee, 2 December 1847, fiche 685, no.19.

He was born in Derbyshire in 1823 and educated at the grammar school in Belper. He joined the Methodist Church in Belper and became a local preacher at an early age. He was accepted as a candidate for the ministry and was sent to Richmond, probably to train at the college there which had been opened in 1843, specifically for those intending to work overseas. Another college at Didsbury had opened in 1842. Gibraltar was Alton's first appointment. He arrived there with his new young wife Amelia (who was known as Amy) on 25 November and both were warmly welcomed. Amy was the daughter of the Rev. Dr Robert Alder, one of the Secretaries of the Missionary Society. In 1817 Dr Alder was sent to Nova Scotia and he later served in Prince Edward Island and Montreal. Amy was probably born in Canada and thus had personal experience of missionary life. Alder was appointed Secretary to the Missionary Society in 1833 and oversaw much of the work in British North America, making several official visits there.

George and Amy Alton sailed on the *Jupiter* with a servant and had a good voyage, although Amy suffered from seasickness. Whilst still on board Alton wrote to the Committee saying,

> The passengers on board are very agreeable. The Captain is a very friendly man, a Roman Catholic and very sincere. I have had a long and interesting conversation with him on religious topics, into which he entered freely and in a good spirit and I trust not without profit ... I shall give myself with all ardour to my great work. God is with us, cheering and blessing us. We both feel much the separation we have experienced from those we love dearly but at the same time feel that we have entered upon a great and glorious undertaking in which we expect to be furthered with the Divine help and blessing.[40]

Once in Gibraltar, Alton immediately began to learn Spanish and made very good progress. He reported that there was a great deal of interest in his appointment and that the work had been continued by Nicholson, 'for many years your faithful and laborious agent ... By his efforts a small Spanish class has been kept together, whilst they have been as sheep without a shepherd; and a service in Spanish on the Sabbath evening has been continued by him to the present and is often numerously attended.' He also felt that the 'schools formed an interesting, important and successful part of the Mission'.[41]

In March 1848 Alton reported on a plan to spend a week in Spain with his wife as a means of improving his Spanish and hoped also to distribute tracts and Bibles. He reported that 'Spaniards want such books. They will read them. They will give anything they have for them'.[42] He also thought

---

[40] Ibid., Alton to Committee, 20 November 1847 from Bay of Biscay, fiche 685, no.18.
[41] Alton to Bunting, 25 December 1847, PLP/2/8/6.
[42] Alton to Bunting, 9 March 1848, PLP/2/8/7.

the visit would be of benefit to his wife whose health had not been good since their arrival. However, overall Alton believed that the climate would suit her constitution and perhaps her pregnancy was the reason for her current poor health. As this plan is not mentioned again the visit may not have taken place, but by June, Alton had made sufficient progress in Spanish to be able to deliver a sermon he had prepared himself.

Alton also did some of the English preaching and he and Dove produced a joint printed report on the Mission schools in May 1848, after holding a public examination of the children. This was presumably a means of publicising the work of the schools both to gain subscribers and pupils.

So the two ministers settled into their appointments at the start of this new phase of the work, but they were soon involved in the first of a number of disputes and difficulties with the authorities in Gibraltar who, over the next few years, seemed particularly ill disposed towards Methodism

CHAPTER 11 OPPOSITION
Retrenchment (1848-52)

The first problem concerned the Methodist burial ground which was part of the main cemetery situated on the neutral ground at North Front, where both Protestants and Catholics were buried. It had been decided that the Jews too must now bury their dead in this cemetery and plans had been drawn up to re-allocate the ground to provide them with a separate part of it. The Church of England and the Roman Catholic Church had been consulted but not the Methodists who only discovered the plans when they became aware of the work already in progress there. They soon realised that a plot of ground for their exclusive use was not part of the plan, which alarmed them, as relationships with the Anglican clergy were still not good, and similar problems to those previously experienced were likely to recur without their own ground.

A small committee was formed and representation made to the Governor, now General Sir Robert Wilson, but despite this, and discussions with various officials in Gibraltar, their rights were completely disregarded. A lengthy report was therefore sent to London in July 1848, signed by both Dove and Alton but in the latter's hand. They urged the Committee to appeal to the authorities in England as a matter of urgency and felt this was their only hope. The Committee did make representations as did the Jews who were most unhappy with the plan and did not want any part of a Christian burial ground. The Home Government eventually ordered a separate area to be prepared for the Jews and the Methodist ground was therefore no longer required.

The Cemetery – the Methodist part is furthest away near the open land
(Picture from the collection of J. Richard Jackson)

163

In September 1848 Dove reported that 'The Governor has had large handsome Iron Gates fixed at the entrance of our Cemetery, and then very politely sent me the Key affixed thereto a large Brass Plate engraved thereon 'Methodist Gate'.'[1] There is one further mention of the cemetery in January 1849, when the leaders requested Dove to write to the Governor to complain that those who ran the washhouse adjoining the cemetery had acquired a key to the Methodist ground and were draping the washing over the tombstones to dry it!

By this time, Alton had informed the Committee that 'Mrs Alton was safely delivered of a very fine son on the 1st [August 1848] at about half past 8 o'clock a.m. Both are doing exceedingly well.'[2] They named the baby Robert Alder after his grandfather. In fact Amy Alton took some time to recover her strength but Robert was reported to be very well and growing rapidly.

The work went on much as before until, in December 1848, Dove wrote to the Committee informing them that his general health had not been good and suggesting 'the necessity, the absolute, necessity of my being removed from this station, at or before the next Conference'.[3] He went on to say that there were 'a few persons in Society, as well as in office, whom I cannot please or even satisfy, by my humble ministry' and, although he mentioned no names, he stated that 'their disaffection and rough treatment' had caused much pain to his predecessor too. He was willing to labour anywhere in the world but felt a removal was imperative and was even willing to pay the whole or part of the removal expenses.

At the request of both Dove and the leaders of the Church, Alton then had the difficult task of writing to try and explain the situation more fully. In his careful and sensitive letter he stated, 'The Leaders, with one exception say, that it is their opinion that by a long residence in Sierra Leone Mr Dove's memory has become impaired, and that in consequence he is not so well qualified to fulfil the duties of the Ministry as at an earlier period of his career'.[4] However, he was anxious to report 'the high regard in which Mr Dove's personal character is universally held' and also expressed the leaders' views that in a station at home, where he would not have to preach to the same people several times a week without a break, his ministry would be more successful and acceptable.

Alton himself refrained from giving his own personal opinion as he felt it was his role to maintain some neutrality in order to fulfil his duty to both the Doves and the Church. However, in a second letter he did comment that he did not think the request for Dove's removal was due to any

---

[1] *WMMS Correspondence,* Dove to Committee, 16 September 1848, fiche 687, no.31.
[2] Ibid., Alton to Committee, 4 August 1848, fiche 687, no.28.
[3] Ibid., Dove to Committee, 30 December 1848, fiche 688, no.43.
[4] Ibid., Alton to Committee, 27 January 1849, fiche 688, no.1.

'factious or merely dissatisfied feelings'.[5] He clearly felt very deeply for the Doves in what was a difficult and distressing situation for them. However, he was also experiencing personal distress himself for in December, at the age of four months and eleven days, his son little Robert Alder died. The cause was in part attributed to the dampness in the house which had become evident once the rain had started. Amy too had been seriously ill and they were being urged by their doctor to move immediately.

For once the Committee responded quite quickly and, by the end of March 1849, Dove had received a letter of recall and Alton was instructed to oversee the whole work until help could be sent. The leaders recorded their thanks for this quick response and their satisfaction with the decisions. It seems the Altons moved into the Mission House to support the Doves and Dove reported, 'my much esteemed friend Mr Alton has kindly and willingly taken part with me in the labour connected with the English work'.[6] One suspects he had had to offer support all along and the maturity with which Alton dealt with such a difficult situation, despite being the younger and junior minister, is very evident, especially when he was also coping with a sick wife and the devastating loss of his son. He accompanied the Doves to their ship and they left Gibraltar at the beginning of May 1849. They returned to England and were stationed at Hitchin. Dove never served abroad again but was appointed to several circuits in England. However, in the spring of 1858 his health began to fail and he died on 1 December 1859 in his 59th year.

Back in Gibraltar, Alton now had the responsibility for all the work and no doubt was glad of Nicholson's help in the Spanish department. Earlier in the year Alton had begun a Spanish evening service during the week. Many of the youths and young men from the schools attended, which he found very gratifying as they were under no obligation to do so. He felt that infant schools ought to be started too as 'without this further agency we must always labour under the discouraging conviction that we have lost some years of valuable opportunity and advantage in arresting the spread of Popish error.'[7] Problems had also developed in the schools because in March 1849 Deacon, who ran the Town boys' and the adult night schools, had become too ill to work. For two weeks Alton had undertaken his duties during the day and Nicholson at the night school, but this situation could not continue because of Nicholson's own health and Alton's increased duties. Deacon's doctor recommended that he should live at the Spanish lines, on the neutral ground, for the summer which was thought to be a healthier place. Alton proposed paying $5 a month towards the rent on the house as Deacon was 'in needy circumstances through long family

[5] Ibid., Alton to Committee, 27 January 1849, fiche 688, no.2.
[6] Ibid., Dove to Committee, 26 April 1849, fiche 689, no.9.
[7] Ibid., Alton to Committee, 1 February 1849, fiche 689, no.3.

affliction'.[8] Not only had his first wife and their two children died, but also two out of the five children born to his second wife. Although Deacon hoped to be able to resume his duties within a month, Alton was not convinced that he would recover so quickly and it is unlikely that he did. The following year, 1850, David Gilchrist took over the night school from Deacon who had resigned on health grounds and Juan Puente, one of their oldest and best trained pupils, became an assistant both in the day and night schools.

Dove had reported the English congregations to be good but in fact numbers had considerably decreased. Many had gone to the Presbyterian church instead but, despite this very real discouragement, Alton felt there 'were pleasing indications of a brighter day approaching'.[9] However, his work load was a heavy one and he was soon involved in another difficult situation with the Gibraltar authorities.

Prior to his departure Dove, with Alton, had sent a memorial to the Governor, now Major-General Sir Robert William Gardiner, as the lease on the chapel and mission house was due for renewal. At this stage they did not expect any opposition but wanted a longer term than twenty-one years because of the considerable debt still existing on the premises ($5,327 or about £1,110). The memorial was to be forwarded to England for a decision and so the Committee's help was requested in support of it. However, opposition soon become apparent and, to Alton's dismay, a plan was suggested that the lease on the chapel should be separated from the one on the house and that the latter should be regarded as an ordinary house and leased to the highest bidder. This was likely to mean that the house rent would be much more expensive and that they would have to buy it on the open market. There were strong reasons to argue against this plan: the history of the property; its usage as a charitable institution; the fact that architecturally the house and chapel were so designed as to be inter-connected. In addition, as Methodist ministers received no stipend from colonial revenues, unlike every other religious body including the Presbyterians, they could argue they deserved at least some support in terms of the lease.

Alton's fears deepened when it became clear that the Governor supported the plan to deal with the two leases separately. None of this information was received through official channels. It came privately from Marcus Costello, Her Majesty's Attorney General, who was friendly with Alton and the Methodists. Alton tried unsuccessfully to obtain an interview with the Governor to put the Methodist case before the mail left but was deliberately stalled and the papers were all sent, presumably without any representation from him other than the memorial. He therefore urged the Committee to take action.

---

[8] Ibid., Alton to Committee, 5 April 1849, fiche 689, no.7.
[9] Ibid., Alton to Committee, 29 June 1849, fiche 670, no.12.

By this time the Altons were rejoicing at the birth of their second child, this time a daughter, Catherine Alder, who was born on 1 July 1849, but at the end of August Alton informed the Committee that the doctor had 'declared it necessary for Mrs Alton to return to England for a short period and she leaves by this packet. We separate for a time by the Providence of God, to meet again I trust after the lapse of three or four months with renewed health'.[10] This must have been a very demanding and worrying time for Alton, but he had been informed that a successor to Dove had been appointed, and he hoped that the new missionary would 'find that, at least, by the blessing of God I have been able to keep our few together and to encourage them in the work of the Lord. What we especially need is "the soul converting power" and for this we are praying'.

The Committee did make representation at the Colonial office and Earl Grey, the Secretary of State for the Colonies, sanctioned a renewal of the lease on both the chapel and mission house. However, it soon became clear in Gibraltar that the Governor was trying to reverse this decision and in October Alton suggested that further representation from the Committee might be necessary in London 'should the Governor's efforts avail with His Lordship with whom I believe he has been in communication some weeks on this subject'.[11] Once again he obtained this information privately from Costello. Perhaps further representation was made in London because the lease was finally renewed in March 1850 on the same terms as before but only for twenty-one years. Twelve trustees were named. Six were connected with the Missionary Society including Dr Alder. Five were resident in Gibraltar including Alton, the new missionary Hilton Cheesbrough and three lay people. The final trustee was Rule.

Cheesbrough reached Gibraltar in mid October 1849 and had to remain in quarantine in the bay for nine days before being allowed to land. He was accompanied by his wife, Sarah Ann, several children and their governess. Cheesbrough was born in Barnard Castle on 18 August 1810. He was brought up in the Church of England but at the age of eighteen began attending the Methodist chapel where he was converted. He offered as a candidate for the ministry and, after being accepted, was appointed to the West Indies in 1833. He served there in several different appointments until 1848 when he returned to England because of bereavement and failing health. After a year's rest he was appointed to Gibraltar.

Soon after his arrival, Cheesbrough was involved in yet another dispute with the authorities, this time concerning the government grant to the Methodist schools. This grant consisted of a third of the amount of money they had raised themselves, which had been allowed on sums raised through subscriptions, tea meetings and their annual juvenile collections. However, early in 1850, Cheesbrough was informed that the grant had been

---

[10] Ibid., Alton to Committee, 25 August 1849, fiche 690, no.19.
[11] Ibid., Alton to Committee, 20 October 1849, fiche 691, no.25.

refused on the latter two amounts collected in 1849, but was not told why. He had for the first time included the sum of £240, the amount of the contribution from the Missionary Society, and the grant was also refused on this sum. There was a precedent for this money to be added because the Catholics included a similar sum in their claim and had received the grant on it. A full report was drawn up by Cheesbrough and Alton on 4 February 1850, for the attention of Earl Grey, but it had to be given to the Governor first for him to send on. Cheesbrough also sent a copy to the Committee explaining that

> The local authorities are ill affected towards us, and will, I fear either delay sending on our letter to Earl Grey or write against us, or in some way or other endeavour to secure from his Lordship a decision adverse to our views and claims. Unless the General Secretaries actively co-operate with us in Downing Street we shall probably be defeated in our present application and exposed in future to greater annoyances than ever. We can get nothing done with the authorities here. If we write them they either delay their answers till they are of no use to us or they decline answering altogether.[12]

He went on to name George Adderley, the Colonial Secretary, as the man chiefly responsible for the opposition to them.

The affair remained unresolved for several years. A year after the memorial had been written Cheesbrough learnt that the grant for 1850 did not include the disputed items either. He tried to discover if a reply had been received to their memorial but, as the answer was rather evasive, he suspected that either the memorial had not even been sent or a favourable decision had been received which the Gibraltar authorities were challenging. He asked the Committee to intervene to put an end to the 'vexatious delay'.[13]

Another year went by and Cheesbrough was informed that Earl Grey had instructed the grant for 1849 to be made on all items on their list. The Gibraltar authorities claimed they had not been told of this decision until January 1852. The additional grant for 1849 was finally paid on 5 April 1852, but the authorities then refused to include the Committee's contribution in their calculations for 1850 and 1851. Cheesbrough was convinced that Earl Grey had intended it to be included in subsequent years but was not allowed to see his letter. He therefore felt that the only course of action left was to send another memorial and he again asked the Committee to help. The schools were an expensive part of the Mission and by this time all pupils were expected to pay a penny a week for stationery. Another memorial was written and passed directly to the Committee in the hope that it could be put safely into the right hands. This was later reported

---

[12] Ibid., Cheesbrough to Committee, 6 February 1850, fiche 692, no.3.
[13] Ibid., Cheesbrough to Committee, 7 February 1851, fiche 693, no.16.

to have been 'partially sucessful' and a further £150 was awarded. However, work was still needed 'to secure some permanent substantial benefit to our schools', as the grant was reviewed every year.[14] Throughout the dispute, the Governor continued to pay his own personal contribution of $25 a year towards the work of the schools.

Meanwhile, back in March 1850, Cheesbrough had sent a full report to the Committee describing the situation in the English department. Congregations had begun to increase and membership had slightly improved. However, he was extremely concerned about the extent of the chapel debt which stood at well over £1,000. He told the Committee, 'The building is a good one, but the debt, viewed in relation to <u>local</u> means of liquidation is so enormous and overwhelming, that unless the Committee make a grant large enough to pay off present deficiencies and liquidate a portion of the principal - the case of this chapel must be utterly hopeless. We shall anxiously await your decision'.[15] However, it seems that the Committee did not agree to help at this stage, although some help was given later.

After Cheesbrough's arrival, Alton could again concentrate on the Spanish work. His wife and baby had arrived back safely on the morning of 6 February 1850 after an absence of over five months and no doubt they were happy to be reunited as a family. The Spanish work had suffered from the loss of Alton's sole attention to it. The congregations had decreased and some members had been lost from the Spanish class, but the schools continued to do well with an increase in numbers and Alton held frequent and careful examinations of the pupils. Since his arrival he felt he had had 'many proofs that with a suitable place our Spanish congregation would be numerous and somewhat respectable. In the present room I have no hope that we shall ever progress much. It is not possible to make you conceive of the wretched place in which we hold our Spanish services, and yet for the present there is certainly no remedy'.[16] He had tried several times to find an alternative without success and added that 'as we can do positively nothing with the Local Government however urgent and reasonable our wants might be, our difficulties are very great.'

In addition Nicholson was feeling unsettled about his future. There were no good employment prospects for his children in Gibraltar where he felt commerce was uncertain and based on immoral principles. He had five children but, as the eldest was still only eight-and-a-half years old, an immediate change was unnecessary. However, Nicholson was concerned enough to write to the Committee to offer his services wherever he could best be employed. He was also having difficulty managing on his salary. He was only paid as a teacher and did not receive any remuneration for his

---

[14] Ibid., Alton to Committee, 27 October 1852, fiche 695, no.34.
[15] Ibid., Cheesbrough to Committee, 4 March 1850, fiche 692, no.6.
[16] Ibid., Alton to Committee, 2 March 1850, fiche 692, no.5.

other work in the Spanish department or, it seems, for his work as Rule's agent. Alton agreed with his views on future prospects for his children as 'a more unfavourable place than Gibraltar could scarcely exist'.[17] He strongly recommended Nicholson to the Committee describing him as possessing 'fervent piety, useful talents and is devoted to his work'. Although his health had been poor at times, Alton felt he was free from constitutional disease. He also stated that he would very much regret Nicholson's removal from Gibraltar because he was 'the only person who can render the Missionary any valuable help' in the Spanish work. He therefore suggested that for the time being the best way forward was to increase Nicholson's salary and possibly give him the status of Assistant Missionary. The Committee did raise his salary which was a great help and Nicholson decided to stay on, although, in his letter of thanks, he asked the Committee to look out for a favourable opening for him.

In July 1850 Alton reported that the Bible Society had made a grant of ninety-two Bibles and Testaments, mainly in Spanish, for use in the schools. In the same month Cheesbrough reported that Alton and others had been making frequent home visits to the Spanish population with the result that the Spanish congregation had somewhat improved and two new members had been added to the Spanish class. The Missionary Society's Report for 1851 referred to 'Bible classes, Tract distribution, domiciliary visitation, and occasional addresses in crowded *patios* and in the public streets'. Alton had thus 'seen and conversed with not fewer than one thousand adults in their own houses, and publicly addressed hundreds more'. Even so, the Spanish congregation was still described as 'unsettled in its character' and the report went on to say, 'Our chief ground of hope on this Mission is, evidently, in the rising population who are being educated in our day-schools'. This was the reason that the Missionary Society continued to support the schools for they hoped through them to be laying 'the foundation of an extensive Spanish work ... by the religious training of so large a number of Spanish children'.[18]

In the autumn of 1850 the Committee asked Cheesbrough for his views on the South property. This sudden interest seems to have been precipitated by the fact that several creditors wanted their money back and Rule did not have the means to pay them. Cheesbrough replied by saying that the school room was the only part of the property that they required. They did also use the upstairs room as a chapel but he felt that one room could be used for both purposes and, if the property was sold, they could probably rent the ground floor for about $10 or $12 a month. A valuation of the entire property was carried out and it was valued at $4,650 which was not good news as the debt was over $9,000. In addition, Dairy Cottage was in urgent need of repair likely to cost between $600 and $700. The

---

[17] Ibid., Alton to Committee, 2 October 1849, fiche 691, no.24.
[18] *WMMS Reports,* vol. xi, 1849-51, 1851, p.17.

Committee decided it was time to sort out the whole business and therefore urged Rule to sell the property. He then wrote to Allen to ask him to do this which upset Nicholson, who was Rule's agent, and the two had a most unfortunate disagreement. Rule did later say that he had intended the two to work together in selling the property but, by this time, Allen had undertaken the task. However, he was very secretive about his actions and was not willing to share any information with anyone. All this put Cheesbrough in a difficult position not least because the creditors were all getting very anxious, knowing that the proceeds from the sale of the property would not cover the loans, although Rule had apparently told Nicholson that the Committee had agreed to pay all his debts. In fact the Committee had agreed to be responsible for the deficiency only temporarily and it would have to be debited in annual instalments from the Gibraltar mission account. Several long letters were written on the subject while Cheesbrough tried to establish what the Committee expected of him.

In the end, the deeds of the property were sent by Rule to Cheesbrough. He refused to part with them because he was suspicious of Allen's actions, as he was being so secretive, commenting, 'Mr Allen's conduct has surprised and perplexed us all'. He went on to say, 'the only conclusion I can come to is, that the intention to become <u>himself</u> the purchaser at a low figure of Mr Rule's Estate, which he thought he might do without injuring Mr Rule inasmuch as the Committee had assumed his liabilities, has temporarily poisoned and perverted this good man'.[19] Cheesbrough made it clear that he would never stand by and allow any action at the expense of the Committee and also informed Allen that the Committee had said, 'We shall hold Mr Rule responsible as long as he shall live' even if it had to pay out in the short term.

There was little interest in the property but eventually the Protestant bishop offered $4,500 for it. However, he was not willing to rent out the schoolroom as he also intended using the premises to incorporate a chapel, school and clergyman's residence. In the end Cheesbrough dared not wait for the Committee's decision, as some of the bishop's friends considered he had offered too much for the property, and Cheesbrough felt it was extremely unlikely that he would get such a good price anywhere else. So, in the middle of June 1851, he agreed to the sale. The property was transferred to the Rt Rev. George Tomlinson, Lord Bishop of Gibraltar on 31 July 1851. The Methodist South schools then closed. The children in them were still mostly English and Mary Nicholson's services had been dispensed with some months earlier, but this still left Nicholson himself without a job and so Cheesbrough suggested some compensation should be paid. In fact it was Nicholson who carried the news of the sale to London. Earlier in the year, he had written to the Committee to ask for paid leave of

---

[19] *WMMS Correspondence,* Cheesbrough to Committee, 6 May 1851, fiche 693, no.21.

absence for three months to visit his 'aged and widowed mother, who through a merciful Providence has just recovered from an attack which it was thought would have proved fatal'.[20] The steam ships were offering reduced fares and, after fourteen years in Gibraltar and the health problems he had experienced, Nicholson felt very much in need of a break and a chance to see his family. Cheesbrough strongly supported his application and he left for Ireland in June 1851, taking a letter from Cheesbrough with him containing news of the sale. Presumably Nicholson knew what information the letter contained and he may therefore have had an opportunity to discuss his own future with the Committee. He was given some compensation and, by this time, his father-in-law had died and he and Mary may have inherited some money because, when their eighth child was baptised in January 1852, Nicholson's occupation was given as store-keeper and merchant.

The proceeds of the sale were used as far as possible to pay off the loans but a sizeable debt still remained. However, Cheesbrough reported that 'the propriety of selling the South Estate no one doubts now that it is done. Had this step been taken long ago, it would have been so much the better'.[21] Several months later he reported that the loss of the South room had not proved detrimental to their cause and he felt it was 'to be deeply regretted that such a property was ever acquired, and having been so acquired, that it was not long since parted with'.[22] He did not realise then how fortunate they had been, for nine years later when the bishop tried to renew the lease, he ran into difficulties. The lease was refused on a third of the property, the best part of it, as it was required for officers' quarters. His claims for compensation were denied and he was told he was lucky to have the lease renewed on the rest of it for fourteen years as he had allowed a portion of the property to become dilapidated. Despite his anger and dismay there was nothing he could do.

In February 1852 Alton wrote to the Committee to ask permission to return to England with his family for a visit. He had three children by this time Catherine, George Alder born on 22 November 1850 and Anna Maria Sophia born on 6 November 1851. Alton's father had recently died, leaving a large family, and his presence was needed to make arrangements for them and to settle his father's affairs. He also felt that 'a short relaxation would be of great benefit to my health and would invigorate and fit me for further usefulness'.[23] By then he had been in Gibraltar for over four years and went on to say that 'since my arrival on the station I have never left it for a day'.

---

[20] Ibid., Nicholson to Committee, 24 April 1851, fiche 693, no.20.

[21] Ibid., Cheesbrough to Committee, 22 September 1851, [papers re South property sale, 1851] fiche 694, no.24.

[22] Ibid., Cheesbrough to Committee, 18 March 1852, fiche 695, no.27.

[23] Ibid., Alton to Committee, 26 February 1852, fiche 694, no.26.

Permission was given and the family left Gibraltar on 5 April 1852. However, before they did so, Cheesbrough received a most unexpected letter from the Committee. Despite the savings already made by the closure of the South schools, the Committee had decided that staffing in Gibraltar should also be reduced, and it was suggested that Cheesbrough should leave the Rock and Alton take sole charge of the work. The reasons for this decision seem to have been purely financial but Cheesbrough was asked for his opinion.

In his reply he stated that the Committee's letter 'has surprised and agitated me so much that for the present I am not able to give it that full consideration which it deserves'.[24] He went on to say, 'I am not surprised that under the circumstances you have named the Committee should have resolved to diminish their operations in Gibraltar ... But what perplexes me is this - that my removal at so early a period should be deemed necessary to the working out of your proposed plan of reduction and economy'. He suggested that Alton could have a year in England and then return to succeed him. He hinted too that Alton's ministry would not be acceptable in Gibraltar and he felt there could be other ways of economising particularly in the Spanish work. He admitted he had a much larger family than Alton. It is not clear how many children he had but two were born in Gibraltar, Elizabeth Farmer on 25 August 1850 and John Beecham on 21 January 1852. However, Cheebrough was quite willing for his allowances to be reduced.

Cheesbrough repeatedly stressed that he felt Alton's ministry was not acceptable in Gibraltar and reported that he had discussed this with him before he left for England. He reported on a discussion at the Quarterly Meeting when

> Every leader spoke his mind fully. They all respected Mr Alton's character very highly, but they all without exception said that Mr Alton's ministry was so little liked, and so unprofitable, that in case of his coming back they saw no prospect of success in the work, but on the contrary, they believed that the cause which had looked up of late, would dwindle and die away. I was then very earnestly requested to state this as the opinion of the meeting, and to beg that in the event of my removal you would make a more suitable appointment for this station.[25]

Cheesbrough went on to say, 'You have already suffered much here from unpopular men and imprudent measures that you might well hesitate again making an appointment which will leave your missionary very slender hopes either of personal comfort, or of prosperity in his work.' He believed one of Alton's friends had already written to him to persuade him not to

---

[24] Ibid., Cheesbrough to Committee, 26 March 1852, fiche 695, no.28.
[25] Ibid.

return.

The account of the Quarterly Meeting in the chapel minute book does not contain any mention of this discussion and it was in fact the last meeting Cheesbrough recorded, leaving a gap in the records. No one else wrote to the Committee to make any representation about the situation and there had been no indications previously that Alton was regarded as in any way unsuitable for the post. Cheesbrough's comments are not very explicit but seem to imply that it was Alton's preaching that was causing the concern. He had already proved himself a sensitive, caring man in his relationship with the Doves in their difficult situation, and to be an able negotiator and administrator with regard to chapel affairs.

There is no surviving record of Alton's views on the situation. Clearly Cheesbrough wanted to stay in Gibraltar. He was by far the more experienced minister, and may have felt a little piqued that Alton was to take charge of the station and not himself. He suggested that Alton was not yet a missionary, although he had the makings of one, and even offered to have him as an assistant on his own next station. However, he did not refer in any of his letters to the one ability that Alton possessed and he did not, which was command of the Spanish language, really a necessity for any missionary stationed in Gibraltar.

So, despite all his representations, the Committee decided to go ahead with its plans even though Cheesbrough wrote again saying that 'the idea of sending Mr Alton here ought really to be abandoned. To send him to Gibraltar will be to condemn him to discomfort and uselessness in the prime of his days, whereas elsewhere he might be honourably and usefully employed. Why persist in a course which cannot end well either for Mr Alton or the work?'[26] He persisted in this view until he left.

The Alton family arrived back in Gibraltar on 6 October 1852 and, at about the same time, Cheesbrough left with his family. They probably overlapped briefly but there is no record of any conversation between them. In his first letter, some three weeks after returning, Alton reported,

> I have now been a sufficient time in Gibraltar since my return to speak with confidence as to the feelings with which I have been received in my new relation to this Station. On all hands I have experienced a very kind reception far exceeding anything I could have expected. The Society and Congregations seem to be quite satisfied with my re-appointment.[27]

They did not immediately move into the Mission House because it had been left in a very unsatisfactory state and needed thoroughly cleaning. Alton declined going into much detail saying that he would not 'trouble you with these unpleasant details. I wish that every allowance should be made for the size of Cheesbrough's family, and the way in which I know

---

[26] Ibid., Cheesbrough to Committee, 28 July 1852, fiche 695, no.32.
[27] Ibid., Alton to Committee, 27 October 1852, fiche 695, no.34.

they were inconveniently crowded in the house'. So the Alton family settled back into Gibraltar and on 7 December 1852 another daughter, Isabella Amelia, was born to them. She was baptised on 12 January by Lewis Irving, the Presbyterian minister.

Cheesbrough went to the Bahamas where he worked as General Superintendent of the District for the next sixteen years, and was reported to be 'an able and eloquent Preacher, a wise administrator, and a kind and sympathetic Pastor.'[28] In 1872 he became a supernumerary in Canada. In 1881 he travelled to England to attend the Methodist Conference. His return was delayed by the death of a son and then a daughter. He eventually travelled to Liverpool to sail for Canada but was taken ill whilst waiting for the ship to sail. He died on 17 May 1883, aged 72.

Meanwhile, in Gibraltar Alton reported on Christmas and New Year services 'of a particularly encouraging character' which had frequently been referred to as 'a season of great spiritual profit'.[29] They had been joined by Irving, the Presbyterian minister, who had preached at one of the services. The annual tea meeting on behalf of the schools had been most encouraging and raised more money than he had expected. Overall he felt there was much to encourage them and he stated,

> I look forward with hope to the year on which we have entered, and this
> I believe is the feeling which animates the Society and Congregations. I
> have received many proofs of kindly regard and I doubt not that with
> God's blessing we shall see His work prosper in our hands.

So Alton carried on with what was to be a long association with Gibraltar in his new status overseeing both departments of the work.

---

[28] *Minutes of the Methodist Conference,* 1884, pp.40-1.
[29] *WMMS Correspondence,* Alton to Committee, 27 January 1853, fiche 695, no.35.

CHAPTER 12   THE MINISTRY OF GEORGE ALTON (1)
INTO SPAIN WITH THE BIBLE SOCIETY
Hopes soon dashed (1853-8)

Little information about the next few months has survived. In March 1853 Alton sent a brief note promising further details and reporting that he was 'labouring with success'.[1] By then, John and Susan Allen had left the Rock after a residence of twenty-four years. A special tea-meeting was held to say farewell to them and a two-page tribute was recorded in the chapel minute book. This particularly mentioned their work as class leaders, Allen's concern for the spiritual welfare of the military, and Miss Allen was thanked as she had 'for several years gratuitously performed on the seraphim'. It seems a rather effusive tribute after their somewhat controversial relationship with Methodism in Gibraltar. It is in marked contrast to the one sentence entry for 27 May which stated, 'Since our last meeting Mr Nicholson has embarked for the United States'. He had done sterling work in the church both as a teacher in the schools and as preacher and leader in the Spanish department and had also acted conscientiously as Rule's agent for the South property. Alton thought highly of him and he was no doubt a great loss to the work. It is not clear why no further tribute is paid to him, which he surely deserved, and to Mary his wife who had also taught in the schools and played her part in the life of the church. They left with seven children.

In America, Nicholson at first ran a clothing store but in 1855 he became a probationary member of the Baltimore Conference of the Methodist Episcopal Church. He was ordained a deacon and elder in 1856 and appointed as a missionary to Buenos Aires where he took charge of a Methodist school, the North American Seminary. A couple of years later this school closed. Nicholson then resigned his connection with the Baltimore Conference and stayed on in Buenos Aires as a local ordained elder instead. He had met up again with Negrotto and they both worked there in the field of education.

In 1858 the Nicholsons and Negrotto sent a donation to Gibraltar which was acknowledged with pleasure because it was 'given in remembrance of spiritual benefits received in this place'.[2] Nicholson wrote again in 1860 recalling his time in Gibraltar where 'most of my happiest and holiest days were spent'.[3] Further donations were sent at Christmas. Nicholson felt that 'the seed sown in Gibraltar is germinating in South America, and promises to yield an abundant harvest', but was sorry that the Missionary Society had not turned its attention to 'this promising field' and that 'as far as American Methodism is concerned I am sorry to assure you that nothing

---

[1] *WMMS Correspondence,* Alton to Committee, 29 March 1853, fiche 696, no.36.

[2] Chapel minute book. (CAG)

[3] *WMMS Correspondence,* Nicholson to Webster, 27 October 1860, fiche 702, no.22.

will be done'.[4] This hint at frustration with Methodism may help to explain why in April 1869 Nicholson resigned his connection with the Methodist Church, although he maintained his belief in Methodist doctrines and polity.

The Nicholsons had a further four children and seem to have prospered well in Buenos Aires. They thus secured good prospects for their children who all seem to have married and settled in Argentina so that there are many direct descendents of Henry and Mary living there to this day. Henry died, aged 54, in a yellow fever epidemic in March 1871 and Mary died in November 1890.

Meanwhile in Gibraltar, towards the end of 1853, there was further persecution within the army. The problem arose in the 44th Regiment commanded by Lieutenant-Colonel Spencer described by Alton as 'a proud and severe man professing great zeal for the Church of England and resolved that there shall be no Methodist heresy in his Regiment'.[5] It seems he was supported by the Governor and Alton reported that 'every means has been resorted to to keep men away from us' and the soldiers were actively discouraged from becoming Methodists. The General Order of 1839 allowed soldiers freedom of worship but the issue in this case was about the right to change denomination. Three men who wished to become Methodists and worship in the Methodist church had been refused permission. Eventually Alton was forced to make representation to the General Commander-in-Chief, which he did via the Missionary Committee, although it seems the Governor backed down after Alton's letters to England were posted. The reply from Horse Guards, dated October 1853, was written in the knowledge of the Governor's change of heart but nonetheless was supportive of the Methodists. It stated that a letter had been sent to the Governor which would 'remove all misunderstanding as to the undoubted right of the soldiers of the Wesleyan persuasion, as well as those of every other religious denomination to change their church as often as they please, and to attend the worship of Almighty God according to the form which they may happen to prefer, when military duty does not interfere'.[6]

However, despite this clear direction, the problems did not end. The Governor did not make these instructions public and Spencer refused to allow any other than the three men Alton had named in his letter to go freely to the chapel. He insisted that other men had to apply for a pass to do so which had to be regularly renewed. Alton was also asked to provide certificates to say that the men were Methodists and others were asked to obtain certificates to say that there would be room in the Methodist chapel if they were allowed to attend services there. Alton refused to provide

---

[4] Ibid., Nicholson to Webster, 27 October 1860, fiche 702, no.22.
[5] Ibid., Alton to Committee, 3 September 1853, fiche 696, no.37.
[6] Copy Brown (Adjutant, Horse Guards) to Beecham (WMMS Secretary), 31 October 1853.

these certificates as they were not required under Queen's Regulations and he knew it was merely an attempt to put obstacles in the way of soldiers who wanted to become Methodists. Alton's attempts to sort things out in Gibraltar were unsuccessful and he was forced to make further representation to England in February 1854. In his letter to the Committee describing developments he said, 'These things will shew you that I have need of patience and prudence. At such times it would be desirable to have your counsel, but I always endeavour to act as I believe you would instruct me to do if I could receive your advice'.[7] It must have been difficult to act in the face of such opposition with no colleague to consult. However, his representations must have been successful because the matter is not referred to again and in the autumn of 1854 Alton reported a revival. He had admitted twenty-two members on trial, more than in any quarter since 1837. Congregations had correspondingly improved and the quarterly meeting minutes for October state, 'we had great reason for thankfulness and praise to God who had so graciously visited our church with the reviving influences of his Spirit, and prospered us'. This was a particular cause for rejoicing because the church had earlier lost forty-two members by removals from the garrison.

Neither Gardiner nor Wilson, his predecessor, were popular governors and Methodism suffered under the administration of both. Gardiner became unpopular because of the action he took to combat smuggling and because he did not accept and enforce the quarantine laws. This resulted in the closure of the border by the Spanish which affected local trade and Alton reported that these measures had caused considerable misery. Prices had risen steeply, some goods were in short supply and commercial interests were much affected. In fact a deputation was sent to England in December 1853 to place Gibraltar's complaints before the Colonial Secretary, the Duke of Newcastle. In February 1854 Alton reported that the troops had refused their now rather meagre rations and seemed to be on the verge of mutiny with the result that the Governor 'yielded in a moment to fear what he had obstinately refused to reason and humanity' and imposed the appropriate quarantine laws which eventually resulted in the re-opening of the border.[8] Gardiner was recalled in 1855, but the Gibraltar economy remained in a depressed state for some time.

In addition to all these difficulties, the Altons were hit hard by personal tragedy at this time. Some of Alton's letters have been lost for the Chronicles he mentions in his letter of 28 September 1853 have not survived. He stated,

> You will see from the Chronicles I sent you how heavy has been our affliction. On the 14th inst. we lost our youngest child and on the 17th

---

[7] *WMMS Correspondence,* Alton to Committee, 10 February 1854, fiche 696, no.3.
[8] Ibid., Alton to Committee, 10 February 1854, fiche 696, no.3.

our next. We are overwhelmed with grief, but we try to seek succour in God. May His dispensation be sanctified to us.[9]

Isabella Amelia was just nine months old and Anna Maria Sophia one year and ten months. They now had only two of their five children left to them - Catherine and George. It is not clear what caused the children's deaths but it may have been cholera which affected Gibraltar and the surrounding area several times in the 1850s. Yet, despite this terrible loss, such was Alton's commitment to the work that only a few weeks later he wrote to report an improvement in the Spanish congregation and added,

> My labours are many and great, but I bend myself to them with cheerfulness for my heart is in the work, and that ever makes labour light. You know the discouragements peculiar to this station but I am from time to time animated by witnessing the good effect of my endeavours to save souls and extend the Kingdom of the Redeemer. His presence is with us in all our assemblies, and by His help the Mission here will be sustained and prospered. I feel the responsibility of the trust you have committed to me, and by God's blessing none of its interests shall suffer or languish under my care. I am most anxious above all things to fulfil my ministry acceptably to the Lord Jesus from whom I have received it, and next by diligence and perseverance to commend myself to the good opinion of the Committee.[10]

However, support was at hand because Dr Robert Alder and his wife, Amy's parents, arrived in Gibraltar. In 1851, after eighteen years as a Secretary to the Missionary Society, Alder retired. However, in 1853, he left Methodism altogether although it is not clear why. He may have been caught up in the problems of the time. In the 1840s there had been further unrest within Wesleyan Methodism to do with a demand for constitutional reform. Several anonymous flysheets were published and eventually in 1849 three ministers were expelled by Conference although their authorship of the sheets had not been proved. The three were James Everett, Samuel Dunn and William Griffith, whose father had been minister in Gibraltar. The expulsions caused further unrest and over the next few years around one third of the Wesleyan membership either left or was expelled and many formed yet another branch of Methodism.

Whatever the reason, Alder too left Methodism and Findlay and Holdsworth recorded that 'he took orders in the Church of England and filled for some time an important pulpit in the city of London'.[11] However, this seems unlikely because by November 1853 Alton reported that Alder was in Gibraltar and later that he had taken orders there. Findlay and Holdsworth stated that 'he remained to the last on friendly terms with his

---

[9] Ibid., Alton to Committee, 28 September 1853, fiche 697, no.5.

[10] Ibid., Alton to Committee, 14 November 1853, fiche 696, no.39.

[11] Findlay and Holdsworth, op. cit., vol. i, p.505 fn.

old colleagues and Methodist associates'. He certainly kept in touch with Elijah Hoole, another of the Secretaries, with whom Alton frequently corresponded. However, the Committee seems to have been concerned about his presence in Gibraltar so Alton wrote, in January 1854, to explain,

> It is quite true that Dr Alder has taken orders in the Established Church, but his having done so does not in the slightest degree affect the interests of Methodism here. And I am sure that no influence will be employed by him in opposition to those interests. Both he and Mrs Alder desire to be affectionately remembered to you. They are comfortably settled here for the <u>present</u> and are quite well.
>
> My diligent attention to the duties of my mission of which you have had the means of judging from time to time, render it unnecessary that on such an occasion I should reassure you of my sincere and conscientious attachment to Methodism, its ministry, its ordinances, and discipline. My firm purpose, as my prayer is, that that attachment should be uninterrupted till death.[12]

Their involvement with different denominations does not seem to have caused any problems and may well have helped the relationship between the two Churches. Alder's work is described in the unpublished history of the Anglican Cathedral as follows:

> Towards the end of 1853 the Bishop admitted a former Wesleyan, Dr Alder ... to Anglican orders and gave him the post of evening preacher in the Cathedral. The following year he was appointed Convict Chaplain on the resignation of the Rev. John Burrow, but he continued to perform the Cathedral duty gratuitously. He was made a Canon in 1855. His fourteen years in the Convict Establishment saw many improvements there. An evening school with special staff was set up, and in 1855 a Scripture reader, Mr John McLoughlin, was appointed. 1858 saw the enlargement of the convicts' chapel in the Dockyard, and a small library was built up under the Chaplain's supervision. Another of his duties was the censorship of letters from convicts, which totalled some 2,500 annually.[13]

Two hundred convicts were sent to Gibraltar in 1842 to extend the south mole and work on Gibraltar's fortifications. Others followed until numbers had increased to about a thousand, but the use of convict labour ended in 1875 as Spanish labour from La Línea was found to be cheaper.

No doubt it was a great support and comfort to the Altons to have the Alders in Gibraltar and when, in March 1854, another daughter, Mary Elizabeth Hepworth, was born, her grandfather baptised her. Alder and Alton also worked together on the Corresponding Committee of the Bible

---

[12] *WMMS Correspondence,* Alton to Committee, 24 January 1854, fiche 696, no.1.

[13] Donald H. Simpson, 'Holy Trinity Cathedral, a History and Description', (unpublished, 1948 with revisions in 1978 and 1988), pp.38-9.

Society which had continued to maintain a depository in Gibraltar but had not been able to find a way of circulating Bibles in Spain. However, this situation was about to change.

In 1854 there had been a further change of government in Spain which had led to the strengthening of the Roman Catholic Church's position but, in the summer of 1854, a revolution took place and the Church once again came under attack. The Catholic faith itself was defended but it was also announced that 'neither Spaniard nor foreigners can be persecuted for their opinions or beliefs as long as these are not manifested by public actions contrary to religion'.[14] There was even some sympathy for full religious toleration but attempts to establish this were defeated. The Church was strongly opposed to it.

The effects of the revolution were felt in Gibraltar and in August 1854 Alton reported to the Bible Society that 'the recent political movements in Spain have afforded an opportunity such as seldom occurs for the introduction of Scriptures into that unhappy country.'[15] The guards and revenue officers at the border were removed for several days and during this time 'the communication with Gibraltar was entirely free.' Alton had 'at once made arrangements for sending into the interior every copy of the Scriptures I could collect ... making a total ... either whole or in part despatched 1,744' and 'with a view to convenient carriage, Scriptures were sewn up in canvas, each package containing an average of thirty copies of all sorts'.[16] After initial difficulties in finding a suitable person, the Corresponding Committee appointed a colporteur, Martin Escalante. Little is known about his background, but he had apparently been educated in the Methodist schools. He immediately went into Spain to commence his work.

Two weeks later, at the end of August, Alton reported that 'the communication by land with Gibraltar and also through the neighbouring port is again closed, but the introduction of things from this place is not at present nearly so difficult as it was before the insurrection'.[17] So, after his return, Escalante was sent on a second tour. He was instructed to sell the books rather than give them away and he planned to visit the fair at Ronda on 15 September to sell there.

In mid September Alton reported that 'the frontiers are again closely watched but communication is free inland. This is favourable to us and we should like to continue our operations until our store at present in Spain is exhausted'.[18] He also suggested that someone should be appointed to visit some of the cities in southern Spain to try and open up channels of

---

[14] Callahan, op. cit., p.199.

[15] *Foreign Correspondence In,* Alton, 14 August 1854, 1854.

[16] Ibid., Alton 13 September 1854, 1854.

[17] Ibid., Alton 29 August 1854, 1854.

[18] Ibid., Alton 13 September 1854, 1854.

communication. The Bible Society responded by asking him to do this himself over the next three months.

Alton had to decline because he could not be absent from Gibraltar for any length of time, although he much regretted this as he felt it was an important mission. He was not sure if there had been any change in the law prohibiting the sale of books printed outside Spain, which in fact there had not, but he thought that Bibles could now be printed and circulated there.

The Missionary Committee was, of course, also aware of the situation. Everyone was enthused and excited by this new opportunity and keen to take immediate advantage of it. In October Sydney Wright, Chairman of the Gibraltar Corresponding Committee, wrote to the Bible Society to suggest the possibility of an arrangement being made between the Bible Society and the Missionary Society to release Alton for this important three-month tour of Spain. He said,

> As regards Mr Alton's qualifications for the work, there is but one opinion in the Committee - His thorough acquaintance with the language of Spain, is an obvious and important advantage. Then, further, the Committee know him sufficiently well and have witnessed enough of his Christian spirit, his enlightened zeal, his energy and tact and judgment, and his familiarity with such operations, to have the utmost confidence, that if he could be set at liberty for this work for a time, it could not possibly be in better hands. Indeed among many providential circumstances which have recently forced themselves upon our notice, we cannot help regarding as one of the most encouraging that an agent in every way so peculiarly qualified for the work is now on the spot, and we trust that circumstances may yet admit him, in the strength of God to enter upon it.[19]

By the time this letter was received, discussions were already under way between the two Societies and arrangements were swiftly made to release Alton from his work in Gibraltar by the appointment of Aaron Edman, a probationer, who would cover for him in his absence.

Edman was born in Bardney, Lincolnshire, on 15 July 1826. His parents were Methodists and he himself was converted at the age of fifteen. He began to preach in 1846 and in 1849 he candidated for the ministry. He was accepted on trial and went to Jamaica in 1850. However, he suffered several bouts of fever there and, after four years, was forced to return to England. He was thus free to go to Gibraltar and seemed in good enough health by then to do so.

Edman arrived on 4 November 1854 and landed the following day. Alton was rather worried about leaving the work as this was the time of the revival. He wrote, 'I have endeavoured to make the best arrangements for my work in Gibraltar during my absence. Nothing has occasioned me so

---

[19] Ibid., Sydney Wright, 31 October 1854, 1854, Box 107.

much anxiety connected with my new duties as leaving my charge in its present flourishing state. But my reliance is in God that he will watch over all.'[20] However, he had some concerns about Edman. 'I earnestly hope that Mr Edman will prove discreet, but I have been grieved to hear remarks made by his fellow passengers as to his ignorance of the most ordinary things. In the pulpit he will do better, and I have no doubt give great satisfaction'. He had however used someone else's sermon for his first attempt in Gibraltar. Alton reported, 'I have spoken with him kindly on this matter and I trust it will prove an exception. He has been well received and will I trust be useful'.

So Alton prepared for his journey into Spain. He had virtually no contacts there and in addition cholera was raging in many parts of the country, which in the end forced him to abandon the route suggested by the Bible Society because there were cordons around some areas. He informed the Missionary Committee that many friends would be praying daily for his success in the hope that a door might be opened into Spain. 'You may rest assured that I will attempt nothing hastily or unadvisedly. Do favour me with some statement of your views and Counsel and guide me'.[21] He was also worried about his family. His departure was delayed by the dangerous illness of his two oldest children, George and Catherine, 'the one with congestion of the brain, and the other inflammation of the bowels' but at the time of writing in mid November they were 'fast recovering'. In the end the Corresponding Committee strongly urged him to take Escalante with him and so they set off together. The two main aims of this exploratory visit were to see if scriptures printed outside Spain could be imported into the country and, if not, to enquire about the possibility of printing Bibles in Spain.

Alton and Escalante set off on Friday 17 November 1854 and travelled through heavy rain to Málaga. The journey took longer than planned because of the weather and difficulties with the cholera cordons. They arrived on Sunday night and the following day contacted Mark who was still the Consul there. He felt that it was impossible to import scriptures but that there was an increasing demand for them so that it was desirable to get editions printed and circulated. Alton visited most of the booksellers in Málaga, who felt that it was possible to print and sell almost anything, though any attempt to sell Bibles was bound to excite priestly opposition. They left Málaga on 23 November and reached Granada the following day. They had hoped to travel to Barcelona but there were no steam ships available because of quarantine measures. They stayed in Granada for four days, meeting only one helpful bookseller who had sold Bibles in previous years. They arrived in Madrid late on 1 December and the next day met a man called Greene, the only contact Alton had there. He had written to

---

[20] *WMMS Correspondence,* Alton to Committee, 13 November 1854, fiche 697, no.7.
[21] Ibid., Alton to Committee, 13 November 1854, fiche 697, no.7.

Alton the previous October about the possibility of preaching to the English residents in Madrid who numbered between sixty and eighty and who had no minister or place of worship. Alton did preach to them on the three Sundays he was there and also took Spanish services. Throughout his journey he took every opportunity to converse with those whom he met, sometimes reading and explaining a chapter from the New Testament and praying with them too. In Madrid he also met Marin and sent on a letter from him to be forwarded to Rule.

Considerable progress was made in Madrid. Greene introduced him to Don Luis Usoz y Río who was sure printing Bibles would be possible but cautioned against publicity and advertising in the distribution of them. Over the next few days, Alton obtained several estimates for printing Bibles. He found the printers eager for the work and not too worried about difficulties. Unfortunately Alton's letters for the next twelve months are missing although some information has survived in the Committee's minute books. He returned to Gibraltar by way of Seville and Cádiz and told the Missionary Committee that he 'heard frequently, and most favourably, of the Mission under Mr Rule in Cádiz. Though its existence was not long, yet it has exerted a wider and more powerful influence than any similar effort in the cause of true religion in Spain'.[22] In the same letter he gave his opinion on the state of things in Spain. There were signs of hope, such as the anticlerical and anti-Catholic feelings he had encountered for himself, but he still felt the country was too unsettled for the establishment of a Mission. However, he thought that 'much may be done by active and prudent evangelists, as well as by means of the press and otherwise, for the advancement of the "truth as it is in Jesus"', and he felt Madrid should be the centre of that work. Overall, he was very pleased with the way things were developing.

Alton and Escalante probably arrived back in Gibraltar at the end of 1854. Alton's youngest child, Mary, then became so ill that for twenty-eight days he despaired of her life but she did eventually recover. The Bible Society was delighted with his progress and entered into further negotiations with the Missionary Society. An agreement was reached that Alton would work for the Bible Society for the next year to oversee the printing of 10,000 scriptures in Madrid, including both Bibles and New Testaments. Alton would retain some responsibilities in Gibraltar as there were matters, such as the government returns, which needed his personal attention.

Alton left again for Madrid in February 1855 and had a rather difficult journey. However, he did arrive safely and immediately opened up discussions with the printers. He had some support in Madrid from Usoz and a Colonel Stopford but Greene seems to have developed other interests.

---

[22] Ibid., Alton to Committee, 27 January 1855, fiche 697, no.10.

This time Escalante did not accompany him but was involved instead in continuing his work of circulating the scriptures in Spain. There was some discussion about the Spanish version of the Bible to be printed. Usoz and Alton favoured that of Valera, rather than Scio, and began working together on improving it which the Bible Society later sanctioned. However, the printer was commissioned to produce Scio's version of the New Testament as his first task.

Alton returned to Gibraltar at the beginning of March but suffered an accident on the journey when the coach overturned. He sustained head injuries and his face was severely cut. It seems that a stop was put on the printing at this time but Alton appears not to have been too concerned at this setback. By then others were interested in Spain, notably Greene and a Spaniard called Hererros de Mora, who went to England to raise awareness about the situation there. The Bible Society was sensibly urging Alton to prudence and caution, but he was well aware of the need for this, and was concerned about the plans of Greene and de Mora. Whilst he was in Gibraltar, a son, Charles William Cooke, was born and later baptised by his grandfather.

At this time the Methodist Church experienced a significant loss for Michael Caulfield died at the age of 78. His funeral was taken by Alton on 21 April 1855. His wife, Sophia, had died in January the previous year aged 66. Once again their loss was not recorded either in letters to England or in the chapel minute book, but their passing marked the end of an era, for they had contributed greatly to the life of the church for many years. Caulfield, along with Davis, had at times been the mainstay of the little Society and the exceptional care and concern for the McMullens from both Michael and Sophia, despite the risk to themselves, should never be forgotten. They were not a wealthy family. Michael's occupation was stated in the baptismal register as teacher, foreman of labourers and store-keeper in the Royal Engineers. He became a local preacher later in life and was still a class leader at the time of his death, attending his last leaders' meeting on 10 April. The Caulfields were survived by four of their eight children, one of whom, also called Sophia, had taught in the Mission school for some years.

Alton returned to Madrid around the middle of May and arrangements for the printing went ahead, so whatever the difficulties had been, they were overcome. However, he was concerned about the activities of de Mora which he felt were political and could prove dangerous to their plans. Unfortunately the details of Alton's concerns are lost with his letters, but he reported to the Missionary Committee that he had written to the Bible Society at length on this subject and suggested that the Missionary Society should also read his letters. He stated that 'really judicious persons here fear that this movement will be more likely than anything else to put an end to our efforts for the printing and circulation of the Scriptures'.[23] He went on to describe the unsettled state of Spain, reporting that the Carlist movement was a serious one and had strong support from many priests. 'What the end will be none can foresee, but a crisis is approaching'. He dared say no more as he was writing from Spain and presumably was worried that his letters might be intercepted. He did report, however, that he conducted worship regularly and 'also make myself useful in Spanish'. He also wrote to the Bible Society to report on a conversation at the British Embassy where he had read 'a despatch from the Earl of Clarendon addressed to Lord Howden, in which an opinion is expressed that the present is a most unfavourable moment for the circulation of the Scriptures in Spain and that should the Government order Mr Alton to withdraw from the country, the English Ambassador might not be able to interfere in his favour'.[24] Alton therefore asked the Bible Society for clear instructions and a few days later reported that he had been advised to withdraw from Madrid for a while but Usoz and Stopford had agreed to oversee the work in his absence. The Bible Society did order the printing to go ahead and asked Alton to continue with his revision of Valera. It is not clear when Alton left Madrid, but in early July he was back in Gibraltar checking on the work there.

There is little information about what was happening in Gibraltar as Edman wrote few letters. He had reported in March 1855 that a few had joined the Society but many had in fact left the Rock to fight in the Crimean War and later in the year, in the membership statistics, twenty-two members were recorded as being 'at the seat of war'.[25] Edman found these circumstances rather discouraging and seems to have wondered if Methodism in Gibraltar was even viable. He was also anxious about his own situation. He wanted to return to England in time for Conference when he hoped to end his probationary period and to marry. He was willing to return to Gibraltar afterwards. Alton reported,

> I have entire confidence as to his Christian and ministerial character, indeed he is one of the most devoted young men I have known.... His pulpit talent is about the average, and I think under my advice he has improved in respect of depending more fully on the fruit of his own study.[26]

He was happy for Edman to return to England but anxious that someone should be sent to replace him. Edman left in July before Alton had received any instructions. He claimed that the Committee had given him

---

[23] Ibid., Alton to Committee, 18 June 1855 from Madrid, fiche 698, no.16.

[24] *Minutes of Committee, No.43,* 25 June 1855, minute 34, p.313.

[25] Chapel minute book.

[26] *WMMS Correspondence,* Alton to Committee, 18 June 1855 from Madrid, fiche 698, no.16.

permission to leave but did not show the letter to Alton. He continued as a probationer because of concerns about his health. However, he soon returned to the West Indies and served there for eight years, returning to England in 1864. He became a supernumerary in 1893 and died in 1899 at the age of seventy-two.

In Gibraltar things were not going well. Alton reported that

> Our Congregation and Society have been nearly broken up by removals ... These are circumstances strongly exercising our faith and patience, and it is indispensable that the Minister should not be desponding. My experience in Gibraltar keeps me from this, for under ordinary circumstances and in a time of peace our Church has been removed about every two years or two years and a half. And with the necessity which you know to exist for every available soldier it will not seem surprising to you that we should be now more than usually reduced. But I am very hopeful. Already two Militia Regiments have arrived, and although they do not bring us one member yet I have set agencies to work which with God's blessing will in a week or two bring many under our influence ... Under God I trust you to send me a young man of judgement, cheerful in his spirit and free to labour, with talent, and at least a fair education, and then with such help as I shall be able to afford we shall undoubtedly advance.[27]

The man sent was Abraham White. He was born in Gillingham in Kent in October 1829. The influence of his father and a school teacher led to an early Christian commitment and he offered for the ministry in 1851. He spent three years at Richmond College before being sent to Gibraltar as his first appointment. He arrived early on Wednesday 25 July 1855 and reached the Alton's house in time for breakfast. He reported that Alton had shown him much kindness and he thought he would work well under him. Once White was settled in, Alton planned to return to Madrid with his family but in the end, because of the extent of the cholera outbreaks, he returned alone in the middle of August.

When Alton arrived in Madrid, he discovered that the printing of the New Testaments was complete and, after receiving further instructions from the Bible Society, the printing of the Bibles began. This was still Scio's version, although Alton continued to press for that of Valera to be printed with the modifications he and Usoz were making. Alton also began cautiously making arrangements for the New Testaments to be bound. He referred in some of his letters to the Spanish Evangelisation Society which had recently been formed in London for the furtherance of religious reform in Spain. Rule was very much a part of this Society, along with Greene and de Mora, and they also seemed to have plans for printing Spanish scriptures. Alton expressed concerns about this Society but, with the loss

---

[27] Ibid., Alton to Committee, 5 July 1855, fiche 698, no.18.

of his letters, it not clear exactly what they were.

In October Alton was unexpectedly summoned to Gibraltar because White was ill. He told the Committee that 'This happened at a moment when my duties are very pressing here, but I shall make the best arrangements in my power and leave on Monday night [15 October]'.[28]

The Committee next received a letter from White saying that his health was tolerably good and, although congregations were small and fluctuating, he hoped God would soon revive his work among them. He was aware that this would conflict with Alton's letters and went on, in a rather convoluted way, to blame Amy Alton for having misrepresented his health for reasons of her own, in wanting her husband to return to Gibraltar. He did not deny that he had been unwell but it seems his illness was largely of a nervous and depressive nature, although he had had some fever. The Altons denied his allegation which does seem rather unlikely. In any case, by then, Alton was feeling the need to consult with the Bible Society, which would mean he could also meet the Missionary Committee, and he must have left Gibraltar almost immediately.

Alton was present at two meetings of the Bible Society's Committee on 12 and 16 November 1855, but the minutes are brief. His work in Spain was discussed and 'while no distinct pledge could be given as to its permanency there was every encouragement to proceed with it, though necessarily with the utmost caution and prudence'.[29] It was decided that when the Bibles were printed Alton would 'take the necessary measures for securing the approval of the Civil Governor of Madrid to its circulation as well as that of the New Testament.' Once approval was obtained, he would look for five or six colporteurs to do the work of distribution. Then, if all went well, he was authorised to print an edition of Valera's translation of the Bible. It was also agreed that the Gibraltar Committee, described now as an Auxiliary, would be given £30 towards the cost of Escalante's work of distribution. There was also discussion about the difficulties likely to arise from the operations of the Spanish Evangelisation Society but no details are given.

Alton must also have met with the Missionary Committee. However, no records have survived apart from a report dated 21 November 1855.[30] In this, Alton described some of the difficulties Methodism was facing in Gibraltar, which had arisen because of the increase in other Protestant work there. He wrote,

> From the years 1809 to about 1832 [when the Anglican Cathedral was built] the Society's chapel was the only Protestant place of worship except the King's Chapel for the use of troops in Garrison, and during

---

[28] Ibid., Alton to Committee, 13 October 1855 from Madrid, fiche 698, no.20.

[29] *Minutes of Committee No.44,* 16 November 1855, minutes 13-4, p.66.

[30] *WMMS Correspondence,* Alton, memo relating to the Gibraltar station, 21 November 1855 from London, fiche 698, no.23.

the same period the Wesleyan Missionary was the only Protestant Minister except the military chaplain. There are now five established chaplains and two curates.

The Presbyterians now also had their own church, St Andrew's, which was formally opened in May 1854. They were all competing for the conversion and allegiance of the same soldiers and the success of any one church inevitably had a negative effect on the strength of the others. The Presbyterian minister received 'a fixed yearly allowance of £120 for services rendered to the military', bringing with it some official recognition and status, which the Methodists did not have. Alton also pointed out that the local authorities had been decidedly unfriendly to Methodism and they also had a large debt 'which cramps all energy'. He urged the Committee to do its best to secure a similar yearly allowance for the Wesleyan minister; to obtain a final settlement of the question of the government grants to the schools which was still dragging on; and to put his personal allowances for the year towards the reduction of the chapel debt.

Alton returned to Gibraltar on 15 December but he

> ... entered a home of great sorrow. During my absence one of our little ones has been taken from us, and owing to previous anxiety and suffering and the present painful loss I found Mrs Alton in a very weakly state. You will not be surprised that my return to Madrid should be delayed a few days.[31]

He does not describe his own feelings at being unexpectedly confronted with the tragic loss of Mary Elizabeth Hepworth at the age of one year and nine months. Her funeral had taken place on 5 December, with Alder officiating. Alton had planned to take his family back to Madrid with him, but now felt that their domestic circumstances were such that he would have to go alone to finish his work there as soon as possible, and then return to Gibraltar to be with his family.

Whilst in Gibraltar, Alton met Pablo Sanchez and reported to the Bible Society 'I think well of him, and he may be a great help to us if all goes well'.[32] Sanchez was born in Spain in 1809 and brought up as a Roman Catholic. He eventually became a novice in a Franciscan Convent and, in 1835, was appointed Superior of a Convent in Toledo, but the following year the monks were expelled by a government decree and Sanchez joined the Carlist movement. In 1840, when the Carlists were defeated, he took refuge in France and later moved to Geneva where, in 1844, through reading the Bible he became convinced of the errors of Roman Catholicism and decided to leave the Church. In 1846 he married a Frenchwoman, Antonia. Some months later, he was employed by the Geneva Evangelical

---

[31] *Foreign Correspondence In,* Alton 21 December 1855, 1856, Box 111.
[32] Ibid., Alton, 29 December 1855, 1856, Box 111.

Society who later described him as a 'colporteur evangelist' and someone who had 'served the Lord faithfully amidst many trials'.[33]   In 1848 he became a naturalized Frenchman and in 1852 the Society sent him to Oran. From then on, he was supported by a Mr John Henderson from Perth in Scotland, described as 'his friend and protector'.   In November 1854 he went to Gibraltar. Henderson offered to support Sanchez in working for the Bible Society and, although Alton could not promise him immediate work as a colporteur, he did promise to remain in contact with him in the hope that he would soon be able to use him in the distribution of the scriptures being printed.

Alton set off for Madrid in January 1856, travelling by way of Valencia in the hope of making useful contacts along the way, but the stops at various ports were not long enough to be of much use. He saw Mark in Málaga, when it was suggested that Escalante should visit to investigate the possibility of opening a depot in the area and he did make some contacts in Alicante and Valencia.

Alton arrived in Madrid late on 1 February and went to see Usoz as soon as possible. The printing of the Bibles had been completed on 29 January in the morning, but in the afternoon the printing establishment had been visited by the police and Alton was soon plunged into delicate negotiations with the authorities. The civil authorities were inclined to be supportive but the Vicar Ecclesiastic opposed the Bibles on the grounds that they had been printed without notes contrary to the law of 1820. Alton and Alegría, the printer, went to see him to argue their case. Alton had studied the law very carefully and based his arguments on the grounds that, while the Vicar did have the right to censor 'writings which treat on the Holy Scriptures, the dogmas of religion or morals', he could hardly claim the right to censor the Bible itself.[34] He suggested therefore that to add notes would give the Vicar the right of censorship. He also claimed that the title page fulfilled all the requirements of the law of the press. Alton presented the two copies of the Bible and New Testament to the authorities that the law required. However, he told the Bible Society that he dared not be too hopeful 'because here everything, under every constitution and every Government is arbitrary'. He added 'I need not dwell on the anxiety I have borne and am bearing. This you will know'.[35]

Alton also contacted the Civil Governor and obtained interviews with deputies in the Cortes and others. The matter was debated in the Cortes but the outcome was inconclusive. The Vicar did ban the books but they remained safe and Alton went ahead with binding the Bibles. He discussed the situation with Lord Howden at the British Embassy in Madrid who

---

[33] Ibid., Alton, 3 May 1856, (enclosing letter from the Evangelical Society of Geneva of 4 April 1856), 1856, Box 111.

[34] Ibid., Alton, 12 February 1856 from Madrid, 1856, Box 111.

[35] Ibid., Alton, 12 February 1856 from Madrid, 1856, Box 111.

suggested that he should obtain a good legal opinion, and gave Alton a letter of introduction to one of the best lawyers in Madrid, to whom he presented a full and clear account of events. By this time, he was feeling the weight of the responsibility upon him and wished that he had the support of Escalante 'as the labour and strain upon me is almost more than I can support'.[36] The legal opinion turned out not to be very helpful, so Alton sought another, but he reported that he was now less sure of Howden's support.

By this time Alton was in touch with another Spaniard called Francisco de Paula Ruet y Roset. He was born in Barcelona in October 1826 and was said to be an advocate and an opera singer so he may have been both. In June 1850 he left Barcelona for Italy. He spent the next four years in Turin where he was befriended by a Christian pastor who encouraged him to study the scriptures. In 1855 he returned to Barcelona wanting to be a missionary in his own country, and in October he wrote to the Bible Society asking for a supply of Bibles. Alton was informed of his letter and began corresponding with him, telling the Bible Society in March 1856 that he had been in touch with Ruet and that

> Considerable noise was being made in Barcelona and also in Madrid about his preaching, and the Government was called upon to put a stop to it. He was made a prisoner for a short time, and otherwise very badly used. In Madrid I tried to sustain him by stirring up some deputies on the subject. Altogether his case has made as much noise as my own about the Bible. It has been generally reported in the newspaper that he has had to leave the country. For all work here with a view to evangelisation the greatest possible caution is necessary, and I fear that our friend Ruet was more zealous than prudent.[37]

Alton had been given permission for Escalante to join him but, in the light of these events, he thought it was sensible to let the storms abate a little first despite his need for support. His own situation remained unresolved despite all his efforts. In March he reported that he had again met with the Governor of Madrid to seek the appointment of a Junta which was needed in order to appeal against the Vicar's ban. He was trying everything within his power but with a frustrating lack of success. He said,

> I have said but little to impress the Committee with a sense of my difficulties. Perhaps I ought to have said more. At times they seem to me overwhelming, at others insurmountable. But it has never been my practice to yield hastily and hitherto when I have seriously pondered my position I have found reason enough to hope and strive on. But no one who does not know Spaniards, nor understand the bearings of the question at issue in relation to the Government, the politics and

---

[36] Ibid., Alton, 3 March 1856 from Madrid, 1856, Box 111.
[37] Ibid., Alton, 10 March 1856 from Madrid, 1856, Box 111.

fanaticism of the nation can form an opinion of the circumstances in which I am placed.[38]

Soon after writing this, Alton discovered that the deputy who was to raise the matter of the Junta in the Cortes would be away for the next few weeks and so, for the time being, there was nothing further he could do. His time of secondment to the Bible Society had expired and he therefore returned to Gibraltar at the end of March, very much regretting that he had been unable to sort matters out despite his best efforts.

Little information has survived about what had been happening in Gibraltar as White wrote few letters to the Committee. However, in April, after Alton's return, White did write to report some improvement in congregations and that he had started a new Bible class for the soldiers encamped outside the garrison. He does not explain why the soldiers were in camp but it may have been part of the efforts to combat cholera which was a considerable problem in Gibraltar and the surrounding countryside in the 1850s. Soon after he arrived, Alton set about completing all the station schedules and reports and sent the Committee a copy of the Bible he had printed in Madrid. He also met Sanchez again and introduced him to the Gibraltar Auxiliary, which sent him to Barcelona to visit various places in Spain on the way and to take some cases of scriptures to Ruet.

Discussions must have taken place in England between the Bible and Missionary Societies for it was eventually decided that Alton should return to Madrid to see if he could resolve the situation there. He himself felt that there was hope saying, 'the issue of the work begun in Spain is in no doubt worth trying, and it cannot possibly be wholly failure - much has already been done, and if the worst comes to the worst the books can be removed to Gibraltar and sent again into Spain'.[39] However, he insisted that if he did return to Madrid, his family should go with him. This was agreed and they prepared to leave at the beginning of May, but their departure was delayed because Alton became ill with severe pains in his head. The doctor decided he 'was suffering from congestion of the brain, attributable mainly to my fall in March 1855 and my subsequent mental anxiety'.[40] The doctor's treatment provided some relief and the family set off for Madrid travelling by way of Cádiz and Seville. They arrived at the end of May after 'encountering many difficulties and delays on account of the great number of persons proceeding from all parts to Madrid.'[41]

Alton wrote a few days later but could report little progress. He was, however, working hard on the revision of Valera's translation and was benefiting from the 'judicious scholarship and matured biblical knowledge'

---

[38] Ibid., Alton, 13 March 1856 from Madrid, 1856, Box 111.

[39] Ibid., Alton, 4 April 1856, 1856, Box 111.

[40] Ibid., Alton, 15 May 1856 from Cádiz, 1856, Box 111.

[41] Ibid., Alton, 30 May 1856 from Madrid, 1856, Box 111.

of Usoz.[42] He reported that Ruet was in prison awaiting trial for apostasy and seeking to overturn the Roman Catholic religion. A newspaper which had advocated his cause had been suppressed and Ruet himself was 'in very distressed circumstances in consequence of the cruel persecution he has suffered.' His house had been searched and papers seized including two letters from Alton, who did not think they could be used against him as he 'had written in anticipation of anything that might happen to my correspondence'. Alton had also received letters from Sanchez who reported good progress in Málaga and Valencia but not in Barcelona, which was not surprising in view of Ruet's situation. Alton also had other correspondents in Spain and reported that two of them had been visited by the police. Only a few tracts had been discovered in the book shop of one of them and he was later acquitted of any charge.

Alton continued his negotiations. Although the civil authorities wanted him to succeed, the Governor of Madrid advised him that any legal battle with the Vicar Apostolic would fail. The authorities would not want to deal with the consequences of opposing him and delaying tactics would ensure that any legal proceedings would never be concluded anyway. The Governor did feel that an order for the removal of the books could be obtained but it seemed that the only way to circulate them would be to do so unofficially. Alton continued to consult with Usoz and Colonel Stopford who wrote to the Bible Society saying that Alton's 'energy is only equalled by his prudence and what these can enable him to accomplish he will effect'.[43]

At the beginning of July, Alton reported that he was ill and had been confined to bed with a severe attack of sickness. He had also heard from Gibraltar that White was ill. The illness was described as a nervous one, but White had obtained a medical certificate advising him not to stay in Gibraltar particularly through the summer. Although Alton accepted that there was a problem, he did not feel White's illness was such that an urgent and immediate removal home was necessary. He told the Committee that he hoped to be able to wind up his affairs in Madrid soon and to return to Gibraltar but added, 'My labours here have been more arduous and harassing than I can well describe'.[44]

At the beginning of August, Alton saw the new Governor of Madrid but 'the result was as unfavourable as could be feared'.[45] In any case, events soon overtook him as another revolution occurred in Spain and martial law was declared. This would have come as no surprise to Alton who had long been reporting the unsettled state of the country but it did of course markedly affect him. He wrote,

---

[42] Ibid., Alton, 4 June 1856 from Madrid, 1856, Box 111.

[43] *Minutes of Committee No.44,* 23 June 1856, minute 47, p.435.

[44] *WMMS Correspondence,* Alton to Committee, 5 July 1856 from Madrid, fiche 699, no.30.

[45] *Foreign Correspondence In,* Alton, 6 August 1856 from Madrid, 1856, Box 111.

After the <u>coup d'état</u> my position and prospects were entirely changed, and it was obvious that during the continuance of the violent and arbitrary rule which it introduced it would be impossible for me to advance my work, and great caution was necessary lest by inconsiderate activity our difficulties should be increased. In these circumstances I consulted freely with Don Luis, Colonel Stopford and Mr Ottway [Chargé d'Affaires at the British Embassy] and our united opinion was that any movement on my part for some considerable time at least might be perilous to our interests, whilst it could not possibly during a state of siege be attended with any favourable result.[46]

It was clearly time for Alton to leave and get his family back safely to Gibraltar. He organised the storage of the books with José Martin Alegría, the printer, before he left and Usoz agreed to oversee things in his absence. However, his departure was delayed because young George developed typhoid and was so seriously ill his parents despaired of his life. Alton sat up with him for nine consecutive nights and the illness then abated, but it was several more days before he was well enough to be moved. Alton reported that things were very unsettled and uncertain in Madrid but he had not been molested.

The family finally set off for Gibraltar and Alton later reported,

> I reached Gibraltar with my family on the 26th August after a long and harrowing journey. We were detained in Valencia eight days waiting for a steamer, and on the voyage Mrs Alton was confined a month earlier than we anticipated and gave birth to twins. This event was hastened no doubt by fright on the breaking out of the Revolution and by fatigue in nursing one of our children who had the typhous fever in Madrid brought on also by fright, and the subsequent fatigue of travelling. I need not tell you how intense was the anxiety through which we passed. But we were called to pass through circumstances so critical not only prematurely but wholly unprepared, and without the assistance of either doctor or nurse and on board a Spanish vessel. God however has been merciful and sustained us through all.[47]

The twins, Sydney Owen and Margarita Luisa, were both very weak and Alton thought they would not survive long. Sydney must have been weaker as Alton himself baptised him in Málaga. He died some weeks later but Margarita survived. The effect on Amy Alton was devastating. Apart from the trauma of the birth itself, she had had to be moved three times within four days after it. Her health was so badly affected that Alton thought he might have to ask for permission to return to England. He felt his own physical health had improved although he mentioned the return of some of his previous symptoms. On arriving in Gibraltar he found that

---

[46] Ibid., Alton, 28 August 1856, 1856, Box 111.
[47] Ibid., Alton, 3 September 1856, 1856, Box 111.

White had already left and stated,

> I found the work here in a deplorable state and it is under some depression of spirit that I buckle on the harness afresh, but with a heart willing to labour, and dedicating myself anew to God I place my faith and hope in him, and with his blessing I trust I shall ere long be able to report to you returning prosperity.[48]

It is amazing that he could find any energy at all to go on after all that had happened, but on his first Sunday back he preached twice in English and once in Spanish and during the week had met with the classes 'in order that I might acquaint myself as soon as possible with the spiritual state of our remaining members'.[49]

White's health throughout his time in Gibraltar had clearly affected his ability to do his job and the work had suffered considerably as a result, with reduced congregations and members. In England White served in two brief appointments and then went to India where he worked for eight years largely doing educational work. Further problems with his health caused his return to England where he served in several appointments. He became a supernumerary in 1894 and died on 8 March 1914 at the age of 84.

During Alton's absence Richard Deacon, the school-teacher, had kept the Spanish work going. He had previously been appointed as a catechist and in the 1855 Missionary report was described as visiting the Spanish-speaking population and conversing with many families about the things of God. The schools generally had kept up their numbers despite some fluctuations.

Alton soon reported a small increase in the congregations but remained very concerned about his wife and, in February 1857, he requested a return to England to avoid the excessive heat of the coming summer. The Committee had already assured him of its willingness to welcome him back to England and to find him a comfortable home circuit. In April he wrote again expressing his anxiety at having received no news about their return which he felt was imperative. In June, having still heard nothing from the Committee, he wrote to say that he had concluded that no successor could be found. He reported his wife's health to be a little improved and stated that, if necessary, he would arrange a change of air for her in the area and they would agree to stay on. The Committee later confirmed that a replacement could not be found and suggested that Amy and the children return, but Amy was not well enough to undertake the journey alone. An offer was then made to send a temporary replacement, but Alton was too committed to the work to allow this saying, 'The Mission has not, and will not soon recover from the disastrous effects of an inadequate supervision during my last year's absence in Spain, and to subject it to similar neglect

---

[48] *WMMS Correspondence,* Alton to Committee, 3 September 1856, fiche 699, no.36.
[49] Ibid., Alton to Committee, 3 September 1856, fiche 699, no.36.

again would be inevitable ruin'.[50]

To add to his problems he lost the help of Deacon who became too unwell to work. Deacon must also have been affected by grief because Sarah, his second wife, had died on 3 April 1857. He was advised to have a complete rest and a change of climate and was given paid leave. He travelled to England in June 1857 taking a letter to the Missionary Committee with him. His loss at this time was hard for Alton not only because of his own personal circumstances but also because it happened 'at a time when a very encouraging work is going on among the military requiring additional care and diligence in order to realise its promising fruits'.[51]

Alton kept in touch with his friends in Madrid but remained concerned about the Spanish Evangelisation Society. He wrote,

> I have many times been pained to see the erroneous statements respecting Spain in religious periodicals; but there is and can be no remedy for such evils and the still more evil consequences which arise out of them, whilst persons will act with the precipitate and infantile credulity which have characterised the movement and plans of individuals and parties both in London and Edinburgh, in relation to Mora and others.[52]

The situation in Spain was extremely difficult and apparently it was believed that de Mora had printed 3,000 copies of a pamphlet when in fact he had not printed any at all. Rule was involved in the Society and seems to have been critical of Alton but perhaps he still had higher hopes for Spain than were realistic. Alton felt Rule had been deceived but added that he would not have been 'had he exercised any judgement at all in the matter'.[53]

Alton was on the spot and had a very good understanding of the delicate nature of the situation in Spain and of the need to proceed cautiously if anything at all was to be achieved. He was not an empire builder but a man genuinely concerned to do all he could to spread the gospel in Spain and because of the need for great caution, he did not publicise his work with the result that little information about it has survived. He was sometimes given books to circulate in Spain and in 1857 he was criticised for not giving greater details of how he had distributed some given to him during 1856. In August 1857 he reported that since receiving them he had circulated

> ... not fewer that 14,000 copies of the Scriptures, Tracts, Pamphlets and Periodicals and since the commencement of the present year very nearly 2,000 copies of the Scriptures alone, chiefly in the interior of Spain.

---

[50] Ibid., Alton to Committee, 27 June 1857, fiche 700, no.45.

[51] Ibid., Alton to Committee, 27 June 1857, fiche 700, no.45.

[52] *Foreign Correspondence In,* Alton, 17 September 1856, 1856, Box 111.

[53] Ibid., Alton, 25 October 1856, 1856, Box 111.

Had I however been writing details of these efforts to everyone it would long ago have been impossible to do anything ... Almost anything will be permitted by Spaniards provided what they call a 'scandal' be avoided. I have therefore striven always to prevent the works of the machine we have had in operation from being heard, which I could not have done had I been informing everybody what was going on.[54]

He thus expressed his feelings unusually strongly and was no doubt frustrated by the unrealistic hopes for Spain and the publicity given to Spanish affairs. As a result of the revolution in 1856 and subsequent events in Spain, things began to get even more difficult. In October 1856 Alton reported that Sanchez could do nothing there and had therefore come to Gibraltar, where 'until something is arranged about him, I have set him to visit from house to house with the permission of the Governor.'[55] Mr Henderson, his sponsor, continued to pay his salary and soon Sanchez took over much of the Spanish preaching in the Methodist chapel and also later became the leader of the Spanish class. His presence was providential as Deacon had not been able to continue his work on his return to Gibraltar and he died on 4 November 1857 at the age of 44. His had been a tragic life with the loss of two wives who between them had borne thirteen children, of whom only four survived. At the quarterly meeting held in January 1858

... reference was made by all present to the great loss the Church had experienced in the death of Mr Deacon, for eighteen years Mission school-master, and for a considerable period a very successful class leader, as also for some years a useful and laborious catechist. In these offices, as well as when Acting Society Steward, Mr Deacon was found faithful and he 'obtained a good report' for 'he was a good man' and numbers were led to 'glorify God in him'.[56]

Soon Sanchez was not the only Spanish preacher in Gibraltar for during 1857 Ruet came to the Rock having been exiled from Spain because of his Protestant activities there. In addition to his contact with Alton, he may also have been in touch with Andrew Sutherland, the Presbyterian minister, for it was in this church that he began preaching, although as Sanchez was preaching in the Methodist church, this may have been the only opportunity for him. Sutherland soon reported a congregation of between 100 and 150 with some forty people wanting to join a Spanish Presbyterian church.

Meanwhile Escalante had continued his work as colporteur both in Gibraltar and Spain. Unfortunately all foreign correspondence to the Bible Society after 1856 has been lost, but the Committee Minutes record some details of letters sent and in July 1857 Alton wrote to say 'successful

---

[54] *WMMS Correspondence,* Alton to Committee, 14 August 1857, fiche 700, no.47.
[55] *Foreign Correspondence In,* Alton 28 October 1856, 1856, Box 111.
[56] Chapel minute book.

attempts have been made by the colporteur to introduce the Scriptures into Cádiz, Seville, Málaga, Granada, Valencia and other places as well as to dispose of them at fairs in Algeciras'.[57] Escalante also visited ships in the bay and collected subscriptions on behalf of the Gibraltar Auxiliary. Altogether, throughout 1857, he made 127 visits to ships

> ... and almost daily employed a portion of his time in visiting the troops and native population and in looking out for strangers entering the garrison for trade or pleasure. He also attended fairs held in Ronda, Algeciras and San Roque, on which occasions, besides the Scriptures circulated, he opened up communications with different parts of Andalucia from which further advantage may be expected.[58]

However, it was still dangerous work and in September 1858 Alton informed the Bible Society that Escalante had been arrested in Spain but 'he had been released after two nights and a day spent in prison'.[59]

As regards the scriptures in Madrid, it was Alegría who ensured their safety by storing them at first in his own home, despite the risks to himself. He had continued with the binding of the New Testaments and eventually placed all the books in cases for storage. There was some concern about the possibility of the books being confiscated, and some hope that they could be removed to Gibraltar, but in the end they remained in Madrid. However it was not possible to put them into circulation. In February 1864 Alegría died and other arrangements were made for their storage.

There are no surviving letters from Alton to the Committee between August 1857 and March 1858, but in November 1857 Charles William Cooke died at the age of two-and-a-half years, the sixth child the Alton's had lost. However, on 19 February 1858 another child, Charlotte Amelia, was born to them. Amy did not recover quickly from the birth and in March, Alton reported that she had 'been for nearly a fortnight in a most precarious state but I trust in God that she will soon be out of danger and recover. For the first few days, indeed ten days, she progressed towards convalescence with rapidity and then was thrown back by an attack of pleurisy, afterwards inflammation of the peritoneum and lastly dysentery. You may imagine how much reduced she is'.[60]

However, their troubles were not over for soon they had to face the greatest loss of all for, in April 1858, their second oldest child Catherine died at the age of 8 years and 9 months. By this age, they must have hoped that she would survive childhood and it is clear that this was a grievous blow to them. She was buried on 12 April and Andrew Sutherland took the funeral on this occasion, perhaps because grandfather Alder was too upset

---

[57] *Minutes of Committee No.46,* 20 July 1857, minute 28, p.47.

[58] Ibid., *No. 47,* 19 July 1858, minute 49, p.41.

[59] Ibid., 20 September 1858, minute 48, p.97.

[60] *WMMS Correspondence,* Alton to Committee, 22 March 1858, fiche 700, no.1.

himself. The April quarterly meeting was delayed and the minutes state that 'Mr Alton explained that the meeting had been held at a later period than was usual in consequence of his severe domestic affliction and bereavement'.[61]

The Altons were now desperate to leave Gibraltar and were most upset to hear that a successor had still not been found. Again a temporary replacement was suggested but Alton felt this would be 'a perilous expedient' and agreed to stay on until proper arrangements could be made.[62] He clearly hoped this would be done soon as his wife was 'in a very debilitated state' and they would have much preferred to avoid the heat of yet another summer. This letter and the next two were written on black-edged notepaper.

In fact, regimental changes at this time meant that the Society was considerably reduced and it must have been very hard to continue at all and contemplate visiting the new regiments that then arrived. Amy went to San Roque to convalesce and two months later, in August, was reported to be much improved having been 'so low when she went out as to be wholly unable to walk, and only with the greatest care could bear the motion of a carriage'.[63] Alton had still heard nothing from the Committee but read in *The Watchman* that a successor had been found and he had been appointed to Ramsgate! He therefore wrote to the Committee for further information, but it was two weeks before he received a reply. The Altons stayed long enough to welcome their successors and left Gibraltar in the middle of October with their remaining three children. After their departure, at the leaders' meeting on 30 October, a special tribute was recorded to George Alton in the following words:

> Mr Alton's pulpit labours have been marked by no ordinary ability and zeal, and they have been extensively blessed to the salvation of souls. But it is not those labours alone that claim our gratitude and command our esteem and respect. It has also been his high and correct sense of public duty, combined with a clear and vigorous intellect successfully employed on our behalf when our interests as a church were in circumstances of unprecedented peril, and when in less skilful hands they must have suffered irreparable injury. We refer especially, though not exclusively, to what transpired at the renewal of the lease of the Mission premises and although it is not necessary to express the particulars here, we, and probably our children, will have cause long to remember them with thankfulness to God, and gratitude to his servant.[64]

Heartfelt good wishes were also expressed for the family's future happiness. This is the only tribute to any minister who had served in

---

[61] Chapel minute book.

[62] *WMMS Correspondence,* Alton to Committee, 4 June 1858, fiche 700, no.4.

[63] Ibid., Alton to Committee, 24 August 1858, fiche 700, no.5.

[64] Chapel minute book.

Gibraltar to be found in the chapel minute book, and it underlines the enormous contribution that Alton had made. His many talents, his dedication to the tasks he was given both in Gibraltar and Spain, his diplomacy and skills in negotiation and his ability to get along with all manner of people, mark him out as a gracious and exceptional minister to whom the church owed a great deal, maybe even its continued existence during a time of great opposition by the authorities. No word or hint of criticism or dissatisfaction from anyone in Gibraltar ever reached the Committee except the opinion of Cheesbrough who was proved so entirely wrong. The cost to George and Amy was incalculable for they left seven children buried in Gibraltar and yet, despite that, they were later willing to return, for this was not to be the end of their ministry upon the Rock.

CHAPTER 13 SPAIN
The Fate of Escalante and the Work in Cádiz (1858-63)

Alton's successor was Joseph Webster. He was born in Bodmin in August 1817 and was converted as a youth during a revival there. In 1847 he was accepted on trial as a missionary and sent to British Honduras. He later worked in Jamaica and San Domingo where he acquired a knowledge of Spanish which was to prove very useful in Gibraltar. He arrived with his wife, Philippa, and their family on the evening of Monday 4 October 1858, after 'a most delightful passage out' and they were given 'a very hearty welcome'.[1]

Webster concentrated his efforts mainly on the soldiers and began by visiting the barracks with some success. 'I found in the 25th regiment about six who were attending our chapel but as the result of my visits to their barracks we had 25 marched on Sunday last, and I am told we shall have about 50 tomorrow'. His Bible class consisted almost entirely of soldiers and on Christmas Eve he invited them to tea. Between twenty and thirthy attended 'and the poor fellows seemed to enjoy themselves so much'. He reported that the soldiers 'seem thankful for any attention that may be shown them.'[2] By July 1859 there were 434 soldiers attending the chapel. So enthusiastic were some of them to meet together that they held daily meetings in a cave which they cleaned up for this purpose. By this time Webster had opened up a reading room at the mission premises, with a library of 600 books, along with newspapers and magazines, as part of a Soldiers' Christian Instruction Society which he advertised in the *Gibraltar Chronicle* in January 1859.

However Webster felt he laboured under some difficulties and like his predecessor he too raised the question of some official recognition of his services. He pointed out that the Presbyterian minister received a stipend of £120 a year from the government as well as 'forage for a horse' and he felt that the Methodist minister had no less a claim on the government. He stated, 'You can hardly conceive the painful position in which I am placed having to labour almost entirely among soldiers, without any recognised position. I am looked upon and treated by the Chaplains and others as an intruder'.[3] He therefore urged the Committee to action.

Meanwhile in England, Rule had continued to fight for the rights of Wesleyan soldiers. He described Gibraltar as 'the chief seat of Methodism in the British army' and felt that elsewhere very little had been done.[4] During the Crimean War he was concerned about the Wesleyan soldiers and suggested that a minister should be sent out to care for their spiritual

---

[1] *WMMS Correspondence*, Webster to Committee, 11 October 1858, fiche 701, no. 8.

[2] Ibid., 27 December 1858, fiche 701, no. 10.

[3] Ibid., 20 July 1859, fiche 701, no. 15.

[4] W.H. Rule, *Wesleyan Methodism in the British* Army, T. Woolmer: London, 1883, p.20.

welfare. The Rev. Peter Batchelor was given a free passage out and permission to work amongst them. He did not have the status of an army chaplain but nevertheless his appointment was a great step forward.

After the Crimean War, a military centre was set up at Aldershot and Rule took it upon himself to visit the camp as soon as a few regiments were stationed there and he drew up a plan to provide ministerial oversight for the Wesleyan soldiers. A Committee was set up by the Conference of 1856 to consider this but there seems to have been no great enthusiasm for the task. According to Rule, he was virtually left to get on with things and to raise funds to build a church outside Aldershot Camp to which Wesleyan soldiers could be marched. Conference suggested that a Committee be formed to receive the money and allocate it. This eventually became the Army Committee. Batchelor was appointed to the work in Aldershot but he soon withdrew so Rule took over and a church and manse were built. Rule spent eight years in Aldershot fighting for soldiers' religious rights against considerable opposition particularly from the Established Church chaplains. He was appointed by the Conference of 1858 to the office of corresponding chaplain and was asked to write to ministers stationed in or near garrison towns to give instruction and advice on soldiers' rights. This became a vast correspondence and Rule was involved in many disputes in different places with problems such as ensuring Wesleyan soldiers were recognised as such and had the right to attend their own services, and have their own chaplains visit them in hospital or prison and marry or bury them as necessary.

Gradually work among soldiers expanded and developed. In 1859 the first minister was appointed to work amongst the troops stationed in India and two ministers were sent to Curragh Camp in Ireland. In 1861 work at Chatham was started and was later developed in other places.

Meanwhile Rule's own workload had become so large that in 1859 Charles Henry Kelly was appointed to assist him, with the result that more and more soldiers wanted to attend Methodist worship which aroused even greater opposition. Difficulties abounded everywhere at this time and the practice of publishing details of Methodist services in Garrison Orders now ceased after twenty-two years. This practice had first been established in Gibraltar and its withdrawal caused considerable problems there. New arrivals found it difficult to find out about Methodism. They did not know the times of services and, on occasion, were marched to them at the wrong time. Webster therefore corresponded with Rule who offered his support adding, in his typically sweeping fashion, his opinion about the Gibraltar station which he believed had been 'dealt with negligently for many years, but which is now reviving under your hand'![5] Representation was made to the authorities both in Gibraltar and in England but was not immediately

---

[5] Rule to Webster, 23 November 1860.

successful.

Webster's position as an unofficial chaplain caused him problems throughout his time in Gibraltar. Shortly after his arrival he was reprimanded for visiting a sick soldier in hospital. It seems the soldier's parents were Methodists but he was officially regarded as belonging to the Church of England for Webster was told that 'if the man in question had really been <u>while a soldier</u> a member of the Wesleyan Church no observation would have been made on your visit'.[6] Presumably this meant that Webster could only visit soldiers officially registered as Wesleyan Methodists and not those who were enquirers or had family links with Methodism. Later Webster was reprimanded for marrying two soldiers who appeared not to have permission from their commanding officers to marry. It seems his every action was closely scrutinised and barely tolerated.

Webster attended to the Spanish work as best as he could. A great deal of opposition from the Roman Catholics had affected the schools, with numbers being reduced to 169, but the work continued and the children were still given a religious education. Sanchez continued to take regular Spanish services in the chapel and was leading a small Spanish class.

It soon became obvious that the Webster family was not finding Gibraltar any healthier than their predecessors and the children were described as suffering much from fever since their arrival. Webster felt the problem might be connected with the premises and in particular the neglected and unhealthy state of the adjacent waste ground. He approached the Governor on this matter and twenty convicts were sent to clear the site. They made it into a nice garden which was a vast improvement. In addition various recommendations were made about the Mission House itself especially with regard to its ventilation. Presumably this work was also carried out although in February 1860, Webster reported his second daughter as so ill with fever that both he and his wife were worried as to whether she would recover. Illness was a continuing problem.

Webster also became involved with the Bible Society Auxiliary. By February 1858 he had taken over from Dr Alder as Treasurer. Alder then became Secretary for a time until a Captain Warden took over. Escalante had been continuing his work of Bible distribution largely in Gibraltar where he visited many ships in the bay, but he also attended fairs in Spain and distributed Bibles there. However, in May 1859 all his work came to an abrupt end when he was arrested in Spain.

Escalante was arrested on 2 May 1859 at Vejer near Cape Trafalgar. The arrest took place at night when he was actually in bed but twenty-seven small Spanish Testaments were found in his possession. He was taken to the prison at Chiclana, south of Cádiz, and charged with 'circulating the

---

[6] Military Secretary's Office to Webster, 8 December 1858.

Scriptures printed in England, without notes, with a view to subvert the religion of the country - and for the second time'.[7] Brackenbury Junior, who had succeeded his father as Consul at Cádiz, was contacted by telegram with the news of the arrest. He promised to do what he could to get Escalante transferred to a prison in Cádiz where it would be easier to help him. He went on to say, 'All legal proceedings are in the country very dilatory, vexatious and expensive but every exertion shall be used by me for the speedy release of Escalante'.[8] However, the fact that this was a second offence - Escalante had briefly been imprisoned before - was likely to count against him.

Escalante remained at Chiclana for three weeks 'confined in a damp and gloomy dungeon' where 'he was seized with rheumatism'.[9] He was then transferred in handcuffs to Cádiz where for a time he shared a cell with several murderers. Money was sent from Gibraltar to Brackenbury to help meet his needs and Brackenbury also engaged a lawyer, Don Pedro Victor y Pico, to defend him. The Gibraltar Auxiliary agreed to pay such sums as were absolutely necessary to defend Escalante but was clearly very concerned about the expense. However, Escalante's salary was paid to his family throughout his imprisonment as without it they would have been in financial difficulty. Contact was also made with Andrew Buchanan, Minister at Madrid, who apparently expressed his willingness to try and obtain a pardon for Escalante should he be convicted. The Governor of Gibraltar was also approached for help but he felt that he could do no more than Brackenbury and Buchanan.

In June Webster travelled to Cádiz 'to advise and console' Escalante whom he described as a 'young man of devoted piety'. He was twenty-six years old at the time and Webster felt he should claim 'the sympathy and prayers of Methodists in England and of British Christians generally'.[10]

The Bible Society was informed of the situation. The reply was a mixture of genuine concern and sympathy for Escalante's plight and anxiety about the effect of his activities on the Society's reputation. It was pointed out that 'In our operations by agents paid by the Society's funds we avoid all systematic violations of national law in the countries where we work ... And we feel that if he carried on the work in defiance of governments we should soon get a bad reputation and very materially damage our labour'.[11] In a later letter, responding to a query as to whether the Society would be willing to pay any fine that might be imposed on Escalante, further comments were made along the same lines. It was felt that payment of a fine would imply responsibility for Escalante's actions when the Society

---

[7] Warden to Bergne, 28 June 1859.
[8] Brackenbury to Warden, 13 May 1859.
[9] *WMMS Correspondence*, Webster to Committee, 20 July 1859, fiche 701, no.15.
[10] Ibid., 20 July 1859, fiche 701, no.15.
[11] Bergne to Warden, 22 July 1859.

had had nothing to do with overseeing his work and would not have sanctioned any illegal acts had it been asked. 'We should compromise the character of the Society in the estimation of many of our friends if it were supposed that we dictated the sort of proceeding which has brought about the present difficulty'.[12]   Clearly the Society's reputation was very important for the future of its work but, although it had not actually directed Escalante's work, it had been aware of what he was doing, had been informed of his earlier imprisonment and does not seem to have queried his activities.

The affair dragged on, with little progress other than the refusal of bail. News of it became public in Britain. Further representations were made to Buchanan but it seems no one could interfere with the course of Spanish justice, although it was hoped that a pardon could be obtained if Escalante was found guilty. In the meantime Escalante's health deteriorated. His family in Gibraltar was also suffering. A daughter was born on 7 August 1859 and ten days later his father, Manuel, suddenly died. A correspondence was maintained with Escalante so he was kept informed of these events and many of his letters have survived. In them he expressed his feelings about his situation and his failing health. He described his attempts to spread the gospel in prison and asked for Bibles to distribute there. He seems to have been able to keep his own for most of the time but it is not clear if he received any for distribution. However, he does seem to have had religious conversations and discussions with fellow prisoners.

He had a variety of visitors, including some from England, but he did not want his wife to visit and see the terrible conditions he was in. In one letter he gave a moving account of the death, in his arms, of another young prisoner whom he regarded as a friend. Escalante also greatly missed George Alton, having shared so much with him in the past. Two of his sons, Manuel Alton and George, were named after him. However, he was very grateful for the support and help he received from Webster and for the support being given to his family in Gibraltar. He also received some financial help from Christians in Vejer. He worried about the expenses being incurred on his behalf believing them to be greater because he was from Gibraltar. He felt that cases like his were prolonged to extract as much money as possible. As time went on, concerns about his health and his desire to be out of prison were more strongly expressed.

In October 1859 Webster went again to Cádiz where he saw Escalante, Brackenbury and some of the Spanish officials. Afterwards, he told the Bible Society that he hoped the matter would now be brought to a speedy conclusion. In fact in December the case was finally heard but Escalante was convicted and sentenced to nine years' penal servitude. However, as his health was causing concern, he was released from prison on bail but

---

[12] Ibid., 2 August 1859.

remained under the surveillance of two guards whose expenses he was expected to pay. Buchanan still hoped he would be pardoned although he also expressed his concerns about Escalante's activities in his letter by saying,

> I hope that the serious punishment to which Mr Escalante has been found liable may deter him and others in future from violating the laws of the country. For however praiseworthy their motives may be, their proceedings not only give rise, as in the present case to embarrassing discussion between Her Majesty's Legation and the Government of Her Catholic Majesty, but have also an injurious influence on the position of British subjects established in Spain by causing their meeting for public worship to be looked upon with suspicion by the ecclesiastical authorities.[13]

Despite the hope of obtaining a pardon, an appeal was lodged with the Audiencia of Seville. In the meantime it seems that money was also raised in England on behalf of Escalante. In spring 1860 Alder visited him and Brackenbury on his way to England. He discussed the situation with the Bible Society and reported to the Gibraltar Auxiliary 'that much misapprehension is entertained in England respecting the case of Escalante' but does not say what this was.[14]

In May 1860, a year after his arrest, Escalante was told he had been acquitted and did not have to pay the court costs. Webster went to visit him as soon as he heard the news. Escalante had to remain in Cádiz until he received formal notification of his acquittal and so he did not return to Gibraltar until the middle of June when he was no doubt warmly greeted by his family and friends. News of his return was reported in the *Gibraltar Chronicle*.

Two developments resulted from Escalante's imprisonment. The first was a renewal of the hope of working in Spain. Whilst he was in Cádiz, Webster spent time investigating the possibility of doing missionary work there and, although few details of his discussions and meetings or how they came about have survived, in June 1860 he told the Committee, 'I hope we shall be able to obtain a footing there. I have formed two classes and have given 18 persons tickets - on trial as members of Society. I believe the Lord is doing a great work at Cádiz. Escalante our brother who has been so long a prisoner has been the instrument of much good to many'.[15] It is not clear who the people were, or if any of the original Cádiz Society were involved, although an article in *Missionary Notices* states that Webster did make the acquaintance of some of Rule's former members as does the

---

[13] Buchanan to Warden, 1 January 1860.

[14] Alder to Warden, 2 June 1860.

[15] *WMMS Correspondence*, Webster to Committee, 7 June 1860, fiche 702, no.20.

Missionary Society's Report for 1860.[16]

It is perhaps surprising that Webster should feel such work had any hope of success in the political climate then existing in Spain, especially after the harsh treatment of Escalante and the reaction of the Bible Society which now insisted that no work at all be attempted there. He did add, 'We shall require great prudence and caution in this matter, and care must be taken not to make it too public', and the Missionary Society's report acknowledged 'an insuperable barrier, it being a penal offence for any Spaniard to profess any religion but the Roman Catholic'.[17] Nevertheless, hope was still entertained that a mission could be re-established in Cádiz.

However, in September 1860, Webster reported on a further visit there when he discovered that, although the people seemed 'ardently attached to the Bible', they were engaging in some spiritualist practices.[18] He now discovered that this had been going on for three or four years but it had been concealed from him on previous visits. He strongly urged them to give up such practices, explaining that he could not recognise them as members of a Methodist Society whilst they continued them. He was doubtful whether they would follow his advice but planned to 'continue to correspond with them and probably I may pay them another visit and will do all in my power to convince them of the delusion into which they have been led.'

The second development concerned Escalante himself. After his release from prison, Escalante continued to work in the town and bay of Gibraltar, but the Bible Society forbad him from working in Spain as it would not be 'justified in employing the funds of the Society to relieve him from any difficulties in which by imprudent and illegal conduct he may be placed'.[19] The Society also asked for a more careful accounting of the cost of the work.

Although Escalante tried to sell scriptures, this was not always possible and more were given away than sold. The Gibraltar Auxiliary had presumed this to be the wish of the parent society because the priority was to spread the Word of God rather than to make money. However, in October 1860, in response to concern from London, the local committee decided as an experiment only to sell books. The result was that by February 1861 it was clear that sales only amounted to about £10 a year and Escalante's salary was £100. It is not clear how much of a change this was although there are hints that, after his imprisonment, the Roman Catholic population was more reluctant to purchase books from Escalante, but it is unlikely that the income generated from sales had ever fully

---

[16] *Missionary Notices,* vol. xvi (1860-2), 1860, p.89.

[17] *WMMS Reports,* 1861, p.13.

[18] *WMMS Correspondence,* Webster to Committee, 11 September 1860, fiche 702, no.21.

[19] *Minutes of Committee No. 49, 2 July 1860 to 17 June 1861,* 23 July 1860, minute 44, p.23.

covered his salary and expenses. However, Captain Warden now wrote to ask if such selling was worthwhile but added that,

> It is believed that he [Escalante] does all that it is in his power to effect for the sale of the Scriptures; he has been now for a very considerable time in the employ of the Society; he has a sickly wife and a large family of young children to maintain and it is difficult to see in what way he could support them if he was deprived of his present employment, moreover he has suffered much from persecution and imprisonment for the cause in which he is engaged.[20]

The Bible Society felt it could not justify such an expense but agreed to place the sum of £50 a year for the next two years at the disposal of the Gibraltar Auxiliary and granted a limited free distribution of the scriptures. This meant that, from October 1861, Escalante's salary was halved but he was unable to find other work and could not make ends meet. He then wrote to people in England saying he was in distressed circumstances and asking for financial help and may also have implied that he felt his treatment by the Bible Society to have been rather harsh. It was not an easy situation to resolve. On the one hand Escalante had done sterling work for the Society at great personal cost but, on the other hand, the Bible Society had a responsibility to its supporters not to waste its resources. In the end, in March 1863, Escalante himself approached the Gibraltar committee with a proposal. He could not support his family on a salary of £50 a year in Gibraltar but felt he could make a living in Lisbon. He therefore asked if he could cease work immediately but be paid until 30 September, which would enable him to move. The Bible Society agreed, and the affair thus seemed to have been satisfactorily resolved.

In the meantime, the idea of attempting missionary work in Spain had not been forgotten despite continuing persecution and further arrests of Spanish Protestants. One of them, Manuel Matamoros, had actually been converted in Gibraltar by the preaching of Ruet. He later spent time in Seville and in Málaga where he founded a small church. He kept in touch with Ruet who seems to have guided him in some of the work. He went on to Granada where José Alhama, a hatter, had also founded a church. Matamoros then went to Barcelona and began working there but, on 9 October 1860, he was arrested as a result of a charge made against him in Granada. His home was searched; various incriminating documents were found and he was imprisoned.

Matamoros was summoned to appear in Granada which meant he would have to travel there on foot, bound with criminals in a gang, staying in prisons along the way. Even at this stage his health was not good and it was likely to be badly affected by such a journey. However, friends in England came to his aid and paid for a sea passage to Málaga. Meanwhile

---

[20] Warden to Bergne, 16 February 1861.

in Granada, a young man studying at the ecclesiastic seminary was found to have some controversial writings in his possession. He was threatened with imprisonment and friends urged him to flee to Gibraltar and thence to England which he did, but Alhama was accused of helping him and was arrested. There were other arrests of Spanish Protestants too including that of Miguel Trigo.

After a long delay, on 13 June 1861, Matamoros, Alhama and Trigo were sentenced to nine years' penal servitude and a further nine years of surveillance. Nine others were sentenced to seven years and one to four. The matter was then referred to a higher court for its judgement. The wait for this was long for it was two years after their arrests before sentence was passed by the higher court. Matamoros was condemned to eight years' penal servitude and had to pay court costs. Alhama was sentenced to nine years and Trigo was pronounced not guilty. However, as they still had the right of appeal, and the fiscal who had wanted them to be sentenced to eleven years was not happy either, the legal process dragged on.

There was an international outcry at these sentences and a great deal of pressure was brought to bear on the Spanish authorities. There was even some condemnation of the intolerance in Spain itself. Overall it was a period of such bitter persecution that some felt it recalled the rigours of the Inquisition.

So, it does seem rather strange that a mission could be contemplated in Spain at such a time. Even the Bible Society seemed to have changed its views for it was in late 1861 that Lieutenant Graydon was sent to Spain on 'a limited tour of enquiry'. Spanish laws had not changed but Captain Warden was told, 'He now goes to observe, enquire and if possible <u>act</u>. I may ask you to keep this piece of information <u>confidentially</u> - plans might be repealed if any publicity were given to them'.[21] Graydon visited several Spanish cities early in 1862 and called at Gibraltar. His letters have been lost but it was reported that 'Lieutenant Graydon gives a dark picture as it respects the prospects of Scripture circulation being promoted in Spain at the present moment' and so no further action was taken.[22]

In the Missionary Society's annual report for 1861, Webster was reported to have 'made missionary tours to *Cádiz*, and to *Tangier* in *Morocco*' but details of these visits have been lost. However, the report went on to say,

> Many circumstances favour the opinion that a better state of things is approaching in Spain, notwithstanding the persecutions to which Bible readers and distributors are still subjected, which indeed may not unreasonably be supposed to express the fears awakened by the spread of scriptural knowledge. The Scriptures have been largely circulated, and have been read in secret by thousands. Not a few meet privately in

---

[21] Bergne to Warden, 21 November 1861.
[22] *Minutes of Committee No.51, 19 May 1862 to 13 April 1863,* 7 July 1862, minute 49, p.80.

various places to read and pray over the sacred page, and, while they watch with eager interest the commotions existing in the chief seats of the Papacy, hope that out of them all some good will arise from their own country. Under these circumstances, the Committee are watching with much solicitude for an opportunity of increasing their agency in this interesting field, and hope before long to send a Minister, who while he in the first place will seek the benefit of the numerous English residents, many of whom were once Methodists, may be of service to many enquiring Spaniards who are desirous of knowing 'the way of God more perfectly'.[23]

Perhaps it was thought that the outcry at the imprisonments would lead to greater toleration but there was little evidence of this in 1861 when George Alton was appointed to undertake the work in Spain. On hearing the news Webster wrote, 'Notwithstanding the restrictive laws which still exist there is plenty of Mission work which may be done by a judicious person'.[24] He went on to say that no one more suitable than Alton could be found. However, he added that, whilst he thought Sanchez could be spared from Gibraltar if necessary, 'I very much question if he would be willing to go to Spain while the present laws are in force'. Of course, as a Spaniard, he would have no protection from Spanish laws but perhaps he also had a better understanding of the situation.

The Alton family set sail in December 1861 on the steamship *Tagus*, bound for Lisbon, as Alton may have been asked to investigate the possibilities in Portugal too. As before, Amy Alton was extremely seasick as were the children and the nurse who accompanied them, though to a lesser extent. It is not clear how many children were on the ship. Two further children had been born, Hepworth Tropolet and Kate Elizabeth, but some of the older three may have stayed in England at school. Alton himself was not seasick and conducted services on board the ship. They arrived in Lisbon on New Year's Day and spent the next two days looking for lodgings. They found suitable apartments in a third class hotel which they took for a fortnight. Alton was pleased when the Captain of the *Tagus* asked him to preach again on board the ship whilst it was still in port and he preached to the whole ship's company numbering seventy-five. He believed there were a good number of English residents in Lisbon and hoped to discover many of them.

Alton stayed a little longer in Lisbon than intended, waiting for a steamer to Cádiz. He preached on the Sundays he was there and visited several people. He reported that there was a degree of religious toleration particularly for foreigners and that there were many ways in which a mission could function with caution and prudence. He was even asked to

---

[23] *WMMS Reports,* 1861, p.13.
[24] *WMMS Correspondence*, Webster to Committee, 5 April 1861, fiche 702, no.26.

stay on as a missionary himself. In the end he did not go on to Cádiz but went straight to Gibraltar where he was given a warm welcome by the Websters and many old friends. No doubt it was good also to be reunited with Dr and Mrs Alder who were reported to be well.

Alton took several Spanish services whilst he was in Gibraltar and also preached to the English congregation. No doubt Webster appreciated having his help and fellowship. The work in Gibraltar had continued much as usual. The chapel had been repaired and painted in the autumn of 1860 at the cost of £50. Regiments came and went as usual and the work with the soldiers continued. A prayer meeting and a Bible class were held weekly, largely attended by soldiers but some sailors were reported to have joined the latter when they were in port. Although membership was only forty-nine, between four and five hundred soldiers regularly attended the Sunday morning services to which they were marched and the evening and week-day services were well attended too. Numbers in the schools had increased slightly to 180 by 1861.

In 1861 the legality of marriages conducted at the Methodist chapel was questioned and a marriage ordinance was drawn up under which a registrar would have to be present. This would have involved a charge for the registrar's services which soldiers could not have afforded. Webster therefore sent a memorial dated 28 May 1861 arguing against this proposal, claiming the precedent of the past twenty years and asking for Methodists to be treated in the same way as Anglicans and Roman Catholics. The memorial was successful and Providence Chapel was licensed for the solemnization of marriages, although the *Gibraltar Chronicle* at first mistakenly announced the licensing of the Mission House and had to correct the mistake in the next day's issue!

After spending several days in Gibraltar, Alton travelled on alone to Cádiz arriving there on the evening of 26 February 1862. He took with him some useful letters of introduction and was well received by Brackenbury. There were few English people in Cádiz itself but more in the surrounding area and Alton spent time investigating all the possibilities. He returned to Gibraltar on 18 March and a few days later wrote to the Committee to report his progress. After meeting several English families he had discovered a kind of semi-consular chaplaincy established at Port St Mary by Charles Campbell, the Vice-Consul there. Services were held in a building adjoining the Vice-Consulate in a room appropriately set up for worship. A few people contributed money for the chaplain's salary but the work was limited to English residents. Two services were held on three Sundays in the month and on the fourth Sunday services had been held at Jerez or San Fernando.

There had been difficulties with this arrangement regarding the financing and the distribution of labour, but there had also been personal relationship difficulties with the result that the chaplain had left. The post was therefore vacant and might provide a suitable temporary opportunity for Alton. The permanent post would have to be filled by a Church of England chaplain. Alton preached several times at Port St Mary where there were six English families who did not all attend worship because they did not agree amongst themselves. He also visited English families at La Carraca, the Spanish arsenal, and at San Fernando where there were twenty-three English families. The chaplain had occasionally taken services there but again there was a problem uniting the people who came from different denominational backgrounds. Alton felt there was a desire for services and also for an English school as there were about forty children of school age. There were also three English families living at Puntales about two miles from Cádiz. In addition there were a considerable number of English and American ships visiting the port of Cádiz which 'would almost alone form an important sphere of properly missionary enterprise'.[25]

Generally speaking the Spanish authorities did not seem to be interfering in such work and Alton felt he was not likely to be greatly opposed and that altogether there was 'a reasonable and useful sphere of labour, if I could succeed with God's blessing in continuing and accommodating it with the ulterior purposes of my mission', which were of course to work with the Spanish.[26]

Alton had managed to converse with a number of Spaniards and found ten or twelve who for several months had been reading the Bible. Between six and eight of them regularly met on 'every Sabbath evening for prayer and reading the Scriptures, and mutual encouragement'. Alton reported, 'I am much pleased with their simplicity and meekness and the warm spirit of brotherly love which existed among them' and felt that 'there is the beginning of a work of grace with many hopeful circumstances.'[27] Only one of these people had been involved in Rule's work but Alton felt it was 'very encouraging to find that after the lapse of so many years and after so many persecutions, there is at least one remaining witness for the truth. God grant in His mercy that this one may prove the germ of a new and enlarged church'. The one was the ever faithful Margarita Barea who was now described as elderly and living in reduced circumstances.

Alton had met with eight Spaniards for private worship and felt it was possible to form a class. It is not clear if any of these people were those with whom Webster had met although Alton did report that at one time spiritualism had affected a large portion of the population but that the practice had now largely ceased.

Alton returned to Cádiz on 2 April with his wife to look for lodgings, leaving the children in Gibraltar for the time being. From Cádiz Alton reported on an incident which had recently occurred in Seville where the

---

[25] Ibid., Alton to Committee, 21 March 1862, fiche 703, no.38.

[26] Ibid., Alton to Committee, 21 March 1862, fiche 703, no. 38.

[27] Ibid, Alton to Committee, 22 March 1862, fiche 703, appended to no.38.

Spanish authorities had put a stop to British Protestant services held there. This had attracted considerable attention and was reported in the *Gibraltar Chronicle* as another example of Spanish intolerance. The services had been held in the British Consulate itself which had been the practice in many Spanish cities for a considerable number of years. An article in *Clamor Publico*, a Madrid newspaper, quoted in the *Gibraltar Chronicle*, attributed the change in attitude to the neo-Catholic party and Alton reported that the usual denunciations of Protestantism during the season of Lent had been stronger than ever.

However, despite this incident Alton decided to undertake the work of chaplain at Port St Mary and San Fernando which he felt would provide him with a legitimate reason for being in Cádiz. He did not make any arrangements for the payment of a salary there as he felt the English residents would not leave him without financial support for long if his services proved acceptable. He had found a house to rent and in the middle of April returned to Gibraltar to organise furniture, which was cheaper there, and to collect his children. It had not been easy to obtain a house and Alton reported,

> I owe it to the kindness of the English Consul and also to my temporary position as Acting Chaplain, that I was able to obtain a house at all. The questions that were put to me about my pursuits and objects were endless, and required almost more vigilance and tact than I could command to avoid embarrassing compromises.[28]

It was clear that Alton's activities would be closely watched.

Alton preached on Sundays at Port St Mary, leaving home at a quarter to six in the morning to do so and returning about four o'clock. In the evening he conducted a Spanish service in his own house which a small number attended. During the week he went to San Fernando where he instructed the children and preached to the adults. Attendances there had not been large 'But with God's help I will try to establish his work and do good notwithstanding numerous family bickerings and social jealousies and religious indifference'.[29] He also began a small Spanish class on Thursday evenings. Amy Alton joined in with this and also a Miss Hamilton who was probably the children's nurse.

Meanwhile, back in Gibraltar in March 1862, Webster had written to the Committee asking for permission to visit England, because his father, aged 79, was in poor health. He also wanted to attend Conference which he had never done before. He planned to leave his family behind though he noted, 'We have had a good deal of sickness in our family during the winter. All the children were down with fever, but at present we are all tolerably

---

[28] Ibid., Alton to Committee, 6 June 1862, fiche 704, no.43.
[29] Ibid., Alton to Committee, 17 June 1862, fiche 704, no.44.

well'.[30]

The Committee was slow in responding to this request and Webster wrote again having heard that his father had had a stroke. By June he had managed to obtain a free passage on a troop ship through the kind intervention of the Governor, Lieutenant-General Sir William Codrington, but had still not heard from the Committee. He wrote yet again asking for permission to visit England and stating that Alton had agreed to oversee the work in his absence. Permission was eventually granted and on 8 July, a few days before he left, Webster wrote to the Committee to recommend Alfredo Giolma as a candidate for the ministry. He and Alton had examined him together and both strongly recommended him.

Giolma was then about twenty-two years old. A native Gibraltarian, his parents had both been Spanish Roman Catholics. He himself spoke English, Spanish, Portuguese, Italian and some French. He was employed as a 'book keeper and manager in a Jewish House of Business'. He had been converted about three years before and for the past two years had been a member of Webster's class. Webster reported him 'to be a young man of consistent piety and anxious in every way within his power to be made useful to his fellow men. He is also a young man of studious habits and has sought to make himself acquainted with the work of our best theological writers so as to qualify himself for future usefulness.'[31]

Shortly after writing this letter, Webster left for England where he visited the Mission House though no records of his meetings there have survived. In his absence on 5 August Alton wrote to the Committee to recommend Sanchez to them and did so in the hope that Webster would be able to discuss his situation with the Committee also. Sanchez was no longer really needed in Gibraltar as Giolma was ready to take over the Spanish preaching, and there was also a Spanish Mission at the Presbyterian church where Ruet preached. In any case his training, background and experience made him suitable for a more challenging position. Alton felt his character and qualifications were of "the highest order" and although he was 'considerably advanced in life, [he was fifty-three!] there is yet promise of some years of useful labour' especially as his health was good.[32] He spoke good French as well as Spanish and felt his wife and two daughters aged fifteen and nine would give him good support. Both his children spoke English, French and Spanish, indeed the elder had begun to teach languages at the age of thirteen. Presumably he was still supported by Henderson. No other correspondence on this subject has survived but Sanchez stayed in Gibraltar, possibly continuing some work there although Giolma does seem to have taken over the Spanish preaching. Giolma was appointed as assistant missionary and, soon after his return, Webster and Alton met with

---

[30] Ibid., Webster to Committee, 13 March 1862, fiche 703, no.37.

[31] Ibid., Webster to Committee, 8 July 1862, fiche 704, no.49.

[32] Ibid., Alton to Committee, 5 August 1862, fiche 704. no.50.

him to discuss his salary, his duties and to plan a course of study for him.

Not long after he returned, Webster's wife and daughter, Mary, became ill. Mary's illness was so severe that the doctor urged an immediate removal from Gibraltar and so Webster decided to send them both back to England, which would leave him with two young children and a baby, Eber Wesley, who had been born on 12 October 1861. However, after consultation with Alton and Alder, it was decided that it would be best for the whole family to return to England. Giolma would go to Cádiz and the Altons would cover the work in Gibraltar. The Committee was asked to send a telegram of authorisation and in the meantime Giolma went to Cádiz no doubt with messages for Amy Alton who had remained there.

Shortly afterwards Webster had second thoughts and decided he ought to stay and suggested instead that his wife and two children returned. This is what the Committee authorised by telegram and, whilst waiting for a ship, Webster took his wife and children to San Roque which he hoped would be healthier. His hopes were short-lived because, although Mary survived, Eber Wesley became ill with bronchitis and died on 9 November 1862 aged thirteen months. Webster wrote,

> We all feel this to be a heavy stroke but we are trying to bow with humble submission to the Divine Will. We know our heavenly Father always afflicts his people in mercy and in love and in this season of deep sorrow we have the consolation of knowing that our dear child is Eternally safe, for ever folded in the bosom of his Saviour.[33]

The ship which they had been waiting for, captained by a friend of theirs, had arrived while Eber was very ill when it was impossible for anyone to leave. In the end the family stayed together in Gibraltar to share their grief and console each other. Alton returned to Cádiz.

The work in Cádiz became increasingly difficult. A few subscriptions were received from English residents towards Alton's salary so clearly some appreciated his services although others declined to contribute on 'ecclesiastical principles'. There was talk of a permanent chaplain being appointed but no-one came. At San Fernando things were gradually improving and Alton felt they would do so even more if there was an appropriate place of worship. Services were held in different houses which was not altogether satisfactory. So far the authorities had not interfered with this work but Alton reported,

> It is quite uncertain how long I may be permitted to continue these services, as the Consul could afford me no protection in case the authorities should interfere. The Ambassador on his late visit here informed the Consul that the British Government would only protect

---

[33] Ibid., Webster to Committee, 12 November 1862, fiche 705, no.58.

services held in a Consulate.[34]

He deeply regretted the fact that he could do so little with the Spaniards many of whom seemed afraid even to speak on religious topics which surprised him as this had not previously been the case. He had thought a lot about the reasons for this, writing that

> As the result of my own enquiries into this state of things I have come to the conclusion that it results chiefly from the widespread influence of the different religious confraternities which during the last eight years have increased beyond all belief. They embrace all classes and all ages, and both sexes, and are entirely under priestly control. It requires some residence in the country with patient investigation especially in this direction in order to get any right view of the extent and ramification of these Societies. They are spread over the whole nation like a closely wrought net, and are inter-laced with almost every family. The principles on which they are conducted are so far as I can learn essentially Jesuitical, and their effect is to create distrust and fear to such an extent as to be all but universal. A state of society is produced by this agency in which sincerity and frankness have no place, and almost every man is by a sort of evil necessity converted into a dissembler or a hypocrite.[35]

Such organisations had existed in Spain for a considerable number of years and although their greatest growth had taken place in the sixteenth and seventeenth centuries, it seems their influence could still be considerable.

Giolma stayed in Cádiz studying under Alton's supervision. He wrote to the Committee to thank them for his appointment and to describe his studies.[36] He reported that he occasionally preached to Alton's Spanish class and visited the members, conversing with others when he could.

In January 1863 Alton reported that, after his latest visit to Gibraltar, he had returned with a number of English books for the English residents, plus some tracts and *Missionary Notices*. He had some Spanish Bibles and some of his own personal books with him too. On landing he noticed unusual customs activity and, realising that he was the object of it, he declared his books. This action surprised the officials but his luggage was still thoroughly searched and his books were all seized for examination by the Governor and the bishop. He was told he could apply to have them returned after this examination had taken place. He later met with the Governor who informed him unofficially and in confidence that a telegram had been received from Gibraltar denouncing him and stating that he was smuggling books into Spain. Without this denunciation no action would have been taken against him although he was now told that he had been

---

[34] Ibid., Alton to Committee, 18 November 1862, fiche 705, no.60.

[35] Ibid.

[36] Ibid., Giolma to Committee, 24 November 1862, fiche 705, no.62.

closely watched for months and note taken of the Spaniards who visited him. The Governor seemed kindly disposed towards him and advised a meeting with the bishop which Brackenbury undertook as he had met him before. This meeting was decidedly hostile, with the bishop making it clear that he regarded Alton's purpose in being in Spain to be the preaching of heresy despite the cover of his chaplaincy work. He knew of his past work with the Bible Society. Alton again met with the Governor who received him kindly as before but could do no more until the bishop made his report. As a precaution Alton suspended his Spanish services as he felt 'it would clearly be perilous to the people to frequent my house' and he sent Giolma back to Gibraltar.[37] He himself remained under observation and was sometimes followed. He had not heard from the Committee for some time and wondered if his letters had arrived. He wrote again towards the end of January saying that he was awaiting their instructions with some anxiety.

> I am entirely shut up to such labours as I can perform in English at Port St Mary's and San Fernando, and watched and followed as I am it is impossible to attempt anything among Spaniards, or to continue what I had hoped was well begun. In the midst of all I feel how necessary it is to place my whole trust and confidence in God, and try to realise the hearty confidence in Him so beautifully expressed in the one hundred and twenty first psalm.[38]

Nearly a month later Alton informed the Committee that the bishop had died before making his report. The Governor was moving on to another post and met with Alton before leaving. Alton's personal books were returned to him but the rest were confiscated.

The Committee did write to Alton on 16 February but seems to have given little advice or instruction as another letter was to be sent a few days later. However, by 27 May Alton had still not heard from London. In the meantime his work had had to be confined to the English residents because of the strict watch still kept upon him. There was then a totally unexpected development which put an end to any lingering hope of continuing his work in Spain for Martin Escalante arrived in Cádiz, with all his family, to denounce Protestantism and return to the Catholic Church. Alton wrote,

> Since his arrival here he has been made much of by the priests, and great efforts have been put forth to create a sensation. If he had been content with his professed conversion there would have been nothing in his case worth a remark. But he has given into the hands of the Priests all his correspondence with everyone both in Spain and other places, and has informed against everyone who has had any communication with him particularly in Cádiz during his imprisonment here as the colporteur of the Bible Society. At that time he became acquainted with many persons

---

[37] Ibid., Alton to Committee, 8 January 1863, fiche 706, no.63.
[38] Ibid., Alton to Committee, 28 November 1863, fiche 706, no.65.

who professed Protestant tendencies. These persons have now been placed in the greatest alarm, and there is too good reason to fear that they will be ruthlessly persecuted either openly or covertly. Indeed such persecution has already begun. Grievous threatenings have been breathed out against everyone known or suspected to be connected with Protestantism, and against myself in particular. I got private information that the Priest who claims the merit of Escalante's conversion was resolved to leave no stone unturned to get my house searched and seize my papers, and therefore as a measure of precaution I have informed the Consul of all that is passing, and deposited all my papers with him. I have ascertained that the person who informed against my books was no other than the wretch Escalante.

The same Priest who seduced Escalante from his duty has also held out sufficiently attractive inducements to our chapel-keeper in Gibraltar, and he is expected here from day to day to make his public recantation also.

Whatever other object the Priests may have proposed to themselves in these seductions, it seems natural to infer that a principal object in bringing them to Cádiz at great expense is to provide a set off against my own efforts, and to excite a fanatical feeling of hostility to my person and work.

These circumstances have made my position far more painful and difficult than it was before and seem to preclude the hope that for some time to come I can do anything among Spaniards with the least prospect of advantage either to Methodism or Protestantism generally. You will judge what will be best to do, so that I have only to await your resolution.[39]

Escalante's betrayal must have been deeply hurtful to Alton when they had shared so much together. Presumably Escalante had felt that he had been badly treated by the Bible Society and perhaps the financial inducements that were undoubtedly offered overcame any scruples he might have had, but it is still hard to understand how he could choose to place people in danger when he knew the trauma of being imprisoned himself. In addition he had deliberately defrauded the Bible Society as his arrival in Cádiz occurred just a short time after he had received his final payment from the Society and his denunciation of Alton's books occurred many weeks before. A letter from Escalante was printed in a Cádiz newspaper 'recounting all his errors and heresies, and professing himself a convert to the Roman Catholic Church.'[40] Presumably he and his family stayed in Cádiz but nothing more is known about his future life there.

There was nothing Alton could do but he had to remain in Cádiz until he received instructions from the Committee. It must have been a very difficult time indeed for him and his family but no accounts of it have

---

[39] Ibid., Alton to Committee, 27 May 1863, fiche 706, no.71.
[40] *Gibraltar Chronicle,* 25 May 1863.

survived. They finally returned to Gibraltar on 10 July 1863. Alton had been instructed to take over the work there and Webster was to return to England.

Whilst these events had been taking place in Cádiz, life had not been particularly easy either for Webster. He was very worried about the health of his family which he described as 'fearfully shattered', and he wanted them out of Gibraltar as soon as possible.[41] In addition further negotiations had been taking place about including Methodist services in Garrison Orders. In England Rule and Kelly had been fighting hard and in June 1862 had finally won some recognition for Wesleyan soldiers. Up to this time soldiers were classified in the official returns under three headings, Church of England, Roman Catholic and Presbyterian. A fourth column entitled 'Other Protestants' was now to be added. Although this may appear to be only a partial victory as Wesleyan Methodism was not actually named, it was regarded as a major step forward for it gave greater rights and recognition to Wesleyan ministers and soldiers than ever before. In Gibraltar Webster negotiated with the Governor and it was agreed that this practice would now be adopted there. So Garrison Orders, which included the times of worship of the three named denominations, now included 'Other Protestants whose ministers are recognised - 10.30'. Webster explained, 'This is the hour at which our service commences, and as the Wesleyans are the only "other Protestants" to which the order can have referred, the arrangement will probably answer our purpose for the present. It is very evident that the Military Authorities design to keep the Wesleyans in the army veiled as long as they are able'.[42]

Soon, however, Webster was asked questions about a printed leaflet which he had used for about two years, giving it to those soldiers and officers who were not sure about the rights of Wesleyan Methodists. It gave details of the Methodist Sunday services and week-day meetings which included class meetings, soldiers' prayer meetings, a weeknight service of worship, a Bible class and a public prayer meeting. However on the third page Webster had printed the following words;

> As misunderstandings are constantly arising among Wesleyan soldiers with respect to their right to attend Divine Service at their own Church on the Sabbath, many of whom not having been registered as belonging to this persuasion on their enlistment, the following letter from the Adjutant-General addressed to one of the General Secretaries of the Wesleyan Missionary Society, is issued for their information and guidance.

The letter printed was the one written in 1853 referring to

> ... the undoubted right of the Soldiers of the Wesleyan persuasion, as

---

[41] *WMMS Correspondence,* Webster to Committee, 21 March 1863, fiche 706, no.68.
[42] Ibid., Webster to Committee, 21 March 1863, fiche 706, no. 68.

well as those of every other religious denomination, to change their Church as often as they please, and to attend the Worship of Almighty God according to the forms which they may happen to prefer, when Military duty does not interfere.[43]

In March 1863 Webster was sent a memo from the Assistant Adjutant General's office asking if he had written the anonymous paragraph printed above. Webster replied, also by memo, saying that he had written it but as the whole sheet clearly bore his signature he could not see how it could be regarded as anonymous. His memo was returned to him because, being in that form, it did not bear his signature! He therefore wrote again this time in letter form, but merely giving the same reply. He was then asked if the second sheet had ever been circulated separately in which case it would have been anonymous. Webster reported three occasions when he had torn off the second page giving it to officers who seemed unsure of their soldiers' rights. It seems that one of them had sent it to the authorities. It was made clear to Webster that anonymous distributions of leaflets would not be allowed, as it was necessary to have control over papers distributed in the barracks.

Webster began preparing to leave Gibraltar although he had not yet been given any information about his next appointment. He hoped to be in London about 20 July and the family probably left Gibraltar shortly after the Altons returned. Webster's interest and experience in working with soldiers was recognised in his next appointments at Shorncliffe Camp, Aldershot Camp, Portsmouth Garrison and Malta. He returned to England in 1880 but the following year his health failed and he became a supernumerary. However, after eighteen months rest, he was asked to become a chaplain to the troops in Egypt and although he was about 66 years old he accepted the appointment which lasted for a year. He then retired to Portsmouth where he died on 19 February 1899 at the age of 81.

---

[43] Copy of leaflet in church archives.

CHAPTER 14   THE MINISTRY OF GEORGE ALTON (2)
GIBRALTAR
Work with the Sanitary Commissioners; Openings in Portugal and Spain (1863 - 9)

George Alton
(With permission from the Oxford Centre
for Methodism and Church History)

So George and Amy Alton returned to Gibraltar to continue their ministry there. They must have had mixed feelings about living again in the place where they had experienced such terrible tragedy, especially knowing that the health of the Webster family had not been good, but it does not seem to have occurred to them to question their orders. Alton wrote, 'In again occupying this station with much fear and trembling we have earnestly implored God's blessing upon us and upon our work'.[1]   Another child, Frank Edward, was born in October 1864 but no more children were lost during these years.

Shortly after taking up their appointment, there were changes in the regiments stationed at Gibraltar. However, in January 1864 Alton sent the following report, indicating success in his work despite continuing opposition.

> You will be pleased to learn that our congregation has quite recovered from the effects of the extensive changes which it has undergone since my arrival here in July. Every available seat in the chapel is now generally occupied on the Sunday morning. On the arrival of three regiments from Malta I employed very active measures to secure as many of the Wesleyans in the Corps as I could, and the result is that we have more soldiers attending our services than has ever been known in Gibraltar. Much yet remains to be done to secure all who ought to attend our ministry but there are many difficulties to be overcome. Men in authority in subordinate positions oppose our efforts in all sorts of ways and one of the Chaplains does all he can against us. Men desiring to attend our Chapel have often to bear a good deal of annoyance, and my own efforts are thwarted.[2]

In addition Alton had begun weekly meetings for the soldiers' children which others joined too, including children from the day schools who

---

[1] *WMMS Correspondence*, Alton to Committee, 17 July 1863, fiche 707, no.74.
[2] Ibid., Alton to Committee, 1 January 1864, fiche 707, no.76.

understood English.

Giolma did much of the Spanish work and, by this time, Gibraltar had become a haven for a number of Spanish Protestant refugees. The Evangelical Alliance had prepared a European deputation, involving nine countries, to protest against the imprisonment of Matamoros and the others and perhaps it was because of this international concern that the sentences were finally commuted to exile. So, on 29 May 1863, Matamoros, Alhama and Trigo left the prison in Granada and were taken to Málaga, along with some family members. They spent the night in prison there. The next day they went on board the warship *Alerta* and were transported to Gibraltar. Others must have joined them there.

In June Webster had written a letter of introduction to the Mission House as Matamoros was due to leave for England. He reported:

> About a week ago Señor Matamoros was sitting with me in my study conversing about his departure for England, when he was seized with a slight cough and immediately commenced vomiting blood. We deemed it prudent to keep him with us at the Mission House until he had sufficiently recovered to undertake a voyage.
>
> Both Mrs Webster and myself have done all in our power to add to his comfort in his affliction and we have been much pleased with his Christian spirit and gentlemanly deportment. We trust his trip to England will, with the Divine Blessing, be the means of restoring his health, which has been fearfully impaired by his long imprisonment.
>
> P.S. Mr Matamoros cannot speak a word of English.[3]

Matamoros left on 22 June arriving in England eight days later. He must have returned to Gibraltar because the *Gibraltar Chronicle* announced that he would preach a farewell address to his friends on 9 August in the Presbyterian chapel. A special service was also held in the Methodist chapel on 11 August when George Alton preached a valedictory address in Spanish. The exiles numbered twenty-one, including women and children. Alton met with them privately to advise and encourage them and did all he could to minister to them. It is not clear how many of them left the Rock at this time. Matamoros certainly did. He spent time in France and Lausanne but he died in July 1866 at the early age of 31. Some of the refugees went to Oran but Alhama stayed in Gibraltar. He was joined there by Juan Bautista Cabrera who was born in Alicante in 1837. After completing his ecclesiastical studies he devoted himself to further biblical research and learnt Greek, Hebrew, English and Italian. He then left his order but had not at this time become a Protestant. However, as he had maintained some correspondence with the prisoners, he went to Gibraltar for his personal safety with his wife, Josefa.

By this time Ruet had left the Rock. He may have gone to Oran for he

---

[3] Ibid., Webster to Committee, 20 June 1863, fiche 707, no.72.

was certainly there as a Spanish pastor in March 1868 when he wrote to the Bible Society asking for some scriptures, but in 1863 it seems to have been Giolma who was doing much of the Spanish work in Gibraltar. He sent an account of it to the Committee.[4] He visited soldiers, conversing with them and distributing tracts. He checked up on the children who were absent from school and often preached to them and to the boys from the night school. He conversed with Spaniards, occasionally giving out Bibles and tracts and sometimes encouraged parents to send their children to the Methodist schools. He held Spanish Bible classes and Spanish services. He tried to persuade some of Ruet's congregation to come to his services and he seems to have preached to the Spanish refugees so successfully that they asked him to preach to them regularly. He reported on two spiritual conversations with Cabrera. He gave him some tracts and it seems that it was during his time in Gibraltar that Cabrera became a Protestant. Two children were born, Rosa Maria and Maria Magdalena and both were baptised by Alton in the Methodist chapel.

Giolma reported some persecution from the Roman Catholic population and also stated that many Spaniards who had once attended their Spanish services still had the Bibles or Testaments given to them by Rule, Deacon or Alton. He went on to say,

> I tried to persuade them again and again to join us at the Spanish services and they have expressed themselves that though they are fully persuaded that the Church of Rome is not the true church of Christ; yet they are afraid to profess openly that one and true faith which was once delivered to the saints, for fear of the world, and of losing their welfare.[5]

He felt little would be done in Gibraltar unless something was first done in Spain. By 1865, despite all his efforts, Giolma only had five Spanish members although more came to his services including the boys from the night school which at times had sixty scholars. However, by then, there was more competition as there were four other workers in the Presbyterian church and one in the Church of England amongst the Spanish-speaking population of the Rock. Giolma was, however, also being visited by people from Spain who took Bibles and tracts to distribute amongst their families and friends. He hoped it would not be long before the scriptures could be freely circulated there.

However, the situation in Spain was not improving. In August 1864 there was further trouble in Cádiz. Only a brief account of events has survived.

> Persecution arose in *Cádiz* in the course of the year, and chiefly against Margarita Barea, who had for many years held fast her profession as a

---

[4] Ibid., Giolma to Committee, 13 Jaunuary 1864, fiche 707, no.78.
[5] Ibid., Giolma to Committee, 11 August 1864, fiche 708, no.85.

Methodist. Her house was ransacked by the Police, and herself and her husband arrested, and although the proceedings were shortly abandoned, there can be no doubt that the painful anxiety they occasioned hastened her end. She maintained her steadfastness to the last, and died in peace. It is due to the Authorities, both Civil and Ecclesiastical, to record that they manifested great unwillingness to be drawn into a persecution of this aged disciple; and after the preliminary investigations, caused the process to be closed, assuring her that she should not be further molested. The miserable informer therefore failed to accomplish the object of his bigoted and cruel zeal. During the course of these events Mr Alton visited *Cádiz* as he thought necessary and prudent, in order to advise and comfort the affrighted flock.[6]

The 'miserable informer' was Escalante, and it seems particularly cruel of him to have denounced Margarita Barea who was 77 years old when she died.

In May 1864, the Committee wrote to Alton about the need to economise because of the Society's financial difficulties. One suggestion was to reduce their children's allowance by twenty-five per cent, which Alton felt would 'press with severity upon our domestic economy, as since the scale of allowances was adjusted to the circumstances of the place, and within the last ten years, every necessary of life has risen in price fully fifty per cent'.[7]

Another suggestion was to set an overall annual budget of £600 for the station which Alton felt was 'as much as the Committee ought to spend on this place. But with the actual staff and liabilities of the Mission it is impossible that the expenditure can be kept within even £700'. Indeed, only a few weeks later, Giolma wrote to Alton to ask for an increase in his salary of £70 a year as 'things are so exceedingly dear that I can scarcely live'. He had not wanted to make the request but 'justice and necessity has compelled me to do it'.[8] Alton sent his letter on to the Committee supporting his request and saying 'no-one could be more economical than Mr Giolma and I believe him to be deserving of this increased allowance'.[9]

Alton made several comments about the work to help the Committee make its decision. First he reported that 'in the English department the civil element has nearly disappeared altogether, and in future the duties of the Missionary will in fact be exclusively those of a military chaplain'.[10] He described the number of other schools now existing in Gibraltar which had led to the reduction of pupils in their schools and an increase in the expense per child. He added, 'These facts indicate that the public necessity for our schools on their present scale is neither so urgent nor so evident as

[6] *Missionary Notices*, vol. xvii (1863-5), 1865, p.91. *WMMS Reports,* 1865.

[7] *WMMS Correspondence*, Alton to Committee, 25 May 1864, fiche 708, no.81.

[8] Ibid., Giolma to Alton, 5 July 1864, fiche 708, no.83.

[9] Ibid., Alton to Committee, 11 August 1864, fiche 708, no.84.

[10] Ibid,, Alton to Committee, 25 May 1864, fiche 708, no.81.

at the beginning'. With regard to the Spanish department, he stated that 'the work is always fluctuating and very uncertain and has hitherto yielded small results. But it is about as difficult and discouraging a field of labour as can be found'.

In July 1866, the Committee expected Alton to return to England so it could send someone to Gibraltar who had fewer children. However, Alton was told of this plan too late to comply and so he was instructed to prepare to leave the following year. The Committee also asked him to make some changes in the running of the schools. The schoolmaster was to be allowed to occupy the premises, to have the government grant, the school fees and £100 a year from the Mission Fund and no more. With respect to Giolma, Alton was told, 'We quite approve of your proposal to send Giolma to this Conference for ordination, if he can arrive in time.'[11] Alton had felt such a visit would also give the Committee an opportunity 'to judge of his general qualifications and his suitability for any other sphere of labour where his services might be better appreciated and more useful than they can be here'.[12]

Giolma did go to England on 20 July and was ordained. He returned to Gibraltar early the following year after receiving some training and broadening his experience of Methodism in England. Alton had previously written, 'it is most desirable that Mr Giolma should have another sphere of labour for several years. I conceive that his usefulness for the future and his value therefore to the Society as an agent, depend upon this'.[13] So, in response to the need to economise, Alton suggested Giolma's services in Gibraltar could be dispensed with.[14] Alton was not impressed with the plan for the schools which he felt would only achieve a saving of £20 a year. He suggested instead the amalgamation of the boys' and girls' schools on the mission premises, which would be cheaper as the boys' school occupied a rented room, but this was not done. The very brief annual report for 1867 merely recorded,

> Great changes in the Spanish people of Gibraltar, and the increase of agencies by Societies established for their special benefit, have led to the conviction of the expediency of lessening our staff at this place, and of principally confining our attention to the military. Meanwhile the regular services, both in English and Spanish, have been carried on with some success, and the Schools have been continued, with some modification of plans, and a small reduction of expenditure.

However, it was not until the following year that Alton informed the Committee that Giolma had left that day, 6 February 1868, for Honduras

---

[11] *WMMS Correspondence Outgoing,* Hoole to Alton, 11 July 1866, fiche 1210.
[12] *WMMS Europe Synod Minutes 1823-76,* Alton, 18 April 1866, fiche 19.
[13] *WMMS Correspondence,* Alton to Committee, 31 July 1866, fiche 708, no.89.
[14] Ibid., Alton to Committee, 31 July 1866, fiche 708, no.90.

where he had been appointed as assistant missionary. He took with him several cases of books including many of Rule's commentaries. He arrived in Belize on 2 April 1868 and travelled on to his station at Corosal, where he preached to English and Spanish congregations and worked in a day school. The Spanish work particularly seemed to prosper, but there were some difficulties in relationships with his colleagues who later complained of his 'ways'.[15] In June 1869 he resigned from Methodism mentioning these difficulties and also the 'stiffness and harshness' of some of the Methodist officials he had met in England at the Mission House.[16] Giolma was then ordained by the Bishop of Kingston, Jamaica, and returned to work in Corosal. The following year the mission was given up and he went to Barbados instead. He later worked in Ponce in Puerto Rico and then moved to England. From 1876 to 1878, he was curate at a church near Chatham but after that his name disappears from the records and what became of him is not known.

Meanwhile, in Gibraltar, Spanish services continued on Sunday evenings presumably with either Alton or Sanchez preaching. A former priest, Antonio Soler, preached in the Presbyterian church. By this time Alton had also become very involved in other work in Gibraltar.

In 1861 the British Government had ordered a Commission of Enquiry into the sanitary state of several of its military stations including Gibraltar. The *Gibraltar Chronicle* gave details of its findings which highlighted the considerable problems that existed. The Commissioners wrote,

> The present mortality is excessive, and the prevailing zymotic diseases are those connected with over-crowding, want of domestic cleanliness and defective ventilation, bad water-supply, bad drainage and sewer gases. The time has certainly arrived when these various questions should be dealt with, and this important garrison placed as far as practicable beyond the influences of epidemic diseases ... The natural disadvantages of the site of the city are very considerable, and without due care as to cleansing and drainage, it must undoubtedly be prejudicial to health and predisposed to fever and other epidemic diseases. The older part of the town has been built without regard to health.[17]

House drainage was extremely poor and it was felt that many homes 'would be considered as unfit for human habitation at home'. The inadequacy of the water supply was of great concern and one major source 'although largely consumed by both the troops and civilians, would not in its present state be a safe water for use during an epidemic'.

The Commission made several recommendations and 'extensive

---

[15] *WMMS Correspondence Honduras 1867-8,* Fletcher to Committee, 19 June 1869, fiche 2131.

[16] Ibid., Giolma to Fletcher, 16 June 1869, fiche 2131.

[17] *Gibraltar Chronicle,* Thursday 19 March 1863.

improvements were carried out in the quarters of the troops, and by the preparation of an Order in Council for enforcing as far as practicable, corresponding improvements in the sanitary conditions of the dwellings of the civil population, and chiefly by the preparation of plans and estimates for a complete system of drainage, and for the better supply of water'.[18] At first a Sanitary Committee was appointed to oversee progress. This was done at a public meeeting of the rate-payers of Gibraltar on 16 June 1865 and amongst the appointments was that of George Alton, who became its secretary. However, Gibraltar was soon plunged into an outbreak of cholera which began in July 1865 and continued until the autumn. The statistics vary as to the number of deaths with the *Gibraltar Chronicle* reporting 575 and the official report, quoted by Benady, giving the death toll as 583.[19] According to Benady, three-quarters of the population suffered from diarrhoea which was described as being very bad and so, although the deaths were nowhere near as numerous as during earlier epidemics, the outbreak still considerably affected much of the population.

In his annual report Alton referred to the effects of the cholera outbreak.

> Every one who could fled from the death-stricken place. The mortality was in proportion to about 3,500 per day for London, so that the alarm of the population was not surprising. Many members of our congregation and several of our church were carried off with awful suddenness but we have reason to hope that not a few of them, in the hour of nature's agony, 'Beheld the Lamb of God which taketh away the sin of the world' ... One of our members Trumpet Major Falkner, Royal Artillery, who with two of his children were carried off within 36 hours, was a valuable and useful man, whose godly conduct had long been admired. His death was felt to be a public loss because of his activity in prosecuting many works of beneficence. He was also Superintendent of our Sabbath School.
>
> Owing to the cause named our congregations have been slightly fewer and there has also been a slight diminution in the church members. The schools also have suffered from the same causes, and there is a decrease of 42 children. Many of the children died during the epidemic and for three months the attendance was exceedingly small.
>
> It is a matter of great thankfulness that all the staff of the Mission have been preserved and are still earnestly prosecuting the work of the Lord.[20]

No doubt it was a great relief that all the remaining Alton children had survived. In the middle of the epidemic, the decision was taken by a draft Sanitary Order in Council to appoint Sanitary Commissioners for Gibraltar which resulted in a more formal body with greater powers than the Sanitary Committee. George Alton became its secretary. Plans went ahead to

---

[18] Ibid., Friday 21 February 1868.
[19] Benady, op. cit., p.92.
[20] *WMMS Europe Synod Minutes 1823-76*, Alton, report for 1865, dated 31 March 1866, fiche 18.

provide a new system of drainage works and a good supply of water.

This position gave Alton scope to use his many talents for the benefit of the community and no doubt he was motivated to do so as a result of the terrible losses he and Amy had sustained. They, more than most, had every reason to want to see conditions in Gibraltar improved and perhaps this was Alton's way of turning personal tragedy into public good. The work was extensive and not always easy for, whereas there seems to have been agreement about the need for improvements, there was a corresponding concern about the cost which had largely to be raised from the rate-payers. A great deal of tact and diplomacy was needed to keep matters progressing.

Alton was, of course, due to leave Gibraltar in the summer of 1867 but it seems representation was made by the Sanitary Commissioners through the Governor for him to be allowed to stay longer. He referred to this in a letter of his own written in January 1867.

> Since my return to Gibraltar it has pleased God to open to me spheres of usefulness, and to make me a means of promoting the public good in a manner which I have not myself sought and to an extent I could not have anticipated. The influence which God has given me with all classes and all creeds of the community I have striven to employ with an earnest and constant aim to His glory for the religious, moral and social welfare of the place. My own advocacy and efforts have I believe contributed more than those of any other individual to the introduction and application of measures which are regarded by Her Majesty's Government and the inhabitants generally as a great blessing to Gibraltar, and I am told that there is a general concurrence in the feeling of gratitude to me on their accomplishment and an equally general desire that I should be permitted to remain for the present to assist in carrying them into full effect.
>
> You will believe that Methodism will have received the full advantage of any influence for good in this community which God has given me and from the frequent changes in the General Staff and among the Heads and other officers of the military and civil departments of the Government impressions will I trust have been carried from Gibraltar to different and distant places in every way favourable to Methodism.[21]

He ended by saying that he was willing to stay on if permission was granted and suggested that it would be helpful for him to visit England to discuss the situation.

By May 1867 Alton had still not heard from the Committee and was very anxious to know what its view was, so he decided to visit England. In his letter notifying the Committee of his intention, he wrote, 'I trust that my doing so will be for the interest of the station'.[22] Little information about his visit has survived, but it was agreed that Alton's appointment in Gibraltar should continue for another year. There are no further letters

---

[21] *WMMS Correspondence*, Alton to Committee, 30 January 1867, fiche 709, no.91.
[22] Ibid., Alton to Committee, 2 May 1867, fiche 709, no.94.

from him until December 1867, when he wrote in response to a request from the Committee to visit Portugal. The Committee had been in correspondence with a small group of Methodists at the Palhal mines near Oporto. They also had contacts in Oporto itself and had recently heard of other denominational work being carried out in Lisbon and Oporto. Alton was therefore asked to visit Lisbon, Palhal and Oporto as soon as possible to report on the prospects for Methodism there saying,

> Your previous acquaintance with some of the leading people at Lisbon renders it unnecessary that we should furnish you with an introduction to them, and our own people at Palhal and Oporto will not fail to receive you as a Methodist minister with affection and delight.[23]

Alton wrote back to say he could not go immediately as there was too much in Gibraltar in the run up to Christmas requiring his attention. He added that, 'We have had Kate Elizabeth very ill, but we hope she is now progressing favourably towards her usual strength'.[24] By February he had still not been able to go to Portugal and he reported on great alarm in Gibraltar as cholera had developed in Morocco and there was concern that it would affect Gibraltar too.

Alton was due to leave Gibraltar that summer but in January 1868, the Governor, now Lieutenant-General Sir Richard Airey, had written to the Committee to ask if he could stay longer. He felt that 'the zeal, tact and ability that he [Alton] has brought to the work have been of incalculable advantage to the community at large' and went on to say, 'The Sanitary Commissioners have made an earnest representation to me to endeavour if possible to retain his services until the completion of the drainage works, which will occupy probably a term of two years'.[25] The Commissioners were quite willing to pay his salary if Alton could be placed on the supplementary list and be replaced by someone else whom, no doubt, he would be able to assist with his valuable local experience.

The Committee wrote to Alton on 19 February to ask for his views. The Governor had been told that no decision could be made until September as the matter would have to be decided at Conference. Clearly it was not an easy decision particularly if Alton was to retire temporarily as a supernumerary. He was told,

> With us it is an unvarying principle that a Methodist Preacher should not leave the work of God for any other occupation whatever - it is for you to decide whether you can reconcile your mind to a partial severance from it, for the sake of an important object which may be supposed to come within the range of another profession.

---

[23] *WMMS Correspondence Outgoing*, Hoole to Alton, 20 November 1867, fiche 1213.
[24] *WMMS Correspondence*, Alton to Committee, 14 December 1867, fiche 709, no.95.
[25] Ibid., Airey to Committee, 31 January 1868, fiche 709, no.98.

The Committee and the Conference may probably give their consent, but there are individual members of the Conference who would disapprove of the arrangement, and whose views might operate to your discomfort in future contingencies.[26]

Alton's reply was delayed because Dr Alder suddenly suffered a stroke which paralysed his right side. By April, it was hoped he might make a partial recovery although he was still described as needing assistance with everything and was confined to bed, though he was 'cheerful and happy and able to converse for short periods'.[27] Poor Mrs Alder was reported at first to be unable to 'believe in the gravity and danger of the attack' and George and Amy were clearly finding the situation very difficult. Alton had actually met with Alder on the morning of the day he was taken ill to discuss his position. He reported, 'Our conversation that morning was entirely spiritual and so intensively so that he might have been conscious that he was giving me his last advice'.[28] As a result of this meeting Alton had resolved to leave the matter entirely in the hands of the Committee and Conference, but now reported that he and Amy 'from feelings both of duty and affection, are naturally desirous of remaining in Gibraltar'. However he did not want to leave the ministry and suggested 'should you deem it to be right to allow me to remain in Gibraltar I should wish to maintain my ministerial position and relations and to devote myself as fully as possible to the work of the Mission and with God's blessing I should be well able to perform a good portion of it.'[29] He felt that with the help of a young man all the work could be done, as it had once before.

In the event, this is what was decided. The Committee wrote to the Governor to inform him that Alton would be staying for at least one year. By this time, he was heavily involved in the work of the Sanitary Commissioners. On 20 February 1868 Lady Airey, the Governor's wife, laid the first stone of the works to form a new system of drainage and water supply. This 'very imposing spectacle' was well attended by troops and civilians. Lady Airey arrived at 3 o'clock in the afternoon and was received by the Sanitary Commissioners, including Alton, the Engineer and the Contractor of the Works. The Governor with his staff and several officers joined the party and inspected a glass bottle full of records and coins which was to be buried with the foundation stone. The party then moved to the site where George Alton, as Secretary, read an address prepared by the Sanitary Commissioners. A photograph was taken, a dedicatory prayer given by the civil chaplain, the Rev. Matthew Powley, and the foundation stone was laid. Lady Airey then replied to the address and the Governor offered his continuing support. The guards of honour presented arms, the

---

[26] *WMMS Correspondence Outgoing,* Hoole to Alton, 19 February 1868, fiche 1213.

[27] *WMMS Correspondence,* Alton to Committee, 18 April 1868, fiche 709, no.102.

[28] Ibid., Alton to Committee, 4 March 1868, fiche 710, no.105.

[29] Ibid., Alton to Committee, 18 April 1868, fiche 709, no.100.

band played the National Anthem, a salute of gunfire followed and events were concluded with 'three hearty British cheers'.

However, the account in the *Gibraltar Chronicle* was not without its more controversial comments. It referred to the building of a breakwater some years before to improve the defences of Gibraltar. The unforeseen result, however, was that it trapped the sewage of the town which could no longer be carried away to sea. Thus the 'work designed to keep enemies out of the fortress threatened also to poison friends within it'. This was the reason why the new drainage works were needed which were going to cost £35,000 of which £25,000 would have to be paid directly or indirectly by the tax-payers of Gibraltar, largely through local rates levied by the Sanitary Commissioners, which the writer felt was rather unfair. He also thought the annual mortality rate quoted by Alton was rather high and went on to say,

> It is perhaps however desirable that the inhabitants of Gibraltar should believe themselves in a very bad sanitary condition and place faith in their physicians the Sanitary Commissioners. People would not take the nasty stuff prescribed by the doctor unless they believed it was to make them better; and the inhabitants of Gibraltar will be reconciled to the distasteful dose offered to them in the shape of greatly increased municipal rates, just in proportion to their belief in the efficacy of the new machinery for improving the public health.[30]

It is clear from this and subsequent articles that the work of the Sanitary Commissioners was far from plain sailing and that all Alton's 'zeal, tact and ability' were needed. In July 1868 a public meeting was called as there were objections to a recent Sanitary Order in Council and the earlier one of 1865 which had paved the way for the works to provide better drainage in Gibraltar, a supply of salt water for sanitary purposes and a supply of good fresh water. In preparation for this meeting and in response to the reasons behind it, Alton wrote a long article for the *Gibraltar Chronicle* which appeared in two consecutive issues on 13 and 14 July. He did not attempt any arguments or offer any opinion but merely stated the history of the developments which had led to the Orders, making it clear that the people of Gibraltar had been fully informed and consulted all along the way. In separate articles within the same issues, the truth of what he was saying was acknowledged and it was agreed that Alton's 'detailed and careful exposition of the facts showed that abundant time was allowed for consideration before the Ordinances passed into law'.[31]

The public meeting still took place and representation was made to the Secretary of State for the Colonies for a revision of the Orders. So the controversies rumbled on but the work continued. In December 1868 Alton

---

[30] *Gibraltar Chronicle*, Friday 21 February 1868.
[31] Ibid., Tuesday 14 July 1868.

wrote another article on the proper principles of drainage to be adopted in parts of Britain, claiming that these were already being followed in Gibraltar. The editor commented,

> In the main we are inclined to agree with Mr Alton in his estimation of our drainage system, and indeed without some faith in the infallibility of the Sanitary Commissioners it would be hard to bear this yoke. We suppose that it is the inevitable lot of suffering humanity to pass though a stage of fiery probation before attaining a state of perfection: a reflection we commend to all readers inclined to grumble at impassable streets, blockaded roads, and more than usually offensive smells.[32]

By this time Alton had been joined by a new young assistant, Henry Richmond. He was born in 1844 to Methodist parents and educated at Taunton College where he was converted. In 1864 he offered for the ministry and was sent to West Africa. Although his health had been affected during his time in Africa, it does not seem to have greatly hindered his work in Gibraltar.

Alton was very busy and had been rather remiss in keeping in contact with the Missionary Committee, although Amy may have taken some messages with her as she and the children visited England at this time. Alton was told, 'We are always expecting to hear from you, but very rarely have that gratification. I hope that you will at least observe the rule of the Society and favour us with a letter or extract from your Journal or both once in three months'.[33] He had not yet had time to visit Portugal but the Committee now had direct contact with a growing work there for, in May 1868, a letter was received from James Cassels in Oporto who had been advised by William Brown to write to the Society.

Brown was born on 26 December 1821 and worked as a clerk for the Missionary Society in London. He was able to speak Spanish and had worked for many years with Spaniards visiting the port of London. He may well have spoken Portuguese too and had met Cassels, who had been brought up in Portugal, though both his parents were English and belonged to the Church of England. James, the manager of a dye works, was twenty-three years old in 1868 and was married to Elizabeth. From about September 1866, he had begun some Christian work amongst the Portuguese and by the end of 1867, he had gathered together a congregation of about 120. There had been some opposition and persecution but the law was more tolerant than in Spain and Cassels had taken legal advice about building a chapel. He was informed 'that although meetings in a private house are liable to be put down, yet that religious worship in a chapel without the exterior form of a Church but set apart for that purpose, and surrounded by a high wall like the English Churchyard in Oporto and

---

[32] Ibid., Wednesday 2 December 1868.
[33] *WMMS Correspondence Outgoing,* Hoole to Alton, 17 October 1868.

Lisbon, is allowed by law'.[34] He had therefore begun to build a chapel, which he wanted to place in the hands of the Missionary Society if a minister could be sent to work in Oporto and also in Palhal amongst the miners. Thomas Chegwin, a Cornish Methodist and captain of the Palhal Mines, had been sending subscriptions to the Missionary Society since 1860 and had formed a small class and Sunday school.

Perhaps because Alton had been unable to visit Portugal, Brown returned to Oporto in autumn 1868 and spent about a month there on an official visit for the Missionary Society. He sent a favourable report on the work and reported that the people were anxiously awaiting a decision about a minister. The Missionary Society's resources were limited and and so, for the time being, it was suggested that Alton should make an occasional visit, although clearly this would not be enough in the long term.

Meanwhile, there were developments in Spain too for in autumn 1868 yet another revolution took place bringing with it the likelihood of religious toleration. In Gibraltar, events were closely watched. Andrew Sutherland, the long-standing minister of St Andrew's church, had died suddenly in October 1867, and Alton had covered the work there from November to December. In September 1868 John Coventry was appointed and, in the same month, Alton and Richmond met with him, Cabrera, Alhama and Sanchez to discuss the situation in Spain. Cabrera was an agent of the Spanish Evangelisation Society and it was decided he would go immediately to Cádiz and also Seville where 'a number of persons so disposed might be called upon to prepare a petition to the Revolutionary Junta regarding authority to hold religious meetings.'[35]

Although Cabrera had not been officially sentenced to exile from Spain, at some stage he, Alhama and another man, Hernandez, met with General Prim, one of the leaders of the Revolution, at Algeciras who assured them that they were at liberty to return to Spain and preach there. Cabrera stayed in Seville and soon established services there. Alton sent Alhama home to Granada with some Bibles and 'instructions how to act as a good man and a Methodist among his friends there whilst furthering his own calling as a Hatter'.[36] Richmond reported that Alhama was 'available for any work our Committee might see fit to employ him in at the present juncture'.[37] Both Alton and Richmond had a high opinion of him and Alton gave him money for his fare to Granada and enough to live on for a few weeks, about £20 in all, but did not make any promises regarding future employment. Richmond later reported that 'Alhama had been sent into Málaga and Granada with several hundred Bibles and Testaments and that on his arrival in Granada a public reception was accorded him, and many tokens of

---

[34] *WMMS Correspondence,* Cassels to Committee, 21 May 1868, fiche 709, no.103.
[35] Ibid., Richmond to Committee, 3 October 1868, fiche 710, no.111.
[36] Ibid., Alton to Committee, 28 December 1868, fiche 711, no.118.
[37] Ibid., Richmond to Committee, 3 October 1868, fiche 710, no.111.

respect paid him by the Revolutionary Local Government'.[38] This is the last reference to Sanchez but he too probably returned to Spain. Ruet moved to Madrid and was preaching there by early 1869 and Antonio Soler, who had preached at the Presbyterian church in Gibraltar, went to Córdoba. Thus the Spanish exiles left the Rock leaving the Spanish work there much depleted. In fact it never recovered from their loss, and virtually dwindled away. In the meantime, Richmond planned an exploratory visit to Cádiz, Seville, Lisbon and Oporto.

The Committee responded quickly, pointing out to Alton that if these decisions had been taken at the expense of the Missionary Society there should have been some consultation first and stating,

> At present the Committee is not prepared to go to any expense on behalf of Spain. If ability is to regulate duty, our present circumstances shut us out from engaging in any new enterprise. If Mr Richmond has not already set out, we wish him not to make the proposed visits to Cádiz, Seville and Lisbon. We thought it might be of service and a comfort to our friends there if you would have visited Oporto. Mr Richmond can perform the various ministerial acts which are required but he is not qualified by a knowledge of the languages or by experience to furnish such a report as the Committee would have expected from you. At the same time it must be allowed that the exciting events which have recently occurred may furnish an apology for sudden and unauthorised proceedings. Madrid has been beside itself, but London and Gibraltar must retain their senses.[39]

Both the Missionary Society and the Bible Society responded to these events with caution. Hopes had been raised before and the problems, failures and expenses of the past were still remembered. The Bible Society was particularly anxious to be seen to respect Spanish law and the Missionary Society was in financial difficulty and unlikely to be able to respond.

However, both Societies were anxious to have information. The Bible Society wrote to several contacts in the area, including Alton, to ask for their views on the situation and extra supplies of scriptures were sent to Gibraltar, at Alton's request, in the hope of getting them into Spain. At the end of December, the Rev. J.G. Curie became the Bible Society's full-time Agent in Madrid and the Earl of Shaftesbury, President of the Bible Society, wrote to General Prim for permission to open a depot there and to circulate the scriptures. Curie met with him and presented the letter to him. Although personally in favour, Prim requested the Society to wait until after the Cortes had met and so, in November, Shaftesbury wrote to *The Times* to explain that the Society proposed

---

[38] *Minutes of Committee No 59, 1 June 1868 to 8 February 1869,* 19 October 1868, minute 40, p.227.

[39] *WMMS Correspondence Outgoing,* Hoole to Alton, 17 October 1868, fiche 1215.

... so to guard our action as not to embarrass the Government, and thereby imperil the ultimate attainments of the object we have in view. In this sense we shall await the assembling of the Cortes, who will give the national confirmation to the decree of the Provisional Government and, at the same time, define in clear and unmistakable language, the rights and limits of 'religious liberty'.[40]

The Missionary Committee was also anxious to hear Alton's views on the subject and wrote both to him and Richmond in the middle of December, rather disappointed not to have heard from either of them before. Alton replied by saying that he had not written earlier because of the difficulty in forming an opinion about what to do.

> I have had daily and nightly anxiety about the so called opening for the Gospel in Spain, and more particularly about the statements and doings of persons professedly interested in its proclamation and in its spread. Mr Richmond and myself have neglected no opportunity that we could prudently embrace for advancing the interests and objects of our own Society and of the British and Foreign Bible Society; but, I am quite sure, we could not safely ten days ago have placed our names to any satisfactory opinion on the openings for work or the manner of seizing them.
>
> I now have no doubt that the time has not yet come for the Committee to incur any serious expense in sending agents to Spain. After the assembly of the Cortes it may be different, if indeed they ever do assemble. Nothing could exceed the agitation of political parties and old factions, and there is too much reason to fear a military dictatorship and a state of siege throughout the nation. As things are going the horrors of Cádiz are likely to be repeated in many cities.
>
> In the meantime several agents belonging to the Spanish Evangelisation Society of Edinburgh and a similar Society in Paris are in Madrid, Seville and Málaga and some agents of the Plymouth Brethren are in there and other places. But they are doing very little so far as we can ascertain. For a few weeks immediately succeeding the revolutionary outbreak they addressed considerable numbers, but the crowds and the feelings and influences were almost wholly political, and they have dwindled almost to nothing.[41]

Richmond had just returned from a brief visit to Málaga and Granada on behalf of the Bible Society and had no doubt met Alhama and reported that there were 600 Protestants in Málaga. However, he agreed with Alton's views adding that he felt many who professed their keenness to evangelise were really only interested in the pay they would receive for doing so, and indeed a number of mistakes were made in these early days in employing

---

[40] *Gibraltar Chronicle,* Wednesday 25 November 1868, quoting the Earl of Shaftesbury's letter to *The Times,* 17 November 1868.
[41] *WMMS Correspondence,* Alton to Committee, 28 December 1868, fiche 711, no.118.

people who turned out to be unsuitable. Alton suggested that if the Committee wanted to do something for Spain, selecting and training Spaniards like Alhama who could be directed from Gibraltar, might be a way forward. They could earn some pay as colporteurs and could travel through Spain making the Gospel known as they went along. Some could work to form congregations. He also felt much could be done through circulating Christian literature particularly short tracts. He also wrote to the Bible Society suggesting Alhama as a suitable person to act as a superintendent of colporteurs under the direction of Curie, but shortly afterwards Richmond announced that Coventry had employed Alhama to engage and direct three colporteurs for the National Bible Society of Scotland which was by then also active in Spain.

The Missionary Committee did not authorise any action and in January 1869 Richmond reported, 'With regard to Spain and Spanish affairs we are still quietly waiting and watching and whilst we hope for good things to come believe that just now our strength is to sit still'.[42] In February 1869 the Cortes did meet and eventually discussed the question of religious liberty. Despite considerable opposition in some quarters, religious toleration was agreed in May 1869.

The Bible Society does not seem to have waited until the Cortes met as by this time Curie had travelled extensively throughout Spain, establishing depots and employing colporteurs. He had also opened a central depot in Madrid. However, finding scriptures for circulation was a problem because the law prohibiting the importation of Spanish books printed outside Spain was still in force. This considerably curtailed activity in Gibraltar but, by January, Curie had begun printing in Madrid. In the meantime, the scriptures Alton had printed in Madrid in the 1850s were available. They had actually been removed to Bayonne for safe-keeping but were now brought back into Spain and put into circulation which must have been of some satisfaction to the Altons. They certainly filled a gap at this time but, by now, the version of Valera was more popular, which was the version Alton had wanted to print all along.

Meanwhile the ordinary work of the Gibraltar Mission continued, with the usual fluctuations in the congregation as regiments came and went. However, Richmond did highlight one issue which was to be raised many times in the coming years. He wrote,

> One thing here is a greater drawback than perhaps it would be in almost any other place, that is the situation of our chapel, the ascent to which is very steep and the position such that it may be frequently passed by without observation. It is the opinion of many that if we but had a building on a level with and near the main street of the city we could depend upon having crowded congregations. Could we but get help in

---

[42] Ibid., Richmond to Committee, 12 January 1869, fiche 711, no.121.

this matter we might soon become a great power for good in this place.[43]

All this time the work in Oporto had been continuing. Although Richmond followed the instructions not to visit Cádiz, Seville and Lisbon, he had gone to Oporto, even though the Committee had wanted Alton to go. Here he opened and dedicated the chapel on Sunday 18 October 1868. He described it as 'neat and substantial' and capable of seating between 200 and 250 people.[44] It was situated at Vila Nova de Gaia, a suburb of Oporto. Richmond met with a small class consisting of James and Elizabeth Cassels and ten Portuguese. The following Sunday he gave out seventeen membership tickets and administered Holy Communion to twenty-four people including some Portuguese. He told Cassels that either he or Alton would visit every quarter. Cassels was grateful for this but still wanted a minister and wrote to the Committee to say that Richmond was just the kind of person they needed. He offered the chapel to the Missionary Society free of debt and guaranteed to provide an annual sum of £100 towards the cost of a minister. By then he had a small Sunday school with twenty children and three teachers and had begun a day school.

Richmond also spent two days at the Palhal Mines, situated some thirty-five miles from Oporto. Here he met Thomas Chegwin and his wife, preached to a very attentive congregation and talked to the Sunday school children about missionary work. Before he left Oporto Richmond promised that he would support their request for a minister, which he did in his report to the Missionary Society.

However, shortly after this visit, Cassels was arrested and charged with proselytising from the religion of the state. He was released on bail but in November he was tried, found guilty and sentenced to six years deportation. He appealed against this sentence but, in the meantime, felt it was best not to hold meetings with the Portuguese either at his home or the chapel. As the legal process dragged on for some time Alton and Richmond felt a visit of support should be made.

So, on 16 April 1869, Richmond sailed for Lisbon and spent nearly a fortnight in Oporto and a few days at Palhal. On 21 June 1869, Cassels' case was heard again and this time resulted in an acquittal. Cassels informed the Committee that he was cautiously continuing his work and pleaded for a minister to be sent.

Meanwhile, from Gibraltar, Alton had kept up a correspondence with Alhama and in May 1869 he reported that Alhama was free if the Committee wished to appoint him as an agent. The Committee did not take up this idea and this is the last reference to Alhama who continued his work and founded several churches. He died in Granada in 1892. Cabrera stayed

---

[43] Ibid.
[44] Ibid., (memorandum of a visit to Oporto and neighbourhood, October 1868. Richmond to Alton attached to Alton to Committee, 28 December 1868, fiche 711, no.118.

in Seville until 1874 when he went to Madrid. In 1880 the Spanish Reformed Episcopal Church was formed and Cabrera became its first bishop. He died in Madrid in May 1916. Ruet, who had begun preaching in Madrid early in 1869, continued his work there until his death which was reported in the Bible Society's report for 1879.

No new work in Spain was initiated from Gibraltar but William Brown was given leave of absence from his work as a clerk and sent on 'a visit of enquiry and observation to Barcelona'.[45] He arrived in February 1869 and soon reported that with patience a Mission could be established. In June he finally managed to obtain a suitable place for worship and before long had a small congregation and links with colporteurs. Spain remained in an unsettled state and Brown tried to keep some financial reserves for he stated, 'It would not be wise to remain without the means of removal in the present state of affairs'.[46] It seems that some oversight had been promised from Gibraltar for he wrote, 'I am glad of the prospect of obtaining tickets and pastoral oversight from Gibraltar until a better arrangement can be made'.[47]

Meanwhile staffing at Gibraltar had come under review. Richmond had only been appointed for a year and in May he wrote to the Committee about his next appointment. He asked for an English circuit as he did not feel his health was good enough to return to West Africa. He probably left Gibraltar in July although Alton had hoped that the Committee might appoint him as the superintendent of the station. He had reported on his popularity and usefulness and stated. 'The more I know of him, the more I am persuaded that it would be an advantage to Gibraltar if he could be continued as Superintendent' but the Committee had other plans and Alton was told that negotiations were under way for a supernumerary to take charge of Gibraltar and he was asked what he wanted to do.[48]

Alton asked the Committee to give him supernumerary status for the coming year so that he could stay in Gibraltar to continue his work with the Sanitary Commissioners. He was also extremely concerned about Dr Alder who had had several epileptic fits. Alton was told that the Committee was likely to agree to his request but was warned that there were people likely to oppose the plan at Conference and he was asked what he wanted to do if this happened. He did not want to leave the ministry but, knowing that representations were being made from Gibraltar, he decided to leave the matter in the hands of the Committee and Conference.

The Sanitary Commissioners had told the Governor that it was 'extremely desirable that Mr Alton's services should if possible be secured for another year'. So the Governor, Sir Richard Airey wrote to Earl

---

[45] *WMMS Correspondence Outgoing,* Hoole to Rule, 15 June 1869, fiche 1216.

[46] *WMMS Correspondence,* Brown to Committee, 23 August 1869, fiche 715, no.161.

[47] Ibid., Brown to Committee, 28 August 1869, fiche 715, no.162.

[48] Ibid., Alton to Committee, 25 June 1869, fiche 714, no.150.

Granville in England who in turn informed the Missionary Society that Airey 'regards it of the greatest importance that Mr Alton should be permitted to remain in Gibraltar for a further period of one year' knowing 'how much the successful prosecution of the measures in progress has been due to his intelligence and the interest he has taken in them from the commencement'.[49]

In the end both Conference and the Committee refused permission and Alton was told that he must choose between his secular appointment and the work of the ministry. Earl Granville was informed of the decision and told that the rules of Methodism did not allow ministers to undertake secular occupations so that even if Alton stayed in Gibraltar, he would be required to confine himself to the work of the ministry. As he had previously been allowed to do this work, a reply was immediately sent from Downing Street saying,

> Looking to the fact that Mr Alton has hitherto been permitted by the Committee of the Wesleyan Methodist Missionary Society to act as Secretary to the Sanitary Commission at Gibraltar, and that the Sanitary Works in progress will be greatly retarded should the Commission be deprived of Mr Alton's valuable experience in all the details connected with these measures, Lord Granville cannot but hope that Mr Alton's case may be allowed to form an exception to the general rule of the Society, and that the Committee will give way to the very urgent representations which have been made in favour of his retention at Gibraltar for another year.[50]

Despite this intervention at such a high level the decision remained unchanged, and so Alton prepared to leave Gibraltar to take up an appointment in Thirsk, and Richard Lyth and his family made their preparations to travel to the Rock.

---

[49] Ibid., Downing Street to Secretary of the WMMS, 30 June 1869, fiche 715, no.163.
[50] Ibid., Downing Street to Secretary of the WMMS, 20 August 1969, fiche 715, no.160.

CHAPTER 15   MARKING TIME IN GIBRALTAR
Developments in Oporto and Barcelona (1869-74)

Richard Burdsall Lyth was born in York in 1810 into a strong Methodist family. He was educated at a small private boarding school and, on his sixteenth birthday, he was apprenticed to a surgeon. After completing his apprenticeship he went to medical school in London, where he qualified and became a Member of the Royal College of Surgeons and a Licentiate of the Society of Apothecaries. However, in 1833, he told his parents of his conversion and, instead of taking up medical work, he became a preacher around Selby and Pocklington. In 1836 he was accepted by Conference, married Mary Ann Hardy and was appointed to Tonga. They later moved to Fiji where cannibalism was rife and living conditions very primitive indeed but, in time, a great work of evangelism swept through the islands and Lyth's medical skills were a big asset to missionary families as well as local people. The family returned to England in 1858 and after several brief appointments, Lyth was seconded to the Bible Society in 1861 to work on a translation of the Bible into Fijian. In 1865 this work was completed and he served one year in circuit and then returned to York as a supernumerary. In 1869 he again volunteered for missionary work and was sent to Gibraltar.

It is not clear why Lyth was appointed. Clearly he and his wife were a remarkable missionary couple, but Lyth had no knowledge of Spanish and little, if any, of military work. He was also the oldest person to have been sent, as he was then aged 59 and had been a supernumerary for three years. Perhaps no-one else could be found or perhaps his appointment was an indication that Gibraltar was no longer a priority. The last three annual reports of the Missionary Society had been brief, referring to the reduction of staff, the continuation of the ordinary work and the fact that it was mainly amongst the military and, although Spain was mentioned, it was more in the context of the failures of the past than the possibilities of the present and future. Indeed it may well be that the Missionary Society had even contemplated ending the work in Gibraltar for in an early letter Lyth wrote, 'Altogether as a garrison chaplaincy the work is too good to be abandoned now that it has been so long established. It is a power for good in this place'.[1]

Both Brown and Cassels were disappointed that Lyth did not call to see them on his way, but he sailed directly to Gibraltar on the steamship *Ripon* arriving on 17 September 1869 at two in the afternoon. With him was his wife, Mary Ann, and three grown-up daughters, Christiana, Martha Octavia and Margaret, the youngest, who was 16 years old. Their voyage had been stormy at first, preventing a service from being held on the Sunday, but

---

[1] *WMMS Correspondence,* Lyth to Committee, 8 October 1869, fiche 716, no.176.

otherwise all had gone well. The Altons had vacated the Mission House but were still in Gibraltar. The Alders were at San Roque as Dr Alder was not well. It had been his cherished hope that he might be able to return to England but he was not well enough to undertake the journey.

The Lyth daughters (photographed in Gibraltar) (With permission from Catharine Crawford)

However, it soon became clear that Alton was in a dilemma about what to do. He had written to the Committee in early September implying that he would leave Gibraltar not later than 1 October, but he had also reported that Alder had had another severe attack the fortnight before and added, 'You may imagine our anxiety at the thought of leaving him in his feeble condition'.[2] The Alders were about to celebrate their golden wedding anniversary. Alton did not discuss his decision with Lyth but the latter reported, 'In all matters relating to the Missionary work here, Mr A. has been most frank and communicative, and has made my introduction to the place and people of all ranks all that could be desired.'[3] He had been sent a telegram to ask what Alton had decided but he was unable to tell the Committee, saying,

> It is no secret that a liberal offer has been made by the authorities here to retain Mr Alton's services which the new Waterworks now in active preparation render (in their opinion) essential to their success ... The little that has passed between Mr Alton and myself in reference to his intention is as I have already stated in the direction of his taking his English appointment, but there are at present I perceive hindrances in his way that occasion delay. These hindrances arise from his connexion with the Sanitary Commissioners and the important services he has been able to render them, services that they have no other man to undertake. Dr Alder's infirm state of health has been another hindrance in his way.[4]

A brief note was sent to Alton from the Committee: 'Your non-arrival is placing <u>us</u> in a false position. The Conference supposed we were acting <u>bona fide</u>, in asking a Circuit for you and there are not wanting persons

---

[2] Ibid., Alton to Committee, 4 September 1869, fiche 715, no.164.
[3] Ibid., Lyth to Committee, 6 October 1869, fiche 716, no.175.
[4] Ibid., Lyth to Committee, fiche 716, no.175.

ready with unfriendly remarks. Do let me hear from you.'[5]

The Altons were in a very difficult situation and obviously agonised over the decision. Alton eventually resigned from the Sanitary Commissioners and they packed their bags. These were placed on board ship but, in the end, they simply could not leave and finally, on 27 November, Alton wrote to the Committee to say that he had written to the President of Conference resigning from the ministry. He wrote to Dr Elijah Hoole, with whom he usually corresponded and who was a personal friend of Dr Alder and a friend to the Altons too.

> It has been impossible for me to relinquish the important undertakings for the social and moral improvement and welfare of this population in which I have been employed without doing violence to the convictions of all classes and all creeds that I had been and still was Providentially called for the present to promote them in the manner in which I have hitherto laboured. Every effort to relieve myself from these duties has resulted in more decisive efforts to retain me. At the same time I cannot myself resist the conviction that my connexion with the Sanitary measures in progress has tended to improve and advance the moral and religious condition of the place in a more efficient manner and in a higher degree than any more directly and exclusively spiritual agency could be hoped to accomplish, and without which, any such agency in the future, as it has been in the past, must be necessarily almost nugatory. But it appears to be no longer possible for me to prosecute these objects, even for a limited time, without relinquishing, as I trust only temporarily, my official relation to the Conference.
>
> I should have been glad if the Conference could have acceded to the application for my remaining another year, and I believe it would have had the cordial esteem of the entire population, as well as of the Government, for conferring a public benefit in so doing, for whilst nothing was desired or asked on any ground personal to myself, almost everyone felt that I had done and was doing what no one else seemed called or able to do, and this, as I believe, not only without detriment to my ministerial office or relations but to the advantage of both in the eyes of the whole community. I cannot however take the step without expressing in the strongest and most heartfelt language I can command my grateful sense of the long and unvarying consideration and kindness of the Missionary Committee, and, above all, of the affectionate interest you have ever shewn in our welfare.
>
> I beg you to assure the Committee that I shall not feel less interest in their work in this place and shall endeavour to promote it so far as my ability and influence may extend ... I do not doubt that you my dear Dr Hoole, will kindly interpret the difficulties domestic as well as public, in which I have been placed during the past three months. After my appointment to Thirsk I was resolved to tear myself away at all risks, but repeatedly when our departure was mentioned Dr Alder had relapse after

---

[5] *WMMS Correspondence Outgoing,* Hoole to Alton, 14 October 1869, fiche 1217.

elapse, and some of them of a very serious nature, so that it became evident that our removal would in all human probability occasion his death.[6]

It does seem a pity that Conference could not have spared the Altons the anguish they clearly experienced in arriving at their decision. Lyth regretted the decision Alton had made but, although he did not really approve of it, he did seem to understand it. He wrote,

> I know Mr Alton well, he has spoken fully and freely to me on these matters, I have observed the difficulty of his position, and can easily conclude how, from his point of view, he should adopt the course he has, as providential.
> With regard to my own line of action toward Mr Alton, his altered position has not made the slightest difference. His deportment and that of his family toward ourselves and Methodism is unaltered. His character in the community stands deservedly high. As a preacher and a Methodist he is looked upon as before. So that, until authoritatively forbidden so to do, I shall heretofore avail myself of his services, always cheerfully rendered.[7]

Richard Burdsall Lyth
(With permission from Catharine Crawford)

Mary Ann Lyth
(With permission from Catharine Crawford)

So the Lyths settled into their new appointment. Most evenings were taken up with meetings. There was a small class meeting on a Monday which was growing and a young people's class had been started. A weeknight service was held on Wednesdays with a Bible class on Thursdays and a prayer meeting every Friday. Congregations were good and Lyth reported that he had visited the military hospital and generally

---

[6] *WMMS Correspondence,* Alton to Committee, 27 November 1869, fiche 717, no.190.
[7] Ibid., Lyth to Committee, 24 December 1869, fiche 718, no.193.

found ready access to patients, but he used 'caution in speaking to such as are not Wesleyans'.[8] However, he soon found this to be unnecessary and reported,

> At the Military Hospital I am always kindly received, and go in and out among patients of all religious persuasions without let or hindrance. In this sphere of labour I have many precious opportunities afforded to sow the seed and implore God's blessing upon it, and his mercy to the afflicted both in mind and body.[9]

One cannot help wondering if this change had anything to do with Methodism's improved status in the community as a result of Alton's work. Lyth also commented on the site of the chapel saying it was 'an unfortunate one being too far removed from the population and too high up the Rock for the convenient access by many that would otherwise attend our services'.[10] However, he was impressed with the schools which had nearly 300 pupils. The schoolmaster, David Gilchrist, kept them 'in very efficient working order' and also ran a night school. Lyth said, 'Mr Gilchrist is a very energetic man, has succeeded well in tuition, and is acknowledged to be doing a good work'.[11] All the children were given religious instruction and Gilchrist took a service on Sunday mornings in Spanish which was attended by about thirty of them. It was no longer the rule that the children had to attend Sunday worship but it is not clear when this change came about. There is no mention of any regular Spanish preaching other than this and it is not clear whether any adults attended Gilchrist's services.

Towards the end of 1869, a deputation from the Bible Society consisting of the Rev. S.B. Bergne and Mr Knolleke was sent to Spain 'to promote the proper management as well as the success and extension of the Society's operations in that country'.[12] By then Curie had established eighty-six sub-depots around the country and opened a new and bigger depot in Madrid. There was still considerable opposition particularly from the priests and on occasion books were seized and destroyed. In Madrid the deputation described a congregation of 800 and later in Seville discovered that the church building capable of seating 400 was no longer big enough. Printing had continued virtually non-stop with new and better editions following the rather hastily produced first copies. However, the deputation was concerned about Curie's 'sadly defective manner' in dealing with his large task and eventually Richard Corfield, who had previously worked in South America and spoke Spanish, took over.[13]

---

[8] Ibid., Lyth to Committee, 8 October 1869, fiche 716, no.176.

[9] Ibid., Lyth to Committee, 7 December 1869, fiche 717, no.191.

[10] Ibid., Lyth to Committee, 8 October 1869, fiche 716, no.176.

[11] Ibid.

[12] *Minutes of Committee No.60, 15 February 1869 to 4 October 1869,* 20 September 1869, minute 13, p.406.

[13] Ibid., *No.61, 18 October 1869 to 9 May 1870,* 13 December 1869, minute 9, p.108.

The deputation also visited Gibraltar 'to infuse fresh life into the Auxiliary' there.[14]   Of course Gibraltar was no longer of strategic importance for getting scriptures into Spain where they could now be freely circulated and were openly being printed.   However, the Committee in Gibraltar was revived, with the aim of circulating scriptures there more widely and it was suggested that a colporteur should be engaged to help in this work.   Lyth was part of the Committee but it was the Rev. John Coventry who became its Secretary.   However, Coventry soon became ill and found his other duties too pressing to continue as Secretary and a Colonel Bent took over for a time.   A colporteur, Miranda, was appointed but the appointment does not seem to have lasted long.   In early 1871 Coventry once again took over as Secretary.

At the beginning of 1870, William Boyce, one of the Secretaries of the Missionary Society, also visited Gibraltar.   Although this was the first Secretarial visit to the Rock, no details of the visit or the reason for it have survived.   It clearly was appreciated and may have been undertaken as part of the thinking about Gibraltar's future.   It seems to have resulted in permission to draw money to pay off some of the debt still existing on the South Estate which Rule had so rashly purchased.   At the end of the year, Lyth asked for permission to settle the debt and, in February 1872 he reported, 'I have paid off the whole of the South Estate' and so at long last the matter was finally settled.[15]

Lyth and Alton settled into their different jobs.   Soon Lyth received a bill for £33 for laying the branch drain connecting the Mission premises to the main sewer, which he felt was rather expensive.   There was another charge, in June 1870, for laying on water to the Mission House and chapel which shows just how far the work undertaken by the Sanitary Commissioners had progressed.

Meanwhile, Cassels had continued his work in Portugal and was disappointed that it was not yet possible to send a minister.   He therefore asked if he could be recognised as a local preacher, and Lyth was asked to visit and assess him.   Whilst he was away, the Committee suggested that Alton took over the work in Gibraltar which does indicate some sympathy for his situation.

Lyth arrived in Oporto on 2 May 1870 and was met at the station by Cassels.   There were about a hundred Portuguese attending the chapel with fifteen children in the Sunday school.   Another preaching place had recently been rented in the city.   Lyth was impressed with Cassels and did approve him as a local preacher.

Lyth went on to Palhal where he visited several English residents and preached twice to small but attentive congregations which contained nearly all those working in the mines.   The children were taught in Sunday school

---

[14] *Reports of the BFBS,* 1870, p.118.
[15] *WMMS Correspondence,* Lyth to Committee, 22 February 1872, fiche 729, no.121.

by Chegwin but, as there seemed little prospect of working with the Portuguese there, Lyth made few comments about the place.

He felt rather differently about Linares in Spain, which he visited on his way back to Gibraltar. This he described as the centre of lead mining in Spain and here he felt there was a real opportunity to work amongst both the Cornish and the Spanish miners. He spent five days there and preached three times to 'small congregations of Methodist people and Methodist sympathisers.' He reported that 'Charles Tonkin, Esq., Director of several of the Mining Companies, himself and wife Methodists at heart, is deeply concerned that the way may be made plain for the support of a minister amongst them; his services to be divided between the English and Spanish.'[16]

Lyth returned to Gibraltar on 21 May and found all well there. In a brief note later, he gave details of the cost of his journey. 'My expenses, three voyages six journeys by rail, three thorough soakings in salt water $110 ... What am I to do for money? A man in Gibraltar without money! Please say!'[17] Presumably the Committee sent him some!

Meanwhile Brown had been continuing his work in Barcelona but there was no contact with Gibraltar. It was really too far away to provide the pastoral oversight that had been suggested. However, in February William Boyce had visited him and suggested that he should have some help but the Committee was unable to find a suitable person and Brown was left to work alone. However, he soon started a school and, by the end of 1870, there were eighty-two children in it and he was even more desperate for help.

The Missionary Society had only limited resources and now had requests for a minister from Barcelona, Oporto and Linares in this part of the world alone. It could not meet all these demands as the report for 1870 made clear: 'Much do we lament our inability to enter upon the openings in Spain. By an annual outlay of about £5,000, several important positions might be occupied by Evangelical Ministers, and good Schools established ... It is most humiliating to us that we cannot take our proper position in this work'.[18]

The work in Gibraltar continued much as usual and in August 1870 Lyth reported that the Mediterranean and Channel Fleets had both been in Gibraltar for a few days. He had written to the Admiral stating Methodist hours of worship with the result that the chapel had been crowded with Wesleyan soldiers and sailors. The soldiers held a tea meeting for the sailors and they also held a lovefeast. Alton and the Presbyterians had joined with them. In this letter Lyth also mentioned that 'No information

---

[16] Ibid., Lyth to Committee, 31 May 1870, fiche 719, no 12.
[17] Ibid., Lyth to Committee, 4 June 1870, fiche 719, no.14.
[18] *WMMS Reports,* vol. xviii, 1870-2, 1870, p.20.

from Conference as respects Mr A's present status has been received'.[19]

Presumably Alton had made some application to Conference but it is not clear exactly what decision was made, as part of Alton's own letter on the subject is too difficult to read. However, he was pleased with the situation and thanked the Committee and Conference for their kindness to him and it seems he was to remain in Gibraltar for another year. He had probably been reinstated into the ministry but without an official position. He did not see his work with the Sanitary Commissioners as a permanent post and said, 'I can sincerely say that my heart is fully in the work of ministry and my greatest happiness is in preaching the Word.'[20]

The work in Portugal continued to grow and in early November 1870 Cassels asked Lyth to visit so that they could have a communion service. Lyth left Alton to oversee the work in Gibraltar and travelled through Spain visiting Linares first. He spent two Sundays there and reported the work to be prospering and that 'hundreds of Spaniards are prepared to listen to the word of truth'.[21]

After leaving Linares, Lyth spent thirty-six hours travelling on to Oporto mostly by ship. He reported, 'I arrived twelve hours earlier than my notice, and without knowing either Spanish or Portuguese found myself, by the good providence of God, passport and all, safely lodged at Mr Cassels, on the morning of the 23rd [November 1870] before coffee was ready'. James was in England but Elizabeth was at home. A preparatory service was held on the Friday evening and a communion service on the Sunday afternoon with ten English people and over twenty Portuguese present. Lyth found it an inspiring occasion and said about the whole work there, 'This is the Lord's doing, it is marvellous in our eyes'. The day after he left some 300 attended the weeknight service and in his report Lyth urged the Missionary Society to act and go into both Spain and Portugal. He ended by saying, 'The land is before you, (it is a goodly land) go up and procure it, for we are well able'.[22]

This time the Society did act and appointed the Rev. Robert Hawkey Moreton to Oporto. He spoke Spanish and had previously offered for the work in Spain. He arrived there on 17 February 1871. Cassels was, of course, delighted but the wider response to the appointment was mixed. Alton wrote, 'I am glad to see you have sent Mr Moreton to Oporto. I wish you had sent Mr Richmond', who had previously expressed his willingness to go.[23] Brown said, 'I think he would have done better here'.[24] He was desperate for help and was doing all he could to establish and expand the

---

[19] *WMMS Correspondence,* Lyth to Committee, 26 August 1870, fiche 720, no.24.

[20] Ibid., Alton to Committee, 2 September 1870, fiche 720. no. 25.

[21] Ibid., Lyth to Committee, 13 December 1870, fiche 722, no.43.

[22] Ibid., Lyth to Committee, 13 December 1870, fiche 722, no. 43.

[23] Ibid., Alton to Committee, 1 April 1871, fiche 724, no.67.

[24] Ibid., Brown to Committee, 7 February 1871, fiche 723, no.56.

work both in Barcelona and its suburbs.

In May, Brown left Barcelona to visit England. He travelled by way of Gibraltar. Lyth commented briefly on his visit there saying, 'We are glad to hear of the progress in Barcelona' but went on to press the case for Linares which he felt was 'the place for the first missionary to Spain, thoroughly open, central and convenient for visiting other parts of the country.'[25] He added, 'Mr Alton thinks with me that Linares is the place for a Missionary. I have perhaps said enough - only one word more - Methodism is the thing for Spain'.

Brown travelled back to Barcelona via Portugal where he spent a few days in Oporto. He wrote,

> The Rev. Mr Moreton I found in his study, engaged with his Portuguese teacher. He appeared to be glad to see me, but much to my amusement suggested that I should wash myself before he presented me to his wife. Sun-burnt and travel-stained, and with clothing rather adapted for work than show, I probably looked unpresentable in polite society, notwithstanding that I had done my best to make myself decent. His young wife seems to be a delicate plant to whom the climes of Eden are more fitted than the fierce blasts and scorching heats of the Peninsula.[26]

Brown went on to say, 'On all hands they have won favour', and he reported that Moreton was already preaching well in Portuguese as he did also in Spanish and English.

From this time on, the work in Portugal developed separately from that in Gibraltar. Moreton devoted the rest of his life to Portugal and gradually saw the church there grow and develop, despite many difficulties and a great deal of opposition. He died on 4 March 1917 and was buried in the British cemetery in Oporto.

In the end James Cassels did not stay within Methodism. In 1880, he left to join the Lusitanian Episcopal Church. He kept on the work at the Vila Nova chapel following an agreement with the Committee which had never taken over ownership of it. In fact, Cassels paid £200 for the privilege of retaining it and relationships with the Methodists seem to have remained amicable once the separation had taken place. At some stage he must have been ordained as the Bible Society's report of 1896 refers to the Rev. James Cassels.

Many other ministers followed, some British and some Portuguese and the work developed in a variety of ways. In 1996 the church became autonomous under its first Bishop, Ireneu Cunha, who has since been succeeded by Sifredo Teixeira.

Meanwhile, in Gibraltar, things had continued much as usual. On 9 December 1870 Lyth memorialised the Government for a renewal of the

---

[25] Ibid., Lyth to Committee, 16 May 1871, fiches 724/5, no.75.
[26] Ibid., Brown to Committee, 30 June 1871, fiche 725, no.77.

lease which was due to expire in a few weeks time. He asked for the unoccupied garden ground alongside to be included. He did not expect any trouble with this. Alton's standing in the community meant that Methodism was no longer in the vulnerable position it had been at the time of the previous application.

In January 1871 Lyth reported that the weather had been unusually cold but services were better attended, meetings were improving and several men had been converted. Alton preached occasionally. Dr Alder was becoming more infirm and in April Alton reported 'in addition to all his previous suffering I fear that he has become the subject of chronic dementia'.[27] That same month Lyth told the Committee, 'Gibraltar is now remarkably healthy - thanks to sanitary improvements'. He went on to say, 'Mr Alton receives £700 per annum for his services: have you an English circuit for him with equal prospects? No doubt from a worldly standpoint he deserves it all for he is the bond and mainspring of the whole - but the ministry of the water of life is an infinitely nobler calling'.[28]

However, by June 1871, Lyth reported smallpox to have broken out in Gibraltar and also some 'cases of a malignant type' which had resulted in several deaths.[29] In 1868 a compulsory vaccination ordinance had become law but, even so, between 29 April and 30 August 1871 there were 204 cases of smallpox with thirty-two deaths.[30] Lyth himself was not well and he and his wife went to San Roque for a few days. In August he reported two of his daughters had gone to Tangier for a week on account of their health. Alton too was not well but planned to visit England in order to attend Conference. He wanted to be restored fully to the work either in a home circuit or as a supernumerary. Lyth suggested that if his health meant he had to have a supernumerary post then what better place than Gibraltar. He felt that this would be 'a pleasure and an advantage to us' but 'of course this means a total separation from his present office of Secretary to the Sanitary Commissioners'.[31]

Alton stayed some time in England and was appointed to Gibraltar as a supernumerary. However, he was allowed to continue some work with the Sanitary Commissioners. One wonders what had changed and why Conference could not have agreed to this in the first place. Lyth wrote, 'The case being an anomalous one - a Supernumerary in business - some instructions for my guidance seem necessary', but no account of any instructions has survived.[32] Lyth was by now also a little concerned about the lease which had still not been renewed but he hoped Alton might help

---

[27] Ibid., Alton to Committee, 1 April 1871, fiche 724, no.67.
[28] Ibid., Lyth to Committee, 15 April 1871, fiche 724, no.70.
[29] Ibid., Lyth to Committee, 1 June 1871, fiche 725, no.76.
[30] Benady, op. cit., pp.93-5.
[31] *WMMS Correspondence,* Lyth to Committee, 14 July 1871, fiche 725, no.79.
[32] Ibid., Lyth to Committee, 4 October 1871, fiche 727, no.89.

with this.

During this time, Brown had continued his work in Barcelona, despite fierce opposition from the priests and the unsettled state of the country. In July 1871 he opened a third school so that he had three school houses and three preaching places, which meant preaching eight times a week. He reported, 'My feet are sore with walking, and my mind and body wearied' but he was not tempted to give up.[33] By August he had 310 pupils in the three schools, most of whom also attended worship.

In September 1871, Brown also visited Mahon in response to an invitation from a Francisco Tudury who had built up a school and congregation there and wanted Brown to take it over. The Committee did not agree because of the cost but Brown decided to start work there himself, using staff from the Barcelona schools. By this time, he also had three local preachers in training. He went to England first, where he was apparently told that a minister would be appointed, and in May 1872, he returned to Mahon to begin work there.

Back in Gibraltar, in spring 1872, Lyth and his wife, with one daughter, had gone to Tangier 'to fortify ourselves for the hot season' and were still healthy in the summer when congregations were reported to be keeping up well.[34] By July Alton had finished working for the Sanitary Commissioners and asked for an appointment in England. By then he had received the news that Dr Hoole had died, which greatly upset him perhaps because he had hoped to see him soon. He told the Committee; 'No event in my ministerial life has affected me so much as the death of dear Dr Hoole whom I revered and loved so much'.[35]

Alton was appointed to Dundee but the family's departure was delayed because Frank developed scarlet fever. Thankfully he made a good recovery and the family finally left Gibraltar for good on 22 September 1872, travelling on the *Kedar* bound for Liverpool. Lyth wrote, 'Mr Alton carries with him the respect of many and those the more respectable and leading members of the community. As regards myself I shall feel his loss. The departure of himself and family will occasion a serious blank in the small circle of our friends to us all. Dr and Mrs Alder feel their removal most acutely.'[36]

There is no account of how the church marked the occasion but the following year, when Lyth intimated that he was contemplating leaving, Gilchrist and others wrote to the Missionary Committee to express their 'earnest desires and wishes for the re-appointment of the Rev. Mr Alton'.[37]

---

[33] Ibid., Brown to Committee, 14 July 1871, fiche 725, no.78.

[34] Ibid., Lyth to Committee, 21 May 1872, fiche 730 no.134 and 25 July 1872, fiche 731, no.147.

[35] Ibid., Alton to Committee, 31 July 1872, fiche 731, no.148.

[36] Ibid., Lyth to Committee, 23 September 1872, fiche 732, no.156.

[37] Ibid., Gilchrist and others to Committee, 24 December 1873, fiche 736, no.51.

They thought that the Committee, from its knowledge of the work in Gibraltar, 'and of the special and high qualifications possessed by Mr Alton will feel with us that no better or more suitable appointment could be made'. Although Alton was not re-appointed, it is clear from this letter that his ministry had continued to be much appreciated by the church.

The wider community had said goodbye at a meeting on 12 September held in the Exchange Rooms 'for the purpose of presenting a testimonial to the Rev. George Alton, late Secretary to the Sanitary Commissioners, on the occasion of his retirement and departure from Gibraltar'. By this time a suitable successor had been found and the appointment of Captain Marillier was reported to have 'met almost universal approval'. Alton was presented with a silver inkstand in an oaken case bearing the arms of Gibraltar and duly inscribed by the merchants and landowners of the city 'In testimony of their esteem and respect'. The report in the *Gibraltar Chronicle* concluded with a tribute to Alton in the following words:

> There are few questions so 'vexed' in Gibraltar as those which relate to the Sanitary Commission, but there can be no doubt that great strides have been made here in sanitary reform, that an immense boon has been conferred upon the place by the provision of a supply of water, and that it needed more than ordinary ability, energy, and perseverance to bring these enterprises to a successful issue. These qualities are most certainly combined in Mr Alton, on whom fell by far the chiefest portion of the labours involved in carrying out undertakings, the importance of which as a whole is but too often lost sight of in consequence of the prominence given to dissensions as to their details. But all, be their opinions what they may, must unite in bearing testimony to the indefatigable industry with which Mr Alton has devoted himself for some years past to the great work of sanitary reform in Gibraltar, and in future years, when the advantages of the work will be more highly appreciated than they are now, his share in it will be had in remembrance and ungrudgingly recognised.[38]

However, although considerable progress had been made, there was still a shortage of good water on the Rock. Eventually water catchments were built and reservoirs constructed within the Rock itself which were ultimately capable of storing sixteen million gallons of water. Even so water shortages still occurred and well into the twentieth century tankers had, on occasion, to bring water out from Britain. In recent years, the water catchments have become obsolete and have been removed. Desalination plants now provide water for Gibraltar so successfully that shortage of water is at last no longer a problem on the Rock.

In 1872, the Alton's long connection with Gibraltar had finally come to an end. The cost to George and Amy had been very high and the health of

---

[38] *Gibraltar Chronicle,* Friday 13 September 1872.

both had been affected by their many trials and tribulations. They left behind the graves of seven of their children and Amy's frail elderly parents. The church had benefited considerably from their ministry but perhaps their greatest achievement was in bringing Methodism out from the shadows into the forefront of Gibraltar's life. Alton was the first Methodist minister to become a respected and valued colleague among the leading members of the community. It is always frustrating that so little information has survived about the role of the missionaries wives. Amy Alton must have been as remarkable a person as her husband, willing to support him in his work both in Gibraltar and Spain, and no doubt taking a leading role in the work with the women of the congregation. She died on 21 December 1877 in Carlisle. News of her death reached Gibraltar and was regarded as important enough to be reported in the *Gibraltar Chronicle* which also stated, 'Mr Alton and his family are well-known in this city where he has many attached friends who will receive with regret and sympathy the above sad notification'.[39] Alton himself had several more appointments and died on 17 July 1887 in the house of his son near Derby. He was 64 years old. He had contributed much to the work in Spain too, despite having to withdraw from the country because of the repressive laws. His revision work on Valera's translation of the Bible was used by the Bible Society in its later editions and he was responsible for circulating thousands of scriptures in Spain. However, the extent of his contribution to the work there will probably never be fully known or appreciated as so much was done in secret. His obituary described him as a man 'endowed with rare gifts' whose 'life was a witness to his whole-hearted devotion to his work'.[40] This was particularly true in Gibraltar where he showed that his work for the community was just as important a part of his Christian witness as his missionary activities, which probably aided the Methodist cause there more than anything else.

The Rock - Eastern side showing the water catchments
(From the collection of J. Richard Jackson)

---

[39] Ibid.,Thursday 3 January 1878.
[40] *Minutes of the Methodist Conference,* 1887, p.34.

The Alders must have felt the Altons' departure keenly. Dr Alder had wanted to return to England but was never well enough to undertake the journey. He died in Gibraltar on 31 December 1873 at the age of 77. His funeral took place the following afternoon at the Cathedral and he was buried in the same cemetery as his seven grandchildren but not in the Methodist part of it. What happened to Mrs Alder is not known; perhaps she returned to England to be reunited with her family.

Soon after the Altons departed, an important issue arose connected with the lease on the Methodist premises. Lyth suggested that the Committee should confer with Alton who 'can supply all requisite information, and no other is so able to do this, or prepared to offer timely suggestions'.[41] The *Gibraltar Chronicle* had printed information about a change in the way Church property was to be held and a sum of money was to be divided among the Anglican and Roman Catholic Churches.[42] In a private conversation, Lyth was given to understand that, as Methodism had merely asked for a renewal of their lease, nothing else would be done for them and that any further representation needed to be made in England. Lyth expressed his own personal opinion 'that the present is a rare opportunity afforded us for placing this Mission and its property on a safe and firm foundation that may not soon if ever occur again' and urged the Committee to action.[43]

The lease was renewed for a period of twenty-one years in November 1872, but the Missionary Society then applied to the Secretary of State for a grant in perpetuity and in May 1873, Lyth was informed that this had been agreed. The grant included the adjoining garden ground, on condition that no buildings were erected there, and the whole property was subject to resumption if required for the defence of the garrison. It is doubtful if any of the money mentioned in the *Gibraltar Chronicle* was given to Methodism, but nevertheless Lyth was delighted and felt, 'the whole being granted to the Society in perpetuity for Mission purposes ... places Methodism here in a most favourable position', especially as rents had been rapidly rising. He added, 'I feel thankful to God to have seen the accomplishment in my time and to leave it unembarrassed to my successor'.[44] One wonders how much Alton's standing in the community had contributed to this change in Methodist fortunes.

Meanwhile, in early 1873, repairs had been made to the Mission premises which had thus been put into good order. Lyth wrote,

> The school Rooms under the Chapel are where all our social means of grace are held, also our Sunday School. Every window had to be taken out and renovated also new window sills in all. A new door was put in a

---

[41] *WMMS Correspondence,* Lyth to Committee, 30 September 1872, fiche 732, no.159.
[42] *Gibraltar Chronicle,* 18 September 1872 and 30 September 1872.
[43] *WMMS Correspondence,* Lyth to Committee, 10 October 1872, fiche 732, no.159.
[44] Ibid., Lyth to Committee, 28 October 1873, fiche 736, no.45.

door way, that had been without a door. Here we have our Mission Library, Bible and Tract depots. So now it is made a most cheerful and compatible Soldiers' Home.[45]

Now that Alton had left Gibraltar, Lyth was alone on the station, but the Committee soon appointed a young man to the Rock 'to prepare for the Spanish work and to enable Mr Lyth to visit the Spanish stations'.[46] Thomas Skelton Dyson arrived in Gibraltar on 31 March 1873, but very little is known about him. He had been accepted on trial at the previous Conference so this was his first appointment.

He went straight into lodgings and it was hoped that the person with whom he lodged would teach him Spanish. Lyth felt he would be suitable for the work to which he had been appointed and said, 'He seems good, and able, and willing and ready,' adding 'to hear another voice than my own in the pulpit is a relief, and will I trust prove, through the supply of the Spirit, a blessing'.[47] No doubt he had been missing Alton's help and support. By this time, Lyth had written to Brown about visiting him but told the Committee that 'The present time, in the existing state of Spain and notably that of Barcelona, does not appear opportune. So I watch and wait for the right opportunity and your instructions'.[48] A Carlist rebellion was the reason for his concern.

However, soon after writing this Lyth did leave for Barcelona travelling by steamer from Algeciras. Dyson was left in charge and in a long letter to the Committee he gave some details of the work. He reported that when the fleet was in they had a full house and that the 'sailors seem to bring with them a fire peculiarly their own and afford us a treat of real downright Methodist feeling'.[49] On other occasions they could not claim a full attendance but, nevertheless, congregations were 'highly encouraging both as to number and behaviour'. Backsliding was common with many temptations to lure the men away but there were frequent meetings for them during the week, class meetings, Bible study, prayer meetings and weeknight preaching so that 'by this plan of constantly affording means of grace we give to our schoolroom the character of a spiritual home and as such the soldiers regard it referring to it repeatedly in their letters from distant stations'. Dyson had been particularly struck by 'the absence of the civilian element'. Those who did attend were never more than hearers and were not seen at other meetings. He spoke highly of the Lyths but felt there was still room for more barrack and hospital visiting. Dyson had started to learn Spanish which he was enjoying and felt that when Lyth returned, they would be in a better position to decide on a future course of action.

[45] Ibid., Lyth to Committee, 21 February 1873, fiche 733, no.7.
[46] *WMMS Reports,* vol. xix, 1873-1875, 1873.
[47] *WMMS Correspondence,* Lyth to Committee, 5 April 1873, fiche 733, no.12.
[48] Ibid., Lyth to Committee, 5 April 1873, fiche 733, no.12.
[49] Ibid., Dyson to Committee, 29 April 1873, fiche 734, no.16.

Lyth may have been instructed to visit other places in Spain but, if so, this did not happen, perhaps because of the unsettled state of the country. He was away from Gibraltar for twenty-eight days but spent twenty of them in travelling. The rest were spent with Brown in Minorca and in Barcelona. Lyth left Barcelona on 14 May. Soon afterwards Brown visited England and so, no doubt, was able to discuss the situation at the Mission House though Lyth's report could not have arrived by then as it was dated 3 June and by 6 June Brown was back in Spain.

However, Lyth strongly recommended 'that a missionary be at once appointed to each place'.[50] By then, Brown had four schools in Minorca, one each for boys and girls in Mahon and Villa Carlos which was about half an hour's walk away. He also ran night schools and Sunday schools and held regular preaching in both places. Lyth had attended a week-night service at Villa Carlos when about 150 people were present and was assured that even more attended on Sundays.

Lyth gave fewer details of the work in Barcelona knowing that this was better known to the Committee but he did state, 'I am convinced that our Barcelona mission is a very important one'. He went on to say, 'With a minister of some experience and standing for Barcelona, a younger one for Port Mahon, and Mr Brown as pioneer, teacher of the language, inspector of schools and translator of religious literature, you would have, I think, all the help from England required for some time'. He ended his letter by saying, 'Glad that I took my journey into Spain, I leave her pressing need with you and our people, and pray that your long cherished hopes may be realised, prayers answered, and plans developed, by seeing Methodism taking her proper place in the evangelisation of Spain'.

In a second confidential letter which has survived, despite Lyth several times remarking that it was 'for the fire', he praised Brown and his work stating that 'Men of the same spirit and zeal and self-denial might do wonders'.[51] Lyth was obviously impressed with him and particularly mentioned the way in which he was training local people to work as teachers and preachers which had involved him in considerable translation work to enable them to benefit from English theological works.

However, even before these letters could have arrived, the Committee told Brown that Dyson would be sent to Mahon to work with him and a minister for Barcelona was promised as well.

Dyson left Gibraltar at the end of June taking with him a considerable number of books, which were probably surplus to the requirements of the local Bible Society Committee. In October 1871 Coventry had suggested opening a 'Bible and Book Depot, conjointly with the National Bible Society of Scotland and the Religious Tract Society, to which should be attached either a boat, by means of which the many ships constantly in the

---

[50] Ibid., Lyth to Committee, 3 June 1873, fiche 734, no.20.
[51] Ibid., Lyth to Committee, 4 June 1873, fiche 734, no.21.

harbour could be visited, or a Bible stand at the Mole, where the sailors land from the ships'.[52] Headquarters had responded with some hesitation but, after receiving a further letter from Coventry, agreed to contribute £100 to the expenses of the first year and also sent some scriptures to a Mrs McCarter, an elderly Methodist, who was in charge of the depot. The Committee also asked Corfield to supervise operations and so in February 1872 he visited Gibraltar. He met with the local Committee and Coventry's plan was adopted. A shop was rented in the main street and a Mr Stephen Fromou was employed to run it and act as colporteur, with his wife running the shop when he was out and about. Mrs McCarter's depot was to be discontinued when she had sold her stock. From this time on the local committee corresponded directly with Corfield in Madrid and so little information has survived in the Bible Society's central records, but the shop remained in Fromou's care for many years and numerous scriptures were sold, though rarely enough to cover costs.

Dyson arrived safely in Minorca and wrote to the Missionary Committee on 12 July to report this and also mentioned that Brown was thinking about extending the work to Palma. A few days later Brown returned to Barcelona to deal with matters there, leaving Dyson alone in Minorca. Then, in August, Brown was informed that Dyson was ill. He immediately returned to Minorca, after informing the Committee of developments and saying, 'You will see the absolute necessity of at once sending help to Barcelona'.[53] On 18 August Dyson had been thrown from his horse twice and, although he did not seem to have sustained any injury, he complained of a bad headache and a few days later was so weak he consented to see the doctor who felt his nervous system had sustained a severe shock. He soon became delirious and was later reported to have developed gastric fever. Brown was desperate for help and, having heard nothing from the Committee since his visit to England in May, he wrote repeatedly to Lyth thinking that the Committee might be regarding him as the Superintendent of the mission. Lyth referred the matter to London but did add, 'Apart from Dyson's illness Barcelona needs a man, who would be as safe there, Spanish affairs notwithstanding, as many others in the wide mission field'.[54]

Dyson died on 24 September 1873. He had had the best care that was available but the doctors do not seem to have really known what was wrong with him. Brown felt his death was due 'to injuries to his system received before his arrival, and a nervous temperament which unfitted him for this climate'.[55] It is not clear what evidence he had for this opinion. Brown may

---

[52] *Minutes of Committee No 64, 21 August 1871 to 18 March 1872,* 20 November 1871, minute 38, p.188.

[53] *WMMS Correspondence,* Brown to Committee, 1 September 1873, fiche 735, no.30.

[54] Ibid., Lyth to Committee, 8 September 1873, fiche 735, no.32.

[55] Ibid., Brown to Committee, 3 October 1873, fiche 736, no.39.

have expressed it because of his despair at losing the only help he had been sent, after such a short time, and because Dyson had not been the experienced minister so often requested. In fact, Dyson had already begun to preach in Spanish, had worked hard in the schools and had taught many new tunes to the children there.

He was buried the next day in the Protestant cemetery situated 'in a quiet nook in the hill-side on the other shore opposite to the village of Villa Carlos'. At 5 o'clock in the afternoon, the boys from the schools formed a procession, and the body in a coffin covered with the Union Jack was carried to the water-front. Four large boats conveyed about forty people to the cemetery where a service took place but not 'without many vexatious interferences' caused by Spanish law. According to Brown,

> The sea was rising, and night coming on apace; I therefore dismissed the friends and remained behind with the corpse, accompanied by four or five persons, until the Spanish officials should sanction the interment. The stars shone out brightly upon us in our lonely watch, and we were cheered by hearing the friends in the boats on their way to the opposite shore singing hymns to some of the beautiful tunes taught them by him whose tongue was now silent in death. At length we buried our dear brother, entered our boat, and in the glorious star-light of this beautiful climate, returned to our homes. Ah! God is present everywhere![56]

Brown continued to urge the Committee to send help without delay, saying, 'From the beginning I have recommended men of standing and age for this Mission, but I trust you will be divinely directed'.

Brown had also informed Lyth of Dyson's death but did not expect any help from Gibraltar in terms of manpower. However, Lyth could and did support him by writing to him and to the Committee. Lyth told the latter that the news had brought sorrow to many hearts in Gibraltar,

> Alas for the bereaved family and Mission that our dear Brother Dyson's course, so promising of results should have been suddenly terminated by death. My fear is lest our valuable agent Mr Brown should sink under his accumulated responsibilities and cares. My opinion is, that two men of experience are required for our work in Spain, which seems urgently to need Missionary help at the present moment.[57]

Finally, on 9 February 1874, Charles Greenway arrived in Barcelona, but he was not the experienced man requested. He was a single man starting his career in this his first post. Unfortunately his health soon began to deteriorate and in August he returned to England. Brown again pleaded for an experienced man in good health to be sent, as did Greenway himself who suggested 'a volunteer if possible' implying that he had not offered for

---

[56] Ibid., Brown to Committee, 3 October 1873, fiche 736, no.39.
[57] Ibid., Lyth to Committee, 8 October 1873, fiche 736, no.40.

the post.[58]

Unfortunately the Committee then sent John Ridgeway Griffin who had already experienced a break-down in health during his first appointment and was later described as only 'having somewhat recovered' when he was sent to Spain.[59] Difficulties in the relationship between Brown and Griffin developed too, possibly because of Brown's frustrations at not being sent the kind of person he so much needed and wanted. In the end, Griffin took over the work in Barcelona and Brown continued the work in Minorca, but no-one else was sent.

Meanwhile the work in Gibraltar continued. In October 1873 Lyth asked the Committee if he could return to England the following year. However, by mid-June he had still not heard from the Committee and wrote to say that he felt very inconvenienced by this. He went on to add,

> From our relations in Lincoln we learn that Mr Richmond when there on Deputation duty informed them that he was expecting to come via Gibraltar on his way to Spain and to wait here for a suitable opportunity to proceed on his journey. From this information I infer that you are probably practically responding to my request and intend to facilitate his coming here at an early date so as to meet my urgent request. Such an arrangement would be most satisfactory … Apart from these considerations my removal from this station is contemplated with sincere regret. The congregations have kept up well and the friends of all classes are kind. Some of the military officers have often dropped in of late and one officer's lady with her husband attends the service every Sabbath evening. And God gives his blessing.[60]

Lyth did eventually receive a letter from the Committee which contained the news that it was not thought advisable for him to serve in a circuit in England. He accepted this decision with equanimity and asked to be made a supernumerary instead. The last letter he wrote from Gibraltar, on 17 August, referred to his plan to leave a few days later 'under the full expectation that my successor will be here to take my place by the earliest opportunity'.[61] In fact his successor did not arrive until early October but it seems that the Rev. John Coventry, the Presbyterian minister, helped out.

Lyth and his family settled in York where he worked as a supernumerary minister. Here 'in pastoral work amongst the residents and soldiers he spent the quiet beautiful evening of a saintly life, respected and beloved of all. Of modest and retiring habits, his real value is only known to those who have seen the fruits of his Missionary life. He died on 27 February 1887, at the age of 77; and at the large gathering at his funeral, the

---

[58] Ibid., Greenway to Committee, 28 May 1874, fiche 738, no.84.
[59] *Minutes of the Methodist Conference,* 1876, pp.27-8.
[60] *WMMS Correspondence,* Lyth to Committee, 23 June 1874, fiche 739, second letter of same date attached to no.88.
[61] Ibid., Lyth to Committee, 17 August 1874, fiche 739, no.96.

Methodists mourned the loss of a true Christian, a faithful minister, and a missionary hero.'[62]

Mary Ann died a few years later in 1890. She had supported her husband throughout his long ministry, endured the dangers and privations of Fiji, and achieved a great deal in her own right. Few details of her contribution to the work in Gibraltar have survived - it was always taken for granted that the missionary's wife would support her husband by working alongside him, but little information about this work is ever given.

Lyth himself had done all that was asked of him in Gibraltar, visiting stations in Spain and Portugal despite the difficulties of travelling abroad at his age and without a knowledge of the languages. He kept the work going in Gibraltar but there is no sense of a dynamic and developing ministry and work. How much he relied on Alton during his years in Gibraltar is not clear, but it was a lonely station and one where preaching to the same congregation for months, even years, without a break could be very daunting. He had however shown that the Gibraltar station was a viable one and there was no further thought of abandoning it, but it was time for a younger man, with more energy to develop the work, to take over.

---

[62] *Minutes of the Methodist Conference,* 1887, p.22.

CHAPTER 16   OFFICIAL RECOGNITION OF THE WORK IN GIBRALTAR
A new school is built (1874-85)

It was Henry Richmond who had been appointed to Gibraltar though not Spain. Since leaving the Rock, he had been ordained, married, and had served in Ipswich and in Kingston, Jamaica. Henry and Anna Louisa arrived in Gibraltar at the beginning of October 1874 and on 19 December a daughter, Beatrice Maud, was born. Two other daughters were born during their stay, Florence Lilian and Ada Ruby.

Shortly after arriving Richmond wrote to the Committee saying that they had received

> … from the very small circle we have here a hearty welcome. On Sunday our congregations were large to an extent which surprised everybody, the chapel being nicely filled both morning and evening. The congregation in the morning being swelled by a number of men from the Fleet which happened to be here.
>
> The military changes which have just taken place have brought our Society proper to a very low ebb. At this moment we number about ten members including three or four who can never present themselves. [Presumably because of their military duties.] On Saturday next my wife and I propose to attend a kind of Levee at Government House so as to be in due relation with the authorities.[1]

The changes meant that many of the troops Richmond had previously known had left, but other Wesleyans arrived with the new troops so that the chapel was pretty full at parade services and the voluntary Sunday evening service was 'better attended than any other in the garrison'.[2] Not only Methodists worshipped with them for Richmond went on to say, 'The handful of persons who may be called our settled congregation are variously Episcopalians, Presbyterians, Independents, Baptists and others, not likely persons to be won to class-meetings though they all seem to get to relish old Methodist doctrine.' They had a small Sunday school and Richmond met the soldiers' children weekly for religious instruction. The week night activities were not so flourishing because of other meetings in the wider community.

At the beginning of February 1875, Richmond reported that he had been very unwell since his arrival. He had been able to get through his duties 'though sometimes in pain and weakness', but felt he had now turned the corner and hoped soon to be 'quite right again'.[3] By then, some 300 men of the military were attached to them so that their congregations were large

---

[1] *WMMS Correspondence*, Richmond to Committee, 15 October 1874, fiche 739, no.100.
[2] Ibid., Richmond to Committee, 16 December 1874, fiche 740, no.107.
[3] Ibid., Richmond to Committee, 2 February 1875, fiche 741, no.117.

and the previous Sunday a hundred men from the Channel Squadron had crowded out the chapel in addition. However, there were problems over naval attendance and Richmond was involved in a lengthy correspondence about this from 1874 to 1877, mostly with Rear-Admiral Beauchamp Seymour who was in charge of the Channel Squadron.

The regulations stated:

> Every facility consistent with the convenience of Her Majesty's Service and the state of the weather is to be afforded by officers in command to enable officers, seamen and others of the fleet of the Roman Catholic persuasion or being Presbyterians or other Protestants not members of the Church of England to attend divine worship according to the forms of their religion in floating chapels where such are established for that purpose or in chapels on shore.[4]

However, when the Channel Squadron was at Gibraltar, Wesleyans were not always allowed to come ashore to worship. Although naval duties had priority, at times the Roman Catholics had been allowed ashore when the Methodists had not. The authorities argued that, as the Methodist service was at 11.00 a.m., the men could not return on board in time for lunch at noon, but Richmond believed that being a little late for lunch was not really a problem and that this was an excuse. He could not easily change the time of morning worship because the military were marched to it. He could have arranged an earlier additional service at 9.30 a.m., but this would have caused him considerable extra work on Sundays and denied the sailors fellowship with others. In addition, the men from some ships were allowed to attend, when others were refused permission, which Richmond felt made a nonsense of the argument that the time of the service was the problem. There were about 300 Wesleyans in the Channel Squadron. At first Richmond thought the problems had been resolved but eventually, in October 1876, when he realised they were continuing, he referred the matter to the Committee. He wrote again in November and in December, when he had still not received a reply, he wrote more strongly saying,

> In view of the probable re-arrival in this port within a few days of the ships of the Channel Squadron I am in anxiety, perplexity and distress at having received no token from you. I am in my work more solitary than almost any man in the Connexion, in many respects my work is difficult and trying and I earnestly and most respectfully appeal to you as to whether upon a matter involving interests so important as my above quoted communications refer to I ought to be left in uncertainty and doubt.[5]

The October letter may not have arrived as it is not in the missionary

---

[4] Addenda to the Queen's Regulations of 1865, article 152, p.51.
[5] *WMMS Correspondence*, Richmond to Committee, 19 December 1876, fiche 755, no.95.

records, although a copy survives in the church archives. However, as Richmond had written in November as well, referring to the earlier letter, he was justified in being angry at not having received a reply. Nevertheless, he was censured both for his letter and for comments he made later to an official visitor to Gibraltar which upset him greatly. He clearly found the Gibraltar station a very lonely and isolated one and in addition often felt unsupported by the lack of correspondence from the Secretaries. He wrote in his defence;

> I think you would be yourself surprised if you knew how many times I have written to the Mission House without receiving any acknowledgement of my letters ... I do not wish to worry or to grieve you but you lay to my charge a lack of 'common courtesy' and I beg you to put yourself for a moment in my place and I think you will withdraw that.[6]

The slowness of response from the Missionary Secretaries was a problem throughout the mission field, but the Secretaries had very heavy workloads and the Rev. George Perks, to whom Richmond's letter was addressed, never received it for he was already dead when it was written. He had died suddenly at the age of 57 and perhaps overwork contributed to his early death.

The Missionary Society did contact the Admiralty. Richmond was not happy with the Admiralty's response and asked the Committee to raise the matter in the House of Commons. In January 1877 he reported that four ships of the Channel Squadron had been to Gibraltar and the men were marched from two of them to the 11 o'clock service which he felt proved his point. As there is no further correspondence on the subject, it is not clear if more representations were made or how the matter was finally resolved. The only other reference is in 1880 when Richmond reported that he held 'an extra Sunday morning service for our men in the ships'.[7]

The usual work had continued but Richmond had appealed for a more realistic consideration of the Christian duty of giving to the church, and pointed out that 'from the whole of this now large and most respectable congregation *not ten pounds a year* is contributed towards the supply of the Ministry in any way'.[8] He placed a collecting box at the back of the church every Sunday for contributions, instead of the previous monthly collection.

Membership in Gibraltar at this time was low, averaging about twenty for the years of Richmond's ministry but this does not give a realistic picture of the size of the church. There were some from non-Methodist backgrounds who regularly attended worship but did not want to be members and the soldiers, being a transient population, often did not

---

[6] Ibid., Richmond to Committee, 1 June 1877, fiche 756, no.4.
[7] Ibid., Richmond to Committee, 9 April 1880, fiche 773, no.19.
[8] Ibid., Richmond to Committee, circular attached to letter 16 March 1875, fiche 742, no. 129.

commit themselves to membership either. The Missionary Society's annual reports give the numbers of 'attendants on public worship' as well as membership. In Richmond's first two years the number was 600, rising to 900 in 1876 and 1,000 in 1877 and 1878 - the highest figure recorded at any time. Of course all soldiers had to be marched to a service and their presence did not therefore mean that they were committed to the denomination they had chosen, but the size of the congregation does give some indication of Richmond's pastoral workload. The Sunday school too gradually grew from forty in 1875 to 140 in 1879.

Almost as soon as he arrived, Richmond reported on the need for repairs to the chapel. He did not get a reply to his first two letters on the subject so in his third letter he wrote to say 'if I do not hear from you to the contrary in immediate reply to this I will proceed'.[9] He was learning fast! He had gathered together a small group of men to advise him, including Gilchrist the teacher, who was also the chapel steward. Repairs were carried out and Richmond drew only two-thirds of the £100 eventually promised by the Committee, raising the rest himself in Gibraltar.

In May 1876 Catherine Herbert, one of the oldest members, died at the age of 89. She was the last remaining creditor of the Methodist property which meant that her estate was owed nearly a thousand pounds after the deduction of a small legacy of just over £20 which she had left to the chapel. As her beneficiaries needed immediate payment, Richmond wrote in haste to the Committee and suggested that if a loan would be necessary it would be more advantageous to borrow the money in England as rates were high in Gibraltar. The Missionary Society was not at all happy when it received the first bills and a note is attached to some of them saying 'cannot accept these bills where supposed to get funds'![10] Richmond was then in trouble for having issued them which he could not understand. He wrote back referring to his letters on the subject and saying that he had given 'due and formal notice as to the amount being required by the estate'. He went on to say,

> To my communication I received no reply which I took to mean that my notice etc. was accepted and I was free to proceed with discretion. I would just note that I have never been accustomed to receive from the Mission House replies to my communications (and knowing the immense pressure of the Secretaries never expected or thought it necessary) and in all straightforward matters of business I have always taken silence to mean that there was no objection and I might proceed. In this present matter there was no course open but to draw the money as it was wanted.[11]

---

[9] Ibid., Richmond to Committee, 24 April 1875, fiche 743, no.145.
[10] Ibid., Richmond to Committee, 12 September 1876, (added note) fiche 752, no.69.
[11] Ibid., Richmond to Committee, 26 September 1876, fiche 753, no.76.

The Committee must have paid the bills one way or another and this meant that the chapel was at long last free of debt.

Throughout his time in Gibraltar, Richmond superintended the work of the school which was still run by David Gilchrist. It now included both boys and girls and there was also a schoolmistress in post. The government grant was still paid in proportion to the amount raised by local subscriptions, the total not being above six shillings a head. This latter proviso had been ignored in 1874, but the following year, the Roman Catholic list of subscriptions was so huge, which 'nobody believed to be genuine' that the rules were being rigidly applied, with the result that the Methodist grant had been reduced by about 15%.[12]

For many years the school had been housed in a variety of rented premises, often liable to a short notice to quit, and Richmond reported that it was at 'present conducted in a room which is very costly to us and far from suitable'. It was really a large loft over stables and he went on to say 'from the stables beneath the effluvium is often sickening, so that only those who have been for some time accustomed to it could endure it'. He suggested instead that 'we might upon a part of the large piece of land which we hold adjacent to the chapel build a well adapted place which would be very useful to us also for collateral purposes.' The annual rental of £40 would thus be saved and Richmond estimated the cost of building at £500. It would also mean that all their work was concentrated on the one site.

Once again the Committee did not respond to this suggestion and Richmond let the matter lie. He returned to the subject in November 1876, when the lease of a nearby property was expiring and he felt that 'the site is the best possible for our purposes'.[13] He asked for a speedy reply as in three or four weeks the opportunity 'will be gone for ever' as others were interested in it. Richmond later reported 'Your permission to me to proceed in the attempt to secure certain premises for the use of our schools did not reach me early enough. When I moved in the matter I was informed by the Colonial Secretary that my application was just two days too late', which must have been very frustrating.[14] Then on 21 March 1877 Richmond met with James Budgett, a lay member of the Missionary Committee who was visiting Gibraltar and again suggested building on the land adjacent to the church. This land had been granted to Methodism in perpetuity but on condition that nothing was built there. However, the fear of epidemics had waned and Richmond had already sounded out the Governor who had no objection to the proposal. There were over 300 children attending the school, virtually all Roman Catholics. They read daily from the Bible in English and Spanish and Richmond felt that their

---

[12] Ibid., Richmond to Committee, 23 March 1875, fiche 742, no.131.
[13] Ibid., Richmond to Committee, 3 November 1876, fiche 745, no.84.
[14] *WMMS Europe Synod Minutes 1876,* Richmond, 22 March 1877, fiche 46.

school was the only means 'to reach with gospel truth the ignorant and debased Roman Catholic population of the Rock' and that 'The seed thus sown cannot all perish'.[15] Yet Gilchrist was no longer taking Spanish services and so no active attempt was being made to convert the children.

It was also to Budgett that Richmond mentioned the problems caused by lack of communication from London and, no doubt, he benefitted greatly from the visit and the rare chance to discuss his work when he so often felt isolated and lonely. Budgett must have reported favourably on the school scheme, for the Committee agreed to it at a meeting in April 1877. Richmond knew the date of the meeting but eighteen days afterwards it he had still not been informed of the decision. He sent a telegram and then received an immediate reply. He felt valuable time had thus been lost but commented, 'such has not been the way of the Mission House since I have known it'.[16]

But was it a wise decision? Back in 1873 Lyth had suggested that when Gilchrist retired, the school should close and the children be educated in the Roman Catholic schools. He wrote,

> The scholars are with few exceptions if any Roman Catholic. The schools have answered a good purpose - more patriotic than Wesleyan. The master has done his work well ... Well trained youths have been sent forth. The schools have given a little prestige to Methodism for which Methodism has paid.[17]

In other words this was no longer a Mission School. Over the years, children had been converted to Protestantism but never in significant numbers. The school gave a good education and training for its day but Lyth, as a missionary, questioned the validity of that as the sole role when there was a cost to Methodism. The Missionary Society's annual report for 1874 stated,

> The Spanish School and the English Ministry and Pastorate are the two claims upon our sympathies which justify the continued occupation of this station. So far as the interests of our branch of the Christian Church are concerned, neither of the two spheres of labour are of much importance to us; but the School educates many enterprising youths, who, for the most part, emigrate to South America, and carry with them an amount of Scriptural knowledge and freedom from anti-Protestant prejudices, which cannot fail to incline them to favour the Protestant Missions now happily established in that part of the world.

It is highly unlikely that it was true to say that 'for the most part' the children emigrated to South America. The school was no longer the

---

[15] Undated draft of a letter from Richmond in the Church archives.
[16] *WMMS Correspondence*, Richmond to Committee, 8 May 1877, fiche 756, no.2.
[17] Ibid., Lyth to Committee, 21 November 1873, fiche 736, no.47.

Mission school it had once been, but it was the only attempt at foreign missionary work and the only thing to justify the Missionary Society's continued support.

Work on the new building went ahead immediately as plans had already been drawn up. The warrant of the Governor to erect the school house, dated 12 May 1877, is in the church archives. Richmond printed a letter appealing for subscriptions, stating that 'general instruction both in Spanish and English, combined with a knowledge of the Holy Scriptures' was given in the school but that it was 'in practical working *undenominational*, no knowledge being taken of distinctions of religious creed'.[18] He also felt that the building would be useful for their work with soldiers and sailors as its rooms would be suitable for evening classes, meetings, lectures and tea meetings.

The School House

(With permission from the Oxford Centre for Methodism and Church History)

The new building was opened on 1 November 1877 in the presence of the Governor, General the Lord Napier of Magdala, and his wife with some two to three hundred others. The Governor addressed the gathering and Richmond thanked him for his presence and interest. After 'three resounding cheers,' he and his wife then left.[19] After tea, entertainment was provided by the Wesleyan church choir and Band-Sergeant Burgess who played two flute solos. Several speeches were given.

Richmond told the Committee,

General satisfaction is expressed with the arrangements and style of the

---

[18] *Wesleyan Schools in Gibraltar* (printed leaflet), Richmond.
[19] *Gibraltar Chronicle,* Friday 2 November 1877.

building in all respects. In addition to the large upper room (55 x 25ft) with paved playground and offices on its level at the back opening upon an upper road, there is a spacious and comfortable class-room below and at the north end a room which for the present I have placed entirely at the disposal of the schoolmaster - from it he has direct access to his place in the school. For other than ordinary school-work, such as tea-meetings or lectures, there is an entrance both to upper and lower rooms from the courtyard of the Church. For day and night school work the access is at the other end of the building so that services and meetings may not be disturbed.[20]

The final cost was about £750. The Committee paid at least £400 and Richmond raised the rest himself so that the building was completed free of debt. It also meant a saving of the school rent and the cost of maintaining the garden.

It is obvious from his letters that Richmond had been instructed to look out for opportunities in Spain too, but at first he reported that he felt nothing could be done. Politically Spain was still in turmoil and he did not feel the time was right to attempt any work there. However, he offered to visit adjacent towns as far as Cádiz, Málaga and Granada 'to make observations and report to you as also to study both the people and the language' if the Committee agreed.[21] Later he mentioned that he might go into Spain for a change of air but, if he did go, no reports of his visit have survived. In June 1875 he said that he had in mind 'a kind of plan for an effort on a small scale and unlike anything I know of as having been attempted yet in Spain. But I will not intrude this upon your ears unless you wish it'.[22] Presumably the Committee did not as there is no further mention of this plan. However, towards the end of the year he felt more hopeful about Spain.

> It appears to me that at this moment the prospect of general liberty, associated of course with religious liberty is growing brighter than it has for a generation ... In view of the approaching election the King [Alphonso XII] has evidently been advised to keep on good terms with the liberal party which augurs well ... In view of all this I am looking around and about with more hope than I have ever had and it seems to me that if these pleasing anticipations be fairly realized our way to cautious extension of missionary operations in the heart of Spain may be clear in a few months.[23]

He planned to make a visit of enquiry to the city and province of Granada where he felt there was 'a fair and unoccupied field'. He asked the Committee to let him know if it wished him to do this but, as little out-

---

[20] *WMMS Correspondence,* Richmond to Committee, 6 November 1877, fiche 758, no.29.
[21] Ibid., Richmond to Committee, 23 November 1875, fiche 742, no.131.
[22] Ibid., Richmond to Committee, 22 June 1875, fiche 744, no.152.
[23] Ibid., Richmond to Committee, 16 November 1875, fiche 746, no.185.

going correspondence has survived, it is not clear what the Committee's response was. A month later Richmond reported, 'My intended journey into the province of Granada I have been obliged to defer another month'.[24] It was a further two months before he wrote again and there was no mention of a visit to Spain in this or subsequent letters, so presumably it was never made. Richmond did not mention Spain again for two years, but in fact by then it was clear that his hopes for the country had not been realised.

The work in Spain had continued in Barcelona under Griffin and in Minorca under Brown. However, in April 1876 Griffin travelled to Madrid to attend a Conference of Portestant pastors. The long cold train journey and bitter weather in Madrid proved fatal and he died there from consumption on 10 May 1876 at the age of 28. Richard Corfield, the Bible Society's agent and a Methodist, made the funeral arrangements. Griffin's loss was keenly felt in Barcelona where he had been doing good work amongst both the English and Spanish. After visiting the city, Brown urged the Committee to send someone out as soon as possible but added, 'You must

John Ridgeway Griffin

not suppose Barcelona to be a suitable station for an invalid but one demanding the entire efforts of the strongest man you can send'.[25]

The Committee appointed Robert Simpson but, yet again, ignored all the pleas for an older experienced man. Simpson had only completed fifteen months training at Richmond College when he was sent to Barcelona as his first appointment. He arrived on 16 October 1876 but plunged into his work with enthusiasm.

By this time the Spanish Constitution had been re-written in a way that made life for Protestants even more difficult. It now stated,

> The Roman Catholic and Apostolic Faith is the religion of the State. The nation agrees to protect its ministers and its right to worship. No one shall be disturbed on Spanish territory for his religious beliefs or form of worship, provided they do not conflict with Christian morality. However, no manifestations or public religious observances will be permitted other than those of the State religion.[26]

---

[24] Ibid., Richmond to Committee, 14 December 1875, fiche 746, no.185.

[25] Ibid., Brown to Committee, 10 July 1876, fiche 751, no. 53.

[26] Jacques Delpech, *The Oppression of Protestants in Spain*, Lutterworth Press: London, 1956, p.19.

This was, of course, deliberately vague - who knew what constituted a 'public manifestation', and it was variously interpreted throughout Spain. In Madrid, the Bible Society had to remove its sign at the shop and depot. The Bibles displayed in the window had to be closed and placed in such a way that the titles could not be read. Colportage was affected because it was 'public' selling but it did continue and opposition to it varied from place to place.

In Minorca, Brown encountered problems when the sub-governor strongly objected 'to our singing, as an "outward manifestation" prohibited by the Constitution'.[27] Brown claimed that, under the Constitution, places of worship were inviolable but he was forced to stop the children singing in the schools. In the end, he had to find separate places for the schools and for worship which increased the cost of the work.

Simpson expected a similar ruling to be made in Barcelona but, in fact, was allowed to carry on there as before which shows just how differently the Constitution could be interpreted. Brown visited him at this time. It was their first meeting. He was impressed with Simpson and reported that he had begun his work in Barcelona 'in an excellent spirit. I bless God for his appointment, and pray that he may long be spared to labour in Spain. With another like-minded, the Mission would be well provided for'[28] But no-one else was sent, despite problems with Brown's health and their united pleas for help. Instead the work continued as before with Simpson covering the work in Barcelona as best he could whilst he learnt the language and Brown remained in Minorca, although he soon extended his work to Palma in Majorca.

In September 1878 the missionaries in Spain, Gibraltar and Portugal were informed that a visitor was being sent to visit all the stations to discuss the work and to examine the five candidates for ministry trained by Brown in the Balearics. The news was greeted with great joy everywhere for each worker often felt isolated and lonely. The official visitor was none other than William Harris Rule.

After Aldershot, Rule had spent three years in Plymouth before moving to Croydon in 1868 as a supernumerary. He retired in 1872. After some weeks of illness Mary Ann Rule died on 26 February 1873 surrounded by her family and friends. Rule married again the following year. His second wife, Harriete, accompanied him on the trip. They left England on 20 September 1878 calling first at Lisbon. They arrived in Gibraltar on Sunday morning 29 September and were met at the ship by Richmond and Gilchrist. They stayed until Thursday 3 October when 'after receiving much personal attention from Mr Richmond, who accompanied us to the ship, we embarked for Cádiz'.[29] They travelled on to Barcelona, via

---

[27] *WMMS Correspondence,* Brown to Committee, 22 August 1876, fiche 753, no.81.

[28] Ibid., Brown to Committee, 28 November 1876, fiche 755, no.91.

[29] Rule, *Recollections,* op. cit., p.280.

Córdoba and Madrid, and spent some time with Simpson visiting the schools and preaching places. They arrived in Minorca on 24 October and also visited Majorca, leaving for Valencia from there on 7 November. They reached Portugal on 10 November and stayed some weeks there, docking at Gravesend on Saturday 7 December. It was quite a strenuous and tiring journey for a man who celebrated his seventy-sixth birthday in the middle of it.

The person who impressed Rule most was Brown who was probably the man most like himself. Rule examined his five candidates for the ministry and recommended that four of them be accepted on probation and their names were then entered in the *Conference Minutes*. The fifth was not thought to be quite ready but Rule did not have any fundamental doubts about him and was altogether impressed with the way Brown had trained these local men, and continued to do so, helping them and supervising their studies. Rule made some general points about the Spanish missions as a whole and felt they should be superintended from a central point, possibly in Madrid or even Cádiz. He felt there should be more than one minister in Barcelona and that preferably the superintendent should be married. One result of his visit was that he spent time producing a suitable Spanish hymn book which the Missionary Society later printed.

It is clear that his visits were greatly appreciated everywhere he went, with the result that everyone continued to correspond with him, which says much about the loneliness and isolation felt on all these stations. His interest in Spain and Portugal continued until his death on 25 September 1890 in Croydon at the age of 87. His obituary referred to his 'crowning work' for the army in securing religious liberty for soldiers, for which 'Dr Rule fought bravely and long; encountering strong opposition, and displaying the rare and peculiar grace that distinguished him in the correspondence it involved'. His 'perseverance and industry were extraordinary. His character was of exceptional force. To those who watched his public work he seemed the embodiment of militant aggressiveness; but those who knew him best discerned the depth of his piety, and the

WILLIAM HARRIS RULE

gentleness of his greatness'.[30] He had certainly done a great deal for Gibraltar but not without mistakes and controversy.

On this tour, Rule was not impressed with the state of Methodism in Gibraltar, largely because of the lack of missionary work there. Indeed, in his autobiography he described it as a 'half-deserted Mission'.[31] This was one of his typically sweeping statements which did not take account of the real efforts made there since he had left, the changing circumstances and the attitude of the Committee. Missionary work in Gibraltar itself had never been very successful and at no time, even under Rule himself, had the Spanish class numbered more than fifteen people.

Rule's written report to the Committee on Gibraltar was as follows:

> I landed at Gibraltar on Sunday morning, 29th September, and remained there until the Thursday following.
>
> Addressed (in Spanish) the Sunday School which chiefly consists of children of the inhabitants. Preached to the English congregation, which is chiefly military, and conducted the evening service, with rather a thin attendance.
>
> During my stay I had much conversation with Mr Richmond whose ministrations are almost entirely confined to such soldiers as are marched from the several Regiments, but he stated that he received no official communications concerning the troops that arrive from England or elsewhere, and has no means of knowing how many of them may be returned as Wesleyans.
>
> There is no Spanish congregation, nor are there any missionary operations in Gibraltar. There are Daily Schools of Boys, Girls and Infants, and a Night School of young men and women, and elder children. The schools of both sexes, both Day and Night meet in the same room under one Master Mr Gilchrist, a Mistress and monitors. This close proximity of sexes is contrary to universal custom in Spain, and is considered objectionable for obvious reasons of morality. The Master's Quarters are the lower floor of the school-house. The instruction is very elementary. The New Testament is the only reading book. The Old Testament is seldom used. No arrangement is made for the assemblage of the children and youths at Divine service on the Lord's Day. There are no Spanish members of Society, nor does Mr Richmond consider that any means are practicable for making the schools conducive to the formation of either Society or congregation. Improved furniture is desired, and in the event of revival of missionary work, would become absolutely necessary.
>
> If there were as formerly, a Spanish Department of such work, under a Minister directly appointed for the benefit of the general population, which is now much larger that it was forty years ago, a school effectively conducted would become the channel of communication with many Spanish-speaking families; a congregation would be assembled, a Society

---

[30] *Minutes of the Methodist Conference,* 1891, p.22. Rule, *Recollections,* op. cit., p.318.
[31] Rule, *Recollections,* op. cit., p.318.

would be gathered, Gibraltar would be centre of a Missionary District (or circuit) comprehending Algeciras, San Roque, La Línea, and many neighbouring places, irrespective of the multitude from many countries continually resorting thither.[32]

Rule seemed quite sure that missionary work would be effective from Gibraltar, although this had never been the case, so Richmond was asked for his comments on separating the boys' and girls' schools and on the possibility of missionary work. He responded by asking if he could visit England to discuss his ideas in person. He also wanted to get his wife and five children out of Gibraltar for the summer, which was always a trying time. His family seem to have kept fairly well throughout their stay except for a very worrying time in September 1876 when their oldest child was dangerously ill with diphtheria. In October their second daughter developed similar symptoms but thankfully they both recovered. They all left Gibraltar in May 1879 and the Presbyterian minister covered the work during Richmond's short absence. His family stayed in England for five months and thus missed an exceptionally hot summer which meant 'they have escaped more or less probable sickness'.[33] Richmond himself only spent two weeks in England and a few days in travelling although he was the one who had been most affected by illness. The only break he had had was in 1877 when the doctor advised him to have a change and he had gone to Oporto where he had been invited to attend some missionary meetings. This visit must have brought back happy memories for him and given him a chance to have some fellowship with Moreton and Cassels.

Just before he left for England, Richmond reported, 'I have thought out a plan of Spanish Mission work in Gibraltar, and two or three towns near at hand, in Spain proper, which I think likely to find some favour with you when I can fully unfold it presently', but in fact no action was taken either to change the schools or to attempt work in Spain.[34] Perhaps the Committee did not feel Richmond was the right person to do this work for in March 1880 he was informed that he was to return to England. Possibly this was the result of Rule's influence as he had not been very impressed with Richmond.

He did not question this decision but wanted, if possible, to leave in time to attend Conference and to avoid the summer. Despite his break in May the previous year, he had suffered much in the October and November 'from debility and consequent severe neuralgia of head and face, and did my work in much pain and weakness'.[35] He was given permission to leave early if he could make arrangements for the work. This he did by arranging with Richmond College to send out a student and so W. Tasker covered the

---

[32] *WMMS Correspondence,* Rule's report to Committee, 1878, fiche 764, no.91.

[33] Ibid., Richmond to Committee, 26 September 1879, fiche 769, no.50.

[34] Ibid., Richmond to Committee, 5 March 1879, fiche 766, no.20.

[35] Ibid., Richmond to Committee, 13 April 1880. fiche 773, no.22.

work when the family left. On 18 June 1880 Richmond delivered 'an able and eloquent Lecture on the "Great Siege of Gibraltar"' in the Wesleyan schoolroom. Following this he and his wife were presented with 'a Gold Watch and a handsome Music Book'. The *Gibraltar Chronicle* reported on the event saying,

> The Rev. gentleman has, by his zealous and able ministry among the members of the Wesleyan Body in this garrison, won their entire confidence and affection. The congregation feel greatly indebted to Mrs Richmond for her efficient and assiduous management of the choir. Mr and Mrs Richmond take with them also the good wishes of a large number of friends outside the circle of their immediate congregation.[36]

Richmond had asked for an ordinary English circuit 'not in any connection with military work' and not too far north because of the cold.[37] He was stationed in Pembroke and then had several other English appointments. In 1891 a Chairman was needed for the work in West Africa and Richmond was asked to go. Believing it to be God's call, he agreed, but a few months later he came back 'broken in health and almost a dying man'.[38] He returned to England as a supernumerary and died in October 1893 at the early age of 49. During his time in Gibraltar, Richmond had felt the strain of the responsibility of the work and had at times felt lonely and isolated, though he did have some fellowship with the Presbyterian ministers. Whatever Rule's opinion, Richmond had served the church well, continuing the work amongst soldiers and sailors and fighting for their rights. He encouraged a greater sense of stewardship within the church and provided versatile premises for the school and other meetings. In one of his last letters, he reported that the Governor, Lord Napier, and Colonel Harvey, the Schools Inspector, had visited the school unannounced and had expressed themselves '"very much pleased indeed" with our work'.[39] He had not developed any work in Spain but he did not get much encouragement from the Committee which was still short of money. Nevertheless, in view of later developments, it is possible that he was recalled to make way for someone else to develop Spanish work.

Richmond's successor was William R.C. Cockill. He was born in Durham in 1832 and began his ministry in 1857 in Madras. After ten years in India, he returned to England where he had a further five appointments before being asked to go to Gibraltar. He hesitated slightly over this appointment 'on account of my boys' but seems to have made arrangements for them to be at school in England.[40] Cockill himself was a

---

[36] *Gibraltar Chronicle,* 19 June 1880.

[37] *WMMS Correspondence,* Richmond to Committee, 30 April 1880, fiche 773, no.26.

[38] *Minutes of the Methodist Conference,* 1894, pp.13-4.

[39] *WMMS Correspondence,* Richmond to Committee, 30 April1880, fiche 773, no.26.

[40] Ibid., Cockill to Committee, 7 July 1880, fiche 774, no.50.

widower and his daughter, Annie, kept house for him.

He must have arrived in the autumn of 1880 but his first letter is dated December. He wrote,

> After giving attention to the duties of the English work, I have since my arrival, devoted myself to the study of the Spanish language, and as far as the reading of the language is concerned I have acquired some mastery over it. For the past month I have gone into the school twice a week and taken all the elder scholars in a Spanish Bible class. This I shall continue to do and go on to more as I am able. I shall not fail to embrace every opportunity that may arise for work amongst Spaniards.[41]

Cockill had obviously been instructed to see what could be done amongst the Spanish in Gibraltar. He continued with his class and, in 1882, reported, 'In addition to my work in the day school I now give some portion of each evening to our night school, in which I take a class of youths and elder scholars in Spanish and English Scripture reading'.[42] Spanish services, conducted by Gilchrist, had been resumed and were held every Sunday morning in the school room. Cockill commented, 'The service is of course quite voluntary and the number of scholars who attend is very encouraging.'[43] The Bible Society contributed 100 English and 100 Spanish New Testaments to the school and the building was repainted.

In early June 1882 Gilchrist's quarters in the school were broken into and some £30 taken which was a considerable loss. Cockill gave him £10 but was unable to do more. By the end of the year Gilchrist was unwell, though managing to do his work, and Cockill helped him out in the night school. In March 1883 he was reported to be much better despite 'suffering from our dreaded Gibraltar fever'.[44] However, the improvement was short-lived for Gilchrist died some weeks later and was buried on 22 June 1883. He was 60 years old and a widower. He had only stopped working about a fortnight before his death and Cockill reported, 'We sustain an unspeakable loss in Mr Gilchrist's death'.[45] He had been the schoolmaster for many years and held office in the church. He was also respected in the wider community.

Unfortunately it soon transpired that Gilchrist's financial affairs were not in order and that in effect he had died bankrupt. In addition to his school work, Gilchrist had been a rent collector but, because he had been unwell, he had been paying the rent over before collecting it from the tenants 'hoping that all would work right in time. It appears that he has lost much in this way'.[46] Cockill and Gilchrist's son were anxious to keep the matter

---

[41] Ibid., Cockill to Committee, 23 December 1880, fiche 778, no.94.

[42] *WMMS Reports,* vol. xxii, 1882-4, 1883, pp.47-8.

[43] Ibid., vol. xxi, 1879-81, 1881, pp.33-4.

[44] *WMMS Correspondence,* Cockill to Committee, 14 March 1883, fiche 787, no.16.

[45] Ibid., Cockill to Committee, 25 June 1883, fiche 788, no.26.

[46] Ibid., Cockill to Committee, 29 June 1883m fiche 788, no.28.

from the public and with some help from the Committee seem to have achieved this. Spanish services had to be suspended which was a great pity as numbers had been improving. It was also 'the only Protestant Spanish service of the kind in Gibraltar' which they had hoped would form 'the nucleus of a more extended work in future'.[47]

By this time, government regulations on education had been changed in an attempt to improve standards. The government grant was no longer given in proportion to subscriptions raised but according to educational results. One aspect of the new rules was to 'encourage a more systematic instruction in singing and twice a week the principal children assemble in the chapel, and are accompanied with the harmonium'.[48] This the children had found most enjoyable and it also meant that they learnt many hymns and spiritual songs. The new regulations also stated that at least one teacher in the school had to be 'trained and certificated'.[49] Not wanting to put anyone out of work, old masters had been allowed to continue but the new one would have to be trained. Cockill sent several letters to England explaining this. In the meantime he covered the work of the school as best he could, on top of all his other work, but felt he could not continue into September. Miss Vecchio, the girls' teacher, also helped out with the assistance of her Spanish monitors.

The Committee recruited Henry Elenor in England. He had been trained at Westminster College. He probably arrived some time in September 1883 as he was in post by the beginning of October. He immediately set about learning Spanish and Cockill and Miss Vecchio helped as best they could. The school was virtually self-supporting at this time depending on the size of the government grant. The children paid a small fee and subscriptions were still raised so that the Missionary Society paid little towards the running costs. Elenor's salary was fixed at £150 per annum but, in addition, he was given one quarter of the government grant awarded over the sum of £120, which was rather like a productivity bonus. It was obviously in his own interest to work hard and improve the efficiency of the school as this would now increase the amount of the government grant. He must have done so, for in August 1884 Cockill reported the grant for the previous year to have been £152, £30 more than they had ever received before. The school inspector's report for 1884 stated,

> I am of opinion that your school has gained much in real efficiency. I found it improved greatly in discipline, order, and system, and I feel justified in awarding to it a special grant (extra) for efficiency. That no other school earned that grant in the past year should encourage you. The singing was very good, and the needlework was satisfactory.[50]

---

[47] *WMMS Reports,* vol. xxii, 1882-4, 1883, pp.47-8.
[48] Ibid., vol. xxii, 1882-4, 1883, pp.47-8.
[49] *WMMS Correspondence,* Cockill to Committee, 5 July 1883, fiche 788, no. 31.
[50] *WMMS Reports,* vol. xxiii, 1885-7, 1885, p.54.

Elenor went back to England in the summer of 1884 and returned a married man. He and his wife, Annie, continued to live in the school building.

Meanwhile, there had been an important development in the army which affected Gibraltar. After the addition of the fourth column 'Other Protestants' in the 'Army Returns of Religious Denominations' in 1862, there had been virtually no opposition to Methodism within the army but ministers still had no status, no rights and no remuneration. However, even so the work spread and developed. The Army Committee was replaced by the Army and Navy Sub-Committee in 1878 with two secretaries, one each from the Foreign and Home Missionary Committees. An assistant secretary to work under these two, the Rev. Richard Watson Allen, was appointed, who later became the sole secretary. There was growing concern over the lack of payment to ministers and, despite some objections that such money was state aid and receiving it might compromise the position of a 'Free Church', negotiations began with the War Office. These culminated in a letter dated 21 January 1881 which announced,

> It has now been decided that, from and after April 1, 1881, Wesleyan ministers shall receive capitation allowances for their services, under the regulations in force for payment to officiating clergymen of the Church of England, Roman Catholic and Presbyterian denominations.[51]

So, on 1 April 1881, William Cockill became the first Methodist minister to be appointed by the War Office as an officiating chaplain to the troops at Gibraltar. This meant that the army returns now included a column for Wesleyans. Apart from the financial benefits, the ministers now had a definite position and status in the army and Cockill reported,

> … the weekly returns which are required from all the corps have had the effect of bringing our men to service in greater numbers … The knowledge of exact numbers returned weekly to the minister has brought a considerable change.[52]

The navy had already been paying capitation fees in some places, but now also added Wesleyans to their official returns and acknowledged Methodism's right to appoint chaplains at all naval ports.

The capitation fee was given on the grounds that services to soldiers were free which meant that they no longer paid seat rents. The fee was greater than the seat rents but the income of the station was very changeable and was still affected by removals. In November 1883 Cockill reported that a Mr Roberts and his family had recently left Gibraltar. He added, 'Mr Roberts for nearly 20 years has been a chief supporter of our

---

[51] Watkins, op. cit., p.103.
[52] *WMMS Correspondence,* Cockill to Committee, 21 March 1882, fiche 782, no.12.

chapel contributing about <u>one third</u> of its income'.[53]

In early 1882 the Rev. George Olver, one of the Secretaries of the Missionary Society visited all the Mediterranean stations. Cockill much appreciated his visit and felt it was of great benefit. No doubt he was glad of the opportunity to talk over the work of the station although there were no particularly pressing issues at the time.

Cockill continued all the usual services and meetings of the church. In the warmer weather, three services were held every Sunday, at other times two. Sometimes, when the sailors were in port, an extra 9.30 a.m. service was provided for them. He gave the English children religious instruction on Friday mornings, undertook hospital and prison visiting as well as calling on people in their homes. Soldiers were converted at services and meetings and Cockill remarked, 'I find the class meeting very much prized by the few more pious soldiers; they speak of it as their greatest help by the way.'[54]

Change, of course, was always happening making life difficult which Cockill highlighted in his annual report;

> In reviewing the year, our first feeling is one of thankfulness to God, that, as a family we have been preserved in health. Owing to late and insufficient rains, the season has been unhealthy; many homes around us have been stricken by fever; but we have been spared. The year has been one of unusual changes in the garrison. All our regiments were called away to the war, and those which took their places have remained very unsettled by the expectation of change. The number of Wesleyans was considerably diminished by the changes, and our few members were reduced one half, so that in Society work among soldiers we have had almost to make a new beginning. The men who left us were followed by our prayers and letters, and it was a joy to us to find that the faith which had given some of them fellowship with us, held them undismayed in the dangers of the field, and in the sickness of the hospital.[55]

However, sometimes the changes were of benefit bringing people with skills that were particularly needed and in 1884 Cockill wrote,

> Miss Cockill and I have kept fairly well, but we very much need a change. We have hitherto not been able, as others do, to get a change, having no one to relieve me in the pulpit. Mr Hipwell a local preacher and officer is now a valuable help. I propose therefore as soon as the weather cools to get away for a week or ten days.[56]

Unfortunately they were unable to have a break as Gibraltar was soon in quarantine because of fears about cholera. However, Cockill reported that

---

[53] Ibid., Cockill to Committee, 29 November 1883, fiche 791, no.60.

[54] *WMMS Reports,* vol. xxii, 1882-4, 1884, pp.55-6.

[55] Ibid., vol. xxii, 1882-4, 1883, pp.47-8.

[56] *WMMS Correspondence,* Cockill to Committee, 11 August 1884, fiche 794, no.30.

he did feel refreshed by the arrival of the cooler weather and hoped to get away in the spring or early summer of 1885.

The soldiers were not the only losses within the church. Towards the end of 1881 Mrs Mary McCarter 'an old member of forty years standing' died at the age of 79, and Mrs Sarah Tasker 'an old seat-holder and kind friend' died in April 1884 at the age of 61.[57] It was hard to lose long-standing members who were part of the small nucleus of more settled members.

Mary McCarter was also a loss to the work of the Bible Society's local committee. She had run a depository for many years and, although it was previously reported as due to close, it seems to have continued or re-opened for the Bible Society's report for 1877 recorded that

> A supply of English Scriptures has been sent to the depot kept by Mrs McCarter, who is an excellent Christian woman, nearly 80 years of age, and who is largely patronised by the red and blue jackets, who constantly come to her shop for Bibles and require them attractively bound.[58]

The main depository was still run by Fromou, a Presbyterian, but altogether sales came nowhere near meeting the expenses. Corfield visited the local committee from time to time and, despite the high cost of the work, it was felt to be too important to abandon. Over a thousand Scriptures were sold most years and the 1880 report described them as being in thirteen different languages, though the majority were English or Spanish.

In the 1883 report, Corfield's retirement, on the grounds of ill health, was announced. He was succeeded by the Rev. E. Reeves Palmer. In 1883 he visited Gibraltar along with Mr Finch, the Society's Assistant Foreign Secretary. Palmer preached in both the Presbyterian and Methodist churches and on 3 December 1883 the Bible Society held its first public meeting in Gibraltar. This was attended by a number of clergymen including the Presbyterian minister, Eneas Mackintosh, Archdeacon Govett and Cockill.

Palmer continued to make an annual visit to Gibraltar and Fromou continued his work in the depot and as colporteur amongst the residents and on the ships in the bay. He did the latter work in conjunction with the Seamen's Mission. They shared the boat and the missioner preached on board ship after which Fromou offered the scriptures for sale. In 1885, 680 ships were visited. The post of Secretary was filled by several different people but eventually Major Hipwell took the job.

Meanwhile Cockill had asked to leave Gibraltar in the summer of 1885. He wrote, 'As far as I am concerned, I shall leave the station with considerable regret, but Miss Cockill's health and my own and other family

---

[57] *WMMS Reports,* vol. xxii, 1882-4, 1882, p.34 and vol. xxiii, 1885-7, 1885, p.54.

[58] *Reports of the BFBS,* 1877, p.83.

considerations, make a further stay here very undesirable'.[59] This is the last letter in the missionary archives from Gibraltar until February 1887, a gap of over two years. Letters must have been written in that time but have presumably been lost. Cockill returned to England in August 1885. He was stationed at Wimborne but the following year he went to Sierra Leone. He returned to England six years later and became a supernumerary the following year. He died on 23 October 1911 at the age of 78. It seems a pity that he left Gibraltar when he was presumably fluent in Spanish. His plans to develop more Spanish work from the school came to a halt with the death of Gilchrist and, as it took time for Elenor to learn Spanish, the Spanish services were not resumed. Cockill had kept the general work going well and was the first minister to be recognised as an official chaplain to the troops, which meant that Methodism's position in Gibraltar was at long last officially recognised.

However, the hope of doing Spanish work from Gibraltar did not die for John Grimshaw, Cockill's successor, soon expressed his concern at the lack of such work.

---

[59] *WMMS Correspondence,* Cockill to Committee, 27 November 1884, fiche 796, no.54.

CHAPTER 17   FURTHER HOPES FOR WORK IN SPAIN
A mission in La Línea (1885-96)

John Grimshaw was born in Rawtenstall, Lancashire on 16 December 1850. His father died when he was four years old but his mother encouraged the development of his faith and he eventually offered for the ministry. After three years at Richmond College he spent eight years in British Guiana before being appointed to Gibraltar. He arrived with his wife, Mary, and their family in August 1885. It is not clear how many children they had but a son, George Herbert, was born during their stay. They arrived at a difficult time in Gibraltar because of cholera. The Bible Society's report gives a description of the regulations imposed.

> ... no person was allowed to enter Spain from Gibraltar without passing a three days' quarantine in a shed upon the Spanish lines. The Governor of Gibraltar issued an order banishing all Spanish visitors from the place, and absolutely prohibiting the entrance of Spaniards so long as the quarantine continued. Thus Gibraltar was shut off almost entirely from communication with its neighbours. Our depot-keeper wrote to me during this time that the streets were utterly deserted and the place desolated to the last degree.[1]

There were thirty-two cases of cholera in Gibraltar with twenty-four deaths, but in La Línea, with a much smaller population, there were 429 cases with 206 deaths.[2] All this had a bad effect on trade and ships stopped calling at Gibraltar. In December, Grimshaw reported, 'Trade has been dull, and is so still and we all in some measure feel it'.[3] For some time soup kitchens were run to feed the poor.

Grimshaw's early letters may not have survived but he did begin to use the chapel minute book, so long neglected. At first he just recorded his annual report to the Missionary Committee but later he included the minutes of leaders' meetings. His first report, for the four months up to December 1885, formed the basis of the Missionary Society's annual report for 1886, carefully edited to conceal Grimshaw's obvious dismay at what he had found in Gibraltar. He wrote of course as a minister whose sole experience to date had been on the foreign mission field. He said,

> After all the expenditure of labour and money for so many years I find on my arrival a church composed of seventeen members, who with one or two exceptions never meet in class. Of these only two are natives of the place, and only one of these can in any sense be claimed as the fruit of past effort on our part, [Miss Vecchio, the school teacher] and this so far as I can find is the only visible fruit of our work among the Spanish

---

[1] *Reports of the BFBS,* 1885, pp.82-3.
[2] Benady, op. cit., pp.92-3.
[3] Chapel minute book.

speaking population. Of course we are doing something in our large school which is very ably conducted by Mr Elenor - the Inspector again gave a special grant for efficiency - but as a matter of fact it does not result in making the children either Christian or Protestant. All this is very distressing and renders my position anything but pleasant from a missionary point of view.[4]

He was also depressed about the lack of giving to the work and planned to make a monthly collection which presumably had lapsed. Subscriptions to the school were also proving more difficult to collect as people felt these were no longer needed because of the government grant.

Grimshaw wrote more positively about the work amongst the soldiers and reported that he had re-opened the Sunday school which now had thirty children and several adults attending it. He had also begun a Bible class which he felt was his most successful effort to date. Members of other churches had joined it along with some army officers.

In his first surviving letter, dated 18 February 1887, Grimshaw responded to a request from the Committee for his views on Spanish work in general and about the work in Gibraltar. He was unhappy that the school was not a mission school and, despite its efficiency as a secular school, he was not even sure if it was going to survive because 'Already the "Christian Brothers" - a band of Roman Catholics devoted to educational work are pursuing us hard and we may expect the priests to do all they can to prevent the attendance of the children at our school'.[5] He wanted to make the school a mission school and to undertake proper missionary work in Gibraltar, believing the premises were ideally suited to this as they were situated in the heart of the Spanish-speaking population.

John Grimshaw

Photograph by John Righton and used with permission from Tom Norgate

He also said,

Gibraltar ought to become the base of our operations in Spain and the key

---

[4] Ibid.
[5] *WMMS Correspondence,* Grimshaw to Committee, 18 February 1887, fiche 797, no.3.

to our Spanish work in general. If with all the disadvantages of Barcelona where we are barely tolerated we obtain success what might we not accomplish here with freedom equal to that of England and all the protection we may require. Within easy reach of Gibraltar there are many Spanish towns and villages where the seed of the kingdom might be sown. One of these we visited on Monday last and in every house found a willingness to hear and a readiness to learn.

He was aware of the situation in Barcelona because the 'we' referred to above included Robert Simpson, who was visiting Gibraltar at the time of writing, along with Sebastian Cruellas, a Spanish school teacher and local preacher in Barcelona.

The work in Spain had continued both in Barcelona and the Balearics but not without considerable opposition which took various forms. Name-calling was common, often accompanied by shouts, jeers and the banging of drums particularly in the streets outside preaching places. Even mud and stone-throwing took place and, although peace could often be restored by appealing to the authorities, it was not always easy to maintain. More serious was the loss of jobs when employers sacked Protestants or made it clear that they would not employ them. In the Balearics, one couple had their adopted child removed from them on the grounds that as Protestants they were unfit parents. Another man was imprisoned for failing to doff his hat when the host was carried through the streets during a religious procession. There were problems with burials, even where a Protestant burial ground had been provided. If the deceased had originally been baptised as a Roman Catholic, the authorities sometimes insisted on Catholic rites whatever the wishes of the dead person or the surviving family.

Although the law allowed for civil marriage, the deliberate delays and requests for documents could result in the process taking so long that couples gave up and submitted to the Roman Catholic ceremony. The treatment of Protestants in hospital in Barcelona was so bad, Simpson and other pastors there opened their own to provide at least more kindly care. There were difficulties in obtaining preaching places and sometimes books were still burnt. All in all it was not easy to be a Protestant in Spain.

Nevertheless the work had progressed. In 1882 after passionate pleas for help from Simpson, whose health had been suffering, Joseph G. Wheatcroft Brown was sent to Barcelona as his first appointment. The two soon expanded the work and an evangelist was also employed to work in Madrid. However in 1884 Simpson fell ill and in July he travelled to England and did not return to Spain until later in 1885. Wheatcroft Brown carried on as best he could and in December 1884 he gained the help of Franklyn G. Smith, a young man in his first appointment. In 1886, after Simpson returned to Spain, Wheatcroft Brown moved to Madrid to oversee and develop the work there.

Meanwhile, Brown had continued to extend the work in the Balearics and in September 1879 he had been ordained into the Methodist ministry himself. He had, after all, been doing the work of a minister for years. No-one was sent to help him and his grant was even reduced by the Missionary Society. However, despite this and problems with his health, he carried on and by 1883 he had four stations in Majorca and two in Minorca and reported that more could be opened if the resources were available. By 1884 he had three ordained Spanish ministers and several local preachers working with him, all of whom he had trained himself.

So, despite all the opposition, a great deal of progress had been made and Grimshaw felt success could be even greater from, and within, Gibraltar where there was more protection. During their visit, Simpson and Cruellas had held meetings in Gibraltar every night for a week which many people had attended. Grimshaw reported, 'We purpose holding a weekly meeting for them forthwith but nothing like permanent work can be thought of unless we have a good man to follow up our efforts.'[6] Simpson was willing to spend a year in Gibraltar and do the work himself, believing he could make arrangements for his work in Barcelona during his absence. He planned to start a Spanish Sunday school and establish Spanish preaching, and also thought there were good openings in La Línea which might spread out to other towns and villages. He and Grimshaw also wanted to turn the school into a proper mission school. Elenor was anxious about this, not because he was unenthusiastic about the plan, but because he wanted reassurance that the Committee would support the work. He felt in the short-term at least there would be opposition, likely to result in a reduction in the number of pupils and in the size of the grant.

Grimshaw and Simpson continued to correspond and sent their thoughts and plans to the Committee, but in the end nothing was done which was extremely disappointing to them both. The chapel minute book states that the special mission was not 'carried out as the Committee could not, on financial grounds, adopt the suggestion of the minister and Rev. R. Simpson who was requested to confer with him on the subject'. This seems a weak excuse, for Grimshaw had already pointed out that the expenses would be low, only involving the extra cost in Gibraltar for the additional worker's accommodation. The Committee must have agreed to, or even proposed, Simpson's visit to Gibraltar which was a pointless exercise if it was not willing or able to finance any kind of future work.

The following year, in his annual report, Grimshaw made another plea for Spanish work believing that an evangelist ought to be appointed to do this. Simpson even offered to find a suitable person and they still felt the school should be more of a mission school. Elenor had by this time learnt Spanish and could have helped with the work, and others were willing to

---

[6] Ibid., Grimshaw to Committee, 18 February 1887, fiche 797, no.3.

offer assistance. Their pleas fell on deaf ears and Grimshaw seems to have had no response at all to his suggestions. However, in 1888, he did re-start the voluntary Sunday morning Spanish service. Attendance was reported to be 'as good as we could expect', but the following year the services were described as having 'met with only partial success'.[7] Grimshaw never stopped pleading for Spanish work to be done but nothing was undertaken during his years in Gibraltar.

In 1887 repairs were carried out to the school, chapel and Mission House. Grimshaw was concerned that the expenditure was always greater than the income and did his best to avoid too much expense for the Missionary Society. In May 1887 he wrote to the Governor about the inequality in pay between the Presbyterian chaplain and himself for ministering to the troops. He explained,

> The civilian element in both congregations being insignificant, the greater part of our time is taken up in communion with the troops, and, so far, our position is identical; but, while the members of Presbyterian troops fall very considerably below those of the Wesleyan denomination, I receive capitation allowance amounting to less than £70 a year only, whereas the Presbyterian minister is paid a fixed salary of £120 a year and a forage allowance at 1/- a day.[8]

He therefore asked for the same rate of pay. This was not given, but he was awarded a fixed salary of £100 a year and a shilling a day in line with that received by the Wesleyan minister in Malta, which was a considerable improvement.

In 1888 Elenor visited England as did Mary Grimshaw and her family who went for health reasons. The following year, Grimshaw himself was given permission to go partly because of the state of his health and partly to attend Conference. He planned to ask one of the missionaries from the North Africa Mission to cover the work during his absence which is presumably what happened. That year Grimshaw reported that Elenor was doing good work in the Sunday school amongst Spanish children and that they had 'a few very promising cases'.[9] In addition, an illustrated article about the work appeared in *Missionary Notices*. In it Grimshaw referred to the problem of location and went on to describe some of their work;

> Our premises are situate in the heart of this thickly built and densely populated town, and are so far removed from the leading thoroughfares, and so shut in by other buildings that even Wesleyan Methodists often visit the Rock and are quite oblivious of our existence. To remedy this, we placard ourselves in the hotels and boarding-houses ...
>   Of the importance of the work done here there can be but one opinion.

---

[7] *WMMS Reports,* vol. xxiv, 1888-90, 1889, pp.31-2; 1890, p.39.
[8] Letter from Grimshaw to Governor, 30 May 1887.
[9] *WMMS Correspondence,* Grimshaw to Committee, 16 May 1889, fiche 797, no.11.

The difficulty of it cannot be exaggerated; for, added to the evils of an ordinary garrison town, are those produced by an effete Romanism, and the temptation to illicit trade.

The English services are supplemented by Bible-classes, temperance meetings, mutual improvement societies, and above all, class-meetings, in which the truly converted soldier greatly delights. Beside these there are the visits to the sick in hospital, and the prison services. The efforts among the Spanish-speaking population are chiefly educational. Upwards of two hundred boys and girls are under our influence in the day-school, besides those who can be induced to attend on Sunday.

Of results it is difficult to speak. They cannot be tabulated. Our English congregation is ever changing, and little visible fruit remains; but we know of some in Egypt, South Africa, the West Indies, Canada, and not a few who have returned to the old country and to civil life, who, burdened and heavy laden, found the Saviour at Gibraltar.[10]

In fact, since Grimshaw's arrival, membership had steadily increased with the highest number, seventy, being recorded in 1888. There were also 'many earnest Christians who although not of our fold delight to worship with us'.[11] There were classes led by Quartermaster Sergeant Dawson, Sergeant-Major Smales, Bombardier Lyttle and Sergeant Smith. Grimshaw may have been new to military work but there was considerable progress under his ministry, despite the frequent regimental changes so frustrating and discouraging for any minister. A tea-service for 150 had been donated by a Mrs Squance and her family and a set of twelve tea urns by personal friends of Grimshaw in Bolton, Lancashire, which helped make the tea meetings and informal gatherings more successful. The Sunday school which had been taken over by Edward Overton of the King's Royal Rifles and other helpers was improving and Grimshaw gave religious instruction to the soldiers' children twice a week.

In January 1890 Grimshaw wrote to the Committee to say he had been approached by the stewards of the Bath circuit to be their second minister and he had agreed. He therefore asked the Committee to make arrangements for a successor and suggested that the change provided an opportunity to reassess the work in Gibraltar. In this letter Grimshaw also referred to the fact that influenza had been causing considerable problems and their annual missionary meeting had had to be postponed.

The influenza is not so fatal as in Spain, but great numbers are prostrated by it. We have had a great deal of diphtheria and the place is very unhealthy just now. We have been mercifully spared, and have cause to be thankful. I think perhaps we have profited largely by our careful attention from time to time, to the drains for while death has taken great numbers of children from our locality:- indeed from a circuit of a few

---

[10] *Missionary Notices,* vol. xxv 1887-9, 1889, pp.86-7.
[11] Ibid., vol. xxiii, 1885-7, 1887, p.54.

yards round us - ours have enjoyed the best of health. Still we are not without anxiety.[12]

He did not state what effect this had had on the school, but in 1888 all schools were closed during an epidemic of measles. Altogether, during Grimshaw's time in Gibraltar, there were several health scares and although these were not on the scale of the massive epidemics earlier in the century, they were nonetheless worrying times.

Grimshaw still wanted the Committee to reconsider the school's position and so he sent a detailed report. He had been a part of a Commission of Enquiry into Elementary Education appointed by the government, and had experienced at first hand the attitude of the Roman Catholics to their school. A large legacy had been left to the Roman Catholic bishop, which was being spent on schools so that 'buildings are rising on every hand, and great numbers of "Christian Brothers" are being brought from Ireland as teachers.'[13] Their numbers had been seriously affected and the Church of England school had already closed, so that the Methodist school was now the only Protestant school in Gibraltar. The bishop had already told Grimshaw that he would empty their school and taunted him with the fact that there was not a single Wesleyan child within it. The new schools also meant that local financial support was harder to obtain as many of the subscribers had been Catholics and they now supported their own schools. Grimshaw felt the school should become a mission school asking, 'What right do we have to spend English missionary money in educating Spanish Roman Catholics if we do nothing more?' He went on to say,

> I should point out that we are missing a splendid opportunity. Our feeble efforts ought to be and might be multiplied, but not until we look our difficulties in the face. If I were asked what ought to be done I would refer you to my communication dated 18 February 1887 which notwithstanding frequent mention, and earnest consideration remains unanswered.[14]

Grimshaw clearly felt very frustrated about the lack of any proper missionary work and the fact that his repeated pleas had been ignored. He did not send a detailed report on the military work, but pointed out, 'The work in this department is more encouraging'. However, the leaders' meeting on 17 June 1890 decided to send a letter of their own on the subject which Grimshaw supported. It was prepared by Overton and was sent to Richard Allen, Secretary of the Army and Navy Committee, who was now involved with the appointment at Gibraltar since it was an officially recognised chaplaincy.

---

[12] *WMMS Correspondence,* Grimshaw to Committee, 22 January 1890, fiche 797, no.15.

[13] Ibid., Grimshaw to Committee, 24 April 1890, fiche 797, no.17.

[14] Ibid., Grimshaw to Committee, 24 April 1890, fiche 797, no. 17.

The leaders wanted at least one chaplain devoted entirely to the army and navy work believing that that was more than enough work for one person. They felt Grimshaw's health had been impaired by trying to work the two branches without help and pointed out that Malta had two ministers when they only had one, although the naval and military strength in Gibraltar was two-thirds of that in Malta. Work in Gibraltar was likely to increase as the Fleet, currently stationed at Vigo, was probably coming to Gibraltar and a new dockyard was proposed for the Rock which would first bring greater numbers of workers and later ships. They also wanted a soldiers' home believing 'that Gibraltar is the largest garrison without one'.[15] There was a soldiers' home in the town and a mission room at the South, but 'they are not worked on Wesleyan lines'. They felt the lack of places to go meant the men were more likely to succumb to the temptations of the beer houses and dancing saloons.

Allen passed the letter on to the Missionary Committee but first asked Major Hipwell, now in England, for his comments and a note from him was attached to the letter. Hipwell demolished all the arguments claiming that Gibraltar was not a mission station; that Grimshaw's health was not affected by the workload but stemmed from his time in British Guiana; that Gibraltar could not be compared with Malta where services were held in several places; and that the proposed dockyard and likely increase in naval work were still under discussion and there was no major need for a soldiers' home. He concluded, 'In short the letter is so full of loose and erroneous statements that it should be ignored'.[16] This arrogant demolition of the leaders' arguments seems quite breathtaking and in fact Hipwell was to be proved wrong on almost all counts, but his intervention may have delayed developments. No copy of any reply has survived and the matter was not referred to again in the minutes of the leaders' meetings.

So Grimshaw prepared to leave Gibraltar. He had the Mission House cleaned and whitewashed and made arrangements with the Presbyterian minister, Thomas Murray, and others including Quartermaster Sergeant Dawson, now a local preacher, to take the services. A farewell meeting was held on Monday 4 August 1890, when a bag of sovereigns was presented to the family as a parting gift. Grimshaw's ministry seems to have been much appreciated and it was pointed out that attendance at the voluntary services was six or seven times higher than it had been five years previously. Certainly the military work seems to have prospered greatly under his care and as events would show, his pleas for Spanish work may not have been as unheeded as he thought. Grimshaw never served abroad again despite his obvious enthusiasm for missionary work and neither did he do any more military work. Instead he served in a further eight English circuits. He died on 8 September 1927 at the age of 76. His obituary stated

---

[15] Ibid., Leaders' meeting, 17 June 1890, fiche 798, no.20.
[16] Ibid., Allen to Olver, with notes from Hipwell, undated, fiche 798, no.19.

that preaching was always a great joy to him and his hearers and that 'he excelled in the homely atmosphere of the class meeting' both of which seem to have been true in Gibraltar.[17]

His successor was W. Terry Coppin. He was born in Chelmsford on 15 April 1854. He was converted at the age of eighteen and four years later was accepted to train for the ministry. He spent two years at Richmond College and then went to Lagos. After eight years in West Africa, he went to Guernsey and from there he volunteered to go to Gibraltar, after reading of Grimshaw's impending departure in the *Methodist Recorder*. He had previously thought he would like to serve on the Rock and had, at some time, met and talked with both Richmond and Cockill. His offer was accepted and he arrived in Gibraltar on 3 September 1890 with his wife, Eva Maria, their young son and a servant.

Apart from a brief note to announce their safe arrival, Coppin was too busy to write fully to the Committee until early November. Despite Grimshaw's attention to the house, the Coppins felt it was in a very poor state. It had been empty for three weeks but, nevertheless, they felt they should not have had so much cleaning to do and were quite upset about it. Coppin reported,

> This, and the discomfort of the drought, the prevalence of a good deal of enteric fever made our incoming to wear a most unfavourable aspect. Mr Grimshaw is an old friend of mine so please take no further notice. But Mrs Coppin and I will never forget our first experiences here and the weariness and fatigue of getting this house habitable under a scorching, sweltering September sun.[18]

He had been forced to buy what he felt were 'essential requisites' including a new bath, coal hole and oilcloth. However, he was much more positive about the work;

> I have been most cordially welcomed. I found a very well organised little Church, a bright and comfortable Sanctuary, a well-attended and well-managed school, and some very fine Christian brethren - men in Christ and eager to work for Him.

It is clear from Coppin's letters that he was aware of Grimshaw's desire to do missionary work from Gibraltar and for the school to be a mission school. He felt the premises were very badly situated for the military work being too remote from the South where many troops were quartered and too out of the way for the rest. However, he did feel they were well situated for Spanish work to be done by a specially appointed agent as one person could not do this and the chaplaincy work.

The school was running well under Elenor's care but in November 1889

---

[17] *Minutes of the Methodist Conference,* 1928, p.97.
[18] *WMMS Correspondence,* Coppin to Committee, 5 November 1890, fiche 798, no.25.

he had told the Committee that he wanted to leave Gibraltar partly because of his own health and that of his elderly father in England. Although he made enquiries about other appointments, he did not leave but, by 1891, he was very concerned about his wife's health. She had had a severe fever and he did not want her to face another hot Gibraltar summer. So Elenor found another appointment and left with his wife Annie and their young daughter, Dora Alice, in mid February 1891. They had taken an active role in church life. Elenor had been chapel steward, treasurer of the contingency fund, poor steward and class leader. At his last leaders' meeting he 'received the hearty thanks of the brethren for the earnest and able and assiduous manner in which for several years he has devoted himself to the welfare of every department of the Church.'[19]

However, a suitable person was on hand to take over the school. John William Righton had also been trained at Westminster College and was currently master of the Jewish school. He and Elenor had been friends and had shared the same Spanish teacher. He was married to Elizabeth Ann and two boys were born to them in Gibraltar, William and George Alfred. Righton already worshipped at the church and now became chapel steward, society steward and a member of the leaders' meeting. The family moved into the accommodation at the school.

The change of master might have been a good time to change the character of the school but Coppin did not think so, for

> ... though I regret the school is not more pronouncedly an Evangelical Mission School, yet until the Committee is prepared to appoint a suitable Spanish agent to prosecute an earnest Spanish Mission that could command the attention and respect and confidence of the Spanish population, it is better for the general welfare of the work (as it is now) to carry on the school on its present lines.[20]

However, before long Coppin wrote to the Committee to say that a suitable Spaniard had been recommended by the Bible Society's agent, now the Rev. John Jameson, to do evangelistic work in Gibraltar. Coppin and the Presbyterian minister, Thomas Murray, wanted to set up a joint mission thus sparing either church from bearing the whole cost but neither church agreed to this plan. However, Coppin was soon told, 'if you can find an earnest godly worker who on Methodist lines could be under your guidance, Bible-man or Bible-woman, we would look carefully at it'.[21]

Meanwhile work amongst the soldiers and sailors had continued. In April 1892 Coppin reported that he had seen little of the Channel Squadron that year because of abnormally rough and wet weather so that 'the men

---

[19] Chapel minute book.
[20] *WMMS Correspondence,* Coppin to Committee, 5 February 1891 fiche 798, no.26.
[21] Ibid., Coppin to Committee, 29 May 1892, fiche 798, no.32, quoting letter from Olver to Coppin, 10 November 1891.

were landed for service at the most twice or thrice'.[22] His plan to hold a series of temperance meetings aboard different ships had also been thwarted by the weather but he hoped for better things during the expected visit of the Mediterranean Squadron in the summer. Work amongst the soldiers had been expanded at the end of 1890 when extra Sunday evening services were begun at the North Front camp and mid-week cottage meetings at Europa. Changes of regiment continued as usual and in September 1891 William Dawson left Gibraltar. The leaders' meeting placed on record its appreciation in the following words:

> It recognises with thankfulness to God the fine fidelity of Brother Quartermaster Sergeant William Dawson who for more than five years has laboured for Christ … in this Garrison notably in the offices of Local Preacher, Class Leader and Steward. It desires also to place on record its appreciation of the valuable services of Mrs Dawson wishing them both Godspeed.

By the beginning of 1892 the school expenses had increased to the point at which Coppin had to ask for extra money from the Committee. He also made several suggestions about the school. The Committee did not reply to them and instead asked for a detailed report. In this, Coppin referred to the unsuitability of the location of their property for the military work feeling that,

> … the premises are almost as badly placed as they can be. We are not only clear away from the one chief thorough-fare (along which the bulk of the traffic streams, in or near which the English civilians chiefly reside and where the military and naval men, when off duty and out, are mostly to be seen), but no short and direct street from the main debouches near us … Hence the confession of almost every stranger, and even residents occasionally, 'we thought we should never find you'.[23]

He felt much was lost as a result as 'Only the few that are sincerely attached to Methodism will find out the premises and attend the means of grace' and he was sure that a better location would more than double their congregations. The premises were better situated for work amongst the Spanish-speaking population, including the school, but even that was dwindling in size now the Roman Catholics had several schools of their own. He therefore recommended that the school become more of a mission school; that an agent be appointed to work amongst the Spanish-speaking residents and that part of the school-house be converted into a Home for soldiers and sailors.

Coppin had already mentioned the need for a soldiers' home to Allen. He did not suggest a new location for it because of the cost involved and

---

[22] Ibid., Coppin to Allen, 21 April 1892. fiche 798, no.31.
[23] Ibid., Coppin to Committee, 29 May 1892, fiches 798/9, no.32.

because he thought the premises, being leasehold and granted solely for church use, could not be sold to finance a move. In any case, there was a 'well-conducted undenominational "home" in good situation in the Main Street.' He also thought that the premises would be well patronised once word got round, and that the magnificent view of the bay was bound to be an attraction. The location was good for the proposed Spanish mission and the now smaller school could be well accommodated in the school building along with the soldiers.

Meanwhile work went ahead to repair the chapel roof. Unfortunately during the execution of this, a cornice unexpectedly gave way dislodging part of the scaffolding and causing one of the labourers to fall. He was seriously injured but Coppin reported 'to the wonder of us all he is progressing favourably in the Colonial Hospital'.[24] He was given twenty shillings and presumably did recover. This meant that more extensive repairs were needed, costing about £180 which was beyond the means of the congregation. The Committee granted £120. Coppin also approached the Governor on the grounds that it was a garrison church and he felt that some of the damage to the roof had been caused by the firing of heavy guns above the church. Fifty pounds was given and then, about 1893, the Admiralty also began to contribute towards the work. All this support was an indication of the improved status of Methodism.

All three of Coppin's recommendations were implemented over the next couple of years. First, Coppin announced,

> After many months of search and a great deal of correspondence we engaged through the agent-general of the British and Foreign Bible Society (the Rev. John Jameson of Madrid) the services of Señor José Rodriguez. He had previously been a colporteur in the Balearic Islands, assisting too at times our Spanish missionary in Majorca, Rev. Franklyn Smith. [He had succeeded William Brown there in 1888.][25]

The Bible Society agreed to pay a small part of the salary on condition that Rodriguez was allowed to do some colportage, which actually fitted in very well with his evangelistic work. The plan was for him to work in Gibraltar and in the nearby towns and villages of Spain. In April 1893 Coppin reported,

> You will also be gratified to learn that our Spanish Evangelist with his wife and family have arrived. They have favourably impressed us. He is now at work. I am rejoiced in seeing that his advent has created no little interest outside of as well as among our church and people. I pray Almighty God to bless his labours in this indifferent and iniquitous city.[26]

---

[24] Ibid., Coppin to Committee, 14 June 1892, fiche 799, no.33.

[25] *WMMS Europe Synod Minutes, Spain 1867-93,* Coppin,, Gibraltar report for year ending 1893, fiche 70.

[26] *WMMS Correspondence,* Coppin to Committee, 19 April 1893, fiche 799, no.1.

The Bible Society work had continued with Fromou acting as depot keeper and colporteur, in conjunction with the Seaman's Mission under Archdeacon Govett. Annual public meetings provided an opportunity for people to hear about the wider work of the Society and to make a contribution to its funds. When Jameson took over from Palmer he felt Fromou's behaviour was not altogether satisfactory. Fromou then decided to leave Gibraltar. He went rather suddenly in the summer of 1889 leaving his house in a poor state and his accounts in some confusion, with several debts unpaid. His work, however, was thought to be of importance and a successor, Mr W. Watson from Inverness, was recruited and sent out. He continued the work of the depot and of visiting ships in the bay.

In the autumn of 1889 Jameson paid a prolonged visit to Gibraltar and thoroughly reorganised the work there. The depot was relocated and a kiosk was also opened which in its first few days attracted quite a crowd of curious people of different nationalities. The kiosk was run by a Mr Moon and both he and Watson wanted to develop the work amongst the Spanish who showed interest in their Bibles. Moon started a Spanish meeting and Watson began to visit Spain to act as a colporteur there too. However, there is no mention of Gibraltar in the following year's report and in 1892 the work seems to have been entirely taken over by a Mr Roxburgh, an old soldier. He ran the kiosk in the morning and visited barracks and married quarters in the afternoon.

The arrival of Rodriguez, an experienced colporteur, may have infused some new life into the work. The Bible Society assisted with the expenses of his removal and Rodriguez and his family travelled to Gibraltar by train from Barcelona. José and his wife, Antonia Maria, settled in with their family and in February 1895, a son was born to them, Ruben Franklyn Melancthon, who was baptised by Coppin.

Detailed accounts of his work have not survived, but Rodriguez probably began by visiting people in their homes and by distributing Bibles. He made little progress in Gibraltar. He held two services a week there, on Sundays at 11.30 a.m. and on Wednesdays at 7.30 p.m., but the size of his congregation is not mentioned. The school had become more of a mission school, within the limitations set by the regulations which required a certain amount of secular teaching in English each day, and Rodriguez spent two days a week there giving religious instruction to the pupils. In addition he began to work in La Línea just across the border and here he fared much better. The Spanish chapel licence, dated 1 June 1893, still exists in the church archives and by November there was a congregation of about ninety which was all the rented room could hold. There were two services a week, at 6.30 p.m. on Sundays and 7.30 p.m. on Thursdays. Rodriguez also visited other nearby towns and villages. In the autumn of 1894, a new and larger preaching hall was opened and on Sunday 14 October, the first communion service was held there in the afternoon. The leaders from the

Gibraltar church were invited to attend. By this time a Sunday school had been formed and Rodriguez also wanted to start a day school. There was surprisingly little opposition from the priests or authorities which was attributed to apathy and religious indifference.

In his report for 1895 Coppin was very enthusiastic about the work;

> There is rarely ever a vacant bench in the preaching hall, and cottage meetings are so frequent in the homes of most of our converts that there is not a district or suburb in Línea in which the Gospel is not preached. Many of the people from the mountain villages in the vicinity, having found employment in the new docks proceeding in Gibraltar, are settled in Línea, and come to hear the Gospel with great interest. Our Evangelist says he is often called to speak to people, who tell him that they are anxious about their souls. Were there room, many stories could be embodied in this report that would set forth the reality of the conversions we rejoice over. Not only could we do with a much larger chapel, but an increased staff, the openings in the country around being numerous and inviting. [27]

There were, by then, twenty-six members, with ten on trial and thirty-six children in the Sunday school. Later Rodriguez himself described a visit to Tarifa in company with three friends from Algeciras. About three hundred people gathered and some expressed a desire for further meetings. Rodriguez ended by saying, 'Let us redouble our efforts, let us not weary in the work ... The will of God is that we finish this work'. [28]

Rodriguez also opened a depot in La Línea for the Bible Society and did colportage work in Spain as time permitted. He also ran the kiosk in Gibraltar and used a room in his own home as a depot.

Meanwhile, in the summer of 1893 Elizabeth Righton, the schoolmaster's wife, had unexpectedly died. She had been suffering from what was described as a Mediterranean-type fever for some three weeks but was not thought to be seriously ill. However, her condition suddenly deteriorated and her death left her husband and three children devastated by her loss. Terry and Eva Coppin too were both extremely upset and Eva herself went down with fever a few days later. They took a house for a few weeks at a nearby Spanish village by the sea and Coppin later reported that he thought the cooler, purer air there had contributed to her speedy recovery. He himself found it a great benefit to spend a day or two a week there preparing for meetings and four Sunday services. He was helping out at the Presbyterian church as their minister was not well. No-one felt it was in the interest of the bereaved family to stay in Gibraltar. So Righton returned to England and soon cabled his resignation to Coppin. He later became a

---

[27] *WMMS Reports,* vol. xxvi 1894-6, 1896, pp.47-9.
[28] Rev. W. Terry Coppin, 'Gibraltar - Spanish Work at the Frontier, in *Work and Workers in the Mission Field,* vol. iv, June 1895, pp.252-4.

photographer and was the connexional photographer from 1904 until his death in 1921. In his absence the military authorities released a young Wesleyan man to take temporary charge of the school.

The photograph was taken by John Righton and is used with permission from Audrey E. Williams, his grand-daughter. It was taken at Catalan Bay around 1892 and shows Terry Coppin (standing); Eva Coppin and their daughter seated; George and William Righton by the post with Elizabeth Righton on the far right.

Coppin tried unsuccessfully to find a suitable replacement in Gibraltar and so asked the Committee to help. He wanted a single man, which would be cheaper, and did not feel that first class qualifications were necessary as the school was 'very much more elementary than the average elementary school in England' and they could not afford to pay a first class salary.[29] He also stated that 'through the peculiar condition of this station I want a Christian brother and helper in the general work as well as just a schoolmaster'. He was 'hoping much from new blood and energy and methods of work'.[30]

Meanwhile the authorities decided that the schoolmaster's quarters in the school house were 'unhealthy and of a fever generating character' and therefore unfit for human habitation.[31] Coppin agreed as no-one living

---

[29] *WMMS Correspondence,* Coppin to Committee, 7 October 1893, fiche 799, no.4.

[30] Ibid., Coppin to Committee, 21 October 1893, fiche 799. no.5.

[31] Ibid.

there had escaped the fever. The rooms had not been intended as living quarters but Gilchrist had been allowed to adapt them for his use and his successors had followed suit. The rooms were greatly needed for church work and Coppin was very keen to use them in this way and let the schoolmaster live off the premises.

The absence of a schoolmaster greatly increased Coppin's workload and towards the end of October he wrote,

> I am also hoping every day to hear you are sending me a master. I have still the work of the Presbyterian chaplain Sunday and week day. My military deputy in the school leaves today for urgent military duties and I have not yet been able to find a man to replace him, and to crown all I am just now afflicted with horrible dyspepsia so you will understand the urgency of my plea.[32]

The Committee appointed Leonard Powlson who arrived in Gibraltar around the end of 1893 or beginning of 1894. He too had been trained at Westminster College. However, he soon expressed some dissatisfaction over his appointment, mainly with regard to his salary. As he was paid in Spanish currency and the exchange rate was not good, he felt he was getting less than he had been promised. In addition he had not been told that he was expected to supervise a night school five nights a week during the winter months and claimed he would have been paid extra for this in England. Coppin suggested he be paid in sterling and be given a proportion of the night school earnings which would also provide him with an incentive to improve it. Powlson himself claimed, 'The school has steadily increased since I took charge of it and as there is a Spanish evangelist doing good work in both school and town I think there is a hopeful future'.[33] The Committee agreed to Coppin's suggestions and he reported that Powlson seemed satisfied.

Powlson also succeeded Righton as chapel steward and organist although he only played on alternate Sundays. However, Coppin soon reported that 'Mr Powlson does not suit me as I had hoped he would. The first impression made upon the School Inspector was unfavourable. My hope is however that he will be an improving quality'.[34]

As Powlson lived in lodgings, Coppin was now able to proceed with his plans to provide better facilities for soldiers and sailors and on 1 December 1893,

> ... a suite of light, cheerful, and airy rooms suitably appointed and furnished for social and recreative purposes was opened upon the Wesleyan Church premises by the Rev. W.T. Coppin. These occupy the basement of the school-house and consist of a sitting

---

[32] Ibid.

[33] Ibid., Powlson to Committee, 16 February 1894, fiche 800, no.10.

[34] *WMMS Correspondence,* Coppin to Committee, 30 March 1894, fiche 800, no.13.

room or parlour, writing and office room, smoking room and lavatory. The erection of a refreshment bar is in contemplation by the Committee. These rooms are at the disposal and for the use of a church club or league entitled 'The Prince Edward's Road Friendly Association' which was inaugurated the same evening.[35]

One hundred people sat down to tea and afterwards the rules of the association were explained. Membership was through nomination and vote by the committee and payment of a minimum subscription of one peseta a month. The association was to be conducted on temperance principles and was undenominational in character. Sixty members were enrolled during the evening.

In March 1894 Coppin asked for permission to visit England with his wife partly on the grounds of health as he felt he and his wife needed 'bracing up', and partly to talk over the work particularly of the Spanish Mission. He reported, 'though we have made scarcely any impression in Gibraltar the work in Línea is promising' but he felt better financial arrangements could be made.[36] He also wanted to visit for 'private family reasons'. Permission was granted and the Presbyterian minister covered for him during his absence.

In October 1894 Coppin reported that a Mr Westall, whom he described later as 'not a member nor even a regular worshipper', had been to the registry office to look over a copy of the church deeds.[37] Coppin was clearly very angry about this, describing Westall as 'a most interfering man in matters that do not concern him'.[38] He believed 'personal animus to me is the root motive'. It seems that all the trustees of the church were now dead - the last survivor had been Gilchrist, and Coppin wondered how this affected their legal position. He later had an unofficial talk with the Attorney General who felt it was a storm in a teacup and did not feel that there was any cause for alarm. Coppin referred the matter to the Committee and eventually the Wesleyan Church Property Ordinance Gibraltar, 1906 was passed. The premises in future were to be held by four trustees - the senior Wesleyan Minister at Gibraltar, the senior Secretary of the Wesleyan Methodist Foreign Missionary Society, the Secretary of the Wesleyan Methodist Home Missions Committee and the Secretary of the Wesleyan Army and Navy Board and their successors in office.

Another difficulty needed resolving at this time, too, for Coppin wanted to change the way in which the soldiers' and sailors' rooms were organised. No specifically Christian work was done in them and the Friendly Association only had thirty members left, of whom seventeen were actually civilians. It seems to have been rather a strange way to organise use of the

---

[35] *Gibraltar Chronicle,* Monday 4 December 1893.

[36] *WMMS Correspondence,* Coppin to Committee, 30 March 1894, fiche 800, no.13.

[37] Ibid., Coppin to Committee, 12 January 1895, fiche 800, no.17.

[38] Ibid., Coppin to Committee, 6 November 1894, fiche 800, no.16.

rooms in the first place but Coppin claimed that it had been a financial expedient and an experiment which he felt had failed. He wanted to make use of the rooms free and for them to 'be a centre of Christian work and activity' and thought it was a good time to make the change as about three-quarters of the garrison was about to leave.[39]   There was opposition to his proposal led by Westall who was the Club's treasurer. So Coppin asked the Committee for a free hand and sole responsibility for making the decisions. This must have been given because the change did take place and Coppin soon reported that it had been 'most wise and right'.[40]

In order to get a speedy response from the Committee, Coppin tended to ask simple questions that required a 'yes' or 'no' answer and ask for a cabled reply, which worked very well.

However, by then, he had yet more problems, as he was not at all happy with Powlson saying, 'By his conduct he has been the cause of much vexation and annoyance to me and Mrs Coppin, and wrought much mischief in the Church, and will continue to do so, such is his character so long as he is identified with us'.[41] Coppin sent two reports, one about the school and another on Powlson. He regretted having to send the letter, but felt it was his 'imperative duty to do so in the interests of the Church and School here'. He felt Powlson had been aware that his post was for a single man, but less than four months after his arrival, a young lady came out from England to join him and they were married. Indeed, she was now pregnant though Coppin did not report that. Coppin felt he had not been consulted over the management of the school as he should have been and that Powlson seemed reluctant to work it on missionary lines. He was often found in the soldiers' reading room when he should have been in the school and Coppin felt, 'He does as little as possible, and is consumed with greed'.

Powlson also seemed reluctant to attend class meetings or to undertake his duties playing the organ. Coppin had not re-appointed him as chapel steward as he considered him 'totally unworthy of trust'. He described him as having thrown in his lot with Westall and stated that one person had wanted to bring a charge against Powlson in the leaders' meeting, but Coppin had dissuaded him, not wanting to add to the existing friction. He had tried to speak to Powlson himself but 'received insult for my pains'. He really wanted to dismiss him but felt this should wait until after the next school inspection and, as he had been engaged at the Mission House, Coppin thought dismissal should come from headquarters.

During 1894 the school had cost the Committee more than twice as much as in 1892 and 1893. Attendance had been dwindling and had fallen to fifty-one and the school fees and government grant were correspondingly reduced. Powlson had had a full year to demonstrate his abilities though he

---

[39] Ibid., Coppin to Committee, 12 January 1895, fiche 800, no.17.
[40] Ibid., Coppin to Committee, 22 February 1895, fiche 800, no.18.
[41] Ibid.

was presumably working under the difficulty of not being able to speak Spanish. Coppin felt the time had come to make a definite decision about the school but did not want the responsibility of closing such an old institution. He therefore asked for one of the Secretaries to visit to discuss the situation and the work of the Spanish mission, as he believed that Gibraltar should be the base from which Spanish work was done.

Coppin also wanted to discuss his own future and hoped to leave Gibraltar in 1896. Like many of his predecessors, he found Gibraltar a lonely station with no colleague to consult. However, he did have some fellowship for he wrote, 'I should say that I fully consult in my difficulties the Presbyterian chaplain [Thomas Murray] a wise good man who has been here ten years, knows our work well and take his advice before taking action'.[42]

One of the Secretaries, the Rev. Frederic W. Macdonald, did visit Gibraltar. In his report he acknowledged the isolation of the station; 'The minister stationed at Gibraltar is in an exceptionally lonely position so far as his relation to the Church and to his brother ministers is concerned' and added that this isolation was part of the reason for his visit especially as it had been twelve years since the last one.[43]

Macdonald had travelled from Madrid by rail to Algeciras and was met there by Coppin who accompanied him across the bay on the steamer on 26 March 1895. A few hours after his arrival, he attended the Tuesday evening class meeting with about twenty-five people present, mostly soldiers but including an artificer from the fleet and two or three women. He reported, 'The testimonies were lively and unconstrained, and the singing - well, robust. Soldiers never seem to tire of singing' and, after the meeting, they continued to sing Moody and Sankey hymns. Not all who came were Methodists. 'Godly men, Churchmen or Presbyterians, see no reason why they should not come and have a good time; neither does anyone else.'

He went on to describe the duties of the chaplain in taking parade services on Sunday mornings and in visiting those who were sick or in prison. 'Of these he receives formal notice, and must fill up his returns of duty done'. Macdonald visited the prison with Coppin where three declared Wesleyans were in trouble. He pointed out that military men could be imprisoned for offences which would not cause civilians to be sent to jail and did not therefore 'imply any great depravity'. He wrote,

> Some thirty-five men were in the prison at the time of our visit. It was a painful sight to me to see them dressed in ignoble canvas suits, breaking stones in a shed under the supervision of three or four warders. Our three

---

[42] Ibid.

[43] F.W. Macdonald, 'A Secretary's Visit to Gibraltar, in *Work and Workers in the Mission Field,* vol. iv, May, 1895, pp.178-81.

erring brethren were called by number, not by name. Each man laid down his hammer, rose, and stood at 'attention' and they were then marched into the prison, where the chaplain could see each man alone. Then comes the opportunity for advice, for kindly reproof, for a word of exhortation and encouragement, and for prayer.

He then described the difficulties and temptations of life for young soldiers and the importance of the chaplain's work and ended this section by saying,

In the admirable premises at our disposal in Gibraltar, Mr Coppin has organised a kind of Soldiers' Institute, which is of great service. There is a reading room, with newspapers and periodicals, a piano, and various appliances for recreation. Religious meetings of various kinds are held, temperance meetings, lectures and the ever-popular tea-meeting. At the bar the soldier's perennial thirst for coffee, ginger-beer, and the like, can be gratified at a very small expense, and a kind of good fellowship is established among those who frequent the rooms which is a wholesome element in their life, and a power to counteract a fellowship which is not good.

He spent the Saturday evening sharing a simple but enjoyable meal with some fifty soldiers as his guests. Sunday 31 March was a busy day and he gave a full description of it.

The Channel Squadron, under the command of Admiral Fitz Roy, had come into the bay on Saturday, and we expected a large muster of blue-jackets at the Parade service on Sunday morning. At half-past ten the body of the chapel was fairly filled with soldiers, about 150 in number, Cameron Highlanders, West Yorkshires, East Lancashires, Engineers, Artillery, and Medical Staff Corps. Some eight or ten were in the choir. There were also between twenty and thirty civilians, men and women. Whilst we were singing the first hymn - very well sung, by the bye - the tramp of many feet was heard outside, and soon the seamen from the fleet, about 170 in number, poured into the chapel, and, trooping upstairs, filled the gallery. We sang a verse or two over again to give them time to settle in their places. The service then proceeded, and I preached to a most attentive congregation, and one that was to me deeply interesting. At the close of the service I baptised the child of a resident English gentleman, a member of the congregation. [Mary Winifred, daughter of Benjamin and Alice Westall.]

In the afternoon Mr Coppin and I went to Línea, the nearest Spanish town immediately beyond the lines, where Señor Rodriguez, the lay evangelist, is at work amongst a poor and ignorant population. It is a squalid little town, in striking contrast with the brightness and smartness of Gibraltar. We found him conducting a Sunday-school single handed, teaching some fifty or sixty children, whose attention he held very well as he taught them by question and answer the primary truths of the Gospel. He had, however, two congregations, for outside the circle of children was a double row of men and women, some of them pathetically old and feeble, who listened to all that was said by teacher and children. Perhaps this mode of instruction was more suitable to them than any other that could have been devised. By-and-by the children were dismissed, and I counted between forty and fifty adults remaining. The door was then closed, and a Communion service was held, six persons partaking of the Lord's Supper with Mr Coppin, Rodriguez, and myself, the others quietly and seriously looking on and listening. Then came a service of hand-shaking and salutations, and we returned to Gibraltar. Here I was expected to take tea with a little company of soldiers who are in the habit of meeting together in this way before the evening service. We had our brotherly cup of tea together, and at half-past six adjourned to the chapel. The evening service differs from that of the morning in being voluntary. There is no parade, no marching of the men to church. The seamen were all on board their ships, so none of them could be with us except a few petty officers on leave. There were, however, about sixty soldiers and forty civilians. I afterwards administered the Lord's Supper to thirty-two communicants, and thus a busy, happy day came to its close.

Macdonald did talk with Powlson during his visit but no account of their discussion has survived. Mention of the school in the article was brief. He merely said,

Our Day School has in the past done good educational work, but it has not been found possible at all events in recent years, to make it effective as a Missionary Agency. Whether under present conditions, it should be continued, is a matter for serious consideration.

What decisions, if any, were made during his visit are not known. The school inspection took place on 29 April. Some time later Coppin met unofficially with the inspector who was still preparing his report, but it was clear that he was dissatisfied. Coppin reported this to the Committee saying also that Powlson had 'grown more apathetic in school and chapel matters' and felt that the sooner he was removed the better.[44] During this time the Powlsons had a daughter but there is no entry in the baptismal register for, as Coppin explained, 'He took advantage of my absence one sabbath in Tangier to have his child baptised in the Presbyterian church'.[45]

In late June Coppin received a memo from the inspector stating, 'Please note that unless considerable improvement in the three elementary subjects is shown at the next examination, it may be my duty in assessing the grant to apply clause 15 of the Education Code'.[46] Under this clause the government grant could be withheld or reduced. Coppin was not surprised by this and reported it to the Committee, but it had already decided that the

---

[44] *WMMS Correspondence,* Coppin to Committee, 22 May 1895, fiche 800/1, no.20.

[45] Ibid., Coppin to Committee, 27 June 1895, fiche 801, no.21.

[46] Ibid., Memo from A. Coll, Inspector of Schools to Coppin, 29 June 1895, fiche 801, no.22.

school should close. The decision had been made with some reluctance and regret. The number of scholars was only four fewer than the previous year and Macdonald wrote,

> Even now if we could find a master with the soul of a missionary willing to devote himself to school work in Gibraltar for the sake of Christ and His Kingdom, I should counsel its continuance. But it is necessary to look facts in the face. We have not such a man at command either now or prospectively. I have satisfied myself that the school is not a missionary school and that it renders no appreciable service to the great cause for which this Society exists, nor has it done so for many years past.[47]

Clearly he did not feel Powlson was the man for the job. He was given three months notice which he accepted 'with satisfaction' and asked for help in finding a new appointment.[48] There is nothing in his letter that shows awareness of any dissatisfaction with him. There may have been personal difficulties in the relationship between Coppin and Powlson, but the inspector's report was an independent assessment and Powlson does not seem to have done a good job in the school. He had certainly not been the co-worker or colleague to Coppin that his predecessors had been, but even if he had been, it is likely the school would have closed eventually anyway. Rodriguez had made little impression in Gibraltar. Catholicism was too strong and had now become the dominant force in education. Nevertheless, it was the establishment of the first Methodist school which had led to the development of so many others and, over the years, Methodism had educated thousands of children which many families acknowledged with gratitude. Powlson returned to England at the end of July.

By then the school had closed for the summer holidays but Coppin soon publicised the fact that it had closed for good. The night school closed as well. He was very pleased to be able to find a post for Miss Vecchio at a Spanish mission school in Tangier which he felt was a happy arrangement.

The closure of the school meant that the building could now be wholly used for the work with the soldiers and sailors. The kitchen, refreshment bar, games, reading and sitting rooms occupied the basement and upstairs the large hall became a useful meeting place. On 28 June 1895 the first picnic to the cork woods had taken place when 116 'soldiers, bluejackets and civilians' set off for the whole day with lunch and tea served to them.[49] This very enjoyable outing was the first of many organised by the Wesleyan Soldiers' and Sailors' Rooms. By October a series of free weekly entertainments had been arranged and advertised in the *Gibraltar Chronicle,* which were for the men of the Forces. The first was a concert organised by the Royal Engineers which took place on 30 October. By

---

[47] Macdonald to Coppin, 2 July 1895.
[48] *WMMS Correspondence,* Powlson to Committee, 9 July 1895, fiche 801, no.25.
[49] *Gibraltar Chronicle,* 29 June 1895.

December, the *Chronicle* reported that nearly all the seats in the hall had been taken. The Missionary Society reported,

> By means of tea-meetings, picnics, Spanish classes, entertainments, and anything that will benefit, we show the men that we take an interest in them and thereby endeavour to gather them about us, keep them from evil places, and attach them to what is good.[50]

A deaconess, Dorothy Coy, visited Gibraltar briefly on a couple of occasions and Coppin reported 'the interest she has taken in our Rooms and soldier's work and the attachment of the men to her have made it very evident how valuable a suitable lady might be for this branch also of our work.'[51] No doubt Eva Coppin helped with this work for her husband reported that he was concerned about her. 'She is wearing herself down to a skeleton with the arduous duties of our home, and in her goodness to make up for any lack of efficient workers, and she suffers much'.[52] As usual no details of the part she played in the life of the church have survived but clearly it was an active part.

Coppin himself reported that he had regained much of the health he had lost in West Africa and that for three years he had been free of 'those weakening attacks of fever which it has taken so long to finally subdue'. He felt now 'that the bracing air of England may make me robust'.[53] For reasons of health, he wanted to leave Gibraltar before the summer but, since the work had developed considerably during his time, he felt it 'in every way desirable that I should hand over my work to my successor on the spot'.

Around this time the future of the Spanish work was discussed and the possibility of withdrawing from Spain altogether considered. Coppin was aware of this for in April 1896 he asked, 'If the Committee should decide to withdraw from Spain, will Línea be surrendered?'[54] He had a particular reason for asking because he went on to say that, 'last week Mr Rodriguez was smitten with a terrible paralytic stroke. He lies very ill unable to speak or understand. The doctor has grave fears he will be unable to regain the full free use of his limbs'. What a tragic blow to the promising work in La Línea this was.

In the short term, Coppin managed to find cover for the work from a neighbouring mission in Algeciras. Details of this mission have not survived but it was organised by a Mrs Todd Osborne. In 1912 the Rev. Alexander Stewart, a Presbyterian minister, began work at a mission in Algeciras which had been begun in 1865 by an Anglican clergyman and

---

[50] *WMMS Reports,* vol. xxvi, 1894-6, 1896, p.48.

[51] *WMMS Correspondence,* Coppin to Committee, 22 May 1895, fiche 801, no.20.

[52] Ibid., Coppin to Committee, 13 February 1896, fiche 801, no.28.

[53] Ibid.

[54] Ibid., Coppin to Committee, 8 April 1896, fiche 801, no.29.

had since been undenominational.[55] This may have been the same mission which in 1896 was under the care of Mrs Todd Osborne. Coppin felt that 'the difficulty of replacing Mr Rodriguez if necessary, will be considerable. If the Committee retire from Spain it is not improbable we might transfer the work to the above Mission' and he asked for the Committee's views on this.[56]

The work was transferred despite the fact that it was so promising being the least opposed of all the Methodist work in Spain. Clearly the loss of Rodriguez was a crippling blow but there seems to have been no attempt or even desire to find a way of carrying on. Perhaps it was partly a matter of timing as Coppin was about to leave Gibraltar and he wanted to sort the problem out before his successor arrived. Perhaps the closure of the school and the failure of Rodriguez to make any real impression in Gibraltar itself contributed to this decision and presumably the Spanish services there ceased when Rodriguez fell ill. The transfer meant a small financial saving but it seems likely that the main reason was that Methodism felt it was time to focus on the army and navy work. MacDonald in his report had written, 'For many reasons Gibraltar is not a place that we should select for a Spanish Mission. Our work at Gibraltar is a military and naval mission, and as such is abundantly justified.'[57]

The mission in La Línea did continue although not with quite the same success as under Rodriguez. He, himself, improved a little and went into Spain for the summer on medical advice. By the beginning of 1897 he had recovered sufficiently to do a little work for the Bible Society, but in March Rodriguez had a second stroke and this time the doctors felt he would never work again. He was by then living in La Línea and would have been destitute without financial support from Methodism. In the end the family returned to the Balearics where presumably they had family and friends. The Bible Society helped Methodism with the cost of the move and a sum of money was given to them to help them resettle, plus the proceeds from a local collection, so that they were as well looked after as was possible in the circumstances.

The Bible Society transferred one of their other Spanish colporteurs from Málaga to La Línea. However, in subsequent annual reports information about Bible Society work in Gibraltar became more sparse. The kiosk remained for a few years but eventually dwindling sales led to a decision to close it. In the end, it was lent to a Mr George Holmes of the South Barrack and Dockyard Mission who continued to sell Bibles from it. From then on, Gibraltar hardly had a mention in the annual reports. A local committee still existed and often the Methodist minister acted as its

---

[55] Alexander Stewart, *In darkest Spain*, Marshall Brothers Ltd.: London & Edinburgh, no date, p.10.

[56] *WMMS Correspondence,* Coppin to Committee, 8 April 1896, fiche 801, no.29.

[57] *Work and Workers*, op. cit., pp.178-81.

secretary or treasurer. An annual meeting took place though these were suspended during the First World War. Methodism in Gibraltar retained an interest in the Bible Society but was no longer actively involved in any work of distribution.

From this time onwards, all attempts at establishing Methodist missionary work in Spain from Gibraltar came to an end and the tenuous links with the work in the north now ceased. Brown had stayed in the Balearics until his retirement in 1888. He was replaced by Smith who moved there from Barcelona. Brown returned to London as a supernumerary but was in failing health. Two years later he moved to Brighton. These later years were spent in 'extreme feebleness'.[58] He had really given his all to Spain. He died on 3 July 1899 at the age of 77. The work in Spain remains a lasting testament to this hard-working man who, without any training or ministerial status, had founded and developed the work both in Barcelona and the Balearics.

Robert Simpson also gave his all to the Spanish work. When Brown retired in 1888, he was designated Chairman of the District and General Superintendent of the Spanish work but two years later failing health led to his return to England 'and he was brought home apparently a dying man'.[59] However he did survive, living as a supernumerary apart from a brief three-year return to full-time work. He died on 29 December 1900 aged 51.

Wheatcroft Brown succeeded Simpson in Barcelona as the Chairman and General Superintendent of the District whilst Smith worked in the Balearics. Madrid was given up at the end of 1894. However, although the Spanish work continued, it was never adequately supported in terms of staff and other resources. Wheatcroft Brown was later recalled and Smith was brought back from the islands to superintend the whole work from Barcelona and stayed there for the next twenty years. Other ministers followed both British and Spanish. The work survived despite the traumas of the Spanish Civil War, the oppressive restrictions imposed on Protestants under the Franco regime and somewhat limited support from the Missionary Society. In 1955 the Methodist churches united with other Protestant Churches, to become part of the Spanish Evangelical Church. Today there are three churches in Barcelona itself and four outlying churches plus two churches in both Majorca and Minorca. So the work of William Brown continues and is a lasting testament to his faith and commitment and to the others who followed in his footsteps.

Meanwhile in 1896 the Coppin family was preparing to leave Gibraltar but stayed on to ensure a good handover to their successors, William and Emily Sarchet, who arrived on Wednesday 27 May 1896 with one child. A combined welcome and farewell meeting took place on 30 May. Coppin had actually met Sarchet before in Guernsey. He wrote,

---

[58] *Minutes of the Methodist Conference,* 1899, pp.41-2.
[59] Ibid., 1901, p.134.

Our friends and successors had a most hearty and sincere reception. My dear wife and I were the recipients of some handsome presents. But what deeply affected us were the expressions, all too kind, and undeserving, that fell from the lips of Colonel Jelf who presided, the Ven. Archdeacon Govet, and other brother chaplains and fellow church-workers who took part.[60]

Clearly ecumenical relationships were much improved and Methodism was now both better respected and established.

The two families spent a fortnight together. Coppin introduced Sarchet to the work and to the various authorities and no doubt the wives discussed their roles as well. On Sunday 14 June the Coppins left Gibraltar. Eva went with their son to London whilst her husband set off via Naples and overland to London taking the opportunity to explore more of the Mediterranean.

After several appointments in Britain, Coppin was appointed to India. On returning to England he served in various circuits before becoming a supernumerary in 1918. He died, at the age of 76 on 22 December 1930.

Coppin had worked hard in Gibraltar but not without some difficulties in relationships. Powlson does not seem to have done a good job, but the difficulties with Westall may have stemmed from a personality clash or different styles of working. However, Coppin's ministry marked a turning point in the work. He had managed to fulfil the desires of several of his predecessors by undertaking Spanish work which, whilst successful in Spain, did not flourish in Gibraltar where Catholicism was just too strong. However, he had not neglected the other work and had really laid the foundations for a new kind of work with the soldiers and sailors. This now became the sole focus of the Methodist Church in Gibraltar, which meant that the Army and Navy Committee, with Richard Allen as its Secretary, became more involved with Methodism on the Rock.

---

[60] *WMMS Correspondence,* Coppin to Committee, 31 May 1896, fiche 801, no.32.

CHAPTER 18   THE SOLDIERS AND SAILORS TAKE PRECEDENCE
The Welcome Home is opened (1896 -1903)

William Henry Sarchet was born in Guernsey in 1862. He began his ministry in France in 1888 and later worked in Britain. He arrived in Gibraltar with his wife, Emily Victoria, and one child at the end of May 1896. In September a second child, Lionel Leslie, was born. They were very grateful for the way the house had been left and for the helpful introduction to the work from the Coppins. Sarchet wrote, 'Our impression so far is that we will like the place and the work.'[1] He felt that the civilian congregation and membership was disappointingly small and that actual membership amongst the military was small too, 'but the opportunities provided by the parade services, hospital and prison visitation and personal intercourse with the men in the Rooms are simply boundless, these I hope to seize and turn to good account.'

Westall wrote to the Committee in February 1897 to say that Sarchet had 'gained the affection of all Methodists in Gibraltar', claiming a massive increase in the voluntary Sunday evening congregation and attendance at class meetings, plus the revival of the Sunday school which he reported had been extinct the year before and now had thirty-five children.[2] This

WILLIAM HENRY SARCHET

statement may be slightly exaggerated as he had not got on with Coppin, and he went on to say how pleased he was now to be able to bear this testimony when on a former occasion he had had to complain about 'the manner in which the affairs of the Church were managed'. Whatever the rights and wrongs at that time, it was good that harmony prevailed now and that the work was going well. However, unlike his predecessors, Sarchet did not have the school to supervise or any Spanish work to consider so that he could concentrate on the English work.

In March 1897 Sarchet reported that the Channel Squadron had been at Gibraltar for the past three weeks. He went on to say that 'we have slept over 300 men since the fleet is in'.[3] He had borrowed some equipment

---

[1] *WMMS Correspondence*, Sarchet to Committee, 23 June 1896, fiche 801, no.33.
[2] Ibid., Westall to Committee, 12 February 1897, fiche 801, no.34.
[3] Ibid., Sarchet to Committee, 23 March 1897, fiche 801, no.35.

from the military and the men camped out in the old school-house, paying a small charge for the service. The naval men, when off duty, were not allowed to return to their ships and without accommodation, the possibilities of getting into all kinds of trouble were endless. Sarchet continued to try and meet this need as best he could. Over a year later, in July 1898, Richard Allen visited Gibraltar. He felt the Sunday he spent there

> ... gave abundant evidence of the vitality and growing usefulness of our Church. The early morning parade service for the Wesleyans of the Channel Fleet with its congregation of some 450 men, the second parade service for the garrison and stationary ships again nearly filling the chapel, the voluntary evening service with more than 100 present, the blessed Sacramental service at the close, and then the crowded Home gathering for praise and prayer and testimony are experiences which will long be remembered.[4]

He went on to say,

> When the fleet was not in, the Home - the converted school premises - we found, was largely frequented, and was the centre of many gracious activities. But when the fleet was in the scenes that were witnessed were both delightful and saddening.
> Mr Sarchet, with admirable ingenuity, strove to meet the demands, and by all kinds of makeshifts - converting tables and forms and the floors even into beds, he provided all possible accommodation for the men who were on leave. But when all had been done by him and by the other two Homes, by far the greater part was left undone. The men crowded into the Home as to a refuge for refreshment and rest, and sorely disappointed, were compelled to go away.

Not long afterwards, Sarchet wrote to the Missionary Committee stating the need for a proper Home in a more accessible and prominent position. He went on to say that he had the 'chance of securing one of the best sites and one of the most ideal buildings imaginable'.[5] In a second letter he wrote, 'Since writing you yesterday it has struck me that perhaps my letter will come to you in the shape of a surprise and seem very abrupt but I wrote under the impression that Mr Allen who visited the station two months ago officially I presume has seen you and talked over the situation'.[6] He went on to say, 'I confess that I do not quite understand where I am in relation to my commanding officers ... The position is not as clearly defined as I would like it to be'. It was indeed rather confusing.

At this time the garrison at Gibraltar consisted of some 5,000 men with a

---

[4] Richard W. Allen, 'Notes of a visit to the Mediterranean Garrisons. II – Gibraltar', in *Missionary Notices,* vol. xxix, 1897-9, October 1898, pp.146-50.

[5] *WMMS Correspondence,* Sarchet to Committee, 11 August 1898, fiche 802, no.38.

[6] Ibid., Sarchet to Committee, 12 August 1898, fiche 802, no.39.

regular naval force of nearly a thousand and the Channel and Mediterranean fleets now visited frequently each numbering from ten to fourteen thousand men. In 1895 work had begun on constructing a proper harbour with a modern dockyard including three dry docks.

> Some twenty two hundred men were employed, many of whom came from Britain ... Others came from Malta, but the majority came from Spain. La Línea grew apace. Housing was so short on the Rock itself that old hulks were again used as accommodation ships, as had to be done in the days of convict labor.[7]

In later years the numbers of labourers employed rose to between four and five thousand and the needs of these workers also became a concern to Methodism.

The building Sarchet had found was situated right in the heart of the town and had been occupied by the Eastern Telegraph Company. He reported, 'There are four flats with splendid, numerous and spacious apartments'. There were many applicants for flats or rooms for offices but the manager wanted to let the whole building and was willing to give the Methodists preference, which was perhaps surprising in view of the accommodation shortage. Sarchet went on to say,

> Mr Westall and I have gone into the whole thing carefully - he is the gas manager and one of the keenest business men in the town and we think, to say nothing of the splendid premises it would give us and the grand opening for philanthropic, social and religious work it presents, as a business operation it would pay well. We will raise more than 200 dollars a month with refreshment bar, baths and beds to say nothing of the flat we could let and rooms for offices ... The site and situation is unique we could not find a better, no structural alteration would be needed. The first storey is so built that the rooms unfold one into the other and give a splendid and great hall in which we could seat 250 to 300 people. What is more is that if we let this slip and do not move out now I don't know where or how we should be able to do in the future.[8]

He wished he could get away to press his case in London but he was just too busy. The Committee must have replied quickly, realising that the offer would not stay open indefinitely, and wanting to know if the new scheme meant abandoning the present premises. Sarchet wrote straight back to reassure them on this point.

> The chapel would remain in constant use as at present, the schoolroom and quarters we propose to sub-let for the present also the minister's house and remove to the top flat of the new place so as to be on the spot for the supervision of the whole work of the Home and the nightly

---

[7] Jackson, op. cit., p.257.
[8] *WMMS Correspondence,* Sarchet to Committee, 11 August 1898, fiche 802, no.38.

meetings. Then as soon as the new Home is fairly started I would propose that we make the old schoolroom the centre of an energetic Spanish Mission. It is right in the centre of a thickly populated Spanish speaking neighbourhood and would succeed.[9]

His last suggestion never came to anything - too many attempts had been made in the past for another to be considered. The Committee was also concerned about the cost but Sarchet felt, 'If we take this place we will command a situation and have premises second to none in Gibraltar. I believe we can do it without putting the Committee to extra expense'. He was clearly very enthusiastic about the scheme and very anxious not to miss this opportunity and so, despite being busy, he wrote,

> If I do not get permission to take the premises I shall always regret that I was not on the spot to give further explanation and plead for the scheme so I am arranging to get away on September 6th. I shall reach London on the 11th and return on the 21st. This will give me ten days to get through with the business. The Headquarters of the Eastern Telegraph Company are in London and it is there that the business will be concluded.[10]

He added, 'I hope I am not doing anything wrong by not waiting for instructions to come'. There were many other issues he wanted to discuss; purchasing furniture for the Home, appointing a manager and the possibility of employing a lady worker. During the past eighteen months they had raised some money 'by means of picnics in connection with our "Rooms" so this money is available either for outfit or lady worker and I see no reason that we should not raise more next year.' He also wanted to visit the Home in Chatham to learn more about running Homes.

The first Wesleyan Methodist Soldiers' Home had been built in 1869 in Aldershot and others had followed in Malta, Portsmouth, Woolwich and Shorncliffe until by 1896 there were twenty-seven at home and abroad, so there was plenty of experience for Sarchet to draw upon.

Sarchet attended a meeting of the Army and Navy Committee on 15 September to plead his case. His application was successful and the Committee voted £500 to the scheme 'provided that on further enquiry it be found that the terms on which the renewal of the lease of the premises can be secured are such as will afford a reasonable prospect of the Home being self-supporting, and are otherwise satisfactory'.[11] £300 was given as a grant and £200 as a loan. The conditions were met and the property at 6, Church Street (now a part of Main Street) was held by the Missionary Society on behalf of the Army and Navy Committee.

Sarchet must have worked extremely hard on his return to Gibraltar to

---

[9] Ibid., Sarchet to Committee, 1 September 1898, fiche 802, no.40.
[10] Ibid.
[11] *Army and Navy Sub-Committee Minutes - October 1896-1898.* Meeting held 15 September 1898, Minute ix, pp.97-8.

appoint a manager and get everything ready in time for the grand opening which took place on Thursday 8 December 1898. A large crowd gathered outside the building to greet the Governor, Sir Robert Biddulph, who arrived at 3 o'clock. He was accompanied by Rear-Admiral Brackenbury, Commander of the Channel Fleet, Major-General Richardson and several other Forces personnel. 'The body of the hall contained many of the Garrison and leading members of Gibraltar Society. There was not room to admit all the soldiers and sailors who assembled later in great numbers'.[12] Several of the other clergy were present and the Ven. Archdeacon Govett took the chair to open the proceedings. He praised Sarchet's hard work in establishing the Home and stressed that it 'was started on no narrow sectarian lines, it was open to all sorts and conditions of men', which was why it was decided to call it '"The Welcome" Soldiers' and Seamen's Home.' Sarchet then gave a detailed history of the work, started by Coppin, which had culminated in this new Home. The building contained 'a refreshment bar, bathrooms, lavatories, lockers and tea room on the ground floor, lecture hall, men's parlour, reading and games rooms on the first floor, and sleeping accommodation on the second floor'.

The Governor then rose to open the Home saying,

> All who are acquainted with Gibraltar know that the several homes we have already got, are not nearly adequate for the numbers who use them. A soldier's life on the Rock is terribly confined; he has no distractions such as those of higher rank can enjoy; he cannot get a change by going into Spain. Soldiers and Sailors have nothing but this congested town to go to, practically one long narrow street, and have no amusements as in other places. The houses of entertainment that exist are not of the highest class, and it is the duty of all to endeavour to provide a proper place of rest for them, a want which this Home so admirably provides for.

He therefore expressed great pleasure in pronouncing the building open. Various votes of thanks followed and then Sarchet read a letter from the Commander-in-Chief, Field Marshal Lord Wolseley which contained the following words:

> Whatever the Wesleyan chaplains undertake prospers. Whilst other sects are busy with preaching up the advantages of incense and tawdry ornaments in Protestant churches and in quarrelling over abstruse questions of consubstantiation and points on which our soldiers take no interest, the Wesleyans are hard at work at good things that benefit the soldiers of all sects.
>
> I wish your new Soldiers' Home success with all my heart.[13]

---

[12] *Gibraltar Chronicle,* 10 December 1898.

[13] *Army and Navy Sub-Committee Minutes.* Meeting held 30 January 1899, Minute ii, pp.17-8.

The Home was then inspected and visitors were invited to make a contribution to the funds. Afternoon tea was served to some 300 people in the refreshment bar and 'Mr Figueras' Mandoline Band provided good music.' A concert took place in the evening when

> ... the Home presented a brilliant appearance, the front being illuminated by a device bearing the words 'The Welcome' and surmounted by a crown and the letters V.R., all worked out with gas jets, whilst the street was gay with a considerable display of bunting.[14]

The Welcome

Sarchet later reported, 'This auspicious opening was followed by a month of decided success in the various branches of work connected with the Home and there is every indication that the site selected was the right one, and that the Home is likely to prove a centre of great usefulness and blessing.'[15]

It did indeed and the Home went from strength to strength. In its first year, 6,253 men slept there and over £2,000 was taken in the refreshment bar. In the second year, 9,389 beds were let and the Home was well used during the day. It became not only self-supporting but began to make a small profit even though the initial costs were over £500. The outings Coppin had started, continued and were quite a feature of the Welcome's organised programme right up to the outbreak of the Spanish Civil War. Sarchet explained that without official trips the 'entire garrison is shut up from January to December; hence to organise a trip across into Spain or

---

[14] *Gibraltar Chronicle*, 10 December 1898.
[15] W.H. Sarchet, 'Soldiers' and Sailors' Home, Gibraltar', in *Missionary Notices,* vol. xxix, 1897-9, April 1899, pp.57-8.

across the Straits to Morocco is to confer a real boon on the men'.[16] With the Governor's permission, now Sir George White, they had run a number of trips, taking in all 1,000 non-commissioned officers and men, or one-fifth of the garrison, across the Straits to Tangier. He described the trips to Tangier as follows:

> We start in the early morning. Breakfast is served on board soon after the excursion boat leaves the harbour; each man is served out with a bag containing a substantial ham sandwich, two eggs, a buttered roll, and a small packet of salt. Tea is placed about the deck in tea-urns, and each man helps himself. Arriving at Tangier, after a three-hours' run, the steamer anchors in the bay, and the party is taken off in rowing-boats by Moorish boatmen. Soon after landing, a cold luncheon of three courses is served at Hotel Cecil. Then, mounting horses and mules and donkeys, and others on foot, the party is soon scattered over the town and adjacent country. At five o'clock we embark for home. Tea is served on board, and by eight o'clock we are back again at Gibraltar. The excursion, including the three meals, boating, pier dues, and trip, costs 6s 6d. Similar picnics take place into Spain, but the Tangier trips are the most popular.
>
> So in many and varied ways we try to make our men know that religion was not intended to make our pleasures less, but that it touches our life in all its parts, and it purifies and ennobles and makes better all that it touches.

The spiritual side was not neglected - conversion was after all the main aim of the work and in his report for 1900 Sarchet wrote,

> Having secured these fine premises in the main street, and right in the heart of the town, we have been able to reach a large number of people hitherto untouched by Methodism at Gibraltar, and as the result - in part - of the various meetings held at the 'Welcome' during the week we now have an increased Sunday evening congregation at the Church; in fact, it has grown so that now the voluntary service is better attended than the parade service, a fact which, as all know who have had to do with military work, is very encouraging.
>
> We have also this winter made a new departure in the shape of a Lime-light Gospel Service on Sunday evenings at the 'Welcome' at 8 o'clock. To keep up a series of this kind so far from any centre where lantern slides may be obtained has been a difficult and expensive work, but the results realised more than repay the output, and indicate that there is a great future for work of this kind at Gibraltar.
>
> In a much larger and better attended class meeting we think we see the most trustworthy evidence that the year's work has not been in vain, but has produced results of the kind for which we have both laboured and prayed, over which every Methodist will rejoice with us.[17]

---

[16] Ibid., vol. xxxi, 1903-4, June 1903, pp.175-7.
[17] *WMMS Reports,* 1902, p.40.

He later wrote that the Lime Light Gospel service 'secures a full house *always*' so they clearly were very popular.[18] Sarchet had the help of a lady worker, Sister Snodgrass, who seems to have been particularly involved with the Bible class and the Sunday school as well as visiting soldiers' wives and families. She was no doubt also a presence in the Home though it is not clear if she actually lived there. Accommodation was provided on the premises for the manager. Sarchet also moved into a flat at the Welcome and on 15 February 1899 a daughter, Irene Hazel, was born there.

All this left much of the property on Prince Edward's Road empty. So the old school-house was let to the Young Women's Christian Association and the manse to Archdeacon Govett (Dean from 1905). He had apparently had to leave his colonial quarters and was unable to find a home anywhere else. He lived there until his death on 1 September 1912 at the age of 85. There is a memorial to him in the Anglican Cathedral where he had ministered for thirty-one years. Decimus Storry Govett seems to have had a wonderful ecumenical spirit and been willing to work alongside the Wesleyans and Presbyterians in Gibraltar. He had a great interest in soldiers and sailors and was involved in the Anglican Seamen's Mission and was a member of the Bible Society's local committee. His occupation of the manse as a tenant, and the changed use of the old school-house, actually broke the conditions of the lease but it seems the authorities were willing to overlook this irregularity. However, after Govett's death, questions were asked and the minister of the day in his correspondence on the subject wrote, 'It was understood that this was irregular, yet the spirit of the Ordinance was kept, in that shelter was afforded the Venerable Dean who was rightly considered the bishop of all denominations ... We shall always feel glad that we had the honour of sheltering for so many years such a distinguished son of the Church of England.'[19] In the end, an Ordinance to amend the Wesleyan Church Property Ordinance, 1906 was drawn up in 1918 to allow the premises to be let out to those whom the trustees regarded as fit persons.

The increased prosperity of the work in the Welcome highlighted one other problem which was the location of the Church itself. In October 1899 Sarchet reported that he had discovered dry rot there and felt it would involve a 'big outlay of money' to eradicate it. He went on to say, 'the question arises has not the time arrived to tackle the long talked of scheme of having our chapel in a more central and more suitable spot?'[20] Allen had, in fact, discussed this issue with the Governor during his visit, but there was a shortage of sites because of the naval work going on in Gibraltar. Although Sarchet had seen the Governor three times since, 'it is plain there is no hope whatever'. He went on to say, 'His Excellency is a

---

[18] Sarchet, *Missionary Notices*, op. cit., pp.175-7.
[19] Sackett to J.B. Crooks, Governor Engineer, 16 June 1914.
[20] *WMMS Correspondence,* Sarchet to Committee, 5 October 1899, fiche 802, no.42.

Christian man and has been exceedingly kind to us throughout our work in connection with the "Home" and I feel quite sure that he would help me if he could but he <u>can't</u>'. He felt their only option therefore was to buy a private property. He recommended a particular central site which he had found with an asking price of £4,500 but this was probably too expensive and was not purchased. However, Sarchet did not give up this plan and some time later wrote,

> There is a great opportunity for Methodism just now in Gibraltar. The creation by the government of a great naval dockyard is bringing to the Rock in large numbers just the class of people who frequent our places of worship at home, and we shall fail in our duty as a Church if we do not make adequate and suitable provision for them. To do this we must have a new church built on a suitable site. The old church, which is in very bad repair, is away up Prince Edward's Road, difficult to reach, and still more difficult to find, hidden away in the midst of the Spanish-speaking population.
>
> There is only one place for Methodism, whether here or elsewhere, and that is not up a side street, but well to the front, right in the main street.[21]

Meanwhile the Sarchets had had their own tragedy to deal with for on 22 February 1900 Irene Hazel died just days after her first birthday. By then Sarchet, who was under the impression that he had been appointed to Gibraltar for five years, was expecting and wanting to leave in 1901. In July 1900 he wrote to the Committee to express his wishes about his next appointment;

> I cannot say that I am altogether in love with military work, although I think it would be very different if the station were not entirely military and naval if there was a fair proportion of the civilian element from which one might receive the help and sympathy that I have so often longed for out here. But while not quite in love with the work I think it would be a pity to remove me from it altogether because my five years experience here has taught me a great deal about military life and routine which puts me in a position to do this kind of work easier.[22]

Overall he was willing to go anywhere. He did not get a response from the Committee and in January 1901 wrote to say 'I may be wrong but I am labouring under the uncomfortable impression that I am not being fairly treated'.[23] He had written to both the Army and Navy and Missionary Committees about his next appointment. Allen had replied to the effect that he had not understood there was a time limit of five years, but the

---

[21] 'Our stations on the Mediterranean. Gibraltar', in *Missionary Notices,* vol. xxx, 1901-2, August 1902, p.229. Also *WMMS Reports,* 1902, p.32.

[22] *WMMS Correspondence,* Sarchet to Committee, 10 July 1900, fiche 802, no.44.

[23] Ibid., Sarchet to Committee, 23 January 1901, fiche 802, no.46.

Missionary Committee had recognised it and offered to bear the matter in mind. Then unexpectedly Sarchet received a letter from the Rev. Dennis Kemp enquiring about the station. Sarchet was very angry and declared, 'What I feel sore about is that matters should have proceeded far enough to be able to open negotiations with Mr Kemp and yet I am kept in entire ignorance even of the fact that I am to be removed.'

The Missionary Committee did not understand the reason for his sense of grievance believing that Sarchet felt slighted by being removed. This was not the case at all as Sarchet hastened to point out, having asked to be removed.[24] It was the fact that the Committee had not informed him of its intentions in response to his request which had annoyed him. Then in February 1901, Sarchet heard that Kemp had accepted the appointment in Gibraltar and was further upset that there had still been no consultation with him about his own next appointment. No further correspondence has survived until April when Westall wrote to the Committee to ask for Sarchet to stay on. He reported,

> Mr Sarchet has had a record of 5 years continual progress of a character that has evoked the admiration of all classes, from the Governor commanding the station to the seamen and private soldiers of the garrison.
>
> He has brought to bear in his work here, untiring devotion, extraordinary effort, and tact of the highest character, and he has been the means of securing for Methodism a very considerable advance towards the position she ought to occupy in a garrison and naval station such as that at Gibraltar, in a church sparing no effort for the spiritual, intellectual and temporal welfare of our soldiers and sailors.
>
> The work has been very arduous and owing to the continual regimental changes, consequent on the South African War the strain has been unusually heavy, yet in face of all this, we have a united congregation, with an attendance at the <u>voluntary</u> services (which are the real tests) of quite 100 per cent more than that of 1896; a flourishing class meeting: the best Sunday School we ever had: a well attended sewing or mother's meeting, and a children's Band of Hope, and a Home which will be hard to beat anywhere.[25]

Westall went on to list the Sunday and midweek services which Sarchet took personally. On Sundays there was an extra 8.30 a.m. parade service in the summer in addition to the main service at 10.30 a.m. Sunday school was at 2.30 p.m. with tea for the service men at 5.00 p.m., and an evening service at 6.30 p.m. was followed by the Lime Light Gospel Service at 8.00 p.m.. On Mondays Sarchet took the Wesley Guild, on Tuesdays the class meeting, on Wednesdays a Lime Light Gospel Service or Temperance Lecture at Europa with the same on Thursdays at the Welcome and on

---

[24] Ibid., Sarchet to Committee,13 February 1901, fiche 802, no.47.
[25] Ibid., Westall to Committee, 16 April 1901, fiche 802, no.49.

Saturdays a prayer meeting. There was also a weekly Mothers' Meeting, Band of Hope and Bible class which he did not take and first aid and Spanish classes. In addition, Sarchet had the hospital and prison visiting, the religious instruction of the army children and the usual pastoral duties and oversight of the Home. Altogether it was a heavy workload.

Overall Westall felt it would be 'calamitous to the work' to remove Sarchet and thought 'every Wesleyan on the Rock' would agree with him. He had not told Sarchet he was writing and was not even sure if he wanted to stay, but he felt that Sarchet had asked to be removed 'when he was thoroughly run down with the strain of overwork'. He suggested that Sarchet be asked to stay on, and if so that he should have a holiday first.

The Army and Navy Committee met on 7 June and recommended that the Missionary Committee extended Sarchet's appointment. So Sarchet stayed on and must have agreed to this, although it was by then getting late to arrange another appointment for him anyway. What Kemp thought of it all is not recorded!

Sarchet was given leave and may well have spent it in England, but he reported 'what we looked forward to as a pleasant holiday turned out to be little else than a protracted sick leave ... It was practically a breakdown resulting from the continuous strain of a busy life in the exhausting climate of this station'.[26] But he was glad to report that he was 'now in splendid health and able to get through a lot of work'. He was pleased also to report the birth of a daughter, Edna Aileen, on 7 October 1901 which perhaps eased a little of their grief at the loss of Irene. There is no record of her baptism in Gibraltar so maybe both her birth and baptism took place elsewhere.

The whole business of Sarchet's appointment really reflected the impossible situation of trying to serve two masters and, although there was communication between the Missionary and the Army and Navy Committees, it was still confusing, as Sarchet had pointed out before. Something had to be done. Gibraltar was no longer a missionary station and so it was decided that oversight of the work should pass to the Army and Navy Committee. Sarchet's last existing letter to the Missionary Committee is dated 2 March 1902. It is a short letter accompanying his annual report. He was in the midst of negotiating for a site for a new church and hoped for a decision soon. He ended the long correspondence from missionaries in Gibraltar on a positive note by saying, 'The Church as well as 'the Welcome' is in a healthy and vigorous condition, we have a splendid opportunity just now if circumstances will only allow us to embrace it'.[27]

The last report on Gibraltar in the Missionary Society's published annual reports referred to the same subject.

---

[26] Ibid., Sarchet to Committee,15 November 1901, fiche 803, no.51.
[27] Ibid., Sarchet to Committee, 26 March 1902, fiche 803, no.53.

The future is full of promise. We see visions of a great and influential Methodist Church here doing a grand work for God and for the soldier and sailor sons of Methodist homes; but if these visions are to crystallise in solid fact, and this possible good be realised, we must adopt a bold enterprising forward policy, and come out from the back street in which we have existed so long, and take that place which is the only fit place for the Methodist Church - whether at Gibraltar or elsewhere - at the front.[28]

So the long association with the Missionary Committee drew to an end, although it was still consulted on some matters, including those relating to the property which it had largely paid for and maintained. The Methodist church had come a long way from the early beginnings when a few soldiers met together for prayer, praise and Bible study under the threat of persecution. Now it was recognised, accepted and respected by the community. The hope of establishing a proper mission in Spain had never been realised but nevertheless there had been some success. Countless lives had also been affected by the circulation of Bibles; some had been changed for ever. The relationships between the ministers, the local church and the Missionary Committee had not always been easy. Mistakes had been made and the difficulties arising from poor communication, especially the slowness of the response from London, had probably been the biggest problem even after the advent of telegrams. This had contributed to the sense of isolation and loneliness that many of the missionaries had felt. Nevertheless the work had been well supported and had grown out of all recognition. The missionary work had begun with soldiers and now ended with soldiers as the work with them and the sailors finally took complete precedence. At the Conference of 1903 oversight of the Gibraltar station officially passed to the Army and Navy Committee.

---

[28] *WMMS Reports*, 1903, p.5

CHAPTER 19   UNDER NEW MANAGEMENT
Increased work and staff (1903-19)

The change of management was part of a wider strategy to unite and improve the efficiency of the army and navy work. In future, this was to come under the care of the Home Missions Committee on the stations, either at home or abroad, where the work was exclusively with the Forces. Consultation with the Foreign Missions Committee would continue for the stations abroad, but the 'control and direction of the work in detail' was to be undertaken by a Board of Managers which became known as the Army and Navy Board. Its members consisted of various officials and included ministers and laymen some of whom were selected 'on the ground of their knowledge of Army and Navy affairs'.[1]

The work of this Board of Managers was to include 'The entire control of all ministers especially set apart to labour under the direction of the Home Missions Committee in garrisons or naval stations at home or abroad'; general oversight of the army and navy work elsewhere by ministers in circuit work or on mission stations; and 'the general oversight and control of all Soldiers' and Sailors' Homes'.

The work was to be supported financially from the War Office and Admiralty payments, the local income such as collections, and the Home Missions Fund. However, Methodist chaplains still had no recognised rank or status, even where their work was exclusively with the Forces, although this was not really the fault of the military and naval authorities. There was a reluctance within Methodism itself for chaplains to be granted commissions because it was thought that this would take away Methodism's control of its own ministers. However, in 1904, it was agreed that the names of ministers exclusively working with the army would be designated as Acting Chaplains in the official Army List.

Unfortunately the Board did not keep all its records and the vast majority of the correspondence from Gibraltar has been lost, although the minute books of Board meetings have survived. The continuing story has therefore been pieced together from minute books, magazines, official reports, newspapers and articles and the occasional surviving letter.

In January 1904, the Mediterranean stations were visited by a deputation of three men including Richard Allen, Secretary of the Board. The morning congregation in Gibraltar averaged some 230 people, of whom about a third were civilians. The evening congregation was not greater than 150 with about half in uniform.

By then the need for accommodation at the Welcome had so increased that Sarchet had moved his family out to create more space there. As Govett was living in the Mission House and they did not want to disturb

---

[1] *Methodist Recorder,* 23 July 1903.

him, the old schoolhouse was altered, renamed Epworth House, and from then on was regarded as the manse.

Methodist premises comprising Epworth House on the left, the Church straight ahead and the old Mission House on the right

(Photograph used with permission from Robert and Edmund Sackett)

The Deputation inspected all the Methodist property in Gibraltar. It was very impressed with the Welcome and the facilities provided there which now included a 'bar, bagatelle room, lecture room capable of seating one hundred people, and neatly furnished, a cosy parlour, a large reading room, and beds for one hundred men including about a dozen cubicles'.[2] It had its own baking ovens. It was felt to be well run and situated and thus 'in every way well suited for the purposes of a Soldiers' and Sailors' Home' and the Deputation recorded that it 'could not speak too highly of its business management by Mr Sarchet'. It was here also that most meetings were held such as the class meeting, the Bible class and also the Sunday school because the church did not have the room to accommodate these. This presented a problem as the building was quite a distance from the church which meant the worship centre was separated from all other activities.

---

[2] Home Missions Department Report. 'Visit to the Chaplaincies of the Mediterranean,' April 1904. Divisonal Records, Box 33 n.d., file 2: Naval History.

The premises on Prince Edward's Road were reported to 'occupy a fairly good position in the town', which was not at all what anyone else had been saying for years. The report went on to say that prior to the visit Sarchet had 'opened negotiations with the Military authorities to secure a portion of a site in the main street on which to build Church, Manse and Soldiers' Home'. The site Sarchet was considering was known as the Spanish Pavilion and was to be granted in exchange for the premises on Prince Edward's Road, but in the end the government refused permission. Since then Sarchet had considered another site but despite all his efforts he was not successful. Allen, at least, seemed to be ready now to accept defeat, which may have been the reason for the more positive statement about the Church's location.

The church however needed considerable repair work. A lot of the woodwork was rotten and 'the ceiling of the Chapel is in danger of falling in as the result probably of heavy gun firing'. The body of the church had been 'repewed' but 'the pews in the gallery are still of the old fashioned type, exceedingly uncomfortable, and quite worn out'! The repairs were regarded as imperative, but once they were done, the Deputation felt the church 'is ample for present wants'.

In the end the Deputation also made a new recommendation to extend the work and meet another need. It reported on

> ... the rapid extension of the population in the direction of Europa Point, [previously referred to as 'The South'] where houses, barracks, and forts are springing up very quickly, and where there is no Protestant place of worship. It is too distant to be ministered to effectively from Gibraltar, and it seems therefore desirable to place, if practicable, a Junior Minister there, and secure a building that would serve for Church, Sunday School, and Soldiers' Home, the latter being, of course, on quite a small scale.
>
> It is also proper to state that the English artizan population of Gibraltar in Government employ, will at no distant date be largely added to when the new Dockyard and Harbour are completed. These extensions will also result in a large Naval force being permanently on the Station.

The Board and the Missionary Committee discussed the report at length and reviewed the way in which the property was held. This was another reason for the passing of the Wesleyan Church Property Ordinance of 1906, already mentioned. The delay meant that the repairs were not immediately done. The Board also decided,

> That no steps be taken in the appointment of an additional minister to the Chaplaincy pending the completion of the Harbour and Dock-yard Works, when it is hoped that the present payments now made to the Naval Chaplaincy by the Admiralty will be greatly increased.[3]

---

[3] *Army and Navy Sub-Committee Minutes - October 1896-1898,* meeting 7 June 1904, minute iii, p.458.

It was perhaps helpful that no great changes took place at this time, because it had been agreed, in November 1903, that Alfred Sackett would replace Sarchet in the summer of 1904, and it was probably best for him to settle into the work first.

So the time drew near for the Sarchet family to leave Gibraltar. A great deal had been achieved during their time on the Rock, with the biggest development of the work being the establishment of the Welcome. Sarchet may well have been disappointed not to have managed to do anything about finding the site for the church premises despite a great deal of effort, but even if the church remained somewhat out of the way, the Welcome was on the main street and had made a big impact on Gibraltar. Methodism was certainly out of the shadows and into the foreground now.

The Sarchet family left Gibraltar at the beginning of September 1904. At a farewell meeting on Friday 26 August at the Welcome, William and Emily Sarchet were presented with a 'Sterling Silver Tea and Coffee Service on a fine oak tray bearing a suitable inscription, which had been subscribed for in a most generous manner by the members and friends of the Wesleyan Church'.[4] A tribute to Sarchet in the *Gibraltar Chronicle* referred to his 'successful work as District Secretary of the Army Temperance Association and the well-known "Welcome" Trips to Tangier and elsewhere' and went on to say,

> But overshadowing everything else in this connection the Welcome Soldiers' and Seamen's Home will ever stand out as the monument *par excellence* of his work on behalf of the Soldier and Sailor. This institution has a reputation throughout the Sister Services. The extent of its benefits can hardly be overestimated and here in Gibraltar it is far too well-known and appreciated to need from us any manner of praise or commendation.
>
> Turning to Mr Sarchet's spiritual work as a pastor and chaplain, this cannot be expressed in words or figures; the record of eight years faithful preaching of the pure Gospel is written deep in the hearts and lives of the great numbers who have come under his influence and within the reach of his words, the majority of whom are now scattered far and wide over the face of the globe. Nevertheless we need only turn to the large and flourishing Church, to which he has ministered for so long and to the earnest band of workers connected with the Welcome, to find ample evidence of his success as a Minister of the Gospel.
>
> ... Mr Sarchet's departure will be a distinct loss not merely to the Wesleyan Church but to Gibraltar generally, and we feel we are voicing the opinion of the whole community when we express our regret that he is leaving us, and it need hardly be said that he will go to his new sphere of labour with the very best wishes of all.

As usual there is little mention of the minister's wife, Emily, who had

---

[4] *Gibraltar Chronicle*, Saturday 3 September 1904.

lived and worked with her husband in Gibraltar and with him mourned the loss of their daughter.

Despite his earlier statement about not being 'altogether in love with military work', Sarchet did in fact devote the rest of his ministry to it, serving at Devonport and Portsmouth and then France from August 1914. Here, he was mentioned in Despatches three times; was awarded the Military Cross for service amongst the wounded and an OBE for special work amongst the troops near the firing line. Two sons died in 1918. Captain Hugh Sarchet, MC who was probably the 'child' who had accompanied them to Gibraltar and Captain Leslie Sarchet, who had been born in Gibraltar. After the war, Sarchet worked on Salisbury Plain until increasing deafness led to his retirement in Guernsey in 1922 where Emily died in April 1924. Despite his deafness, Sarchet continued preaching until he died on 27 August 1936 at the age of 74.

Sarchet's successor, Alfred Barrett Sackett, was born on 6 July 1862. He was converted as a young boy and started work as an office boy at the age of twelve. At thirteen he was secretary of the Sunday school with his father as superintendent. He became a Sunday school teacher and a class leader and began preaching when he was nineteen. He was accepted for the ministry in 1886 and went to Richmond College to train. His first appointment was in London as Chaplain to the Guards, assistant to the Rev. Richard Allen, Secretary of the Board. He was there for four years serving his probationary term and was then ordained which meant he was free to marry Lydia Anne Sandford, who had waited three-and-a-half years to marry him under the Methodist rules. After serving in four circuits in England, he was appointed to Gibraltar.

Alfred Barrett Sackett
(With permission from the family)

Lydia Anne Sackett
(With permission from the family)

Alfred and Lydia sailed for Gibraltar in the summer of 1904 with their two children, a son who shared the same name as his father, but was known as Barrett to avoid confusion, and a daughter, Dorothy May. Barrett later became headmaster of Kingswood School and put together a short account of his father's life including some of his own memories, although both he and Dorothy returned to England to school and to work.

Lydia with Barrett and Dorothy May

(With permission from the family)

They sailed on a cargo ship which carried only a few passengers. Lydia was very seasick. On landing they went to a hotel which Barrett remembered; 'It is infested with bugs: the mosquito nets are faulty and we are so bitten that Mother is sure we have chickenpox or worse'.[5] The Sarchets were still in Gibraltar so that introductions could be made and the work properly handed over. On Sunday 3 September 1904 Sackett took the morning parade service and Sarchet the evening service, presumably his last on the Rock.

Barrett described the Methodist property including Epworth House, the manse.

Mother is there, too much alone; there is a Spanish maid, Concha. Water is scarce: milk is goat's milk. The market is a good walk away, down a long ramp and through the main street: there, fruit is abundant, grapes, large long and succulent and crackling and translucently green, are a penny a pound. Probably there is a soldier or two or a dockyard worker coming for a meal who must be fed.[6]

He did not give much information about his mother's role, other than referring to hospitality, but mentioned also her worries about her husband's work-load and the difficulties of his job.

The amount of work generated by the Welcome continued to increase despite the fact that another Home had been opened in November 1903. The number of beds let in a year had increased to over seventeen thousand by 1905. The charge was a shilling a bed and fourpence for tea apparently known by the sailors as 'a shilling dosser and fourpence buster'![7] There were a hundred beds provided at the Welcome but sometimes even that was not enough as the 1906 report stated,

The Games Room, with its marble floor and bagatelle tables, easily accessible from the street, is well patronised by men of both services, while at night it often has to become the asylum of intoxicated sailors who find even in that state no refusal of admission.[8]

[5] Barrett Sackett's memoirs of his father, p.69.

[6] Ibid., p.69.

[7] Ibid., p.70.

[8] *The Welcome Soldiers' and Seamen's Home,* Annual Report 1906-7, p.5.

When even that was full, Barrett recorded, 'Those who could stagger up hill found their way on to the pew seats in the Methodist Chapel! When that was full they slept in Father's study. When that was full they slept on our stairs. Poor mother! How she must have suffered and loved'.[9] It was not always easy work and Barrett records at least one occasion when his father returned home with a black eye. Drunken men could be quite destructive too to furniture and fittings.

Sackett also became the Secretary of the Royal Army Temperance Association, well supported by the authorities in Gibraltar for obvious reasons. Of course the spiritual side of the work was not neglected either and there was a full programme of meetings at the Welcome. This was in addition to the Sunday services, the visits to hospitals and prisons and the religious instruction of the army children. The most popular event of the whole week was the Sunday evening social, the successor to Sarchet's Lime Light Gospel Services. Sackett reported that it 'meets a growing need as a centre for good comradeship after Church hours. From eight till eleven on Sunday evenings the Lecture Hall is crowded, hymns chosen by the men are sung, solos enjoyed, light refreshments supplied, concluding with family worship'.[10] It meant that Sundays were very busy for the chaplain.

Indeed there was so much work to do that the time seemed to have come to appoint a second minister. Allen wrote to the Admiralty in May 1905 referring

> ... to the great increase in the Naval establishment at Gibraltar resulting from the completion of the Dock Yard and Harbour Extension and the fact that for the future Gibraltar is to be the base of the Atlantic Fleet, and the consequent large and permanent increase in the number of Wesleyans on the station belonging to His Majesty's ships and the Dock Yard staff.[11]

The Board wanted to appoint a second minister 'for duty as Acting Wesleyan Naval Chaplain' and asked that 'a salary of £200 per annum be substituted for the capitation payments at present received'. The Admiralty generally approved of the scheme but was only prepared to grant £150 a year as salary. The Board had already recommended the appointment of a second minister to Conference 'on the understanding that no additional charge come upon the Home Missions Committee' and so, with this undertaking from the Admiralty, Conference agreed and Robert Coutts was appointed.[12]

He was born in Banff in 1875 and worked for a year in the South Hants Mission before going to Richmond College to train for the ministry.

---

[9] Memoir, op. cit., p.12.

[10] Welcome Report, p.11.

[11] Divisional records, box 33 n.d. file 3 *History of the Methodist chaplaincy at Gibraltar.* Letter dated 3 May 1905 from Allen to the Admiralty.

[12] *Army and Navy Committee vol. iii, 1904-1911,* meeting 11 April 1905, minute v, p.48.

Gibraltar was therefore his first appointment and presumably he went as a single man not yet ordained. Very little is known about his work in Gibraltar as no correspondence at all from him has survived. No doubt it was a great help to Sackett to have a colleague to share some of his heavy duties and with whom he could discuss the work. Coutts probably arrived in late August or early September 1905. It is not clear where he lived at first but by then other developments were being considered.

In June 1905 Sackett asked the Board for permission to acquire the lease on the Empire Theatre for 'a Central Hall for Evangelistic Services, and for the social work which is so urgently needed on the station'.[13] Presumably he too did not feel the Church's situation was ideal but the Board did not agree to this plan. However, it was more interested in Sackett's later proposal to obtain a site on Naval Hospital Road to use as a branch of the Welcome. Sackett asked for £300 from the reserve Gibraltar Fund, which the Board had set aside, to adapt the premises and furnish them. This was agreed though the cost turned out to be nearer £400. A lease for twenty-one years at the cost of £50 a year 'terminable at twelve months notice on either side' was signed on 31 January 1906 and thus the South Branch of the Welcome came into being.[14] The 1906 report stated, 'The ground floor consists of refreshment Bar, Games Room, Men's Parlour, while the rooms above are available as quarters for Junior Chaplain and Manager, and the grounds above are open to the use of the soldiers.' Presumably Coutts moved in.

The Welcome, South Branch

[13] Ibid., meeting 27 June 1905, minute iv, p.56.
[14] Ibid., meeting 8 November 1905, minute ix, pp.86-7.

There were other attempts to meet the men's needs wherever they were too, for the report also mentioned, 'The Coffee Van at the North Front during the Firing season, and the Tent at the annual rifle meeting, have again done excellent work' and added, 'At the request of the authorities a small "Welcome" Kiosk is about to be opened at the North Front for the supply of wholesome refreshments at football and cricket matches'.[15]

By coming alongside the men in all situations the church was trying to show its care for them physically as well as spiritually and no doubt there were many opportunities for conversation in these situations. In May 1906 two evangelists visited Gibraltar to conduct a mission there. Preparations for their coming seem to have been considerable, with a good degree of co-operation between the Protestant churches. Choir practice had involved the choirs of the Cathedral, the King's Chapel, the Methodist and Presbyterian churches. Preaching took place in various venues and the mission continued every night for a week. The crowds were so large some services were moved to the Theatre Royal to accommodate them. There is no record of the longer term results of this week but a couple of years later an American evangelist who had worked with Moody and Sankey was invited to spend a week in Gibraltar and preached in many places including both the Methodist church and the Welcome.

Ecumenical relationships between the Protestant churches had greatly improved over the years but there were still occasions when friction could occur. In May 1907 there was some correspondence over the religious instruction of the children in the army school.[16] This was given by the individual chaplains to their own church children, in addition to the religious instruction given at the school under the school regulations. The Wesleyan children were taken out of the school and taught either at the Welcome or the South Branch. On this occasion, the Anglican chaplain wanted to change the time of his visit to the school because of other duties but the time he wanted was not convenient to the school and its curriculum. The schoolmistress, a Wesleyan, was then accused of favouritism and the Anglican chaplain threatened to report her to the War Office. This upset her greatly as she felt her own personal religion was a private matter and she strove hard to fulfil the regulations fairly. In the end, the Colonel in charge of the school sorted matters out and intended to report the Anglican chaplain to the Governor if he had indeed written to the War Office. The chaplain seems to have acted in a rather high-handed way but the response of the authorities shows that denominational rights were much more fairly regarded than in the past.

Meanwhile the famous Welcome trips had continued and became larger and longer over the years. They were often advertised in the *Gibraltar*

---

[15] Welcome Report, p.13.
[16] Bundle of letters dated from 24 April to 18 May 1907.

Chronicle where accounts of many of them also appeared. On 9 August 1906 a combined military and dockyard picnic party including wives and girl friends set out for Ronda. Special permission had been obtained from the Governor for the military to attend and the party travelled by steamer and train on this first trip there. They set off early arriving at 9 o'clock in the morning. 'At Jimena the Colonel Commandant of Ronda, who clearly intended that the visit of so many British soldiers should be a happy and enjoyable one very kindly met and accompanied the party to Ronda'.[17] Here they breakfasted at the station restaurant with music provided by a band. Lunch and tea were eaten there too and at lunchtime several 'Spanish officers, including the affable captain of the Guardia Civil', joined the party. It is not clear how the language problem was surmounted as Sackett spoke no Spanish. Indeed his son wrote, 'How he managed the Spanish end is a mystery for he could not bring himself to learn one word of Spanish and that he horribly mispronounced. It was a joke in the family.'[18] Perhaps an interpreter went on the trips. On departure from Ronda, 'Three hearty ringing British cheers was the form of recording the gratitude of the departing company'. The commandant travelled with them back to Jimena and the party arrived back in Gibraltar at 10 o'clock, tired after an outing of some fifteen hours.

Ronda Party

These outings were all so successful that eventually they were extended so that places further afield could be visited. On Friday 7 August 1908 over a hundred people set off on a weekend trip to Granada. In reporting it,

---

[17] *Gibraltar Chronicle,* 11 August 1906.
[18] Memoir, op. cit., p.78.

the *Gibraltar Chronicle* felt that Sackett 'certainly has a genius rivalling that of the renowned Cook, for the organisation of these pleasure trips which do so much to alleviate the monotony which attends existence on the Rock during the summer months'.[19] Following this successful trip, another one was organised to Seville which began on 6 November 1908. 'The party was composed principally of Ladies, Naval and Military Officers, Heads of Civil departments and Dockyard staff and employees', 146 people in all.[20] This was a very well organised trip with a special train waiting at Algeciras to take the party to Ronda and refreshment stops organised along the way. They travelled overnight arriving at Seville at 7.15 a.m. to find thirty coaches and carriages waiting to take them to their hotels. Various tours were organised including a trip to the theatre to see some 'graceful Spanish dancers'. On Sunday morning they went to the Cathedral to watch the celebration of high mass and later climbed the Giralda Tower, with further visits arranged in the afternoon and on the Monday morning to a variety of venues. Their train left at 3.30 p.m. on the Monday afternoon. 'Both at the Hotel and Station large crowds of people were looking on and we are sure the visit of so large a number of Britishers to the town caused no little excitement'. It was reported to have been 'one of the most pleasant excursions one could wish for, and the thanks of the whole community are due to the Rev. Sackett for his kindness and thoughtfulness for all, for we are sure this undertaking was not taken in hand without a certain amount of brain worry, may he be spared to arrange many more'.

The trips also made some money. The Welcome was expected to be self-supporting which was not always easy. The facilities there were all provided free apart from food and accommodation. Drunks sometimes caused damage. There was rent and upkeep on the building and the wages of the manager to find. Barrett recorded, 'The Finances were always a terrible worry. I remember the labour involved in this: the Home Church was not wealthy, and he seemed to be forgotten so far away. He had to make both ends somehow meet'.[21]

One on-going problem was the fact that the grants from both the army and navy fluctuated which made forward planning very difficult. The allowances were sometimes paid as fixed grants and sometimes as capitation allowances based on the number of declared Wesleyans. In 1909 the Admiralty grant was reduced to a capitation allowance because the Atlantic Fleet and a Cruiser Squadron were no longer to be based at Gibraltar. Some of the correspondence arguing against this decision has survived. It was felt that the need for staff and facilities remained much the same despite the changes and the Wesleyan chaplains also cared for members of other denominations and for the dockyard workers. In the

---

[19] *Gibraltar Chronicle,* 7 August 1908.
[20] Ibid., 11 November 1908.
[21] Memoir, op. cit., pp.71-2.

end, this was to be a continuing problem leading to considerable correspondence over the years in trying to achieve fair payments to ensure financial support for the work.

In 1907 Robert Coutts returned to England having decided that he did not want to stay a third year in Gibraltar as he had been invited to do. He continued to work in various circuits until he retired in 1944. He died in February 1959 in his eighty-fourth year.

His replacement was Frederick Edmund Brown who was to have a long association with Gibraltar. He was born at Earby on 25 April 1877 into a Methodist family. He attended Earby Grammar School where he later became a pupil teacher. He was converted during a mission and began local preaching. In 1899 he volunteered to become a missionary with the China Inland Mission and spent two years at a Bible Training College. The Boxer rebellion put an end to this plan and he offered for Methodist missionary work instead. He was accepted and went to Secunderabad as an army chaplain. He also had some responsibility for Indian Christians. Whilst on holiday from India, he visited China and Japan which helped to develop his interest in oriental art. In 1907 he was sent to Gibraltar as Sackett's assistant. He lived at the South Branch.

> For five years they worked together and developed a great friendship. The younger man appreciated the way his Superintendent won the confidence of the toughest of sailors, and those five years were formative in their influence. He grew in confidence in his service to soldiers and sailors, and he began to develop that love for Gibraltar, and for Spain, which provided him with his sphere of greatest influence.[22]

Around this time decisions about the church building were finally made. The attempts to find a more suitable location had been strenuous but they had all failed. The development of the dockyard and harbour meant Gibraltar was now much busier and property even scarcer. The church repairs, regarded as imperative in 1904, had not been carried out while discussions went on about the best way forward. Something clearly had to be done and eventually it was decided to undertake a major renovation. Estimates were drawn up and a renovation fund was launched with various events taking place to raise money. The naval and military authorities were asked to help with the cost as some of the damage was thought to have been caused by the firing of heavy guns.

The final cost was just over £2,000. The Missionary Society contributed £450, the War Office £120, the Admiralty £100 and the Board the £200 remaining in the Gibraltar reserve fund. Other contributions began to come in from subscribers in England and Gibraltar as a result of fund raising and appeals for help.

---

[22] Ernest R. Taylor, *Padre Brown of Gibraltar*, Epworth Press: London, 1955, p.19.

The old church (decorated for harvest) before the renovation

The work began around June 1908 and services were held in the Assembly Rooms until it was finished. The work was extensive and the chapel described as 'for so long in a sad and dirty condition' was brought to life again. 'The windows have been entirely renewed, the plaster ceiling is replaced by a new one in pitchpine, the gallery has been renewed and enlarged and by throwing out behind the pulpit an organ and Choir Chamber and erecting an entrance porch, additional accommodation has been provided for the congregation'.[23]

The grand re-opening took place in January 1909 amidst a great deal of publicity. The *Gibraltar Chronicle* published a series of articles on the history of Methodism in Gibraltar and reported fully on the re-opening and what were regarded as the centenary celebrations although, in fact, the chapel had not been built until 1810. A deputation of three men was sent out from England and a reception was held for them at the Welcome on Wednesday 27 January 1909. 'The room was crowded with a very enthusiastic company' and both Brown and Sackett made the introductions.[24] Musical items followed. The actual re-opening and dedication of the church took place the following day in the presence of a large group of dignitaries, including commanders from the army and navy, leading citizens of Gibraltar and a number of fellow clergymen. The Governor unfortunately was ill and unable to attend so the Deputy Governor, Sir Frederick Evans, performed the opening ceremony.

---

[23] *Gibraltar Chronicle,* 19 January 1909.
[24] Ibid., 30 January 1909.

The opening of the renovated church
(Photograph used with permission from Edmund and Robert Sackett)

A brief dedication service was led by Sackett with the Rev. John Bell, from the deputation, giving a short address in which he referred to a letter from the Lord Bishop of Gibraltar, the Rt Rev. William Edward Collins who sent his good wishes. He had read the articles in the *Gibraltar Chronicle* which had mentioned the difficulties between the Methodists and Anglicans in earlier years, and wrote,

> It is hard, now, to believe that such intolerance was ever possible, and one can only think of it with shame and sorrow. It may be that there are things in the present day hardly less bad, which we share in with no greater realisation of what it is that we do - But at least we have learned, I trust, that the fulfilment of Our Lord's prayer that 'they may all be one' must depend very largely upon our learning to be like Him in our dealings with one another. And it is to me the first fruits and the pledge of that

331

unity that you and we alike long for the fulfilment of that prayer, not in our own way but in His.[25]

Musical accompaniment was provided by the band of the Second Bedfordshire Regiment and afterwards tea was served at the Welcome. In the evening, a 'very hearty meeting' was held in the church. The chair was taken by Westall who had been part of the renovation committee appointed to oversee the work. He was also 'financial adviser and accountant without remuneration' of the Welcome and his work in this respect was much appreciated.[26]

Renovation Committee
Back row from the left: Mr Westall; Rev. F.E. Brown; Mr Roccia (contractor)
Front row from the left: Lieut Crombie R.E. (Hon Architect); Rev. A.B. Sackett
and Sergeant Major Boulter R.E. (Hon Foreman of Works)

Speeches and musical items followed and a collection was taken. By the end of the day, only £54 still needed to be raised. Special services were held on the Sunday at which the men of the deputation preached. A small booklet written by Richard Allen was later published to mark the occasion. It gave a short history of Methodism in Gibraltar and mentioned some of the on-going work including the two Sunday schools which had 180 children and twelve teachers.

A further £500 was spent on the other two buildings on the Prince Edward's Road site, on the recommendation of the deputation, and the

---

[25] Memoir, op. cit., p.75.
[26] Welcome Report, p.17.

manse furniture described as meagre and worn out was renewed. Two memorial windows were later placed in the church and were dedicated on Sunday 9 May 1909. These were gifts from Methodists in England. One pictured 'Christ and the Centurion' and was in memory of Corporals James Lamb and Richard Russell who had been flogged over a hundred years before. The other pictured 'The Centurion welcoming Peter to Caesarea' and was in memory of Dr Rule who had fought so hard for religious liberty in the army.

The Memorial Windows
(Photograph used by permission from Edmund and Robert Sackett)

Gradually money was also raised for a proper pipe organ which cost £425 10s 0d and replaced a 'harmonium of ancient origin'![27] A brief dedication service followed by an organ recital was held in the church on Thursday 29 January 1914 and the celebrations continued at the following Sunday services.

Meanwhile, back in 1909, the deputation had returned to England to give its report. Overall it was impressed with the way the work was being carried out and with the good local working relationships. It was felt that both in Gibraltar and Malta, the Methodist position 'has been immensely extended and strengthened' and 'that nothing seems neglected that ought to come within the sphere of a Christian Minister's duty'.[28] Congregations tended to fluctuate according to the strength of the garrison and the ships in port but civilian numbers were reported to be largely increased and the evening congregation much improved. However, concern was expressed that the Sunday school and all week-night meetings had to be held at the Welcome. Various suggestions were made to remedy this, but none proved

---

[27] *Home Missions Report,* 1914, pp.114-6.

[28] Ibid., 1909, pp.110-4, 'Report of the visit to the chaplaincies of the Mediterranean'.

possible.

The work at the South was going well. 'The parade service is held in a military schoolroom, but an admirable Sunday School meets at the Soldiers' Home. Altogether the stationing of a Minister at this part is answering its purpose well and is full of promise'.[29] The 'South Welcome' seemed to be paying its way well but things were not so good at the main Home, where income had declined, because of the reduction in the garrison strength, more frequent absences of the fleet and the increased value of Spanish currency. The latter markedly affected the rent which was now much higher. It also affected wages and the cost of supplies.

The Renovated Church

The deputation also reported, 'There are two other Homes in the place, but ours is the only one that is paying, notwithstanding the heavy rent, and it is certainly the most popular and best attended'. A valuable addition to the income came from the excursions which continued. In the summer of 1908, parties were organised to 'Ronda, Tangier, Tarifa, Málaga, Seville and Granada, with advantage and delight to 3,500 men and their friends'. The profits from these trips had become indispensable which must have added to Sackett's burden of work and worries.

The deputation ended the report by saying that Sackett was hoping for leave before commencing a second term of duty in Gibraltar, five years being now the accepted term. This was granted and in September 1909 he attended a Board meeting in England. By then Richard Allen had retired and been succeeded by the Rev. Joseph H. Bateson. The main point of discussion was Sackett's suggestion that the Welcome should be purchased which he felt could be done for £10,000 and would be cheaper in the long run, saving them the heavy cost of the rent. 'The Board heartily recommended the scheme, and wished Mr Sackett every success', which implies that the matter was mostly left up to him.[30] However, despite the Board sanctioning an appeal for the purchase, it was reported the following year that 'little advance has been made, owing to so many other urgent cases before our people'.[31]

On Sunday morning 23 May 1910, the Governor, Sir Frederick W.E.F.

---

[29] Ibid.

[30] *Army and Navy Committee vol.iii, 1904-1911,* meeting 27 September 1909, minute xii, pp.328-30.

[31] *Home Missions Report,* 1910, pp.164-7.

Forestier-Walker, paid an unexpected visit to the Methodist church which was 'as far as is known the only occasion on which the Governor has been to the Wesleyan Church here'.[32] His visit no doubt caused quite a stir but it does show how far Methodism had come since its early days on the Rock.

The heavy rent of the Welcome continued to be a big burden and financial resources were strained to the limit whenever there was a sudden influx of men. In 1910 with only forty-two hours notice, such an occasion arose and Sackett reported,

> ... we were unable to cope with the demand on our social resources. A sudden addition of between 3 or 4 thousand men in a comparatively small place like Gibraltar leads to a startling sense of responsibility in those who have for years past provided bed accommodation. As the evenings wore away, bluejackets in hundreds were seen in a home to home pilgrimage in vain for shelter, and were obliged to sleep beneath the stars. All beds at the Welcome were booked early, and every inch of room used - on the roof, landings, patio, on and under the billiard tables, on mats and straw. Many were sent to the bedless South Welcome for shelter, while both ministers used studies and dining rooms for sheltering others.[33]

The trips continued, relieving the monotony of Gibraltar which Sackett described as 'a prison, practically, to hundreds of men, who cannot go beyond the barriers unless in organised parties, and it has fallen to my happy lot and privilege to do this work for the men. It undoubtedly gives me a great advantage, and helps to fill our church, indirectly doing much more good than appears'.[34]

Cork Woods Outing - with permission from Edmund and Robert Sackett

---

[32] Ibid.
[33] Ibid.
[34] Ibid.

The trips improved morale, encouraged the soldiers to save their money and apparently had even helped to reduce the suicide rate, as well as placing the men under some Christian influence. They were much appreciated by everyone, the participants, the commanding officers and the Governor.

Sometimes there was more tangible evidence of the appreciation of all the work Sackett did. In 1912 the Second Battalion of the Queen's Regiment left Gibraltar and their Colonel, J.G. King-King, wrote to Sackett on behalf of all ranks,

> ... to convey to you the expression of their gratitude for the kindness and pleasure which they have experienced at your hands, and to ask your acceptance of the accompanying token which but faintly expresses their appreciation of all you have done to make their sojourn on the Rock what it has been through your instrumentality. I need hardly say that I personally more than endorse their sentiments.[35]

The token was a silver tea-set which was presented by the very regiment which had flogged the Methodist soldiers so many years before.

In 1912 Frederick Brown left Gibraltar. He had come as a probationer and had now been fully accepted into the ministry. In 1911 he was invited to stay on by the Board, provided he continued to receive a probationer's allowances which was all the station could afford. It is not clear if this is why he left or whether he felt it was time to widen his experience but in 1912 he left Gibraltar and was replaced by Ernest Pickard.

Ernest Richard Pickard was born in 1888 in Cowbridge, Glamorgan. He was accepted for the ministry in 1908 and went to Headingley College but, before his training was finished, he was called to help with the work on Salisbury Plain amongst the soldiers there. He enjoyed the work and thus came to Gibraltar in 1912 with a little experience of work with the military. He must have lived at the South Branch but little is known of his work as no letters have survived.

The heavy work load eventually took its toll and Sackett became ill. On 12 January 1913 he left Gibraltar with his wife on medical advice. Best wishes were sent to him through the pages of the *Gibraltar Chronicle* which also recorded his return in March when he was reported to have 'thoroughly recuperated and come back full of vigour and energy and we trust that he may enjoy good health and be enabled to continue his work at the Rock for many years to come'.[36]

The plan to buy the Welcome had not been forgotten and in January 1913 the Board put aside some £600 for this purpose. A sub-committee was appointed in May 1914 which included Sarchet, but the outbreak of war altered everything and purchasing the Welcome was no longer a

---

[35] Memoir, op. cit., p.81.
[36] *Gibraltar Chronicle,* Tuesday 11 March 1913.

priority despite its worsening finances. By 1914, the numbers sleeping at the Welcome had reduced because the fleets had been absent from Gibraltar for some two years and 'despite severe economy and careful work,' the Welcome showed an abnormal loss.[37] Around this time, the Board agreed that Sackett should return to England in 1915, as he had requested, but the war changed that too and he stayed on.

During the First World War, Gibraltar provided a naval base for supplying coal and provisions and a repair yard for damaged ships in the new dry docks. From 1915, hospital ships arrived frequently carrying the wounded from Gallipoli. Many were landed at Gibraltar for treatment, too many for the naval and military hospitals to cope with, and an auxiliary hospital was opened at Europa. From 1917 Gibraltar became an assembly point for convoys and the harbour was constantly filling up and emptying as convoys formed and sailed on. All this had an effect on the economy and there were some shortages and increased prices. There was insufficient water on the Rock to meet the increased demand and, after somewhat lengthy negotiations, Spain supplied water from Algeciras and Ceuta, but only on condition that it was loaded at night. A food rationing system for the working people of Gibraltar was introduced to enable them to buy essential foods at reduced prices. All this inevitably meant added expense at the Welcome at a very hectic time there.

In May 1918, influenza affected Gibraltar with 600 cases reported causing twenty-one deaths. A more severe form struck in September with some 3,000 cases resulting in 111 deaths. Over 300 merchant seamen arrived in Gibraltar with the illness and were treated there. Bodies were taken in special vehicles directly to the cemetery to try and prevent the spread of infection. Just two days before the Armistice was signed, the battleship HMS *Britannia* was torpedoed off Cape Trafalgar with the eventual loss of about one thousand lives. Many died from their injuries in Gibraltar's hospitals and joy at the end of the war was somewhat dampened by the resulting funerals.

It was against this background of events that Sackett continued his work. Proper commissions were still not being given to Methodist chaplains, but their work was recognised by the award of honorary ranks. Sackett was probably at first appointed honorary chaplain fourth class because his promotion to third class, in recognition of the valuable work he was doing, was reported in June 1918. Both he and Pickard were given the necessary military passes to ensure access around the Rock so that they could carry on their usual work. Despite the difficulties, it was even possible to continue the trips into Spain but they had to be made out of uniform because of Spanish neutrality. The burden of visits to the sick in hospital at times must have been heavy and Sackett also kept up a correspondence with

---

[37] *Home Missions Report,* 1914, pp.114-16.

many who had spent time on the Rock and travelled on. In spring 1915 he received a letter from a George Scott serving in the trenches who wrote,

> The mud and cold are the worst enemies. Many times in the cold of the night the boys said, 'I wish I was out in Gib once again' ... If the worst does come I am glad to be able to say that the help I got at Gib will enable me to face it more bravely than if I had never been with you and I thank you for the bit you did toward showing me which duty comes first. The duty of man to God and man to man.[38]

Sackett also received requests from prisoners of war to send them supplies and in November 1915 he organised a concert in the Church to raise money for this purpose, which was at least the second occasion on which he had done this.

By this time, Sackett was alone in Gibraltar for Lydia had sailed for England during the last days of 1914 as she was much in need of a break. Sackett was too busy to accompany her and was also trying to deal with the worsening financial problems at the Welcome. Bateson had written to him 'assuring him of the sympathy of the Board in the financial difficulties of the Gibraltar "Welcome" Home', but there seemed to be no question of offering practical or financial support and Sackett seems to have been left to carry the burden himself.[39] Of course, the Board's resources were limited and stretched beyond the limits by the needs of the war. Camp homes were opened in Britain, France and elsewhere; many chaplains served with the Forces; the needs were great and Gibraltar could have no priority. On the other hand it was a lonely and distant station and the burden for Sackett must sometimes have felt intolerable. However, help was at hand from a completely unexpected and unlikely source.

Charles Stephenson lived in Birmingham. He was a semi-invalid and, through a friend of Sackett's, he heard about the problems in Gibraltar. Being unable to go out to work, he devoted his time to helping good causes and he took up the Gibraltar cause with great enthusiasm. Sackett always felt his help to be an answer to prayer and one wonders indeed if the work in Gibraltar would have survived without it. Stephenson wrote to anyone and everyone he could think of, companies, firms and individuals, to ask for help, using information Sackett sent him about the work. Sometimes goods were sent in kind and as often as possible, he managed to arrange for them to be taken to Gibraltar by ship, carriage free. Sometimes money was donated. Queen Alexandra sent £25 in 1914, the first year of his activities, and more in later years. Between 1914 and 1920, he raised a staggering £11,380 for the Welcome. Barrett recorded the wonderful job he did and noted too that 'Father was also sore about his treatment by the Army and

---

[38] Memoir, op. cit., p.85.

[39] *Minutes of the Army and Navy Board vol. iv, 1911-1918,* meeting 23 March 1914, minute v, p.132.

Navy Board: and rightly on the whole'.[40] However, the Board was aware of Stephenson's activities and very grateful to him, sending him letters of appreciation and acknowledging his help publicly.

Sometime in 1915, the manager of the Welcome left and Sackett had to cover his work as well until a replacement could be found. Meanwhile Barrett had volunteered for service in England and called at Gibraltar briefly on his way to Gallipoli in September. A little later, Lydia returned to the Rock and wrote to Barrett saying that 'nearly all the men in hospitals here are suffering from diseases brought on by bad food and water not wounds' and in December she wrote of 'the poor frost-bitten men who were landed here on Sunday'.[41] Sackett had visited some of them. How they must have worried about Barrett, seeing at first hand the results of service in Gallipoli. They sent him letters and parcels too. In his turn, Barrett was concerned about both his parents, feeling their health was being affected by the volume of work. He wrote, 'Do try and rest and give up having sailors and tommies and people at all hours. I don't consider it fair on Mother at all to have all these crowds in for meals and things'.[42] However, some help was at hand for, from June to August 1916, a Mr T.G. Lomas from Llanfairfechan helped out.

> Mr Lomas wished to undertake some war work for his Church and most kindly volunteered to go to Gibraltar, where Mr Sackett was bearing very heavy responsibilities. Mr Lomas assisted in pulpit duty, preaching with much acceptance, and, as Mr Sackett says, 'did us all good'. He has now returned home, but his services will not be forgotten by the many sailors and soldiers who came under his influence.[43]

Around this time the Rev. Richard Hall and Mr Isaac Holden visited Gibraltar on behalf of the Board because of 'the serious state of the Current Account of the "Welcome" Home', but no first-hand account of their visit has survived.[44] They recommended that some work should be done to the building and in 1917 it was reported that the Home 'had been renovated and repainted, and put in a satisfactory condition'.[45] This was only possible because of Stephenson's help and in 1918 he was formally appointed as the Welcome's official fund-raiser and his accounts were properly audited. Barrett stated 'Hall (one of the Army and Navy Board men sent to inspect, I suppose) seems to have sent in a "nasty" report. Father was never a "yes"

---

[40] Memoir, op. cit., p.83.

[41] Ibid., p.87.

[42] Ibid., p.88.

[43] *Methodist Recorder,* 31 August 1916, "War work at Gibraltar", under heading 'Stories from the Rev. J.H. Bateson's mail-bag'.

[44] *Minutes of the Army and Navy Board vol. iv, 1911-1918,* meeting 29 May 1916, minute x, p.317.

[45] *Management Committee,* meeting 11 September 1917, minute iv, pp.119-20.

man'.[46]

Barrett felt that the Board disapproved of the way his father ran the Home and that they 'would not help him run the "Welcome" for the physical well being (as opposed to spiritual well being) of the Forces'. There were problems at times with fights, and drunken men damaging the property, even throwing furniture out of the upstairs windows of the Welcome into the street on one occasion, but Barrett stated 'Father believed he must be seen to help in any way open to him' and he certainly did not neglect the spiritual side of things.[47] Hundreds of soldiers and sailors had spent the Christmas of 1915 at the Welcome and a petty officer writing from a battleship in February 1916 remembered how,

> I, with others from this ship, had grand, refreshing spiritual times with the soldier brothers at the Wesleyan Chapel and the 'Welcome'. The Rev. A.B. Sackett has especially been a good friend to us, and his encouraging words have been a great help to us. We have had grandly joyous uplifting times at the prayer meetings on Tuesdays, and at the sing-songs after the Sunday evening services at the chapel.[48]

Later he wrote about the Christian work on board the ship saying,

> I am glad to say that God is blessing us. We have now twelve on board here, and we have a gathering on the upper deck at night time. We begin with a quiet word, and then sing hymns and many gather round us, and join in the singing ... I give one or two words of encouragement to those who are saved, and also to those who are close to us. One is greatly encouraged, for, through the grace of God, four have surrendered to our blessed Saviour ... On Wednesdays we have a Bible class, and are studying the Life of Christ. The Rev. Mr Sackett here is a great friend of ours, and he gave me the opportunity of taking the prayer meeting at the chapel. All twelve of us attended and we were all abundantly blessed.[49]

In May 1917 Sackett himself reported that,

> ... the work is heavy and absorbing. Our Parade Services are well attended considering that our men are scattered all over the Rock. But the evening voluntary service is always crowded, and is a wonderful means of grace, looked forward to by many men who are hazarding life on minesweepers, secret service ships etc., and who eagerly gather at the hour of worship.[50]

In 1917 Ernest Pickard left Gibraltar as his five-year term of duty was

---

[46] Memoir, op. cit., p.88.

[47] Ibid., p.88.

[48] *Methodist Recorder,* 3 February 1916, "The Welcome at Gibraltar", under heading 'Bateson's army correspondence'.

[49] Ibid., 10 February 1916, 'A Petty Officer at Gibraltar'.

[50] Ibid., 31 May 1917, 'The Welcome at Gibraltar'.

completed. He was not replaced and so Sackett was left without a colleague, although the volume of work had not diminished. Perhaps there was simply no-one available to send with so many chaplains on active service. Pickard himself served briefly as a chaplain in France before a breakdown in health caused his return to England. He then served in various circuits before retiring in 1954. He died in 1971.

Lydia with Barrett
after the amputation in 1918
(With permission from the family)

The heavy work load took its toll on both Sackett and his wife and in August 1917 they returned to England for a short break. They went via France and actually managed to meet up with Barrett there who was serving in the trenches. Barrett was wounded soon afterwards and spent some time in hospital. Sackett was back in Gibraltar in early September.

At the end of March 1918 the Governor, now Lieutenant-General Sir Herbert Miles, granted Sackett a month's leave in order to visit Barrett who had been wounded again, this time more severely and his leg had been amputated. He left on 1 April and travelled overland via Madrid and Paris. Lydia probably travelled with him as she definitely went to Barrett's aid and stayed in England until the following year. Sackett travelled on to England and must have met with Bateson who wrote in the *Methodist Recorder* that the Welcome was 'well used, not only by British sailors and soldiers, but every evening American sailors come crowding in. It is customary to sing at the Parade Service, "My Country 'tis of Thee" as well as our own National Anthem'.[51]

In 1918 there were difficulties with the manager and in the middle of the year it seems he left leaving Sackett for several months with no colleague, no manager and no wife, for Lydia was still in England. This was a very busy year too with over 20,000 men sleeping at the Home. Barrett recorded that, 'In July I write wishing I could get a job in Gibraltar and be with him: he must be having a terrible time'.[52] Several times he urged him to press Bateson to send him a colleague but, if he did, no-one was sent.

In October 1918 the *Methodist Recorder* reported that Sackett was having a 'strenuous time in Gibraltar' and went on to say,

He has been greatly helped by the service which Local Preachers

---

[51] Ibid., 18 April 1918.
[52] Memoir, op. cit., p.91.

belonging to the Services have been able to render him. The mates of a stoker, who had previously read the lessons in Church, sent a request that their comrade might be allowed to preach. Mr Sackett arranged to meet their wishes at an evening service, to the edification of the congregation. Among other preachers is a candidate for the ministry, who was with his ship in Gibraltar, and is now going further east. The Governor of Gibraltar, General Sir H.L. Smith-Dorrien, G.C.B., G.C.M.G., D.S.O. [newly arrived on the Rock] recently paid an official visit to our Home, 'The Welcome'. His Excellency expressed his astonishment at the size of the place and the measure of the work, and delight that so much is being done for the moral and spiritual welfare of soldiers serving on the Rock and sailors visiting the port. During August no fewer than 2,500 Service men slept at the Home.[53]

Christmas was reported to be 'the busiest and biggest the Welcome has ever known. On New Year's Day no less than 1,252 meals were served to sailors and soldiers and more than 800 servicemen used the games and recreation room'.[54] By February, Barrett was even more concerned about his father writing to him to say, 'If the worst comes about, go into hospital and Bateson will <u>have</u> to send somebody out'.[55] Somehow Sackett continued and at Easter, Barrett took his mother back to Gibraltar travelling overland. This must have led to a happy and most welcome reunion for all three. On 3 June 1919 the Governor informed Sackett, 'The king has bestowed on you the OBE in today's Gazette and I send you my hearty congratulations'.[56] It was awarded in recognition of the work Sackett had done with the Forces in Gibraltar - he had certainly earned it.

In August 1919 Benjamin Westall left Gibraltar after thirty-three years there, thirty-one of which he had spent as manager of the Gibraltar Gas Company. His retirement was due to the prolonged illness of his daughter. A lengthy tribute appeared in the *Gibraltar Chronicle* for he had been involved in many different aspects of Gibraltar life and, whatever his difficulties had been with Coppin, he had worked tirelessly for the Welcome acting as its honorary accountant. The *Chronicle* reported that, 'Since its opening he has systemised and audited the accounts, whilst during the past fifteen years he had been the guide, philosopher and friend of the Hon. Superintendent, the Rev. A.B. Sackett, who permits me to say that the services thus voluntarily rendered for so many years are beyond all praise'.[57] He was also 'the oldest resident member of the congregation and his loss is already greatly felt'.

By this time Sackett too was preparing to leave. Appreciations of his

---

[53] *Methodist Recorder,* 10 October 1918.

[54] Ibid., 16 January 1919.

[55] Memoir, op. cit., p.93.

[56] Ibid., p.94, quoting letter dated 3 June 1919 from Smith-Dorien to Sackett.

[57] *Gibraltar Chronicle,* 13 August 1919.

work were printed in both the *Gibraltar Chronicle* and the *Methodist Recorder*. In the latter, a soldier wrote describing the Welcome as a real 'home from home' and mentioning some of the facilities, including the roof, where on the terrace 'in the summer teas are served and concerts held'.

A concert was held every Saturday evening at the Welcome and overall the soldier felt, 'But for this Home, there would not be anything for a soldier to do to while away his time'.[58] He felt Sackett was a 'splendid man' adding that he was 'now under orders to proceed home, and the soldiers and sailors here regret that he is going, and will miss him much'. He went on to write about the church.

> The Church is a fine building, and in it is the finest organ on the Rock. I am proud to say that I have been the organist for eight months. How Mr Sackett is appreciated this will show - the church holds 550, so it is rather large; every Sunday it is packed from floor to ceiling, and many a time before I took over the organ have I had to sit either on the floor or on the stairs leading to the gallery, no seat or even an extra chair being available. You may imagine what the singing must be like. It is a credit to the Church and people of every denomination come to hear it. The harvest festival services were so successful that the people wanted the whole evening service repeated on the following Sunday. The collection amounted to £11 10s. We sent it to the National Children's Home and Orphanage. Strange, to say, in the choir we had a young fellow who was brought up in the Home; he was ashore from one of the cruisers.

On Wednesday 19 November 1919, a joint farewell and welcome meeting took place at a crowded Welcome. Members of 'all religious denominations in the community' were present including the Dean of Gibraltar. His presence 'was greatly appreciated by all present as showing the sympathy existing between the Ministers of the Churches'.[59] There were also 'Naval, Military and Civilian representatives' there. Sackett was presented with a purse containing £45. Various speeches were given and musical entertainment followed. There was no mention of Lydia Sackett in the report.

The following morning Sackett called on the Governor, Sir Horace Smith-Dorrien, to say farewell and introduce his successor. In the *Gibraltar Chronicle*, the Governor was reported to have said, 'It is impossible for me to express how much we all owe to you for what you have done in Gibraltar'.[60] The article ended with the words, 'Mr and Mrs Sackett are posted for duty to the Portsmouth Garrison, and fortunate are the people who will enjoy their ministrations'. This is the only reference to

---

[58] *Methodist Recorder,* 11 December 1919.
[59] *Gibraltar Chronicle,* Saturday 22 November 1919.
[60] Ibid., Tuesday 30 December 1919.

Lydia Sackett despite her able support for her husband when she was with him in Gibraltar and her kindness to so many through the provision of hospitality.

They left the Rock on 20 November 1919, travelling on the *Kashmir*. They had achieved an enormous amount in their fifteen years in Gibraltar. The church had been completely renovated and the work of the Welcome had grown and was much respected. Sackett's trips had been particularly appreciated and he obviously had a gift for organising them, sometimes even writing informative booklets for the participants. The spiritual side of the work had also been much appreciated and it is clear that Sackett gave a great deal of support, comfort and encouragement to all those serving in the Forces and particularly so in the war years when life itself was uncertain. He maintained contact with many through correspondence showing his continuing concern for them. It is amazing that he was able to keep going, particularly in 1918, with the enormous pressures of his very heavy work load.

Sackett went to the Portsmouth area but, according to Barrett, the manse in Southsea was situated in a suburban area and Sackett found 'only one weak church and no troops', with the result that 'a very unhappy time followed'.[61] After a year they moved to Shorncliffe Camp and in 1920 he joined the Board, along with Sarchet who had been a member for some

years. Sackett retired to Gloucestershire in 1929 and later he and Lydia moved to Kent to live with their daughter, Dorothy May. Lydia died in 1949, but Alfred continued his work and 'commenced a remarkable ministry ... At eighty-eight years of age he was still canvassing for Jesus, in which holy occupation his familiar figure was seen distributing tracts to cinema queues and visiting business houses and homes in the city.'[62] He died on Sunday 28 January 1951 in his eighty-ninth year.

Alfred Barrett Sackett in retirement
(With permission from the family)

---

[61] Memoir, op. cit., p.99.
[62] *Minutes of the Methodist Conference*, 1951, p.137.

CHAPTER 20   THE WELCOME IS FINALLY PURCHASED
Brown returns to the Rock (1919-36)

After the First World War the Board became the Wesleyan Royal Navy, Army and Air Force Board following the formation of the latter service. In addition Methodism's contribution to the war, through the work of its chaplains, had been too significant to be ignored and the Conference of 1918 appointed a special committee to consider whether permanent commissions should now be accepted. This was agreed, on the understanding that the service authorities would deal with chaplains in their capacity as officers and the church authorities would deal with them in their role as ministers of the gospel. However, as the chaplain in Gibraltar was not exclusively attached to the Forces, he was designated as an honorary chaplain. Allowances towards the cost of the work there continued to be granted by the army and navy authorities but the minister was paid by Methodism.

After the war, the harbour was less busy and the naval establishment at Gibraltar was reduced. However, naval ships still visited and each spring the Home and Mediterranean Fleets exercised from there, but Methodism decided that one minister was now sufficient and appointed William Thomas Sharpley, the son of a Methodist minister. He was born at Haddenham near Ely in 1880 and was educated at Kingswood School. After training at Handsworth College, he served in Malta and England. In 1916 he went to France and was back in England in September 1918, after being invalided home. After working as a chaplain at a demobilisation centre, he was sent to Gibraltar. Before his departure, Sackett introduced him to the Governor and the work. There is no mention of any wife or children so Sharpley may well have come alone.

Few details of his work have survived. The Welcome was still very much appreciated and supported by the authorities and the Governor, Sir Horace L. Smith-Dorrien, wrote to Sharpley in April 1920 to express his high opinion of the work and to say, 'Although it is not possible for me to visit the "Welcome" very often, I should like you to feel that you have in the Governor one who appreciates the work, and that you will always find him sympathetic if in need of help or advice'.[1]

The trips continued, proving as popular as ever but commercial organisations also began arranging some, no doubt seeing them as lucrative opportunities. In 1920 the Board gave permission for electric light to be installed at the Welcome and collections were taken in Gibraltar to raise money towards the cost.

A brief mention in the 1921 Home Mission report merely stated, 'In Gibraltar, the Rev. W.T. Sharpley reports "the best Sunday evening

---

[1] Memoir, op. cit., p.93.

congregation" on the Rock. The Class Meetings are "alive", three Sunday Schools are well attended, and a series of services in Holy Week were "a great inspiration".[2]

In spring 1921 Sharpley wrote to the Board about a site adjoining the Welcome and next to the Bristol Hotel, suggesting this might be purchased. It seems that once again the possibility of uniting all the work on one site was considered. However, the plans came to nothing when Sharpley was informed that the site could not be offered to him. Instead the purchase of the Welcome was once again seriously considered, especially as the rent was now about £500 a year and the Home was only making ends meet because of Stephenson's continuing help.

In September 1921 Sharpley visited England and had some discussion with the Board about the finances, the management of the Home and the possibility of purchasing the Welcome. In October it was reported that Mr Ferdinand Schott, its owner, was willing to sell for £15,000. An official visit to Gibraltar was due and so the deputation was asked to consider whether to secure a site on which to build or to purchase the Welcome.

By this time, Stephenson had already raised £6,000 towards the cost of purchase and, on 17 December 1921, he launched a special campaign to raise the rest although the decision to purchase had not yet been made. He referred to the crippling rent and reported,

> No Institution of this kind in all Europe is more beloved by our brave soldiers and seamen than the Welcome 'Home from Home' at Gibraltar.
>
> We have been able to keep the Home open every day for twenty two years, and it has proved a mighty blessing to countless thousands of our gallant men of both services and the Mercantile Navy.[3]

From the end of December 1921 to the beginning of January 1922, Bateson and the Rev. Richard Hall visited the Mediterranean stations, ending their tour at Gibraltar where the main concern was the Welcome. It was felt that, 'The condition of the building was not satisfactory, owing, doubtless, to the difficulty of getting things done during the War'.[4] An estimate was obtained for a thorough renovation of the premises and the deputation recommended the work be done without delay and reported that 'a certain amount of refurnishing' would also be necessary.

They met with Mr Schott who refused to reduce his price of £15,000 and insisted on a decision within three months or else he would sell the building elsewhere. However, as the lease was secure until 1927 there was no immediate danger of losing the use of it. Hall and Bateson consulted with the authorities, including the Governor, and 'ascertained definitely that it is

---

[2] Home Missions Report, 1921, p.20.

[3] Memoir, op. cit., p.94.

[4] Divisional Records Box 33 n.d. File 2: *Naval History.* Report on a visit to Egypt, Palestine and the Mediterranean Stations, Bateson and Hall.

absolutely impossible to secure a site, or even to erect a building for the purposes of a Home'. They were also told that the military and naval situation in Gibraltar was not likely to be greatly changed in the future and felt it would be a calamity to be without a property to continue the work 'in view of the past record of the "Welcome" and the testimonies we have heard to its moral value to the Fleet and the garrison of the Rock'.

They therefore recommended the purchase of the building, which would save five years rental, and reported that 'facts were brought to our notice which show that the price asked for the "Welcome" is not so exorbitant as might appear'. As the building was in such a good situation, they felt it would always command a high price.

They visited the South Branch and felt it was 'doing exceedingly good work'. They also met the congregation at a social gathering at the Welcome and took a service on the Sunday, reporting, 'We were impressed with the enthusiasm of the friends and delighted with the tone of the services ... We were particularly pleased with the good work of our people in the Choir, the Guild and three Sunday Schools'.

After hearing the deputation's report, the Board decided to buy the building and Hall agreed to return to Gibraltar to effect the purchase. The building cost £14,500 and £558 was allocated to cover the cost of the renovations. Slightly over £9,000 was available and the rest of the money was provided by a loan from the Home Missions Department.

On hearing the news, Westall wrote an angry letter to Sackett. He felt Hall and Bateson had bungled the affair and should have appointed a local negotiator to see Schott saying, 'There would have been a very different price if the enquiry had been put in the hands of a broker, with the name of the proposed purchaser kept secret'.[5] As regarded Schott's threat to sell elsewhere, Westall commented, 'Who would buy the place and pay £15,000, knowing that they would have to wait five years for possession?' Altogether he felt the whole transaction was 'abominable' and added, 'I suppose that the deputation did not even think of spending five guineas on getting an expert Surveyor's Report of the value'. Overall, he felt the purchase had been enormously to the seller's advantage, commenting, 'Won't Schott be rubbing his hands?' In later years it did indeed become clear that the price paid had been too high.

On Wednesday 14 June 1922, the Welcome was officially re-opened by the Governor with the usual representatives from the army, navy and other churches present. Sharpley opened the proceedings with an appreciation of the Governor's interest in the work and gave some details of its history paying particular tribute to Sackett, his predecessor; to Stephenson for his help with the fund raising; and to Major W.R. Syer who had acted as Honorary Superintendent in his absence on leave in 1921. The Governor

---

[5] Memoir, op. cit., pp.94-5.

then responded by stating his appreciation of the work of all Wesleyan Homes and offering his congratulations to Sharpley and to Mr Orman, the manager, on the 'successful restoration, re-arrangement and decoration of the Home'. He felt that both Sackett and Westall would rejoice to hear that the Welcomes' future was assured. He said,

> When I arrived here three and a half years ago I first became acquainted with Mr Sackett. The harbour was crowded with ships of War, the streets were crowded at night, the temptations were great and uncontrolled and it is impossible to exaggerate the enormous benefit of Mr Sackett's work at that time. He lived for the Home. From 6 a.m. to 1 a.m. he was here every day, a wonderful enthusiast who endeared himself to all.[6]

He wished the Welcome an even more successful future. A group photograph was taken on the roof; the Governor inspected the building and broke off on the new full-sized billiard table. The Royal Engineers Bijou Orchestra provided 'a pleasing selection of music' during the evening.

Not long afterwards, on 10 August 1922, the *Gibraltar Chronicle* published an article entitled, 'Departure of a well-known clergyman', which stated,

> The many naval, military and civilian friends of the Rev. W.T. Sharpley, the Honorary Superintendent of the 'Welcome' Home, will regret to learn that he left the Garrison yesterday for England on termination of his tour of duty. He was an indefatigable worker and during his stay amongst us instituted many trips to Málaga, Granada, Algiers, Tangier and other places. He carries the good wishes of everyone with him for his future success in life.

There is no account of a farewell meeting and no reason given for Sharpley's departure after only three years in Gibraltar. He seems to have done good work and to have had the approval of the Board which had unanimously invited him to stay on the previous year. Perhaps he had wanted to leave. He returned to England and served in a variety of different circuits until his retirement in 1945. He died on 30 May 1950, in his seventieth year.

His successor was Frederick Edmund Brown who now returned to Gibraltar after an absence of ten years. When war broke out, he had volunteered to serve as a chaplain and went to France in December 1914. In 1917 he was awarded the DSO because 'As Senior Chaplain of his Division he was conspicuous for his initiative, habitual gallantry, and personal influence amongst the troops'.[7] He continued to serve throughout the war and afterwards would have liked to stay on as a regular chaplain but was apparently considered too old. He lived for a while with his

---

[6] *Gibraltar Chronicle,* 16 June 1922. *Methodist Recorder,* 13 July 1922
[7] Taylor, op. cit., p.22.

mother and worked in Surrey before being sent to Hartlepool. He did not find it easy to settle into the work of an English circuit and was therefore glad of the opportunity to return to Gibraltar.

It is not clear exactly when he arrived, but presumably he did so before Sharpley left to ensure a proper hand-over of the work, which seems to have continued with little change, except for a reduced need for beds at the Welcome as described in the following account:

Frederick E. Brown

> The Atlantic Fleet is visiting Gibraltar. The men are attending the services of our Church in large numbers, and many of them are making the 'Welcome' their home when ashore. The Home has been greatly improved since the last visit of the Fleet, and the newly opened supper-room and tea-room are very popular. The social hour on Sunday evenings attracts large numbers of men, and the picnics which are arranged on the Rock are appreciated. All-night leave is not given to men of the Fleet so freely as in previous years, so there is not the same demand for sleeping accommodation. Nevertheless, a goodly number of men who sleep ashore avail themselves of the accommodation provided.[8]

On 23 March 1923, Charles Arthur Stephenson died in England at the early age of 48. The Board paid tribute to his support for Gibraltar in the *Methodist Recorder* and in the Home Mission Report for that year. He was a loyal member of his local church, and vice-president of the Birmingham Philatelic Society. 'For many years suffering with a weakness which resulted in his death, he has continually exhibited a cheerfulness and courage which was remarkable, and his whole life was graced with a gentleness and consideration for others which made him what he was, a "Christian gentleman"'.[9] The Home Mission Report stated that the total cost of the purchase and renovation of the Welcome had eventually amounted to £17,000 but, thanks to Stephenson's help, by 1923 a debt of only £4,000 remained. His support for Gibraltar had been truly remarkable and it seems perfectly possible that the Welcome would not have survived without it. His work did not end for Miss E. Law, who had been associated with him in it, carried on the work of his collecting scheme.

The report for 1923 also stated,

> There have never, in living memory, been so few sailors and soldiers at Gibraltar as during the past year. There have also been considerable

---

[8] *Methodist Recorder,* 10 February 1923.
[9] Ibid., 9 April 1923.

reductions in the dockyard establishment. Nevertheless the work of our Church and the 'Welcome' Home has been maintained, and there has been much to encourage the Chaplain ... The garrison was brought up to strength by the arrival of troops from Constantinople, and the outlook for the winter's campaign is promising.[10]

The ever changing population of Gibraltar continued to be a problem, not only in planning the work, but also because the fluctuating allowances from the army and navy made financing the work more difficult.

The following year's report, 1924, told a similar story;

Some of the shore establishments, at the Rock, have been cut down almost to vanishing point, entailing an unusually large number of removals. Ships of war are less frequent in port, the garrison has been reduced, but 'Providence Chapel', as our Wesleyan Church used to be called, is still a centre of Christian activity and spiritual influence. Methodism is being worked, the fellowship meeting is a strength and inspiration to many Christian confessors, the Wesley Guild flourishes, the Sunday evening Social Hour is attractive, good work is being done in the Sunday School.[11]

On 29 March 1925 an unveiling ceremony took place in the church when a plaque in memory of Henry Ince was placed there. This was not a specially advertised event but the Governor, now General Sir Charles C. Monro, and his wife were present along with members of his staff. The ceremony had originally been planned for 8 March. However it had been postponed after the Governor fell from his horse at the end of February as it was thought he might not be recovered in time. He and his wife obviously took an interest in the work for Brown reported,

Lady Monro called and spent an hour here yesterday morning, and was, as always, very friendly. She is really interested in our work and would do everything possible to help us ... She thinks our congregations and hearty services - small as they sometimes seem to us, very wonderful, and has come to the conclusion that the Wesleyans are a live people. I suppose the congregations do seem large to her compared with the ones she is familiar with.[12]

The plaque stated that Ince had given his house to be the first Methodist meeting place on that site. This is now known not to be true, although Brown did not state his reasons for thinking this. He had prepared a history of Methodism for the Governor prior to the ceremony. Nevertheless, the plaque still has a place in the church today in tribute to Ince. It had been

---

[10] Home Missions Report, 1923, p.69.

[11] Ibid., 1924, pp.57-8.

[12] Divisional Records 33 n.d. File 3, *History of the Methodist Chaplaincy at Gibraltar,* letter from Brown to Bateson, 28 February 1925.

paid for by Syer and other Methodists and was unveiled by the Governor amidst a large congregation. Brown reported that when he thanked him, the Governor replied, "'It is I who am grateful to have been present at such a beautiful service" ... Lady Monro was also very appreciative and said some very kind things. I am glad for the work's sake'.[13]

Later that year Brown had leave in England. There is little of note to report over the next few years. On 1 April 1927 the lease on the South Branch was renewed for a further twenty-one years. Some repairs had to be made in order to put it into the condition required by the authorities. In October 1927 Brown wrote to the Board about the difficulty of making the Welcome pay its way. He suggested that a room there should be let out for business purposes, which would not harm the work of the Home, and that the flat at the South Branch should also be let. The authorities gave permission and the flat was let for £100 a year, which was double the rent of the whole of the South Branch.

In 1928 Major Syer left Gibraltar. He had clearly been an active member of the church and a great help to both Sharpley and Brown. The Board thanked him for all he had done and later, on his return to England, he became a member of the Board himself.

The year 1932 was a significant year for Methodism itself as its various branches united. Although this was a huge change for Methodism as a whole it had little impact in Gibraltar which had always been Wesleyan. Indeed so little changed there that it was not until 1934 that the word Methodist was substituted for Wesleyan in the *Gibraltar Chronicle* in the details of church services. However, the composition of the Board changed to include representatives of the three main branches. The last meeting of the Wesleyan Board took place on 19 September 1932 and the first meeting of the Methodist Church Board was held on 10 October 1932. Bateson continued as secretary.

In Gibraltar, in 1932, the South Branch closed temporarily to consider its future, probably because it was not paying its way. Letting it was considered but in the end it was re-opened as an extension of the Welcome rather than an independent Branch which saved the expense of employing a separate manager. However, even this plan did not last long for in October 1935, Brown was given permission by the Board and the Governor to let the whole building out which he seems to have done in early 1936. So the South Branch closed but the work at the Welcome continued.

However, there were changes there too. In November 1932 the YMCA decided not to renew its lease on the King Edward VII Institute which was situated on the main street near the Convent. Brown immediately wrote to the Board to suggest that Methodism buy the building and move the Welcome into it. He felt that the Welcome had many drawbacks. It was

---

[13] Ibid., letter from Brown to Bateson, 30 March 1925.

dark so that artificial light was always needed in several rooms. It had too many floors and too many small rooms with no outside windows. The kitchen facilities were poor. There was only one bath and no hot water system. In addition it was situated in the narrowest part of Main Street with no pavement in front of it which Brown felt was dangerous. He went on to say, 'And standing where it does men are not allowed to visit it unless properly dressed, and it is the only place of its kind to which this order applies'.[14] The noise from a large nearby café made it impossible to hold meetings in the Lecture Hall. It was an old building and would continue to need work doing to it. However, despite these drawbacks, Brown felt the building would sell, being well situated for business purposes.

In contrast, the Institute had 'two large halls, five kitchens, baths etc., a bar, a tea lounge and behind, three self-contained flats which could be let. It also had a number of rooms for boarders, and bedroom accommodation for sailors, also manager's quarters.' Brown also pointed out that nearly all the men were stationed in the South District and had to pass the Institute to get into town.

King Edward VII. Soldiers' and Sailors' Institute.

From the collection of J. Richard Jackson

The Board appointed a special committee which included Syer to consider the matter. The business negotiations took place between the Board and the Institute's trustees who were Christian men who wanted the building to be used for Christian purposes. One of them was A.G. Hipwell,

---

[14] Copy of a letter from Brown to Bateson, 14 November 1932.

now a colonel. As ever, the finances were of prime concern. Brown thought the Welcome was worth about £10,000 but the price of the Institute was less at around £8,000, possibly because it was less adaptable for other uses. However Brown thought the Institute would be profitable and in any case the closure of it by the YMCA would reduce their competition.

Correspondence continued over the next few months. The Institute was offered to Methodism at the price of £8,000 but the Board wanted about £13,000 for the Welcome. In February 1933 Brown reported,

> The Governor's private secretary has just telephoned to ask us what we are doing in the matter. He is anxious to know. If we are not going to acquire this building some other means will be sought to keep it open. I do hope the question will be decided with as little delay as possible. Personally, of course, it is a matter of no consequence to me, but from the standpoint of our ministry to the Garrison it means much. If this opportunity is lost such a chance will never recur.[15]

He wrote again to say that he felt the original purchase price of the Welcome had been much too high, commenting, 'The property cost £14,500 but it was never worth that'.[16] The best offer Brown could get was for £9,500, which he urged the Board to accept believing that the only important consideration was whether the new premises would be an advantage to their work. He felt they would be.

So the Board agreed to the price of £8,000 for the Institute and paid a £500 deposit to seal the transaction. Bateson wrote to Brown, 'I want to congratulate you on the fact that the King Edward VII Institute becomes ours! How thankful you will be, and with what hope you will enter on this new development. I know, from all our correspondence, how you have set your heart upon this purchase, and how devoutful thankful you will be'.[17] Brown signed an agreement to sell the Welcome, was given a deposit and banked it. He began to make plans to buy some of the YMCA's furniture and for the move.

Then an unexpected blow fell. Brown discovered that the Governor, now General Sir Alexander J. Godley, was in fact patron of the YMCA but the decision to end the work at the Institute had been taken without consulting him, and he was rather displeased about being ignored. He had examined the Deed of Trust which had been granted on condition that the building be used for a Soldiers' and Sailors' Institute. Only if it was decided that the premises were no longer required for this purpose could they be sold. The Governor had therefore sent a telegram to the Institute's trustees on 9 February to inform them that, as the building was still required for this purpose, he could not sanction the transfer of the deeds.

---

[15] Copy of a letter from Brown to Bateson, 7 February 1933.
[16] Ibid., 13 February 1933.
[17] Letter from Bateson to Brown, 24 February 1933.

The trustees had failed to inform Bateson of this telegram and went ahead with the agreement to sell. When Bateson was finally informed. he was horrified and wrote to Brown saying, 'It seems as though the earth has fallen from under my feet. I had the absolute assurance that the site of the King Edward Institute was freehold, and that there were no restrictions or encumbrances'.[18] He had called an emergency meeting of the Gibraltar Committee and felt he would have sleepless nights until it had met.

Brown does not seem to have been quite so concerned. Methodism had not been at fault in agreeing to the sale, as it was the Institute's trustees who had failed to inform them of the Governor's views. In addition Brown felt the authorities in Gibraltar had always been very friendly to him personally and that the Governor's interpretation of the deeds was definitely open to question. Brown spoke at length to the Colonial Secretary who seemed quite sympathetic to his views and hopeful that the sale could go ahead and so Brown told Bateson, 'I have no doubt the difficulty can be overcome'.[19]

However, the Gibraltar Committee decided to withdraw the offer to purchase. Brown was told that there was absolutely no question of buying the building with any restriction in place, as the future use of it could not be predicted. The Committee therefore began to consider the possibility of renting the building instead. Whilst these negotiations were going on, there was the problem that the purchaser of the Welcome was expecting to take possession of that building. He was John Mackintosh a local business man and philanthropist. Brown explained the situation to him and he agreed to wait a week or so.

Brown had a further conversation with a government official who 'considered the Governor's position untenable'. He went on to say,

> It seems to me his [The Governor's] attitude is largely personal ... The course to be pursued is this. The Trustees must establish their right to sell, and if after that he should hold out, to say that the matter will be referred to the Colonial Office in London. That would have a good effect on him. The government here are not anxious to have any matter referred to the home authorities.[20]

Meetings and discussions went on. Telegrams and letters flew back and forth. The Governor refused to consent to anything until he heard from the Institute's trustees who were rather dilatory in communicating with him. In March Brown met with the Governor himself and reported,

> Of course the Governor is simply doing his best to obstruct the whole business although he says we are not to blame in the matter. I think however if the Trustees will satisfy him that they are willing to let the premises to us, and with our assurance as to their use he may withdraw

---

[18] Ibid., 3 March 1933.
[19] Copy of a letter from Brown to Bateson, 3 March 1933.
[20] Ibid., 11 March 1933.

his objection.

Legally I think his whole position is untenable, and I am advised that that is so … But he leaves in July and the Attorney General very soon also so it might be well to get into the building as tenants and then put forward the sale documents when the new Governor comes. The Supreme Court is the legal authority, all the Governor has to do is attach his signature, and I hardly think a new Governor would think it worthwhile to carry on the quarrel of his predecessor.[21]

Discussions went ahead to fix the rent and conditions of the lease. The Institute was surveyed. Brown felt that it had been well built and was in a good state of repair but that 'the cubicles are small, dark and unwholesome and should be removed. More rooms might be made in the refreshment bar also and will be needed when the ships are in'.[22] The Medical Officer of Health agreed with him about the cubicles, which then had to be discussed with the trustees. Brown was not clear if the three flats were to be included. A lease was drawn up but Brown objected to it as it stated that the work would be solely with soldiers and sailors. He commented, 'We have always, of course, given preference to service men, but for years past civilians have lived on the premises of the Welcome'.[23] The suggested annual rental of £375, including the flats, he considered to be far too high. He too was obviously feeling exasperated by this time, writing, 'This Board of Trustees is the most futile and unbusinesslike collection that I have ever heard of. Every move they make seems to be the worst possible'.

Things dragged on so long that the Welcome's new owner, Mackintosh, not surprisingly asked for a monthly rental as compensation for the prolonged wait for possession, but at least he was prepared to wait so that the work of the Welcome could continue. The trustees continued to drag their heels and Brown wrote to Bateson to say, 'I strongly feel that they ought to be compelled to compensate us for all the loss and expense to which they have put us'.[24]

In mid April, a telegram from the trustees to the Governor enraged him even further, and the Colonial Secretary told Brown that the Governor then 'went off the deep end entirely' and had said 'I will not be browbeaten by these people … Before I consent to anything I shall demand an assurance in writing that the Methodists will offer the same social activities that the YMCA have offered. I am advised that if they take over the place they will run it as a psalm-singing, tea-drinking shop, and I won't have that'. Brown went on to say, 'I was very angry, and there was a good deal of plain speaking especially on my side. I asked what H.E. thought we were trying to do … If we were seeking to establish a brothel no greater difficulty could

---

[21] Ibid., 17 March 1933.

[22] Ibid., 21 March 1933.

[23] Ibid., 11 April 1933.

[24] Ibid., 18 April 1933.

be put in our way'.[25] The Colonial Secretary planned to see the Governor again the next day and would see what he could do.

Shortly afterwards Bateson informed Brown that, as they could not get any further forward with the Institute's trustees, the Board had placed the matter in the hands of solicitors. The anxiety was beginning to tell on everyone.

Brown saw the Colonial Secretary again and reported, 'H.E. is absolutely unreasonable about the whole matter'.[26] All they could do was wait. Mackintosh was charging a justifiable £70 a month rent but had at least agreed to an even longer wait for possession.

By the beginning of May, the Governor was still refusing to be rushed! Even Brown felt that 'The strain and worry is very trying'.[27] At last in mid May, the Governor gave way and consented to the new lease. Brown sent a telegram saying 'Matter settled' to which Bateson responded, 'Thankful beyond words'. The lease was finally signed on 1 June 1933 and plans went ahead to vacate the Welcome on 15 June. Brown must have worked incredibly hard to get everything done in so short a time. He reported, 'The new place is in a frightful muddle. Nearly every room is stacked with things, and the workmen are busy still. We expect to see the bar and kitchen ready for occupation tomorrow [12 June] and we shall have to exercise patience, and gradually get the other parts of the building finished as the workmen go out'.[28]

The move did take place but, hardly surprisingly, there was no big opening ceremony. On this occasion the Governor would have been the last person they wanted to perform one and so the event passed without any reporting at all. In any case, there was still much to be done in the building. The problems were not over as it took time to get everything ready and negotiations continued as to who paid for what. Brown discovered the boiler in the kitchen range to be defective and the flues in the bakery were choked up. The electric light installation was in such an appalling state he felt it was a wonder the building had not burnt down. Gradually order was restored and the work was done. A few weeks later, Brown sent Mr and Mrs Pearce, the manager and his wife, on holiday to Cádiz for a few days, after all their hard work, but does not seem to have been able to take a break himself until November when he too spent some time in Spain. Bateson had hoped to visit Gibraltar but was unable to do so on health grounds. In March 1934 the Board pressed Brown to take some leave but he did not want to go to England. A Mr Linton spent some weeks in Gibraltar in July and was reported to have been a help to Brown and it may be that Brown took some local leave at this time. In May 1935 he agreed to

---

[25] Ibid., 25 April 1933.
[26] Ibid., 26 April 1933.
[27] Ibid., 2 May 1933.
[28] Ibid., 11 June 1933.

take three months leave and the Board arranged a supply to cover the work in his absence. On this occasion he did visit England and, whilst there, had the opportunity to discuss the work with the Board.

The whole affair shows just how much power the Governor still had. However, the move did turn out to be a good one and there was increased patronage of the Welcome. The large concert hall also proved a popular venue for other organisations which helped with the finances. However, even with the arrival of a new Governor, General Sir Charles H. Harington, no further attempts were made to buy the building. He seems to have delayed visiting the Home and did not do so until October 1934 when he was reported to have been pleased with what he saw.

The rent was set at £280 a year, excluding the three flats which the Institute's trustees retained. Some of the £9,500 received for the Welcome was used towards the cost of the move and to pay off the remaining debt which was by then just over £2,000. The balance of £6,453 7s 10d was invested on behalf of the Gibraltar Account.

The work of the Birmingham collecting scheme had been continuing but not very successfully and so Bateson visited Birmingham at the end of 1933 to discuss the situation. It was decided to dispense with the services of Miss Law's assistant thus cutting down the overheads. This improved things for a while, but in 1937 it was agreed that the scheme should close. Miss Law had apparently expected this decision which allayed the Board's anxiety about her. The list of subscribers was passed to Brown for him to continue the work. He was happy to do this but eventually it came to an end and no further appeals were made.

In the last five months of 1933, the Welcome made a small profit, despite competition from other organisations. As Brown wrote, 'We can never hope to do the business that the old Welcome did years ago when these homes were the only places of entertainment in the town. Still we are paying our way, and hope to continue to do so.'[29] However, it seems he was only referring to the day-to-day expenses of the Welcome; part of the annual rent was sometimes paid by the Board. Brown felt the interest on the money received from the old Welcome should be used for this purpose but it is not clear if this happened.

The need for accommodation was now much less. The Welcome only had some thirty beds and a few rooms were occupied by boarders who provided a more reliable income. Bateson wrote to Brown in May 1934 in reply to a letter from him which has not survived.

> You certainly enlighten me on one point, viz., that even when the Fleet is in the 'good men' prefer to return to their ships at night. I think they thereby show very great discretion; though I am sorry that they are thus deprived of the hospitality and environment which awaits them in the

---

[29] Ibid., 14 May 1934.

Home.

I understand the state in which a 'drunk' can leave his room - but when one thinks what might have happened to a 'drunk' had there not been this refuge for him, one cannot but be thankful that we are able to do this work for the saving of the men, in body and soul.[30]

Bateson's next letter, again in reponse to one from Brown now missing, refers to the fact that Brown had had to call out the naval police one night and that at the subsequent court-martial, two men had been convicted and discharged from the navy. The details of the incident have not survived but it illustrates the fact that at times the work was far from easy. Bateson supported Brown's actions saying, 'It was imperative that strong action should be taken, that our reputation might be defended'.[31]

One of the other changes Brown made at the Welcome was the provision of a small chapel there, knowing that the church was somewhat out of the way and that not everyone could be bothered to seek it out. In mid 1935 he wrote the following report which gives a good picture of all the changes.

> The religious and social work of the 'Welcome' is still carried on in the Institute, true to the traditions which made the old 'Welcome' in Main Street so widely known.
>
> The Institute offers better facilities for the work than the old building did, and it is a pleasure to be able to say that the past year has been a better one than some former years were.
>
> Much more is done in barracks and on board ships for the comfort and entertainment of Service men than in the past; notwithstanding this, need still exists for such places as the 'Welcome'. Certainly this applies to Gibraltar, with its very limited space, and congested town. Conditions here have changed greatly during the past few years, and the men enjoy greater liberty; but the restricted area induces monotony, and lays men all the more open to the temptations that abound. Many men never take advantage of what we have to offer, but on the other hand many do; and it may mean more than we think that there are places where a man can find clean entertainment, good food and kindly fellowship, and where if he feels his need of spiritual help and guidance, he can find it. A man said to the writer the other day, 'This place and the Church Services are the only things I really look forward to in Gibraltar'; and it would not be difficult to multiply testimonies to the usefulness of the Institute.
>
> The Games and reading Rooms are well furnished and very comfortable, and the little Chapel is open all day for private prayer and meditation. Services are held there also during the week, and many during the year find it a 'Bethel'.[32]

This account was actually part of a report entitled 'King Edward VII

---

[30] Letter from Bateson to Brown, 15 May 1934.
[31] Ibid., 14 June 1934.
[32] King Edward VII Soldiers' and Sailors' Institute, Gibraltar, 1934.

Soldiers' and Sailors' Institute, Gibraltar' for 1934 which was published by the Institute's trustees and reads as if they were responsible for the work there. Relationships between the trustees and Methodism continued to pose some problems. Brown felt Mr H.F. Yearsley, the Army Scripture Reader who lived in one of the flats, reported all his doings to the Committee. In March 1934 a complaint was made about Brown for failing to ask permission for two small brackets to be fixed to the walls to carry wires without asking permission. Brown was having wireless installed at the Welcome and reported, 'The company has been carrying its wires all over the city and I have heard of no objections having been raised ... It is generally recognised that this company is bringing the pleasures of modern life to many people who otherwise would not be able to enjoy it'.[33] No harm had been done to the building and Brown had not thought it necessary to seek permission first.

The trustees also stated that the Institute's patron was the King and the vice-patron the Governor. In 1936 when George VI became king, the trustees asked him to become patron in succession to his father, but did this without reference to Methodism or the Governor. When Brown heard about it he asked,

> What is the king to be patron of? Just a building presumably. The Trustees are now just landlords of a set of premises which they let at a rental - nothing more ... Sir Charles seemed to know nothing about his being Vice Patron of the Institute. I do not suppose he has ever been approached about the matter ... The whole thing seems to me ridiculous, and the handling of the matter is just on a par with their bungling in the past.[34]

The Board responded, 'This is another illustration of dual control which sometimes becomes exasperating' and there was concern that the Institute's trustees were trying to pass Methodism's work off as their own.[35] The trustees apologised to the Governor who graciously accepted the apology and it seems the king did agree to be Patron!

By this time, there was a new Secretary of the Board for in October 1935, Bateson died following a heart attack. His health had been causing concern for some time but, nevertheless, his death came as a shock. The person eventually appointed to succeed him was the Rev. H. Beverley Dodd.

At the end of 1936, Mr Pearce, the manager of the Welcome, asked to be relieved of his post because his wife's health was poor and he felt she needed to return to England. A Mr Scott, who had been working at the Devonport Home, was recruited in England as Pearce's replacement. He

---

[33] Copy of a letter from Brown to Bateson, 20 March 1934.
[34] Ibid., 20 May 1936.
[35] Letter from Standing to Brown, 7 May 1936.

arrived in Gibraltar in early 1937.

The Methodist work in Gibraltar had now been carrying on for many years without any regard for affairs in Spain. Apart from the visits there from the Rock, no interest had been taken in the country and the work in Gibraltar was more than enough to occupy all the time and energy of the ministers appointed there. However, the Spanish civil war changed that and Brown found himself, to some extent at least, caught up in Spanish affairs.

There had been considerable unrest in Spain over a long period of time and in July 1936, the Spanish army based in Morocco took over Ceuta and Melilla. Similar revolts occurred in Spain itself as nationalist forces rose up against the republican government. Early action took place around Gibraltar and many Gibraltarians, who were attending the La Línea fair at the time, fled back to the Rock along with refugees from Spain. About a thousand refugees came to Gibraltar on the day the war started and many more came later. They all had to be accommodated somewhere and the police ordered various places, including the Welcome, to take them in. Sheer numbers meant that for a time the frontier gates were closed to enable a screening process to be set up. Those who did enter Gibraltar were encouraged to leave as soon as possible. Some people from Gibraltar, and other British subjects, were trapped in Spain by the outbreak of the war but the navy came to the rescue and brought them out from ports such as Málaga and Almería.

The civil war affected Gibraltar in several other ways. It affected the labour force as some two thousand workers had been coming in from La Línea on a daily basis before it began. Supplies of fresh fruit, vegetables and fish brought in from Spain were reduced which led to shortages and increased prices. In addition Gibraltarians supported different sides, which created unrest and dissension in Gibraltar itself. Relationships at the border were affected too, and never really returned to the pre-war state of co-operation and understanding.

Padre Brown, as he came to be known, was caught up in these events. On 23 July 1936, shortly after the start of the war, he wrote,

> Every possible place in Gibraltar is crowded ... It is a pitiable business. I have been down at the gates handing cocoa, etc., through the railings to the women and children. The folk behaved splendidly ... The crowd was great all day and all night, and it was impossible to do all one would have liked. The native people have been splendid. They have allowed people to crowd their already full houses and have shared their food with them. I know one family of six that only had four chairs and a three foot table, and they took in eight or ten people! I sent them some chairs and an additional table. I thought they deserved them. All this is so hard upon the women and children. I found a woman the other evening with a three days old baby, and there was another woman with a baby two days old!
>
> You will have read of the engagement in the Bay. It was quite thrilling, but very terrifying to the people still remaining in the towns near, and it caused a new rush to the fortress gates. Refugees from Málaga say that the place is in ruins. The Communists have just gone mad, and have looted, burned and murdered in true Communist style. I have just had a lady to see me who along with others was evacuated by

the 'Shamrock' and she escaped with nothing at all but the clothes she was wearing. I am arranging to send her to friends in England.[1]

At first Brown's sympathies lay more with Franco and his men, believing that they might do more for the Christian cause than the republicans but, as the war progressed with bitter fighting and cruelty, his attitudes began to change. It was one of Franco's officials who ordered him out of Spain at gun-point when he tried to take in supplies to relieve some of the suffering. He sheltered as many refugees as he could, from both sides, often looking after them in his own home.

A year after the war began the *Methodist Recorder* described his work as follows:

> The past year has been a new experience to all. Access to Spain had been easy aforetime: men on leave had moved in and out at will: and the picnics and trips, for which Mr Brown is famous throughout the Services, helping to break the monotony of life on the Rock, were the consequences. The civil war since last July, has completely changed conditions, for since then no military permits to Spain have been granted, with the result that all have felt the restrictions of life in Gibraltar.
>
> Nevertheless, there has been much work to do. Ships on duty in Spanish waters have been in and out constantly, and our 'Welcome' Home has been catering for their general welfare. Mr Brown comments that the work of the British ships during these troubles has been beyond praise. At one time all the sleeping accommodation at the 'Welcome' was given over to refugees, and the work generally was to some extent disorganised. This period has passed, but there is seldom a week that does not see refugees on the premises. Two cases may be of interest.
>
> A young Hungarian landed in Gibraltar some nine months ago and, being destitute, was compelled to leave the Colony. The only course open to him was to go into Spain. A long story can be condensed into these few sentences. He was sentenced to be shot three times - twice by the insurgents and once by the Government. In his despair he attempted suicide whilst in prison at Málaga, and very nearly succeeded. On coming out of hospital he was sent to La Línea, the nearest Spanish town, to be dealt with there; and one night, in an almost miraculous manner, he escaped back to British territory. Word was sent to Mr Brown that the man was hiding on the beach. Apart from intervention he would have been sent back to Spain on being discovered, and that would certainly have resulted in his death. Mr Brown was allowed to deal with the case on condition that he would look after the man until passage could be secured. As he had no passport it took over two months to achieve this, but happily in the end it was possible to get him home. His comment as he left was to the effect that his experiences in Morocco and Spain had cured him of any 'wandering spirit'!
>
> The second case related to three Protestant ladies from Málaga - a

---

[1] Taylor, op. cit., pp.30-1.

widow and two daughters - who had continued to reside in the city all through its occupation by the Government Forces, but, after its fall to the insurgents, life had become too precarious and, in their fear, they left and managed to get through to Gibraltar. They were completely destitute, as no money is allowed to pass out of the country. They had literally nowhere to go and no one to turn to but, as the lady said, to God. At the end of three months care, Mr Brown was able to get them away to Valencia and to arrange for their reception there.[2]

There were many other refugees including a Catholic monk.

> He had been 'drafted' from his convent to the army 'fighting for Christianity'. His mind had almost given way amid the battles and massacres of political prisoners he had witnessed. At length he deserted. He made his way to Gibraltar, by the simple but effective ruse of wearing his habit, and booking a series of return tickets on the railway, though never using the return half. When he made his way over the frontier and into the Fortress, he dared not turn to his own folk, but, in his trouble he found unexpected help from a Protestant minister. When he later passed on through Tangier, he was ill-advised enough to broadcast a tribute to his 'Samaritan' friend, and this led to a warning from the Spanish Consul in Gibraltar that 'Padre Brown would not be safe in the parts of Spain controlled by General Franco'.[3]

This must have curtailed his activities and he did not again visit Ronda, his favourite Spanish town, until 1942. In December 1937 the Rev. J. Oliver Hornabrook visited the Mediterranean stations including Gibraltar and no doubt Brown benefited from some fellowship and the opportunity to discuss the work. In January 1938 Dodd, the Secretary of the Board, died suddenly after only two years in the post. He was eventually succeeded by the Rev. George Standing.

In February the naval authorities complained that as civilians were living at the Welcome, two naval men, who had landed for two months' duty, had to sleep in dormitories. Brown replied by saying that there were eleven single rooms at the Welcome which were occupied by a civilian employed in the army, a naval rating, four men employed in the dockyard, one Naafi employee and four ordinary civilians. Some had been living there for years, others for months. Brown reported, 'The accommodation for naval ratings is very rarely in full use and if some of these private rooms were not let to civilians they would remain empty throughout the year'.[4] In fact, the two men had not had to sleep in a dormitory, but had been given exclusive use of a shared room capable of sleeping five and two of the extra beds had been removed to give them more space. Brown went on to say, 'The

---

[2] *Methodist Recorder,* 1 July 1937, 'A Chaplain at Gibraltar'.
[3] Taylor, op. cit., p.35.
[4] Brown to Admiral's Secretary, 9 February 1938.

Welcome has forty years of good service for troops behind it, and it has always been run in the interests of the men of the navy and army. What other purpose could we have in carrying on the work? Every year I have to raise a considerable sum to keep things going and civilians who are accommodated help to pay the expenses of the place'. He also pointed out that the two men had been 'very objectionable to the manager who works hard to be of service and gets no appreciation from the majority of the men, but often a great deal of vile abuse'. He ended by saying, 'We are prepared at all times to do all that is possible, and I regret that it is impossible to provide any other accommodation for these ratings than that already given'. That appears to have been the end of the matter but it illustrates some of the difficulties associated with the work.

Shortly afterwards, a Mr Joe Brice visited Gibraltar. He later wrote about his visit saying,

> A little while ago several ex-Presidents of Conference said that they had not known of the existence of a Methodist Church at Gibraltar. But the Roman Catholic docker knew all about it. I asked him to direct me to Padre Brown. 'Yes, sir', he replied, 'He's an institution here'.[5]

Brice found it a 'toilsome climb' to the church but felt the fellowship received from Brown 'was worth ten times the effort'. Brice attended the 10.30 a.m. service, which followed an earlier parade service, and they lunched at the Welcome where 'throughout the week, with the genial help of Mr and Mrs Scott, the Padre carries on a most beneficent, spiritual and social ministry'. He went on to describe the facilities there;

> Within are the café, baths, reading-room, parlour, games-room, writing-room, and a whole floor of bedrooms. At the centre is a sanctuary with a beautiful altar-piece, which is exquisitely lighted by old Salamanca lamps. Here the mid-week devotional meetings are held and much-tempted men find grace to help in time of need.
>
> Scores of men frequent 'The Welcome' for clean fellowship, recreation and home comforts; and not a few of them remain for quiet talks in the Padre's room opposite the chapel. I heard several moving stories of salvation by friendly counsel. It is a beautiful work, and its influence has gone throughout the world.

Brown was offered home leave that year but declined it. However, he apparently spent a month at the Convent instead, staying with Sir Charles and Lady Harington with whom he was friendly. Taylor records,

> He was happy in this friendship; but much of the conduct of affairs in the colony depressed him. His letters expressed his sense of uneasiness about colonial housing conditions, about inadequate preparation for defence;

---

[5] *Methodist Recorder,* 26 May 1938.

above all, about the careless social life that went on, as in days of peacetime soldiering.[6]

The year 1939 was a momentous one. In March, the war in Spain ended in victory for General Franco who had received powerful help from Germany and Italy. It had been a bitter civil war which had divided friends and families and left much of the country in ruins. There had been terrible atrocities on both sides and around a million Spaniards were dead. In September the Second World War began and Spain remained neutral although Franco expected and wanted Germany to win. However, he also wanted to keep Spain independent and if possible take possession of Gibraltar. An offer had previously been made to exchange it for Ceuta which Britain declined, but Gibraltar's defences had been strengthened and the docks enlarged to accommodate the modern larger ships. In 1933 a small grass airstrip had been constructed and in 1938 work began to make this a proper runway.

At first it was thought that Gibraltar's role would be similar to that during the First World War and convoys began assembling there. However, as the war progressed, Gibraltar was felt to be of much more strategic importance in guarding the entrance to the Mediterranean and as a naval base and, as it was thought that the Rock was likely to come under attack, it was decided that the civilian population must leave. Service families were evacuated directly to England leaving in mid May 1940. At the same time, the first group of Gibraltarians left for French Morocco and by the end of June over 13,000 people had been evacuated there. A few with relatives in Spain or Tangier, who could afford to be independent, saw to themselves. The Indian community decided to return to India but their ship was attacked and captured by the Germans.

Meanwhile there had been considerable developments in the war with the fall of France, the British evacuation from Dunkirk, and the entrance of Italy into the war. There was also concern about Spain for Franco changed his position from one of neutrality to one of non-belligerency. Might Spain too enter the war? Difficult decisions had to be made; one of which was to bomb the French ships at Oran to prevent the Germans using them. This was carried out with the loss of some 1,300 French sailors. This resulted in a great deal of anti-British feeling and meant that the Gibraltar evacuees were no longer welcome. When a convoy of British ships arrived carrying French troops the authorities impounded them and refused to let them leave without taking the evacuees. There was no time to clean the ships or re-provision them. The Gibraltarians were herded aboard at short notice, after standing for hours in the hot sun not knowing what was happening. Gibraltar's Governor did not want them back; Britain did not want them either, but Commodore Creighton felt he had no choice and took them back

---

[6] Taylor, op. cit., p.38.

to Gibraltar anyway. The Governor at first refused to let them land, fearing difficulties in getting them away again, but there was such a public outcry that he had to give way. In due course, the evacuation began again and this time in even greater numbers. Only those in essential work were allowed to remain behind. All the rest had to leave with no exceptions. Many had never left the Rock before and families were split up. The total number evacuated was 16,700. Some died on the journey and others were born. About 2,000 people went to Madeira and around 1,600 to Jamaica but the vast majority were taken to London and the blitz! The same convoy ships were used to transport them. They had been hastily cleaned and adapted but were still not very suitable. It was a long and uncomfortable voyage of seventeen days as a circuitous route was taken to try and minimise the danger of attack from German U-boats. In mid 1944 they were mostly moved to Northern Ireland to await repatriation. The story of the evacuation is told in Finlayson's book with its apt title, *The Fortress came first*.

Brown was involved in all of this. In a letter to his sister, which refers to the initial evacuation, he wrote,

> The evacuation goes on as speedily as possible. This afternoon another 1200 or so were got away, and I think I never saw as many babies and young children gathered together anywhere in such a small space as a ship. It takes some time to get the people aboard, as certain particulars have to be taken by the French authorities as each family passes, and it means that the evacuees have to stand for quite a long time in the sun. A good number of helpers were present and they handled the babies; but some of them yelled blue murder and made one wonder how long they could carry on. The noise on the mess decks below was almost deafening, but the Gibraltar people are well accustomed to noise, and would not mind that.
>
> I was amused a good many times as I was carrying babies and bundles down when men came up and offered to carry them for me, and two or three times someone pointed to a pram that had been brought aboard and asked me if it were mine and if they could get it down for me!
>
> It did not occur to me until afterwards that they could not understand a man dressed as a Major doing such work.[7]

Brown had, by this time, been given a proper commission as a war-time chaplain which he held for the duration of the war. No doubt he helped when the people returned from Morocco and set off again but no details have survived. However, it seems that many people sought his advice and some even left their keys with him. The heavy work load took its toll and he wrote, 'Today I am not going home to lunch and am going to be invisible all afternoon if I can. I feel just about the end of my ability to

---

[7] Ibid., p.42. (Quoting letter from Brown to his sister Sallie, 5 May 1940.)

advise and "do something".[8] Elsewhere he noted, 'All that can be done here in the way of defence is being done, but if war comes our way, as I fear it will, we shall have to face a difficult time. It does not worry me much: we live a day at a time, and it is no use crossing bridges before we reach them.'[9]

In the meantime, in the uncertain situation, extensive work began to prepare Gibraltar to defend itself. Air-raids began before the evacuation was completed and a few civilians were killed. They continued over the next two or three years but tended to be sporadic and were not too devastating in their effects. Later attacks included under-water attempts on ships in the bay which sank and damaged a number of them. Extra guns were sent to Gibraltar and more men including tunnellers, some of whom were Canadian. So much tunnelling was done that by the end of the war virtually a whole town had been created within the Rock including a barracks, a hospital and all necessary facilities for living, with ample room for stores and equipment. Some thirty miles of tunnels now exist. Work continued on the airfield at North Front, probably encroaching slightly on the cemetery which may explain why some of the early Methodist graves can no longer be found. Spain too prepared defensive works in the vicinity of Gibraltar, no doubt adding to the anxiety about a possible attack.

A new naval force, called Force H, was stationed at Gibraltar including the *Ark Royal*. Its job was to guard the entrance to the Mediterranean and its ships were used to escort convoys to the beleaguered island of Malta. The 8th Submarine Flotilla was also based at Gibraltar and the dockyard was kept busy with repair work.

Meanwhile, Hitler developed a plan, code-named 'Operation Felix', to take the Rock, but he wanted Franco's agreement and support. The two met at Hendaye on the Spanish-French border in October 1940 to discuss the plan, but the meeting ended without agreement and, in the end, Hitler did not attack Gibraltar. By this time the Rock had become a haven for escaped prisoners of war and other servicemen separated from their comrades. Brown was occasionally involved in offering support to them as they waited to return to Britain.

The threat of attack led to an anxious time in Gibraltar and a busy one too. Of course this was a Gibraltar as never experienced before. There were no children, very few women, apart from the two thousand Spanish women who came in daily to work there, and far more men in uniform. Some Spanish labourers also came in daily to work in the dockyard and elsewhere. There was restricted access to many parts of the Rock and a curfew was imposed. There was no black-out. Generally speaking life was rather monotonous and boredom in off-duty hours difficult to combat. Hard drinking sessions sometimes led to fighting and the overall crime rate

---

[8] Ibid., p.43. (Quoting letter from Brown, July 1940.)
[9] Ibid., p.42 (Quoting letter from Brown to his sister Sallie, 5 May 1940.)

increased. All sorts of attempts were made to provide entertainment and activities. The Welcome, of course, was very busy indeed but the work was not always easy for the open-doors policy continued, although the Gibraltarians themselves were not allowed to use the facilities there. In December 1940 the building was inspected following an application for an admiralty grant. The inspector felt the Welcome struck a rather gloomy note and needed redecoration. In his reply, Brown agreed that it did, but went on to say, 'it appears to me to be rather a waste of money to repaint a place that may be destroyed tomorrow. Few people, I think, would do it to their private property'. He went on to describe the expenses of running the Welcome adding that,

> ... many of the men show very little respect for the property and sometimes I wonder if it is worthwhile. What can be done where men deliberately break off the ivory keys of a valuable piano; make latrines of vases on mantels and drive the points of billiard cues through pictures, urinate in passages and down the stairwell, to say nothing of other things! I am not suggesting of course that such men compose the services, but they exist, and not in any particular rank, and they spoil things for other men.[10]

He also stated, 'We are facing great difficulties in these days where staff and food are concerned, and if the men would appreciate that and make even a little allowance for it things would go on more happily'. The naval reply was sympathetic, hoping that he would not become too discouraged and pointing out that 'such a place as the Welcome is of invaluable use these days'.[11]

There were of course many men who did value and appreciate what was on offer and congregations had grown much larger. In November 1941 Brown reported,

> Services are good and hearty and, as the weather changes, numbers will doubtless be larger ... The house is very crowded afterwards, and Anna and Teresa have a big party to cater for. They don't seem to mind, however; indeed, they seem to enjoy it. It does the men good to spend an hour or two in a house again, and as the house is full of interesting things the men enjoy it all the more.[12]

As Brown was a bachelor, he employed two Spanish sisters, Anna and Teresa, who looked after him and the manse very well. His interest in antiques had grown over the years and he had furnished the manse with many old and interesting things which he liked to show to others.

November 1941 was a sad time in Gibraltar for *Ark Royal* sank at sea

---

[10] Letter from Brown to Captain in the Royal Navy, 13 December 1940.

[11] Letter from Captain in the Royal Navy to Brown, 23 December 1940.

[12] Taylor, op. cit., p.46. (Quoting a letter from Brown, 5 November 1941.)

only twenty-five miles from the Rock. She had been hit by a torpedo some time earlier. Brown must have been affected by this and other losses for he had made friends of many of the sailors.

Soldiers at the Manse

In 1942 there was a new development at the Welcome when 'The Club' was formed. The story is best told in the words of one of its founder members, John Ross, who lives today in Hartlepool with his wife Connie.

I arrived in Gibraltar on Thursday, 24 July 1941. On the following Sunday, 27 July I went with two other companions to have tea at the Welcome where a number of Christian fellows usually gathered. There I met Rev. Brown, Methodist Padre, and we talked together. I soon found out I had an extra affinity with the Padre as he had been a minister at the Westbourne Methodist Church in my home town of West Hartlepool for a short time some years earlier. After tea I played for the fellows singing hymns. It was a grand piano, German and good. Then the meeting ended and the fellows went to their respective churches. Some to the Church of Scotland, one to the Cathedral and I to the Methodist Chapel where Rev. Brown was the preacher. After the service he invited some of us into his home. The Manse was wonderful, containing antique furniture with ornaments and pictures and decorations of beauty. Here we sat talking and had some supper.

And so began a wonderful association with the charismatic person of Padre and the Methodist Chapel.

I became organist at the Chapel and soon we had formed a choir of men's voices. The attendance at both morning and evening services was good and grew so that at times the Chapel was full to capacity of service men - no ladies, of course, as during the war years there were very few ladies living on the Rock. Padre Brown was a very good preacher and very well liked and respected by so very many of the large numbers of

Service personnel. I held weekly choir rehearsals and they sang anthems occasionally during the services in the Chapel.

In January 1942 about four of us sat talking together voicing ideas of the possibility of forming a Club from the fellows attending the Welcome Sunday teas and the Chapel. We were looking for a 'little home comfort'; somewhere to go during the week days for Christian and social companionship away from the otherwise inevitable bars and such like. We four approached the Padre and he sympathetically listened to our expressions and asked us to leave the subject with him. It was with much astonishment and pleasant surprise that we went to the Welcome at Padre's request and he showed us what he had done. On the second floor of the Welcome he had transformed two rooms, having them redecorated and very well furnished, much of the furniture coming from his own possessions. He handed these over to us and said carry on and form your Club. The Club was opened on Monday 2 February 1942 and a formal meeting took place when Norman Finnegan was elected Secretary, Syd Gleave Steward and myself Treasurer together with a general committee. Padre accepted the Presidency. The meeting proceeded with discussion of subscriptions and possible future activities. And so began a splendid fellowship for a group of Service personnel away from home. There was a quiet area where we could sit and read and reflect. We played table board games; had an organised evening, mostly on Tuesdays, when a speaker would be invited to talk to us on their special subject and many of these proved to be very interesting. The Concert Room was put to dual use; it was lined out as a badminton court and many of us used this to good advantage; and we arranged concerts given by ourselves of music and drama.

In the Club we had a small well-furnished Chapel and we held a closing Epilogue each evening, these being taken by a member of the Club. The Padre was connected with the local radio broadcasting station giving Epilogue Services commencing at 21.25. There was a prayer, a lesson and a short sermon. I sang bass in a male quartet for the three hymns that were sung. These short Epilogue services were given almost every Sunday evening with the same singers but occasionally a minister of another denomination would lead it.

Brown took the epilogue at the Club once a week and a full service was held on Saturday evenings. The Club went from strength to strength. Members paid a subscription and were issued with properly printed membership cards stating the rules. There was something to do every night of the week. Various games were available, a dark room was set up, there were books and magazines to read, and of course the use of the canteen and other facilities of the Welcome which were still open to all servicemen. Only the Club rooms were for the exclusive use of its members and here life-long friendships were formed.

Sundays were particularly busy. In October 1942 Brown described his Sunday programme as starting with a 10.30 a.m. service in the church followed by Upper Rock services at 11 o'clock. In the afternoon he was at the hospitals at the South, followed by family tea at the Welcome, an evening service at 6.30 p.m., a communion service at 7.30 p.m. and a social gathering from 8.15 to 9.30 p.m. when he ended the day with a broadcast service. He went on to say that 'It used to be considered that two services on a Sunday made the parson feel very tired, and in need of rest on Mondays. One smiles at that now! Monday just begins another round of duties.'[13]

Of course those on duty were not able to attend the services in the church so Brown went out to them instead, holding his Upper Rock services, but also visiting the men and talking with them during the week. Obviously his workload was much increased during the war years with so many men stationed in Gibraltar and with the sailors who came and went with their ships. Some correspondence took place about getting some help for him but, for one reason or another, this was not possible. There were problems too in getting equipment for the Welcome.

Founders of the Gibraltar Club with Padre Brown
(John Ross is on the left of the front row)

In 1941 the Board had suggested Brown took home leave and offered to send a supply, but he wrote to his family saying,

> I don't like the thought of leaving things now. I would rather be on the spot if anything happens, as I know more about things than anyone coming out would. So I am saying thank you, and declining.
> I never get off the Rock now; indeed, I have not been over the border

---

[13] Ibid., p.49. (Quoting a letter from Brown, 26 October 1942.)

for many months past. The old carefree happy trips to Spain are just a memory, but a very happy one. Fortunately, I am not much given to worry. My philosophy of life is to do the best I can and leave the results in higher hands - and it is a good one.[14]

However, in May 1942, he did manage to spend two weeks in Ronda with a Gibraltarian friend which gave him a much needed break. It was probably just as well for his work load increased even more in the autumn when the manager of the Welcome resigned. Local circumstances seem to have prevented a replacement being sent from England although the Board had made progress in finding someone. In the meantime Brown slept at the Welcome trying to cover the work as best he could. There was obviously great concern about him in England. The Secretary of the Board was now the Rev. Joseph Firth who took over from Standing in 1942. He wrote to Brown in November that year expressing his concern about his heavy workload and saying, 'Do take care of yourself and if possible do not overwork. As you know, we are ready to do anything at any time at this office for you. You have only to make your request'.[15] But it was difficult to know what they could do. There were hints that life at the Welcome was actually easier in some ways without a manager, for in another letter Firth wrote, 'It is interesting to hear that the staff are working better now that the Manager is away'![16] But it still meant more work for Brown, at what was also a particularly hectic time in Gibraltar.

One way of reducing the threat to the Rock was to establish bases in North Africa from which a more powerful assault could also be made against Italy. Plans to launch 'Operation Torch' from Gibraltar were therefore made. The preparations, especially the build-up of air support, could hardly be hidden from the Spanish and concern was expressed as to how they might react, but in the event Spain did nothing. More than four hundred aircraft were brought to Gibraltar. American pilots came to fly them alongside the RAF. On 5 November 1942 Eisenhower arrived to take command and over the next few days the landings took place.

After this, the threat to Gibraltar largely receded but it was still a busy place and a base for operations. Many people visited the Rock including Churchill and the unfortunate Polish leader, General Sikorsky, who died when his plane crashed into the sea off Eastern beach.

Life for Brown continued to be very busy and Firth wrote in February 1943, 'I sympathise with the special difficulties that you are having in these days. Unfortunately there is practically nothing which we can do at this end to help you'.[17] However, the suggestion was soon made that a probationer or lay agent might be a help. Firth explained the difficulties

---

[14] Ibid., p.44.

[15] Letter from Firth to Brown, 18 November 1942.

[16] Ibid., 1 December 1942.

[17] Ibid., 11 February 1943.

even with this plan by saying, 'Such men are hard to come by these days, in view of my constant pleas for chaplains, though Lay Agents are not required for commissions, they are necessary to fill the places of ministers taken from circuits'.[18] However, before long, Robert Henry Emerson was appointed. He was born in County Durham on 27 September 1904. His family later moved to Whitby and, as a teenager, it became Robert's job to drive the local preachers to their appointments in the family's horse and trap. If the preacher failed to arrive, Robert took his place and later, in his early twenties, he was accepted as a full-time lay pastor. He had served in several appointments before being sent to Gibraltar in early summer 1943. Taylor records that a reading of Brown's letters home 'shows with what relief and gratitude he received the loyal and persevering assistance of Pastor 'Robbie' Emerson ... Whilst he did not work any less in consequence he could consider a short absence from his duties without the fear that the work would collapse'.[19] Emerson seems to have worked hard and well in Gibraltar. He also took an interest in the Club and his flat became a meeting place for many.

In autumn 1943, Brown was again offered extended leave which he declined, proposing instead to take local leave in Spain or Tangier, which is presumably what he did. There were continuing problems in getting supplies for the Welcome. A consignment of crockery seems to have gone missing altogether.

In spring 1944, in the continuing absence of a manager, it was suggested that a woman might be able to do the job instead. The Rev. George Standing suggested Mary Jane Halsey, who was then about forty-five years old. She had earlier approached him to see if he could obtain some war work for her and, through him, she had begun work as a leader of the YWCA in Chelmsford. Standing described her to Brown as 'an excellent business woman ... She can control and manage splendidly'.[20] Standing was aware that making the appointment would not be easy. 'The arrangements would be considerable. Release from YWCA. Uniform. War-office permission, passage and so on.' However, the arrangements did go ahead and Miss Halsey started her journey to Gibraltar on Monday 22 January 1945. She arrived safely and, in April 1946, it was reported that 'since the arrival of Miss Halsey to take over the management of the Home, there had been a remarkable improvement; the small deficiency of last year had been turned into a credit balance'.[21]

During this time of course many changes had been taking place in Gibraltar. Once the threat to the Rock had receded, thoughts went to the

---

[18] Letter from Firth to Brown, 9 March 1943.

[19] Taylor, op. cit., pp.49-50.

[20] Letter from Standing to Brown, 23 June 1944.

[21] *Minutes of Soldiers' and Sailors' Homes Management Committee, 1926-1955,* meeting 10 April 1946, minute iv, p.279.

evacuees still far from home, but there were huge problems over their return. There was now no educational establishment in Gibraltar; medical services were thought to be insufficient to meet the likely demands and above all there was a shortage of suitable housing. Many properties, including both the South Welcome and the old Mission House, had been requisitioned. Some properties had been demolished or damaged by air-raids; others were no longer considered suitable. In addition it was not easy to find ships to transport the evacuees and so, for all these reasons, they had to return gradually, but priority was given to those who had relatives in Gibraltar. The first group returned from England in April 1944 with another group arriving from Madeira the following month. Some never returned at all as they had died in the intervening years. Some chose not to return and some young children born in exile had never seen the Rock before. Many had to live in temporary accommodation at first whilst a building programme was undertaken. Some found the rooms containing their personal belongings, sealed by the government before departure, had been broken into and goods stolen. The very last family did not return until August 1951.

Change, after all this, was inevitable and not just with housing and education for probably the most significant change was to the Gibraltarians' view of themselves and their rights. Often made to feel inferior in the past, there was now a desire to be heard and to have some influence in their own land. In 1942, an Association for the Advancement of Civil Rights (ACCR) was formed with a young lawyer, Joshua Hassan, taking a leading role. The city council, suspended at the outbreak of war, was eventually revived and later a legislative council was formed. Hassan became chairman of the City Council in 1945. The Governor still had the power of veto and there were both elected representatives and colonial officials on the councils, but it was nevertheless a move towards self-government and as such it alarmed Spain for Franco still very much wanted Gibraltar.

A major change which affected church attendance was the abolition of the compulsory parade service and the extension of leave granted to the services. The parade service had provided a point of contact with those who chose to attend Methodist services and now different ways of working were developed instead, including Padre's Hours and Moral Leadership Courses. In Gibraltar the Welcome still provided a useful point of contact. As many of the servicemen left the Rock, congregations inevitably decreased as did the numbers attending the Club and the Welcome, but there was still plenty to do. As women and children returned, the Sunday school re-started and a few women even joined the Club! After the war-time difficulties and shortages, a certain amount of equipment was needed at the Welcome which also badly needed redecorating. There were some difficulties with the building's owners in getting this done and it was a long time before the work was finally completed. Club members helped with some of the internal decorating. Repairs to the other Methodist buildings were also needed. Brown reverted to his position as an honorary chaplain and gradually life became more normal.

In spring 1946, Emerson spent some time in England on leave and met with Firth, who wrote to Brown saying, 'Emerson has warmed my heart by what he has told me about the work in Gibraltar. I congratulate you once again on all that you are able to do in the Garrison'.[22]

Brown himself took local leave at this time. Miss Halsey too was due for leave and in July 1946 it was agreed that she should have an assistant who could then also cover her work when she was away. Miss Covington arrived in autumn 1946. Around this time a Mr Carter of Liverpool died. As he was described as a 'constant subscriber' to Gibraltar's funds he may well have been one of the remaining subscribers from the Birmingham scheme.[23] He left £450 to Gibraltar, after tax, which meant that the Welcome made an overall profit of £1,500 that year.

Meanwhile the Club had become a very well-developed organisation with different committee members overseeing the various activities. Brown continued as President and as such provided a strong guiding hand. Activities were many and varied and after the war included picnics and outings both in Gibraltar and Spain. Brown led many rambles around the Rock and Miss Halsey often provided the refreshments. Refreshments and special meals were clearly much appreciated and 'big eats' are occasionally mentioned in the magazines! As members left the Rock, contact was maintained by letter and through the regular magazines. Emerson became corresponding secretary, organising replies to the many letters received.

Brown himself kept up an extensive correspondence. For some considerable time, a reunion was talked about but the plans did not come to fruition until February 1947. The venue was Willersley Castle in Derbyshire, a reasonably central place, and both Brown and Miss Halsey attended it.

The winter of 1947 was one of the worst on record. Taylor recorded,

The weather was appalling; thick snow prevented the arrival of many of his [Brown's] friends at the first Club Reunion at Willersley Castle, and he wrote afterwards that he had only felt half alive in the bitter English winter after years of Gibraltar's sunshine.[24]

Miss Halsey cutting the cake at the first reunion

---

[22] Letter from Firth to Brown, 12 April 1946.

[23] Ibid., 25 November 1946.

[24] Taylor, op. cit., p.55.

However, some twenty-eight members did gather together and, despite the weather, felt the event was a success and planned another reunion for the following year.

Emerson had remained in Gibraltar to oversee the work there, but later in 1947 he left to return to work in England. The reduced numbers stationed on the Rock meant there was no longer need for extra help. He served in a variety of appointments and married Mildred in March 1950 who joined him in maintaining his links with the Gibraltar Club. Eventually the lay pastorate was phased out and in 1964 Emerson was finally accepted into the ministry. He became a supernumerary in 1970 and settled at Great Ayton in North Yorkshire. He died in February 1991 in his eighty-seventh year, after a battle with Alzheimer's disease.

A gift for Robbie and Mildred Emerson

In the summer of 1947, Miss Leveridge succeeded Miss Covington as assistant to Miss Halsey, and was at first reported to be settling down happily to the work but, by February 1948, it was clear that she was not happy and wished to return to England. Firth wrote to Brown to say he would look for a successor commenting, 'We will definitely say this time that she is assistant to Miss Halsey, though I thought that was understood before' which implies that there had been some difficulties in the relationship.[25] Miss Halsey clearly did sterling work in the canteen, and her contribution to the life of the Club and church was much appreciated but few people found her an easy colleague. So Miss Leveridge left and was

---

[25] Letter from Firth to Brown, 9 March 1949.

replaced by Miss Strachan.

In 1948 Brown returned to England to attend the second reunion at Willersley Castle. Afterwards he wrote in the Club magazine that,

> It was an event that could not be fully recounted, for in order to know all that it meant, one would need to have experienced it. One could relate the incidents connected with it but one could not pass on the feelings and emotions that I believe all who were there shared. To us, it was an experience of the high places of fellowship not to be forgotten.[26]

Soon afterwards the canteen was extended and Miss Halsey reported,

> I still get help from Club members when the need arises. I remember how my morning trade commenced with small takings. Now we take up to £9 on a Saturday morning.
> Those of you who helped me in those early days will I am sure be interested. We have the Home Fleet with us at present for twelve days and expect the American Fleet to arrive in a few days time. So you will know I shall be busy for the coming weeks.[27]

However, by the end of 1948 Miss Halsey had decided it was time to leave Gibraltar. The Board recruited a replacement for her in England. This was Captain P. Squelch of the RAOC. He was a local preacher and his wife had some experience in catering. They sailed from Liverpool on 22 February 1949 with their eleven-year-old daughter, Sheila. A joint party was held to welcome them and say farewell to Miss Halsey on 8 March. Miss Halsey was presented with a travelling clock and a handbag by Club members and she left Gibraltar on 12 March. Squelch became Vice-President of the Club in her place. Soon Brown handed over the canteen accounts to Squelch which may have been an indication of his need to do a little less. His decision was accepted with the comment, 'I can only say that I hope Mr Squelch will send us the very clear and helpful statements which we have had from you for so many years'.[28] Miss Strachan, who had wanted to leave Gibraltar, did stay on and fulfilled her one-year contract, though when she left she was not replaced.

Brown did not attend the 1949 Club reunion but Miss Halsey and Emerson did. By this time, it had been decided that it was time to make an official visit to Gibraltar as it was fifteen years since the last one. So, on 26 May 1949, Firth arrived. Club members met him at Epworth House and Firth commented that 'a delightful evening was had by all'.[29] Firth spoke at the Club on 31 May. He later reported that 'Roman Catholicism, the religion of the civilian inhabitants, seems to have gradually absorbed by

---

[26] *The Club Bulletin,* March 1948.
[27] Ibid.
[28] Letter from Hartley to Brown, 25 August 1949.
[29] *The Club Bulletin,* vol. i, June quarter, 1949, no 2.

marriage or otherwise, most of the Gibraltarian families who belonged to us'.[30] One exception was Richard Cavilla, a young man to whom Brown had offered a home for some twelve years. In March 1949 he was married in the Methodist chapel by Brown and he with his wife, Lourdes, and later their daughter, Arabella, remained part of the Methodist community until they finally left Gibraltar over twenty years later. They live today in London. The vast majority though were either in the services or connected with them which brought the continuing problems of an ever-changing congregation. The number of servicemen in Gibraltar was now much lower and average attendance at morning and evening services was between forty and sixty. The Sunday school numbered between thirty and forty children.

The work of the Welcome of course continued but with far less need for the accommodation there. Firth described the building as follows;

> The ground floor provides lounge and writing room as well as restaurant, kitchen, and other offices. The first floor provides games room - with two excellent billiards tables and two table tennis tables - padre's office, chapel and three other rooms. The second floor consists of concert room with stage, club lounge, club quiet room, club workshops etc. On the top floor there is the manager's flat and bedrooms for letting ... All parts of the Home except the club rooms are public.

Firth ended by saying, 'My visit was a grand experience. Methodists vied with each other in making me happy and comfortable. Nothing was too good for me. The only thing I lacked during my visit was sleep'.

During the visit Brown's future was discussed. By then he was 72 years old, well over retirement age, and the strain of the war years was beginning to tell. It was decided therefore that a probationer would be sent out the following year, and Brown would become a supernumerary.

Another result of his visit was an invitation to Firth to attend the fourth Club reunion in March 1950. Brown managed to get away for it and over seventy members were present including some wives. Firth clearly enjoyed himself and later reported, 'The enthusiasm of the weekend revealed that our work is not so fleeting as it often seems', which turned out to be a far more prophetic statement than anyone realised at the time.[31]

Meanwhile, plans went ahead to appoint a Headingley student, Frank W. Wilson, to Gibraltar. It seems that Firth was aware that Brown had some health problems and wanted to ensure that he could stay in Gibraltar until he died, as he did not want to go anywhere else. Wilson sailed on the *Empress of Australia*, a kind of troopship taking service people and ancillary workers to the various Mediterranean stations. He arrived on 13

---

[30] *Methodist Recorder,* 23 June 1949, 'A Healthy Look about Methodism in Gibraltar', Joseph Firth.

[31] *Minutes of the Board, vol .iii, May 1945 - Febraury 1955,* meeting 16, May 1950, minute xii, p.244. Also in *Over to You,* vol. ii, no.4, spring 1950, p.129.

August 1950 and a reception was held at Epworth House to welcome him.

Wilson was born in Hull and educated there. After leaving school he worked in an insurance company and then spent five years in the RAF when he offered for the ministry. In 1946 he went to Lincolnshire for two pre-collegiate years and entered Headingley College in 1948.

Frank Wilson and Padre Brown

Brown made it clear that he expected his assistant to be suitably attired to take worship and Wilson was measured for a cassock which cost the princely sum of £10 - rather a lot for a probationer. As the manse was filled with antiques and *objets d'art*, there was only one bedroom which Brown occupied and Wilson's quarters were in an outside annexe. Wilson found Brown's appearance and manner rather aristocratic. One was unlikely to be on first name terms with him but this did not cause any barriers in his relationships with people from all kinds of backgrounds. He also had some independent means and did not have to rely on his salary alone. Brown seems to have been happy with the help he had been sent. He wrote as follows to Harry Twine who was at that time editor of the Club Magazine;

> At the end of last month I officially retired from the active ministry. A young padre (Rev. Frank Wilson) arrived a fortnight ago and has settled in nicely. He is twenty eight years of age and spent some years in the RAF during the war in India, so he knows the service background quite well. He is a fine fellow, and will, I believe, do good work. The change has not made much difference to me however for although he has taken over things that formerly I had to do, I can still occupy my time. We are hoping that as he gets about he may be able to get some new Club members.[32]

Wilson did take an active part in the life of the Club but by this time much had changed. There were now far more other interests and activities available. There were fewer servicemen and more women, children, civilians and also National Service youngsters. Needs were different too and the Club magazines and minute book indicate that it was not always easy to accommodate all this change; sometimes there was tension in trying to meet the needs of the different groups and ages. Membership fluctuated greatly as people came and went, but overall it declined and at the Annual

---

[32] Letter from Brown to Harry Twine, Editor of the Club Bulletin in England, 9 September 1950.

General Meeting in January 1951 local membership was only twenty-two, though there were still over four hundred on the overall membership roll, including those who had left Gibraltar. There had been difficulties at times in raising numbers for sports teams and in ensuring reasonable support for activities. Brown's counsel and guidance was still much appreciated, but by this time his health had begun to decline.

Towards the end of 1950, he was diagnosed as suffering from jaundice which had affected his heart. After a stay in Ronda, he began to feel better, but he was unable to chair the Club's AGM on 30 January 1951 and, in February, at the time of the Club reunion, he was in hospital. After five weeks there he was allowed home but after only a few days he was confined to bed again and reported the doctor to have diagnosed him as suffering from severe heart strain. He was well looked after by Anna and Teresa and his room was kept bright with flowers, some of which were sent as a gift from the reunion.

However, disaster was about to strike the Rock for on Friday 27 April 1951 the ammunition ship, *Bedenham*, blew up. Ammunition was being unloaded from the ship on to a lighter alongside which caught fire and caused a massive explosion. Pieces of debris showered the area with the largest piece of metal, said to weigh nearly half a ton, landing on the garrison library roof; some pieces were reported to have blown right over the Rock into Catalan Bay. Almost every window in Gibraltar was broken by the blast and even some in La Línea across the border. Many buildings were very badly damaged including the Convent and King's Chapel and both the Anglican and Catholic cathedrals which were virtually put out of use. Wilson later wrote of his experiences that day.

> The day was gloriously sunny and I left the Manse for the 'Welcome' at the usual hour. At that time Mr Brown was far from well, and was in bed. The Canteen was open when I arrived, and our regulars were being served with tea and coffee. Shortly before ten Mrs Squelch shouted from the flat 'Come up, Padre, there's a fire'. In a matter of moments the 'Welcome' was rocked by an explosion greater than any I had experienced during the War. Window frames blew in, doors blew out, plaster dropped from walls and ceilings and familiar fixtures and fittings could be seen hanging awry through the rising cloud of dust. After a brief silence the wailing of some of the staff was heard and I stumbled downstairs to find Captain Squelch regaling the more hysterical ones with cognac.
>
> (I may say, in digression that within an hour beverages were being served in a canteen which resembled a blitzed cafe, and it is to the credit of the Manager and his helpers that the work of the 'Welcome' was never halted despite the severity of the damage.)
>
> … It was difficult for me to decide where my duty lay. I decided to go first to the Manse and when I arrived I realised that the house had received the full impact of the blast. Windows were out, plaster fragments littered the carpet and many of the Manse treasures were

dislodged. Amidst the wreckage stood Padre Brown, with a cut on his forehead, in his dressing gown, surveying the scene with characteristic calmness. Anna was feverishly sweeping up the debris and Teresa rendered what assistance she could. Mr Brown told me that the church had suffered similarly and that the memorial windows were destroyed.[33]

Soon Wilson received a telephone call to say that one of their members a Mr James Keen was in hospital and so he immediately went to see how he was. Jim Keen, the Naval Armament Supply Officer, was near the ship when the explosion occurred and was blown into the sea. He was lucky to be alive. Altogether thirteen people were killed, most of whom had been on the ship or the lighter. On the following Monday the *Gibraltar Chronicle* reported forty people to be still in hospital including two children and six women.

Although Brown seems to have been calm at the time there is no doubt that the damage to the buildings and to his treasures and, most of all, the loss of the stained glass windows upset him greatly. As soon as Firth heard the news, he dropped everything to visit Gibraltar, to offer his support and make plans for the future. He later reported that for nearly a fortnight Keen lay between life and death in hospital, a very worrying time for his wife who was the church organist. However, he did recover and was awarded the George Medal.

Firth inspected the damage. The roof of the church had just been repaired but was now damaged again and leaking. All the Methodist properties needed repair, the Welcome most of all, 'But scarred though it is, it is open and has been kept open all the time. A souvenir is a piece of ship's plate which crashed through the door'.[34] Firth provided some money in the hope that there would be little delay in getting the necessary work done. He thought that at least £1,000 would be needed to put everything in order. During his visit he discussed Brown's position with him too and it was decided that a successor would be appointed at the Conference of 1952. In the meantime Wilson agreed to carry on and was by then doing most of the work.

Firth preached at the church on Sunday 12 May, despite the lack of windows and the damaged roof. The following day Brown wrote again to Twine saying that he was feeling better and hoped, if the doctor agreed, to go to Ronda. He needed to get away from the damaged manse which was not suitable for someone in poor health. He had been given some priority and had already been able to get 'the scores of window panes and broken frames repaired', but 'doors and their frames have been moved and interior walls buckled and cracked'.[35] Work could hardly be done quickly when so many buildings in Gibraltar were similarly affected; indeed many were

---

[33] *The Club Bulletin,* March 1950, vol. viii, no.1.

[34] Firth, 'Gibraltar', *Over to You*, vol. iv, no.2, autumn 1951, pp.31-2.

[35] Letter from Brown to Twine, 13 May 1951.

much worse.

In England the Board appointed a Committee 'to consider our future work on the Rock'.[36] It met on 7 June 1951 and decided to approach the Church of Scotland to explore the possibility of joint work, but it was not interested in the proposal so Methodism decided to carry on alone. However, local co-operation between the two churches was still much valued.

Then Captain Squelch asked to return to England because of his wife's health. He had taken an active part in the life of the church and Welcome, often giving talks to the Club and involving himself in its activities. His departure meant that Wilson, a probationer, was left with a sick colleague and no manager. Two mainstays in his life were Reg and Dorothy Nodder and George Pillidge and his wife. Both men worked in the dockyard and Pillidge was also a local preacher. Wilson wrote, 'These families thought I was undernourished by the fare provided in the manse by Anna and Teresa and were determined to supplement my rations with their more substantial luncheons' and he obviously appreciated their help and support.[37]

The picture features from the top left Clarice Carlyle, Dorothy Nodder, Harry Cadogan and Reg Nodder. Then Frank Wilson and Richard Cavilla with Constance Brown and Joy Cadogan seated.

It was in fact Miss Halsey who now returned to take over as manageress of the canteen and she soon considerably improved the situation at the Welcome. Towards the end of October Brown, who was visiting Ronda, sent his Christmas message to the Club. He planned to return to Gibraltar the following day and reported that the damage had all been repaired and the Welcome redecorated throughout so that it now looked bright and cheerful. At the time of writing the fleet was in and the Welcome extra busy.

In the end the Admiralty paid £2,823 10s 11d in compensation for the damage to the Methodist property which the Board felt was most generous.

---

[36] *Minutes of the Board, vol .iii, May 1945 - February 1955,* meeting 23 May 1951, minute v, pp.293-4.

[37] Letter from Wilson to the author, 10 January 1994.

All the repairs were done but the stained glass windows were not replaced.

Brown returned to Gibraltar but his health worsened. By early December it was clear that he was dying so Firth flew out to Gibraltar to be with him. He died on 9 December 1951 aged 74, and was buried the same day. His family was represented by his two nieces, Constance Brown and Clarice Carlyle. The Governor, Lieutenant-General Sir Kenneth Anderson, and Lady Anderson were present and the church was filled with members and friends. The other Protestant clergy all came as well as the Vicar-General of the Roman Catholic Church and the Jewish rabbi. Wilson and Firth conducted the service with Firth paying tribute to Brown's long ministry in Gibraltar.

Many tributes and obituaries appeared. The Conference obituary stated,

> It is difficult to reveal his personality in words. Scholarly, cultured in the widest sense, a connoisseur of the fine arts, a preacher of outstanding ability, austere in habits and sometimes in manner, yet with a warm heart and a capacity for great friendship. He was an intimate friend of a succession of Governors and yet was no less a beloved friend of the humblest soldier. He loved Gibraltar and Gibraltar loved him. To walk through the town with him was a tremendous experience, for almost every inhabitant knew him. His work has been rich and fruitful.[38]

His popularity in Gibraltar is best summed up by the heading of the announcement of his death in the *Gibraltar Chronicle* which simply stated, 'Gibraltar mourns the passing of a real friend'.[39] He had always taken an interest in the history of the Rock and was Chairman of the Museum Committee. In addition, he was Honorary Treasurer of the St John's Ambulance Association, Honorary Secretary and Treasurer of the Protestant Poor Fund and District Chaplain General of the English Constitution of Freemasons in Gibraltar.

At the AGM of the Club held in Gibraltar in January 1952 the secretary, James P. Jones, wrote the following tribute to Brown:

> He served the Club faithfully and indeed was more than a President to us, he was a friend, a guide, who with his profound knowledge of human affairs, was ever ready to do all he could to help serve the community. By his death the Club has suffered a great loss, and we shall always remember our Padre as one who bore the mark of greatness.[40]

The news travelled to England to the Club members there who shared their tributes to Brown in the pages of the magazine, particularly remembering his preaching and conduct of worship; his willingness to help and advise; his hospitality at the manse which was often full of servicemen

---

[38] *Minutes of the Methodist Conference,* 1952, p.132.
[39] *Gibraltar Chronicle,* Monday 10 December 1951.
[40] Club Minute Book.

particularly during the war years; his ability to get on with people from all walks of life; and the fact that his faith was seen in his actions thus sharing the love and presence of God with those whom he met. At the reunion in March 1952, a memorial service was held on the Sunday morning conducted by Emerson. There was talk of memorials but the overall feeling was that the best tribute was to keep the Club going and so maintain 'that great spirit of Christian fellowship which we knew on the Rock'.[41]

The Club did carry on far longer than anyone, including Brown, could have foreseen. It continued to hold its annual reunions and contact was maintained through magazines, letters and telephone calls. Wives, children, grand-children and even great-children are now involved and share in the fellowship. In 2002 the Club celebrated its sixtieth anniversary, meeting as ever at Willersley Castle. Altogether eighty-one people attended part or all of the weekend, including nine of the original members. The warm fellowship remains as strong as ever but, as Brown himself once said, it cannot be explained or described, only experienced. It is indeed a tribute to a padre who cared for all.

Altogether Brown had spent thirty-four years in Gibraltar and it was to be no easy task to succeed him as Methodist minister on the Rock.

---

[41] *The Club Bulletin,* June 1952, vol. viii, no.9.

CHAPTER 22   A SUCCESSOR TO BROWN
The work unites on one site (1952-61)

The Board already had a successor in mind; John Frederick Jackson who was born on 13 March 1913 in Hull. After attending Hull Grammar School he started working for a wholesale provision merchant where he experienced a sudden and most unexpected call to the ministry. After four terms at Cliff College, he candidated for the ministry and entered Headingley College in 1935. In April 1939 he was sent to Nottingham, to cover a short-term vacancy, and there he met Irene Emma Antoinette Bancroft (Rene). In September he moved to the Pickering circuit where he joined the Home Guard and later volunteered to serve as a chaplain with the Forces. After he was accepted, a special ordination service was held in Pickering on 16 January 1942, and he began basic training almost immediately afterwards. His ordination meant that, under Methodist rules, he was now free to marry and he and Rene were married on 3 June 1942 in Nottingham. By then, Rene was serving in the ATS and so they only had a short honeymoon and embarkation leave together in the October before Jackson sailed for North Africa to take part in the landings there.

After nearly two years in North Africa and Italy, Jackson returned to England on a hospital ship. Following a short stay in hospital, he was posted to Lincoln but was unable to set up home with Rene until August 1945 because of their separate postings. Jackson was refused a permanent commission as an army chaplain because he was graded 'B' medically and so he accepted an appointment in the Nottingham East circuit.

In 1951 Jackson met Firth at the Methodist Conference and jokingly said that he was missing the sun and wondered if there was a vacancy in Malta. Firth suggested Gibraltar instead and, as he was interested, further discussion took place immediately. Jackson went home to tell Rene, who thought he was joking! However, they both went down to London to discuss things further and plans went ahead to move following the Conference of 1952. Brown's death altered these plans and, because Wilson needed to return to England for ordination, it was decided that an earlier appointment was necessary. Arrangements were therefore made to take over Jackson's responsibilities in Nottingham, including his role as Synod Secretary, and the packing began. By then there were four children to consider too, Richard, Susan, Dorothy and Carolyn who were all under five years of age; the youngest were twins just a few months old.

The family set sail from Tilbury on the S.S. *Orcades* on 20 March 1952 arriving in Gibraltar on Sunday 23 March. Fog delayed disembarkation but finally they left the ship and were met by Reg Nodder and escorted to the manse. The weather was exceptionally warm for the time of year and everything felt strange. Brown's maids had left, but another Spanish maid, Ana, was already installed at the manse. She lived in but spoke no English.

Food for the day had been provided along with the bill! The manse had been the home of a bachelor for many years and it was not well equipped for young children. The babies slept the first night in drawers. The manse was well furnished and decorated and most of Brown's antiques had been removed, but nevertheless some of his personal effects were still there and many of the cupboards and drawers were full.

The Jackson family taken just before leaving for Gibraltar

It was no easy task following Brown who had been in Gibraltar for so long and had earned everyone's respect. He had been in charge of the Protestant Poor Fund doling out money on a regular basis. Wilson carried this out when Brown was ill. Once a week, a queue formed at the Welcome for the weekly handout. As Wilson later reported, 'How many were genuinely Protestant was a matter of doubt. None of them ever attended services of worship to my knowledge'.[1] One of them even lived in Ronda. By the time Jackson arrived, the administration of the Poor Fund had moved into other hands but, nonetheless, local people still expected him to have money available. It was also assumed that he would be a Mason and it was made clear in some quarters that life would be easier for him were he to join which he never did. All in all, there were moments when both of them wondered if they had made a mistake in coming. However, the view from the manse across the bay was a great compensation and the frequent changes to the congregation on the Rock meant that Brown's ministry, like that of others before him, was soon forgotten.

Gradually the family settled into the manse which was situated up a steep hill. Without a car or a double pram, it was hard for Rene to go far though

---

[1] Letter from Wilson to the author, 10 January 1994.

she soon discovered the shops and the market, but they were both dismayed by the high cost of everything. It was some weeks before anyone thought to offer Rene a tour of the Rock and she long remembered the joy she felt at stepping on to the beach that first time. In the autumn, a family friend visited bringing a double pushchair which made a big difference despite the steep hill. Rene soon decided to learn Spanish and enrolled at an evening class so that she could begin to talk to Ana and later, as her fluency increased, to the other Spanish staff at the Welcome. In these early days, she and John saw little of each other as all the weekly activities took place at the Welcome. A welcome meeting was held for them at the end of their first week, when they were able to meet the church folk and the other clergy. The church was at rather a low ebb. Congregations were small and the Sunday school virtually non-existent. Rene soon revived that, holding it in the manse as there were no rooms at the church.

Wilson was a tower of strength in these early days, introducing Jackson to the work and to the relevant people. He met the Governor, Lieutenant-General Sir Gordon H.A. McMillan, as was customary and found him to be friendly and supportive as were his successors. Soon it was time for Wilson to leave Gibraltar and he travelled to England overland through Spain and France, accompanied by his cousin. He was ordained at Conference that year and was then stationed at Blyth in Northumberland. He had done a great deal in Gibraltar to keep the work going. Firth paid tribute to him as follows:

> Two years ago I invited a young Probationer to become assistant to Padre Brown. Unfortunately, his arrival coincided with a deterioration in the health of Padre Brown and the full burden fell upon the Rev. Frank W. Wilson. The illness itself complicated matters. The Soldiers' Home fell on difficult days. The *Bedenham* explosion with all its disastrous results to our property and its form-filling and general anxieties. Above all the maintenance of the pulpit and probationary studies. But he has survived it all with tremendous credit. We are proud of Frank Wilson and all he has done.[2]

Wilson stayed in the north of England serving in several appointments before retiring in 1987 to Ampleforth where he still lives today.

Back in Gibraltar life was quite hectic for Jackson, overseeing the work of the Welcome, preaching, visiting and getting to know the people. Gradually congregations did build up and occasional exchanges with the Church of Scotland minister, Ronald Torrie, relieved the burden of preaching twice every Sunday to the same congregation. Occasionally visiting naval chaplains took a service too, but there were few local preachers throughout his time on the Rock.

In June the church was closed for redecoration, when morning services

---

[2] *Over to You,* vol.iv, no. 3 winter 1951-2, pp.28-9.

were held at the Welcome and the evening ones at St Andrew's. The Nodders gave new light fittings to the church and took the Jacksons up to Málaga to buy them which gave them an opportunity to see a little of Spain.

Jackson became President of the Club and a welcome was extended to him in the pages of the Club Bulletin. This was printed in England but it also included news of the Club's doings in Gibraltar. In October Jackson reported on the service of re-dedication held in the church on 21 September 1952 after its refurbishment. A communion table and chairs as well as a pulpit chair had been purchased and specially dedicated in memory of Brown. But the problems with the Club continued as John Tall, the Secretary in Gibraltar, explained,

> All we need now is a sufficient number to support us and that is a problem which will have to be faced when the summer has cooled sufficiently for us to think clearly. For some reason the servicemen are 'backward in coming forward' at the moment, but you may be sure we shall do everything possible in the winter months to effect a greater attendance.[3]

Eventually it was decided to reorganise the Club into a Methodist Guild. A new thing was needed for post-war Gibraltar. Tall explained this in the next magazine.

> A Guild, you may remember, is divided into four committees, each responsible for a meeting once every four weeks. These take the form of a Devotional evening, Christian service, Literary and Social evenings. The increase in attendance has been most marked and has certainly justified our efforts to create a wider interest for servicemen and civilians on the Rock.[4]

Jackson sent his greetings to the Club Reunion for 1953 saying that he hoped at a future date to be able to attend one himself but that was never possible because of the limited leave he was allowed - a visit to England every two years in the school summer holidays which did not coincide with reunion dates. He also explained the re-organisation of the Club 'with the result, I am thankful to say, of more than doubling the attendance. So there should be a continuation of the stream from the Welcome to the Club at Home which is what we all desire'.[5] However, this did not happen perhaps because there was no link person who knew both past and present members. New members were unlikely to attend a reunion with people they had never met and gradually less news was sent from Gibraltar. The Club in England continued as already described and the Guild in Gibraltar

---

[3] *The Club Bulletin*, vol. viii, no. 10, October 1952.
[4] Ibid., vol. viii, no. 11, February 1953.
[5] Ibid.

continued to flourish too.

Many of those frequenting the Welcome were young people doing National Service who also formed a large part of the congregation. There were also civilians from the dockyard, Forces personnel and a very small number of local people, including the Cavilla family. Later on women from the ATS and the WAAF arrived too. The Welcome provided a useful meeting place with its canteen and other facilities. It was now open to all, as it had been since the war, but local people saw it primarily for the Forces and rarely ventured in. Outings and visits around the Rock and into Spain were organised and older church members and families, including the Jacksons, often offered hospitality to the younger ones. Jackson organised some bus trips into Spain, taking groups away for a few days. He had a guide for the first one but managed the rest himself, visiting many of the major cities in southern Spain.

The photo is of a later trip and was taken in Ronda in 1959
(Jackson is on the far left)

He was also kept busy with hospital visits, and regular Padre's Hours, which were discussion groups with the various units on the Rock, as well as preaching on Sundays and speaking at or leading meetings at the Welcome. It often meant Rene was left alone at the manse for long periods of time.

Soon there was another development in the work. At some stage the religious education of Methodist children had ceased. It may be that it never resumed after the war-time evacuation or it may have stopped even earlier but, by this time, all the Protestant children were taught by the

Anglicans. Torrie and Jackson together sought permission from the Governor to teach their own church children which was granted. The result was that the girls from the Loreto Convent came down to the Welcome every morning, except Thursday, for a fifty-minute lesson, following a specified course of study. Torrie took the boys from the Christian Brothers' school, the split being decided solely on the grounds of geographical location. As far as the junior school, St Christopher's, was concerned, they shared the work, with weekly lessons being given either at St Andrew's or at the Welcome. Rene played a part in this too going occasionally to the infant school, St George's. As a result of this, both chaplains eventually sat on the education committee, but only after a further appeal to the Governor.

Ecumenical relationships were good but the closest one was between Torrie and Jackson. From a Methodist point of view, it was still an isolated post with no Methodist colleague anywhere near. However, not long after their arrival, an unexpected visitor called at the manse. This was Roy Dalton who was working for the American Assemblies of God Church in Ronda. Protestant work, started there before the Spanish civil war, had been abandoned during it. However, for fifteen years a small group had met together behind closed doors and in 1950 a couple had gone to Ronda to work with them. Illness had forced them to leave and in September 1951 Dalton, who had previously been a missionary in Cuba, replaced them. He lived in the middle of Ronda and converted one room of his house into a chapel. It was hard and lonely work for,

Roy Dalton

since the civil war, being a Protestant in Spain was almost as difficult as it had ever been. Protestant services could not be advertised, no notice boards were allowed and buildings could not have the outward appearance of a church although they could be appropriately furnished within. Proselytism was forbidden. Ownership of Bibles was still frowned upon and parcels sent to Dalton through the post often went missing or were tampered with. Individual Protestants were much persecuted and it was particularly difficult to find employment. Poverty in Spain was still considerable, particularly so amongst the Protestants, many of whom found that the only way to earn a living was to be self-employed. The vicar had issued a handbill in December 1950 speaking out against the Protestant false prophets and accusing them of being agents of 'Judaism, Freemasonry and International Communism'. He went on to state, 'I also call the attention of the dwellers of certain houses, whose names I am keeping for future reference, but which I am not publishing today, but if needs be I will publish publicly, to the danger they incur by attending secret meetings in which they threaten and defy the official religion of the state'.[6] In 1955 the Bible Society estimated that there were about 26,000 Protestants in the whole of Spain amongst a population of around twenty-nine million.

So Dalton visited the Methodist manse looking for fellowship. There he found it for a close friendship was formed with Jackson which embraced the whole family and was to their mutual benefit in providing fellowship and support. By this time, Jackson had bought a car and so could now take supplies to Ronda directly, even on occasion smuggling in Bibles. Once or twice they did this for the Bible Society too, stacking them on the back seat of the car, covering them, seating the four children on top and taking them to an address in La Línea.

At the beginning of 1953, Miss Halsey left Gibraltar to take up a post in Malta. A local person, Mrs Jones, who had some relevant experience, took over temporarily until the Board appointed Miss Hilda Southey who had done similar work in Germany. She arrived in September 1953.

Before she left, Miss Halsey told Jackson one day that the army scripture reader wanted to show a friend round the Welcome. Jackson agreed to this but insisted on accompanying them and soon realised that a potential buyer was being shown round! Jackson immediately informed Firth of this development. In October 1952 Firth had written to Colonel Clarke, one of the trustees, about an extension of the lease. He had received a reply asking if the Board would consider a lease of seven years if the trustees felt this was desirable, but also stating that the question of selling might be considered. Firth had replied saying he would prefer a twenty-one-year lease and that any question of purchase would have to go to the Board as the Welcome had lost about £3,000 over the last five years.

Clarke himself now visited Gibraltar and went over the Welcome with Jackson and another two people, who also seemed interested in the building. Jackson wrote, 'I rather gathered this feeling. That they would sell the building in preference to a lease and that they are not very interested in our having it again. I hope I am wrong there'.[7] He also pointed out that the Welcome was a considerable asset and that if Methodism lost it, it would be very difficult to find anything else. In his reply it is clear that Firth was rather annoyed at the way the trustees were behaving and felt they should have discussed the option of buying with them before entering into negotiations with anyone else. He did not want to lose the building and remarked that the financial returns for the last twelve months had been excellent 'and revealed that in spite of certain weaknesses Miss Halsey is a most excellent manageress. You have an idea of what we have lost in previous years and what we can easily lose in the

---

[6] Translation of a handbill in Spanish issued to the people of Ronda, by the Vicar to the Bishop, December 1950. (in author's possession.)

[7] Box 1, Gibraltar Property Files 1953-6, letter from Jackson to Firth, 17 December 1952.

future unless we have someone of Miss Halsey's calibre in charge'.[8]

Firth then received a letter from the trustees saying that they wished to sell the building and had given first refusal to the Sandes Soldiers' Home organisation. On hearing this, Jackson decided to discuss the matter with the Governor. Property in Gibraltar still could not be sold without his permission and he was willing to support the Methodist right to have first refusal as sitting tenants. However, it seems in the end his help was not needed as the Sandes organisation turned down the offer. Methodism then offered £16,000 for the property without the annexe at the back which could easily be separated from the rest. Jackson felt a little aggrieved at the way decisions were being made in London without much consultation with him, pointing out that he would be the one to bear the consequences of any decisions. The Welcome needed to be self-sufficient if possible and losing the annexe would mean losing revenue. His offer to fly home had been rejected. The trustees turned down the offer of £16,000 but an increased offer of £18,000 was accepted. It was agreed that the purchase would not be completed until 25 March 1954 when the lease ran out. When Firth informed Jackson of this decision he also suggested a consultation as he was wondering about structural alterations to the top floor of the Welcome to maintain their standards of letting. Jackson was only too happy to agree because by then, he had his own ideas about the property. He wrote,

> When the Welcome becomes ours it seems to me that we shall have far too much property in Gibraltar. It will be a real burden to maintain, a burden we shall never be able to meet at this end. The Welcome premises need painting outside, it will have to be done the minute they are bought, and in any case the Queen is visiting Gibraltar and staying three or four days, so we must look reasonable for that. I doubt if the premises have been painted for the last eight or nine years.
>
> In a nutshell my suggestions are these:
>
> That all our work be centred in the Welcome, that the second floor be made into the Church. This would give us the most central position in Gibraltar. All the buses stop outside our door, there are two car parks within 20 yards.
>
> That all our Prince Edward's Road property be sold ... That of course would leave me without a home, but either we could have a flat in the Welcome, or build a manse. But in any case something will have to be done, there are six of us and two and a half bedrooms, and I have a number of friends etc. visiting.
>
> Now obviously the above is something I could never discuss in a public meeting. But I have talked privately with Nodder and one or two others, in confidence of course, and I find they all agree. There is with us a feeling of sentiment to the old church. I love the place dearly and I don't want to leave Epworth House, but nevertheless I feel, for the sake of

---

[8] Ibid., letter from Firth to Jackson, 23 December 1952.

the future we ought to make these moves.[9]

Jackson wished Colin Roberts, head of the Home Missions Department, could come out with Firth to consult with him but, as it was his presidential year, this was not possible. However, Firth quickly saw the possibilities of this suggestion and sent Jackson's letter to Roberts. Both of them thought the idea was well worth considering. The Welcome was nowhere near as busy as it had been in former years even when the Fleets were in. The need for accommodation for the navy had gone and the rooms were nearly all let to long-standing occupants. The loss of the rooms would mean a loss of revenue but this would be more than off-set by the savings gained by not having to pay for, and maintain, all the property on Prince Edward's Road and the Welcome was big enough to accommodate all the church activities including the church itself.

Meanwhile Jackson was busy with the coronation celebrations in Gibraltar. These included a united service with a congregation of about 3,000 in which all the ministers took part. He had also held a general church meeting which about forty people attended. He reported, 'We appointed a new committee which includes three ladies now. I managed to get the Church on more Methodist lines, we have a poor steward now, and the meeting confirmed the appointment of a chapel steward'.[10] Things were going well at the Welcome and Mrs Jones was described as 'doing excellently'. On 16 June 1953, a farewell party was held for Reg and Dorothy Nodder who were leaving after six years in Gibraltar. They were presented with an oil painting of the Rock. Later Nodder joined the Board in England.

In early summer a Mr W.H. Gunton, who was the principal of a large firm of architects in London, was on holiday in the Mediterranean. His ship was due to call at Gibraltar and he agreed to visit the Welcome and give his opinion on the plan to unite the work on one site. The visit took place in July 1953 and Gunton saw no problems with the scheme reporting back favourably to the Board. The Board then appointed a committee to consider the matter. It met on 19 October 1953. It considered the history of the work in Gibraltar, its present situation and likely future developments. Two things were clear;

> That the present Church was from a geographical point of view most unsuitable to meet the present need. It is difficult of access and not easy to find even when the seeker is directed to it … That the Home, being in the centre of the Garrison and opposite Government House and the Headquarters, has none of these shortcomings. Not only is it easy to find but is difficult to miss. Moreover it is large enough to enable a Church to be recreated within it, and the Architect's advice is that a Church could be

---

[9] Ibid., letter from Jackson to Firth, 19 May 1953.
[10] Ibid., 8 June 1953.

made worthy, both in size and dignity of our Church.[11]

A problem remained though, for the scheme depended on money from the sale of the property on Prince Edward's Road and, as it was leasehold, it was not clear if Methodism had the right to sell it. Jackson went again to see the Governor and reported on a cordial meeting with him, saying that he would help them all he could, although a definite decision was not possible at this first meeting. Jackson also met a local surveyor and went round the building with him. He too could see no problems with the scheme.

In January 1954 Colin Roberts did visit Gibraltar and was able to see all the properties for himself and discuss the situation with Jackson, the Governor and the Church Committee. The latter, whilst 'not actively opposing the idea was not exactly enthusiastic about it'.[12] Change is never easy. The Governor was very helpful and it was agreed that the property could be sold on the understanding that 5% of the sale price would go to the government and the Governor's consent would be required as to the purchaser. This meant the property really became freehold and it was a very generous concession. The Board was delighted. So was Jackson who wrote to Roberts afterwards to say how thrilled he was with the way things had gone. He went on to say, 'My most urgent requirement is the architect as I really can't get much further without him. I don't mind who, so long as he will do the job well'.[13] It seems too that Roberts' visit had had other effects. He must have been there for a Sunday service and the new people who came that day had not missed attending since then. Jackson wrote, 'Much good was done in that evening service which wasn't manifest openly'.

A problem then arose with Miss Southey, the new manageress, who had not been happy since her arrival on the Rock. Everyone had hoped she would settle but she failed to do so and eventually a dispute with one of the waiters brought matters to a head. In the end Jackson felt it would be best if she left, a conclusion she had herself reached. So Mrs Jones returned to the work in her place.

Jackson could not find a suitable architect in Gibraltar so Gunton's firm in London was appointed. Jackson gave notice to the residents at the Welcome who were living in the annexe, as he expected the sale to go through at the end of March as planned. It did not. It had been decided that local solicitors should be employed to do the conveyancing which took time to arrange. It was agreed that the terms of the lease would continue in the meantime, although of course this meant a loss of revenue from the

---

[11] *Minutes of the Board, Vol.III May 1945-February 1955,* minutes of committee to consider the possible concentration of our work in Gibraltar held on 19 October 1953, pp.440-2.

[12] Box 1, Gibraltar Property Files 1953-6, letter from Jackson to Firth, 8 February 1954.

[13] Ibid., letter from Jackson to Roberts, 25 January 1954.

rooms given up. Various legal difficulties arose and the solicitors seemed to be taking their time over everything and, although there was an acknowledgement that the delay was not on the Methodist side, that did not compensate them for the loss of income.

Other events were taking place in Gibraltar itself which were also to affect matters. The Queen was due to visit the Rock as part of her coronation tour in May. In January, news of her planned visit caused anti-British riots in Spain and Britain was asked to cancel it. Even so, the newly-appointed Spanish military Governor of the Campo de Gibraltar paid an official visit to Gibraltar at this time as was customary. He was given a seventeen-gun salute. There were no problems but more demonstrations were reported in Spain and an estimated 30,000 students marched through Madrid calling for the return of Gibraltar. The British ambassador protested about damage done to British property in Madrid, Barcelona, Huelva and Málaga. Feelings were obviously running high.

The visit did take place and on 10 May, Jackson was presented to the Queen along with the other clergy on the Rock, though for some reason he was the one she chose to speak to briefly. The whole of Gibraltar was decorated with bunting, including the Welcome. The Spanish closed the border but did allow their domestic workers to stay overnight in Gibraltar whilst the gates were closed. However, the British refused entry to some four hundred Spanish workers describing them as a security risk.

The repercussions did not die down. The Spanish Consul was withdrawn from Gibraltar. Only Spaniards with work permits were allowed to visit the Rock and British passport holders were only allowed one visit a day through La Línea. The *Gibraltar Chronicle* published an open letter to the government in Spain, referring to the fact that,

> ... because of the visit of H.M. the Queen the Spanish frontier authorities and the radio and press of our neighbouring country has unleashed a 'cold' war - a cold war which has for its aim the re-establishment of Spanish sovereignty over Gibraltar ... The Spanish authorities seem to think that a blockade of Gibraltar, accompanied by a policy of annoyance and unneighbourliness will benefit them - a policy directed against us who have always visited their great country in cordial and friendly circumstances.

It went on to say, 'Actions which may diminish the commerce of Gibraltar will in no way affect the British sovereignty over it.'[14]

Whilst all this was going on, it was time for the Jackson family to return to England on leave. A student from Headingley College, Arthur Mottashed, was sent out as supply. The day set for departure was 1 July 1954. Rene and the children were flying to England. John was going with Roy Dalton and two others by car. They were both taken aback on arriving

---

[14] *Gibraltar Chronicle*, 26 June 1954.

at the airport to find a crowd waiting to see them off! Very few people flew to England at this time and no-one wanted to miss the occasion. The plane left at 11.40 a.m. for Madrid where a meal was served and passengers transferred to another plane which arrived at Heathrow at 6.30 p.m. There were no problems at customs where the official, in a somewhat surprised tone, asked Rene, 'Are they all yours?' and when she replied 'Yes', waved her through! Although the roads in Spain were quite appalling at this time, Jackson arrived safely and had so enjoyed the trip that he decided the whole family should return by car. They eventually set off from Nottingham in a Triumph Mayflower crammed with luggage, with their oldest child, Richard, sitting on a biscuit tin. It all sounds highly dangerous these days but in fact the journey was enjoyed by all. It took eight days, averaging 195 miles a day. From then on, the family always went on leave by car taking at least a week on the journeys and using the opportunity to visit places of interest along the way. The journeys became a highlight for them all.

Whilst in England, Jackson was able to meet Firth and talk over the work. It was clear that the political situation in Gibraltar was going to delay the sale of the Prince Edward's Road property. It was agreed therefore that the £8,000 in the Gibraltar account, from the sale of the old Welcome, would be used to purchase the new one and the remainder would be loaned from the Property and Development Fund.

Jackson's return to Gibraltar was somewhat marred as he explained in a letter to Firth,

> Well I arrived back to a somewhat stormy welcome. The house had been broken into three times. We lost some money and some of our things were damaged. I had let some of our people use the house whilst we were away and they lost money too. I have had to have two new doors fitted and new locks to make the place secure again. The local police are on the job and have taken up a whole lot of my time but as yet we are no nearer finding who did it.
>
> Mottashed [who had stayed at the Welcome] has had a very good time here and has done well in the Church - the people have liked him very much indeed, and he certainly held things together remarkably well.
>
> Unfortunately for me personally he was not too good with the accounts and I have had a real job sorting things out. I managed to complete the Welcome accounts this morning and I will send them off to London in a day or so - and now I have the Church accounts to sort out.[15]

He found the political situation in Gibraltar unchanged and was very concerned about the Welcome. 'After another summer the outside appearance is dreadful - we are losing custom now because the place looks so bad. It can't have had any paint for years and years - much of the

---

[15] Box 1, Gibraltar Property Files 1953-6, letter from Jackson to Firth, 22 September 1954.

woodwork has rotted'.[16] But nothing could be done until the property had been bought. However there was good news too for he reported,

> The Church at the moment is really healthy we are getting 50 and more to both services - with more children coming too. There were 40 at the guild last night and we are hoping to start a cub pack for boys next week. Then something for girls will follow - we never had so many children as we have at the moment.[17]

The purchase of the Welcome was at last nearing completion. The trustees, whose signatures were needed, were the Methodist minister in Gibraltar, the Secretary of the Board, the Secretary of the Home Missions Committee and the Senior Secretary of the Foreign Missionary Committee who was actually in India at the time! Somehow the document was safely sent out to him and returned and the purchase finally went through on 17 November 1954. Work could not go ahead at the Welcome though until the other property was sold.

By May 1955, a prospective buyer was in the offing and so plans were drawn up for the alterations to the Welcome. Jackson wanted the part to be used for the church to take up two floors which would give it much needed height in the hot weather. The Board did not agree. The Governor, now Lieutenant-General Sir Harold Redman, very kindly arranged a flight with the RAF and so Jackson flew to London to argue his case. Firth reported to the Board that 'the suggestions for the reconstruction of the present premises proposed by Mr Jackson did not seem possible at present, as they would weaken the structure of the building'.[18] Jackson however persisted in his arguments and eventually it was agreed that Gunton would visit and give his opinion. Jackson had, of course, already discussed his ideas with qualified people in Gibraltar and on his visit Gunton agreed that the plan was entirely feasible.

The property on Prince Edward's Road eventually went to three separate purchasers. The Masons bought the church and two private buyers bought Epworth House and the old Mission House. The price paid, along with the money from the old Welcome, was more than sufficient to cover the cost of the Welcome but not enough to cover the cost of the alterations. The shortfall was paid by the Property and Development Fund.

So, at long last the work began. Mrs Jones' husband was appointed the local clerk of works and it was hoped that the work would be finished by March 1956 when the Rev. Dr W. Edwin Sangster, who had replaced Roberts as head of the Home Missions Department, would visit Gibraltar to dedicate the new church. Unfortunately the work was not finished by then.

---

[16] Ibid.

[17] Ibid.

[18] *Minutes of the Board, Vol.IX, May 1955-April 1969,* meeting 20 September 1955, minute 10, p.28-9.

Apart from delays, the contractors eventually went bankrupt before the work was completed and it proved difficult to find anyone else willing to finish off the job. However, Sangster's visit went ahead as planned. He was one of the most outstanding Methodist ministers of his day and his visit was a great joy to the whole Jackson family and to the Methodist community. He insisted on staying at the manse and was interested in everything and everybody. His wholehearted support for the work was a great boost and it was a wonderful opportunity to talk things over with him. When he realised the extent of the hospitality provided at the manse, knowing how expensive this could be, he made sure that a hospitality grant was given in future to help with the cost.

He took both the morning and evening services on 25 March and spoke at the Guild. Although he could not dedicate the church formally, on visiting it in its unfinished state, he conducted a short act of devotion there, which was so inspiring that those present always regarded it as the real dedication of the church. Jackson also took him into Spain for a brief visit to see the Alhambra, lending him a jacket as he had only brought his frock coat with him. On his return to England, he wrote most favourably of the work. There were those who were critical of the changes and his public support was good to have. He wrote,

Jackson and Sangster in Granada

> We are leaving our old Church and Manse, and bringing all our work under one roof in Main Street ... Many service men knew where we provided tea but not where we provided worship. Now a radical alteration of our Central building unites on the same spot of earth all our many activities in this famous fort. The ground floor is still the canteen. The first floor is the Church and Sunday School. The next floor has a fine Recreational and Guild Room, etc. The top of the building is the minister's flat.
>
> The Rev. John Jackson is to be congratulated on the vision and drive which has brought this transformation to pass. Sad as many feel to leave the old Church, no one seriously doubts that the new arrangements will make for more effective work and I invite all who love our Lord to remember in prayer our Methodist witness at the Gate of the Mediterranean.
>
> ..... Nor is it the Chaplain only. It often happens - as at Gibraltar - that his devoted wife doubles the value of his work by her comradeship and hospitality - and even the children play their part in illustrating to lonely lads far from England, the loveliness of a Christian home.[19]

---

[19] *Joyful News,* Thursday 10 May 1956.

The building also contained a small flat for the manageress and the only disadvantage was the lack of a lift which was too expensive to install. This meant that there were seventy steps up to the manse.

Firth too wrote about the changes in a similar vein, pointing out that the church had become even more isolated once compulsory parade services ended and the men were no longer shown the way by being marched there.

The woodwork for the new church was all made and carved in Ronda with the help of Dalton. By this time his church had grown. Despite their poverty, the members of the congregation tithed their income and the money was set aside for a proper church. In 1955 a farm on the edge of the town was offered to Dalton. The barn and the house were badly run down but even so, the money saved was not sufficient. However, after much prayer, he decided to go ahead and a deposit was accepted on the property. Repair work began with Dalton and others doing as much as they could themselves to keep the costs down. Somehow, a year and a half later, the debt was paid and a proper church provided. The friendship with Jackson had continued and he took some catalogues up to Ronda. Dalton introduced him to wood workers who copied what he wanted, including the surround for the fire-place in the manse. It was all brought down to Gibraltar and installed. Esparto grass mats were also made to measure in Ronda for the aisle. The large lights were bought in Málaga and the organ and pews were brought down from the old church. By this time a choir had been formed and a series of organists had accompanied it. The organ builder had to come from London to install it but his visit was made in co-operation with other churches in Gibraltar so that he also tuned their organs whilst he was on the Rock.

New Church at Wesley House

One further addition was a stained glass window to replace the memorial windows lost in the *Bedenham* explosion. Unfortunately the first one was damaged before it ever got to Gibraltar but, after repair, it arrived safely and was finally installed at the end of 1957.

The last services in the old church were held on 10 June 1956. Soon afterwards the Jackson family moved down to the Welcome now renamed Wesley House. They were due to go on leave and the Rev. and Mrs Middleton Brumwell were appointed to cover the work in their absence. The Jacksons left on 26 June arriving back in Gibraltar on 29 August. By this time, Firth had retired from the post of Secretary to the Board and so it was his successor, the Rev. F. Wilfred Hilborne, who came out to dedicate the church on 14 October 1956. The Governor and Lady Redman were present along with the mayor and senior representatives of the services. The event was reported fully in both the *Gibraltar Chronicle* and the *Methodist Recorder.*

So, at long last, the work was united on the same site. It was nearly ninety years since Henry Richmond had first put into words the concern about the inaccessibility and unsuitability of the site on Prince Edward's Road. It was sad to leave the old buildings, where so much had happened but the change probably did ensure Methodism's future in Gibraltar for today the old site is even more inaccessible and there is no parking whatsoever. There was an immediate improvement in the size of the congregation and the Sunday school. Rene now had several helpers with the latter and it was good to have the improved facilities at Wesley House.

Sunday School Outing – John and Rene are at the top of the picture
(With permission from Brian Adamson)

The move also meant that Rene was far less isolated and the hospitality work grew even more. She started a women's meeting and later it provided the two small stained glass windows at the front of the church and a new pulpit Bible. By then, Rene's Spanish was fluent which was a help with the Spanish canteen staff at Wesley House. A few women actually lived in and rarely a day went by without one or other coming up to the manse for a chat. They were kind to her in return, helping her to carry her shopping up the seventy steps! There was also one lady in the congregation who spoke no English and Rene was able to find the lesson for her in her Spanish Bible and talk with her. Occasionally she helped with marriages too. On one particular occasion, a young Protestant couple from Madrid turned up in Gibraltar wanting to get married there as it was so difficult for them to do so in Spain. On arrival, they discovered they did not have enough money for the special licence. Then to make matters worse the girl was rushed into hospital with appendicitis. Her fiancé was desperate and needed to get back to Madrid or else he would lose his job. An appeal was made to the church congregation and enough money was raised for them to cover all the costs. Jackson married them in the hospital on Easter Monday with Rene reading the service in Spanish.

Fellowship and friendship was always good in Gibraltar. Perhaps because people were far from home and had no relatives nearby, more effort was made. There was more than one occasion when someone brought their child to Sunday school and met with such a welcome they stayed on for the service themselves. Large parties were often held particularly at times like Christmas, Easter and Harvest so that no-one spent the important seasons alone. In addition to the regular Tuesday evening guild meeting and Thursday fellowship group, there were endless organised activities from concerts and plays to outings and trips round the Rock and into Spain. People came to the canteen both to eat and chat and the hospitality offered at the manse continued. So the church grew and thrived in its new setting.

Picnic in the cork woods   (With permission from Brian Adamson)

Another unexpected result of the move was the offer of fresh milk from the Governor. He had young children too and had a cow and several goats. The Jacksons had had to use dried milk and evaporated milk like everyone else in Gibraltar until then, but now, living opposite the Governor, the two oldest children were able to go across the road with their jugs every morning to collect fresh milk. In 1958 a new Governor was appointed, General Sir Charles F. Keightley, and soon Rene received a letter from his wife to say that the cow and the goats were to be disposed of! She was told, 'It has been increasingly difficult to get fodder and cow cake out from England and hay from Spain. This, together with the fact that the milk obtainable in Gibraltar is now much improved, has led to the decision not to keep them any more'.[20] Delivery stopped on 14 June 1958 but it had been enjoyed while it lasted.

Shortly after the move, a somewhat different 'Welcome' was purchased. The naval cinema gave an annual grant of £100 to the work at the Welcome

On the Welcome

and continued to do so after the change over. After the war, a number of old ships in the harbour were used for storing oil and some of them still had their lifeboats. When these were sold off, Jackson used the £100 to buy one. He sold a number of the fittings which paid for a small cabin to be built. It had a small petrol engine and the following year he used the £100 to replace it with a more efficient diesel engine. Permission had of course to be sought from the Board and it was given. He named the boat *The Welcome* and it was used for church outings, bathing parties, and hymn-singing on summer Sunday evenings after the service. On occasion, when there was trouble at the border, it was possible to give a list of names to the Spanish authorities and to sail across to Getares beach where the boat would be met by a member of the Guardia Civil who checked the names and allowed people to land for an afternoon on the beach. The boat brought a great deal of pleasure to many and a little seasickness to the unlucky few. There were also some mishaps leading to the occasional naval rescue!

In 1956 a bookshop had been opened in the canteen and Miss Addy Dryland came out for a while as assistant manageress. This new venture

---

[20] Letter from Major T.L. Gossage, Assistant Military Secretry to the Governor, on behalf of Lady Keightley to Mrs Jackson, 9 June 1958 (in author's possession).

was successful and in autumn 1957 alterations were made to provide a larger display area for the books. Later a local artist painted a magnificent mural along the wall. Around this time Mrs Jones had to resign as manageress because of her husband's ill health. She was eventually replaced by Mrs Freda Sneezum, who was a local preacher and could therefore relieve Jackson in the pulpit from time to time. Latterly Rene helped out in the canteen one day a week to give Mrs Sneezum a day off. She had previously helped out with the baking too when the chef was ill. Another development was the broadcast of services on the radio and the Methodist church took its turn with these along with the other denominations.

The canteen showing the book section on the left

In January 1958 the government finally took back the South branch property which had been let to a Methodist family for years. They were able to stay in it and it saved the church the administration of a property it no longer needed. It does not exist today as a large block of flats was later built on the site.

In 1958 Jackson again returned to England on leave and the Rev. Albert S. Hullah supplied for him. Departure was delayed as the children were recovering from chickenpox. In addition there was a good deal of polio in Spain at this time. Indeed there had been cases in Gibraltar. A polio vaccine had just become available to all Forces personnel but the Jackson children did not officially qualify for this. However, a Methodist nurse managed to arrange for doses to be given and the family set off on leave on 7 July returning to Gibraltar on 4 September with a caravan in tow! This made the journeys in Spain much cheaper and far more fun, for in those days it was perfectly permissible to stop for the night by the side of the road and Rene's Spanish was a great help if problems did arise.

On his return Hullah met with the Board and 'gave a vivid picture of the Methodist witness on the Rock and paid tribute to the devotion of our workers and the excellence of our premises'.[21] As a result a letter of appreciation was sent to Mrs Sneezum.

So the work progressed with little out of the ordinary to report. In 1959 Sister Mabel Todd spent time in Gibraltar so that Mrs Sneezum could take a well-earned rest. It was reported that 'there are thriving week-night fellowships and the church is so well-filled that there is talk of opening the gallery'.[22]

At Christmas, a toy service was held in Gibraltar and one year a terrible storm hit Spain almost destroying a Spanish village not far from the Rock. The church decided to give the toys to the children there. Contact was made with the priest and a car-load of toys was taken to his house for distribution. Much joy was given to the children despite the hardship and poverty in the village.

Then, at Christmas 1959, it was decided that the toys should go to the Protestant children in Ronda. The poverty amongst the members there was such that many children had no toys at all. Traditionally Spanish children receive their presents at Epiphany when the three wise men bring the gifts. So, on 5 January 1960, the Jacksons set off in their caravan, despite the dreadful road to Ronda, with a large consignment of toys. When they explained that the toys were for Spanish children, they were waved through customs.

Dalton had returned to the United States in the summer of 1957 and, whilst there, married Adele Flower who returned to Spain with him. There were at this time around sixty children in the Sunday school at Ronda and it took some time to divide everything up as fairly as possible, wrap the presents in Christmas paper and label them

Adele and Rene in Ronda

with each child's name. Three men from the church dressed up as the three

[21] *Minutes of the Board, Vol.IX, May 1955-April 1969,* meeting 7 October 1958, minute 6, p.169.

[22] *Over to You,* vol. xii, no. 2 winter 1959, pp.12-13.

kings. At 11 o'clock on 6 January everyone crowded into the church. Carols were sung with gusto to the accompaniment of Roy Dalton's accordion and the Christmas story was told using a flannelgraph. When the story of the three kings was reached, the three men came into the church with the gifts for the children. After the service was over the children unwrapped their presents. Some were so thrilled with the pretty paper that they needed encouragment to unwrap the parcel and discover that there was something even better inside. There was much joy amongst the children and their parents too. The following year the toys were again taken to Ronda.

After the Toy Service, Ronda

In the summer of 1960, the Jacksons returned to England on leave and this time the person sent out as supply was Rene's uncle, the Rev. Donald Godfrey, who came out with his wife, Dorothy, and spent some extra time there on holiday with the family.

In 1961 the church was reported to be thriving with nine new members added. By this time Mrs Sneezum had left and Miss Halsey returned temporarily until a successor could be found. She had, in fact, officially retired in 1956 and was awarded the MBE in the Queen's Birthday Honours in 1957.

After a great deal of thought, Jackson had reluctantly decided it was time to leave Gibraltar. Despite the rather difficult start, these had been happy years and at one stage he was offered the chance to make Gibraltar his life's work, but he had to consider the needs of his family. He was concerned about secondary education in Gibraltar and neither he nor Rene wanted the children to go to boarding school. In addition Rene was looking forward to seeing more of her family. So, plans were made to leave Gibraltar in the summer of 1961. The Board appointed a successor, Richard Cleave, who arrived with his wife and daughter before the Jacksons left to ensure a proper handover was effected. The Jacksons vacated the manse on 1 July and went to stay in a bungalow at San Diego on the Spanish coast - the caravan had been sold. Tourism was just beginning and this was one of the first self-catering developments. It is still there today. It was well equipped with a calor gas cooker and a paraffin refrigerator. Lamps were brought down each evening as there was no electricity. Fruit sellers rode up to the door on their donkeys and the sea was just across the road.

The family returned to Gibraltar on 2 July for the farewell services when various presentations were made to them all including a book for each of the children. Several other visits to Gibraltar took place to help the Cleaves settle in. On 15 July the family finally set off on the journey back to England. Jackson was later invited to meet the Board and report on the work which he did in October 1961 when he was thanked for his contribution to the work in Gibraltar.

Jackson's main achievement in Gibraltar was to unite the Methodist work on the one site. The result was a bigger and improved congregation and Sunday school and a stronger witness on the main street at the forefront of Gibraltar life. He had been ably supported by his wife who had made a significant contribution of her own as no doubt many of her predecessors had done too, if only their stories had survived to be told. It was not easy settling back into English life after more than nine years away. There had been many changes and to the children England was a foreign country! After several appointments, Jackson was asked to be the Warden of Wesley House in Berlin, where there was a full-time job for Rene too. They went in 1975, the year after their son Richard began training for the ministry, and retired from there four years later to Lincolnshire. Here they continued to take an active part in church life and were able on several occasions to return to Gibraltar to act as supplies. They moved into very sheltered accommodation in Suffolk in autumn 2000 where Rene died on 27 July 2002 at the age of 83 after a long and brave battle with progressive supranuclear palsy. John continued to attend the Methodist church in Stowmarket which had warmly welcomed them both. The last occasion was on Christmas morning 2003. He died the following day at the age of 90.

CHAPTER 23   PROBLEMS WITH SPAIN
The border is closed (1961-81)

There were no major developments in the work over the next few years although there were changes to the congregation with the end of National Service. The new minister, Richard Henry Cleave, was born in Cornwall on 18 April 1918. He trained for the ministry at Didsbury College and served in four appointments before going to Gibraltar with his wife, Doris, and their young daughter, Elizabeth. They had travelled by ship but unfortunately their heavy luggage was somehow left on board and it was some weeks before it came back.

News of their arrival was published in *Over to You*, the magazine of the Forces Board, which also reported,

> Then there was the tale of the Board - the Wesley House boat which has given such pleasure to generations of picnicers in recent years. Before Mr Cleave had been in Gibraltar many days he was informed that the boat had had rough usage at the hands of a too-happy sailor and was in need of extensive repairs. Repaired, the boat was returned to her moorings. A few days later the Padre went down to see her only to be told she was lying at the bottom of the harbour! She is now in position again, but - Mr Cleave writes - 'In these torrential rains of the last couple of weeks I have been pumping out 6 to 8 inches of rain water every two or three days.'[1]

It did continue in use before finally being sold some years later. Links were maintained with Ronda and, although there were no more toy services, supplies including toys were taken there. A few years later, Roy and Adele Dalton travelled to England and spent a few days with the Jackson family. By then Roy was ill and he died in Ronda towards the end of the 1960's. He was buried in the Spanish cemetery there, a significant mark of respect for a Protestant in Catholic Spain. Adele stayed on in Spain until 1975 when she returned to the States to look after her elderly mother. She did re-visit Ronda in later years and the church continues to this day on a different site now, but at last openly identifiable as a Protestant church.

Hilborne visited Gibraltar soon after Cleave arrived and, whilst there, interviewed Doris's mother, Mrs F.G. Townsend, and offered her the job of manageress. Miss Halsey returned to England with the thanks of the Board for having helped out.

Cleave, a musical man and a good organist, may have been the inspiration behind a new venture early in 1962.

> Unlike most Church choirs, that at Wesley House has a preponderance of male voices. There was, in fact, one occasion when no women at all were

---

[1] *Over to You,* vol. xiv, no. 3, winter 1961, p.28.

present at choir practice! Seizing this opportunity the men conspired to form a Male Voice Choir - not, we are assured, to 'take the place of the Church choir, but to encourage the men to learn some sacred and secular music which could be given at concerts.'

That, at any rate, is the story, and our informant tells us that the first concert should be given around Eastertide.[2]

In August that year, a successful conference was held for Sunday school teachers and friends. It was well attended despite the heat and the unexpected visit of one of the apes!

Services were still regularly broadcast over the radio and in Spring 1963 'Sunday Half Hour' programmes were added which came from the Methodist church every six weeks. These were transmitted to all barrack rooms and were reported to be greatly appreciated by service personnel. The choir too was recorded at times and that Easter its rendition of 'Olivet to Calvary' was broadcast on Good Friday.

Around this time Mrs Townsend returned to England, having resigned her post on health grounds. Her place was taken by Miss M. Taylor but she did not stay long for, in February 1964, Miss Halsey once again returned as manageress.

In the summer of 1963 the Cleaves returned to England on leave and their place was supplied by the Rev. Harry Breakspear. By this time the Board had a new secretary, the Rev. Roland Hamblin, who had taken over from Hilborne in 1962.

The festivities of Christmas 1963 were much affected by a fire aboard the liner *Lakonia*. Although this happened some five hundred miles from Gibraltar, the ship had to be abandoned and the survivors were picked up by numerous ships which had responded to the distress signals. On Christmas afternoon, fifty-eight bodies were brought to Gibraltar and a mass funeral took place on Boxing Day. Two services were held, one at the Roman Catholic Cathedral and one at the Anglican Cathedral where the Dean was assisted by other ministers including Cleave. After the service the clergy of all denominations were involved in the burials at the cemetery. Twenty-nine of the victims were British and many local people attended the services as a mark of respect and sympathy.

The year 1964 was special as it was the first time the President of the Methodist Conference had visited Gibraltar during his year of office. The Rev. Dr Frederic Greeves, accompanied by Hamblin, flew into Gibraltar on Friday 17 April 1964 on a four-day visit. Dr Greeves stayed at the Convent with General Sir Dudley and Lady Ward. He visited all three services; taking a Padre's Hour with the army, chatting with some of the Methodists in the navy, after a tour of the harbour and dockyard, and visiting RAF units. There was an opportunity to meet the other clergy including the

---

[2] Ibid., no. 4, spring 1962, p.9.

Roman Catholic bishop and the Jewish rabbi. He was also welcomed by the mayor of Gibraltar, Sir Joshua Hassan, and interviewed on Gibraltar television.

Sunday was a busy day. A large congregation assembled in the morning including the Governor and his wife, Sir Joshua Hassan and the heads of the three services. Cleave conducted the service, Worsley led the prayers and both the Governor and Hassan read a lesson. Greeves preached and the service was broadcast on Gibraltar radio. Later in the day a special service was held to receive several new members into the church. In the evening the President went to the television studios to broadcast the epilogue and then returned to the manse for an informal gathering with hospitality provided by Doris Cleave. On Tuesday evening, a final 'At Home' was held just for the Methodist community. All in all, the visit went well and was felt to be a very encouraging experience for Methodism in Gibraltar.

However, during the visit, events occurred which necessitated Cleave's immediate return to England. Fortunately there was a young man in the congregation, David Kinch, who was in the process of candidating for the ministry. He took over the preaching and kept the work going. On his return to England, Cleave was stationed in Nottingham but then seems to have left the ministry. However, in 1978 he began working in the Liskeard and Looe circuit but he died there suddenly on 18 March 1985 at the age of 66, leaving a wife, Lyn, and three young children.

Meanwhile in August 1964, David Kinch left Gibraltar to start his ministerial training and the Rev. Owen Roebuck visited the Rock. He reported to the Board in October 1964 referring to the 'very successful Presidential visit'.[3] Concern had previously been expressed about the cost to the Board of maintaining the work, which had averaged £1,000 a year for the last few years, but it was felt that the work was too important to be discontinued. Roebuck also introduced the new minister, Henry Bentley, to the work. He was born in County Durham on 3 March 1907. He was first appointed as a Lay Pastor but in 1939 he entered the ministry starting work in Cornwall. In 1942 he became a chaplain to the Forces and served throughout the rest of the war. He then served in several circuits in the north-east of England.

Henry and Ena Bentley arrived in early September. They only stayed for two years during which time the work continued much as before with little of note recorded. In June 1965 Miss Halsey finally left Gibraltar for good, having helped out for the last time and Ena took over her duties in the canteen. The Board sent Miss Halsey a letter of thanks for all she had done both in Gibraltar and Malta for service men and women over the years. She returned to England to continue her retirement. She died on 20 December 1977 on the Isle of Wight.

---

[3] *Minutes of the Board, Vol.IX May 1955-April 1969,* meeting on 13 October 1964, minute 2, pp.344-5.

During these years there may have been little change within Methodism but it was affected by other developments. Spain had continued to press its claim to Gibraltar. Discussions had taken place within the United Nations which was urging decolonisation and a solution to the problem. Over the next few years there was constitutional change in Gibraltar. The number of elected representatives on the councils increased and eventually a ministerial system was developed and, following elections in 1964, Hassan became Gibraltar's first chief minister. In 1969 a new constitution was published. The Legislative and City Councils merged into the House of Assembly. Most domestic matters were delegated to the chief minister and his council of ministers but the Governor was still the chief executive and had responsibility for external affairs. These moves towards internal self-government alarmed Spain but the changes did not mean Gibraltar had become independent. Spain pressed its claim hard, hoping to win by gaining international support and through the use of economic pressure on Gibraltar itself. The story of the negotiations is long and complicated but gradually Spanish attitudes hardened. In the absence of any agreement with Britain, Spain began by tightening restrictions at the border, at first on the pretext of cracking down on the smuggling. This resulted in a considerable reduction of the traffic across and there were long delays for those who did go through. The daily Spanish labour force lessened. The war-time high of about 13,000 had dropped to around 9,500 by 1963 and continued to decline.

In March 1965 Spain issued orders that Spaniards alone could be given worker's passes and refused to recognise the passports issued by Gibraltar's government. As a result large numbers of non-Spaniards living in Spain, but working in Gibraltar, had to decide where to live and work. Gibraltar already had a housing shortage and so could only provide temporary accommodation for those choosing to live there. In August 1966 the border was closed to the Spanish female workers. By the beginning of 1967, the number of men coming into Gibraltar had reduced to around 5,000 and the border was only open to pedestrians.

In September 1967 a referendum was held in Gibraltar which was overwhelmingly in favour of retaining the links with Britain but Spain continued to press its case. Spain did have a considerable amount of international support, but the British government refused to discuss anything other than the border restrictions. Then, shortly after the publication of Gibraltar's new constitution, the Spanish closed the border gates completely and a short time afterwards, on 27 June 1969, the Algeciras ferry service ceased.

All of this, of course, affected Gibraltar dramatically. Families were split up and sometimes relatives would gather on opposite sides of the border gates to wave to each other. Telephone communication was also cut off and Gibraltar's airspace limited. The Rock's economy was affected.

There was a shortage of fresh meat, fish, fruit and vegetables which had been imported from Spain. Eventually some 3,000 Moroccan workers came to Gibraltar to fill the gap left by the Spanish workers but this arrangement was not so satisfactory and they were also housed in very poor conditions. The Spanish workers were affected too. They lost their jobs. Over the next few years, there was a great deal of investment and development in the Campo area but this took time and in the short term many of Gibraltar's former employees must have ended up unemployed.

The resilience of the Gibraltarians came to their aid and a new sense of community and independence was forged. Different activities and interests were developed to compensate for the confinement to the Rock. Methodism was of course affected too and it is against this background of events that it continued its work. The Board watched developments anxiously wondering what the future held and recorded in October 1965, 'The frontier restrictions were causing certain difficulties to the property in Gibraltar but trading in Wesley House was better than for many years, and the life of the Church was strong and vigorous'.[4]

At Easter 1966 Hamblin and the Rev. Dr L. Davidson, head of the Home Mission Department, visited Gibraltar and were 'impressed by all that was being done in our Wesley House'.[5] Tribute was paid to the work of both the Bentleys 'despite the difficulties the frontier restrictions had imposed on those on "The Rock"'. The Bentleys were, by then, preparing to leave Gibraltar and their last services were held on Sunday 19 June with a farewell meeting later in the evening. They returned to England on holiday before going on to Berlin to take charge of the Wesley House there. Nine years later they retired to the north-east of England where Henry died in 1983 and Ena some time later.

The Bentleys had left Gibraltar early as they were due for leave. The gap before their successor arrived was covered by the Rev. John Haswell and his wife. It turned out to be a very difficult time indeed because during their stay the border was closed to the female Spanish workers. This much affected Wesley House where several Spanish women had been employed, some for many years. It must have been extremely hard for everyone that loyal staff should lose their jobs through no fault of their own. Finding replacements was not easy either with so many women lost as workers on the Rock. The Board paid tribute to the Haswells 'who had done holiday duty under extremely difficult conditions'.[6] The Finance Committee had given 'long consideration' to the work in Gibraltar since the future seemed so uncertain, but it was decided that Wesley House should continue as before and that a manageress would be appointed for two years in the first instance. The post was eventually filled by Mrs Hague who had had

---

[4] Ibid., meeting on 12 October 1965, minute 3. pp.373-4.
[5] Ibid., meeting on 26 April 1966, minute 4, p.394.
[6] Ibid., meeting on 11 October 1966, minute 2, pp.406-9.

previous experience of work amongst the Forces.

The minister now appointed to Gibraltar was Keith Roy Jefferies. Around this time it became more usual to call the ministers by their Christian names and he was known on the Rock as Roy. However, for the sake of continuity, surnames will continue to be used in this narrative. Jefferies was born on 31 August 1928 and brought up as an Anglican, but he joined the Methodist Church in 1944. He became a local preacher and was accepted for the ministry, entering Richmond Theological College in 1949. After ordination he married Patricia Lewis on 7 August 1954. By then he had been accepted as a Forces' chaplain and, after training, he served briefly in Egypt before being sent to Cyprus. In 1957 he returned to circuit work. A chance meeting with Roland Hamblin led to a conversation about Gibraltar and Jefferies expressed interest. He flew out to meet Bentley and discuss the work and, as a result, he and Pat agreed to go.

They arrived in Gibraltar at the end of August 1966 with their two children, Katharine aged eight, and Richard who was just eight months old. Their first services were taken on Sunday 4 September and they were welcomed to the work. Jefferies thought that the Bentleys had limited the canteen to service people only. He opened it up to all and saw its use as a valuable aid to pastoral work. The Board had discussed its future and considered closing it but Jefferies pointed out that it was a 'useful and indispensable bridge between the church and the public'. He went on to say,

> It is in the canteen that contact is made with the Servicemen and the Dockyard worker and their families. It is in the Canteen that mention is made of Church services and youth and Sunday School activities. It is in the Canteen that people come to seek out the chaplain. It is in the Canteen that customers have access to Christian literature ... It is from the Canteen as a base that the Chaplain and the Manageress make contact not only with Service and Dockyard personnel but also tourists, undergraduates, 'teddy boys' and the like, and the general public.[7]

As a result, a team was sent out to consider the way forward. It made several recommendations and eventually the canteen was refurbished. John Hague, the manageress's husband, rebuilt the counter and Jefferies returned to England to buy kitchen equipment. The result was that, in due course, the canteen became a meeting point for local as well as service people and became both busy and profitable. Indeed it was possible in later years to send sums of money to England from the profits.

Ecumenical relationships were also important to Jefferies and he developed closer links with the Roman Catholics than ever before. So, in early 1967, the Week of Prayer for Christian Unity was launched by a television programme when Jefferies joined in dialogue with Father

---

[7] Gibraltar Property File, 1967-9, Letter from Jefferies to Hamblin, 29 August 1967.

Bernard Linares on the subject of Christian unity and the following Sunday, history was made when Linares preached in the Methodist church.

So Jefferies began to forge closer links with the Gibraltar community which must have been recognised because, in September 1967, he was asked to act as an observer during the referendum. Shortly after this, Hamblin visited Gibraltar. He reported to the Board that,

> He had been glad to meet many members of the congregation at an informal gathering. The church is alive and thriving, and many of its members help in the work in the canteen. The emotions aroused by the referendum had much impressed the British people stationed on the Rock and showed the confidence of the Gibraltarians that Great Britain would accept responsibility for their future. Methodism is strategically placed to do its work as long as it is required. Canteen returns have been at a high level over recent months and Mr Jefferies is convinced of its value as an expression of the activity of the Church. The Secretary said that because of the amount of trade, as well as the illness of the Manageress, undue weight had fallen on Mr and Mrs Jefferies. The staff would therefore be increased.[8]

In summer 1968 the Jefferies returned to England on leave and the Rev. Elphin Ellis and his wife were sent as supplies. On their return, Ellis too reported to the Board paying tribute to both the Jefferies and stating 'that the Church, which is fortunate in its officers, is in a very healthy state, and doing excellent work among service and dockyard families ... The standing of Church and Canteen is high in the life of the town and among the Services'.[9]

By then the Jefferies were preparing for a major event in the life of Methodism in Gibraltar as the bicentenary was approaching. A booklet entitled 'Upon this Rock' was produced outlining the church's history. The Post Office was approached about a bicentenary stamp. This was not possible, but a special franking was authorised which was the first time the Gibraltar post office had used a commemorative postmark to recognise a special event. The envelopes all contained a card giving information about Methodism in Gibraltar. In due course, the money raised from the sale of these envelopes, supplemented by a few other donations, was sufficient to purchase four wheelchairs for use by the Physically Handicapped Society in Gibraltar. These were handed over as 'a thank offering for 200 years of Methodism on the Rock'.[10] An exhibition was carefully prepared using items from the Methodist archives and went on public display in the John Mackintosh Hall not far from Wesley House.

The President of Conference, the Rev. Dr Gordon Rupp, who had been

---

[8] *Minutes of the Board, Vol. IX May 1955-April 1969,* meeting on 10 October 1967, minute 5, pp.442-3.

[9] Ibid., meeting on 8 October 1968, minute 4, p.473.

[10] *Over to You,* vol. xxv, no. 1, summer 1972, p.30.

specially invited, flew into Gibraltar on the evening of Friday 11 April 1969. The official programme began the following evening with a reception held at the RAF officers' mess which had been lent to the Methodists for the evening. Invited guests included local civic, Forces and church leaders, as well as representatives of the Gibraltar Club, including Miss Halsey.

After a meal Jefferies introduced the President and called on Sir Joshua Hassan to welcome him on behalf of the people of Gibraltar. In his speech of welcome, Hassan spoke of the religious tolerance that existed in Gibraltar referring to the presence at the reception of the Roman Catholic bishop, the Jewish rabbi, the acting dean of the Church of England and the Presbyterian minister. Dr Rupp replied by expressing his appreciation of the warmth of his welcome and by congratulating the Methodist Church on its anniversary.

On Sunday 13 April the Methodist church was filled to capacity for the service 'in which the people gave thanks for their great inheritance and dedicated themselves afresh to the service of God and the community'.[11] The deputy fortress commander, Brigadier Wingate-Grey, read from Fortress Orders dated 3 June 1769, the first official reference to Methodism. Hassan and Mr Thomas Oates, the Acting Governor, read the lessons and Rupp preached referring frequently to the history of the church. Coffee was served afterwards in the canteen.

In the afternoon, a short service was held at the cemetery remembering those who had gone before. A church tea was held at Wesley House and an evening service of Holy Communion followed. Finally the President appeared on Gibraltar television to give the Sunday message.

Monday was an equally busy day, beginning with official calls on the various civic, church and Forces' leaders. Later in the afternoon, the President opened the exhibition in the John Mackintosh Hall and in the evening a special service was held in the old church on Prince Edward's Road. Finally the President was interviewed on Gibraltar television.

On Tuesday visits were made to service establishments around the Rock when the President had the opportunity to meet with sailors, soldiers and airmen. A special tea was held in the afternoon for the Sunday school children and young people at which everyone sang 'Happy birthday to us' and enjoyed a piece of birthday cake. The President then had a brief hour of relaxation before a meeting at the John Mackintosh Hall on the subject of Christian unity. Jefferies acted as chairman to a packed hall with the Roman Catholic bishop, the Anglican acting dean and the Church of Scotland minister all present with him. Dr Rupp spoke at length on the subject of Christian unity and there was plenty of opportunity for questions and other contributions. The *Gibraltar Chronicle* reported on the meeting,

---

[11] Account of centenary celebrations written by Pat Jefferies (in author's possession).

which ended with everyone joining together in saying the Lord's Prayer, and described the occasion as 'the most inspiring meeting yet seen at the John Mackintosh Hall'.[12] What a long way Methodism had come from the early days of soldiers meeting together often persecuted and despised by other Christians. It was indeed fitting that the bicentenary celebrations not only celebrated the history of Methodism on the Rock but also the history of the growth in understanding and toleration.

After such a hectic few days, a relaxing day followed with a sea trip round the Rock and visits to places of interest including Ince's Farm. In the evening a final 'At Home' took place in the Manse. The President left Gibraltar the following day. His visit had been a memorable one and a great encouragement to Methodists who could still feel far from home. The celebrations were reported at length in the *Gibraltar Chronicle* and Dr Rupp wrote, via its pages, a special letter of thanks to all those who had made his visit such a happy and successful one.

In all of these events, Dr Rupp did not fail to support and encourage the Jefferies family in their work. Seeing how tired they were after all the planning and preparations that had gone into such successful anniversary celebrations, he authorised payment for a short holiday in Spain which was much appreciated. The family crossed to Algeciras on the ferry, hired a car and spent a few days in Málaga.

They returned to Gibraltar not long before the border gates were finally closed and the ferry service ceased. These were difficult days, for now two men who had worked long and faithfully in the canteen, Antonio and Frankie, lost their jobs too. The Spanish workers were warned of the planned closure of the gates and given time to collect their tools and no doubt say goodbye to colleagues remaining on the Rock. The two men were given a gratuity which may have helped but was unlikely to have compensated them for the uncertain future they now faced.

Spanish workers had been employed in the canteen for a very long time and their loss meant considerable changes. Service wives and others helped out but they came and went and there was no longer a stable, long-term staff as before, apart from the manageress. A Moroccan lady was appointed for a while and Pat Jefferies helped out in the canteen when the need arose. Altogether four manageresses were sent out from England and there were at times quite long gaps before the replacements arrived, when Pat took over as best she could. This meant a lot of hard work and on one occasion, for several weeks, she got up at five o'clock in the morning to prepare an early breakfast for some twenty dockyard workers.

So the general work continued with the usual round of preaching and visiting, Padre's Hours and fellowship groups. There was always a welcome at Wesley House for visitors and the ministry of hospitality

---

[12] *Gibraltar Chronicle,* 17 April 1969.

continued and became more important now that everyone was confined to the Rock. Sunday was a particularly busy day when visitors for lunch were always present at the manse. In fact some people stayed all day, attending the morning service, staying for lunch and taking advantage of organised outings and activities in the afternoon. After the evening service, fellowship was offered in the manse when thirty or more people might gather especially if naval ships were in port. There was a Bible study on Thursday nights, a coffee morning on Tuesdays, a monthly ladies meeting which Pat ran and a large Sunday school and Bible class. Days were full and busy particularly when ships called at Gibraltar.

The educational work continued too but in a different form. The girls from the Loreto Convent no longer came to Wesley House; instead Jefferies visited the school a couple of times a week and paid occasional visits to other schools, sometimes taking assemblies there. Latterly Pat, a trained teacher, obtained a part-time teaching post at St George's school.

By this time, local television was established in Gibraltar and Jefferies felt this to be a useful medium as well as the continuing radio broadcasts of services. During his second Easter, he organised a brains trust with Bernard Linares and other clergy. In order to do the work better, he and Linares decided to undergo training in London organised by the Catholic church. In the event, Linares was unable to go and Jefferies went alone on what proved to be quite a gruelling course but it certainly helped with the television work. This continued on a regular, though not very frequent basis, and involved interviews and discussions. Services were not yet televised although a brief Sunday message was shown and he took his turn with that. One Easter the church produced its own Easter play which was broadcast and other plays were occasionally performed but not televised.

In addition to all the hospitality, Pat helped with the crèche on Sundays, worked in the canteen when necessary, ran the women's meeting and found time to help with the work of the Save the Children Fund and the Women's Guild of Prayer. Katharine too played her part in the life of the church, helping her mother with the hospitality and acting as organist for their last two years on the Rock. She also took an active part in life in Gibraltar, making local friends at the Loreto school which she attended and playing in the Gibraltar Youth Orchestra and Gibraltar's Symphony Orchestra.

In 1973 another presidential visit was planned but the President was unable to go at the last minute because of illness. The previous President, the Rev. Kenneth Waights, stepped in at short notice, and on this occasion was the guest of the navy, staying with Rear-Admiral H.W.E. Hollins and his wife. A full programme had been arranged and during the Sunday evening service a number of young people were received into church membership. Waights was interviewed on television and visited all three services. Once again it seems to have been a most successful visit, encouraging the Methodists in Gibraltar and providing an opportunity to report back to the Board on the thriving work going on at Wesley House.

In March 1974 the Secretary of the Board, the Rev. A. Douglas Spear, who had taken over from Hamblin in 1970, visited Gibraltar. By this time the Jefferies were preparing to leave the Rock. For various reasons, including family ones, they felt it was time to move on. On his return, Spear paid tribute to the work they had done, referring to the border closure and the sense of fellowship and community which had been created at Wesley House. He also referred to Pat's support and wrote, 'It is virtually impossible to express adequately the gratitude that many feel for all that the ministry of friendship and service rendered by the Jefferies has meant to them'.[13]   A lengthy tribute to the family appeared in the *Gibraltar Chronicle* too which referred to their 'Team Ministry', stating that their 'partnership of caring' had been the keynote of their ministry. Other clergy also paid tribute to them in this article. The Jefferies had carried out their ministry during difficult times in Gibraltar. Hospitality had played an important part but the television work and desire for good ecumenical relationships had brought far more of the local people into contact with Methodism. The Methodist church had become less of a Forces' church and more of a church for everyone.

The Jefferies family on their last Sunday in Gibraltar

---

[13] *Over to You,* vol. xxvii, no. 1, summer 1974.

A farewell meeting was held at Wesley House on 12 July 1974 and the family left the Rock the following Friday. Jefferies went into the sector ministry working as a teacher, but still took services on Sundays and led a Bible study and discussion group. He retired from teaching in 1993 and became a full-time industrial chaplain with pastoral oversight of two small churches. After four years he took a part-time supernumerary post. In January 1999 Pat died at the age of 67 and in 2000 Jefferies retired and went to live in Upminster where he lives today still taking an active part in church life.

Meanwhile in Gibraltar, the Rev. George Harker had been doing holiday duty until the arrival of the new minister, John Bland, who was born in Warrington on 11 December 1937. After working as a cost accountant, he candidated for the ministry and trained at Hartley Victoria College. He married Margaret Bleasdale in May 1961 as Methodism no longer required its ministers to complete their training before marriage. Appointments followed in Scotland and Tadcaster where, in addition to circuit duties, Bland was a part-time RAF chaplain. He was thinking about full-time chaplaincy work when Gibraltar was suggested and he flew out to talk with Jefferies. He and Margaret accepted the appointment and they arrived in Gibraltar on Wednesday 28 August 1974 with their two young daughters, Janet and Elaine. A service of induction and welcome was held on Friday 30 August with representatives from other churches and members of the congregation taking part.

In the early 1970's there was unrest in Gibraltar because of low wages resulting from high inflation. Union activity increased seeking higher wages and better working conditions until in August 1972, a general strike took place. No agreement was reached and industrial action continued into early 1975. At times this affected postal, telephone and power services. An interim agreement calmed things down for a while but later, in the absence of a final agreement, the campaign was resumed and the unrest continued until July 1978 when a settlement was made. Many of the union leaders met unofficially in the Wesley House restaurant and were known to the Methodist ministers during this time. This was regarded as neutral ground and the ministers maintained an impartial position throughout the dispute.

Methodism was also affected because the wages of the Wesley House restaurant staff had to be increased. As a result the manageress, Miss Joyce Holmes, felt that prices would have to be raised. Bland understood her concerns but felt there might be another way and, promising to take full responsibility himself, suggested prices stayed as they were. In no time at all, the restaurant was full as it was the cheapest eating place on the Rock. Queues formed for lunches priced at fifty pence. By the end of the year a profit of several thousand pounds had been made and sent to England, but more important was the contact with the wider community.

One day Bland visited a Roman Catholic man in prison whom he had met at Wesley House. He was later informed by letter that an old law, which stated that only chaplains of the prisoner's denomination could visit, had never been repealed. The days of religious intolerance were long past and it was not a condemnatory note, but it did suggest that in view of the existence of the law it would be better if he did not visit again. As the man himself asked for another visit, Bland discussed the matter with the Roman Catholic bishop and also with Sir Joshua Hassan and it was agreed that steps would be taken to rectify the situation. Unfortunately Bland himself was not able to see this through because problems with Margaret's health meant that he only stayed a year on the Rock. They went to Derby but, in 1979, John himself had to become a supernumerary on health grounds.

Back in Gibraltar the Jefferies family had gone out to cover the gap. They arrived on 28 July 1975 and the *Gibraltar Chronicle* reported on their 'very welcome return' to the Rock.

Bland's successor was Norman Berryman. He was born on 25 December 1923 in Scarborough. After working in a grocery business he volunteered for the RAF and in February 1942 began training as a flight engineer. After the war he returned to Scarborough to work in the civil service. He became a local preacher and went to Hartley Victoria College in 1951 to train for the ministry.

In 1954 he went to Armadale in West Lothian where he met Isobel Russell Graham and, after ordination, they married on 10 August 1957. Other appointments followed and in 1969 Berryman became chaplain and welfare officer at the Queen Victoria Seaman's Rest in London. In 1975 he called at the Forces' Board headquarters to discuss the future of the Seamen's Mission. He met with Spear, and found to his surprise that his appearance was seen as a possible answer to prayer. Bland's appointment to Gibraltar had, of course, been expected to last much longer than a year and his unplanned return to England had led to difficulties in finding a successor. The situation was therefore discussed with both the Berrymans who went away to consider the possibility. They did have an opportunity to talk things over with the Jefferies and decided to accept.

Norman and Isobel Berryman arrived in Gibraltar at the beginning of September 1975, before the Jefferies left and it was the Jefferies who organised their welcome. A special induction service was held on Wednesday 10 September. Five other clergymen were present representing all the denominations then in Gibraltar, the Roman Catholic, Anglican, Presbyterian, Pentecostal and evangelical churches. After the service there was an informal get-together in the Wesley House restaurant. Jefferies introduced Berryman to the work and gradually he got to know the heads of the Forces' departments, local leaders and the Governor, as well as the local congregation.

The continuing industrial unrest had led to an equal pay agreement for men and women which meant that prices in the restaurant did have to increase. In June 1976 the Secretary of the Board, the Rev. Gordon Briggs, who had taken over from Spear in 1975, visited Gibraltar with his wife and did holiday duty whilst the Berrymans were in England. He wrote, 'We were surprised and delighted to discover that a large Church posse had turned out at the airport to greet us - and their immediate welcome into the Church's family was to be a continuing feature of our three week stay'.[14] He referred to the restaurant saying it was 'still very popular with all-comers, but is feeling the draught through the very high cost of living, and from the fact that fewer Royal Navy ships are calling into Gibraltar'. In due course, as staff left, it was possible to reduce staffing levels a little to compensate for the increased costs. There were around fourteen staff members consisting of Gibraltarians, service wives and expatriates. Although the profits decreased, the restaurant was still viable and well patronised.

Berryman was also called upon to help with community welfare

Norman and Isobel Berryman after a baptism

problems. On one occasion two young people arrived without papers and he and Isobel accommodated them in the manse until matters were sorted out. One never quite knew what the day would bring and there was always an open door at the manse.

On Sundays coffee was served after the morning service and an informal fellowship met in the manse after evening services. Occasional services were broadcast on the radio and sometimes a Sunday Message and Thought for the Day. There were also occasional interviews on television. The Thursday night Bible study continued and was known throughout the Forces so that naval lads turned up for it when their ships were in port.

There was a good Sunday school with no shortage of teachers and regular planning meetings were held. On Monday mornings people would gather at the manse for coffee and a chat and to watch the changing of the guard at the Convent which for many years had taken place every week with the band accompanying the guards. There was a more formal coffee morning on Tuesdays and a fortnightly women's meeting which Isobel helped with. All these activities opened up pastoral opportunities. Some of

---

[14] Ibid., vol. xxix, no. 2, winter 1976.

the service wives found the confinement to the Rock very claustrophobic and a few left, unable to cope with it. Generally speaking though the warmth of the fellowship in Gibraltar continued and helped to compensate for the restrictions.

Ecumenical relationships were good and on 5 January 1977, the clergy all met together on the initiative of Father Caruana to sign a letter to the Spanish authorities asking for the telephone links with Spain to be permanently restored. They had been temporarily reconnected over Christmas. The reply arrived at the Spanish border gates. The English guards were called over and Father Caruana sent for. Only after he had proved his identity was the reply handed over. In it he was thanked for his letter and told that the matter was under review by the authorities in Madrid.

As leave arrangements had not been discussed with the Berrymans before their appointment, they chose to return to Britain for three weeks every year which, after their first leave, meant that no supply was necessary. By this time the Forces too tried to ensure that everyone had a regular break from the confines of the Rock. Of course, this was not so easy for the Gibraltarians themselves. It was difficult for the Berrymans to get away even for a few hours in so small a place, but they did manage occasional trips across to Tangier.

In summer 1977 there was a new development in the catering work. The dockyard advertised for tenders to staff two small canteens there. In fact Wesley House did not originally send in a tender, but when those which were submitted were felt to be unsatisfactory Wesley House was approached and asked to tender. This was done and the tender was accepted. The dockyard provided the canteens themselves and Wesley House did the rest which increased the profitability of the whole catering operation.

By this time there was another secretary to the Board as the Rev. C.R. Wolsey Gilbert had taken over in 1977. His first visit to the Rock was in March 1978 when he reported that 'He was most impressed by the work being done by the Rev. Norman Berryman and his wife' and went on to say 'The congregation and Church fellowship seems an ideal example of unity for it includes Baptists, Pentecostals, Brethren and Methodists'.[15] He visited again in spring 1979.

By this time problems had arisen in the building itself. In 1977 Berryman was reported to be ''working hard to make Wesley House as attractive as limited funds will allow.' He was 'facing a pretty heavy builder's bill as a result of corrosion to steelwork at the rear of our building' although it was also reported that some of the congregation had 'saved us a lot of heavy repair costs through skilful "DIY" operations.'[16] Some of the

---

[15] Ibid., vol. xxxi, no. 1, summer 1978.
[16] Ibid., vol. xxx, no. 2, winter 1977.

woodwork had become infested and the Berrymans did their best to treat this. They felt the building needed a re-fit but the Board did not authorise this. They did send out some fifty new stacking chairs for the restaurant but that is all.

In spring 1978 a new manager, John Capurro, was appointed. He was a local man and a member of the congregation along with his wife Daisy. Joyce Homes left the Rock after a good few years of service there.

Both the Berrymans found their days full and busy with church meetings, pastoral work, hospitality, preaching, visiting and Padre's Hours in addition to supervising the restaurant and dockyard canteens. It was very difficult to get a day off. Isobel did the accounts. She kept the books, paid the wages, and sorted out the income tax and insurance. She was eventually allowed £1 an hour for ten hours a week for her services but worked much longer than that. The Board set exacting standards for stocktaking and account-keeping. However, they both found time to be involved in the Dockyard Drama Group and in the Drama Festival of 1980, Berryman won the Magnolia Cup for Best Supporting Actor.

There was one note of controversy during this time. When Berryman received a cheque made out to him personally for the chaplaincy work he had done, he discovered the Board expected him to pass it to them to be used for his salary which was paid at the basic rate for superintendent ministers. This was, in fact, how his predecessors had been paid but this had not been discussed with him on appointment and he felt that he was entitled to the money for work he had done. The matter was never satisfactorily resolved. Berryman continued to question his right to the money as a matter of principle, knowing that officiating chaplains in England were paid an additional allowance.

In due course, the Board informed Berryman that his appointment would end in the summer of 1981. A farewell meeting was held at the beginning of August when various presentations were made to them. Sir Joshua Hassan had been invited but was unable to attend as he was away at the royal wedding in London. In his letter explaining this he wrote,

> I would, however, wish to avail myself of this opportunity to say how much the Reverend Berryman and his wife have endeared themselves to the people of Gibraltar, during their stay here. They have always taken a very great interest in the welfare and the future of our community and I personally have found great comfort by talking with him about our problems.
>
> My wife and I would therefore, in our absence, wish to express our regret at the departure and express Gibraltar's gratitude for their service to the community.[17]

---

[17] Letter from Sir Joshua Hassan to Mr David Dolding, Church Steward, 21 July 1981 (in author's possession).

The Berrymans returned to England to an appointment in Seahouses. In 1989 they retired to York where they live today, still taking an active part in church life. Norman continues his chaplaincy work too, as part-time chaplain to 2434 Air Training Corps at Church Fenton and as honorary chaplain to several squadron associations.

The next two ministers who had both been full-time army chaplains and subject to compulsory retirement at the age of fifty-five, did eventually get extra allowances for their work in Gibraltar and, during their ministries, there were further changes which affected the Methodist work on the Rock.

CHAPTER 24   CHANGES IN GIBRALTAR
The border reopens and the troops begin to leave (1981-97)

The Berrymans left Gibraltar before their successors arrived and holiday duty was done by John and Rene Jackson. The new minister was Douglas Allan Dennis (known in Gibraltar as Dougie) who was born on 21 February 1927 in East Ham. He attended a Methodist church with his family and left school at the age of fifteen to begin an apprenticeship in plant engineering. He then became a local preacher. In 1946 he was called up for War Emergency Service and served as an engine fitter with the RAF. During this time he successfully candidated for the ministry. After a pre-collegiate year in circuit work, he went to Richmond College. He was ordained in 1954 after completing his period of probation and was thus free to marry Anne Manuell his fiancée. By this time Dennis had been accepted for chaplaincy work and, after training, he was sent to Egypt. The following years were busy and varied with service all over the world. Sometimes Anne was able to accompany him, at other times she stayed in England. Three children were born - Allan, Martin and Hilary.

During service in Germany, Dennis became Director of Religious Broadcasting in Germany, and was well known for his 'Padre's Pops' when he pointed listeners to the messages in popular songs. In June 1978 he went to Bagshot as Deputy Chaplain General, the highest position a non-Anglican could then attain. He was appointed as honorary chaplain to the Queen and awarded a CBE for services to the church in the army.

On compulsory retirement from the army, the Board suggested he went to Gibraltar. He and Anne flew out to meet the Berrymans to discuss the work and agreed to go. They arrived in August 1981, with their daughter Hilary, and an induction service was held on 7 September led by members of the congregation.

It soon became obvious that the building was indeed in need of a refit. In due course the manse flat was renovated and re-decorated. The case of the restaurant was more complex and there was much discussion about its future with the Board.

It was clear by then that the border was likely to re-open. There is little doubt that the Spanish had expected Gibraltar to buckle under the pressures caused by its closure, but the Gibraltarians did not and neither did they waver in their desire to be under British sovereignty. However, discussions had continued between the Spanish and British, with hopes of a solution fluctuating with changes of minister and the death of Franco in November 1975. Towards the end of 1977, things began to move forward as Spain wanted to join the EEC and Nato, and felt it would be easier to do so with Britain's support. Meetings and discussions took place culminating in the Lisbon agreement, following a meeting there in April 1980, in which both governments agreed to start negotiations to overcome the Gibraltar problem. Spain restated its territorial claim and Britain its commitment to honour the wishes of the Gibraltarians, but they did agree to consider any proposals each might make. Many Gibraltarians were alarmed by this and felt a closed border might be preferable to discussions about Spanish sovereignty. Things were unsettled in Spain too, with the resignation of the Prime Minister and an abortive military coup in February 1981, which led to concerns in Gibraltar about safety and security if the border gates re-opened. Negotiations continued but the Falklands invasion delayed things further. Eventually the gates opened at midnight on 14 December 1982 for pedestrians only. It was not until 5 February 1985 that the border opened fully and traffic could once again pass across although delays, restrictions and queues continued. At first, the border opening was greeted with some trepidation but the advantages soon overcame the concerns.

It was against this background of events that Methodism continued its work. It was eventually decided that the restaurant should continue. Its fortunes had fluctuated in the past but it had mostly proved financially viable and had provided a useful meeting place and a bridge between the church and the community. It was thought that the expected re-opening of the border would increase tourism and thus improve trade too. So, it was completely re-designed, renovated and furnished at a cost of around £40,000. It was re-named Ince's Restaurant and had two different floor levels to simulate a Galleries effect. It was big enough to seat 104 customers. The restaurant was officially opened on 1 December 1983 by Lady Williams, the Governor's wife, who poured the first cup of tea for her husband, Admiral Sir David Williams. Also present was the Rev. George Sails, head of the Home Missions Department, who had been largely responsible for the funding of the project, via the Forces Board, although some money had been raised locally. The *Gibraltar Chronicle* covered the event and stated that the restaurant had 'unlike others in trade, done remarkably well as a result of the pedestrian opening of the frontier'.[1] This success was thought to be due to the fact that the restaurant specialised in simple but wholesome food at reasonable prices (£2.85 was the cost of a three-course lunch) which was what servicemen, visiting families and local people seemed to like. In addition, staff were 'known for their friendliness and helpfulness'. John Capurro continued as the manager. The Christian bookstall had ceased some time before but from time to time Christian books were available on the premises. Work at the dockyard expanded with a third canteen and the number later increased to five.

This work provided many evangelistic opportunities. Dennis had always believed in coming alongside people rather than waiting for them to come to him. So early in the morning, he was often to be found at the dockyard talking to the workers queuing up at the canteens for refreshment and later

---

[1] *Gibraltar Chronicle*, 3 December 1983.

in the day in the restaurant. Padre's Hours continued and Dennis visited families from all the services. Apart from Sunday services, he held a weekly fellowship group called 'Talking it Over' in the manse and started a weekly prayer meeting for the men which was held at 6.30 a.m. before work began and was followed by breakfast. There was a weekly women's meeting which Anne attended plus a Sunday school and a youth club. The strong fellowship within the church continued and a warm welcome was always given to strangers. In August 1984 a long article about the work appeared in the *Methodist Recorder*. The reporter who visited the Rock wrote,

> At the evening service I attended during my visit I spoke to two naval men, one a ship's doctor and the other a NAAFI worker from the same ship … Both had been to lunch with one of the church members and both said that although neither were church members or even Methodists, they needed to go to church when away from home. The Methodist Church in Gibraltar was the place to find hope and comfort in such a situation.[2]

As Dennis himself said in the same article, one of the main functions of the church was to provide care for Christians away from their home churches of whatever denomination, but they also had an opportunity 'of bringing people to a faith in Christ who have never felt a need at home'.

Once the border opened, another group of people began to appear too. They were mostly young people who turned up in Gibraltar without a clear purpose and often needing support and guidance. Dennis developed a welfare fund to help in times of real need.

As a result of this policy of reaching out to people, congregations increased and soon a new development occurred. Dennis, like his predecessors, was involved in the radio and television broadcasting of services, the Sunday Message, Thought for the Day and occasional discussions, but his reputation had gone before him and soon he was asked to do holiday relief, producing a weekly two-hour concert music programme on the radio. The holiday relief turned into seven-and-a-half years! During the programmes he was able to slip in occasional Christian references. Other one-off programmes also made him well known. Many programmes could be received on the Costa del Sol and early in 1983, one was heard by Mike and Elsie Godman, two Methodists living near Estepona. They then wrote to Dennis and asked to meet him. As a result of this meeting, a monthly weekday fellowship was formed, with Dennis acting as its chaplain. Initially the group consisted of eight Methodists but numbers increased to about twenty-four including people from different denominations and countries and soon a monthly communion service began. Once the border was fully open some of the members visited Gibraltar to share in the fellowship there and faith lunches were organised

---

[2] *Methodist Recorder*, 16 August 1984.

on Sundays so that visitors could spend the day on the Rock.

Dennis also became a regular visitor to Gibraltar's schools. He took assemblies at the junior schools usually accompanied by Uncle Holy Bear - a ministerial teddy bear! He also visited the secondary schools taking religious education sessions and once a year he took a leading role in a quiet day organised for sixth formers who were about to leave school.

Anne played her part in all of this, providing hospitality in the manse and a listening ear as well as by supporting her husband. She also helped with the commercial side of things, being responsible for the staff's wages, dealing with the bank and coping with insurance stamps and tax forms. She helped out with the Sunday school and the women's meeting and was church organist on Sunday evenings. She joined a new group that started in the church making banners as an aid to worship which were most effective. She was involved in organising the Women's World Day of Prayer when it was the turn of the Methodist church to host it and still found time to be on the Save the Children Fund Committee.

All in all it was an extremely busy life and by 1985 both Anne and Dougie were ready for some extended leave. This was agreed by the Board and the first few weeks of supply duty were done by John and Rene Jackson and the last few weeks by John Bland, but unforeseen developments were to affect the latter's time there.

By then the navy had been reduced and in 1981 the decision to close the dockyard in 1983 had been announced. This was a blow as around 750 Gibraltarians were employed there. After consultation and discussion, it was decided that most of the dockyard, apart from a small section to be used by the navy, would be handed over to the Gibraltar government for a commercial ship-repair yard with substantial aid to help the new company establish itself. The unions campaigned vigorously against this plan, hoping the British government would change its mind. However, their activity ceased in 1982 during the Falklands crisis when the dockyard rallied round to prepare ships for action, many of which happened to be in Gibraltar on exercises at the time. The *Uganda* was refitted at Gibraltar as a hospital ship. Everyone worked flat out to achieve the conversion in as short a time as possible and the Wesley House canteens worked non-stop to feed the workers. One church member, Ian Bishop, collected as many paperbacks as he could to form a ship's library. All of this delayed the closure of the dockyard but it still took place at the very end of 1984. Labour disputes continued and the repair yard operated at a considerable loss. It was closed in 1991 and leased a few months later to a Norwegian company instead.

The changes at the dockyard affected Methodism because the canteen contracts had been agreed with the navy and the new authorities decided they wanted to run what was seen to be a lucrative business themselves. In 1985 they invited Bland to a discussion about this, knowing Dennis was away. Bland managed to stall things until Dennis got back but the change went ahead, although Wesley House continued to run the two remaining canteens situated in the naval part of the dockyard.

This reduction in the work affected the viability of the whole Wesley House catering operation as it became clear that the returns from the restaurant and two canteens could not cover the expenditure. Other factors were involved too: the availability of cheaper eating places in Spain once the border was fully opened; the fact that Wesley House was not a licensed restaurant and never could be; and the considerable regulations imposed by the unions regarding staff. Reluctantly the Board decided the restaurant would have to close. The unions tried to prevent this and several articles appeared in the *Gibraltar Chronicle*. Redundancy payments were made and, as some staff including John Capurro had secured other jobs, it was more difficult for the union to argue against closure. Of course, the union was concerned for its members, but it did not understand that the function of the restaurant was not purely a commercial one. Its primary role was to be a part of the church's outreach programme and, if it was not succeeding well on either count, it was too big a drain on resources to continue. It closed on 4 December 1986 and Wesley House also ceased to run the naval canteens.

When the Methodist work united at Wesley House, with an eye to future options, Jackson had designed the ground floor, where the restaurant was situated, to be a separate unit with its own entrance. So it was decided that this part of the building could now be let. The Board arranged this and the rent was paid directly to England to be used in the general cost of the work.

This reduced the work load but there was still more than enough to do. At some time, the church acquired a caravan on the Costa del Sol not far from Gibraltar which proved useful in offering short breaks from the Rock for those in need. Anne and Dougie used it occasionally and found it so beneficial they bought one of their own which enabled them to have short breaks away from the constant demands of the work, visitors and the telephone.

One of the pressures was the constant comings and goings which meant that church officers changed frequently. Another pressure was the lack of local preachers meaning that the ministers had mostly to preach two sermons every Sunday to the same congregation. Gradually however a small nucleus of more settled members was beginning to gather which brought some stability and continuity to the life of the church.

In January 1971 David and Mary Dolding had come to Gibraltar, with their three children, responding to a suggestion made at a missionary conference that working abroad in an ordinary job, whilst supporting a local church, was one way of doing missionary work. David had been offered an eighteen-month's contract as a quantity surveyor in Gibraltar and when this ended, he joined a local engineering firm and they stayed on.

In due course Mary took several 'O' levels and began training as a nurse. She later worked at St Bernard's Hospital, as a District Nurse and, from 1982, as a Macmillan nurse for which she was awarded an MBE in 1997. Both their jobs meant that they were in contact with local people as well as the Forces. Over the years they have done many jobs in the church, Sunday school and youth club and in 1993 Mary qualified as a local preacher. Since retirement they have continued to be actively involved in church life.

Another couple were Sheila and Fidelio Patron. Fidel, a Gibraltarian, was brought up as a Roman Catholic. In 1971 he met Sheila Kite, who had come to Gibraltar as a naval nurse. They used to meet outside the Methodist church and one day Sheila asked him to go in and he was struck by the sermon and the enjoyment of the congregation. He began to attend and eventually became a church member. On 26 December 1972 he and Sheila were married. Some time later they met a missionary couple who had a profound effect upon them both and through them they experienced a much deeper Christian experience which changed their lives. They began to think of doing more specifically Christian work possibly in Spain. They left the Methodist church for a while, finding the focus on the Forces a little exclusive. On returning Fidel began to train as a local preacher and both began to take an active part in church life.

Meanwhile a young man, Patrick Aldred, who had come to Gibraltar with the navy, linked up with the Methodist church. As there were few young people of his age at this time, Dennis suggested he joined the youth group at Bethel church. This church held services in both Spanish and English and Patrick went along with them to help with outreach work in Estepona. Here a group of Christians had gathered together, meeting mostly in their own homes, including the Zambrano family who had moved there from Ronda where they had worshipped at the Assemblies of God church. Indeed Juan Zambrano had worked there in the very wood-carving co-operative where the woodwork for the Methodist church had been carved and, with his wife Pepa, had been at the services when the toys from Gibraltar were distributed to the Sunday school children. Patrick soon became friendly with their daughter Lidia and a romance blossomed with the aid of a large dictionary! They were married in Estepona on 18 July 1987 and went to live in Gibraltar as Patrick was still in the navy. They worshipped in the Methodist church, but for the first six months dashed off after morning service there to catch the Spanish service at Bethel but eventually they decided to settle within Methodism. By this time Patrick was thinking about his future and wondering about full-time Christian work. He began training as a local preacher. In February 1989 he left the navy, planning to go to Cliff College for a year with Lidia, to train as a lay assistant and then return to Gibraltar. The cost was covered by a joint grant from the Forces Board and the Aldershot Trust with very generous support from the local church who saw their potential and were anxious to encourage it.

Meanwhile, the British government had announced its plans to withdraw most, if not all, the British battalion in Gibraltar by the early 1990's. The Secretary of the Board, the Rev. C.R. Wolsey Gilbert, stated that there would be no Methodist withdrawal and that the work would continue in Gibraltar even if it had to change.[3] In any case the congregation consisted of civilians, expatriates, and Gibraltarians as well as Forces' people.

In the summer of 1989, Patrick and Lidia went to Cliff College and Anne and Dougie Dennis also left Gibraltar, having decided it was time to move on. They retired in 1992 and later moved to Melton Mowbray where they live today. Here Dougie took on new work as chaplain to the Royal Naval Association, the British Legion and the Gibraltar Club and as honorary member of 218 Parachute Regiment. He also undertook some broadcasting work with BBC Leicester and both of them remain actively involved at Sage Cross Methodist church and in the circuit. During their years in Gibraltar, the work had developed and changed considerably and it continued to do so in the coming years.

Dougie and Anne Dennis in retirement

The Board appointed Paul Mears to Gibraltar. He was born on 19 January 1936 in Croydon where he attended the local Methodist church with his family. He joined the RAF and during this time several experiences, when his personal resources seemed inadequate, led him to think more deeply about matters of faith. As time went on, he found himself more and more drawn to the idea of ministry and eventually left the

[3] Ibid., 9 February 1989.

RAF and went to Cliff College for two years. In 1958 he began ministerial training at Handsworth College in Birmingham.

In August 1961 he married Leila, the daughter of a Methodist minister, and they moved to their first appointment in the Wensleydale circuit. Here Mears met several of the chaplains at Catterick Camp and eventually offered for chaplaincy work himself. Various postings followed in England and abroad including Deputy Assistant Chaplain General in Cyprus, staff chaplain at BAOR in Rheindalen and Deputy Assistant Chaplain General of the 4th Armoured Division in Germany.

When the Board approached him to ask if he would consider leaving the army to go to Gibraltar, he and Leila flew out to meet Anne and Dougie Dennis and discuss the work. After much thought and prayer, they felt it right to accept and so Mears resigned from the army. Their two daughters, Althea and Wendy, did not accompany their parents to Gibraltar but did come out on visits.

When they arrived in summer 1989, a new development was already underway. The loss of the restaurant had meant the loss of the opportunity to have Christian literature available to the public, so a small Christian bookshop was opened on the premises, situated at the end of the entrance to Wesley House. It was constructed by Chief Petty Officer Colin Lupton and his wife Sue. A local couple, Michael and Mary Grech, stocked and ran it. Michael, a teacher in Gibraltar, with Mary and their family were part of the developing group of settled church members. The book shop was seen as part of the outreach programme of the church and Mary, who manned it, often found opportunities to engage in conversation with the customers.

The loss of the restaurant had also meant the loss of the bridge between the service community, the local population and the church and the idea of providing a non-alcoholic bar, suggested some time earlier, was now considered more carefully. Suitable rooms were available but the conversion was likely to cost about £80,000; nevertheless planning went ahead.

In September 1990 Patrick and Lidia Aldred returned to Gibraltar where Patrick was to work as the lay assistant. They lived on the premises in the old manageress's flat. As Patrick wrote later,

> I remember our first day back in Gibraltar as Lay Worker. The workmen were still decorating our flat, we had no furniture, our belongings hadn't arrived from England, it was raining and I had my very first 'welfare case' banging on the flat door wanting food and clothing. This wasn't supposed to happen but it did give us a clue of things to come.[4]

He went on to say, 'I was given three main areas of responsibility. The alcohol-free bar (which still wasn't built!) setting up work in Spain among

---

[4] *Church magazine,* June 1993.

expatriates, and some work in the British Forces'.

In January 1991 the church was pleased to welcome Princess Piluleva Tuita, a Methodist from Tonga, to the Sunday morning service which was the annual covenant service. During the service the Princess presented Patrick with a certificate and Bible in recognition of having qualified as a lay worker.

Work continued on the Costa del Sol, building on the start which had already been made there. This eventually led to the formation of a small ecumenical congregation at Sotogrande with Methodists taking two services a month, alternating with the Anglicans.

Work also went ahead on the planned bar and Paul Farrell, a soldier serving in the Royal Green Jackets, suggested the name, 'The Carpenter's Arms'. It was dedicated on 6 April 1991. The Rev. Colin G. Rowe, Chairman of the London South-West District and also Chairman of the Forces Board, came out for the occasion. Various representatives of the Forces were present and took part in the service along with several church members. The Governor unveiled a commemorative plaque. The *Gibraltar Chronicle* reported on the occasion and expressed the local church's gratitude 'to the Methodist Church, the British Sailors' Society and International Transport Federation, the local Service Community and local businessmen who have made this venture possible' by helping with the cost.[5]

As Patrick later wrote, 'you can't put into words seeing the alcohol-free bar (The Carpenter's Arms) up and running. It serves the whole community and has led many people into a living faith. It has satellite television, a pool table, music, telephones and attracts lots of Gibraltar's youth'.[6] It was open from 10.00 a.m. to 2.00 p.m. and from 7.00 p.m. to 10.00 p.m. Mondays to Fridays and on Saturday night from 7.00 p.m. to 10.00 p.m. A young man from Northern Ireland, Trevor Wilson, ran it for the first few months with the help of volunteers including Marie-France Bishop. When Trevor returned to Northern Ireland it was her daughter, Johanne Bishop, who took over. After leaving school, she had spent a year, in 1990, in America working with Teen Missions. The local church gave her some financial support and she gained much valuable experience of Christian outreach work. On returning to Gibraltar she eventually took charge of the Carpenter's Arms, which soon became as well-known in Gibraltar as the restaurant had been. It is situated on the first floor of the building and to get to it, customers pass the Christian bookshop and the entrance to the church itself which is kept open so that visitors may enter and spend time in prayer and meditation if they wish.

The welfare work continued and developed. Over the years, Wesley House had built up quite a reputation and so people in distress and those

---

[5] *Gibraltar Chronicle*, 6 April 1991.
[6] *Church magazine,* June 1993.

arriving at the border in need of help were often advised to go there. Many were young people travelling in Europe who had got into difficulties. Contact was made with family or friends to arrange a flight home. Others came to Gibraltar on boats or were living rough. A bedsitter flatlet was constructed in the building for those in need of urgent accommodation and a shower was installed in the basement for those who were living rough, with soap and towels provided. Free food could be given in the Carpenter's Arms. Mears offered a counselling service, with back-up from Leila, which was also used by service personnel and members of the local population. There were several remarkable stories of lives being changed as a result of help received at Wesley House. On one occasion, two travellers re-varnished and polished the church floor as a thank-you for the help and support they had received. There were failures too, and even thefts from the building but the positive outcomes far outweighed the negative ones.

The ordinary work continued too, through fellowship meetings, youth club, Sunday school, Sunday services, pastoral work and visits to homes, hospital and ships, taking school assemblies and the radio and television work. As the members of the congregation came from different backgrounds, different needs had to be met so babies were sometimes dedicated and sometimes christened and some new adult Christians were baptised by full immersion in the sea. Mears also performed marriages for the Protestant United States Navy personnel stationed in Spain who were not allowed to marry there. The American chaplain carried out the marriage preparation and the couple then went to Gibraltar with their relatives and friends to be married with only twenty-four hours notice given. American sailors had used and appreciated Wesley House for years and the Welcome before it.

Paul and Leila Mears

Wesley House housed other activities ensuring that the building was well used. There were keep-fit classes, a physiotherapy surgery, a nursery school, piano lessons and a lunch club for children with working parents.

All in all it was a very busy life. Leila played her part helping with the women's fellowship and Bible study group, working in the Carpenter's Arms and by providing hospitality. She helped with the youth club, was the church organist on Sunday mornings and organised the flower rota. Lidia too played an active role in the life of the church.

Soon there were changes in the church sanctuary itself. The organ took up a lot of room and was in need of renovation but one Sunday Lidia was asked by a Spanish visitor if they were thinking of selling it. The man concerned was prepared to organise the dismantling of the organ, its exportation into Spain and its rebuilding there, so his son could learn to play it! He was willing to pay £11,000 for it. It was too good an opportunity to miss and the sale was agreed. This meant that there was more space at the back of the church and the gallery, which had rarely been used, was made into an extra meeting room. In the course of the work, a picture was found under the pews in the gallery of Jesus with Joseph in the carpenter's shop. It therefore seemed appropriate to hang it in the Carpenter's Arms. The money gained from the purchase of the pipe organ was used to replace the old pews with more comfortable seats and to buy an electronic organ.

By 1992 Patrick had successfully candidated for the ministry and he and Lidia were preparing to leave Gibraltar. Lidia qualified as a local preacher before they left and their first child, Reuben, was born on 24 August. A few weeks later Patrick left to begin his training at Wesley College in Bristol whilst Lidia and Reuben first spent some time in Spain with her family. After training, Patrick was appointed to Nottingham and three years later he became an army chaplain. Some time earlier, whilst on holiday in England, he and Lidia had visited Cliff College to see if they could find a successor. John and Jill Chitty were interested and, after an interview in Gibraltar, they began work there in 1992. They too worked hard and made a significant contribution to the life of the church, introducing drama into the worship. John was mainly responsible for the Carpenter's Arms and the youth work but also found time to play football for a Forces' team. Jill became the presenter of the 'By the Way' religious programme on Gibraltar television.

In 1993 Mears informed the Board that he wished to leave the following year to go back into ordinary circuit life. So the Board began to look for a successor and the man appointed was Frank Elmer Sykes who was born on 28 March 1935 in Bradford where he was educated. Although he was taken to Sunday school it was through the influence of the Boys' Brigade that he later joined the Church. After working as an apprentice coach-builder he was called up for National Service in the RAF. During this time, he began training as a local preacher and in 1955 he went to Cliff College for a year and then worked for a year as a student lay pastor. He candidated for the ministry and was bitterly disappointed not to be accepted.

He returned to Bradford where he took a clerical job and in 1958 he because a Missioner with the Newcastle upon Tyne City Mission which was an interdenominational body. In May 1959 he married Mavis Atkins and, after losing their first child, they adopted Ian and later Joy was born. Work in North Shields amongst delinquent young people followed and time as an insurance salesman, but he still felt a call to the ministry and this time he was accepted and started training at Queen's College in 1970.

After several circuit appointments, he went to Berlin in 1989 as the Warden of Wesley House. At that time, no-one could have foreseen the dismantling of the wall but when it did occur, the whole nature of the work had to change. There was no longer a need for Wesley House and its welfare work and, in any case, the building was requisitioned and did not belong to Methodism. Sykes was therefore involved in setting up an English-speaking church to ensure that church life continued. These developments made him redundant and in 1994, when he discussed his next appointment with the Board, Gibraltar was suggested as he already had the experience of guiding a church through change imposed upon it by outside events.

The naval presence on the Rock had already been reduced, as described earlier, and now that Gibraltar had its own regiment, the British army was to leave and the RAF would be reduced. This affected the Methodist church because service families, who had worshipped there, left. This reduction of the Forces also meant that it was no longer appropriate for the Forces Board to oversee the work.

It gradually became clear that various ideas were being considered by the Board. These included an amalgamation with the Church of Scotland; the possibility that Wesley House would become independent and part of the Methodist Church in Portugal; that the premises be sold and the work cease or move elsewhere. All this created a climate of uncertainty and even suspicion. Over the years the Forces Board had appointed all the ministers and nearly all the canteen or restaurant managers in England without any involvement from the local church. Views had been sought about property and policy decisions, but ultimately all these decisions had also been made by the Board. There were good reasons for doing this, at first, with the transient nature of the congregation. However, in more recent years this rather paternalistic approach was less suitable with the increased number of settled members who wanted a greater say in their own church affairs.

Sykes had wanted to visit Gibraltar before his interview with the Board. As this was not agreed, he and Mavis did not visit until January 1994 after they had been appointed. The local church had been led to believe that it would have some say in this appointment and Sykes, on realising this, insisted that he would not go unless the church council unanimously agreed, which it later did. Unfortunately he had also been recommended as having done a good job in 'closing down Berlin' and so some suspicions remained. Meanwhile, during a visit to Gibraltar, the Rev. Michael F. Hucker, now secretary to the Board, had informed the church that it would have to become self financing. However, this was to be done without the rent money received from the letting of the ground floor which continued to be paid directly to the Board. Some weeks later, Mears informed the congregation of this through the pages of the church magazine. He wrote,

We shall shortly have to become self financing and not rely on the Forces Board of the English Church. Our premises are the envy of other churches in Gibraltar, but the upkeep is expensive. We have now heard that the Trust which has financed our Lay-Assistant will no longer be able to provide the support. Our Church Council and the congregation have made it plain that it would not be in keeping with what we understand to be God's will to allow the ministry of Wesley House to decrease. Therefore, believing that God will provide in response to our obedience in these ever changing times, we will go forward in the name of Jesus Christ.[7]

None of this helped with the anxiety about the future but plans for a new lay assistant did go ahead. By this time John Chitty had successfully candidated for the ministry and was returning to England for training. However, in 1992, the church had paid for Johanne Bishop to go to Cliff College and, whilst there, she met Peter Goodhall. They now planned to go to Gibraltar together, where Peter would be the lay assistant and Johanne would resume her job at the Carpenter's Arms. Once Johanne had finished her time at Cliff, the church paid for another young man, Trevor Addison, to go. He had arrived in Gibraltar after travelling through Europe and had experienced a life-changing conversion there. The church was very generous in its support of so many young people, several of whom went on to become ministers.

In April 1994 when the church in Gibraltar celebrated its two hundred and twenty-fifth anniversary, the President of Conference, the Rev. Brian E. Beck, paid an official visit to the Rock. He visited all three services; seeing round the RAF's control tower, going on patrol with the navy and

Brian Beck and Paul Mears with the RAF

---

[7] *Church magazine,* May 1994.

touring the Rock, including some of the tunnels, with the army. He also went to Ince's Farm. The President preached at a special thanksgiving service at Wesley House which was attended by Mr Andrew Carter, the Deputy Governor, and Rear Admiral Jeremy Sanders, the Commander of British Forces at Gibraltar. Other clergy and visitors, including representatives of the Gibraltar Club, were also present. The history of the church was remembered as well as the ongoing work and the challenge of the gospel for the present day. A Chief Petty Officer gave a personal testimony of faith. He had recently felt a heart-warming experience similar to that of Wesley himself. It was a successful and encouraging presidential visit and it was clear that there was a thriving work still going on at Wesley House.

In the summer of 1994, Paul and Leila Mears returned to England and went to an appointment in the Poole and Swanage circuit where Paul continued to do some chaplaincy work. They retired in 2001 to Wimborne in Dorset where they both remain active in local church and community life. Under their ministry in Gibraltar, the work had developed embracing people outside the Forces which meant that there was now a stable nucleus of members to ensure that the church had a future even if the Forces were leaving.

Frank and Mavis Sykes flew to Gibraltar on 18 August 1994 and were met by John and Jill Chitty who welcomed them to the Rock and gave them a meal. A few weeks later the Chittys returned to England for John to begin ministerial training at Wesley College in Bristol and Peter and Johanne took their places. Johanne lived in the flat and Peter the bedsit which was no longer needed for emergency accommodation as the need for the welfare work had gradually reduced. Peter took up the general duties of the lay assistant but his main area of responsibility was the youth work. He and Johanne ran the Discovery Group which met twice a week in the Carpenter's Arms and consisted of some twenty young people, mainly boys. Johanne resumed her duties as manageress of the Carpenter's Arms but soon realised that the evening opening was no longer viable as so few customers came in. So the hours were reduced to 10.00 a.m. to 2.00 p.m. This meant the Arms could be used for the Discovery Group and any other evening activities. They were also involved in the Naval Christian Fellowship. The local contacts for this were Annie and Ian Holmes who worshipped at the Methodist Church and provided fellowship and hospitality to naval personnel passing through Gibraltar.

By the time the Sykes arrived, the work had changed even more as he was no longer to be an officiating chaplain to the Forces. As there was not sufficient chaplaincy work for both the Church of Scotland and Methodist ministers, it had been agreed that they would cover the work in turn beginning with the Church of Scotland minister. When he left Gibraltar, the Methodist minister took over and this practice continues today.

However, as fees for this work had been promised to Sykes at his interview, the Board did eventually pay them as there were still some members of the Forces in the congregation, along with local people, expatriates, MOD workers and holiday-makers. The local church paid both Sykes' and Peter's salary.

The radio work continued with regular broadcast services and Thought for the Day programmes and the local preachers were now encouraged to help with the latter. The television work largely ceased as did the educational role in the Forces' schools. However Mavis, a trained teacher, was asked to do some religious education work at St Christopher's school which she did on a voluntary basis. General church life continued much as before with the weekly Bible study group and an intermittent women's meeting. Gradually a new ministry began to develop in offering support to missionary organisations working in the area, such as Horizons and Operation Mobilisation. Plans also began to come together for using the building as a base for a radio ministry. It was also still used for other purposes such as the nursery and the physiotherapy surgery.

A core of local preachers, with some still in training, now existed to help cover the preaching at Wesley House and also at Sotogrande. One of those in training at this time was Sheila Lee who had come to Gibraltar in 1991 with her husband, Peter, who worked for the MOD. Sheila later obtained a teaching job at the Loreto Convent school.

By this time Fidel Patron had decided he wanted to commit himself to the life of the church in a new way and offered for the ministry in local appointment. This process was already under way when Sykes arrived but he supported Fidel in his training for this post. As a Gibraltarian, Fidel provided a link with the local community and also with the Protestant community in Spain as he attended a monthly fraternal of evangelical pastors in the Campo area. Sheila too had always worked hard for the church, helping in the Carpenter's Arms, the women's meeting and taking responsibility for the maintenance of the polished floor in the church itself. They also provided a great deal of hospitality in their own home.

Mavis was also busy helping in the Carpenter's Arms and occasionally the bookshop, supporting the women's meeting, providing hospitality and doing some baking for the Arms. She was also the covenant secretary for the church. During these years, the church archives, which had somehow survived in an odd assortment of boxes, were finally catalogued and placed on permanent loan in the Gibraltar Government Archives on the understanding that they still belonged to Methodism.

At the end of 1995 the church rejoiced with Peter and Johanne on the occasion of their marriage. This took place in Nottingham on 9 December 1995 with Patrick Aldred officiating, but a church blessing was held on the Rock so that their church family could share in the celebrations too.

The uncertainty about the future continued and the fear that Wesley

House might be sold remained. Eventually it was decided at the Methodist Conference of 1995 that a Commission, under the chairmanship of the Rev. Dr Richard G. Jones, would be set up to consider the options. The Commission consisted of two members of the Overseas Division - the Rev. Dr Kathleen Richardson and the Rev. Dr Stephen Plant; three members from the Forces Board - the Rev. Martin Broadbent, its chairman, Mr Alex Cloke, its treasurer, and the Rev. Brian Sherrington, its secretary designate; two independent members appointed by the President's Council - the Rev. Gerald Burt and Mr Derek Cargill plus five people from Gibraltar - Frank Sykes, David Dolding, Michael Grech, Fidel Patron and Sheila Lee. The first meeting of the Commission took place in London in January 1996 when the Forces Board and the Gibraltar Church, through Sheila Lee, each presented its views. Sykes was unable to be present as he was on sabbatical. It was then decided that the whole Commission would spend a weekend in Gibraltar and this took place from 3 to 6 May 1996. The weekend included a Rock tour and opportunities to meet members of the congregation, and representatives of other churches, to worship at the church and to hear a little about the church's history during a service at the cemetery on the Sunday afternoon, remembering the legacy of the many faithful people who had gone before. During the weekend, the Commission met together for further discussion and a final meeting was held in London in July. It was agreed that the Methodist Church in Gibraltar would become a circuit in its own right as part of the London South-West District and would pay the Forces Board £40,000 over a period of time in recognition of the support it had given to the work. The recommendations were to be presented to the Conference of 1997.

After the meeting, Sykes indicated that he wished to leave Gibraltar in the summer of 1997 to enable a new minister to be appointed to take the work forward in this new way. It had been a very difficult time for him, often caught in the middle between the views of the Forces Board and the local church, but he had appreciated the support he received from Martin Broadbent.

The work of the church continued as before with the addition of an Alpha course which led to the formation of house groups. However, in the summer of 1996 Peter and Johanne Goodhall left Gibraltar. Peter had been accepted to train for the ministry at Wesley College in Bristol and afterwards, in September 1999, they moved to their first appointment in the Horsham and Dorking circuit. No lay worker was appointed to take Peter's place as there were now sufficient lay people in Gibraltar. The work of the Discovery Group continued under Warwick Danks who had come to Gibraltar sponsored by Youth for Christ. A succession of managers continued the work of the Carpenter's Arms along with many hard-working volunteers including Mary and David Dolding.

In the spring of 1997 Sykes took part in a sponsored cycle ride from

Ronda down to Gibraltar raising £1,500 for cancer home care nursing in Gibraltar. He and Mavis were getting ready to leave the Rock when Conference met that summer and the Commission report was presented. It was agreed that Gibraltar should become a circuit in its own right as part of the London South-West District, but it was felt that £40,000 was too big a burden for a small church to bear and so that part of the recommendations was not agreed. The news travelled quickly to Gibraltar where it was well received. It relieved them of a debt that would have taken some time to pay even though they would now have the rents from the ground floor at their disposal. However, at a subsequent Church Council, it was felt that something should be done in recognition of the work of the Forces Board in Gibraltar and the church offered to set up a bursary fund for anyone from the Forces who wished to pursue a course of study at Cliff College.

So Frank and Mavis Sykes left Gibraltar after what had been a rather difficult three years, but they left a church ready and able to embark upon a new phase in its long existence. They returned to the north-east of England and retired in 2000 to West Moor on the outskirts of Newcastle upon Tyne, accompanied by Wesley, a West Highland terrier purchased with money from the gift they received when they left Gibraltar, whose kennel name is Gibraltar Laddie! They remain very involved in local church and circuit life.

Frank and Mavis Sykes taken in retirement

So, once again, the Methodist Church in Gibraltar embarked on a new phase in its life and, for the first time in its history, the local church had a say in the appointment of its new minister.

CHAPTER 25   ANOTHER NEW BEGINNING
Into the future (1997 onwards)

The new minister was Ivor Wilfrid Pearce who arrived in Gibraltar with his wife, Doreen, in August 1997. He had begun his training at Headingley College and, when it closed, he moved to Wesley College in Bristol and later completed a three months' course at Kingsmead College, Selly Oak, for those intending to work overseas. He and Doreen spent five years in Nigeria in the early 1970's, followed by several appointments in Britain.

Soon after their arrival, a special weekend was held to welcome them to the Rock and to mark the inauguration of the Gibraltar circuit. On Saturday 6 September 1997 a service of welcome and induction was held. The Rev. Dr Richard Jones, assisted by Fidel Patron, took the service and was the preacher. Peter Caruana, the Chief Minister, was also present. David Dolding, the church steward, welcomed Doreen and Wilf on behalf of the local congregation and the Rev. John Page, the Church of Scotland minister, welcomed them on behalf of the Gibraltar Clergy Fraternal. The following day another special service was held which reflected on the past, the present and the future. The church welcomed the Rev. Brian Sherrington, the Secretary of the Forces Board, to this service and Michael Grech, as circuit steward, presented him with a framed picture of the stained glass window for the Forces Board. This window, which had replaced those lost in the old church, when the *Bedenham* explosion occurred, has the Forces' badges incorporated within it. It seemed fitting therefore for a copy of it to be given in remembrance and gratitude for all the Board had done in overseeing the work at Gibraltar over a period of ninety-four years. As with the Missionary Society, the relationship had not always been easy, the difficulties of communicating at a distance and understanding the local situation had occasionally hindered understanding on both sides. Sometimes the work in Gibraltar had needed to draw on the funds at home; at other times it had contributed to them, but without the Board and its support for the work, it might well not have been able to continue at all. So gratitude for the past was expressed to the Forces Board as the church began to look to its future and the congregation committed itself afresh to the work of the gospel in Gibraltar.

The work continued to thrive under the ministry of Wilf and Doreen Pearce supported by an able group of lay workers, including several local preachers, and also by Fidel and Sheila Patron. Fidel was ordained as a minister in local appointment in the summer of 1998. A special service was first held in Gibraltar on Sunday 31 May when the Rev. Martin Broadbent, Chairman of the London South-West District, visited Gibraltar and Fidel was ordained in Grimsby on 21 June 1998. It was fitting that the Rev. Dr Richard Jones was the preacher and that the Rev. Dr Kathleen Richardson took part. Frank Sykes was the assisting minister.

The congregation continued to fluctuate as people came and went, but gradually a nucleus of some twenty or thirty settled members formed. On one Sunday in 2001 there were fourteen nationalities represented in the congregation and that year twenty-six new members joined the church, eleven of whom were Gibraltarian. For a time, the building housed a radio ministry and it still provides a spiritual home for people working for a variety of missionary organisations in the area. Each year large numbers gather together in Spain for a residential church weekend with teaching and activities provided for all the church family.

Under the ministry of Wilf Pearce the church has become less and less a Forces' church and more and more a Methodist church for all the people of Gibraltar. Both the Pearces worked hard in the Carpenter's Arms and also provided hospitality in the manse. Doreen was the church treasurer. The congregation benefited greatly from Wilf's teaching and his concern for, and interest in, people of all ages including the children and young people. He explained Methodist principles, ensuring the work continued on Methodist lines whilst acknowledging and rejoicing in the diversity of denominational backgrounds of the members which brings a richness to the life and worship of the church. Throughout their time people have continued to come and go as always in Gibraltar and it was sad to lose friends but good to gain others. The whole congregation was greatly saddened by the sudden death of Peter Lee in May 2004. The church was packed for the thanksgiving service with a large number of people also on the stairs outside. Sheila Lee was a further loss to the congregation when she left Gibraltar the following year.

Wilf and Doreen Pearce in Australia

Over recent years worship has become less formal as modern hymns and worship songs are sung alongside the more traditional ones. There is a music group to accompany the singing and the use of a digital projector brings a new dimension to worship. The installation of air conditioning in June 2006 soon proved of benefit in the hot summer months. Shortly afterwards the congregation said farewell to Wilf and Doreen, who left Gibraltar in July 2006, when they retired. They have since joined their family in Australia.

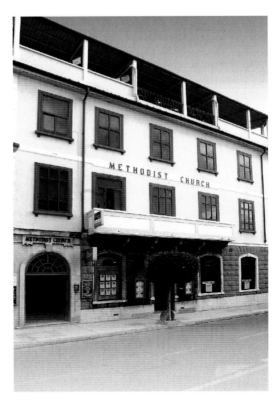

The Methodist Church building with the entrance on the left.
The Church and Carpenter's Arms take up the middle two floors with the manse on the top floor. *The Christian bookshop* "Words Aflame" is situated at the end of the entrance hall.

In the Carpenter's Arms are customers, members of the congregation including Doreen Pearce and David Dolding, staff and volunteers. *The Church* can be entered through the Arms and features the stained glass window commissioned to replace the Memorial Windows in the old Church destroyed by the Bedenham explosion.

Church photos taken by Anselmo Torres

Sheila and Fidel Patron, *taken at Fidel's induction service*

The group photograph was taken at the **Church Weekend at Antequera in 2009**. *In the front group is David Russell, second from the left, with his wife Pilar. Behind them is Dougie Cumming (standing) then Mary and David Dolding, Rosi (Dougie's wife) Olivia and Martin Bates (seated). Sheila Patron is kneeling on the left with Fidel on the back row on the right in the blue shirt.*

Group photo taken by Stephen Reeve

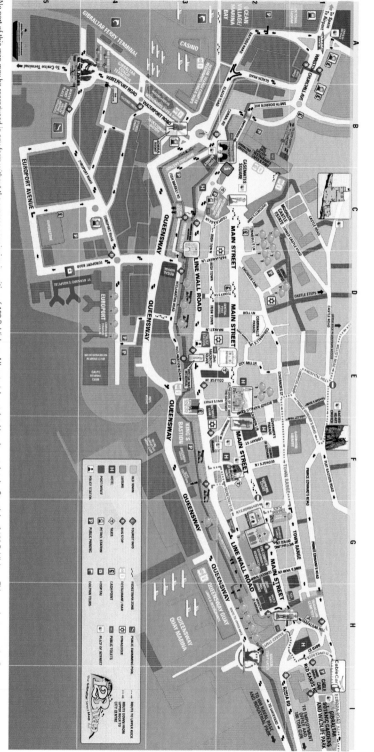

When the stationing process was completed, the announcement that the new minister was to be Fidel Patron was made to the congregation who greeted the news with spontaneous applause. So for the first time in its history a Gibraltarian has become the minister in pastoral charge. A special service of induction was held on Wednesday 30 August 2006 conducted by the Rev. Sheila Foreman, Assistant Chair of the South-East District which Gibraltar now comes under following the reorganisation of the London Districts. Representatives from the other churches were present and refreshments were served afterwards in the Carpenter's Arms.

The following weekend in England, the church was represented by Dougie Cumming, a local preacher and circuit steward, at the inauguration of the new South-East District. He carried the Gibraltar church's beautiful new banner which had been made by Mary and David Dolding's daughter, Sue.

Fidel took charge of a small but thriving church, keen to spread the gospel to all who will listen. The building is still well used. The bookshop, now run by Maggie Hosken and staffed by volunteers, is the first thing people see as they enter the building. The Carpenter's Arms is still busy and provides a bridge between the church and the community and opportunities for conversation. It is largely staffed by volunteers and for part of the week currently benefits from the cooking skills of Freddie and Brenda Sardeña who have done sterling work there in the past too. The worship sanctuary alongside is always open at the same time as the Arms and many people do take time to pause in quietness there.

The Little Twinkles nursery rents a large room and meets each weekday so that there are always children going up and down the stairs! The Gibraltar branch of Children's Aid, which was set up to work in Gibraltar and North Africa, has a storeroom on the premises for clothes which are primarily sold to raise money for the North African projects. Other goods are collected for distribution. This is a practical Christian mission and its presence on church premises brings people of other faiths into the building. One of the trustees, Martin Bates, is a member of the church.

The Gideon stock is kept on the premises and nearly all the members of the Gideon Camp are Methodists who organise regular Bible distribution around the Rock so that Bible distribution is still part of the church's ministry as it has been since its earliest days. There are three active local preachers – Mary Dolding, Dougie Cumming and David Russell and one retired preacher, John Capurro. Olivia Bates is in charge of the Sunday school which has eight teachers working in pairs. There are about twenty children plus a few of younger ages. Dougie Cumming is in overall charge of the youth work which consists of several groups including a post-Alpha youth group and a youth Bible study group. There are several adult house groups and Alpha courses are run from time to time.

Mary and David Dolding, at the door of the church in Spain before Mary took the service

Services are still taken fortnightly in Spain though the congregation has moved from Sotogrande to Torreguadiaro where they worship in a Roman Catholic church kindly lent to them each Sunday. The Methodist congregation meets there every fortnight with the Anglican congregation meeting on the alternate Sundays. There is another Anglican congregation at San Pedro and together they form the Anglican Church of the Costa del Sol West in the care of the Rev. Canon Dr Alan Maude. However as some people are now attending the services at Torreguadiaro each week, it may be that there will be an opportunity for closer Methodist-Anglican work in the future.

So the Methodist witness continues and Fidel hopes to build on the warm sense of fellowship and church family which already exists and to continue to share the gospel with all who will listen to it. He hopes that the church will be active in the wider community and provide a spiritual home for all who want to worship there, whether they be visitors, expatriates, missionaries, Gibraltarians, Forces workers or others who are spending time on the Rock thus continuing to point people to that other Rock – the living God. Already there are more Gibraltarians in the congregation than ever before and in 2007, for the first time ever, a woman minister, the Rev. Frances Blood, officiated at a wedding when Joanna Patron married James Bell with her father, Fidel, giving her away.

The Methodist Church in Gibraltar has existed for well over two hundred years despite its humble beginnings and the fierce early persecution. Over these years, it was able to change and adapt its work to meet different needs. It began with soldiers and then moved out to the local community making significant contributions in the fields of education and community health. It tried to establish missions in Spain itself and, although it largely failed, at least it made the attempt and was the first Protestant church to do so at that time. The emphasis moved back to the soldiers and the sailors who so needed the accommodation provided at the Welcome where all servicemen and later servicewomen were made welcome as the name implied. The welfare work was a recognition of the fact that physical and spiritual needs are both important and those who used the Welcome and later Wesley House were always encouraged to think about the deeper things of life. When the Forces largely left Gibraltar, the work had to change again and become more of a community church than a Forces' church though that process had already begun some years before. Change is often difficult but perhaps it was easier in Gibraltar because of the more transient nature of the congregation so that there were few people to say, 'but we've always done it this way'!

Over the years a great many people have played a part in the life of the church; some names have not been recorded for lack of space, and there are some whose names have been forgotten. Nevertheless it is a remarkable story of courage and commitment, of triumph over opposition and adversity, of steady perseverance, of constant change because of life in the shadow of that other Rock, the Rock of Gibraltar. Mistakes were made and human frailties exposed but despite that, the work went on and sometimes the cost was great. Many ministers served in Gibraltar. They came with different talents, interests and styles of ministry but generally they came with a passionate commitment to the work as did their wives, the unsung heroines of Methodism, who quietly got on with the job of supporting their husbands and often made significant contributions of their own in their different ways. Sometimes the cost to the men, their wives and their children was great. It cost some their health and a few their lives. Yet, if their sacrifice continues to challenge and inspire us today then that is indeed a lasting memorial and a foundation on which to build future work.

Early Leaders and Ministers of the Gibraltar Methodist Church

Sergeant Henry Ince
Brother Morton
Sergeant Henry Hall
Sergeant Andrew Armour   1769-1804
John Byrn
Robert Brand and other soldier preachers

Michael Caulfield	1802-55
Thomas Davis	1803-41
James Lyon	1836-41
Henry Nicholson	1841-53
James McMullen	1804
William Griffith	1808-11
James Gill	1812-14
Benjamin Wood	1814-16
Thomas Davis	1816-19
Owen Rees	1819-21
William Croscombe	1821-4
James Dixon	1824-5
William Barber	1825-8
Joseph Pratten	1825-8
Joseph Stinson	1829-32
William H. Rule	1832-42
John Garrett	1833-5
Edward M. Sweetman	1836-9
George Dowty	1838-9
Thomas T.N. Hull	1842-7
Thomas Dove	1847-9
George Alton	1847-58
Hilton Cheesbrough	1849-52
Aaron Edman	1854-5
Abraham White	1855-6
Joseph Webster	1858-63
George Alton	1861-72
Alfredo Giolma	1862-8
Henry H. Richmond	1868-9
Richard B. Lyth	1869-74
Thomas S. Dyson	1873
Henry H. Richmond	1874-80
William R.C. Cockill	1880-5
John Grimshaw	1885-90
W. Terry Coppin	1890-6

William H. Sarchet	1896-1904
Alfred B. Sackett	1904-19
Robert Coutts	1905-7
Frederick E. Brown	1907-12
Ernest R. Pickard	1912-18
William T. Sharpley	1919-22
Frederick E. Brown	1922-51
Frank W. Wilson	1950-2
John F. Jackson	1952-61
Richard H. Cleave	1961-4
Henry Bentley	1964-6
Keith R. Jefferies	1966-74
John D. Bland	1974-5
Norman Berryman	1975-81
Douglas A. Dennis	1981-9
Paul A. Mears	1989-94
Frank E. Sykes	1994-7
Ivor W. Pearce	1997-2006
Fidelio R. Patron	1998-

Bibliography and Source Material

Books

Allen, Rev. R.W., *Gibraltar Wesleyan Mission 1809-1909*, no publisher, no place, no year.

Archer, E.G. and Traverso, A.A., *Education in Gibraltar 1704-2004*, Gibraltar Books: Gibraltar, 2004.

Barber, Aquila, *A Brother's Portrait or Memoirs of the late Rev. William Barber Wesleyan Missionary to the Spaniards at Gibraltar*, no publisher: London, 1830.

Baker, Frank, *A Charge to Keep - An Introduction to the People called Methodists*, Epworth Press: London, 1954.

Barrass, Tine, 'The Catalan New Testament and the British and Foreign Bible Society 1820-1888', PhD. Girton College, Cambridge, 1968.

Benady, Sam, *Civil Hospital and Epidemics in Gibraltar*, Gibraltar Books Ltd.: Northants-Gibraltar, 1994.

Bigland, Eileen, *In the Steps of George Borrow*, Rich and Cowan: London, 1951.

Borrow, George, *The Bible in Spain*, London, Collins, no date.

Bowmer, John C, *Pastor and People*, Epworth Press: London, 1975.

Callahan, William J., *Church, Politics and Society in Spain 1750-1874*, Harvard University Press: Cambridge, Massachusetts, London, 1984.

Canton, William, *A History of the British and Foreign Bible Society,* John Murray: London, 1904, 5 vols.

Caruana, Charles, *The Rock under a Cloud*, Silent Books: Cambridge, 1989.

Collie, Michael, *George Borrow, Eccentric*, Cambridge University Press, 1982.

Connolly, T.W.J., *History of the Royal Sappers and Miners*, Longman, Brown, Green, Longmans and Roberts: London, 1857, 3 vols.

Crofts, B.D., Stanley A.K., Jefferies P. and K.R., *Upon this Rock. A Short History of Methodism in Gibraltar*, no publisher, Gibraltar, 1969.

Cuming, G.J. and Baker, Derek (eds), *Popular Belief and Practice, Studies in Church History*, Cambridge University Press, 1972, vol. viii.

Curnock, Nehemiah, *The Journal of John Wesley*, Epworth Press: London, 1938, 8 vols.

Darlow, T.H. (ed.), *Letters of George Borrow to the British and Foreign Bible Society*, Hodder and Stoughton: London, 1911.

Davies, R. and Rupp, G. (eds), *A History of the Methodist Church in Great Britain*, Epworth Press: London, 1965, vol. i; 1978, vol. ii; 1983, vol. iii.

Delpech, Jacques, *The Oppression of Protestants in Spain*, Lutterworth Press: London, 1965.

Drinkwater, John, *A History of the late Siege of Gibraltar*, no publisher: London, 1835.

Ellicott, Dorothy, *Our Gibraltar*, Gibraltar Museum Committee: Gibraltar, 1975.

Findlay G.G. and Holdsworth W.W., *The History of the Wesleyan Methodist Missionary Society*, Epworth Press: London, 1921, 5 vols.

Hempton, David, *Methodism and Politics in British Society 1750-1850*, Hutchinson: London, 1987.

Hills, George, *Rock of Contention; a History of Gibraltar*, Robert Hale and Co: London, 1974.

Howes, H.W., *The Gibraltarian - the Origin and Development of the Population of Gibraltar from 1704*, Mediterranean Sun Publishing Co. Ltd. [Reprint]: Gibraltar, 1991.

Jackson, Sir William G.F., *The Rock of the Gibraltarians; a History of Gibraltar*, Associated University Presses: London and Toronto, 1987.

Jenkins, Herbert, *The Life of George Borrow*, John Murray: London, 1924.

Kamen, Henry, *The Spanish Inquisition, an Historical Revision*, Phoenix: London, 1997.

Knapp, William I., *Life, Writings and Correspondence of George Borrow*, John Murray: London, 1904, 2 vols.

Lannon, Frances, *Privilege, Persecution and Prophecy: The Catholic Church in Spain 1875-1975*, Clarendon Press: Oxford, 1987.

Lawson, William D., *Wesleyan Local Preachers*, W.D. Lawson: Newcastle upon Tyne, 1874.

Martin, Arturo Gutiérrez, *El Campo de Gibraltar en la Obra Evangélica Española*, Ediciones Evangélicas Europeas: Barcelona, 1969.

Martin, Arturo Gutiérrez, *Gibraltar and the Spanish Evangelical Movement*, no publisher: Gibraltar, 1994.

McKendrick, Melveena, *A Concise History of Spain*, Cassell and Co. Ltd: London, 1972.

Mews, Stuart (ed.), *Religion and National Identity, Studies in Church History*, Basil Blackwell: Oxford, 1982, vol.xviii.

449

Moister, Rev. William, *Conversations on the rise, progress and present state of Wesleyan Missions in various parts of the world*, Hamilton, Adams and Co: London, 1869.

Norgate, Tom, *From Pedagogy to Photography: The Life and Work of John William Righton*, 613 Books: Petersfield, 2008.

Philip, Robert, *The Life and Times of the Rev. George Whitefield, M.A.*, George Virtue: no place, 1837.

Pollock, John, *George Whitefield and the Great Awakening*, Lion Publishing, Oxford, 1986.

Pudney, John, *John Wesley and his World*, Thomas and Hudson: London, 1978.

Rule, W.H., *An Account of the Establishment of Wesleyan Methodism in the British Army*, T. Woolmer: London, 1883.

Rule, W.H., *Memoir of a Mission to Gibraltar and Spain*, John Mason: London, 1844.

Rule, W.H., *Recollections of my Life and Work at Home and Abroad*, T. Woolmer: London, 1886.

Sawchuck, L.A. & Benady, S., *Diary of an Epidemic: Yellow Fever in Gibraltar, 1828*, Gibraltar Government Heritage Division: 2003.

Smith, John T., *Methodism and Education 1849-1902*, Clarendon Press: Oxford, 1998.

Spilsbury, Captain, *A Journal of the Siege of Gibraltar 1779-1783*, Gibraltar Garrison Library: 1908.

Stewart, Alexander, *In Darkest Spain*, Marshall Brothers Ltd: London and Edinburgh, no date.

Taylor, Ernest R., *Padre Brown of Gibraltar*, Epworth Press: London, 1955.

Traverso, Albert A., 'A History of Education in British Gibraltar 1704-1945', M.A. University of Southampton: 1980.

Vickers, John, *Thomas Coke, Apostle of Methodism*, Epworth Press: London, 1969.

Vincent, Mary, *Catholicism in the Second Spanish Republic: Religion and Politics in Salamanca, 1930-1936,* Clarendon Press: Oxford, 1996.

Watkins, Owen Spencer, *Soldiers and Preachers Too*, Methodist Church: Reprint, 1981.

Whitefield, George, *Journal of a Voyage from London to Savannah in Georgia*, no publisher: no place, 1826.

Whitefield, George, *Letters of George Whitefield for the period 1734-1742*, The Banner of Truth Trust: Edinburgh, 1976.

Williams, David, *A World of his Own - The Double Life of George Borrow*, Oxford University Press: 1982.

Yale, R., *A Story in Stone, being a History of the King's Chapel, Gibraltar*, no publisher: no place, 1948.

Anonymous, *Some Account of the Opposition made to the Religious Instruction of the Soldiers at Gibraltar*, Butterworth: London, 1805.

Guide books

Ellicott, Dorothy, *Cathedral of the Holy Trinity, Gibraltar.*

Lewington, J.E.L., *A Church was built*, Gibraltar 1955.

Philip, D. Stuart, (updated) *A History of the Church of Scotland,* after 1978.

A brief History of the King's Chapel, Gibraltar.

Journals and Periodicals

The Cornish Methodist Historical Association Journal, October 1975.

The Sapper, October 1937.

D.B.U. Journal, Reprint April 1941.
Proceedings of the Wesley Historical Society, 1979; October 1986; May 1996.

Gibraltar Heritage Journal, no.1 1993; no.2 1994; no.3 1996.

British and Foreign Bible Society records, Cambridge University Library

Annual Reports from 1808.

Occasional Monthly Extracts of published letters from agents etc.

Foreign Correspondence in and out from 1808.

Committee Minute Books especially from November 1836 when Graydon's correspondence is missing, during 1855 when Alton's letters are missing, and after 1857 when all incoming correspondence is missing.

School of Oriental and African Studies, London

Annual reports of the Wesleyan Methodist Missionary Society from 1804.

Missionary Notices from June 1817.

Methodist Church (MMS Archives) on microfiche:
- Home and General Minutes 1798-1837.
- Gibraltar Correspondence from 1804.
- Home and General Correspondence Outgoing 1816-1914.
- Special Series (biographical) Europe I 1817-20.
- Malta Correspondence 1827-9.

John Rylands Library, Manchester

Some correspondence e.g. Thomas Coke, February 1810.

The Arminian Magazine, February 1784.

The Methodist Magazine from 1802.

The Wesleyan Watchman from April 1840.

Minutes of the Methodist Conferences from 1744.

Garrison Library, Gibraltar

Gibraltar Directories and complete set of the *Gibraltar Chronicle* from the first edition in 1801.

Land Property Services, Gibraltar

Large record books and files about property leases, alterations to property, changes of ownership, property plans etc. from 1788.

Government Archives, Gibraltar

Crown lands registers, registers of deeds and leases, letter books, Gibraltar's blue books of statistics and miscellaneous files.

Church Archives, Gibraltar

Registers of births, marriages and deaths, minute book of the leaders' and stewards' meetings 1829-95, numerous records and miscellaneous documents such as those relating to leases, official correspondence, minute books etc.

(Since sorting all the material and cataloguing it for the purposes of this research, most of the material, apart from the registers and minute book, has been placed on permanent loan at the Government Archives in Gibraltar. In addition, all the documents relating solely to the work with the Bible Society have now also been catalogued and deposited in Cambridge.)

25th Regiment 201
26th Regiment 35, 38, 50-1
27th Regiment 50
28th Regiment 11
44th Regiment 177
46th Regiment 11, 130
51st Regiment 11
61st Regiment 11
64th Regiment 49-50
67th Regiment 35
80th Regiment 50

Adderley, George, Colonial Secretary
  168
Addison, Trevor 436
Admiralty *see also* allowances and
  capitation allowances 97
  dispute with 262
  grants from 291, 318, 320, 324, 328- 9,
    368, 382
advertisements
  Graydon's 111-3, 123
  use of 90, 110, 201, 301, 326, 421
Airey, Lady 230
Airey, Lieutenant General Sir
  Richard, Governor 229, 238-9
Alameda 34, (56)
Alder, Mrs 179-80, 211, 230, 241, 250,
  253
Alder, Rev. Dr Robert
  as Missionary Society Secretary 161,
    167
  in Gibraltar 179-80, 189, 198, 211,
    215, 242, 250
  illness 230, 238, 241-2, 249, 253
  work with the Bible Society 203, 206
Aldershot camp 202, 220, 269, 309
Aldred, Lidia née Zambrano 429-31,
  433-4
Aldred, Patrick 429-32, 434, 438
Alegría, José Martin 190, 194, 198
Algeciras 58, 198, 233, 254, 272, 293,
  298, 328, 337
  mission work there 142-3, 155, 302
Algeciras ferry 410, 415
Alhama, José 208-9, 222, 233, 235-7
Allen, John 79-80, 127-8, 134, 149-50,
  153, 155-7, 159, 171, 176
Allen, Mrs Susan 127, 176

Allen, Rev. Richard Watson,
  Secretary to the Board 276, 286-7, 290,
    305, 307, 313-4, 318, 320, 322, 324,
    332, 334
allowances from the army to the cost of
  Methodist work *see also* Admiralty
  and capitation allowances
  lack of 166, 201
  paid 276
  problems with 284, 328-9, 350
Almería 64, 74, 361
Alpha course 439, 443
Alton, Anna Maria Sophia
  birth 172
  death 179
Alton, Catherine Alder 172, 179, 183
  birth 167,
  death 198
Alton, Charles William Cooke
  birth 185
  death 198
Alton, Charlotte Amelia 198
Alton, Frank Edward 221, 250
Alton, George 172, 183, 194
Alton, Hepworth Tropolet 210
Alton, Isabella Amelia
  birth 175
  death 179
Alton, Kate Elizabeth 210, 229
Alton, Margarita Luisa 194
Alton, Mary Elizabeth Hepworth
  birth 180
  death 189
Alton, Mrs Amelia (Amy) 161, 164-5,
  179, 188, 194-5, 198-200, 210, 213,
  215, 221, 228, 230, 232, 251-2
Alton, Rev. George 137, 205, 259
  in Gibraltar 160-70, 172-81, 195- 200,
    221-39, 245-54
  in Spain 210-20
  with the Bible Society 181-94
  with the Sanitary Commission 227-32,
    238-9, 241-53
Alton, Robert Alder
  birth 164
  death 165
Alton, Syney Owen
  birth and death 194
Amat, Don Félix Torres, Bishop of
  Astorga 91
American Assemblies of God church
  in Ronda 390, 399, 404-5, 407, 429

American ships/Fleet 49, 101, 212, 377
American weddings 433
Americans 101, 341, 372, 433
Anderson, Lady 383
Anderson, Lieutenant General Sir
  Kennneth, Governor 383
Anna 368, 380-2
Anthony, Brother Thomas 89
anticlerical views in Spain 99, 184
apocrypha and the Bible Society 58
  and Spanish law 99, 111-2
Ark Royal 367-8
Armour, Andrew 10, 13
Army Committee 202, 276
Army and Navy Board 318
  and Air Force 345
  Methodist Church Board 351
  as trustees of the property 296, 320,
    397,
  involvement with
    appointment of staff 372-3, 377, 391,
      435
    canteen/restaurant 412, 422, 424-5,
      428
    finances of the work 325, 329, 336,
      338-9, 346, 349, 351, 357, 382, 391,
      409, 422, 425, 428, 435-6
    Institute 351-7, 359
    problems at the border 411
    purchase of the Welcome 334, 336,
      346-7, 391, 393-4, 397
    relinquishment of oversight 435, 438-
      9, 441
Army and Navy Board Secretaries see
  Allen, Bateson, Dodd, Standing, Firth,
  Hilborne, Hamblin, Spear, Briggs,
  Gilbert, Hucker, Sherrington
  Secretarial visits to Gibraltar 318-20,
    377-8, 381, 383, 408, 411, 413, 417,
    420-21
Army and Navy Committee 276, 286,
  305, 309, 314, 316-7, 309, 316-7
army returns 219, 276, 298
Assembly Rooms 330
Association for the Advancement of
  Civil Rights 374
Atlantic Fleet 324, 328, 349
Audiencia of Seville 206
Auxiliary see Bible Society
Auxiliary Missionary Society 40, 51, 58,
  94

Bailey, Lieutenant John William 42, 46-
  9, 51, 58
Baird, Rev. Dr 158, 160
Balearics, Methodist work there
  269, 282-3, 303-4
Baptism controversy 32
Barber, Aquila 54-5
Barber, Rev William 54-70
Barcelona
  base for Graydon 98-100, 122-3
  home of Ruet 191-3
  visited by
    Lyth 254-5
    Matamoros 208
    Rule 269-70
  work there of
    Brown 238, 246, 248, 250, 256
    Greenway 257
    Griffin 258, 268
    Simpson 268-9, 282-3
    Wheatcroft Brown & Smith 282, 304
Barea, Margarita 117, 133-5, 152, 212,
  223-4
Barleta, Manuel 90, 92, 102-3, 108
Barnard, Mrs 69
Barnard, Robert G. 40, 46, 62, 66, 69
Barnard, Robert the younger 64, 72
Barnett, Major-General Charles 10, 14-
  5, 17, 20
Batchelor, Rev. Peter 202
Bates, Martin 443
Bates, Mrs Olivia 443
Bateson, Rev. Joseph H., Secretary
  to the Board 334, 338, 341-2, 346-7,
  351, 353-9
Beck, Rev. Brian E. 436
Bedenham explosion 380, 387, 400
Bell, James 444
Bell, Mr, Deputy Receiver General 63
Bell, Rev. John 331
Benlisha, Solomon 145
Bent, Colonel 245
Bentley, Mrs Ena 409, 411
Bentley, Rev. Henry 409, 411-2
Bergne, Rev. S. B. (Bible Society) 244
Bergnes, Antonio 99-100, 122-3
Berryman, Mrs Isobel 419-22
Berryman, Rev. Norman 419-22
Bethel flag 49, 103
Bethel Society 49, 54, 56-8
Bible class 170, 192, 201, 211, 219,
  243, 281, 285, 313, 316, 319, 340, 416

Bible depots
  Bible Society's 236, 244
    main depot see also Madrid 236, 244
  depositories in Gibraltar 49, 74,
    86, 157, 181, 204, 206, 207-8, 245,
    278
  Borrow's 110
  Graydon's 98, 111, 113, 123
Bible printing in Spain
  Alton 182-8, 190-4, 236
  Bible Society 236, 244
  Borrow 100-1, 110, 123
  Graydon 98-9, 100, 123
  other attempts 159
Bible Society see also Alton & Fromou
  formed 22
  Auxiliary 188, 192, 198, 203, 206-8
  Bible distribution 22-4, 29, 31-2, 36,
    43, 48-9, 89-90,
  Bibles given for school work 107, 170,
    274
  Corresponding Committee 48-9, 58,
    73, 137, 157, 180-3
  official visits to Gibraltar 245, 256,
    278, 292
  Rodriguez' work 291-3, 303
  Rules's links with 97, 107
  worries about the work in Spain 121-2,
    204-5, 234 see also Escalante
Bible Society Agents see Borrow,
  Graydon, Curie, Corfield, Palmer and
  Jameson
Bible Society kiosk 292-3, 303
Bible Society's first public meeting 278
  later public meetings 292, 304
Bible Society Reports 238, 248, 278,
  280, 292, 303
Bicentenary see Methodist Curch
Biddulph, Sir Robert, Governor 310
Birmingham Collecting Scheme 357,
  375 see also Stephenson and Law
Bishop of Cádiz see also Cádiz 102,
  104, 118, 142, 216-7
Bishop, Ian 427
Bishop, Johanne 432, 436-9
Bishop, Mrs Marie-France 432
Bland, Mrs Margaret 418-9
Bland, Rev. John 418-9
Blood, Rev. Frances 444
blue books of statistics 116, 154
Board see Army and Navy Board
books at Wesley House 402-3, 425
bookshop at Wesley House 431-2, 438,
  443

border
  closure 410, 415, 417
  problems at 21, 23, 178, 181, 361, 395,
    402
  re-opening 424-5
Borrow, George 98-8, 100-01, 108-13,
  115, 121-4
Boyce, Rev. William, Missionary
  Society Secretary 245-6
Boyd, Lieutenant General Sir Robert,
  Governor 11,13
Brackenbury, John, Consul in Cádiz 90,
  108, 114, 118-9, 121-2,
Brackenbury, Rear-Admiral 310
Brackenbury, John, Vice Consul in
  Cádiz 90, 101, 104, 106, 204-6, 211,
  217
Brand, Robert 13-5, 17, 20
Brandram, Rev. Andrew, Secretary
  to the Bible Society 97-9, 110, 113
Breakspear, Rev. Harry 408
Brice, Joe 364
Briggs, Rev. Gordon, Secretary to the
  Board 420
British and Foreign Bible Society see
  Bible Society
Broadbent, Rev. Martin 439, 441
Brooks, Rev. Mr (Baptist) 158
Brown, Constance 382-3
Brown, Rev. Frederick Edmund
  as junior minister 329-30, 332, 336
  in pastoral charge 348-88
Brown, Rev. Joseph G. Wheatcroft
  282, 304
Brown, William (later Rev.) 232-3, 238,
  240, 246-8, 250, 254-8, 268-70, 283,
  291, 304
Brumwell, Mrs 400
Brumwell, Rev. Middleton 400
Buchanan, Andrew, Minister in Madrid
  204-6
Budgett, James 264-5
Bull, Mrs 157
burial ground
  concerns about 32, 36-7, 163-4
  encroached on 367
  services at 414, 439
Burrow, Rev. John (Anglican) 180
Burt, Rev. Gerald 439
Butterworth, Joseph 16, 22-3, 26
Byrn, John 13-5, 17, 20

455

Cabrera, Juan Bautista 222-3, 233, 237-8
Cabrera, Señora Josefa 222
Cádiz *see also* Governor & Bishop of
 Bibles taken there 90, 159-60, 198
 British raids 2
 Escalante's imprisonment 203-6
 Methodist work
  under Alton 211-3, 215-9
  under Lyon 102-8, 113, 119, 132-4, 140-1
  under Rule 114-9, 124
   with Dowty 115, 117, 125
  plans for future work 134-6, 143, 152, 158, 206-7, 209, 270
  persecution there 223-4
  Quirell's final home 83
  Spanish Protestant work there 233, 235
 visited by
  Alton 184, 192
  Borrow 101, 113, 121-2
  Graydon 110-1, 123
  Hull 158
  Pratten 60
  Rule 90-1, 101-2, 108, 142
Cádiz school 103-4, 106-9, 113-20
Camp Homes 338
Campbell, Charles, Vice Consul at Port St Mary, 211
Campbell, Major General Sir Colin, Governor 26,28
canteen *see also* restaurant, dockyard
 canteens and Carpenter's Arms
 at Welcome 370, 376-7, 380, 382, 389
 at Wesley House 398, 401, 403, 407, 412-6
capitation allowances *see also*
 allowances and Admiralty 276, 284, 324, 328
Capurro, John 422, 425, 428, 443
Cargill, Derek 439
Carlists 96, 102, 186, 189, 254
Carlyle, Clarice 382-3
Carpenter's Arms 432-4, 436-9, 442-3
Carter, Mr 375
Carter, Mr Andrew, Deputy Governor 437
Caruana, Father 89, 156, 421
Caruana, Peter, Chief Minister 441
Cassels, Mrs Elizabeth 232, 237, 247
Cassels, James 232, 237, 240, 245, 247-8, 272
Castaños, General 21
Catalan New Testament 98-100

Caulfield, Michael 13, 18-24, 27, 29, 40, 42, 45-9, 63, 69-71, 75, 79, 131, 159, 185
Caulfield, Miss Sophia 185
Caulfield, Mrs Sophia 20, 185
cave meetings 3, 24, 201
Cavilla, Arabella 378, 389
Cavilla, Mrs Lourdes 378, 389
Cavilla, Richard 378, 382, 389
cemetery *see* burial ground
censorship of Christian books 98, 190
Channel Fleet 246, 307-8, 310
Channel Squadron 261-2, 289, 299, 306
chapel *see* Methodist church, Providence Chapel and Wesley House
chapel at the Welcome 358, 364
Chapel minute book 71, 78, 137-8, 174, 176, 185, 200, 280, 283
Chatham 202, 309
Chatham, Earl of, Governor 33
Cheesbrough, Mrs Sarah Ann 167
Cheesbrough, Rev. Hilton 167-75, 200
Chegwin, Thomas, Captain of the Palhal Mines 233, 237, 246
Chiclana 203-4
Chitty, Mrs Jill 434, 437
Chitty, John 434, 436-7
cholera in Gibraltar 88, 179, 192, 227, 277, 280
cholera in Spain 183, 187, 192, 280
Christian Brothers *see also* schools 89, 281, 286, 390
Church bookshop *see* bookshop
Church of Scotland *see also* St Andrew's and Presbyterian Church 369, 382, 387, 435, 437, 441
Churchill, Winston 372
City Council 374, 410
Clarendon, Earl of *see* Sir George Villiers
Clarke, Colonel 391
Clarke, Henrietta 121
Clarke, Mary 121-2
Class leaders 40, 70, 79, 88, 129, 138, 157, 176, 185, 197, 289-90, 322
Class meetings 5, 7, 10, 24, 30, 36, 42, 45, 47, 70, 75, 86, 94, 148, 156, 195, 214, 219, 243, 254, 260, 277, 285, 288, 297-8, 306, 312, 315, 319, 346
 in Cádiz 83, 117, 132-3, 135, 142, 206, 212-3, 216
 in Palhal 233
 in Portugal 237

Spanish class 56, 58, 93, 128, 148,
    153, 155, 161, 169-70, 197, 203, 294
class tickets 135, 142
Cleave, Mrs Doris 405-7, 409
Cleave, Rev. Richard Henry 405-9
Cloke, Alex 439
Club, The
  founded and developed 369-71, 373-80,
    382-4, 388
  later links 414, 430, 437
Club chapel 370
Club Reunions 375-8, 380, 384, 388
Cockill, Annie 274
Cockill, Rev. William R.C. 273-9, 288
Codrington, Lieutenant General Sir
  William, Governor 214
coffee van 326
Coke, Dr Thomas 16-8, 20, 23, 33
Coldstream, Dr 35, 38, 41-3, 45-6,
  48-50
Collins, Rt Rev. William Edward,
  Bishop of Gibraltar 331
Colonial Office 3-4, 167, 354
colonial revenues 166
Colonial Secretary (Gibraltar) 168, 264,
  354-6
colporteur 181, 188, 190, 197-8, 217,
  236, 238, 245, 256, 278, 291- 2, 303
Columbine, Lieutenant General Francis,
  Lieutenant Governor 4
Commander-in-chief 16, 129, 177, 310
Commission of Enquiry into the Sanitary
  State of Gibraltar see also Sanitary
  Commission 226
Commission re future of Methodism
  439-40
Commission to settle titles to land in
  Gibraltar 34
commissions for Methodist chaplains
  318, 337, 345
Committee, The see Wesleyan Methodist
  Missionary Society
Committee of Finance and Advice 16-7,
  20, 22, 32
communication difficulties with
  Missionary Society see Wesleyan
  Methodist Missionary Society
congregational change 276-7, 386, 407,
  428, 445
  due to troop removals 11-12, 22, 24,
    49-51, 153, 178, 186-7, 19, 221, 260,
    277, 285, 290, 315, 350, 378
Constitution of Spain 105-6, 111, 118-9,
  133, 136, 268-9

Conference see Methodist Conference
constitutional change in Gibraltar 410
Convent 2, 8, 128, 157, 351, 364, 380,
  408, 420
Convict Chaplain 180
convict labour 180, 308
Coppin, Mrs Eva Maria 288, 293-4, 302,
  305
Coppin, Rev. W. Terry 288-306, 310-1,
  342
Corcoran, Brother Francis 89
Córdoba 234, 270
Corfield, Richard, Bible Society Agent
  244, 256, 268, 278
Cornish miners 233, 246
Corresponding Chaplain 202
Corresponding Committee see Bible
  Society
Cortes 106, 190, 192, 234-6
Costello, Marcus, Attorney General
  166-7
cottage meetings 290, 293
court martial 15
Courtois brothers 97-8
Coutts, Rev. Robert 324-5, 329
Coventry, Rev. John (Presbyterian) 233,
  236, 245, 255-6, 258
Covington, Miss 375-6
Coy, Deaconess Dorothy 302
Craddock, General Sir John, Governor
  25
Creighton, Commodore 365
Crillon, Duke de 8
Crimean War 186, 201-2
Croscombe, Mrs Ann 46
Croscombe, Rev. William 46-52
Crown Colony status 34
Cruellas, Sebastian 282-3
Cumming, Douglas 442-3
Cunha, Bishop Ireneu 248
Curie, Rev. J.G., Bible Society Agent
  234, 236, 244
Curragh Camp 202

Dalrymple, General Sir Hew, Governor
  21
Dalton, Mrs Adele 404, 407
Dalton, Roy 390-1, 395, 399, 404-5, 407
Danks, Warwick 439
Davidson, Rev. D.L. 411
Davis, Mrs Jane 33, 38-9
Davis, Mrs Mary Anne 95
Davis, Rev. Thomas 33-40, 45

Davis, Thomas 20-7, 33, 36, 40-3, 46-9, 57, 59-60, 63, 65-6, 69-72, 83, 86, 95, 129, 138, 185
Dawson, Quartermaster Sergeant 285, 287, 290
Deacon, Mrs Mary Ann 128, 146
Deacon, Richard 128, 146, 149, 155, 165-6, 195-7, 223
Deacon, Mrs Sarah 196
deaths on the station
  children 79, 116, 127, 165, 179 (2), 189, 194, 198 (2), 215, 314
  ministers 19, 69, 383
  wives 20, 59
debt on main premises 26
  added to 28, 47, 86
  concerns about 31, 36, 40, 63, 85, 143, 166, 169, 189
  lessened by Tripp's legacy 34
  paid off 263
debt on South property 143-4, 149-50, 170-2
  paid off 245
Dennis, Mrs Anne 424, 426-8, 430-1
Dennis, Rev. Douglas Allan 424-431
depository/depots see Bible Society
deputation
  about the state of Gibraltar 178
  about the Spanish prisoners 222
  from the Bible Society 244-5
  from Methodism 318-20, 330-4, 346-7
diphtheria 272, 285
Didsbury College 161, 407
discipline (internal) 12, 73-5, 79
Discovery Group 437, 439
division in the Church
  Rees 40-8, 52
  Rule 78-80, 84, 126-8, 139
  under Coppin 296-7, 305-6
  with Allen 155, 157, 173
Dixon, Eliza 57
Dixon, Mrs Mary 53, 57
Dixon, Rev. James 52-8, 71
dockyard 287, 308, 314, 320, 329, 356, 367, 408, 427
dockyard canteens see also canteen, restaurant and Carpenter's Arms 421-2, 425, 427-8
dockyard mission 180, 303
dockyard workers 314, 320, 323, 327-8, 363, 367, 382, 389, 412-3, 415
Dodd, Rev. H. Beverley, Secretary to the Board 359, 363
Dolding, David 428, 439, 441, 443

Dolding, Mrs Mary 428-9, 439, 443
Don, Lieutenant General Sir George, Lieutenant Governor, 32-7, 39, 56, 61, 63, 67, 70-2, 80
Dove, Mrs 160, 165
Dove, Rev. Thomas 160, 162-7
Dowty, Rev. George 115, 117, 124- 6, 135, 140
drainage/sewage works 227-32
Dryland, Miss Addy 402
Duck, Miss Eliza 61-4, 67, 69
Dyson, Rev. Thomas Skelton 254-7

ecumenical relationships 305, 313, 326, 330-2, 343, 383, 386, 390, 408-9, 412, 417, 419, 421, 436, 441
Edman, Rev. Aaron 182-3, 186
education see schools
Edward, Prince, Duke of Kent, Governor 10, 13-4, 33, 80
Elenor, Henry 275-6, 279, 281, 283-4, 288-9
Elenor, Mrs Annie 276, 289
Eliot, Lieutenant General George, Governor 7-8
Ellis, Mrs 413
Ellis, Rev. Elphin 413
Elms, Mr 86
Emerson, Robert Henry (Robbie) 373, 375-7, 384
epidemics see yellow fever
Epworth House see also school-house 319, 323, 377, 379, 392, 397
Escalante, Martin
  as colporteur 181, 183-5, 188, 190-1, 197-8,
  imprisonments 198, 203-8
  treachery 217-8, 224
evacuation of Gibraltarians 365-7
  return 374
Evans, Sir Frederick, Deputy Governor 330
evening school see night school
Exchange Rooms 251
excommunication , threats of 87, 154

Falkner, Trumpet Major 227
Farrell, Paul 432
fever see also yellow fever 33, 40, 52, 277, 288
  brain fever 152, 154
  concerns about 226

deaths from at the mission 19, 20, 69,
274, 293
fever-generating 294-5
precautions against 34-5, 73
sufferers at the mission 158, 188, 203,
213, 289,
fever season 30
Finch, Mr 278
Finnegan, Norman 370
First World War 304, 337-42, 345, 365
Firth, Rev. Joseph, Secretary to the
Board, 372, 375-8, 381, 383, 385, 387,
391-3, 396-7, 399-400
Fitz Roy, Admiral 299
flogging 15
Fluccard, John 15
Force H 367
Foreign Missions Committee 276, 296,
318, 397
Foreign Office 121, 124
Foreman, Rev. Sheila 442
Forestier-Walker, Sir Frederick W.E.F.,
Governor 335
Fox, Lieut. General the Honourable
Henry Edward, Governor 21
Franco, General 304, 362-3, 365, 367,
374, 424
Fromou, Stephen 256, 278, 292

Galleries *see* Ince's Galleries
Gallipoli 337, 339
Gardiner, Major-General Sir Robert
William, Governor 166, 178
Garrett, Major 130-1
Garrett, Rev. John 84-6, 90, 92-5
Garrison Library 18, 32, 380
Garrison Orders 7, 15, 67, 132, 202,
219
Garrison schools 34
Garrison town 2, 34, 202, 285
General Order re soldiers' worship rights
129-31, 177
Gibraltar Chronicle 206, 211, 213, 222,
226, 231, 251-3, 273, 321, 328, 330-1,
336, 342-3, 348, 351, 381, 383, 395,
400, 414-5, 417, 419, 425, 428, 432
adverts in: 83-4, 157, 201, 301
re fever 20, 67, 69-70, 227
Gibraltar Club *see* Club
Gilbert, John 40, 46-7
Gilbert, Rev. C.R. Wolsey, Secretary
to the Board 421, 430

Gilchrist, David 166, 244, 250, 263-5,
269, 271, 274, 279, 295-6
Gill, Mrs Catharine 28-30
Gill, Rev. James 28-30
Gillfilang, Richard 29, 40, 45-6
Gilpin, Dr 30
Giolma, Rev. Alfredo 214-7, 222-6
Gleave, Syd 370
Glenelg, Lord 116
Godfrey, Mrs Dorothy 405
Godfrey, Rev. Donald 405
Godley, General Sir Alexander J.,
Governor 353-6
Godman, Mike 426
Godman, Mrs Elsie 426
González, Federico 117, 152-3
Goodhall, Peter 436-439
Gourly, Captain 24
Governor of Cádiz *see also* Cadiz 102,
107, 118, 133
government grant to Methodist schools
*see also s*chools 116, 167-9, 189, 225,
264, 275, 281, 283, 297, 300
Govett, Archdeacon Decimus Storry
(Dean from 1905) 278, 292, 310, 313,
318
Grain, Mr 145
Granada
Bibles taken to 90, 159, 198
outings to 327, 334, 348
Spanish Protestants there 208-9, 222,
233, 237
visits to
Alton 183
Barber 64
Richmond 235, 267-8
Rule 101-2
Granville, Earl 239
Graydon, Lieutenant James Newenham
97-102, 104-5, 107, 110-13, 121-4, 209
Great Siege 7-10
Grech, Michael 431, 439, 441
Grech, Mrs Mary 431
Green, William , Senior Engineer 7-8
Greene, Mr 183-5, 187
Greenway, Rev. Charles 257
Greeves, Rev. Dr Frederic 408-9
Grey, Earl, Secretary of State for the
Colonies 167-8
Griffin, Rev. John Ridgeway 258, 268
Griffith, Mrs Ann 23
Griffith, Rev. William 23-8, 43
Griffith, William 23, 179

Grimshaw, Mrs Mary 279, 284
Grimshaw, Rev. John 279-88
Guilbert, Mr 86, 140
Guild meetings 315, 347, 350, 388, 397-8, 401
Gunton, Mr W.H. 393-4, 397

Hague, John 412
Hague, Mrs 411
Hall, Henry 7
Hall, Rev. Richard 339, 346-7
Halsey, Miss Mary Jane 373, 375-7, 382, 391-2, 405, 407-9, 414
Hamblin, Rev. Roland, Secretary to the Board, 408, 411-3, 417
Hamilton, Miss 213
Hampton, James 15
Harington, General Sir Charles H., Governor 357, 364
Harington, Lady 364
Harker, Rev. George 418
Harvey, Colonel, Schools Inspector 273
Hassan, Sir Joshua 374, 409-10, 414, 419, 422
Haswell, Mrs 411
Haswell, Rev. John 411
Hatchman, Rev. Robert, Garrison Chaplain 67
health difficulties at Mission House
  Altons 165, 167, 183-4, 189, 192-5, 198-9, 229
  Barber 54, 56-7, 61, 64, 68-9
  Cockills 278
  Coppins 293, 295, 296
  Croscombe 52
  Davis, Jane 38
  Dixon family 53, 57
  Garrett 84, 86, 92
  Grimshaws 284, 287
  Hulls 151, 153, 157-8, 160
  McCrindell, Miss 141
  Prattens 59-60, 62, 64
  Rees, Mrs 43, 45
  Richmond 260, 272
  Rules 79-80, 104, 114-6, 133, 139, 46-7
  Sackett 316
  Stinsons 74-5
  Sweetman, Sarah 127
  Websters 215
  White 188, 193, 195
Hennen, Dr John, Principal Medical Officer 59-60, 62-4, 67-70, 72
Herbert, John 40, 46, 49, 63, 69, 71-2

Herbert, Mrs Catherine 69, 263
Hernandez, Señor 233
Hesse-Darmstadt, Prince George of 2
Hilborne, Rev. F. Wilfred, Secretary to the Board 400, 407-8
Hill, General Lord, Commander-in-Chief 129-31, 134
Hipwell, Major 277-8, 287, 352
Hitler 367
Holden, Mr Isaac 339
Hollins, Rear-Admiral H.W.E. 416
Holmes, Ian 437
Holmes, Miss Joyce 418
Holmes, Mr George 303
Holmes, Mrs Annie 437
Holy Club 3
Holy Communion dispute 13-4
Holy Trinity Cathedral 34, 83, 180, 188, 253, 313, 326, 369, 380, 408
Home Fleet 377
Home Missions Committee 296, 318, 324, 397
Home Missions Department 347, 393, 397, 425
Home Missions Fund 318
Home Missions Reports 334, 345, 349-50
Hoole, Rev. Elijah, Missionary Society Secretary 180, 242, 250
Hornabrook, Rev. J. Oliver 363
Horse Guards 130-1, 177
Hosken, Maggie 443
hospital visitation
  difficulties with 36, 202-3
  practice of 243-4, 254, 277, 285, 306, 316, 324, 338-9, 371, 389, 433
hospitality 323, 344, 383, 389, 398, 401, 415-7, 422, 427, 433, 438, 442
House of Assembly 410
Houston, Lieutenant General Sir William, Governor 34, 81
Howden, Lord 186, 190-1
Howell, Anne 54
Hucker, Rev. Michael F., Secretary to the Board 435
Hughes, Dr Henry 153
Hughes, Rev. Mr, Garrison Chaplain 153
Hull, Mrs 105, 149, 151-2, 158, 160
Hull, Rev. Thomas T.N. 105, 148-60
Hullah, Rev. Albert S. 403-4
Humphries, Mr 86

Ince, Henry 5-10, 13, 20, 350
Ince's Farm 9-10, 415, 437
Ince's Galleries 8
Ince's Restaurant *see* restaurant
influenza 285, 337
Irving, Rev. Lewis (Presbyterian) 175
isolation of ministers 126, 151, 153,
178-9, 191, 254, 259, 261-2, 265, 269-
70, 273, 277, 298, 314, 317, 338, 390-1,
415
Isturitz 99, 101

Jackson, Mrs Irene Emma Antoinette
(Rene) 385-7, 389-90, 395-6, 400-7,
424, 427
Jackson, Rev. John Frederick 385-407,
424, 427-8
Jameson, Rev. John, Bible Society Agent
289, 291-2
Jefferies, Katharine 412. 416
Jefferies, Mrs Patricia (Pat) 412, 415-8
Jefferies, Rev. Keith *Roy* 412-9
Jenkins, Rev. John 148-9, 152
Jerez 90, 103, 158, 211
Jones, James P. 383
Jones, Mr 397
Jones, Mrs 391, 393-4, 397, 403
Jones, Rev. Dr Richard G. 439, 441
Junta of Elders 89, 153, 157

Keeling, Rev. John (Malta) 62, 69
Keen, James 381
Keightley, General Sir Charles F.,
Governor 402
Kelly, Rev. Charles Henry 202, 219
Kemp, Rev. Dennis 315-6
Keys, Mr Thomas 84, 86
Kinch, David 409
King Edward VII Institute 351-9
King Edward VII Institute's Trustees
352-7, 359, 391-2
King's Chapel 3-4, 9, 20, 34, 69, 188,
326, 380
King-King, Colonel J.G. 336
Knolleke, Mr 244

La Línea 272, 280, 283, 361-2, 380,
391, 395
Mission there 292-3, 299-300, 302-3
workers from 180, 308
lady worker 309, 313

Lakonia 408
Lamb, Corporal James 15, 20, 333
Law, Miss Elizabeth 349, 357
lay workers *see also* Emerson,
Aldred, Chitty, Goodhall 372-3, 376,
429, 431-2, 434, 436-7, 439, 441
lease on Methodist premises *see also*
trustees
acquired 25-6
amended 86
renewed 63-4, 72, 166-7, 199, 49-50
perpetuity 253
leasehold nature of premises 291, 313,
394
Ledger, Zacharias 21, 24-5
Lee, Mrs Sheila 438-9, 442
Lee, Peter 438, 442
Legislative Council 374
Lent (and action against
Protestantism) 83, 87, 117, 132, 154,
213
Leveridge, Miss 376
liberal views in Spain, 87, 91, 96, 99,
267
library for the Methodists 12, 36, 151,
201, 254
Lime Light Gospel Service 313, 315,
324
Linares 246-8
Linares, Father Bernard 413, 416
Linton, Mr 356
Lisbon 60, 78, 100, 208, 234, 237, 269
Alton's visit 210
Protestant work there 229, 233
local preachers 19, 83, 131, 141, 157,
341, 387, 428, 438, 441
Aldred, Lidia 434
Aldred 429
Armour 10
Byrn 13
Capurro 443
Caulfield 131, 185
Cumming 443
Davis 20, 33, 36, 40, 83, 138
Dawson 287, 290
Dolding, Mary 429, 443
Hipwell 277
Lee, Sheila 438
Lyon 89
Pilledge 382
Quirell 72
Russell 443
Sneezum, Freda 403
Squelch 377

local preachers (in Spain) 250, 282-3
location of Methodist property
  concerns about 236, 244, 284, 288,
    290, 313-4, 358
  efforts to find new location 313-4, 317,
    320, 329, 346-7, 392-4
  relocated 400
Lomas, Mr T.G. 339
loneliness of ministers *see* isolation
Loreto nuns arrival *see also* schools 156
Loreto Convent School 390, 416, 438
love-feast 35, 246
Lovero, Nicolas 93
Lupton, Chief Petty Office Colin 431
Lupton, Mrs Sue 431
Lyon, James 88-9, 102-8, 113-6, 119-
  120, 122, 132-4, 137-41, 143-4
Lyth daughters 240, 249-50
Lyth, Mrs Mary Ann 240, 249-50, 259
Lyth, Rev. Richard Burdsall 239-41,
  243-50, 253-9, 265
Lyttle, Bombardier 285

Macdonald, Rev. Frederic W.
  Missionary Society Secretary 298, 301,
  303
Mackereth, Rev. Mr, Garrison Chaplain
  32
Mackintosh Hall 413-5
Mackintosh, John 354-6
Mackintosh, Rev. Eneas (Presbyterian)
  278
Madrid 21, 29, 88, 90-1, 93, 118, 204,
  213, 234-5, 238, 268, 270, 298, 341,
  395-6, 401, 421
  Alton's work there 183-94, 196, 198
  Bible Society HQ 234, 236, 244, 256,
    68-9, 291
  Borrow, Graydon and Rule in Madrid
    98-101, 107-12, 121-3
  Methodist work there 113, 115-7, 124-
    5, 135-7, 282, 304
Magdala, General the Lord Napier of,
  Governor, 266
Mahon 250, 255
Majorca, Methodist work there 269
  70, 283, 291, 304
Málaga 91, 101-2, 159, 183, 194, 222,
  267, 303, 361, 388, 395, 399, 415
  and the civil war 361-2
  Graydon's visits 110-12, 122-3
  Protestant work there 208, 235

supplying Bibles to 43, 190, 193, 198,
  233
trips to 334, 348
Malta 50, 60-4, 67, 69, 77, 84, 105, 148,
  220-1, 284, 287, 308-9, 333, 345, 367,
  385, 391, 409
managers of the Welcome and Wesley
  House *see also* Orman, Pearce, Scott,
  Capurro, Squelch 309-10, 313, 328,
  339, 341, 348, 352, 356, 359, 364, 372-
  3, 378, 380, 382, 422, 425, 431, 435
manageresses of the Welcome and
  Wesley House *see also* Halsey,
  Southey, Jones, Sneezum, Townsend,
  Hague and Holmes 382, 391, 394, 399,
  403, 408, 411- 3, 415, 418
  assistant manageresses *see also*
  Covington, Dryland, Leveridge 375-6,
  402
managers of the South Welcome 325,
  351
marching of troops to worship *see also*
  Parade services 132, 138, 201- 2, 211,
  261-3, 271, 300
  abolished 374
Marillier, Capt. 251
Marin y Candado, Don Pascual 105-6,
  109-10, 112-17, 124-5, 135-7, 184
Mark, William, Consul in Málaga 102,
  111, 122-3, 183, 190
marriage law 137, 211
Martínez, Enriqueta 117
Martínez, Josefa 117, 133
Matamoros, Manuel 208-9, 222
Maude, Rev. Canon Dr Alan (Anglican)
  443
McCarter, Mrs Mary 256, 278
McCrindell, Miss 128-9, 141
McLoughlin, John 180
McMillan, Lieutenant-General Sir
  Gordon H.A., Governor 387
McMullen, Annie 17, 20
McMullen, Mrs Susanna 17, 20
McMullen, Rev. James 17-21
Mears, Mrs Leila 431, 433, 437
Mears, Rev. Paul 430-7
measles 52, 286
Mediterranean Fleet 246, 308, 345
Mediterranean Squadron 290
memorials to the Governor
  about land and leases 25, 63, 85, 88,
    104, 166, 249
  about marriage law 211

about right to worship 11, 13-4, 21
about school grant 168
request for burial ground 37
memorial services 70, 384
memorial windows 333, 381, 400
Mendizábal, Juan Alvárez 99, 101
meningitis 152
Methodist Centenary celebrations 129
Methodist Church *see also* Providence
  Chapel and Wesley House
  chapel 12, 21-2, 25-6
  closed during epidemics 19, 30, 66
  new chapel
    built 25-7
    enlarged 84-6
    used as a hospital 67-70
    poor state of 313-4, 320
    repaired 263, 284, 291,
    renovation 329-32
    damaged by explosion 381
    repaired 382
    sold 397, 400
    third chapel at Wesley House 400
Methodist Church bicentenary
  celebrations 413-5
Methodist Church Board *see* Army and
  Navy Board
Methodist Conference *see also*
  Presidents of Conference, Minutes of
  Conference
  about appointments 16, 53-4, 62, 64,
    94-5, 135, 138, 153, 156, 158, 164,
    179, 186, 202, 225, 229-30, 238-43,
    247, 249, 254, 324, 381, 385, 387
  Conference Commission 439-40
  Conference Committee 202, 345
  Conference decisions 13, 26, 33, 317
Methodist Missionary Society *see*
  Wesleyan Methodist Missionary
  Society
Methodist Recorder 288, 341, 343, 349,
  362, 400, 426
Methodist schools *see* schools, night
  school and South schools
Miles, Lieutenant-General Sir Herbert,
  Governor 341
Minorca, Methodist work in 256, 258,
  268-70, 283, 304
Minutes of Conference 39, 44, 47, 128,
  132, 141, 270, 383
Miranda, Mr 245
Mission budget 154
Mission House, Cádiz 108

Mission House, Gibraltar *see also* lease
  and library
  altered/repaired 28, 47, 203, 284, 287
  built 25-7
  centre of epidemic 66
  depository at 49, 90
  let to Govett 308, 313, 318-9
  poor state of 72, 85, 174-5, 203, 288
  rebuilt 104-5
  requisitioned 374
  school at 86, 154
  sold 397
  water supply at 51, 245
Mission House, London 33, 46, 145,
  214, 222, 226, 255, 262-3, 265, 297
Missionary Notices 33, 40, 51, 53, 206,
  216, 284
Missionary Society *see* Wesleyan
  Methodist Missionary Society
Monro, General Sir Charles C.,
  Governor 350
Monro, Lady 350-1
Moon, Mr 292
Mora, Herreros de 185, 187, 196
Moral leadership Courses 374
Moroccan workers 411, 415
Moreton, Rev. Robert Hawkey 247-8,
  272
Morton, Brother 7
Mottashed, Rev. Arthur 395-6
Murray, Rev. Thomas (Presbyterian)
  287, 289, 298

National Service 379, 389, 407, 434
Naval Hospital Road 325
Negrotto, Mrs Catherine 88
Negrotto, Salvador 88, 114-5, 128, 149,
  155, 176
neutral ground
  camp at 35, 66-8, 73, 152, 165
  centenary celebrations at 129
  site of cemetery 19, 163
  source of water 51
New Lights 3-4
Nicholson, Corporal Henry Richard
  army career 130
  children 142, 148, 156, 172, 177
  concern for his future, 169-70
  departure and future 176-7
  health 142, 155, 165, 170
  marriage 137
  school teacher 146, 148-9, 153-6, 165

visit to England 171-2
work in the Spanish department 155, 161, 165, 170
Nicholson, Mrs Mary 137, 146, 171-2, 176-7
Nicklin, John 64, 72
Nicklin, Mrs Caroline 31, 43, 48-9, 59, 90, 95
night (evening) schools, Methodist 128, 142, 149, 154-5, 165-6, 223, 244, 267, 271, 274, 295 closed 301
Nodder, Mrs Dorothy 382, 388, 393
Nodder, Reg 382, 385, 388, 392-3
North Front 163, 367
coffee van and kiosk 326
services there 290

O'Flaherty, Brother Patrick 89
O'Hara, Lieutenant General Charles, Governor 11
Oates, Mr Thomas, Acting Governor 414
OBE awarded to Sackett 342
Ofália, Conde de 109, 121
official recognition of Methodist chaplains 276, 278, 345
Olver, Rev. George, Missionary Society Secretary 277
Operation Torch 372
Oporto (now Porto) 229, 232-4, 237, 245-8, 272
opposition see also persecution
against Rule's work with Catholic children 82-4, 87, 89, 105-6, 109
at the South schools 153-4
against the school 281, 286
Oran 190, 222, 365
organ see also pipe organ (seraphim 176), 297, 330
Orman, Mr, Welcome manager 348
Osborne, Mrs Todd 302-3
Osler, Mr 86
'Other Protestants' 219, 261, 276
Ottway, Mr, Chargé d'Affaires in the British Embassy at Madrid 194
outings see trips and picnics
Overton, Edward 285-6

Padre's Hours 374, 389, 415, 422, 426
Page, Rev John (Presbyterian) 441
Palhal Mines 229, 233, 237, 245-6
Palma 256, 269

Palmer, Rev. E. Reeves, Bible Society Agent 278, 292
Palmerston, Lord, Foreign Secretary 121-2, 124, 132-4
Parade Services see also marching
of troops to worship 260, 298-300, 306-7, 312, 315, 323, 334, 340-1, 364, 374, 399
Parker, Dr 43, 48-9
Parody, Catalina 116
Patron, Joanna 444
Patron, Mrs Sheila 429, 438, 441
Patron, Rev. Fidelio 429, 438-9, 441, 443-4
Pearce, Mr and Mrs, Welcome manager and wife 356, 359
Pearce, Mrs Doreen 441-2
Pearce, Rev. Ivor Wilfred 441-2
penal servitude 205, 209
Perez, José María 114, 132
Perks, Rev. George, Missionary Society Secretary 262
Perpignan 98-9
Persecution see also opposition
early persecution 6,7, 11-2, 13
events re the flogging 14-7, 21
in connection with
burials and baptisms 32, 36, 163-4
lease renewals 63, 166-7
religious education 326
school grants 167-9, 189
soldiers' rights 177-8, 201-3, 219-21
the work at the South 49-50
petty opposition 75
towards
Christian officers 56
soldiers 129-32, 137
the navy 261
Pickard, Rev. Ernest Richard 336-7, 341
picnics see also trips 301-2, 309, 312, 327, 349, 362, 375, 407
Pillidge, George 382
pipe organ see also organ 333, 343, 399, 433-4
Plant, Rev. Dr Stephen 439
Port St Mary 103, 133, 158, 211-3, 217
Portugal 100, 210, 229, 232-3, 245, 247-8, 259, 269-70, 435
Powley, Rev. Matthew (Anglican) 230
Powlson, Leonard 295, 297, 300-1, 305
Powlson, Mrs 297
Prat, Mr 98
Pratten, Mrs Fanny 57, 59, 69
Pratten, Rev. Joseph 57-64, 72

prayer meetings 12, 30, 36, 75, 79, 129, 160, 219, 254, 340
Presbyterian church *see also* St Andrew's and Church of Scotland 137, 166, 189, 222, 278, 300, 326
Presbyterians 246, 260-1, 276, 313
  allowances for Presbyterian ministers 189, 201, 284
  collaborative work with Methodists 151, 175, 198, 246, 258, 272-3, 289, 293, 295-6, 298, 387
  use of Methodist chapel 138, 150-1
President of Conference 16, 20, 57, 76, 242
Presidential visits to Gibraltar 408, 413-5, 436
Prim, General 233-4
Prince Edward's Road property 9, 25, 31-4, 320, 332, 392-4, 396-7, 400, 414
Prince Edward's Road Friendly Association 296
prison visiting 202, 277, 285, 298-9, 306, 316, 324, 419
Protestant Poor Fund 383, 386
Providence Chapel *see also* Methodist Church 27, 211, 350
Puente, Juan 166
Puntales 212
Pyne, John 40-42, 46-9, 51, 53, 55, 58-61, 63-4, 67-8, 72

quarantine
  Gibraltar under quarantine 30-1, 277, 280
  personal quarantine 78, 84, 167, 280
quarantine laws and measures 178, 183
Quarterly Meeting 173-4, 178, 197, 199
Queen's Regiment 6, 14, 336
Queen's Regulations 178
Queen's visit to Gibraltar 392, 395
Quirell, John 51-4, 56-61, 71-5, 82-3
Quirell, Señora Antonia 53, 57, 83

radio broadcasts 370, 403, 408-9, 416, 420, 424, 426, 433, 438
radio ministry 438, 442
Radley, John 97-8
Ramírez 91
Ramsay, Lieutenant Colonel 14-5
ration given 30, 31, 36
Razola, Señor 98, 108
reading room 201, 297, 299, 319, 358

Redman, Lady 400
Redman, Lieutenant General Sir Harold, Governor 397, 400
Rees, Mrs 39, 43, 45
Rees, Rev. Owen 38-48, 51, 80, 138
Reeves, John 15
referendum 410, 413
refugees
  Spanish Protestants 222-3
  from the Civil War 361-3
regimental changes *see* congregational changes
Religious Book and Tract Society 157
religious confraternities 216
religious education of children 260, 277, 285, 316, 324, 326, 389-90, 416, 427, 438
religious toleration in Spain
  lack of 106, 181, 210
  hope of 233
  granted 236
  problems with 268-9, 282, 304, 390-1
restaurant *see also* canteen, dockyard canteens and Carpenter's Arms 418-20, 422, 424-5
  Ince's restaurant 425-6
  closed 428
revival 50, 178, 182
  prayers for 151, 160
revolutions in Spain
  1854 181
  1856 193-4, 197
  1868 233-5
Richardson, Major-General 310
Richardson, Rev. Dr Kathleen 439, 441
Richmond College 161 187, 268, 272, 280, 288, 322, 324, 424
Richmond, Mrs Anna Louisa 260, 272-3
Richmond, Rev. Henry 232-8, 247, 258, 260-9, 271-3
Righton, John William 289, 293-5
Righton, Mrs Elizabeth Ann 289, 293
Roberts, Mr 276
Roberts, Rev. Colin 393-4, 397
Rodriguez, José 291-3, 299-303
Rodriguez, Señora Antonia Maria 292, 303
Roebuck, Rev. Owen 409
role of ministers' wives
  importance of 61
  relating to
    Alton, Amy 252
    Bentley, Ena 409
    Berryman, Isobel 422

Coppin, Eva 302, 305
Dennis, Anne 426-7
Jackson, Rene 387, 390, 398, 400-1, 403, 406
Jefferies, Pat 413, 415-7
Lyth, Mary Ann 259
Mears, Leila 433
Patron, Sheila 438
Pearce, Doreen 442
Rule, Mary Ann 81, 104, 146
Sackett, Lydia 324, 339, 343-4
Sarchet, Emily 321-2
Sweetman, Sarah 94
Sykes, Mavis 438
Roman Catholicism *see also* Christian Brothers, Loreto Nuns, Constitution of Spain, opposition, St Mary the Crowned
improved relationship with 412, 414-5
religion of Spain 96
Romero, Juan 2
Ronda
Bible selling there 181, 198
Brown's visits there 363, 372, 380-2
Protestant work there 390-1, 399, 404-5, 407, 429
trips to 327, 328, 334
Rooke, Admiral Sir George 2
Rosia Bay 22
Ross, John 369, 371
Ross, Mrs Connie 369
Rowe, Rev. Colin G., Chairman of the Board 432
Roxburgh, Mr 292
Royal Artillery 35
Royal Order (Spanish)
against Graydon 122
against Rule and Lyon 119, 133, 143
about Spanish schools 118
to seize Bibles 112-3, 123
Ruet y Roset, Francisco de Paula 191-3, 197, 208, 214, 222-4, 238
Rule, Barrow 80, 146-7
Rule, Martin Luther 86, 147
Rule, Mary Ann 147
Rule, Melancthon 104, 116
Rule, Mrs Harriete 269
Rule, Mrs Mary Ann 60-61, 77-8, 80-1, 84, 88, 102, 104, 107, 114-7, 146. 269
Rule, Philip Melancthon 147
Rule, Rev. William Harris
first visit 60-1
in Gibraltar 77-89, 91-5, 97, 100-7, 113, 124-33, 137-41, 144-6

in Spain (Cádiz) 114-23, 133-6, 142-3
plans for Algeciras 142-3
South property 148-53, 154-8, 167, 170-1
subsequent fight for soldiers' rights 201-2, 219
visit to Gibraltar and Spain 269-72
Rule, Ulric Zuinglius
Rule's commentaries 91, 143-4, 226
Rupp, Rev. Dr Gordon 413-5
Russell, Corporal Richard 15, 333
Russell, David 443

Sabine, Lieutenant General Joseph, Governor 3-4
Sackett, Alfred *Barrett* 322-4, 328, 339-42, 344
Sackett, Dorothy May 322-3, 344
Sackett, Mrs Lydia Anne 322-3, 338-9, 341, 343-4
Sackett, Rev. Alfred Barrett 321-45, 347-8
sailors *see also* Soldiers' and Sailors' Rooms, Welcome and South Welcome
at the church when in port 211, 246, 254, 266, 277, 299, 340
difficulty over hours of worship 261-2
need for accommodation 306-7, 323-4
Sails, Rev. George 425
Salinas, Don Diego de 2
San Fernando 211-3, 215, 217
San Pedro 443
San Roque 2, 28
Bible selling there 103, 198
English living there for health reasons 39, 43, 45, 57, 155, 199, 215, 241, 249
hope of Methodist work there 52, 93, 102, 272
Sanchez, Mrs Antonia 189
Sanchez, Pablo 189-90, 192-3, 197, 203, 210, 214, 226, 233-4
Sanders, Rear Admiral Jeremy 437
Sangster, Rev. Dr W. Edwin 397-8
Sanitary Commissioner(s) *see also*
Commission of Enquiry 227-32, 238-9, 241-2. 250
Sanitary Commission Secretary 227-32, 238, 241-2, 247, 249-51
Sanitary Committee 227
Sarchet, Irene Hazel
birth 313
death 314

Sarchet, Mrs Emily Victoria 304-6,
  321-2
Sarchet, Rev. William Henry 304-16,
  318-24, 327, 344
Sardeña, Brenda 443
Sardeña, Freddie 443
scarlet fever 52, 250
school for young ladies 128-9, 141
Schools, Methodist *see also* South
  schools, Christian Brothers and Loreto
  nuns, night schools and government
  grant
  background 29, 80
  begun 81-2
  general work of 87-8, 104-5, 116, 149,
    154, 156-7, 159, 161-2, 170, 203, 224-
    5, 244, 264, 280-1, 284-5
  need to be more of a Mission school
    281, 283, 286, 289, 290, 292
  opposed by Christian Brothers 281,
    286, 290
  problems with Powlson 297, 300
  work ended 301
school-house *see also* Epworth House
  and Soldiers Rooms 264, 266, 271,
  290, 294-5, 307
  let out 308, 313
Schott, Ferdinand 346-7
Scio's version of the bible 185, 187
Scott, George 338
Scott, Mr, Welcome Manager 359, 364
Seamen's Mission *see also* Bethel
  Society 278, 292, 313
Second World War 365
settled numbers/members 260, 278, 428,
  431, 435, 442
Seville 96, 158, 184, 192
  Borrow's visits 11, 121-2,
  Protestant work there 208, 212, 233-5,
    238, 244
  Rule's visits 90-1, 108
  Scriptures taken there 159, 198
  trips to 328, 334
Seymour, Rear-Admiral Beauchamp
  261
Shaftesbury, Earl of 234
Sharpley, Rev. William Thomas 345-9,
  351
Sherrington, Rev. Brian, Secretary to the
  Board 439, 441
ship visitation *see also* Bethel Society
  12, 48, 54, 157, 198, 203, 255-6, 278,
  292
Shorncliffe Camp 220, 309, 344

sieges *see also* Great Siege 1
Sikorsky, General 372
Simpson, Rev. Robert 268-70, 282-3,
  304
Smales, Sergeant Major 285
smallpox 34, 249
Smith, Rev. Franklyn G. 282, 291, 304
Smith, Sergeant 285
Smith-Dorrien, General Sir Horace L.,
  Governor 342-3, 345
Sneezum, Mrs Freda, Manageress of the
  Welcome 403-5
Snodgrass, Sister 313
Soldier Artificer Company 7-9
Soldiers' and Sailors' Home *see also*
  sailors, Welcome and South Welcome
  requested 287, 290
  Soldiers' and Sailors' Rooms 295-7,
    299, 301-2, 306, 309
  plans to develop the work 308-10
Soldiers' Christian Instruction Society
  201
soldiers' right to worship *see* persecution
Soler, Antonio 226, 234
Sotogrande 432, 438, 443
South, The 29, 56-7, 66, 80, 86, 151,
  159, 287-8, 352, 371
  preaching there 25, 35, 50-1, 70, 73,
    138, 148
  Spanish preaching there 54, 83
  Methodist premises there 143-50, 153,
    170-3, 176, 245
South schools 128, 146, 148, 153-7, 171
South Welcome 320, 325-6, 329, 334-6,
  347, 351, 374, 403
Southey, Miss Hilda 391, 394
Spanish speaking work in Gibraltar,
  Methodist
  suggested 43, 51-2
  under
    Alton 161-2, 165, 169-70, 179, 226
    Barber 53-60
    Deacon 195
    Giolma 214, 222-3, 225
    Nicholson 148, 153, 155, 161
    Quirell 71-5
    Rodriguez 291-2, 296, 303
    Rule 82-3, 86, 88, 104-5, 113, 124,
      128, 132, 138, 141
    Sanchez 197, 203, 214, 226
  work continues with varying fortunes
    265, 271, 274-5, 280-4, 289-90, 296
  work stops 303
Spanish Civil War 304, 311, 360-4

467

Spanish commentary (Rule's) 91, 143-4, 225
Spanish Constitution 105-6, 111, 118-9, 133, 136, 268-9
Spanish Evangelical Church 304
Spanish Evangelisation Society 187-8, 196, 233
Spanish hymn book 85, 270
Spanish Inquisition 96, 209
Spanish labour 180, 367, 410
Spanish law 121, 124, 204, 234, 257, 282
  and Bibles 49, 101, 182, 190, 236
  and education 106
  and Protestantism 93, 102, 106, 118-9, 133
Spanish Presbyterian work in Gibraltar 197, 214, 222-3, 226, 234
Spanish Protestants
  persecution of 191, 193, 208-10
  exiled in Gibraltar 222-3
  return to Spain 233-4
Spanish Reformed Episcopal Church 238
Spanish watchnight service 59
Spear, Rev. A. Douglas, Secretary of the Board 417, 419, 420
Spencer, Lieutenant-Colonel 177
spiritualist practices 207, 212
Squelch, Captain P., Manager of the Welcome 377, 380, 382
Squelch, Mrs 377, 380, 382
St. Andrew's see also Presbyterian Church and Church of Scotland 189, 233, 388, 390
St Christopher's Junior School 390, 438
St. George's Infant School 390, 416
St Mary the Crowned, RC Cathedral 2, 8, 156, 380, 408
Standing, Rev. George, Secretary of the Board 363, 372-3
Steward, Captain Robert 140, 143
Stephenson, Charles 338-9, 346-7, 349
Stewart, Rev. Alexander (Presbyterian) 302
Stinson, Mrs. Hannah 71, 74-5
Stinson, Rev. Joseph 71-6, 78-9, 81
Stokes, Henry 64, 72
stone laying
  chapel 26
  new drainage system 230
Stopford, Colonel 184, 186, 193-4
Strachan, Miss 377

Strauchan, Rev. William (Presbyterian) 137-8, 151, 157
Sunday school 51, 58, 74, 94, 129, 253, 260, 263, 281, 285, 306, 313, 315, 319, 332-4, 346-7, 350, 374, 378, 387, 400-1, 406, 408, 414, 416, 420, 426-7, 433, 443
  for Spanish children 74, 82, 89, 271, 283-4
  in Palhal 233, 237, 246
  in Portugal 237, 245
  in Spain 255, 293, 404
supernumerary
  Alton 229, 238, 249
  Brown 378-9
  Lyth 238, 240, 258
Sutherland, Rev. Andrew (Presbyterian) 197-8, 233
Sweetman, Edward Merson
  birth and death 127
Sweetman, Mrs Sarah 94, 127
Sweetman, Rev. Edward 94-5, 103, 106, 108, 116, 124, 126-8
Syer, Major W.R. 347, 351-2
Sykes, Mrs Mavis 434-5, 437-8, 440
Sykes, Rev. Frank Elmer 434-5, 437-41
Symons, Rev. Dr, Garrison Chaplain 31-2

Tall, John 388
Tangier 2, 49, 122, 209, 249-50, 300-1, 363, 365, 373, 421
  trips to 312, 321, 334, 348
Tarifa 28, 293
  trips to 334
Tarn, Joseph (Bible Society) 22
Tasker, Mr. W. 272
Tasker, Mrs Sarah 278
Taylor, Miss M. 408
tea meetings 129, 246, 266, 285
  for missionary work 159
  for the schools 167, 175
Teixeira, Bishop Sifredo 248
Temperance meetings 285, 290, 299, 315
Temperance Society or Association 126, 321, 324
Teresa 368, 380-2
Thompson, Rev. Dr James, Bible Society 159
Todd, Sister Mabel 404
Tomlinson, Rt Rev. George, Lord Anglican Bishop of Gibraltar 171

Tonkin, Charles 246
Toreno, Count de 98
Torreguadiaro 443
Torrie, Rev. Ronald (Presbyterian) 387, 390
Townsend, Mrs F.G. 407-8
toy service 404-5, 407, 429
tract depots 86, 254
tract distribution
  by Graydon 112-3, 122-3
  in Gibraltar 35-6, 49, 129, 132, 151, 157, 170, 223
  in Spain 43, 52, 74, 103, 133, 152, 159, 161, 196, 216, 223, 236
Tract Societies 151, 157, 255
translation work 91, 255
Treaty of Utrecht 2
Treffry, Rev. Richard 77
Trigge, Major General Sir Thomas, Lieutenant Governor 10, 14, 19
Trigo, Miguel 209, 222
Tripp, Captain 35, 38, 40-2, 45, 47
trips see also picnics 301, 311-2, 321, 326-8, 334-7, 344-5, 348, 362, 372, 375, 389, 401-2, 416
Trustees of the Methodist property see also lease 25, 47, 63, 72, 86, 143, 150, 167, 296, 313, 397
Tudury, Francisco 250
Tuita, Princess Pululeva 432
tunnels see also Ince's Galleries 367, 437
Twine, Harry 379, 381
typhoid 194

Unification of Methodism 80, 351
Upper Rock Services 370-1
Urquinaona, Don Pedro 102, 106
Usoz y Río, Don Luis de 101, 109, 184-7, 190, 193-4

Valencia 190, 193-4, 198, 270, 363
  Graydon's work there 98, 105, 111
  Marin's home 105-6, 108-9, 125, 136
Valera's version of the bible 185-8, 192, 236, 252
Vecchio, Miss 275, 280, 301
Vejer 203, 205
Vicar Apostolic
  in Gibraltar 87, 105
  in Spain 93, 193
Vicar Ecclesiastic 190

Victor y Pico, Don Pedro 204
Victor, Antonio 154
Vila Nova de Gaia 237, 248
Villa Carlos 255, 257
Villiers, Sir George, later Earl of Clarendon, British Minister in Madrid 98, 101, 108-10, 112, 118, 121
voluntary services ie evening ones 287, 315

Waights, Rev. Kenneth 416
Ward, General Sir Dudley, Governor 408
Ward, Lady 408
Warden, Captain 203, 208-9
Watchman, Wesleyan 32, 199
water, scarcity and supply of 18, 34, 51, 323, 337
  quality of 226-8, 230-1, 241, 245, 251
Watson, Mr R. 292
Weatherburne, Sergeant 137
Webster, Eber Wesley
  birth and death 215
Webster, Mary 215
Webster, Mrs Philippa 201, 203, 215
Webster, Rev. Joseph 201-7, 209-15, 219-22
Welcome boat 402, 407
Welcome chapel 358, 364, 370, 378
Welcome Kiosk 326
Welcome Soldiers' and Sailors' Home
  see also South Welcome
  opening of 310-13
  purchase and re-opening 346-8
  use of 315-6, 318-9, 321, 323-4, 326, 328, 330, 332-45
  used for refugees 361-2
  Welcome relocated 352-9
  work continues 349. 350-1, 363-4, 368-75, 378, 380-2, 386-97, 400
Wesley House see also canteen, dockyard canteens and restaurant 400-1, 407, 411, 413- 9, 421, 428, 431-3, 435- 8, 444
Wesley, John 2-6, 13, 16, 40, 59, 80
Wesleyan Church Property Ordinance Gibraltar, 1906 296, 320
  amended 1918 313
Wesleyan Methodist Missionary Society
  established 33
  financial constraints of 64, 115, 134, 144, 153-4, 160, 173, 224, 233-4, 246, 273, 283

oversight of Gibraltar 124, 144-5, 150, 168, 170, 182, 184-5, 234, 239-40, 253, 262
ceased 317
staff as trustees of Gibraltar property 72, 167, 296
Wesleyan Methodist Missionary Society Committee 33, 39
difficulties in communicating through it 44, 47, 63, 85, 106-7, 113-5, 126, 147, 195, 199, 213-4, 217, 225, 228, 258, 261-5, 286, 314-5
helped through use of telegrams 297
involvement with
Alton and Sanitary Commission 228-30, 238, 241-2
Barber's request to marry 62-4
burial ground dispute 163
Cheesebrough and staffing 173-4
lease renewal 166-7, 253
Lyon's leaving 139-41
Rees dispute 42-8
reviving Spanish work 283
Revolution in Spain 234-6, 239
Richmond's problem with navy 262
Rule's deteriorating relationship with 119-20, 124-5, 128, 132, 134-5, 141-7, 158
schools grant 167-9
schoolteacher appointment 294-5
soldiers' rights 131-2, 177-8
South property 145-55, 156, 170-2
Wesleyan Methodist Missionary Society Reports 22, 30, 40, 170, 195, 207, 209, 225, 240, 246, 263, 265, 280, 302, 316
Wesleyan Methodist Missionary Society Secretaries see also Alder, Hoole 33, 39,
asked to visit 153
visits to Gibraltar 245, 277, 298-300
Wesleyan Methodist Missionary Society Treasurers 33, 86,149
Wesleyan Royal Navy, Army and Air Force Board see Army and Navy Committee
Wesleyan Watchman 32, 199
West, Mrs 44, 47
Westall, Mr Benjamin 296-7, 299, 305-6, 308, 315-6, 332, 342, 347-8
Westall, Mrs Alice 299
Westminster College 275, 289, 295
Wetherall, Revd Mr, Garrison Chaplain 13-4
White, Rev. Abraham 187-8, 192-3, 195

White, Sir George, Governor 312
Whitefield, George 3-4
Willersley Castle 375, 377, 384
Williams, Admiral Sir David, Governor 425
Williams, Lady 425
Wilson, General Sir Robert, Governor 163, 178
Wilson, Rev. Frank W. 378-83. 385-7
Wilson, Trevor 432
Wingate-Grey, Brigadier 414
wireless installed 359
Wolff, Joseph 61
Wolff, Lady Georgiana 61-2
Wolseley, Field Marshal, Commander-in-Chief 310
women's role see ministers' wives
Wood, Mrs Esther 30-31
Wood, Rev. Benjamin 30-3, 37
Woodford, General Sir Alexander, Governor 129
Words Aflame bookshop see books
Wright, Sydney 182

Yearsley, Mr. H.F. 359
yellow fever epidemic see also fever 18-20, 29-31, 66-71

Zambrano, Juan 429
Zambrano, Señora Pepa 429
Zino, Father, Vicar Apostolic 87-89